KU-022-623

CONTENTS

EVERYMAN'S LIBRARY

WITHDRAWN

EVERYMAN,
I WILL GO WITH THEE,
AND BE THY GUIDE,
IN THY MOST NEED
TO GO BY THY SIDE

W. B. YEATS

The Poems

Edited and introduced by Daniel Albright

EVERYMAN'S LIBRARY

103

This book is one of 250 volumes in Everyman's Library
which have been distributed to 4500 state schools
throughout the United Kingdom.
The project has been supported by a grant of £4 million
from the Millennium Commission.

First included in Everyman's Library, 1992
© J. M. Dent & Sons Ltd., 1990

ISBN 1-85715-103-8

A CIP catalogue record for this book is available from the
British Library

Published by David Campbell Publishers Ltd.,
Gloucester Mansions, 140A Shaftesbury Avenue,
London WC2H 8HD

Distributed by Random House (UK) Ltd.,
20 Vauxhall Bridge Road, London SW1V 2SA

821 YEA
10054335

Luton Sixth Form College
Learning Resources Centre

INTRODUCTION

I

Neath Ben Bulben's buttoks lies
Bill Yeats, a poet twoice the soize
Of William Shakespear, as they say
Down Ballykillywuchlin way.
(Ezra Pound, *Pavannes and Divagations*, p. 228)

Yeats's size is difficult to measure. Pound's mean parody of 'Under Ben Bulben' suggests that Yeats appears to be twice the size of Shakespeare only because Ireland is a quarter the size of England. Today Ireland is not a small country – such modern Irishmen as James Joyce, Samuel Beckett, Bernard Shaw, and Yeats himself have so powerfully shaped European literature that Ireland looms as large as France or Germany on the cultural map. But when William Butler Yeats was born, in 1865, Ireland had little tradition of imaginative literature written in English – to an ambitious poet unacquainted with Gaelic, Ireland might have seemed a cramped, remote, ingrown island. To some extent Yeats suffered from this insularity:

Great hatred, little room,
Maimed us from the start.
('Remorse for Intemperate Speech')

Yeats was born into a culture in which poetry was (in popular caricature) the occasion for sentimental tears, or an arouser of patriotic emotion. Yeats sometimes feared that his work would be distorted by the restrictions of Irish culture.

And yet, there is a sense in which Yeats was extraordinarily lucky to have been born an Irishman. Because the English-speaking culture was so spatially confined, it was possible for a young man to be exposed to the whole of it. Yeats's father, John Butler Yeats – a voluble, energetic, unself-confident man – was a well known painter, and his household attracted the leading cultural figures of the day; Edward Dowden, the Professor of English at Trinity College, Dublin, whose Shakespearean criticism is still studied, was a regular guest of the Yeatses. Yeats's father was also involved with the British artistic world – he corresponded with D. G. Rossetti (the pre-Raphaelite painter and poet), and he was commissioned to illustrate Robert Browning's *Pippa Passes.* The peculiar concentration of Irish culture was useful to the young Yeats, who found easy connections everywhere: in 1888 he spent Christmas in London with his fellow Irishman Oscar Wilde (though Yeats felt that his yellow shoes marked him a provincial [*A: FY* 10]), and a few years later he met Paul Verlaine and other literary figures in Paris.

The interconnectedness of Irish life also proved to be an advantage in Yeats's mature work. W. H. Auden, attempting to account for the fact that a better poem had been written about a small Irish uprising in 1916 than any about the whole of World War II, wrote:

> To write a good poem on Churchill, a poet would have to know Winston Churchill intimately, and his poem would be about the man, not about the Prime Minister. All attempts to write about persons and events, however important, to which the poet is not intimately related in a personal way are now doomed to failure. Yeats could write great poetry about the Troubles in Ireland, because most of the protagonists were known to him personally and the places where the events occurred had been familiar to him since childhood. (*The Dyer's Hand*, p. 81)

In 1929, Yeats advised Ezra Pound, 'Do not be elected to the Senate of your country' (*AV*, p. 26). Yeats did not understand that under no circumstances could Pound, or perhaps any poet of stature, have been elected to the American Senate; for he himself had just completed a six-year term in the Senate of the Irish Free State. The artistic, political, and social lives of Ireland were integrated in a way difficult to reproduce elsewhere; and Yeats benefited from that integration.

II

Yeats also benefited from the depth of focus of Irish culture. Not long before Yeats's birth, scholarly English translations of the ancient Irish mythological texts started to appear; and it was clear that a richly detailed but not fully defined lore awaited assimilation into the imagination of modern Europe. Yeats often insisted that only Greece rivalled Ireland in the exuberance and power of its mythology. Greece, of course, had found its Homer, its summary poet, in 800 BC; but in Ireland the role of Homer was open to any great poet who might appear. When Lady Gregory's *Cuchulain of Muirthemne* appeared in 1902, Yeats appointed her to the role – he wrote in the Preface to that book, 'she will have given Ireland its *Mabinogion*, its *Morte d'Arthur*, its *Nibelungenlied*'. But it is clear that Yeats himself thought of being Ireland's epic poet – and not only its Homer, but its Sophocles and its Sappho as well. *The Wanderings of Oisin* (1889) measures itself against the *Odyssey*; *On Baile's Strand* (1904) measures itself against *Oedipus Rex*; and any number of Yeats's lyrics strive for the chiselled perfection of classical verse. Few poets have ever had what Ireland gave to Yeats: the sophistication of a mature culture combined with the openness, the freedom of action of a immature one. In America, Walt Whitman enjoyed some of these advantages, but lacked the vast body of unused myths available to Yeats.

When Yeats considered the Ireland of his youth, he was struck by its malleability. In his autobiography he wrote that 'the sudden certainty that Ireland was to be like soft wax for years to come, was a moment of supernatural insight' (*A: IP* 1). A few pages later he noted that his literary associates 'had come under the seal of Young Ireland [an important nationalistic movement] at that age when we are all mere wax' (*A: IP* 3); later, 'Now that he [John O'Leary, the noble fierce old leader of the Irish independence movement] is dead, I wish I could question him ... but I doubt if I would have learnt anything, for I think the wax had long forgotten the seal' (*A: IP* 5); and a little further still, Yeats referred to Dr Douglas Hyde, the leader of the Gaelic language movement, as 'Proteus' (*A: IP* 6). Wherever Yeats looked, he saw softness, a culture accepting whatever form was imposed upon it. He found in Ireland great energy, but no clear definition of purpose. Yeats took it upon himself to impress shape upon this wax, to compel these Proteuses to assume a form. Much of his work as a Senator pertained to the design of coins – as if he saw himself as a stamper of images in the most literal way.

III

In his own art Yeats hated vagueness. He spent years in editing an edition of William Blake's poetry (published in 1893), and he quoted with approval Blake's expostulation against chiaroscuro – his hatred of 'blot and blur' and his preference for 'firm and determinate outline' (*EI*, p. 126). Blake learned this from his master, the engraver James Basire; and Yeats might have learned a similar lesson from his father, who partly followed the pre-Raphaelite style, a style in which shallow fields were often constructed from profuse fine detail. But his father's style changed, to his son's horror:

> My father began life a pre-Raphaelite painter; when past thirty he fell under the influence of contemporary French painting. Instead of finishing a picture one square inch at a time, he kept all fluid, every detail dependent upon every other, and remained a poor man to the end of his life, because the more anxious he was to succeed, the more did his pictures sink through innumerable sittings into final confusion. (*A: DP* 16)

Yeats himself originally intended to be a painter – his grades were too poor to attend his father's alma mater, Trinity College, so he went to art school instead. He saw in his father's evolution a glimpse of an evolution in his own work that he feared and avoided – a poet as well as a painter may cultivate a thick, turbid, wavering style, and Yeats was determined to resist such infirmity:

> The Irish bards any way, always were explicit rather than suggestive in dealing with the supernatural ... They surround the vague with the definite. (*L* I, p. 284)

> Above all I avoid suggesting the ghostly (the vague) idea about a god, for it is a modern conception. All ancient vision was definite and precise. (*L*, p. 343)

Much of the advanced contemporary poetry of Yeats's youth (such as that of Oscar Wilde and Arthur Symons) was influenced by Whistler and by French impressionistic painting. Yeats, then, found himself in a world where art was smear or blur, and politics and society were wax; and he countered them by striving towards hardness, purity, definition.

IV

But Yeats wanted precision and security of outline, not in order to specify what his physical eye saw, but to specify what his imagination saw. Yeats hated realism. For Yeats, as for the Romantic poets he loved, there were two chief species of art: one mimetic and factual, the other subjective, luminous; one the mirror, the other the lamp:

> He [Arthur Symons] thought to spend his . . . artistic life, in making the silver mirror without speck, and I thought to see it fused and glowing. (*Mem*, p. 36)

> The greater the subjectivity, the less the imitation. Though perhaps there is always some imitation. . . . In fact, imitation seems to me to create a language in which we say things which are not imitation. (*L*, p. 607)

As a poet, Yeats hoped to subvert a language created for the description of the everyday world, in order to embody visions of the extra-terrestrial. The mirror of his art must not merely reflect, but kindle, start to burn with images hitherto unseen.

Yeats's poetry shows a lifelong search for such images, images that were not reflections but illuminations. He sought them in translations of old Irish myths. He sought them in visionary poetry, especially that of Blake and Shelley. He sought them in the fairy-tales told by Irish peasants – he heard many as a boy, when his family spent summers in Sligo, in the far west of Ireland, and later he made a systematic investigation of folk-beliefs. He sought them in séances, alchemical research, spiritualistic societies, telepathic experimentation, hashish-dreams, meditations on symbols. When old, he sought them in philosophy, from Plato to Berkeley to the Indian Upanishads. Wherever anyone purported to find revelation – even the most disreputable places – Yeats was willing to look.

As he contemplated these multifarious sources of transcendental images, he came to the conclusion that there was in fact one source, a universal warehouse of images that he called the Anima Mundi, the Soul of the World. Each human soul could attune itself to revelation, to miracle, because each partook in the world's general soul. Most of us had blinded our spiritual eyes, in order to maintain our little privacies, in order not to be disturbed by truths that violated logic and the evidence of the five senses; but the real principles that governed life were these:

> (1) That the borders of our mind are ever shifting, and that many minds can flow into one another ... and create or reveal a single mind, a single energy.
>
> (2) That the borders of our memories are as shifting, and that our memories are a part of one great memory, the memory of Nature herself.
>
> (3) That this great mind and great memory can be evoked by symbols. (*EI*, p. 28)

As best he could, Yeats tried to discipline his imagination, to cultivate a detachment from the normal world, to smooth and empty his mind until it could flame with images from the world beyond our own.

V

What sort of image did Yeats seek? In general, he favoured images of extravagance. He assumed the world of experience comprises puny, deformed, incomplete, perishing things; whereas the world of imagination comprises things that are excessive, immeasurable, autonomous, triumphant. What he especially esteemed in the old Irish literature was a quality of superhuman abundance: he wrote of some translations of Gaelic love songs 'they seem to be continually straining to express a something which lies beyond the possibility of expression' (*UP* I, p. 377). And Yeats incorporated into his own poetry such old Irish images as a river running over with beer ('The Happy Townland'). He tried to create in his poetry a domain of the indefatigable and the exorbitant, where passion intensified, became perpetual – where a warrior could battle a demon for a hundred years (*The Wanderings of Oisin* II), where ideal lovers were transformed into swans, eternally linked by a golden chain (*Baile and Aillinn*), where a man in love with the infinite could sail his ship so far out on the ocean that he sailed right out of the world (*The Shadowy Waters*). Such was the inspiration of Celtic mythology, although some of these poems have no direct source in old Irish texts.

Yeats's folklore research helped him to define the relation between these vast fluent dreams and ordinary life. Yeats seemed best to like those peasant stories of kidnappings – stories in which the faeries snatched away brides, babies, and handsome boys, and kept them in some unearthly realm, sometimes never to return. Something of the frenzy, the high pitch of life in faeryland was suggested by this account: 'A woman, said still to be living, was taken from near a village called Ballisodare, and when she came home after seven years she had not toes – she had danced them all off' (*UP* I, p. 177; compare *M*, p. 76). In many of the stories Yeats collected, the faeries were marked by a strange irresponsible playfulness, as if they made the cruellest mischief for their own aesthetic delight. The faeries of peasant superstition were presumably the old pagan gods, dwindled and in retreat from the Christian ethos, but something of the brutal splendour of the gods of the ancient myths remained in them. Furthermore, one might hope to join them in their revels – at some risk to body and soul. It was as if, in Ireland, a region of invariant ecstasy were all around, hovering invisibly in certain sacred places. Yeats expressed this co-presence of the physical and the spiritual in some memorable lines:

> Is Eden far away, or do you hide
> From human thought, as hares and mice and coneys
> That run before the reaping-hook and lie
> In the last ridge of the barley? Do our woods
> And winds and ponds cover more quiet woods,
> More shining winds, more star-glimmering ponds?
> (*The Shadowy Waters*, Introductory Rhymes)

All the mind's eye needs is a slight adjustment of focus, and paradise is right there.

Yeats's researches into myth and folklore helped him to construct a habitation where enormous bodily appetites would be enormously gratified – where the muscles that swing the sword or lift the dancing leg could develop amazingly. Yeats's occult researches helped him to construct similar gratifications for the spirit. The theosophical and Rosicrucian societies that Yeats joined from 1887 to 1890 taught that the material world is a low emanation of the spiritual world; and that mankind struggles slowly upward through many reincarnations towards enlightenment, the spiritual One. The great spiritualist in those days was Madame Helena Petrovna Blavatsky; and among his reminiscences of this startling woman Yeats recorded the following:

'The most devout and learned of all her following said to me, "H. P. B. has just told me that there is another globe stuck on to this at the north pole, so that the earth has really a shape something like a dumbbell"' (*A: FY* 19). In the Society for Psychical Research, as in Irish peasant beliefs, Yeats found corroboration (sometimes less ludicrous than the present example) for the existence of an anti-world, an invisible complement to the earth, keener and greater than ours, where the dead could think with superhuman speed and sureness.

VI

Yeats thought that through the work of great poets – especially the Romantic poets – the Anima Mundi could also display some of its stock of images. He even wondered whether such great lyrics as Keats's 'Ode to a Nightingale' pre-existed in the Anima Mundi – whether Keats was nothing more than an accidental vessel through which the poem passed (*MAV* II, p. 356). And Yeats tried to sum up Shelley's career in a single sentence, a general coordination of the symbols that governed his work:

> A single vision would have come to him again and again, a vision of a boat drifting down a broad river between high hills where there were caves and towers, and following the light of one Star; and that voices would have told him how there is for every man some one scene, some one adventure, some one picture that is the image of his secret life, for wisdom first speaks in images ... (*EI*, pp. 94–95).

Every poet, it seems, enjoys a limited access to the Anima Mundi – only a certain range of meaningful images is open to him. The images granted to Yeats constituted a somewhat different assortment: in 1921 Yeats enumerated his 'main symbols' to the designer of his book covers: 'Sun and Moon (in all phases), Tower, Mask, Tree (Tree with Mask hanging on the trunk)' (*TSMC*, p. 38); to that list one might add shell, rose, sword, bird of gold. But every poet uses elements from the stock of images legible in the work of previous poets. The building-stuff for constructing a more significant, more intense world has been available from the beginning of time. As Yeats wrote, 'I am very religious, and deprived by Huxley and Tyndall [Darwinian rationalists and atheists], whom I detested, of the simple-minded religion of my childhood, I had made a new religion, almost an infallible church of poetic tradition' (*A: FY* 2).

And yet, despite Yeats's unworldliness, his concentration on art, it is a mistake to think of Yeats as an aesthete. No poet believed less in art-for-art's sake; far from exalting style, he exalted the subject matter of art: 'I was so angry with the indifference to subject, which was the commonplace of all [recent] art criticism ... that I could at times see nothing else but subject' (*A: FY* 17). In his great essay on Cavalcanti, Pound stated an opinion about art, an opinion with which Yeats agreed:

> The best Egyptian sculpture is magnificent plastic; but its force comes from a non-plastic idea, i.e. the god is inside the statue.
>
> I am not considering the merits of the matter, much less those merits as seen by a modern aesthetic purist. I am using historic method. The god is inside the stone ... (*Literary Essays*, p. 152).

What matters is not the art but the god embodied in the art. In the story 'Rosa Alchemica' (1896), Yeats's narrator is a caricature of the modern aesthetic purist – he dwells in a sealed room where he gluts his senses on Renaissance paintings and sculpture, incense, gorgeous books, peacock tapestries:

> I had gathered about me all gods because I believed in none, and experienced every pleasure because I gave myself to none, but held myself apart, individual, indissoluble, a mirror of polished steel. (*M*, p. 268)

But at last his friend Michael Robartes induces him to visionary trance: the peacocks on the tapestries start to turn three-dimensional, and (as in Tennyson's 'The Lady of Shalott') the mind's disengagement starts to falter – the mirror cracks:

> I heard a voice over my head cry, 'The mirror is broken in two pieces' ... and a more distant voice cry with an exultant cry, 'The mirror is broken into numberless pieces'. (*M*, p. 276)

Here is another assault on the mirror, on the passive model of mental action. Art is not an end but a means – a means for images, images more real than we ourselves, to swell and grow heavy, to enter human experience.

Yeats was, in a sense, a professional fabricator of idols. He once read in a pamphlet on Japanese art of

> an animal painter so remarkable that horses he had painted upon a temple wall had slipped down after dark and trampled the neighbours' fields of rice. Somebody had come into the temple in the early morning, had been startled by a shower of water drops, had looked up and seen painted horses still wet from the dew-covered fields, but now 'trembling into stillness'. (*A: FY* 20; compare *JSD*, p. 115)

This was the sort of art that Yeats envied – an art that realizes images of extreme potency. In the course of 'Rosa Alchemica' the pagan gods step out of the petals of a mosaic rose and begin to dance with the human celebrants of a ritual; and Yeats hoped that the readers of his poems would feel the shudder of a god's physical presence. Zeus's rape of Leda – the subject of one of Yeats's greatest poems – is a model for reader-response. His poems are properly read as such conjurings of hyperrealities. Furthermore, to make an idol is to magnify the strength of the god idolized: as Yeats wrote in 1929, in a diary entry that seems almost a commentary on Pound's Cavalcanti essay, 'I recall a passage in some Hermetic writer on the increased power that a God feels on getting into a statue' (Ellmann, *IY*, p. 240). The poet and the sculptor assist godhead by providing a body for it.

VII

At the beginning of Yeats's career, the gods only occasionally make a personal appearance; most of the divinity is embodied in landscapes, not in human figures. The development of Yeats's landscapes can be illustrated with the following passages:

> As when upon her cloud-o'er-muffled steep
> Oenone saw the fires of Troia leap,
> And laugh'd, so, so along the bubbling rills
> In lemon-tinted lines, so blaze the daffodils.
> (*The Island of Statues* I i)

> See how the sacred old flamingoes come,
> Painting with shadow all the marble steps:
> Aged and wise, they seek their wonted perches
> Within the temple, devious walking, made
> To wander by their melancholy minds.
> ('Anashuya and Vijaya')

Do you not hear me calling, white deer with no horns?
I have been changed to a hound with one red ear;
I have been in the Path of Stones and the Wood of Thorns,
For somebody hid hatred and hope and desire and fear
Under my feet that they follow you night and day.
('He mourns for the Change ...')

I know where a dim moon drifts, where the Danaan kind
Wind and unwind their dances when the light grows cool
On the island lawns, their feet where the pale foam gleams.
No boughs have withered because of the wintry wind;
The boughs have withered because I have told them my dreams.
('The Withering of the Boughs')

In the first example (from a juvenile poem published in 1885, when Yeats was twenty) the landscape is decorous and harmless – though even here a certain mythological exuberance is latent in it. The word *daffodil* is disconcerting in a poem by Yeats, not only because it is a trademark registered to William Wordsworth, but also because Yeats almost never used the names of flowers (other than the rose) in his poetry; botanical accuracy tends towards the world we all know, whereas Yeats usually wrote of a world few of us know. A friend of Yeats's who liked to garden remarked 'how strongly Yeats disliked flowers, almost an active obsession ... it does in my opinion dim most poems of his concerned with Nature' (*DWL*, p. 173). In the second example, written not long after the first, the poet deliberately moves to the exotic and flamboyant, the moody and pensive; such a distant landscape has no pedestrian detail to distract from the emotion it reifies.

In the third example, from 1897, the landscape is simply a stylization of emotions – there is little sense of a specific locale, for the path, the wood, are only the balsa stage-props of a lyrical cry. We are not in Ireland, or Arcadia, or India, but in a wash of moods. Through the first part of his career, Yeats's landscapes grow increasingly weightless; they are evacuated into significance. In the fourth example, from 1900, the scene contains scarcely more than a wisp of moonshine; and the poet suggests, disturbingly, that the dream-world's strengthening is a direct function of the real world's weakening. In 'Village Ghosts' there is a ghost that begins 'to swell larger and larger' as the spectator feels 'his own strength ebbing away, as though it were sucked out of him' (*M*, p. 16); and similarly the antiworlds in Yeats's poems seem to thrive by making the natural world wither. The other globe, on top of the north pole, seems to drain all the air from our globe, making it collapse like a balloon.

VIII

The young Yeats thought that modern art had triumphed by a steady emptying of its contents. He believed that Wordsworth, Tennyson, Browning had all erred by overinclusion – by trying to absorb into their work science, politics, philosophy, ethics, until their poems became hopelessly heavy, distended (*UP* II, p. 39). By contrast, Yeats announced (in 1898, in 'The Autumn of the Body') that he belonged to a movement, including D. G. Rossetti and Mallarmé, that worked towards disembodiment and purity:

> Man has wooed and won the world, and has fallen weary ... with a weariness that will not end until the last autumn, when the stars shall be blown away like withered leaves. He grew weary when he said, 'These things that I touch and see and hear are alone real', for he saw them without illusion at last, and found them but air and dust and moisture.... The arts are, I believe, about to take upon their shoulders the burdens that have fallen from the shoulders of priests, and to lead us back upon our journey by filling our thoughts with the essences of things, and not with things. (*EI*, pp. 192–93).

Yeats's faint but highly saturated landscapes present such essences, such distillations of reality. As the sensuous world fumes away, another, keener world shivers into being.

But after the turn of the century, a countermovement begins to be felt in Yeats's work. Instead of cultivating disembodiment, Yeats argued in favour of a new physicalness, a new solidity of gesture. In a letter of 1903, he wrote:

> I am no longer in much sympathy with an essay like 'The Autumn of the Body' ... The close of the last century was full of a strange desire to get out of form, to get to some kind of disembodied beauty, and now it seems to me the contrary impulse has come. I feel about me and in me an impulse to create form, to carry the realization of beauty as far as possible. (*L*, p. 402)

And the next day, he restated this:

> I have always felt that the soul has two movements primarily: one to transcend forms, and the other to create forms.... I think I have to some extent got weary of that wild God Dionysus, and I am hoping that the Far-Darter [Apollo, the god of forms] will come in his place. (*L*, p. 403)

Ecstasy is no longer enough; its secret cause must materialize, must present itself in forms apprehensible to the senses.

When Yeats wrote these letters, he was helping to found the Abbey Theatre; and, for the next seven years (until 1910), most of his artistic energies went into play-writing and theatre-management, not poetry-writing. This work in drama may have hastened his development towards a more sensuous, more immediate sort of art. His imagination increasingly turned to the human body as it sought an ideal image. In 1906 he claimed that the body was a better organ for thinking than the brain:

> Those learned men ... have followed some abstract reverie, which stirs the brain only and needs that only, and have therefore stood before the looking-glass without pleasure and never known those thoughts that shape the lines of the body for beauty or animation ... [No art] could move us at all, if our thought did not rush out to the edges of our flesh, and it is so with all good art, whether the Victory of Samothrace which reminds the soles of our feet of swiftness, or the *Odyssey* that would send us out under the salt wind ... (*EI*, p. 292)

Yeats came to make his own art similarly kinesthetic, carnal; and he came to esteem its bodily potency more than its beauty. Far from banishing the sensations of the flesh, his later work seems to appeal to the whole inner whorl of the body's nerves:

> O body swayed to music, O brightening glance,
> How can we know the dancer from the dance?
> ('Among School Children')

> But Love has pitched his mansion in
> The place of excrement ...
> ('Crazy Jane talks with the Bishop')

lad and lass,
Nerve touching nerve upon that happy ground,
Are bobbins where all time is bound and wound.
(*The King of the Great Clock Tower*)

He that sings a lasting song
Thinks in a marrow-bone ...
('A Prayer for Old Age')

Yeats's later poetry strives for the fullest possible representation of physical experience, as if words could be the magical equivalent of a human body.

Yeats was not the only modern writer who tried to heighten the corporality of his work. Indeed certain poets in the later nineteenth century had already laboured to make art more vibrant, more physically stimulating. The passage about the Thinking of the Body, cited above, is almost a paraphrase of Oscar Wilde's *De Profundis* (1897, published 1905):

> I discern great sanity in the [ancient] Greek attitude. They never chattered about sunsets ... But they saw that the sea was for the swimmer, and the sand for the feet of the runner.... We have forgotten ... that the Earth is mother to us all. As a consequence our Art is of the Moon and plays with shadows, while Greek art is of the Sun and deals directly with things. (*Complete Works*, ed. Holland, p. 954)

Many of Yeats's later contemporaries also contributed to the literature of the body – D. H. Lawrence and James Joyce, with the exact descriptions of engorged tissue and intestinal upheavals. Even T. S. Eliot, often fastidious about bodily functions, commended poets whose 'words have often a network of tentacular roots reaching down to the deepest terrors and desires' (*Selected Essays*, p. 135); and further wrote that a poet is not looking deep enough if he obeys the old advice 'to look into our hearts and write': 'Racine or Donne looked into a good deal more than the heart. One must look into the cerebral cortex, the nervous system, and the digestive tracts' (p. 250). And yet Yeats's interest in the body differs from Joyce's and Eliot's, and perhaps from Lawrence's, in that every body is an embodiment of something – a vehicle chosen by a spirit for external expression.

IX

This fascination with the body required a poetry in which human presences were more vivid, less dispersed, than in his early work. In a letter to his father (5 August 1913), Yeats suggested the change in his poetry from landscape-architecture to personal drama:

> All our art is but the putting our faith ... into words or forms and our faith is in ecstasy. Of recent years instead of 'vision', meaning by vision the intense realization of a state of ecstatic emotion symbolized in a definite imagined region, I have tried for more self portraiture. (*L*, p. 583)

As Yeats grew older, he wanted to realize divinity less in haunted and moody landscapes than in himself – and in a few other select human images.

Yeats's poetry has an unusually restricted cast of characters. It is rich in dead people: dead poets (Lionel Johnson, Ernest Dowson, John Synge), dead relatives (George and Alfred Pollexfen), dead friends (Robert Gregory and MacGregor Mathers), dead warriors (those executed in the 1916 Easter Rebellion), and beautiful dead women (Florence Farr, Eva Gore-Booth, and Con Markiewicz) – as if in death the soul became fit for refashioning with a verbal body.

Among the living, there are three people who predominate in Yeats's poetry: Maud Gonne, Iseult Gonne, and Georgie Hyde-Lees. Maud Gonne (1866–1953) was the great love of Yeats's life. She was nearly six feet tall, imperial in demeanour, and by many accounts the most beautiful woman in Ireland. He met her in 1889, when she called at his house, ostensibly to meet his father; it was the season of apple-blossoms; she walked (Yeats wrote) like a goddess. He never quite recovered. There is a frequent motif in Yeats's work, of a man who is touched by a faery queen and whose life is forever blighted – as in the *Stories of Red Hanrahan* and 'The Queen and the Fool'. And Yeats regarded himself as a man whose emotional life was half-crippled by his obsession with Maud Gonne:

> A romantic, when romanticism was in its final extravagance, I thought one woman, whether wife, mistress, or incitement to platonic love, enough for a life-time: a Parsifal, Tristram, Don Quixote, without the intellectual prepossessions that gave them solidity. (*A: DP* 14)

But if his life was deformed by his love for her, his art was much quickened – though he did not like to hear her say that posterity would be grateful to her for refusing him, because he wrote so many fine poems about it.

Maud Gonne was attracted to radical politics; she was, for example, part of a scheme to blow up British troops on boats bound for South Africa during the Boer War. According to Yeats's description, she seemed physically aroused by violence: when glass was being everywhere shattered during street rioting in Dublin, 'Maud Gonne has a look of exultation as she walks with her laughing head thrown back' (*A: SB* 5). Yeats, though alarmed by her bloodthirsty politics, contrived to implicate himself in her emotional life in odd ways. She was interested in Yeats's occultism, and studied with him; Yeats evoked for her a 'past personality', a vision of a life in which she had been an Egyptian priestess (*Mem*, p. 49). In the mid-1890s, Maud Gonne became the lover of a French anarchist editor, Lucien Millevoye; she bore him a child, who died in infancy; and she decided to assist the baby's reincarnation by sleeping with Millevoye in the vault under the dead child's grave (*Mem*, p. 133).

In this fashion was Iseult Gonne (1895–1954) conceived. Yeats continued his hopeless wooing of Maud Gonne; in 1898 she told him that, though they could never be physically married, she had had a dream in which 'a great spirit' put her hand into Yeats's and married them; and she kissed him on the lips – for the first time – and confessed to him her sordid relations with Millevoye. Then they had a remarkable double vision:

> She thought herself a great stone statue through which passed flame, and I felt myself becoming flame and mounting up through and looking out of the eyes of a great stone Minerva. Were the beings which stand behind human life trying to unite us, or had we brought it by our own dreams? (*Mem*, p. 134)

Yeats always considered Maud Gonne a kind of complement to himself:

> My outer nature was passive – but for her I should never perhaps have left my desk – but I knew my spiritual nature was passionate, even violent. In her all this was reversed, for it was her spirit only that was gentle and passive ... (*Mem*, p. 124)

The double vision of statue and flame seemed to embody their complementariness, their interdependence – as if together they added up to a single, animate, monumental thing.

When, in 1903, Yeats heard the news that Maud Gonne had married a soldier, John MacBride – he described the report as a blast of lightning – he felt that she had betrayed her mystical marriage of 1897. She and MacBride soon quarrelled, and separated in 1905. MacBride in 1916 was executed by the British for his part in the Easter Rebellion – and Maud Gonne was again free to marry. Once again Yeats pestered her with proposals; once again she refused; and then Yeats proposed to Iseult Gonne. To Yeats, this playful, impetuous girl represented youth and spontaneity – he often pictured her by the sea, singing or dancing, with the wind blowing in her hair. In 1915, at the age of twenty, Iseult had suggested to Yeats that they marry – Yeats was a frequent guest of her mother's at their home in Normandy; but at the age of twenty-two she was unwilling to marry the fifty-two-year-old poet. Despairing, Yeats asked another attractive woman, Georgie Hyde-Lees (1892–1968) – little older than Iseult Gonne – to marry him; and she said yes.

Yeats's black mood did not immediately lift. He worried that, by marrying, he was merely involving yet another person in the squalor of his emotional life. As he wrote in a letter to Lady Gregory on 29 October 1917, a few days after his marriage:

> Two days ago I was in great gloom, (of which I hope, and believe, George knew nothing). I was saying to myself 'I have betrayed three people;' then I thought 'I have lived through all this before'. Then George spoke of the sensation of having lived through something before (she knew nothing of my thought). Then she said she felt that something was to be written through her. She got a piece of paper, and talking to me all the while so that her thoughts would not affect what she wrote, wrote these words (which she did not understand) 'with the bird' (Iseult) 'all is well at heart ...' (*L*, p. 633)

But Mrs Yeats's automatic writing soon started to offer much, much more than words of consolation from the great beyond about Yeats's treatment of Iseult Gonne. Thereafter Mrs Yeats found – to her own surprise – that she could easily enter a mediumistic state, and write or speak messages from dead or unborn spirits. Over the next few years she filled thousands of pages with automatic writing – often in response to questions from Yeats – and gave the poet the rudiments of the system elaborated in *A Vision* (1925): a general system for explaining history, personality, and the progress of the soul after death. But the first purpose of the automatic writing was to elucidate Yeats's personal relations with Maud Gonne, Iseult Gonne, and his wife.

According to one of Mrs Yeats's favourite Controls, Thomas of Dorlowicz, Yeats and his 'three birds' (the three woman) formed a kind of tetrad: Yeats was Heroic, Iseult Good, Maud Beautiful, George True; Yeats represented the Fall (the loss of unity of being), Iseult the Heart, Maud the Head, George the Loins; Yeats was Instinct, Iseult Desire, Maud Intellect, George Emotion; Yeats's element was Earth, Iseult's Water, Maud's Air, George's Fire – and so on (*MAV* I, pp. 149–50). William Blake – an edition of whose poetry Yeats published in 1893 – conceived the Fall of Man as the division of a single giant, Albion (the whole human race), into four Zoas, representing the various faculties of the soul, bickering, impeding one another, working fractiously towards reunion. Similarly, it seems that Yeats and his wife, Iseult and Maud Gonne, together constituted a single complete human identity. Yeats believed that, for centuries, he and these women had known one another, sometimes as 'brother and sister' (*Mem*, p. 46), sometimes in sexual relations, twisting, writhing through a thousand incarnations, exploring every conceivable permutation of relationship:

> We all to some extent meet again and again the same people and certainly in some cases form a kind of family of two or three or more persons who come together life after life until all passionate relations are exhausted, the child of one life the husband, wife, brother or sister of the next. (*AV*, p. 237)

Thus Yeats's poems about Iseult and Maud Gonne and his wife are simply a form of extended self-inquiry. The women are not autonomous beings, but portions of that fourfold being in which Yeats himself is comprised.

In addition to these three, Yeats celebrated other living women in his verse. In 1896 Olivia Shakespear, a gentle and attractive married woman, had become Yeats's first lover; in 1914 her daughter Dorothy married Ezra Pound. Yeats's liaison with her lasted only a year, but they were to remain lifelong friends; he explained their unsuitability as lovers as follows:

> she was too near my soul, too salutary and wholesome to my inmost being. All our lives long, as da Vinci says, we long ... for our destruction, and how, when we meet [it] in the shape of a most fair woman, can we do less than leave all others for her? Do we not seek our dissolution upon her lips? (*Mem*, p. 88)

Olivia Shakespear was Yeats's like, but he craved his opposite, a more devastating relation.

Another vital presence in Yeats's poetry was an Irish noblewoman, Isabella Augusta Persse Gregory (1852–1932). A widow older than Yeats, deeply involved in the revival of Irish literature, a folklorist and playwright, she provided (beginning in 1897) a tranquil environment in which Yeats could work, could take refuge from the tumult of passion. At her home, Coole Park, County Galway, Yeats spent many a pleasant month; and he frequently turned to her for literary collaboration (such as the play *The Unicorn from the Stars*) and personal advice. After she died, in 1932, Yeats endured a period of creative sterility; he feared that the 'subconscious drama that was my imaginative life end[ed]' at Lady Gregory's death (*VP*, p. 855).

Imaginative life returned to the elderly Yeats, partly in the form of a number of younger women, some of whom were his lovers. In 1934 he underwent the Steinach rejuvenation operation, a kind of vasectomy supposed to restore sexual potency; and he began a period of sexual swagger and passionate poetical effusions. One such poem, 'The Three Bushes', was a collaborative effort between Yeats and Dorothy Wellesley (1889–1956) – Yeats wrote her a stirring letter about his revision of her ballad:

> Ah my dear how it added to my excitement when I re-made that poem of yours to know it was your poem. I re-made you and myself into a single being. We triumphed over each other ... (*DWL*, p. 82)

Afterwards Yeats added to 'The Three Bushes' sequence a lyric full of explicit phallic imagery, and mailed it to Dorothy Wellesley; in the same letter he wrote:

> My dear, my dear – when you crossed the room with that boyish movement, it was no man who looked at you, it was the woman in me. It seems that I can make a woman express herself as never before. I have looked out of her eyes. I have shared her desire. (*DWL*, p. 108)

And he soon wrote her another letter about Greek statues of hermaphrodites. Again, Yeats's imagination laboured to compound and confound, to merge the poet and the beloved into a single entity. When Yeats wrote of a woman, he wrote of his Muse, his own creative faculty, his anima, his female self.

X

One species of 'self portraiture' in Yeats's verse is the depiction of the carnal self, intricately involved with many women – the Wild Old Wicked Man, as Yeats called him in one late poem. But there is another kind of self-portraiture, harder and purer, eerie, sexless:

> Once out of nature I shall never take
> My bodily form from any natural thing,
> But such a form as Grecian goldsmiths make
> Of hammered gold and gold enamelling
> To keep a drowsy Emperor awake . . .
> ('Sailing to Byzantium')

Yeats, as man and as poet, was unusually afraid of incoherence, the sensation of being soft wax; and such images as the golden bird in this famous poem (written in 1926) offer an aesthetic refuge from the shapelessness of commonplace life. In 1906 Yeats described the evolution of his art as a turning-away from his ordinary self:

> I had set out on life with the thought of putting my very self into poetry . . . I thought of myself as something unmoving and silent living in the middle of my own mind and body . . . Then one day I understood quite suddenly, as the way is, that I was seeking something unchanging and unmixed and always outside myself, a Stone or an Elixir that was always out of reach, and that I myself was the fleeting thing that held out its hand. The more I tried to make my art deliberately beautiful, the more did I follow the opposite of myself . . . (*EI*, p. 271)

It is important to note that, for Yeats, Art is not self-expression – the self is too shifty, evanescent – but a search for impersonal beauty. By 1909 this feeling that the proper subject matter of art is the opposite of oneself developed into the doctrine of the Mask.

In the poem 'Ego Dominus Tuus' (1915) and the essay *Per Amica Silentia Lunae* (1917), Yeats expounded the belief that every man has an ideal counterpart, an intimate double, an anti-self in whom every trait is the opposite of his own. Poets, according to this doctrine, gain imaginative intensity through the struggle to realize in their poems a vision of this Mask. Thus the lecherous Dante laboured to create a 'Dante' of austere and unforgiving purity, the poet as we infer him from the poem. The irritable and intense William Morris elaborated a vision of peaceful bucolic indolence. The penniless Cockney Keats dreamed of unparalleled luxury and splendour. The reader of Yeats's work must try to suspend some of his Freudian convictions, such as the postulate that a man's fundamental self is the birth-self, the baby, an incoherent monster of appetite. To Yeats, the fundamental self is what a man strives to become, not what he originally is.

Yeats tried to define his own character according to this model:

> I know very little about myself and much less of that anti-self: probably the woman who cooks my dinner . . . knows more than I. It is perhaps because nature made me a gregarious man, going hither and thither looking for conversation, and ready to deny from fear or favour his dearest conviction, that I love proud and lonely things. (*A: FY* 18)

The random, restless, compromising Yeats was driven by fantasies of impossible solitude, integrity, focus. Little wonder, then, that he should present himself in his poems as a golden bird, or a statue of a triton. Often he wrote of the anti-self as a tutelary spirit, or even as a kind of god hovering just beyond the range of vision, 'that dazzling, unforeseen, wing-footed wanderer' (*M*, p. 332). To realize a vision of the anti-self is to evoke the private divinity that lies behind each fragmentary incarnation of self. The golden bird of 'Sailing to Byzantium' is the idol of Yeats's personal godhead, always tempting, always out of reach.

Several times Yeats recorded the sensation that he was petrifying, turning into an image. Yeats gathered many folk tales about surrogates – logs, leaves, heaps of wood-shavings arranged into human likeness – that the faeries left behind when they snatched people away. Such surrogates appear in Yeats's plays *The Land of Heart's Desire* (1894) and *The Only Jealousy of Emer* (1919); and once Yeats awoke from sleep to hear a voice, not his own voice, speaking through his lips: 'We make an image of him who sleeps, and it is not him who sleeps but it is like him who sleeps, and we call it Emmanuel' (*Mem*, p. 126; compare *M*, p. 366 and *AV*, p. 233). In his novel *The Speckled*

Bird, abandoned around 1902, Yeats ascribed this shiver of involuntary speech to the chief character, who feels his body becoming impersonal, magical, a kind of tomb-sculpture (*LTMSB*, pp. 69–70). To be the dummy of supernatural ventriloquists was perhaps Yeats's closest approximation to his Mask. He had almost become a savage idol, stark and hieratic, a block of wood crudely cut into human shape.

XI

Yeats's fullest participation in the world of images – the occult world, full of such outrageous entities as walking mummies, metal birds that scorn flesh, flames begotten of flame, the whole supernatural apparatus of such poems as 'Byzantium' – came through his wife's trances, her bouts of automatic writing and speech. The wisdom, the fund of images bestowed by the spiritual Controls, were systematized in *A Vision* (1925, revised 1937). Many a reader of Yeats's poetry is so gratified by the poems themselves, with their astonishing metrical energy, their teasing and wondrous images, that he feels no need to investigate the poet's private sources, the principles of correspondence that govern the movement from image to image. And yet some knowledge of that laboured and vexatious, but rewarding book, *A Vision*, may improve the reader's pleasure.

The fundamental principle is that of the double gyre (a word Yeats pronounced with a hard *g*). Imagine two interlocked spinning cones, the point of each screwing into the centre-point of the base of the other. Now imagine a cross-section of this contraption, oscillating slowly from one base to the other and back. A cinematic image of this cross-section would show two concentric circles (let one be black, the other white) expanding and contracting reciprocally. As the white circle grows larger, the black circle grows smaller, until the white circle reaches its maximum size, and the black circle dwindles to a point. Then the white circle starts to shrink, and the black circle starts to widen. As Yeats said of one of his diagrams, there are 'two pulsations, one expanding, one contracting. I can see them like jelly fish in clear water' (*AV*, p. 200).

The double gyre was a handy model for defining many different relationships. Yeats had long conceived of the spiritual reality as something 180 degrees out of phase from normal reality: the lambs of faeryland were born in November while ours were born in spring (according to *The Hour-Glass*); the boughs withered when we told them our dreams. The gyre of the spirit (faeryland, fantasy, art) expands as the gyre of commonplace life contracts. Throughout *A Vision* there chimes Yeats's favourite sentence of Heraclitus': gods and men are always 'Dying each other's life, living each other's death' (*AV*, pp. 68, 197, 275).

The double gyre could also be used to specify the dynamic of human personality. In western philosophy, most models of the psyche are dualistic – based on the conflict of two principles. In Freudian psychology, for example, the id (undifferentiated lust and greed) is hampered or channelled by the superego (conscience, internalized restriction of conduct). In Plato's *Phaedrus* – a text that was an inspiration for the whole of *A Vision* (*MAV* I, p. 10) – the Soul's chariot is pulled by two horses, a black horse hankering for earthly pleasure, snorting, difficult to control, and a white horse driving upwards towards divine ideals. Yeats's model is equally dualistic; and the two opposing principles that tug at us, vex us, almost tear us in two, he called the subjective (or *antithetical*), and the objective (or *primary*). Yeats's simplest formulation of the opposition is as follows: 'The *primary* is that which serves, the *antithetical* is that which creates' (*AV*, p. 85). Therefore the two basic drives of mankind are the urge to fantasize, to wish, to gratify wishes, and the urge to rest content in received reality. The balance between these competing urges describes the identity of each of us.

Yeats discovered 26 basic personality types, which he plotted on the calendar of the lunar month, 28 days long. Two days were missing because an absolutely subjective personality (symbolically, the full of the moon, the 15th night – Phase 15, in his technical term) was impossible to find on earth; we are all of us mixed, imperfect creatures. Similarly, an absolutely objective personality (the dark of the moon, Phase 1) was only a supernatural abstraction, never actually born. As the soul progressed from one incarnation to the next, it was usually reborn in the next Phase; so after 28 deaths and rebirths the soul returned to its starting-point on the Great Wheel of human personality. Each of us, therefore, has been everyone; I have been a farmer, a politician, a hero, a poet, a preacher, a pedant, as I have worked my way around the wheel.

The objective gyre is at its maximum at Phase 1; the subjective gyre at Phase 15. Highly subjective people (such as Keats at Phase 14, Blake at Phase 16, Yeats at Phase 17) live in a state of creative fury; while highly objective people (Queen Victoria at Phase 24, John

Calvin at Phase 25, cloddish farmers at Phase 2) submit themselves to external codes of behaviour, or to nature itself. All predominantly subjective people (Phases 9–21) are driven to create, to chase a vision of themselves as unlike as possible to their birth-selves: the *Mask*. The diameter of the Great Wheel conveniently shows the relation between *Will* (the Ego, the birth-self) and *Mask*: a man of Phase 17 discovers his *Mask* at Phase 3 (exactly half way around the Wheel), the Shepherd, a sophisticated poet's unattainable dream of rustic simplicity and ease. All predominantly objective people (Phases 23–7), on the other hand, must flee from the *Mask*, must cure themselves of dreams; they must love reality as it is, not as it might be. Here are found realistic artists (such as Rembrandt, Phase 23), who dote on ugliness. The task of an objective man is self-effacement; the task of a subjective man is self-enhancement. All this is explained more fully in the poem, 'The Phases of the Moon'.

In another part of *A Vision*, Yeats described how history is governed by a similar scheme. Subjective and objective eras alternate; and on the largest scale (periods of 2000 years) each era is inaugurated by the birth of a god. The Christian era has provided mankind with 2000 years in which the objective virtues were taught: obedience, pity, chastity, self-abnegation before an abstract and rigid God. But before the birth of Christ came a subjective age, Greek antiquity, which prized the opposing virtues: beauty, aristocracy, sexual prowess, heroic splendour of conduct. The Christian era was begun by a virgin birth; but the classical era was begun by a swan's rape of a girl (according to 'Leda and the Swan'); and the subjective age that will annihilate Christian virtue will come in AD 2000, when a rough beast slouches towards Bethlehem to be born (according to 'The Second Coming'). At the beginning of an era, the new force is intense but narrow; in AD 1, for example, the energy behind the whole Christian age is focused, brought to bear, on one small town in Palestine. By the end of an era, the original energy has realized itself completely, conquered the world; when the objective Christian gyre has expanded to its outermost bound, the whole world is Christian – but Christianity is lax and spent, a bore, and we await a new influx of strength. Every civilization achieves itself by diminishing the capital of fantasy and force that inspired it; as it becomes substantial, it becomes 'a spider smothered in its own web' (*Ex*, p. 403).

But the mathematics of Yeats's historical system is much complicated by the existence of gyres within gyres, wheels within wheels –

some periods of 1000 years, other periods of 500 years. Just as Ptolemy could describe any planetary motion by his unwieldy system of epicycles, so Yeats could account for any inconvenient deviations in history from circular perfection by appealing to some subsidiary system. He would have liked to name Charlemagne as the demigod initiating a subjective era beginning in AD 1000, but such finagling was difficult even for Yeats, since Charlemagne was crowned emperor on Christmas day, AD 800.

It is noteworthy that Yeats defines both human identity and human history with terms derived from literary criticism and art criticism. The terms *subjective* and *objective* seem to come from Browning's essay on Shelley (1852), which describes literary history as a cyclical pattern: heaves of creative energy from *subjective* artists (such as Shelley) overturn established concepts, seize the world's imagination, are particularized and elaborated by *objective* artists, finally decay into stock truths, until some new *subjective* visionary appears to refresh the world's image of itself. In the tradition of Shelley ('Poets are the unacknowledged legislators of the world') and Browning, Yeats believed the artistic faculties were fundamental to mankind. *A Vision* is an exposition of the rhythm of creativity, according to which man makes, accepts, and unmakes the world.

Yeats's gyres can, then, be seen as a representation of nineteenth-century ideas about historical surges of creativity – Hallam's and Pater's as well as Browning's. But behind Yeats's system there also lies the Vorticism of Ezra Pound. Pound argued in 1914 that the nucleus of every creative act was what he called a vortex:

> The image is the poet's pigment ... The image is not an idea. It is a radiant node or cluster; it is what I can, and must perforce, call a VORTEX, from which, and through which, and into which, ideas are constantly rushing. In decency one can only call it a VORTEX. (*Ezra Pound and the Visual Arts*, pp. 203–7)

Yeats was equally excited by the notion that amazing energies, at once artistic and sexual, could be whirled into tight focus, brought to bear on one small spot. Yeats's poetry continually strives to embody the processes through which the imagination receives images, as if a poem could be a funnel delivering symbols from the Anima Mundi. Sometimes Yeats even tried to make his poems literal concretions of the gyres – as in 'A Dialogue of Self and Soul', where the *antithetical* gains strength in exact measure as the *primary* grows feeble. It might even be said that Yeats managed to establish his household inside a gyre, for (as he shows in 'Blood and the Moon') the tower where he lived, Thoor Ballylee, had a winding staircase easy to see as a reification of the spiral motion that governs all things. Yeats wished to facilitate the transit of images to him, by all means available from philosophy, poetry, and domestic architecture.

XII

Yeats enjoyed much respect from his contemporaries; but he also suffered much derision. It is easy to laugh at a man so superstitious that he once cut a piece out of his fur coat, rather than disturb a sleeping cat; so absent-minded that he once started to eat his own flowing hair when he twirled it onto a spaghetti-fork; so peculiar that he once appeared at a public gathering with thick woollen socks on his hands. *A Vision* is in some ways a fatuous book, but it is not negligible. If Yeats had lived to read *Of Grammatology*, by Jacques Derrida (the philosopher of deconstructionism), he would have been delighted to find the ultimate expression of objectivity, exactly appropriate for gyre's end: for Derrida drains human personality from every literary act, reduces all texts to anonymous expressions of culture. If Yeats was right, the year 2000 will bring a new self-assertion, to counteract this extreme self-surrender.

Yeats's prophecies have been partly vindicated in other ways as well. In an interview he once said:

> Technically we are in a state corresponding to the time of Dryden . . . The position of the young poet to-day is not unlike that of the young Swift in the library of Sir William Temple. At that time, they were moving away from the Elizabethans and on towards Pope. To-day, we are moving away from the Victorians and on towards the modern equivalent of Pope. We are developing a poetry of statement as against the old metaphor. The poetry of to-morrow will be finely articulated fact. T. S. Eliot fascinates us all because he is further on towards this consummation than any other writer. (Mikhail, *IR* II, p. 200)

The comparison of Eliot with Pope is intriguing, all the more so because Yeats could not have known that Eliot deleted from *The Waste Land* a long Popean pastiche in heroic couplets. And Yeats probably did not know the poetry of William Carlos Williams, who seriously began the attack on metaphor that Yeats described. How many poems written after Yeats's death could properly be described as 'finely [or clumsily] articulated fact'? Because most modern poets cannot accept the legitimacy of systems of correspondence – whether the Medieval Great Chain of Being, or *A Vision* – metaphor has become pallid, or tentative, or simply bewildered. Yeats's silliness ('You were silly like us', Auden wrote in his elegy on Yeats) was the source of much of his strength. 'We have come to give you metaphors for poetry', said the Communicators who spoke through Mrs Yeats (*AV*, p. 8); and metaphors he received. No poet of recent centuries received a greater profusion.

Yeats conceived his work as an end, not a beginning: 'We were the last romantics', he announced to Lady Gregory ('Coole and Ballylee, 1931'). And in many ways Yeats's poetry has seemed to be an end. Few poets followed his example, either in theme or style. The great poets of the next generation regarded him suspiciously. Ezra Pound, who spent the winters of 1913–16 in Yeats's company, attempted to reform Yeats into a Modernist, as if Yeats were Tradition personified, susceptible to modification according to a new aesthetic. Though Pound praised much of Yeats's work, he turned increasingly hostile, dismissing *The King of the Great Clock Tower* with the single word 'Putrid' (*VPl*, p. 1310). And although the Cantos contain a few attractive reminiscences of Yeats – 'Sligo in heaven murmured uncle William / when the mist finally settled down on Tigullio' (77/473) – some of the later Cantos can be seen as a deliberate undoing of Yeats's creative work. For example, Canto XCVI (1959) quotes genuine documents of Justinian's Constantinople ('Mr Yeats called it Byzantium', 96/661), setting forth the penalties for selling wine at false measure, or for building a wall that falls down – as if Pound were showing that civic magnificence could be achieved honestly through a good law code, instead of existing precariously in the dreams of an ignorant poet.

Eliot and Auden were equally perplexed in their relation to Yeats. Eliot gave a gracious lecture shortly after Yeats's death, full of praise for Yeats's impersonal (that is, Eliot-like) virtues. But in 'Little Gidding' II (1942), a caricature of Yeats appears as an anguished ghost, giving advice (based partly on 'The Tower' I, 'Swift's Epitaph', and 'Vacillation' V) of the sort that people least like to hear:

> Let me disclose the gifts reserved for age
>   To set a crown upon your lifetime's effort.
>   First, the cold friction of expiring sense
> Without enchantment, offering no promise
>   But bitter tastelessness of shadow fruit
>   As body and soul begin to fall asunder.
> Second, the conscious impotence of rage
>   At human folly, and the laceration
>   Of laughter at what ceases to amuse.
> And last, the rending pain of re-enactment
>   Of all that you have done, and been; the shame
>   Of motives late revealed . . .
> (*Collected Poems, 1909–62*, p. 204)

In early drafts Eliot's anonymous ghost referred specifically to Yeats's political situation as well. Auden, too, evidently regarded Yeats as a monster looming behind his work. His elegy on Yeats, while not exactly warm, presents Yeats as a great man; but in a strange essay published in the year of Yeats's death, 'The Public v. the Late Mr. William Butler Yeats', Auden's 'Public Prosecutor' says, 'In 1900 he believed in fairies; that was bad enough; but in 1930 we are confronted with the pitiful, the deplorable spectacle of a grown man occupied with the mumbo-jumbo of magic and the nonsense of India' (*The English Auden*, p. 391); and even asserts that no one could remember a line of Yeats's poems. And the protagonist of Auden's and Kallman's libretto to Hans Werner Henze's *Elegy for Young Lovers* (1961) is a wicked poet, clearly half-modelled on Yeats, who visits séances in order to be inspired, takes hormones to rejuvenate himself – and at last provokes the death of his mistress and her new companion in order to stimulate interesting aesthetic emotions. The poets who followed Yeats tried first to demote him to an inane ghost, then to exorcize him. Only now perhaps can Yeats's influence be salutary once again; Seamus Heaney's mind echoes and reechoes with Yeatsian cadences, yet he does not seem to fear the encroachment of the dead master.

XIII

If, as Yeats said of Shelley, 'there is for every man some one scene, some one adventure, some one picture that is the image of his secret life, for wisdom first speaks in images' (*EI*, p. 95) – what is Yeats's one scene, one adventure? Perhaps it is this: a frustrated man seeks escape from an inadequate world – escape from nature, escape from society, escape from history, escape from himself; in pursuit of the Eternal Beauty that lies beyond, he immerses himself in dreams of supersensual splendour; he dwells in an austere and symbolical tower and tries to transmute himself to metal or stone, in order to assume a permanence equal to that of the beauty he seeks; but in the end (as in 'The Circus Animals' Desertion') he finds that what he has painfully sought, what he has painstakingly constructed, is nothing but an image of his own simple perishing face.

A NOTE ON THE TEXT

Editing is a task that requires all resources of attention and imagination. This is especially true when an author has poor handwriting, and Yeats's handwriting resembles a mouse's electrocardiogram. But the exasperations have been much eased by two books: *The Variorum Edition of the Poems of W. B. Yeats*; and Richard J. Finneran's *Editing Yeats's Poems*. The latter book justifies the decisions made in Finneran's *The Poems of W. B. Yeats: A New Edition*.

Finneran's scholarship is a great contribution to the study of Yeats. He has cogently demonstrated that the soundest basis for Yeats's texts (for poems up to *The Winding Stair and Other Poems*) is *The Collected Poems of W. B. Yeats* (London, 1933) – and not Yeats's earlier construction (1931) of his canon for the 'Edition de Luxe' (used as the basis for the Variorum Edition). And he has adduced unpublished correspondence with publishers, corrected typescripts, and corrected page-proofs, some of which is extremely helpful in guessing at Yeats's intentions for poems written near the end of his life. My constructions of Yeats's poems of 1938–39 differ from Finneran's in some important details; but I am grateful for his clear and intelligent exposition of the textual problems.

I part company from Finneran in two ways. First, he is more respectful of Yeats's punctuation than I. He supposes (as did Curtis Bradford) that Yeats's punctuation was rhetorical rather than grammatical, an imaginative attempt to notate breath-pauses, stresses, and so forth; and that the bizarre punctuation in some of Yeats's later poems is due to the influence of experimental modernists such as T. S. Eliot and Laura Riding (*EYP*, p. 52). I suppose that Yeats was too ignorant of punctuation to make his deviations from standard practice significant. Although Yeats surely wished to make his canon a text worthy of reverence, he conceived poetry as an experience of the ear, not of the eye. He could not spell even simple English words; he went to his grave using such forms as *intreage* and *proffesrship*. His eyesight was so poor that he gave up fiction-writing because the proof-reading was too strenuous. Finally, Yeats himself admitted, 'I do not understand stops. I write my work so completely for the ear that I feel helpless when I have to measure pauses by stops and commas' (*L*, p. 598). Like Yeats, I prefer light punctuation. But where the lack of 'stops and commas' seemed clumsy, I have made small changes. Often these changes were identical to those introduced by Thomas Mark and by Mrs Yeats, the first comprehensive editors of Yeats's poems. An inattentive, half-blind, possibly dyslexic poet must rely on his editors, and in fact Yeats was often happy to do so. Yeats had a strong sense of decorum and propriety; he wanted his poems to look finished, indeed burnished, but he could not fulfil this wish without aid.

Among Yeats's punctuational quirks were these: he rarely used hyphens; he did not like to enclose vocatives in commas; and he often neglected to put commas before quotations, or to capitalize the first word in a quotation. As to quotations, I have usually changed the texts to follow standard practice. As to vocatives, I have usually followed Yeats's usage, except where a misreading was likely (as in the first line of 'A Drunken Man's Praise of Sobriety'). As to hyphens, I have added them in the cases of compound adjectives. In a famous line in 'Among School Children' (l. 61), Yeats called a tree a 'great rooted blossomer'. Did Yeats then mean that the tree was great, and not its roots? This seems unlikely; in 'Crazy Jane on the Mountain' Yeats used the term 'Great bladdered Emer', in which it is certain that *great* modifies *bladdered*; and he also wrote of 'Deep-rooted things' ('The Municipal Gallery Re-visited' V 5).

In order to punctuate Yeats's texts, I believe, one must first try to divine the purpose that punctuation must serve. I will mention two difficult cases. The first is the transition between stanzas V and VI of 'The Municipal Gallery Re-visited', which Yeats left as follows (and which Finneran doggedly retains):

> And now that end has come I have not wept;
> No fox can foul the lair the badger swept.
>
> VI
>
> (An image out of Spenser and the common tongue)
> John Synge, I and Augusta Gregory thought . . .

I take it that Yeats wanted the punctuation to accomplish three goals: to close stanza V firmly (Yeats believed in 'complete coincidence between period and stanza' [*EI*, p. 522]); to demote the first line of stanza VI to the status of an aside or a footnote; and to connect the first line of stanza VI to stanza V, since the 'image out of Spenser and the common tongue' refers to fox and badger. Yeats succeeded in the first two goals, but failed at the third; in the Variorum text, Mark and Mrs Yeats, by putting a dash after 'swept' and a full stop after the end-parenthesis, accomplished the second and third but failed at the first. I have hoped, by leaving Yeats's punctuation, but inserting a full stop inside the end-parenthesis, to accomplish all three – this is the same solution used in *Last Poems and Plays* (1940).

There are passages, however, in which Yeats asked punctuation to do more than punctuation can:

> That is no country for old men. The young
> In one another's arms, birds in the trees,
> – Those dying generations – at their song ...
> ('Sailing to Byzantium' I 1–3)

Here 'generations' is in apposition to 'The young' and to 'birds' (and to other entities later in the stanza); but only the birds, and not the young lovers, are 'at their song'. The punctuation must therefore show the strong connectedness of 'birds in the trees at their song'; but it must sufficiently disrupt that clause to allow the 'dying generations' to point backwards to 'The young'. The authoritative punctuation does not accomplish this; but I have been unable to contrive any punctuation that could.

My second disagreement with Finneran lies in the matter of obedience to authority. Sometimes he has poorly chosen which authority to obey: for example, he prints 'Brown Penny' (1910) from a revised version (circa 1937) intended for a never-realized edition of Yeats's poems; but the revised version (reprinted in the notes to this edition) seems tentative, repetitious, and ill-considered, and I doubt that Yeats would have allowed its printing – he frequently rejected experimental revisions. Similarly, Finneran prints 'John Kinsella's Lament for Mrs. Mary Moore' from a smoothed version Yeats intended for singing aloud.

Sometimes the authority is good, but the result of obedience is disappointing. No editor wants to be a Tottel, rewriting great poetry to make it please a conventional taste. But sometimes the most reputable of Yeats's texts seem to be impossible to construe. I am unable, for example, to accept that l. 19 of 'Hound Voice' is 'That stumbling to the kill beside the shore':

> Some day we shall get up before the dawn
> And find our ancient hounds before the door,
> And wide awake know that the hunt is on;
> Stumbling upon the blood-dark track once more,
> That stumbling to the kill beside the shore;
> Then cleaning out and bandaging of wounds,
> And chants of victory amid the encircling hounds.

This text has a fine pedigree, but it must be garbled; if *That* is changed to *Then* (as Mark and Mrs Yeats proposed), it is grammatical.

Sometimes every modern text is mistaken. 'The Gift of Harun Al-Rashid', l. 28, reads, according to Mark and Finneran alike: 'As air under a wing, can give birds' wit.' However, in an early magazine printing, the apostrophe is absent. The apostrophe ought to be absent; *birds* must be dative, not genitive; in fact in an early draft this line read, 'Even as the air has given a bird wits' (Stallworthy, *BL*, p. 68), where the genitive construction is impossible.

It is possible that there are many cases in which early printings are preferable to the important collected editions over which Yeats's eyes must have glazed again and again. If the last word in 'Among School Children' I 4 were *histories* (as a magazine had it) instead of *history*, the rhyme would be improved. A similar improvement in rhyme would result (though here there is no sanction from an early printing, only from a printing after Yeats's death) if *stairs* were changed to *stair* in 'The Tower' II 67. I have made neither emendation; I have not been bold; but I can see room for a bolder editor to tackle these texts. My intention has been to take a middle course, to be neither lord over the text nor slave to it.

I must also describe the order of the poems here. Harold Macmillan persuaded Yeats to separate his poetry into two divisions (Lyrical; and Narrative and Dramatic), so that an edition intended for the popular market did not begin with a forbiddingly long poem, *The Wanderings of Oisin* (*EYP*, p. 14). The second section consisted of six poems: *The Wanderings of Oisin*; *The Old Age of Queen Maeve*; *Baile and Aillinn*; *The Shadowy Waters*; 'The Two Kings'; and 'The Gift of Harun Al-Rashid'. This division can in part be justified: the Narrative and Dramatic section constitutes (except for the final poem) a kind of short epic centred around the love-god Aengus and the catastrophes that over-great love wreaks on human life. But the division is still arbitrary – why should 'The Two Kings' be severed from *Responsibilities*, when the almost-as-long 'The Grey Rock' (thematically related to 'The Two Kings') remains? The advantages of a roughly chronological sequence, carefully arranged by Yeats, are many. And few browsers in bookstores are now likely to pick up a volume of Yeats's poetry, then replace it in disgust at the discovery of a long poem on the first page.

Another editorial difficulty concerns Yeats's excisions of certain poems from his canon. Should these poems simply be omitted (in the manner of the *Collected Poems*), or printed in an appendix (in the manner of the Variorum Edition and Finneran's)? One can argue for the former by citing a quatrain that Yeats printed in the final volume of the Collected Works of 1908:

> Accursed who brings to light of day
> The writings I have cast away!
> But blessed he that stirs them not
> And lets the kind worm take the lot! (*VP*, p. 779)

But since this curse on editors was itself consigned to the worm, it can be invoked only by an editor willing to flout it.

I have thought it best to omit those poems that Yeats wished to omit – on the grounds that the poet has the authority to unwrite his poems as well as to write them. This volume presents Yeats's canon as (according to available evidence) Yeats might have wished it to be constructed. But I have taken some liberties. I have included the poems from *On the Boiler*, for reasons discussed in the headnote to that section; and I have printed 'The Hero, the Girl, and the Fool' instead of 'The Fool by the Roadside', in the belief that Yeats's wavering between these two versions justified the longer, more interesting text. In order to illustrate Yeats's methods of revision, I have printed both an early and a late version of two poems, 'The Sorrow of Love' and 'The Lamentation of the Old Pensioner'. And I have put in the notes complete texts of some rejected or uncollected poems – those that illuminate other poems (such as 'Mourn – And Then Onward' with respect to 'To a Shade', and 'Let images of basalt, black, immovable', with respect to 'The Statues'), and those unpublished to avoid embarrassment to the living (such as 'Reprisals', suppressed to avoid offence to the Gregory family, and 'Margot', celebrating adulterous love). But Yeats was a good judge of the merits of his own work, and many of his juvenile works deserve oblivion. Those who wish to dredge Lethe may consult the Variorum Edition, or Finneran's.

A NOTE ON THE GLOSSES

The most comprehensive annotation that exists on Yeats's poetry is A. Norman Jeffares, *A New Commentary on The Poems of W. B. Yeats* (Stanford: Stanford University Press, 1984). He has done much of the basic work of finding the cross-references between Yeats's poetry and his prose, and of reporting the findings of other scholars. I have had to repeat some of his labour in order to write the present glosses, and I know what a large task it is. I am indebted to his learning in many ways. I have been able to supplement my annotations from a number of sources, including some recently published texts of Yeats's work not then available to Jeffares. I have added a number of cross-references among Yeats's plays, poems, letters and rough drafts of poems, and have connected Yeats's poems to the work of other authors, from Sir Thomas Wyatt to W. H. Auden. In preparing these glosses I have been so substantially helped by Wendy Bashant of the University of Rochester, that it has not always been easy to tell whether she was my research assistant, or I hers.

Some readers may find these glosses too elaborate, too long, or too prescriptive; but my view is (1) that, as Blake thought, too much is better than too little; (2) that no glossing wholly devoid of interpretative bias is possible, no matter how hard the glosser strives to confine himself to the denotative core of the poem; (3) that the number of interpretations possible to a poem is not strictly infinite, and that interpretative cues may prove valuable to the reader, if only to inspire a counter-thesis; and (4) that Yeats believed that the theme of his poems was original sin (see 'Vacillation' VII), and therefore it follows that his poems have much to confess.

After each poem there appears a date in the right margin – the year of the poem's first publication. If, above that date, there is an italicized date, that is the date Yeats wished to append to the poem. If there is a bracketed date in the left margin, it is a supposition on the date of the poem's composition.

CHRONOLOGY OF YEATS'S LIFE

1865 Birth (13 June, in Sandymount Avenue, Dublin) of William Butler Yeats, the first child of John Butler Yeats and Susan Mary Pollexfen Yeats.

1866 Birth (25 August) of Susan Mary (Lily) Yeats, the poet's sister.

1867 Yeats's father gives up the study of law in order to paint; he and his family move to Regent's Park, London.

1868 Birth (11 March) of Elizabeth Corbet (Lollie) Yeats, a second sister. The family spends a summer holiday in Sligo (in the west of Ireland, where Susan Yeats's parents lived) – a practice common in subsequent years.

1871 Birth (29 August) of John Butler (Jack) Yeats, the poet's brother.

1872 Susan Yeats and her children move from London to Sligo, in the west of Ireland.

1874 Family moves to West Kensington, London.

1876 Father abandons portrait-painting for landscapes.

1877 Yeats enrolled (until 1881) at the Godolphin School, Hammersmith, London, 'a cheap school . . . an obscene, bullying place' (*A: R* 5–6), where he is teased and beaten for being Irish and delicate. He at last earns some respect by his prowess at high-diving.

1879 Family moves to Bedford Park, London.

1881 Father's finances worsen, and the family moves to Howth, near Dublin (in 1884 the family will be compelled to move to another house in the Dublin area). Yeats enrolled (until 1884) at the Erasmus Smith High School, Dublin.

1882 Yeats enamoured with Laura Armstrong, who becomes the subject of some juvenile verse. But she marries another in 1884.

1884 Yeats enrolled at Metropolitan School of Art, Dublin. There he will meet George Russell (AE), who will be a lifelong friend.

1885 Yeats's first publications, including the long Spenserian idyll *The Island of Statues*. Yeats helps to found the Dublin Hermetic Society. He meets several people important to his career, including John O'Leary (see 'September 1913'), Douglas Hyde (see 'At the Abbey Theatre'), and Kathleen Tynan (a minor Roman Catholic poet, who helps to introduce him to the literary world).

1886 He begins to write *The Wanderings of Oisin*, about the conflict between Christianity and its predecessor. Publication of *Mosada*, a dramatic poem about the clash of visionary paganism and flesh-denying Christianity.

1887 Yeats and his family rejoin father in London (South Kensington), where the poet is unhappy. He begins to visit the spiritualist Madame Blavatsky, and to attend the William Morris household (active in handicrafts and politics; in 1888 Lily Yeats begins to work as an embroidress for the Morrises). Yeats's mother suffers two strokes.

1888 Yeats attends a séance where he twitches so violently that he breaks the table (*A: R* 31). He accepts a commission to edit *Fairy and Folk Tales of the Irish Peasantry* (published later in 1888). He joins the Esoteric Section of the Theosophical Society (devoted to the discovery of the absolute truth behind all systems of religious thought). He spends Christmas with Oscar Wilde (*A: FY* 10).

1889 Memorable first meeting (30 January) with Maud Gonne (*A: FY* 5; also see Introduction IX). Yeats begins work with Edwin Ellis on their three-volume edition of William Blake (later this year they discover the MS of Blake's *Vala*). Yeats begins to write his play *The Countess Kathleen*. Publication of *The Wanderings of Oisin and Other Poems*.

1890 Yeats ill with influenza. Unknown to Yeats, Maud Gonne gives birth to an illegitimate son, George (the father is a French anarchist newspaper editor, Lucien Millevoye); the baby dies in 1891. In London, Yeats and Ernest Rhys found the Rhymers' Club (see 'The Grey Rock'), active until 1894. Yeats is initiated into the Hermetic Order of the Golden Dawn (a Rosicrucian society – see the headnote to *The Rose*); later in the year the Esoteric Section of the Theosophical Society asks him to resign. Yeats's health poor – a heart ailment. Charles Parnell, the leader of the Irish delegation to Parliament (see 'To a Shade'), is named co-respondent in a divorce trial; this splits the Irish political movement working for independence from England.

1891 Marriage proposal to Maud Gonne, repeated at intervals until 1903. Yeats plans to revive literature in Ireland by founding various societies. Publication of *Representative Irish Tales* (an anthology) and *John Sherman and Dhoya* (a novella and a story, published under the pseudonym Ganconagh).

1892 Yeats tries to establish a Library of Ireland, to make important new Irish books and reprints generally available – despite Yeats's strenuous efforts, he eventually loses control of the Library to Sir Charles Gavan Duffy, a respectable statesman and politician who ruins the scheme. *The Countess Kathleen* receives a single performance, to establish copyright. Publication of *Irish Fairy Tales*; of *The Countess Kathleen and Various Legends and Lyrics* (containing most of the poems later assembled in *The Rose*); also of the first two Hanrahan stories (concerning a wandering poet), 'The Devil's Book' (rewritten as 'The Book of the Great Dhoul and Hanrahan the Red', not reprinted in *Mythologies* [1959]) and 'The Twisting of the Rope' – six Hanrahan stories were ultimately collected in *The Secret Rose* (1897).

1893 After a ritual examination, Yeats is inducted into a higher order of the Golden Dawn. Publication of *The Works of William Blake* and *The Celtic Twilight*; and of three stories to be collected in *The Secret Rose*, 'Out of the Rose', 'The Heart of the Spring', and 'The Curse of the Fires and of the Shadows'.

1894 After some years of regular movement between Ireland and London (which would continue to be a pattern for most of his life), Yeats visits Paris, where he stays with a leader of the Golden Dawn, MacGregor Mathers (see 'All Souls' Night', l. 61). He meets the decayed poet Verlaine (*A: TG*

18). With Maud Gonne, he attends a performance of Villiers de l'Isle-Adam's *Axël*. Back in Sligo, Yeats experiments in telepathy and symbol-evocation with George Pollexfen, his astrologer uncle (see 'In Memory of Major Robert Gregory' V). In London, *The Land of Heart's Desire* becomes Yeats's first play in regular production. He begins work on *The Shadowy Waters*. In Sligo, he revises his poems for a collected edition. He thinks of proposing marriage to Eva Gore-Booth (see 'In Memory of Eva Gore-Booth . . .'). Publication of two more Hanrahan stories, 'Kathleen-ny-Hoolihan' and 'The Curse of O'Sullivan the Red upon Old Age'; and of 'A Crucifixion' (titled 'The Crucifixion of the Outcast' in *The Secret Rose*) and 'Those who Live in the Storm' (titled 'The Rose of Shadow' in *The Secret Rose*, not reprinted in *Mythologies*).

1895 Yeats visits Castle Rock, in Lough Key, where he wishes to live with Maud Gonne and George Pollexfen, studying occult truths (*Mem*, p. 123–25). In Dublin, he offers his support to Oscar Wilde during his trial for sodomy. Unknown to Yeats, Maud Gonne gives birth to a second child by Millevoye, Iseult Gonne (see Introduction IX). Publication of his collected *Poems*, and of two stories later collected in *The Secret Rose*, 'Wisdom' (later called 'The Wisdom of the King') and 'St. Patrick and the Pedants' (later called 'The Old Men of the Twilight).

1896 First sexual experience, a year-long affair with Olivia Shakespear (see Introduction IX). A visit to the Aran Islands. Yeats starts work on his visionary, somewhat autobiographical novel, *The Speckled Bird* (abandoned around 1902). In Paris, Yeats meets J. M. Synge (see 'In Memory of Major Robert Gregory' IV) – Yeats alters the course of Synge's career by suggesting that a visit to the Aran Islands might help him to break out of his creative impasse. Publication of two more Hanrahan stories, 'The Vision of O'Sullivan the Red' and 'The Death of O'Sullivan the Red'; of four other stories to be collected in *The Secret Rose*: 'The Binding of the Hair' (not reprinted in *Mythologies*), 'Where there is Nothing, there is God', 'Rosa Alchemica' (the first Michael Robartes story), and 'Costello the Proud, Oona MacDermott, and the Bitter Tongue'; of 'The Tables of the

Law', a pendant to 'Rosa Alchemica'; and of the uncollected story 'The Cradles of Gold'.

1897 Yeats spends two months at Coole with Lady Gregory (see Introduction IX), who was collecting folklore; they discuss the establishment of a theatre congenial to their taste – he often visits her in future years. Publication of *The Secret Rose* (including 'Rosa Alchemica') and *The Tables of the Law. The Adoration of the Magi* (two Rosicrucian stories associated with 'Rosa Alchemica').

1898 'Mystic marriage' with Maud Gonne: she confesses her tangled relations with Millevoye, affirms her affection for Yeats, but says she can never marry him in the flesh (*Mem*, pp. 132–34).

1899 In Paris, Yeats again proposes to Maud Gonne. In London, rehearsals of the Irish Literary Theatre (precursor to the Abbey Theatre) with the actress Florence Farr (see 'All Souls' Night', l. 41) and the author George Moore. At the theatre's opening night, the first regular performance of *The Countess Cathleen* (henceforth spelled with a *C*, not a *K*) – already accused of heresy by Cardinal Logue (*A: DP* 10). Difficult collaboration with George Moore on the play *Diarmuid and Grania*, finished in 1900 (*A: DP* 16). Publication of *The Wind among the Reeds.*

1900 Death of Yeats's mother. Yeats writes letters to newspapers denouncing Queen Victoria's visit to Dublin. Yeats vexed by bitter struggles for control of the Golden Dawn – Yeats sides with anti-Mathers faction. Publication of the first version of *The Shadowy Waters.*

1901 Yeats sees Gordon Craig's production of Purcell's *Dido and Aeneas* – Craig's abstract decor becomes a lasting influence on his dramaturgy. Première of Yeats's and George Moore's *Diarmuid and Grania.* Yeats begins to coach Florence Farr in chanting his poems to a psaltery (see 'The Players ask for a Blessing ...').

1902 First production of Yeats's play *Cathleen ni Houlihan* – Maud Gonne plays the title role, a personification of Ireland. Plans for an Irish National Theatre. Yeats meets James Joyce (who tells Yeats that he is too old to be of any use to younger writers). Yeats begins a serious study of Nietzsche.

1903 Yeats is devastated when Maud Gonne marries John Mac-

Bride. Yeats begins affair with Florence Farr, thus ending seven years of celibacy. Yeats's first American lecture tour. First productions of *The Hour-Glass* (in a prose version) and *The King's Threshold*. Publication of the final Hanrahan story, 'Red Hanrahan' (see 'The Tower' II); of *Ideas of Good and Evil* (a collection of essays); and of *In the Seven Woods* (the first publication of the Dun Emer [later called Cuala] press, run by Lollie Yeats).

1904 First production of *The Shadowy Waters* and *Where There is Nothing*. Opening (27 December) of Abbey Theatre, which will consume most of Yeats's energies for the rest of the decade; at the opening *On Baile's Strand* is given its première.

1905 Maud Gonne separates from John MacBride. Yeats attracted by Hugh Lane's proposal for a Dublin gallery of modern art (see 'To a Wealthy Man . . .).

1906 Publication of *The Poems of Spenser* (a selection) and another collection, *Poems 1899–1905*. Première of *Deirdre* at the Abbey Theatre.

1907 Riots at the première of Synge's *The Playboy of the Western World* (see 'On those that hated . . .'). Yeats's love-affair with Maud Gonne is evidently consummated (in 1907 or 1908). Visit to Italy with Lady Gregory and her son – Yeats sees the great Byzantine mosaics at Ravenna. Yeats's father departs for New York, where he will remain.

1908 Affair with Mabel Dickinson. In Dublin, the famous actress Mrs Patrick Campbell plays in Yeats's *Deirdre*; première of *The Golden Helmet* (later revised as *The Green Helmet*). In Paris, Yeats works on his interminable project *The Player Queen*. Publication of Yeats's eight-volume *Collected Works*.

1909 Death of Synge. Death of Swinburne – Yeats tells his sister that he supposes that now 'I am the King of the Cats' (*WBY*, p. 230).

1910 Mabel Dickinson disturbs Yeats by sending him a telegram accusing him (falsely) of making her pregnant (see 'Beggar to Beggar Cried' and 'Presences'). The principal backer of the Abbey Theatre, Annie Horniman, is outraged when the Abbey remains open on the day of Edward VII's death; this ultimately leads to a different financial arrangement. Yeats begins slowly to extricate himself from the Abbey Theatre. Yeats accepts a pension of £150 from the British government – this makes him unpopular with some Irishmen. Publication of *The Green Helmet and Other Poems*.

1911 Yeats meets Ezra Pound in Paris.

1912 Publication of *The Cutting of the Agate* (a second book of essays).

1913 Yeats makes hospital calls to the dying Mabel Beardsley (see 'Upon a Dying Lady'). Death of Edward Dowden, Professor of English at Trinity College, Dublin, and an old family acquaintance of Yeats's; some possibility that Yeats might be appointed to his Chair. In the winter, Yeats and Pound rent a cottage in Sussex (where they will spend the next two winters as well) – they study poetry together and Pound acts as Yeats's amanuensis.

1914 Yeats is irritated by George Moore's 'outrageous article' (in *Hail and Farewell* III), lampooning Yeats's aristocratic pretensions (see the Introductory and Closing Rhymes to *Responsibilities*). Yeats begins writing a memoir of his childhood (published in 1916). Another American tour. In July, Parliament passes a bill granting Home Rule to Ireland but suspends it because of tensions on the Continent – and in August the Great War indeed begins. Publication of *Responsibilities*.

1915 Hugh Lane dies when the Germans sink the *Lusitania*. Yeats persuades the Royal Literary Fund to offer a grant to Joyce. Yeats refuses a knighthood. Probably in this year (or 1914) Yeats writes a dialogue with his Anti-self, Leo Africanus, a boisterous ghost who had been exhorting Yeats in séances for some years. As a sequel to his memoir of childhood, Yeats writes his autobiography from 1887 to 1898 – this suppressed original version was published posthumously in *Memoirs*.

1916 A private performance of *At the Hawk's Well*, Yeats's first play written in the style of the Japanese Noh drama – the fruit of his study of Oriental texts with Pound. At Easter, rebels seize central Dublin and hold it for a few days until they are overwhelmed by the British (see 'Easter, 1916'). The British execute the rebel leaders, including Maud Gonne's husband, John MacBride. On 1 July, Yeats proposes marriage to Maud Gonne; soon afterwards he discusses marriage with Iseult Gonne (and he will do so again in 1917). Yeats and Lady Gregory urge the removal of Hugh Lane's collection of French Impressionist paintings from London to Dublin (see 'To a Wealthy Man . . .'). Publication of *Reveries over Childhood and Youth*.

1917 Purchase of a Norman stone tower in Co. Galway, which Yeats names Thoor Ballylee. In September, he proposes marriage to Georgie Hyde-Lees, who accepts him (see Introduction IX); on 20 October they are married in a civil ceremony; a few days later his wife begins the automatic writing later digested in *A Vision* (see Introduction XI). Zeppelin raids drive Yeats from London to the countryside. Publication of *The Wild Swans at Coole*.

1918 Robert Gregory killed when his plane is shot down over Italy (see 'In Memory of Major Robert Gregory' and 'An Irish Airman Foresees his Death'). End of Great War. In December, a General Election in Ireland.

1919 Birth of Anne Yeats (26 February). Première of *The Player Queen* at the Abbey Theatre. Terrorism in Ireland – see 'Nineteen Hundred and Nineteen'.

1920 American lecture tour.

1921 Truce in Anglo-Irish war. Birth of Michael Yeats (22 August). Publication of *Michael Robartes and the Dancer*, and *Four Years* (more autobiography).

1922 The Dáil (Irish legislature) ratifies the Anglo-Irish treaty, creating the Irish Free State but annexing Ulster to England – this leads to full civil war (see 'Meditations in Time of Civil War'). Yeats establishes household at Merrion Square, Dublin. Death of Yeats's father. On 19 August, the bridge to Ballylee is blown up by the Irish Republican Army. Dinner with T. S. Eliot, who has recently published *The Waste Land*. On 11 December, Yeats is appointed a Senator of the Irish Free State. Publication of *The Trembling of the Veil* (more autobiography).

1923 Further campaigns in London for Irish possession of the Lane bequest. In November, Yeats awarded Nobel Prize, and travels to Stockholm (see *A: BS*).

1924 In autumn, Yeats suffers from high blood pressure.

1925 In January, a visit to Italy – Yeats sees Byzantine art in

Sicily. Yeats (following Milton's model) gives notorious speech in Senate advocating divorce.

1926 Yeats chairs Senate committee on coinage design. More agitation in London over the Lane bequest. Publication of a limited edition of *A Vision* (dated 1925).

1927 Arthritis and influenza. Kevin O'Higgins assassinated (see 'Death'). Visit to southern Spain and France. Serious lung congestion.

1928 Visit to Rapallo, where Pound lives (see *AV*, pp. 3–7). Back in Dublin, Yeats resigns from the Irish Senate. Publication of *The Tower*.

1929 Visit to Rome. Abbey Theatre gives première of *Fighting the Waves* (a revised version of *The Only Jealousy of Emer*). In November, a lung haemorrhage delays a visit to Rapallo; when Yeats arrives there in December, a bout of Malta fever so debilitates him that he makes an emergency will (witnessed by Pound and Basil Bunting). Publication of *A Packet for Ezra Pound*, which will become prefatory material for *A Vision* (1937).

1930 Première of *The Words upon the Window-Pane* at the Abbey Theatre.

1931 Yeats delivers to Macmillan the poetry MS for a projected 'Edition de Luxe' of his works. Yeats studies the philosophy of Berkeley. Publication of his last prose fiction, *Stories of Michael Robartes and His Friends*, to be included in *A Vision* (1937).

1932 Death of Lady Gregory. Yeats establishes a household at Riversdale, near Dublin (see 'An Acre of Grass'). Last American tour. Publication of *Words for Music Perhaps*.

1933 Yeats intrigued by O'Duffy's fascist Blueshirts, (see 'Parnell's Funeral' II and 'Three Marching Songs'). Publication of *The Winding Stair and Other Poems* and *Collected Poems*.

1934 Yeats undergoes Steinach rejuvenation operation – a kind of vasectomy supposed to restore sexual potency. Thus emboldened, he soon establishes intimate friendships with young women, including Margot Collis (a minor poet) and Ethel Mannin (a novelist). Première of *The King of the Great Clock Tower* at the Abbey Theatre. Publication of *Collected Plays*.

1935 In sickbed from January to early March, due to more lung congestion. First visits to the Sussex home of Dorothy Wellesley (see 'The Three Bushes' and 'To Dorothy Wellesley'). Death of George Russell. Operation to remove lump on tongue. Yeats travels to Majorca, where he and Shri Purohit Swāmi collaborate on a translation of the Upanishads. Publication of *A Full Moon in March* and *Dramatis Personae* (the last instalment of autobiography).

1936 Georgie Yeats flies to Majorca after Yeats collapses from nephritis and heart irregularities. Margot Collis goes insane in Barcelona; Yeats travels there to help her and to pay for her care (see 'Sweet Dancer'). Publication of Yeats's anthology *The Oxford Book of Modern Verse*, widely criticized for the capriciousness and eccentricity of its choices of poems.

1937 Yeats vexed by a poorly produced radio broadcast of his poetry from the Abbey Theatre stage. He contemplates a voyage to India in the company of Lady Elizabeth Pelham (see 'The Wild Old Wicked Man'). He begins close relations with Edith Shackleton Heald, 'the best paid woman journalist in the world' (*L*, p. 910). Yeats makes several BBC radio broadcasts (he had done this sporadically for some years). He announces his retirement from public life. Publication of *The Ten Principal Upanishads*, the second edition of *A Vision*, and *Essays 1931–36*.

1938 Visit to southern France. In Dublin, trouble over the Abbey Theatre's première of the un-Christian play *Purgatory* (10 August). Death of Olivia Shakespear. At the end of the year, another visit to southern France. Publication of *New Poems*.

1939 Death of Yeats (28 January), at Roquebrune. Posthumous publication of *Last Poems and Two Plays* and *On the Boiler*.

1948 Yeats's remains moved to Drumcliff churchyard, Sligo.

A NOTE ON GAELIC NAMES

Yeats knew very little Gaelic, and prided himself on the eccentricity of his spelling and pronunciation of Gaelic names. It may be that his pronunciation of certain names is forever lost. But it is possible to make reasonable guesses about some pronunciations, based on English transliterations he used, on the lists of dramatis personae in his plays, on his metrical practice, and on Lady Gregory's pronunciation guides. Since Yeats also said that he wished to follow her orthography, except for a few favourite spellings, such as *Aengus* and *Edain* (*VP*, p. 840), I have generally followed Lady Gregory's usage where Yeats had difficulty in making up his mind – especially in the cases of names spelt with (or without) a terminal *h*.

Aedh: Ae (rhymes with *day*) (*CM*, p. 269).
Aillinn: Alyinn (*L*, p. 353).
Aoife: Eefa (*CM*, p. 269).
Conchubar: Conohar (*VPl*, p. 344). Accent on antepenult.
Cruachan: Crockan (*VP*, p. 180).
Cuchulain: Cuhoolin (*VPl*, p. 420). Accent on penult.
Echtge: Aughty (*PN*, p. 45).
Emer: rhymes with *schemer* (*VPl*, p. 557).
Eochaid: Yohee (*VP*, p. 276).
Gabhra: Gavra (*VP*, p. 1).
Maeve: rhymes with *save*.
Mocharabuiee: Mockrabwee (*VP*, p. 178).
Muirthemne: Mur-hev-na (*CM*, p. 269). The first two vowels are short. But also see *CM*, p. 268.

Niamh: Neave (*VP*, p. 1); Nee-av (*CM*, p. 269). Accent on penult.
Oisin: Usheen (*VP*, p. 1). Probably a faint accent on the penult, since Yeats put the name in trochaic positions.
Sidhe: Shee.

SELECT BIBLIOGRAPHY AND KEY TO ABBREVIATIONS

Primary Texts

BOOKS BY YEATS

(Published by Macmillan unless otherwise specified)

A — *The Autobiography*. (The title *Autobiographies* also appears.) Because this book exists in several editions with different paginations, I print references not by page number but by division and chapter numbers. Its divisions are *Reveries over Childhood and Youth* (*A: R*); *Four Years: 1887–91* (*A: FY*); *Ireland after Parnell* (*A: IP*); *Hodos Chameliontos* (*A: HC*); *The Tragic Generation* (*A: TG*); *The Stirring of the Bones* (*A: SB*); *Dramatis Personae, 1896–1902* (*A: DP*). Yeats wrote no formal memoirs of the years after 1902 – the rest of *The Autobiography* consists of two groups of selections from his diary begun in 1908, *Estrangement* (*A: E*) and *The Death of Synge* (*A: DS*); and *The Bounty of Sweden* (*A: BS*), a description of Yeats's sojourn in Stockholm after receiving the Nobel Prize, including his speech *The Irish Dramatic Movement* (*A: IDM*).

ASD — *Ah, Sweet Dancer: W. B. Yeats and Margot Ruddock*. A correspondence edited by Roger McHugh (1970).

AV — *A Vision* (1925, 1937). This book describes occult relations among human personality types, occult patterns in history, and an account of what befalls the soul between death and rebirth. All citations are from the revised edition, unless marked *AV* (1925).

CEAV (1925) — *A Critical Edition of Yeats's 'A Vision' (1925)*, ed. G. M. Harper and W. K. Hood (1978).

CP — *Collected Poems* (with year of publication in parentheses).

DWL — *Letters on Poetry from W. B. Yeats to Dorothy Wellesley*. London: Oxford University Press, 1964.

EI — *Essays and Introductions*. This comprises *Ideas of Good and Evil* (1903), *The Cutting of the Agate* (1912), and later essays on philosophy and poetry.

Ex — *Explorations*. This medley, assembled by Yeats's widow in 1962, contains some book prefaces; Yeats's occasional pieces of 1901–8 setting out his hopes and intentions for the Abbey Theatre; speculations on the historical era soon to come (including excerpts from his 1930 diary); and the bulk of *On the Boiler*, his polemic on eugenics.

Fairy and Folk Tales of Ireland, ed. W. B. Yeats. London: Colin Smythe, 1973.

JSD — *John Sherman and Dhoya*, ed. Richard J. Finneran. Detroit: Wayne State University Press, 1969. A mild-mannered novella and a wild short story, first published pseudonymously in 1891.

L I — *The Collected Letters of W. B. Yeats*, vol. I, 1865–95, ed. John Kelly and Eric Domville. Oxford: Clarendon Press, 1986.

L — *The Letters of W. B. Yeats*, ed. Allan Wade. London: Rupert Hart-Davis, 1954. Outdated, but, until more of the Kelly edition is published, necessary.

LNI — *Letters to the New Island*, ed. Horace Reynolds. Cambridge: Harvard University Press, 1934. A collection of pieces that Yeats wrote as Irish correspondent to two American newspapers, 1888–92.

LTMSB — *Literatim Transcription of the Manuscripts of William Butler Yeats's 'The Speckled Bird'*, ed. William H. O'Donnell. Delmar: Scholars' Facsimiles & Reprints, 1976. What remains of Yeats's unfinished novel (1896–1902), treating an artist's visionary youth, unhappy love, and induction into mystical ritual.

M — *Mythologies* (1959). This comprises *The Celtic Twilight* (1893 – economical retellings of folktales concerning the old gods); *The Secret Rose* (1897 – ornate visionary short stories), *Stories of Red Hanrahan* (1897 – a collection of six stories about a wandering poet, written in collaboration with Lady Gregory); 'Rosa Alchemica', 'The Tables of the Law', and 'The Adoration of the Magi' (1897 – the three chief Michael Robartes stories, about a mystagogue who founds a pagan sect); and *Per Amica Silentia Lunae* (1917 – not fiction, but a statement of Yeats's beliefs in the anti-self and the Anima Mundi – a book important in the prehistory of *A Vision*).

Mem — *Memoirs*, ed. Dennis Donoghue (1972). This contains the suppressed autobiography written in 1915–16, and a much fuller version of the journal begun in 1908, excerpts of which appeared in *The Autobiography*.

OBMV — *The Oxford Book of Modern Verse 1892–1935*, chosen by W. B. Yeats. Oxford: Clarendon Press, 1936.

PNE — *The Poems of W. B. Yeats: A New Edition*, ed. Richard J. Finneran (1983).

SSY — *The Senate Speeches of W. B. Yeats*, ed. Donald R. Pearce. Bloomington: Indiana University Press, 1960.

TPU — *The Ten Principal Upanishads: Put into English by Shree Purohit Swāmi and W. B. Yeats*. London: Faber & Faber Ltd, 1937.

TSMC — *W. B. Yeats and T. Sturge Moore: Their Correspondence 1901–37*, ed. Ursula Bridge. New York: Oxford University Press, 1953.

UP — *Uncollected Prose by W. B. Yeats*, vol. I, ed. John P. Frayne (1970), vol. II, ed. John P. Frayne and Colton Johnson (1975).

VP — *The Variorum Edition of the Poems of W. B. Yeats*, ed. Peter Allt and Russell K. Alspach (1957).

VPl — *The Variorum Edition of the Plays of W. B. Yeats*, ed. Russell K. Alspach (1966).

VSR — *The Secret Rose, Stories by W. B. Yeats: A Variorum Edition*, ed. Phillip L. Marcus, Warwick Gould, and Michael J. Sidnell. Ithaca: Cornell University Press, 1981.

BOOKS NOT BY YEATS

EYP — Finneran, Richard J. *Editing Yeats's Poems*. New York: St Martin's Press, 1983.

LTY — *Letters to W. B. Yeats*, in two vols., ed. R. J. Finneran, G. M. Harper, and W. M. Murphy (1977).

CM Gregory, Lady Augusta. *Cuchulain of Muirthemne.* London: Colin Smythe, 1970. A skilful retelling of the Red Branch cycle of Old Irish mythology – a book extravagantly praised by Yeats.

——. *Gods and Fighting Men.* A companion to her *Cuchulain of Muirthemne*, treating the Fenian cycle.

MacBride, Maud Gonne. *A Servant of the Queen: Reminiscences.* Woodbridge: Boydell Press, 1983.

PN McGarry, James P. *Places Names in the Writings of William Butler Yeats.* Gerrards Cross: Colin Smythe, 1976.

IR Mikhail, E. H. *W. B. Yeats: Interviews and Recollections*, in two volumes. New York: Barnes and Noble Books, 1977.

O'Shea, Edward. *A Descriptive Catalog of W. B. Yeats's Library*. New York: Garland Publications, 1985.

LS Yeats, J. B. *Letters to his son W. B. Yeats and others*, ed. Joseph Hone. London: Faber & Faber, 1944.

Secondary Texts

Yeats was a lucky man – even his disappointments were usually useful to him – and he has remained lucky after death. Few authors of any age have attracted the attention of so many gifted critics and scholars – I must omit many important names to keep this list manageable. Most gifted of all was the late Richard Ellmann, a critic in whose company Dr Johnson and Hazlitt would have felt stimulated and at ease. But he was also happy to discuss poetry with less distinguished men. A conversation about a poem of Yeats's with Richard Ellmann was like a stroll through a forest with an agreeable companion who not only knows the names of every bird, bush, lichen, and bug, but also hears sounds usually audible only to bats.

I. COMPREHENSIVE STUDIES OF YEATS'S WORK

YMM Ellmann, Richard. *Yeats: The Man and the Masks*, revised edition. New York: W. W. Norton, 1979.

IY ——. *The Identity of Yeats.* London: Faber & Faber; New York: Oxford University Press, 1954.

NCP Jeffares, A. Norman. *A New Commentary on The Poems*

of *W. B. Yeats*. Stanford: Stanford University Press, 1984.

SS Whitaker, Thomas R. *Swan and Shadow: Yeats's Dialogue with History*. Chapel Hill: University of North Carolina Press, 1964.

II. YEATS AND THE RENAISSANCE

Salvadori, Corinna. *Yeats and Castiglione: Poet and Courtier*. Dublin: Allen Figgis, 1965.

III. YEATS AND THE EIGHTEENTH CENTURY

Torchiana, Donald T. *W. B. Yeats & Georgian Ireland*. Evanston: Northwestern University Press, 1966.

IV. YEATS AND THE NINETEENTH CENTURY

Bloom, Harold. *Yeats*. New York: Oxford University Press, 1970.

YS Bornstein, George. *Yeats and Shelley*. Chicago: University of Chicago Press, 1970.

V. YEATS AND THE TWENTIETH CENTURY

ED Ellmann, Richard. *Eminent Domain: Yeats among Wilde, Joyce, Pound, Eliot, and Auden*. New York: Oxford University Press, 1967.

SC Longenbach, James. *Stone Cottage: Pound, Yeats, and Modernism*. New York: Oxford University Press, 1988.

VI. YEATS AND THE VISUAL ARTS

Loizeaux, Elizabeth Bergmann. *Yeats and the Visual Arts*. Rutgers: Rutgers University Press, 1986.

LT Henn, T. R. *The Lonely Tower: Studies in the Poetry of W. B. Yeats*. London: Methuen, 1965.

VII. YEATS'S OCCULTISM

Harper, George Mills. *Yeats's Golden Dawn* (1974).

VIII. *A VISION*

MAV Harper, George Mills. *The Making of Yeats's 'A Vision': A Study of the Automatic Script*, in two volumes. Carbondale: Southern Illinois University Press, 1987.

Raine, Kathleen. *From Blake to 'A Vision'*. Dublin: Dolmen Press, 1979.

YVLP Vendler, Helen. *Yeats's 'Vision' and the Later Plays.* Cambridge: Harvard University Press, 1963.

IX. DRAFTS OF YEATS'S MANUSCRIPTS OF POEMS

WPQ Bradford, Curtis B. *The Writing of 'The Player Queen'*. DeKalb: Northern Illinois University Press, 1977.

YW Bradford, Curtis B. *Yeats at Work*. New York: The Ecco Press, 1978.

DC Sidnell, Michael J., George P. Mayhew, and David R. Clark. *Druid Craft: The Writing of 'The Shadowy Waters'*. Amherst: University of Massachusetts Press, 1971.

BL Stallworthy, Jon. *Between the Lines: Yeats's Poetry in the Making*. Oxford: The Clarendon Press, 1963.

VR ——. *Vision and Revision in Yeats's 'Last Poems'*. Oxford: The Clarendon Press, 1969.

The New Yeats Papers of the Dolmen Press (Ireland) offer a number of manuscript transcriptions; and the Cornell University Press (America) has undertaken a comprehensive series of facsimile editions. Important titles other than those mentioned have appeared and will be appearing. Eventually all extant manuscript drafts of Yeats's poems will be considered by the editors of the Cornell Yeats – *The Early Poems* I: *Mosada* and *The Island of Statues*, ed. George Bornstein, was published in 1987.

X. BIOGRAPHY

WBY Joseph Hone. *W. B. Yeats 1895–1939* (1965). A book that should prove not difficult to supersede.

THE WANDERINGS OF OISIN
1889

'Give me the world if Thou wilt, but grant me an asylum for my affections.' – Tulka

TO EDWIN J. ELLIS

Book I

S. Patrick. You who are bent, and bald, and blind,
With a heavy heart and a wandering mind,
Have known three centuries, poets sing,
Of dalliance with a demon thing.

Oisin. Sad to remember, sick with years,
The swift innumerable spears,
The horsemen with their floating hair,
And bowls of barley, honey, and wine,
Those merry couples dancing in tune,
And the white body that lay by mine;
But the tale, though words be lighter than air,
Must live to be old like the wandering moon.

Caoilte, and Conan, and Finn were there,
When we followed a deer with our baying hounds,
With Bran, Sceolan, and Lomair,
And passing the Firbolgs' burial-mounds,
Came to the cairn-heaped grassy hill
Where passionate Maeve is stony-still;
And found on the dove-grey edge of the sea
A pearl-pale, high-born lady, who rode
On a horse with bridle of findrinny;

And like a sunset were her lips,
A stormy sunset on doomed ships;
A citron colour gloomed in her hair,
But down to her feet white vesture flowed,
And with the glimmering crimson glowed
Of many a figured embroidery;
And it was bound with a pearl-pale shell
That wavered like the summer streams,
As her soft bosom rose and fell.

S. Patrick. You are still wrecked among heathen dreams.

Oisin. 'Why do you wind no horn?' she said.
'And every hero droop his head?
The hornless deer is not more sad
That many a peaceful moment had,
More sleek than any granary mouse,
In his own leafy forest house
Among the waving fields of fern:
The hunting of heroes should be glad.'

'O pleasant woman,' answered Finn,
'We think on Oscar's pencilled urn,
And on the heroes lying slain
On Gabhra's raven-covered plain;
But where are your noble kith and kin,
And from what country do you ride?'

'My father and my mother are
Aengus and Edain, my own name
Niamh, and my country far
Beyond the tumbling of this tide.'

'What dream came with you that you came
Through bitter tide on foam-wet feet?
Did your companion wander away
From where the birds of Aengus wing?'

Thereon did she look haughty and sweet:
'I have not yet, war-weary king,
Been spoken of with any man;
Yet now I choose, for these four feet

Ran through the foam and ran to this
That I might have your son to kiss.'

'Were there no better than my son
That you through all that foam should run?'

'I loved no man, though kings besought,
Until the Danaan poets brought
Rhyme that rhymed upon Oisin's name,
And now I am dizzy with the thought
Of all that wisdom and the fame
Of battles broken by his hands,
Of stories builded by his words
That are like coloured Asian birds
At evening in their rainless lands.'

O Patrick, by your brazen bell,
There was no limb of mine but fell
Into a desperate gulph of love!
'You only will I wed,' I cried,
'And I will make a thousand songs,
And set your name all names above,
And captives bound with leathern thongs
Shall kneel and praise you, one by one,
At evening in my western dun.'

'O Oisin, mount by me and ride
To shores by the wash of the tremulous tide,
Where men have heaped no burial-mounds,
And the days pass by like a wayward tune,
Where broken faith has never been known,
And the blushes of first love never have flown;
And there I will give you a hundred hounds;
No mightier creatures bay at the moon;
And a hundred robes of murmuring silk,
And a hundred calves and a hundred sheep
Whose long wool whiter than sea-froth flows,
And a hundred spears and a hundred bows,
And oil and wine and honey and milk,
And always never-anxious sleep;
While a hundred youths, mighty of limb,
By knowing nor tumult nor hate nor strife,

And a hundred ladies, merry as birds,
Who when they dance to a fitful measure
Have a speed like the speed of the salmon herds,
Shall follow your horn and obey your whim,
And you shall know the Danaan leisure;
And Niamh be with you for a wife.'
Then she sighed gently, 'It grows late.
Music and love and sleep await,
Where I would be when the white moon climbs,
The red sun falls and the world grows dim.'

And then I mounted and she bound me
With her triumphing arms around me,
And whispering to herself enwound me;
But when the horse had felt my weight,
He shook himself and neighed three times:
Caoilte, Conan, and Finn came near,
And wept, and raised their lamenting hands,
And bid me stay, with many a tear;
But we rode out from the human lands.

In what far kingdom do you go,
Ah, Fenians, with the shield and bow?
Or are you phantoms white as snow,
Whose lips had life's most prosperous glow?
O you, with whom in sloping valleys,
Or down the dewy forest alleys,
I chased at morn the flying deer,
With whom I hurled the hurrying spear,
And heard the foemen's bucklers rattle,
And broke the heaving ranks of battle!
And Bran, Sceolan, and Lomair,
Where are you with your long rough hair?
You go not where the red deer feeds,
Nor tear the foemen from their steeds.

S. Patrick. Boast not, nor mourn with drooping head
Companions long accurst and dead,
And hounds for centuries dust and air.

Oisin. We galloped over the glossy sea:
I know not if days passed or hours,

And Niamh sang continually
Danaan songs, and their dewy showers
Of pensive laughter, unhuman sound,
Lulled weariness, and softly round
My human sorrow her white arms wound.
We galloped; now a hornless deer
Passed by us, chased by a phantom hound
All pearly white, save one red ear;
And now a lady rode like the wind
With an apple of gold in her tossing hand;
And a beautiful young man followed behind
With quenchless gaze and fluttering hair.

'Were these two born in the Danaan land,
Or have they breathed the mortal air?'

'Vex them no longer,' Niamh said,
And sighing bowed her gentle head,
And sighing laid the pearly tip
Of one long finger on my lip.

But now the moon like a white rose shone
In the pale west, and the sun's rim sank,
And clouds arrayed their rank on rank
About his fading crimson ball:
The floor of Almhuin's hosting hall
Was not more level than the sea,
As, full of loving fantasy,
And with low murmurs, we rode on,
Where many a trumpet-twisted shell
That in immortal silence sleeps
Dreaming of her own melting hues,
Her golds, her ambers, and her blues,
Pierced with soft light the shallowing deeps.
But now a wandering land breeze came
And a far sound of feathery quires;
It seemed to blow from the dying flame,
They seemed to sing in the smouldering fires.
The horse towards the music raced,
Neighing along the lifeless waste;
Like sooty fingers, many a tree

Rose ever out of the warm sea;
And they were trembling ceaselessly,
As though they all were beating time,
Upon the centre of the sun,
To that low laughing woodland rhyme.
And, now our wandering hours were done,
We cantered to the shore, and knew
The reason of the trembling trees:
Round every branch the song-birds flew,
Or clung thereon like swarming bees;
While round the shore a million stood
Like drops of frozen rainbow light,
And pondered in a soft vain mood
Upon their shadows in the tide,
And told the purple deeps their pride,
And murmured snatches of delight;
And on the shores were many boats
With bending sterns and bending bows,
And carven figures on their prows
Of bitterns, and fish-eating stoats,
And swans with their exultant throats:
And where the wood and waters meet
We tied the horse in a leafy clump,
And Niamh blew three merry notes
Out of a little silver trump;
And then an answering whispering flew
Over the bare and woody land,
A whisper of impetuous feet,
And ever nearer, nearer grew;
And from the woods rushed out a band
Of men and ladies, hand in hand,
And singing, singing all together;
Their brows were white as fragrant milk,
Their cloaks made out of yellow silk,
And trimmed with many a crimson feather;
And when they saw the cloak I wore
Was dim with mire of a mortal shore,
They fingered it and gazed on me
And laughed like murmurs of the sea;
But Niamh with a swift distress

Bid them away and hold their peace;
And when they heard her voice they ran
And knelt there, every girl and man,
And kissed, as they would never cease,
Her pearl-pale hand and the hem of her dress.
She bade them bring us to the hall
Where Aengus dreams, from sun to sun,
A Druid dream of the end of days
When the stars are to wane and the world be done.

They led us by long and shadowy ways
Where drops of dew in myriads fall,
And tangled creepers every hour
Blossom in some new crimson flower,
And once a sudden laughter sprang
From all their lips, and once they sang
Together, while the dark woods rang,
And made in all their distant parts,
With boom of bees in honey-marts,
A rumour of delighted hearts.
And once a lady by my side
Gave me a harp, and bid me sing,
And touch the laughing silver string;
But when I sang of human joy
A sorrow wrapped each merry face,
And, Patrick! by your beard, they wept,
Until one came, a tearful boy;
'A sadder creature never stept
Than this strange human bard,' he cried;
And caught the silver harp away,
And, weeping over the white strings, hurled
It down in a leaf-hid, hollow place
That kept dim waters from the sky;
And each one said, with a long, long sigh,
'O saddest harp in all the world,
Sleep there till the moon and the stars die!'

And now, still sad, we came to where
A beautiful young man dreamed within
A house of wattles, clay, and skin;
One hand upheld his beardless chin,

And one a sceptre flashing out
Wild flames of red and gold and blue,
Like to a merry wandering rout
Of dancers leaping in the air;
And men and ladies knelt them there
And showed their eyes with teardrops dim,
And with low murmurs prayed to him,
And kissed the sceptre with red lips,
And touched it with their finger-tips.

He held that flashing sceptre up.
'Joy drowns the twilight in the dew,
And fills with stars night's purple cup,
And wakes the sluggard seeds of corn,
And stirs the young kid's budding horn,
And makes the infant ferns unwrap,
And for the peewit paints his cap,
And rolls along the unwieldy sun,
And makes the little planets run:
And if joy were not on the earth,
There were an end of change and birth,
And Earth and Heaven and Hell would die,
And in some gloomy barrow lie
Folded like a frozen fly;
Then mock at Death and Time with glances
And wavering arms and wandering dances.

'Men's hearts of old were drops of flame
That from the saffron morning came,
Or drops of silver joy that fell
Out of the moon's pale twisted shell;
But now hearts cry that hearts are slaves,
And toss and turn in narrow caves;
But here there is nor law nor rule,
Nor have hands held a weary tool;
And here there is nor Change nor Death,
But only kind and merry breath,
For joy is God and God is joy.'
With one long glance for girl and boy
And the pale blossom of the moon,
He fell into a Druid swoon.

And in a wild and sudden dance
We mocked at Time and Fate and Chance
And swept out of the wattled hall
And came to where the dewdrops fall
Among the foamdrops of the sea,
And there we hushed the revelry;
And, gathering on our brows a frown,
Bent all our swaying bodies down,
And to the waves that glimmer by
That sloping green De Danaan sod
Sang, 'God is joy and joy is God,
And things that have grown sad are wicked,
And things that fear the dawn of the morrow
Or the grey wandering osprey Sorrow.'

We danced to where in the winding thicket
The damask roses, bloom on bloom,
Like crimson meteors hang in the gloom,
And bending over them softly said,
Bending over them in the dance,
With a swift and friendly glance
From dewy eyes: 'Upon the dead
Fall the leaves of other roses,
On the dead dim earth encloses:
But never, never on our graves,
Heaped beside the glimmering waves,
Shall fall the leaves of damask roses.
For neither Death nor Change comes near us,
And all listless hours fear us,
And we fear no dawning morrow,
Nor the grey wandering osprey Sorrow.'

The dance wound through the windless woods;
The ever-summered solitudes;
Until the tossing arms grew still
Upon the woody central hill;
And, gathered in a panting band,
We flung on high each waving hand,
And sang unto the starry broods.
In our raised eyes there flashed a glow
Of milky brightness to and fro

As thus our song arose: 'You stars,
Across your wandering ruby cars
Shake the loose reins: you slaves of God,
He rules you with an iron rod,
He holds you with an iron bond,
Each one woven to the other,
Each one woven to his brother
Like bubbles in a frozen pond;
But we in a lonely land abide
Unchainable as the dim tide,
With hearts that know nor law nor rule,
And hands that hold no wearisome tool,
Folded in love that fears no morrow,
Nor the grey wandering osprey Sorrow.'

O Patrick! for a hundred years
I chased upon that woody shore
The deer, the badger, and the boar.
O Patrick! for a hundred years
At evening on the glimmering sands,
Beside the piled-up hunting spears,
These now outworn and withered hands
Wrestled among the island bands.
O Patrick! for a hundred years
We went a-fishing in long boats
With bending sterns and bending bows,
And carven figures on their prows
Of bitterns and fish-eating stoats.
O Patrick! for a hundred years
The gentle Niamh was my wife;
But now two things devour my life;
The things that most of all I hate:
Fasting and prayers.

S. Patrick. Tell on.

Oisin. Yes, yes,
For these were ancient Oisin's fate
Loosed long ago from Heaven's gate,
For his last days to lie in wait.

When one day by the tide I stood,

I found in that forgetfulness
Of dreamy foam a staff of wood
From some dead warrior's broken lance:
I turned it in my hands; the stains
Of war were on it, and I wept,
Remembering how the Fenians stept
Along the blood-bedabbled plains,
Equal to good or grievous chance:
Thereon young Niamh softly came
And caught my hands, but spake no word
Save only many times my name,
In murmurs, like a frighted bird.
We passed by woods, and lawns of clover,
And found the horse and bridled him,
For we knew well the old was over.
I heard one say, 'His eyes grow dim
With all the ancient sorrow of men';
And wrapped in dreams rode out again
With hoofs of the pale findrinny
Over the glimmering purple sea.
Under the golden evening light,
The Immortals moved among the fountains
By rivers and the woods' old night;
Some danced like shadows on the mountains,
Some wandered ever hand in hand;
Or sat in dreams on the pale strand,
Each forehead like an obscure star
Bent down above each hookèd knee,
And sang, and with a dreamy gaze
Watched where the sun in a saffron blaze
Was slumbering half in the sea-ways;
And, as they sang, the painted birds
Kept time with their bright wings and feet;
Like drops of honey came their words,
But fainter than a young lamb's bleat.

'An old man stirs the fire to a blaze,
In the house of a child, of a friend, of a brother.
He has over-lingered his welcome; the days,
Grown desolate, whisper and sigh to each other;

He hears the storm in the chimney above,
And bends to the fire and shakes with the cold,
While his heart still dreams of battle and love,
And the cry of the hounds on the hills of old.

'But we are apart in the grassy places,
Where care cannot trouble the least of our days,
Or the softness of youth be gone from our faces,
Or love's first tenderness die in our gaze.
The hare grows old as she plays in the sun
And gazes around her with eyes of brightness;
Before the swift things that she dreamed of were done
She limps along in an aged whiteness;
A storm of birds in the Asian trees
Like tulips in the air a-winging,
And the gentle waves of the summer seas,
That raise their heads and wander singing,
Must murmur at last, "Unjust, unjust";
And "My speed is a weariness," falters the mouse,
And the kingfisher turns to a ball of dust,
And the roof falls in of his tunnelled house.
But the love-dew dims our eyes till the day
When God shall come from the sea with a sigh
And bid the stars drop down from the sky,
And the moon like a pale rose wither away.'

Book II

Now, man of croziers, shadows called our names
And then away, away, like whirling flames;
And now fled by, mist-covered, without sound,
The youth and lady and the deer and hound;
'Gaze no more on the phantoms,' Niamh said,
And kissed my eyes, and, swaying her bright head
And her bright body, sang of faery and man
Before God was or my old line began;
Wars shadowy, vast, exultant; faeries of old
Who wedded men with rings of Druid gold;
And how those lovers never turn their eyes
Upon the life that fades and flickers and dies,

Yet love and kiss on dim shores far away
Rolled round with music of the sighing spray:
Yet sang no more as when, like a brown bee
That has drunk full, she crossed the misty sea
With me in her white arms a hundred years
Before this day; for now the fall of tears
Troubled her song.
I do not know if days
Or hours passed by, yet hold the morning rays
Shone many times among the glimmering flowers
Woven into her hair, before dark towers
Rose in the darkness, and the white surf gleamed
About them; and the horse of Faery screamed
And shivered, knowing the Isle of Many Fears,
Nor ceased until white Niamh stroked his ears
And named him by sweet names.
A foaming tide
Whitened afar with surge, fan-formed and wide,
Burst from a great door marred by many a blow
From mace and sword and pole-axe, long ago
When gods and giants warred. We rode between
The seaweed-covered pillars; and the green
And surging phosphorus alone gave light
On our dark pathway, till a countless flight
Of moonlit steps glimmered; and left and right
Dark statues glimmered over the pale tide
Upon dark thrones. Between the lids of one
The imaged meteors had flashed and run
And had disported in the stilly jet,
And the fixed stars had dawned and shone and set,
Since God made Time and Death and Sleep: the other
Stretched his long arm to where, a misty smother,
The stream churned, churned, and churned – his lips apart,
As though he told his never-slumbering heart
Of every foamdrop on its misty way.
Tying the horse to his vast foot that lay
Half in the unvesselled sea, we climbed the stair
And climbed so long, I thought the last steps were
Hung from the morning star; when these mild words
Fanned the delighted air like wings of birds:

'My brothers spring out of their beds at morn,
A-murmur like young partridge: with loud horn
They chase the noontide deer;
And when the dew-drowned stars hang in the air
Look to long fishing-lines, or point and pare
An ashen hunting spear.
O sigh, O fluttering sigh, be kind to me;
Flutter along the froth lips of the sea,
And shores the froth lips wet:
And stay a little while, and bid them weep:
Ah, touch their blue-veined eyelids if they sleep,
And shake their coverlet.
When you have told how I weep endlessly,
Flutter along the froth lips of the sea
And home to me again,
And in the shadow of my hair lie hid,
And tell me that you found a man unbid,
The saddest of all men.'

A lady with soft eyes like funeral tapers,
And face that seemed wrought out of moonlit vapours,
And a sad mouth, that fear made tremulous
As any ruddy moth, looked down on us;
And she with a wave-rusted chain was tied
To two old eagles, full of ancient pride,
That with dim eyeballs stood on either side.
Few feathers were on their dishevelled wings,
For their dim minds were with the ancient things.

'I bring deliverance,' pearl-pale Niamh said.

'Neither the living, nor the unlabouring dead,
Nor the high gods who never lived, may fight
My enemy and hope; demons for fright
Jabber and scream about him in the night;
For he is strong and crafty as the seas
That sprang under the Seven Hazel Trees,
And I must needs endure and hate and weep,
Until the gods and demons drop asleep,
Hearing Aedh touch the mournful strings of gold.'

'Is he so dreadful?'
'Be not over-bold,
But fly while still you may.'
And thereon I:
'This demon shall be battered till he die,
And his loose bulk be thrown in the loud tide.'
'Flee from him,' pearl-pale Niamh weeping cried,
'For all men flee the demons'; but moved not
My angry king-remembering soul one jot.
There was no mightier soul of Heber's line;
Now it is old and mouse-like. For a sign
I burst the chain: still earless, nerveless, blind,
Wrapped in the things of the unhuman mind,
In some dim memory or ancient mood,
Still earless, nerveless, blind, the eagles stood.

And then we climbed the stair to a high door;
A hundred horsemen on the basalt floor
Beneath had paced content: we held our way
And stood within: clothed in a misty ray
I saw a foam-white seagull drift and float
Under the roof, and with a straining throat
Shouted, and hailed him: he hung there a star,
For no man's cry shall ever mount so far;
Not even your God could have thrown down that hall;
Stabling His unloosed lightnings in their stall,
He had sat down and sighed with cumbered heart,
As though His hour were come.

We sought the part
That was most distant from the door; green slime
Made the way slippery, and time on time
Showed prints of sea-born scales, while down through it
The captive's journeys to and fro were writ
Like a small river, and where feet touched came
A momentary gleam of phosphorus flame.
Under the deepest shadows of the hall
That woman found a ring hung on the wall,
And in the ring a torch, and with its flare
Making a world about her in the air,
Passed under the dim doorway, out of sight,

And came again, holding a second light
Burning between her fingers, and in mine
Laid it and sighed: I held a sword whose shine
No centuries could dim, and a word ran
Thereon in Ogham letters, 'Manannan';
That sea-god's name, who in a deep content
Sprang dripping, and, with captive demons sent
Out of the sevenfold seas, built the dark hall
Rooted in foam and clouds, and cried to all
The mightier masters of the mightier race;
And at his cry there came no milk-pale face
Under a crown of thorns and dark with blood,
But only exultant faces.

Niamh stood
With bowed head, trembling when the white blade shone,
But she whose hours of tenderness were gone
Had neither hope nor fear. I bade them hide
Under the shadows till the tumults died
Of the loud-crashing and earth-shaking fight,
Lest they should look upon some dreadful sight;
And thrust the torch between the slimy flags.
A dome made out of endless carven jags,
Where shadowy face flowed into shadowy face,
Looked down on me; and in the self-same place
I waited hour by hour, and the high dome,
Windowless, pillarless, multitudinous home
Of faces, waited; and the leisured gaze
Was loaded with the memory of days
Buried and mighty. When through the great door
The dawn came in, and glimmered on the floor
With a pale light, I journeyed round the hall
And found a door deep sunken in the wall,
The least of doors; beyond on a dim plain
A little runnel made a bubbling strain,
And on the runnel's stony and bare edge
A dusky demon dry as a withered sedge
Swayed, crooning to himself an unknown tongue:
In a sad revelry he sang and swung
Bacchant and mournful, passing to and fro
His hand along the runnel's side, as though

The flowers still grew there: far on the sea's waste
Shaking and waving, vapour vapour chased,
While high frail cloudlets, fed with a green light,
Like drifts of leaves, immovable and bright,
Hung in the passionate dawn. He slowly turned:
A demon's leisure: eyes, first white, now burned
Like wings of kingfishers; and he arose
Barking. We trampled up and down with blows
Of sword and brazen battle-axe, while day
Gave to high noon and noon to night gave way;
And when he knew the sword of Manannan
Amid the shades of night, he changed and ran
Through many shapes; I lunged at the smooth throat
Of a great eel; it changed, and I but smote
A fir-tree roaring in its leafless top;
And thereupon I drew the livid chop
Of a drowned dripping body to my breast;
Horror from horror grew; but when the west
Had surged up in a plumy fire, I drave
Through heart and spine; and cast him in the wave
Lest Niamh shudder.

Full of hope and dread
Those two came carrying wine and meat and bread,
And healed my wounds with unguents out of flowers
That feed white moths by some De Danaan shrine;
Then in that hall, lit by the dim sea-shine,
We lay on skins of otters, and drank wine,
Brewed by the sea-gods, from huge cups that lay
Upon the lips of sea-gods in their day;
And then on heaped-up skins of otters slept.
And when the sun once more in saffron stept,
Rolling his flagrant wheel out of the deep,
We sang the loves and angers without sleep,
And all the exultant labours of the strong.
But now the lying clerics murder song
With barren words and flatteries of the weak.
In what land do the powerless turn the beak
Of ravening Sorrow, or the hand of Wrath?
For all your croziers, they have left the path

And wander in the storms and clinging snows,
Hopeless for ever: ancient Oisin knows,
For he is weak and poor and blind, and lies
On the anvil of the world.

S. Patrick. Be still: the skies
Are choked with thunder, lightning, and fierce wind,
For God has heard, and speaks His angry mind;
Go cast your body on the stones and pray,
For He has wrought midnight and dawn and day.

Oisin. Saint, do you weep? I hear amid the thunder
The Fenian horses; armour torn asunder;
Laughter and cries. The armies clash and shock,
And now the daylight-darkening ravens flock.
Cease, cease, O mournful, laughing Fenian horn!

We feasted for three days. On the fourth morn
I found, dropping sea-foam on the wide stair,
And hung with slime, and whispering in his hair,
That demon dull and unsubduable;
And once more to a day-long battle fell,
And at the sundown threw him in the surge,
To lie until the fourth morn saw emerge
His new-healed shape; and for a hundred years
So warred, so feasted, with nor dreams nor fears,
Nor languor nor fatigue: an endless feast,
An endless war.

The hundred years had ceased;
I stood upon the stair: the surges bore
A beech-bough to me, and my heart grew sore,
Remembering how I had stood by white-haired Finn
Under a beech at Almhuin and heard the thin
Outcry of bats.

And then young Niamh came
Holding that horse, and sadly called my name;
I mounted, and we passed over the lone
And drifting greyness, while this monotone,
Surly and distant, mixed inseparably
Into the clangour of the wind and sea.

'I hear my soul drop down into decay,
And Manannan's dark tower, stone after stone,
Gather sea-slime and fall the seaward way,
And the moon goad the waters night and day,
That all be overthrown.

'But till the moon has taken all, I wage
War on the mightiest men under the skies,
And they have fallen or fled, age after age.
Light is man's love, and lighter is man's rage;
His purpose drifts and dies.'

And then lost Niamh murmured, 'Love, we go
To the Island of Forgetfulness, for lo!
The Islands of Dancing and of Victories
Are empty of all power.'

'And which of these
Is the Island of Content?'

'None know,' she said;
And on my bosom laid her weeping head.

Book III

Fled foam underneath us, and round us, a wandering and milky smoke,
High as the saddle-girth, covering away from our glances the tide;
And those that fled, and that followed, from the foam-pale distance broke;
The immortal desire of Immortals we saw in their faces, and sighed.

I mused on the chase with the Fenians, and Bran, Sceolan, Lomair,
And never a song sang Niamh, and over my finger-tips
Came now the sliding of tears and sweeping of mist-cold hair,
And now the warmth of sighs, and after the quiver of lips.

Were we days long or hours long in riding, when, rolled in a grisly peace,
An isle lay level before us, with dripping hazel and oak?
And we stood on a sea's edge we saw not; for whiter than new-washed fleece
Fled foam underneath us, and round us, a wandering and milky smoke.

And we rode on the plains of the sea's edge; the sea's edge barren and grey,
Grey sand on the green of the grasses and over the dripping trees,
Dripping and doubling landward, as though they would hasten away,
Like an army of old men longing for rest from the moan of the seas.

But the trees grew taller and closer, immense in their wrinkling bark;
Dropping; a murmurous dropping; old silence and that one sound;
For no live creatures lived there, no weasels moved in the dark:
Long sighs arose in our spirits, beneath us bubbled the ground.

And the ears of the horse went sinking away in the hollow night,
For, as drift from a sailor slow drowning the gleams of the world and the sun,
Ceased on our hands and our faces, on hazel and oak leaf, the light,
And the stars were blotted above us, and the whole of the world was one.

Till the horse gave a whinny; for, cumbrous with stems of the hazel and oak,

A valley flowed down from his hoofs, and there in the long grass lay,
Under the starlight and shadow, a monstrous slumbering folk,
Their naked and gleaming bodies poured out and heaped in the way.

And by them were arrow and war-axe, arrow and shield and blade;
And dew-blanched horns, in whose hollow a child of three years old
Could sleep on a couch of rushes, and all inwrought and inlaid,
And more comely than man can make them with bronze and silver and gold.

And each of the huge white creatures was huger than fourscore men;
The tops of their ears were feathered, their hands were the claws of birds,
And, shaking the plumes of the grasses and the leaves of the mural glen,
The breathing came from those bodies, long warless, grown whiter than curds.

The wood was so spacious above them, that He who has stars for His flocks
Could fondle the leaves with His fingers, nor go from His dew-cumbered skies;
So long were they sleeping, the owls had builded their nests in their locks,
Filling the fibrous dimness with long generations of eyes.

And over the limbs and the valley the slow owls wandered and came,
Now in a place of star-fire, and now in a shadow-place wide;
And the chief of the huge white creatures, his knees in the soft star-flame,

Lay loose in a place of shadow: we drew the reins by his
side.

Golden the nails of his bird-claws, flung loosely along the
dim ground;
In one was a branch soft-shining with bells more many than
sighs
In midst of an old man's bosom; owls ruffling and pacing
around
Sidled their bodies against him, filling the shade with their
eyes.

And my gaze was thronged with the sleepers; no, not since
the world began,
In realms where the handsome were many, nor in glamours
by demons flung,
Have faces alive with such beauty been known to the salt
eye of man,
Yet weary with passions that faded when the sevenfold seas
were young.

And I gazed on the bell-branch, sleep's forebear, far sung
by the Sennachies.
I saw how those slumberers, grown weary, there camping
in grasses deep,
Of wars with the wide world and pacing the shores of the
wandering seas,
Laid hands on the bell-branch and swayed it, and fed of
unhuman sleep.

Snatching the horn of Niamh, I blew a long lingering note.
Came sound from those monstrous sleepers, a sound like the
stirring of flies.
He, shaking the fold of his lips, and heaving the pillar of his
throat,
Watched me with mournful wonder out of the wells of his
eyes.

I cried, 'Come out of the shadow, king of the nails of gold!
And tell of your goodly household and the goodly works of your hands,
That we may muse in the starlight and talk of the battles of old;
Your questioner, Oisin, is worthy, he comes from the Fenian lands.'

Half open his eyes were, and held me, dull with the smoke of their dreams;
His lips moved slowly in answer, no answer out of them came;
Then he swayed in his fingers the bell-branch, slow dropping a sound in faint streams
Softer than snow-flakes in April and piercing the marrow like flame.

Wrapt in the wave of that music, with weariness more than of earth,
The moil of my centuries filled me; and gone like a sea-covered stone
Were the memories of the whole of my sorrow and the memories of the whole of my mirth,
And a softness came from the starlight and filled me full to the bone.

In the roots of the grasses, the sorrels, I laid my body as low;
And the pearl-pale Niamh lay by me, her brow on the midst of my breast;
And the horse was gone in the distance, and years after years 'gan flow;
Square leaves of the ivy moved over us, binding us down to our rest.

And, man of the many white croziers, a century there I forgot

How the fetlocks drip blood in the battle, when the fallen on fallen lie rolled;
How the falconer follows the falcon in the weeds of the heron's plot,
And the name of the demon whose hammer made Conchubar's sword-blade of old.

And, man of the many white croziers, a century there I forgot
That the spear-shaft is made out of ashwood, the shield out of osier and hide;
How the hammers spring on the anvil, on the spearhead's burning spot;
How the slow, blue-eyed oxen of Finn low sadly at evening tide.

But in dreams, mild man of the croziers, driving the dust with their throngs,
Moved round me, of seamen or landsmen, all who are winter tales;
Came by me the kings of the Red Branch, with roaring of laughter and songs,
Or moved as they moved once, love-making or piercing the tempest with sails.

Came Blanaid, Mac Nessa, tall Fergus who feastward of old time slunk,
Cook Barach, the traitor; and warward, the spittle on his beard never dry,
Dark Balor, as old as a forest, car-borne, his mighty head sunk
Helpless, men lifting the lids of his weary and death-making eye.

And by me, in soft red raiment, the Fenians moved in loud streams,
And Grania, walking and smiling, sewed with her needle of bone.

So lived I and lived not, so wrought I and wrought not, with creatures of dreams,
In a long iron sleep, as a fish in the water goes dumb as a stone.

At times our slumber was lightened. When the sun was on silver or gold;
When brushed with the wings of the owls, in the dimness they love going by;
When a glow-worm was green on a grass-leaf, lured from his lair in the mould;
Half wakening, we lifted our eyelids, and gazed on the grass with a sigh.

So watched I when, man of the croziers, at the heel of a century fell,
Weak, in the midst of the meadow, from his miles in the midst of the air,
A starling like them that forgathered 'neath a moon waking white as a shell
When the Fenians made foray at morning with Bran, Sceolan, Lomair.

I awoke: the strange horse without summons out of the distance ran,
Thrusting his nose to my shoulder; he knew in his bosom deep
That once more moved in my bosom the ancient sadness of man,
And that I would leave the Immortals, their dimness, their dews dropping sleep.

O, had you seen beautiful Niamh grow white as the waters are white,
Lord of the croziers, you even had lifted your hands and wept:
But, the bird in my fingers, I mounted, remembering alone that delight

Of twilight and slumber were gone, and that hoofs impatiently stept.

I cried, 'O Niamh! O white one! if only a twelve-houred day,
I must gaze on the beard of Finn, and move where the old men and young
In the Fenians' dwellings of wattle lean on the chessboards and play,
Ah, sweet to me now were even bald Conan's slanderous tongue!

'Like me were some galley forsaken far off in Meridian isle,
Remembering its long-oared companions, sails turning to threadbare rags;
No more to crawl on the seas with long oars mile after mile,
But to be amid shooting of flies and flowering of rushes and flags.'

Their motionless eyeballs of spirits grown mild with mysterious thought,
Watched her those seamless faces from the valley's glimmering girth;
As she murmured, 'O wandering Oisin, the strength of the bell-branch is naught,
For there moves alive in your fingers the fluttering sadness of earth.

'Then go through the lands in the saddle and see what the mortals do,
And softly come to your Niamh over the tops of the tide;
But weep for your Niamh, O Oisin, weep; for if only your shoe
Brush lightly as haymouse earth's pebbles, you will come no more to my side.

'O flaming lion of the world, O when will you turn to your rest?'

I saw from a distant saddle; from the earth she made her
moan:
'I would die like a small withered leaf in the autumn, for
breast unto breast
We shall mingle no more, nor our gazes empty their
sweetness lone

'In the isles of the farthest seas where only the spirits come.
Were the winds less soft than the breath of a pigeon who
sleeps on her nest,
Nor lost in the star-fires and odours the sound of the sea's
vague drum?
O flaming lion of the world, O when will you turn to your
rest?'

The wailing grew distant; I rode by the woods of the
wrinkling bark,
Where ever is murmurous dropping, old silence and that
one sound;
For no live creatures live there, no weasels move in the dark;
In a reverie forgetful of all things, over the bubbling ground.

And I rode by the plains of the sea's edge, where all is barren
and grey,
Grey sand on the green of the grasses and over the dripping
trees,
Dripping and doubling landward, as though they would
hasten away,
Like an army of old men longing for rest from the moan of
the seas.

And the winds made the sands on the sea's edge turning and
turning go,
As my mind made the names of the Fenians. Far from the
hazel and oak,
I rode away on the surges, where, high as the saddle-bow,
Fled foam underneath me, and round me, a wandering and
milky smoke.

Long fled the foam-flakes around me, the winds fled out of the vast,
Snatching the bird in secret; nor knew I, embosomed apart,
When they froze the cloth on my body like armour riveted fast,
For Remembrance, lifting her leanness, keened in the gates of my heart.

Till, fattening the winds of the morning, an odour of new-mown hay
Came, and my forehead fell low, and my tears like berries fell down;
Later a sound came, half lost in the sound of a shore far away,
From the great grass-barnacle calling, and later the shore-weeds brown.

If I were as I once was, the strong hoofs crushing the sand and the shells,
Coming out of the sea as the dawn comes, a chaunt of love on my lips,
Not coughing, my head on my knees, and praying, and wroth with the bells,
I would leave no saint's head on his body from Rachlin to Bera of ships.

Making way from the kindling surges, I rode on a bridle-path
Much wondering to see upon all hands, of wattles and woodwork made,
Your bell-mounted churches, and guardless the sacred cairn and the rath,
And a small and a feeble populace stooping with mattock and spade,

Or weeding or ploughing with faces a-shining with much-toil wet;

While in this place and that place, with bodies unglorious, their chieftains stood,
Awaiting in patience the straw-death, croziered one, caught in your net:
Went the laughter of scorn from my mouth like the roaring of wind in a wood.

And because I went by them so huge and so speedy with eyes so bright,
Came after the hard gaze of youth, or an old man lifted his head:
And I rode and I rode, and I cried out, 'The Fenians hunt wolves in the night,
So sleep thee by daytime.' A voice cried, 'The Fenians a long time are dead.'

A whitebeard stood hushed on the pathway, the flesh of his face as dried grass,
And in folds round his eyes and his mouth, he sad as a child without milk;
And the dreams of the islands were gone, and I knew how men sorrow and pass,
And their hound, and their horse, and their love, and their eyes that glimmer like silk.

And wrapping my face in my hair, I murmured, 'In old age they ceased';
And my tears were larger than berries, and I murmured, 'Where white clouds lie spread
On Crevroe or broad Knockfefin, with many of old they feast
On the floors of the gods.' He cried, 'No, the gods a long time are dead.'

And lonely and longing for Niamh, I shivered and turned me about,
The heart in me longing to leap like a grasshopper into her heart;

I turned and rode to the westward, and followed the sea's
old shout
Till I saw where Maeve lies sleeping till starlight and
midnight part.

And there at the foot of the mountain, two carried a sack
full of sand,
They bore it with staggering and sweating, but fell with
their burden at length.
Leaning down from the gem-studded saddle, I flung it five
yards with my hand,
With a sob for men waxing so weakly, a sob for the Fenians'
old strength.

The rest you have heard of, O croziered man; how, when
divided the girth,
I fell on the path, and the horse went away like a summer
fly;
And my years three hundred fell on me, and I rose, and
walked on the earth,
A creeping old man, full of sleep, with the spittle on his
beard never dry.

How the men of the sand-sack showed me a church with its
belfry in air;
Sorry place, where for swing of the war-axe in my dim eyes
the crozier gleams;
What place have Caoilte and Conan, and Bran, Sceolan,
Lomair?
Speak, you too are old with your memories, an old man
surrounded with dreams.

S. Patrick. Where the flesh of the footsole clingeth on the
burning stones is their place;
Where the demons whip them with wires on the burning
stones of wide Hell,
Watching the blessèd ones move far off, and the smile on
God's face,

Between them a gateway of brass, and the howl of the angels
who fell.

Oisin. Put the staff in my hands; for I go to the Fenians, O
cleric, to chaunt
The war-songs that roused them of old; they will rise,
making clouds with their breath,
Innumerable, singing, exultant; the clay underneath them
shall pant,
And demons be broken in pieces, and trampled beneath
them in death.

And demons afraid in their darkness; deep horror of eyes
and of wings,
Afraid, their ears on the earth laid, shall listen and rise up
and weep;
Hearing the shaking of shields and the quiver of stretched
bow-strings,
Hearing Hell loud with a murmur, as shouting and mocking
we sweep.

We will tear out the flaming stones, and batter the gateway
of brass
And enter, and none sayeth 'No' when there enters the
strongly armed guest;
Make clean as a broom cleans, and march on as oxen move
over young grass;
Then feast, making converse of wars, and of old wounds,
and turn to our rest.

S. Patrick. On the flaming stones, without refuge, the limbs
of the Fenians are tost;
None war on the masters of Hell, who could break up the
world in their rage;
But kneel and wear out the flags and pray for your soul that
is lost
Through the demon love of its youth and its godless and
passionate age.

Oisin. Ah me! to be shaken with coughing and broken with
old age and pain,
Without laughter, a show unto children, alone with
remembrance and fear;
All emptied of purple hours as a beggar's cloak in the rain,
As a hay-cock out on the flood, or a wolf sucked under a
weir.

It were sad to gaze on the blessèd and no man I loved of old
there;
I throw down the chain of small stones! when life in my
body has ceased,
I will go to Caoilte, and Conan, and Bran, Sceolan, Lomair,
And dwell in the house of the Fenians, be they in flames or
at feast.

[1886–87] 1889

CROSSWAYS
1889

'The stars are threshed, and the souls are threshed from their husks.' – William Blake.

TO A. E.

The Song of the Happy Shepherd

The woods of Arcady are dead,
And over is their antique joy;
Of old the world on dreaming fed;
Grey Truth is now her painted toy;
Yet still she turns her restless head:
But O, sick children of the world,
Of all the many changing things
In dreary dancing past us whirled,
To the cracked tune that Chronos sings,
Words alone are certain good.
Where are now the warring kings,
Word be-mockers? – By the Rood,
Where are now the warring kings?
An idle word is now their glory,
By the stammering schoolboy said,
Reading some entangled story:
The kings of the old time are dead;
The wandering earth herself may be
Only a sudden flaming word,
In clanging space a moment heard,
Troubling the endless reverie.

Then nowise worship dusty deeds,
Nor seek, for this is also sooth,
To hunger fiercely after truth,
Lest all thy toiling only breeds
New dreams, new dreams; there is no truth
Saving in thine own heart. Seek, then,
No learning from the starry men,
Who follow with the optic glass
The whirling ways of stars that pass –
Seek, then, for this is also sooth,
No word of theirs – the cold star-bane
Has cloven and rent their hearts in twain,
And dead is all their human truth.
Go gather by the humming sea
Some twisted, echo-harbouring shell,
And to its lips thy story tell,
And they thy comforters will be,
Rewording in melodious guile
Thy fretful words a little while,
Till they shall singing fade in ruth
And die a pearly brotherhood;
For words alone are certain good:
Sing, then, for this is also sooth.

I must be gone: there is a grave
Where daffodil and lily wave,
And I would please the hapless faun,
Buried under the sleepy ground,
With mirthful songs before the dawn.
His shouting days with mirth were crowned;
And still I dream he treads the lawn,
Walking ghostly in the dew,
Pierced by my glad singing through,
My songs of old earth's dreamy youth:
But ah! she dreams not now; dream thou!
For fair are poppies on the brow:
Dream, dream, for this is also sooth.

[1885] 1885

The Sad Shepherd

There was a man whom Sorrow named his friend,
And he, of his high comrade Sorrow dreaming,
Went walking with slow steps along the gleaming
And humming sands, where windy surges wend:
And he called loudly to the stars to bend
From their pale thrones and comfort him, but they
Among themselves laugh on and sing alway:
And then the man whom Sorrow named his friend
Cried out, *Dim sea, hear my most piteous story!*
The sea swept on and cried her old cry still,
Rolling along in dreams from hill to hill.
He fled the persecution of her glory
And, in a far-off, gentle valley stopping,
Cried all his story to the dewdrops glistening.
But naught they heard, for they are always listening,
The dewdrops, for the sound of their own dropping.
And then the man whom Sorrow named his friend
Sought once again the shore, and found a shell,
And thought, *I will my heavy story tell*
Till my own words, re-echoing, shall send
Their sadness through a hollow, pearly heart;
And my own tale again for me shall sing,
And my own whispering words be comforting,
And lo! my ancient burden may depart.
Then he sang softly nigh the pearly rim;
But the sad dweller by the sea-ways lone
Changed all he sang to inarticulate moan
Among her wildering whirls, forgetting him.

[1885] 1886

The Cloak, the Boat, and the Shoes

'What do you make so fair and bright?'

'I make the cloak of Sorrow:
O lovely to see in all men's sight

Shall be the cloak of Sorrow,
In all men's sight.'

'What do you build with sails for flight?'

'I build a boat for Sorrow:
O swift on the seas all day and night
Saileth the rover Sorrow,
All day and night.'

'What do you weave with wool so white?'

'I weave the shoes of Sorrow:
Soundless shall be the footfall light
In all men's ears of Sorrow,
Sudden and light.'

1885

Anashuya and Vijaya

A little Indian temple in the Golden Age. Around it a garden; around that the forest. Anashuya, the young priestess, kneeling within the temple.

Anashuya. Send peace on all the lands and flickering corn. –
O, may tranquillity walk by his elbow
When wandering in the forest, if he love
No other. – Hear, and may the indolent flocks
Be plentiful. – And if he love another,
May panthers end him. – Hear, and load our king
With wisdom hour by hour. – May we two stand,
When we are dead, beyond the setting suns,
A little from the other shades apart,
With mingling hair, and play upon one lute.

Vijaya [entering and throwing a lily at her]. Hail! hail, my Anashuya.

Anashuya. No: be still.
I, priestess of this temple, offer up
Prayers for the land.

Vijaya. I will wait here, Amrita.

Anashuya. By mighty Brahma's ever-rustling robe,
Who is Amrita? Sorrow of all sorrows!
Another fills your mind.

Vijaya. My mother's name.

Anashuya [sings, coming out of the temple].
A sad, sad thought went by me slowly:
Sigh, O you little stars! O sigh and shake your blue apparel!
The sad, sad thought has gone from me now wholly:
Sing, O you little stars! O sing and raise your rapturous carol
To mighty Brahma, he who made you many as the sands,
And laid you on the gates of evening with his quiet hands.
[Sits down on the steps of the temple.]
Vijaya, I have brought my evening rice;
The sun has laid his chin on the grey wood,
Weary, with all his poppies gathered round him.

Vijaya. The hour when Kama, full of sleepy laughter,
Rises, and showers abroad his fragrant arrows,
Piercing the twilight with their murmuring barbs.

Anashuya. See how the sacred old flamingoes come,
Painting with shadow all the marble steps:
Aged and wise, they seek their wonted perches
Within the temple, devious walking, made
To wander by their melancholy minds.
Yon tall one eyes my supper; chase him away,
Far, far away. I named him after you.
He is a famous fisher; hour by hour
He ruffles with his bill the minnowed streams.
Ah! there he snaps my rice. I told you so.
Now cuff him off. He's off! A kiss for you,
Because you saved my rice. Have you no thanks?

Vijaya [sings]. Sing you of her, O first few stars,
Whom Brahma, touching with his finger, praises, for you hold
The van of wandering quiet; ere you be too calm and old,
Sing, turning in your cars,
Sing, till you raise your hands and sigh, and from your carheads peer,
With all your whirling hair, and drop many an azure tear.

Anashuya. What know the pilots of the stars of tears?

Vijaya. Their faces are all worn, and in their eyes
Flashes the fire of sadness, for they see
The icicles that famish all the North,
Where men lie frozen in the glimmering snow;
And in the flaming forests cower the lion
And lioness, with all their whimpering cubs;
And, ever pacing on the verge of things,
The phantom, Beauty, in a mist of tears;
While we alone have round us woven woods,
And feel the softness of each other's hand,
Amrita, while –

Anashuya [going away from him]. Ah me! you love another,
[Bursting into tears.]
And may some sudden dreadful ill befall her!

Vijaya. I loved another; now I love no other.
Among the mouldering of ancient woods
You live, and on the village border she,
With her old father the blind wood-cutter;
I saw her standing in her door but now.

Anashuya. Vijaya, swear to love her never more.

Vijaya. Ay, ay.

Anashuya. Swear by the parents of the gods,
Dread oath, who dwell on sacred Himalay,
On the far Golden Peak; enormous shapes,
Who still were old when the great sea was young;
On their vast faces mystery and dreams;
Their hair along the mountains rolled and filled
From year to year by the unnumbered nests
Of aweless birds, and round their stirless feet
The joyous flocks of deer and antelope,
Who never hear the unforgiving hound.
Swear!

Vijaya. By the parents of the gods, I swear.

Anashuya [sings]. I have forgiven, O new star!
Maybe you have not heard of us, you have come forth so newly,
You hunter of the fields afar!
Ah, you will know my loved one by his hunter's arrows truly,
Shoot on him shafts of quietness, that he may ever keep
A lonely laughter, and may kiss his hands to me in sleep.

Farewell, Vijaya. Nay, no word, no word;
I, priestess of this temple, offer up
Prayers for the land.

[Vijaya goes.]

O Brahma, guard in sleep
The merry lambs and the complacent kine,
The flies below the leaves, and the young mice
In the tree roots, and all the sacred flocks
Of red flamingoes; and my love, Vijaya;
And may no restless fay with fidget finger
Trouble his sleeping: give him dreams of me.

1889

The Indian upon God

I passed along the water's edge below the humid trees,
My spirit rocked in evening light, the rushes round my knees,
My spirit rocked in sleep and sighs; and saw the moorfowl pace
All dripping on a grassy slope, and saw them cease to chase
Each other round in circles, and heard the eldest speak:
Who holds the world between His bill and made us strong or weak
Is an undying moorfowl, and He lives beyond the sky.
The rains are from His dripping wing, the moonbeams from His eye.
I passed a little further on and heard a lotus talk:
Who made the world and ruleth it, He hangeth on a stalk,
For I am in His image made, and all this tinkling tide
Is but a sliding drop of rain between His petals wide.

A little way within the gloom a roebuck raised his eyes
Brimful of starlight, and he said: *The Stamper of the Skies,*
He is a gentle roebuck; for how else, I pray, could He
Conceive a thing so sad and soft, a gentle thing like me?
I passed a little further on and heard a peacock say:
Who made the grass and made the worms and made my feathers
gay,
He is a monstrous peacock, and He waveth all the night
His languid tail above us, lit with myriad spots of light.

[1886] 1886

The Indian to His Love

The island dreams under the dawn
And great boughs drop tranquillity;
The peahens dance on a smooth lawn,
A parrot sways upon a tree,
Raging at his own image in the enamelled sea.

Here we will moor our lonely ship
And wander ever with woven hands,
Murmuring softly lip to lip,
Along the grass, along the sands,
Murmuring how far away are the unquiet lands:

How we alone of mortals are
Hid under quiet boughs apart,
While our love grows an Indian star,
A meteor of the burning heart,
One with the tide that gleams, the wings that gleam and
dart,

The heavy boughs, the burnished dove
That moans and sighs a hundred days:
How when we die our shades will rove,
When eve has hushed the feathered ways,
With vapoury footsole by the water's drowsy blaze.

[1886] 1886

The Falling of the Leaves

Autumn is over the long leaves that love us,
And over the mice in the barley sheaves;
Yellow the leaves of the rowan above us,
And yellow the wet wild-strawberry leaves.

The hour of the waning of love has beset us,
And weary and worn are our sad souls now;
Let us part, ere the season of passion forget us,
With a kiss and a tear on thy drooping brow.

1889

Ephemera

'Your eyes that once were never weary of mine
Are bowed in sorrow under pendulous lids,
Because our love is waning.'

And then she:
'Although our love is waning, let us stand
By the lone border of the lake once more,
Together in that hour of gentleness
When the poor tired child, Passion, falls asleep:
How far away the stars seem, and how far
Is our first kiss, and ah, how old my heart!'

Pensive they paced along the faded leaves,
While slowly he whose hand held hers replied:
'Passion has often worn our wandering hearts.'

The woods were round them, and the yellow leaves
Fell like faint meteors in the gloom, and once
A rabbit old and lame limped down the path;
Autumn was over him: and now they stood
On the lone border of the lake once more:
Turning, he saw that she had thrust dead leaves
Gathered in silence, dewy as her eyes,
In bosom and hair.

'Ah, do not mourn,' he said,
'That we are tired, for other loves await us;
Hate on and love through unrepining hours.
Before us lies eternity; our souls
Are love, and a continual farewell.'

[1884] 1889

The Madness of King Goll

I sat on cushioned otter-skin:
My word was law from Ith to Emain,
And shook at Invar Amargin
The hearts of the world-troubling seamen,
And drove tumult and war away
From girl and boy and man and beast;
The fields grew fatter day by day,
The wild fowl of the air increased;
And every ancient Ollave said,
While he bent down his fading head,
'He drives away the Northern cold.'
They will not hush, the leaves a-flutter round me, the beech leaves old.

I sat and mused and drank sweet wine;
A herdsman came from inland valleys,
Crying, the pirates drove his swine
To fill their dark-beaked hollow galleys.
I called my battle-breaking men
And my loud brazen battle-cars
From rolling vale and rivery glen;
And under the blinking of the stars
Fell on the pirates by the deep,
And hurled them in the gulph of sleep:
These hands won many a torque of gold.
They will not hush, the leaves a-flutter round me, the beech leaves old.

But slowly, as I shouting slew
And trampled in the bubbling mire,

In my most secret spirit grew
A whirling and a wandering fire:
I stood: keen stars above me shone,
Around me shone keen eyes of men:
I laughed aloud and hurried on
By rocky shore and rushy fen;
I laughed because birds fluttered by,
And starlight gleamed, and clouds flew high,
And rushes waved and waters rolled.
They will not hush, the leaves a-flutter round me, the beech leaves old.

And now I wander in the woods
When summer gluts the golden bees,
Or in autumnal solitudes
Arise the leopard-coloured trees;
Or when along the wintry strands
The cormorants shiver on their rocks;
I wander on, and wave my hands,
And sing, and shake my heavy locks.
The grey wolf knows me; by one ear
I lead along the woodland deer;
The hares run by me growing bold.
They will not hush, the leaves a-flutter round me, the beech leaves old.

I came upon a little town
That slumbered in the harvest moon,
And passed a-tiptoe up and down,
Murmuring, to a fitful tune,
How I have followed, night and day,
A tramping of tremendous feet,
And saw where this old tympan lay
Deserted on a doorway seat,
And bore it to the woods with me;
Of some inhuman misery
Our married voices wildly trolled.
They will not hush, the leaves a-flutter round me, the beech leaves old.

I sang how, when day's toil is done,
Orchil shakes out her long dark hair
That hides away the dying sun
And sheds faint odours through the air:
When my hand passed from wire to wire
It quenched, with sound like falling dew,
The whirling and the wandering fire;
But lift a mournful ulalu,
For the kind wires are torn and still,
And I must wander wood and hill
Through summer's heat and winter's cold.
They will not hush, the leaves a-flutter round me, the beech leaves old.

[1884] 1887

The Stolen Child

Where dips the rocky highland
Of Sleuth Wood in the lake,
There lies a leafy island
Where flapping herons wake
The drowsy water-rats;
There we've hid our faery vats,
Full of berries
And of reddest stolen cherries.
Come away, O human child!
To the waters and the wild
With a faery, hand in hand,
For the world's more full of weeping than you can understand.

Where the wave of moonlight glosses
The dim grey sands with light,
Far off by furthest Rosses
We foot it all the night,
Weaving olden dances,
Mingling hands and mingling glances
Till the moon has taken flight;
To and fro we leap
And chase the frothy bubbles,

While the world is full of troubles
And is anxious in its sleep.
Come away, O human child!
To the waters and the wild
With a faery, hand in hand,
For the world's more full of weeping than you can understand.

Where the wandering water gushes
From the hills above Glen-Car,
In pools among the rushes
That scarce could bathe a star,
We seek for slumbering trout
And whispering in their ears
Give them unquiet dreams;
Leaning softly out
From ferns that drop their tears
Over the young streams.
Come away, O human child!
To the waters and the wild
With a faery, hand in hand,
For the world's more full of weeping than you can understand.

Away with us he's going,
The solemn-eyed:
He'll hear no more the lowing
Of the calves on the warm hillside
Or the kettle on the hob
Sing peace into his breast,
Or see the brown mice bob
Round and round the oatmeal-chest.
For he comes, the human child,
To the waters and the wild
With a faery, hand in hand,
From a world more full of weeping than he can understand.

1886

To an Isle in the Water

Shy one, shy one,
Shy one of my heart,
She moves in the firelight
Pensively apart.

She carries in the dishes,
And lays them in a row.
To an isle in the water
With her would I go.

She carries in the candles,
And lights the curtained room,
Shy in the doorway
And shy in the gloom;

And shy as a rabbit,
Helpful and shy.
To an isle in the water
With her would I fly.

[October 1886] 1889

Down by the Salley Gardens

Down by the salley gardens my love and I did meet;
She passed the salley gardens with little snow-white feet.
She bid me take love easy, as the leaves grow on the tree;
But I, being young and foolish, with her would not agree.

In a field by the river my love and I did stand,
And on my leaning shoulder she laid her snow-white hand.
She bid me take life easy, as the grass grows on the weirs;
But I was young and foolish, and now am full of tears.

[1888] 1889

The Meditation of the Old Fisherman

You waves, though you dance by my feet like children at play,
Though you glow and you glance, though you purr and you dart;
In the Junes that were warmer than these are, the waves were more gay,
When I was a boy with never a crack in my heart.

The herring are not in the tides as they were of old;
My sorrow! for many a creak gave the creel in the cart
That carried the take to Sligo town to be sold,
When I was a boy with never a crack in my heart.

And ah, you proud maiden, you are not so fair when his oar
Is heard on the water, as they were, the proud and apart,
Who paced in the eve by the nets on the pebbly shore,
When I was a boy with never a crack in my heart.

[June 1886] 1886

The Ballad of Father O'Hart

Good Father John O'Hart
In penal days rode out
To a shoneen who had free lands
And his own snipe and trout.

In trust took he John's lands;
Sleiveens were all his race;
And he gave them as dowers to his daughters,
And they married beyond their place.

But Father John went up,
And Father John went down;
And he wore small holes in his shoes,
And he wore large holes in his gown.

All loved him, only the shoneen,
Whom the devils have by the hair,
From the wives, and the cats, and the children,
To the birds in the white of the air.

The birds, for he opened their cages
As he went up and down;
And he said with a smile, 'Have peace now';
And he went his way with a frown.

But if when anyone died
Came keeners hoarser than rooks,
He bade them give over their keening;
For he was a man of books.

And these were the works of John,
When, weeping score by score,
People came into Coloony;
For he'd died at ninety-four.

There was no human keening;
The birds from Knocknarea
And the world round Knocknashee
Came keening in that day.

The young birds and old birds
Came flying, heavy and sad;
Keening in from Tiraragh,
Keening from Ballinafad;

Keening from Inishmurray,
Nor stayed for bite or sup;
This way were all reproved
Who dig old customs up.

[1887] 1888

The Ballad of Moll Magee

Come round me, little childer;
There, don't fling stones at me
Because I mutter as I go;
But pity Moll Magee.

My man was a poor fisher
With shore lines in the say;
My work was saltin' herrings
The whole of the long day.

And sometimes from the saltin' shed
I scarce could drag my feet,
Under the blessed moonlight,
Along the pebbly street.

I'd always been but weakly,
And my baby was just born;
A neighbour minded her by day,
I minded her till morn.

I lay upon my baby;
Ye little childer dear,
I looked on my cold baby
When the morn grew frosty and clear.

A weary woman sleeps so hard!
My man grew red and pale,
And gave me money, and bade me go
To my own place, Kinsale.

He drove me out and shut the door,
And gave his curse to me;
I went away in silence,
No neighbour could I see.

The windows and the doors were shut,
One star shone faint and green,
The little straws were turnin' round
Across the bare boreen.

I went away in silence:
Beyond old Martin's byre
I saw a kindly neighbour
Blowin' her mornin' fire.

She drew from me my story –
My money's all used up,
And still, with pityin', scornin' eye,
She gives me bite and sup.

She says my man will surely come,
And fetch me home agin;
But always, as I'm movin' round,
Without doors or within,

Pilin' the wood or pilin' the turf,
Or goin' to the well,
I'm thinkin' of my baby
And keenin' to mysel'.

And sometimes I am sure she knows
When, openin' wide His door,
God lights the stars, His candles,
And looks upon the poor.

So now, ye little childer,
Ye won't fling stones at me;
But gather with your shinin' looks
And pity Moll Magee.

1889

The Ballad of the Foxhunter

'Lay me in a cushioned chair;
Carry me, ye four,
With cushions here and cushions there,
To see the world once more.

'To stable and to kennel go;
Bring what is there to bring;
Lead my Lollard to and fro,
Or gently in a ring.

'Put the chair upon the grass:
Bring Rody and his hounds,
That I may contented pass
From these earthly bounds.'

His eyelids droop, his head falls low,
His old eyes cloud with dreams;
The sun upon all things that grow
Falls in sleepy streams.

Brown Lollard treads upon the lawn,
And to the armchair goes,
And now the old man's dreams are gone,
He smooths the long brown nose.

And now moves many a pleasant tongue
Upon his wasted hands,
For leading aged hounds and young
The huntsman near him stands.

'Huntsman Rody, blow the horn,
Make the hills reply.'
The huntsman loosens on the morn
A gay wandering cry.

Fire is in the old man's eyes,
His fingers move and sway,
And when the wandering music dies
They hear him feebly say,

'Huntsman Rody, blow the horn,
Make the hills reply.'
'I cannot blow upon my horn,
I can but weep and sigh.'

Servants round his cushioned place
Are with new sorrow wrung;
Hounds are gazing on his face,
Aged hounds and young.

One blind hound only lies apart
On the sun-smitten grass;
He holds deep commune with his heart:
The moments pass and pass;

The blind hound with a mournful din
Lifts slow his wintry head;
The servants bear the body in;
The hounds wail for the dead.

[1889] 1889

THE ROSE
1893

'Sero te amavi, Pulchritudo tam antiqua et tam nova! Sero te amavi.' – S. Augustine

TO LIONEL JOHNSON

To the Rose upon the Rood of Time

Red Rose, proud Rose, sad Rose of all my days!
Come near me, while I sing the ancient ways:
Cuchulain battling with the bitter tide;
The Druid, grey, wood-nurtured, quiet-eyed,
Who cast round Fergus dreams, and ruin untold;
And thine own sadness, whereof stars, grown old
In dancing silver-sandalled on the sea,
Sing in their high and lonely melody.
Come near, that no more blinded by man's fate,
I find under the boughs of love and hate,
In all poor foolish things that live a day,
Eternal beauty wandering on her way.

Come near, come near, come near – Ah, leave me still
A little space for the rose-breath to fill!
Lest I no more hear common things that crave;
The weak worm hiding down in its small cave,
The field-mouse running by me in the grass,
And heavy mortal hopes that toil and pass;
But seek alone to hear the strange things said
By God to the bright hearts of those long dead,

And learn to chaunt a tongue men do not know.
Come near; I would, before my time to go,
Sing of old Eire and the ancient ways:
Red Rose, proud Rose, sad Rose of all my days.

1892

Fergus and the Druid

Fergus. This whole day have I followed in the rocks,
And you have changed and flowed from shape to shape,
First as a raven on whose ancient wings
Scarcely a feather lingered, then you seemed
A weasel moving on from stone to stone,
And now at last you wear a human shape,
A thin grey man half lost in gathering night.

Druid. What would you, king of the proud Red Branch kings?

Fergus. This would I say, most wise of living souls:
Young subtle Conchubar sat close by me
When I gave judgment, and his words were wise,
And what to me was burden without end,
To him seemed easy, so I laid the crown
Upon his head to cast away my sorrow.

Druid. What would you, king of the proud Red Branch kings?

Fergus. A king and proud! and that is my despair.
I feast amid my people on the hill,
And pace the woods, and drive my chariot-wheels
In the white border of the murmuring sea;
And still I feel the crown upon my head.

Druid. What would you, Fergus?

Fergus. Be no more a king
But learn the dreaming wisdom that is yours.

Druid. Look on my thin grey hair and hollow cheeks
And on these hands that may not lift the sword,

This body trembling like a wind-blown reed.
No woman's loved me, no man sought my help.

Fergus. A king is but a foolish labourer
Who wastes his blood to be another's dream.

Druid. Take, if you must, this little bag of dreams;
Unloose the cord, and they will wrap you round.

Fergus. I see my life go drifting like a river
From change to change; I have been many things –
A green drop in the surge, a gleam of light
Upon a sword, a fir-tree on a hill,
An old slave grinding at a heavy quern,
A king sitting upon a chair of gold –
And all these things were wonderful and great;
But now I have grown nothing, knowing all.
Ah! Druid, Druid, how great webs of sorrow
Lay hidden in the small slate-coloured thing!

1892

Cuchulain's Fight with the Sea

A man came slowly from the setting sun,
To Emer, raddling raiment in her dun,
And said, 'I am that swineherd whom you bid
Go watch the road between the wood and tide,
But now I have no need to watch it more.'

Then Emer cast the web upon the floor,
And raising arms all raddled with the dye,
Parted her lips with a loud sudden cry.

That swineherd stared upon her face and said,
'No man alive, no man among the dead,
Has won the gold his cars of battle bring.'

'But if your master comes home triumphing
Why must you blench and shake from foot to crown?'

Thereon he shook the more and cast him down

Upon the web-heaped floor, and cried his word:
'With him is one sweet-throated like a bird.'

'You dare me to my face,' and thereupon
She smote with raddled fist, and where her son
Herded the cattle came with stumbling feet,
And cried with angry voice, 'It is not meet
To idle life away, a common herd.'

'I have long waited, mother, for that word:
But wherefore now?'

'There is a man to die;
You have the heaviest arm under the sky.'

'Whether under its daylight or its stars
My father stands amid his battle-cars.'

'But you have grown to be the taller man.'

'Yet somewhere under starlight or the sun
My father stands.'

'Aged, worn out with wars
On foot, on horseback or in battle-cars.'

'I only ask what way my journey lies,
For He who made you bitter made you wise.'

'The Red Branch camp in a great company
Between wood's rim and the horses of the sea.
Go there, and light a camp-fire at wood's rim;
But tell your name and lineage to him
Whose blade compels, and wait till they have found
Some feasting man that the same oath has bound.'

Among those feasting men Cuchulain dwelt,
And his young sweetheart close beside him knelt,
Stared on the mournful wonder of his eyes,
Even as Spring upon the ancient skies,
And pondered on the glory of his days;
And all around the harp-string told his praise,
And Conchubar, the Red Branch king of kings,
With his own fingers touched the brazen strings.

At last Cuchulain spake, 'Some man has made
His evening fire amid the leafy shade.
I have often heard him singing to and fro,
I have often heard the sweet sound of his bow.
Seek out what man he is.'

One went and came.
'He bade me let all know he gives his name
At the sword-point, and waits till we have found
Some feasting man that the same oath has bound.'

Cuchulain cried, 'I am the only man
Of all this host so bound from childhood on.'

After short fighting in the leafy shade,
He spake to the young man, 'Is there no maid
Who loves you, no white arms to wrap you round,
Or do you long for the dim sleepy ground,
That you have come and dared me to my face?'

'The dooms of men are in God's hidden place.'

'Your head a while seemed like a woman's head
That I loved once.'

Again the fighting sped,
But now the war-rage in Cuchulain woke,
And through that new blade's guard the old blade broke,
And pierced him.

'Speak before your breath is done.'

'Cuchulain I, mighty Cuchulain's son.'

'I put you from your pain. I can no more.'

While day its burden on to evening bore,
With head bowed on his knees Cuchulain stayed;
Then Conchubar sent that sweet-throated maid,
And she, to win him, his grey hair caressed;
In vain her arms, in vain her soft white breast.
Then Conchubar, the subtlest of all men,
Ranking his Druids round him ten by ten,
Spake thus: 'Cuchulain will dwell there and brood
For three days more in dreadful quietude,

And then arise, and raving slay us all.
Chaunt in his ear delusions magical,
That he may fight the horses of the sea.'
The Druids took them to their mystery,
And chaunted for three days.
                                        Cuchulain stirred,
Stared on the horses of the sea, and heard
The cars of battle and his own name cried;
And fought with the invulnerable tide.

[November 1891–April 1892] 1892

The Rose of the World

Who dreamed that beauty passes like a dream?
For these red lips, with all their mournful pride,
Mournful that no new wonder may betide,
Troy passed away in one high funeral gleam,
And Usna's children died.

We and the labouring world are passing by:
Amid men's souls, that waver and give place
Like the pale waters in their wintry race,
Under the passing stars, foam of the sky,
Lives on this lonely face.

Bow down, archangels, in your dim abode:
Before you were, or any hearts to beat,
Weary and kind one lingered by His seat;
He made the world to be a grassy road
Before her wandering feet.

[1891] 1892

The Rose of Peace

If Michael, leader of God's host
When Heaven and Hell are met,
Looked down on you from Heaven's door-post
He would his deeds forget.

Brooding no more upon God's wars
In his divine homestead,
He would go weave out of the stars
A chaplet for your head.

And all folk seeing him bow down,
And white stars tell your praise,
Would come at last to God's great town,
Led on by gentle ways;

And God would bid His warfare cease,
Saying all things were well;
And softly make a rosy peace,
A peace of Heaven with Hell.

1892

The Rose of Battle

Rose of all Roses, Rose of all the World!
The tall thought-woven sails, that flap unfurled
Above the tide of hours, trouble the air,
And God's bell buoyed to be the water's care;
While hushed from fear, or loud with hope, a band
With blown, spray-dabbled hair gather at hand.
Turn if you may from battles never done,
I call, as they go by me one by one,
Danger no refuge holds, and war no peace,
For him who hears love sing and never cease,
Beside her clean-swept hearth, her quiet shade:
But gather all for whom no love hath made
A woven silence, or but came to cast
A song into the air, and singing passed
To smile on the pale dawn; and gather you
Who have sought more than is in rain or dew,
Or in the sun and moon, or on the earth,
Or sighs amid the wandering, starry mirth,
Or comes in laughter from the sea's sad lips,
And wage God's battles in the long grey ships.

The sad, the lonely, the insatiable,
To these Old Night shall all her mystery tell;
God's bell has claimed them by the little cry
Of their sad hearts, that may not live nor die.

Rose of all Roses, Rose of all the World!
You, too, have come where the dim tides are hurled
Upon the wharves of sorrow, and heard ring
The bell that calls us on; the sweet far thing.
Beauty grown sad with its eternity
Made you of us, and of the dim grey sea.
Our long ships loose thought-woven sails and wait,
For God has bid them share an equal fate;
And when at last, defeated in His wars,
They have gone down under the same white stars,
We shall no longer hear the little cry
Of our sad hearts, that may not live nor die.

1892

A Faery Song

Sung by the people of Faery over Diarmuid and Grania, in their bridal sleep under a Cromlech.

We who are old, old and gay,
O so old!
Thousands of years, thousands of years,
If all were told:

Give to these children, new from the world,
Silence and love;
And the long dew-dropping hours of the night,
And the stars above:

Give to these children, new from the world,
Rest far from men.
Is anything better, anything better?
Tell us it then:

Us who are old, old and gay,
O so old!
Thousands of years, thousands of years,
If all were told.

1891

The Lake Isle of Innisfree

I will arise and go now, and go to Innisfree,
And a small cabin build there, of clay and wattles made:
Nine bean-rows will I have there, a hive for the honey-bee,
And live alone in the bee-loud glade.

And I shall have some peace there, for peace comes dropping slow,
Dropping from the veils of the morning to where the cricket sings;
There midnight's all a glimmer, and noon a purple glow,
And evening full of the linnet's wings.

I will arise and go now, for always night and day
I hear lake water lapping with low sounds by the shore;
While I stand on the roadway, or on the pavements grey,
I hear it in the deep heart's core.

[December 1888] 1890

A Cradle Song

The angels are stooping
Above your bed;
They weary of trooping
With the whimpering dead.

God's laughing in Heaven
To see you so good;
The Sailing Seven
Are gay with His mood.

I sigh that kiss you,
For I must own
That I shall miss you
When you have grown.

[January 1890] 1890

The Pity of Love

A pity beyond all telling
Is hid in the heart of love:
The folk who are buying and selling,
The clouds on their journey above,
The cold wet winds ever blowing,
And the shadowy hazel grove
Where mouse-grey waters are flowing,
Threaten the head that I love.

1892

The Sorrow of Love

The brawling of a sparrow in the eaves,
The brilliant moon and all the milky sky,
And all that famous harmony of leaves,
Had blotted out man's image and his cry.

A girl arose that had red mournful lips
And seemed the greatness of the world in tears,
Doomed like Odysseus and the labouring ships
And proud as Priam murdered with his peers;

Arose, and on the instant clamorous eaves,
A climbing moon upon an empty sky,
And all that lamentation of the leaves,
Could but compose man's image and his cry.

[October 1891] 1892; 1925

When You are Old

When you are old and grey and full of sleep,
And nodding by the fire, take down this book,
And slowly read, and dream of the soft look
Your eyes had once, and of their shadows deep;

How many loved your moments of glad grace,
And loved your beauty with love false or true,
But one man loved the pilgrim soul in you,
And loved the sorrows of your changing face;

And bending down beside the glowing bars,
Murmur, a little sadly, how Love fled
And paced upon the mountains overhead
And hid his face amid a crowd of stars.

[21 October 1891] 1892

The White Birds

I would that we were, my beloved, white birds on the foam of the sea!
We tire of the flame of the meteor, before it can fade and flee;
And the flame of the blue star of twilight, hung low on the rim of the sky,
Has awaked in our hearts, my beloved, a sadness that may not die.

A weariness comes from those dreamers, dew-dabbled, the lily and rose;
Ah, dream not of them, my beloved, the flame of the meteor that goes,
Or the flame of the blue star that lingers hung low in the fall of the dew:
For I would we were changed to white birds on the wandering foam: I and you!

I am haunted by numberless islands, and many a Danaan shore,
Where Time would surely forget us, and Sorrow come near us no more;
Soon far from the rose and the lily and fret of the flames would we be,
Were we only white birds, my beloved, buoyed out on the foam of the sea!

1892

A Dream of Death

I dreamed that one had died in a strange place
Near no accustomed hand;
And they had nailed the boards above her face,
The peasants of that land,
Wondering to lay her in that solitude,
And raised above her mound
A cross they had made out of two bits of wood,
And planted cypress round;
And left her to the indifferent stars above
Until I carved these words:
She was more beautiful than thy first love,
But now lies under boards.

1891

The Countess Cathleen in Paradise

All the heavy days are over;
Leave the body's coloured pride
Underneath the grass and clover,
With the feet laid side by side.

Bathed in flaming founts of duty
She'll not ask a haughty dress;
Carry all that mournful beauty
To the scented oaken press.

Did the kiss of Mother Mary
Put that music in her face?
Yet she goes with footstep wary,
Full of earth's old timid grace.

'Mong the feet of angels seven
What a dancer glimmering!
All the heavens bow down to Heaven,
Flame to flame and wing to wing.

1891

Who Goes with Fergus?

Who will go drive with Fergus now,
And pierce the deep wood's woven shade,
And dance upon the level shore?
Young man, lift up your russet brow,
And lift your tender eyelids, maid,
And brood on hopes and fears no more.

And no more turn aside and brood
Upon love's bitter mystery;
For Fergus rules the brazen cars,
And rules the shadows of the wood,
And the white breast of the dim sea
And all dishevelled wandering stars.

1892

The Man who Dreamed of Faeryland

He stood among a crowd at Drumahair;
His heart hung all upon a silken dress,
And he had known at last some tenderness,
Before earth took him to her stony care;
But when a man poured fish into a pile,
It seemed they raised their little silver heads,
And sang what gold morning or evening sheds
Upon a woven world-forgotten isle

Where people love beside the ravelled seas;
That Time can never mar a lover's vows
Under that woven changeless roof of boughs:
The singing shook him out of his new ease.

He wandered by the sands of Lissadell;
His mind ran all on money cares and fears,
And he had known at last some prudent years
Before they heaped his grave under the hill;
But while he passed before a plashy place,
A lug-worm with its grey and muddy mouth
Sang that somewhere to north or west or south
There dwelt a gay, exulting, gentle race
Under the golden or the silver skies;
That if a dancer stayed his hungry foot
It seemed the sun and moon were in the fruit:
And at that singing he was no more wise.

He mused beside the well of Scanavin,
He mused upon his mockers: without fail
His sudden vengeance were a country tale,
When earthy night had drunk his body in;
But one small knot-grass growing by the pool
Sang where – unnecessary cruel voice –
Old silence bids its chosen race rejoice,
Whatever ravelled waters rise and fall
Or stormy silver fret the gold of day,
And midnight there enfold them like a fleece
And lover there by lover be at peace.
The tale drove his fine angry mood away.

He slept under the hill of Lugnagall;
And might have known at last unhaunted sleep
Under that cold and vapour-turbaned steep,
Now that the earth had taken man and all:
Did not the worms that spired about his bones
Proclaim with that unwearied, reedy cry
That God has laid His fingers on the sky,
That from those fingers glittering summer runs

The Lamentation of the Old Pensioner

Although I shelter from the rain
Under a broken tree,
My chair was nearest to the fire
In every company
That talked of love or politics,
Ere Time transfigured me.

Though lads are making pikes again
For some conspiracy,
And crazy rascals rage their fill
At human tyranny;
My contemplations are of Time
That has transfigured me.

There's not a woman turns her face
Upon a broken tree,
And yet the beauties that I loved
Are in my memory;
I spit into the face of Time
That has transfigured me.

1890; 1925

The Ballad of Father Gilligan

The old priest Peter Gilligan
Was weary night and day;
For half his flock were in their beds,
Or under green sods lay.

Once, while he nodded on a chair,
At the moth-hour of eve,
Another poor man sent for him,
And he began to grieve.

'I have no rest, nor joy, nor peace,
For people die and die';
And after cried he, 'God forgive!
My body spake, not I!'

He knelt, and leaning on the chair
He prayed and fell asleep;
And the moth-hour went from the fields,
And stars began to peep.

They slowly into millions grew,
And leaves shook in the wind;
And God covered the world with shade,
And whispered to mankind.

Upon the time of sparrow-chirp
When the moths came once more,
The old priest Peter Gilligan
Stood upright on the floor.

'Mavrone, mavrone! the man has died
While I slept on the chair';
He roused his horse out of its sleep,
And rode with little care.

He rode now as he never rode,
By rocky lane and fen;
The sick man's wife opened the door:
'Father! you come again!'

'And is the poor man dead?' he cried.
'He died an hour ago.'
The old priest Peter Gilligan
In grief swayed to and fro.

'When you were gone, he turned and died
As merry as a bird.'
The old priest Peter Gilligan
He knelt him at that word.

'He Who hath made the night of stars
For souls who tire and bleed,
Sent one of His great angels down
To help me in my need.

'He Who is wrapped in purple robes,
With planets in His care,
Had pity on the least of things
Asleep upon a chair.'

1890

The Two Trees

Beloved, gaze in thine own heart,
The holy tree is growing there;
From joy the holy branches start,
And all the trembling flowers they bear.
The changing colours of its fruit
Have dowered the stars with merry light;
The surety of its hidden root
Has planted quiet in the night;
The shaking of its leafy head
Has given the waves their melody,
And made my lips and music wed,
Murmuring a wizard song for thee.
There the Loves a circle go,
The flaming circle of our days,
Gyring, spiring to and fro
In those great ignorant leafy ways;
Remembering all that shaken hair
And how the wingèd sandals dart,
Thine eyes grow full of tender care:
Beloved, gaze in thine own heart.

Gaze no more in the bitter glass
The demons, with their subtle guile,
Lift up before us when they pass,
Or only gaze a little while;
For there a fatal image grows
That the stormy night receives,
Roots half hidden under snows,
Broken boughs and blackened leaves.
For all things turn to barrenness
In the dim glass the demons hold,
The glass of outer weariness,
Made when God slept in times of old.
There, through the broken branches, go
The ravens of unresting thought;
Flying, crying, to and fro,
Cruel claw and hungry throat,

Or else they stand and sniff the wind,
And shake their ragged wings; alas!
Thy tender eyes grow all unkind:
Gaze no more in the bitter glass.

1892

To Some I have Talked with by the Fire

While I wrought out these fitful Danaan rhymes,
My heart would brim with dreams about the times
When we bent down above the fading coals
And talked of the dark folk who live in souls
Of passionate men, like bats in the dead trees;
And of the wayward twilight companies
Who sigh with mingled sorrow and content,
Because their blossoming dreams have never bent
Under the fruit of evil and of good:
And of the embattled flaming multitude
Who rise, wing above wing, flame above flame,
And, like a storm, cry the Ineffable Name,
And with the clashing of their sword-blades make
A rapturous music, till the morning break
And the white hush end all but the loud beat
Of their long wings, the flash of their white feet.

1895

To Ireland in the Coming Times

Know, that I would accounted be
True brother of a company
That sang, to sweeten Ireland's wrong,
Ballad and story, rann and song;
Nor be I any less of them,
Because the red-rose-bordered hem
Of her, whose history began
Before God made the angelic clan,
Trails all about the written page.
When Time began to rant and rage

The measure of her flying feet
Made Ireland's heart begin to beat;
And Time bade all his candles flare
To light a measure here and there;
And may the thoughts of Ireland brood
Upon a measured quietude.

Nor may I less be counted one
With Davis, Mangan, Ferguson,
Because, to him who ponders well,
My rhymes more than their rhyming tell
Of things discovered in the deep,
Where only body's laid asleep.
For the elemental creatures go
About my table to and fro,
That hurry from unmeasured mind
To rant and rage in flood and wind;
Yet he who treads in measured ways
May surely barter gaze for gaze.
Man ever journeys on with them
After the red-rose-bordered hem.
Ah, faeries, dancing under the moon,
A Druid land, a Druid tune!

While still I may, I write for you
The love I lived, the dream I knew.
From our birthday, until we die,
Is but the winking of an eye;
And we, our singing and our love,
What measurer Time has lit above,
And all benighted things that go
About my table to and fro,
Are passing on to where may be,
In truth's consuming ecstasy,
No place for love and dream at all;
For God goes by with white footfall.
I cast my heart into my rhymes,
That you, in the dim coming times,
May know how my heart went with them
After the red-rose-bordered hem.

1892

THE WIND AMONG THE REEDS
1899

The Hosting of the Sidhe

The host is riding from Knocknarea
And over the grave of Clooth-na-Bare;
Caoilte tossing his burning hair,
And Niamh calling *Away, come away:*
Empty your heart of its mortal dream.
The winds awaken, the leaves whirl round,
Our cheeks are pale, our hair is unbound,
Our breasts are heaving, our eyes are agleam,
Our arms are waving, our lips are apart;
And if any gaze on our rushing band,
We come between him and the deed of his hand,
We come between him and the hope of his heart.
The host is rushing 'twixt night and day,
And where is there hope or deed as fair?
Caoilte tossing his burning hair,
And Niamh calling *Away, come away.*

[29 August 1893] 1893

The Everlasting Voices

O sweet everlasting Voices, be still;
Go to the guards of the heavenly fold
And bid them wander obeying your will,
Flame under flame, till Time be no more;

Have you not heard that our hearts are old,
That you call in birds, in wind on the hill,
In shaken boughs, in tide on the shore?
O sweet everlasting Voices, be still.

[29 August 1895] 1896

The Moods

Time drops in decay,
Like a candle burnt out,
And the mountains and woods
Have their day, have their day;
What one in the rout
Of the fire-born moods
Has fallen away?

1893

The Lover tells of the Rose in his Heart

All things uncomely and broken, all things worn out and old,
The cry of a child by the roadway, the creak of a lumbering cart,
The heavy steps of the ploughman, splashing the wintry mould,
Are wronging your image that blossoms a rose in the deeps of my heart.

The wrong of unshapely things is a wrong too great to be told;
I hunger to build them anew and sit on a green knoll apart,
With the earth and the sky and the water, re-made, like a casket of gold
For my dreams of your image that blossoms a rose in the deeps of my heart.

1892

The Host of the Air

O'Driscoll drove with a song
The wild duck and the drake
From the tall and the tufted reeds
Of the drear Hart Lake.

And he saw how the reeds grew dark
At the coming of night-tide,
And dreamed of the long dim hair
Of Bridget his bride.

He heard while he sang and dreamed
A piper piping away,
And never was piping so sad,
And never was piping so gay.

And he saw young men and young girls
Who danced on a level place,
And Bridget his bride among them,
With a sad and a gay face.

The dancers crowded about him
And many a sweet thing said,
And a young man brought him red wine
And a young girl white bread.

But Bridget drew him by the sleeve
Away from the merry bands,
To old men playing at cards
With a twinkling of ancient hands.

The bread and the wine had a doom,
For these were the host of the air;
He sat and played in a dream
Of her long dim hair.

He played with the merry old men
And thought not of evil chance,
Until one bore Bridget his bride
Away from the merry dance.

He bore her away in his arms,
The handsomest young man there,
And his neck and his breast and his arms
Were drowned in her long dim hair.

O'Driscoll scattered the cards
And out of his dream awoke:
Old men and young men and young girls
Were gone like a drifting smoke;

But he heard high up in the air
A piper piping away,
And never was piping so sad,
And never was piping so gay.

[1 October 1893] 1893

The Fish

Although you hide in the ebb and flow
Of the pale tide when the moon has set,
The people of coming days will know
About the casting out of my net,
And how you have leaped times out of mind
Over the little silver cords,
And think that you were hard and unkind,
And blame you with many bitter words.

1898

The Unappeasable Host

The Danaan children laugh, in cradles of wrought gold,
And clap their hands together, and half close their eyes,
For they will ride the North when the ger-eagle flies,
With heavy whitening wings, and a heart fallen cold:
I kiss my wailing child and press it to my breast,
And hear the narrow graves calling my child and me.
Desolate winds that cry over the wandering sea;
Desolate winds that hover in the flaming West;

Desolate winds that beat the doors of Heaven, and beat
The doors of Hell and blow there many a whimpering ghost;
O heart the winds have shaken, the unappeasable host
Is comelier than candles at Mother Mary's feet.

1896

Into the Twilight

Out-worn heart, in a time out-worn,
Come clear of the nets of wrong and right;
Laugh, heart, again in the grey twilight,
Sigh, heart, again in the dew of the morn.

Your mother Eire is always young,
Dew ever shining and twilight grey;
Though hope fall from you and love decay,
Burning in fires of a slanderous tongue.

Come, heart, where hill is heaped upon hill:
For there the mystical brotherhood
Of sun and moon and hollow and wood
And river and stream work out their will;

And God stands winding His lonely horn,
And time and the world are ever in flight;
And love is less kind than the grey twilight,
And hope is less dear than the dew of the morn.

1893

The Song of Wandering Aengus

I went out to the hazel wood,
Because a fire was in my head,
And cut and peeled a hazel wand,
And hooked a berry to a thread;
And when white moths were on the wing,
And moth-like stars were flickering out,
I dropped the berry in a stream
And caught a little silver trout.

When I had laid it on the floor
I went to blow the fire aflame,
But something rustled on the floor,
And some one called me by my name:
It had become a glimmering girl
With apple blossom in her hair
Who called me by my name and ran
And faded through the brightening air.

Though I am old with wandering
Through hollow lands and hilly lands,
I will find out where she has gone,
And kiss her lips and take her hands;
And walk among long dappled grass,
And pluck till time and times are done
The silver apples of the moon,
The golden apples of the sun.

1897

The Song of the Old Mother

I rise in the dawn, and I kneel and blow
Till the seed of the fire flicker and glow;
And then I must scrub and bake and sweep
Till stars are beginning to blink and peep;
And the young lie long and dream in their bed
Of the matching of ribbons for bosom and head,
And their day goes over in idleness,
And they sigh if the wind but lift a tress:
While I must work because I am old,
And the seed of the fire gets feeble and cold.

1894

The Heart of the Woman

O what to me the little room
That was brimmed up with prayer and rest;
He bade me out into the gloom,
And my breast lies upon his breast.

O what to me my mother's care,
The house where I was safe and warm;
The shadowy blossom of my hair
Will hide us from the bitter storm.

O hiding hair and dewy eyes,
I am no more with life and death,
My heart upon his warm heart lies,
My breath is mixed into his breath.

[1894] 1894

The Lover mourns for the Loss of Love

Pale brows, still hands and dim hair,
I had a beautiful friend
And dreamed that the old despair
Would end in love in the end:
She looked in my heart one day
And saw your image was there;
She has gone weeping away.

1898

He mourns for the Change that has come upon him and his Beloved, and longs for the End of the World

Do you not hear me calling, white deer with no horns?
I have been changed to a hound with one red ear;
I have been in the Path of Stones and the Wood of Thorns,
For somebody hid hatred and hope and desire and fear

Under my feet that they follow you night and day.
A man with a hazel wand came without sound;
He changed me suddenly; I was looking another way;
And now my calling is but the calling of a hound;
And Time and Birth and Change are hurrying by.
I would that the Boar without bristles had come from the West
And had rooted the sun and moon and stars out of the sky
And lay in the darkness, grunting, and turning to his rest.

[1895–June 1897] 1897

He bids his Beloved be at Peace

I hear the Shadowy Horses, their long manes a-shake,
Their hoofs heavy with tumult, their eyes glimmering white;
The North unfolds above them clinging, creeping night,
The East her hidden joy before the morning break,
The West weeps in pale dew and sighs passing away,
The South is pouring down roses of crimson fire:
O vanity of Sleep, Hope, Dream, endless Desire,
The Horses of Disaster plunge in the heavy clay:
Beloved, let your eyes half close, and your heart beat
Over my heart, and your hair fall over my breast,
Drowning love's lonely hour in deep twilight of rest,
And hiding their tossing manes and their tumultuous feet.

[24 September 1895] 1896

He reproves the Curlew

O curlew, cry no more in the air,
Or only to the water in the West;
Because your crying brings to my mind
Passion-dimmed eyes and long heavy hair
That was shaken out over my breast:
There is enough evil in the crying of wind.

1896

He remembers Forgotten Beauty

When my arms wrap you round I press
My heart upon the loveliness
That has long faded from the world;
The jewelled crowns that kings have hurled
In shadowy pools, when armies fled;
The love-tales wrought with silken thread
By dreaming ladies upon cloth
That has made fat the murderous moth;
The roses that of old time were
Woven by ladies in their hair,
The dew-cold lilies ladies bore
Through many a sacred corridor
Where such grey clouds of incense rose
That only God's eyes did not close:
For that pale breast and lingering hand
Come from a more dream-heavy land,
A more dream-heavy hour than this;
And when you sigh from kiss to kiss
I hear white Beauty sighing, too,
For hours when all must fade like dew,
But flame on flame, and deep on deep,
Throne over throne where in half sleep,
Their swords upon their iron knees,
Brood her high lonely mysteries.

1896

A Poet to his Beloved

I bring you with reverent hands
The books of my numberless dreams,
White woman that passion has worn
As the tide wears the dove-grey sands,
And with heart more old than the horn
That is brimmed from the pale fire of time:
White woman with numberless dreams,
I bring you my passionate rhyme.

[1895] 1895

He gives his Beloved certain Rhymes

Fasten your hair with a golden pin,
And bind up every wandering tress;
I bade my heart build these poor rhymes:
It worked at them, day out, day in,
Building a sorrowful loveliness
Out of the battles of old times.

You need but lift a pearl-pale hand,
And bind up your long hair and sigh;
And all men's hearts must burn and beat;
And candle-like foam on the dim sand,
And stars climbing the dew-dropping sky,
Live but to light your passing feet.

[before August 1895] 1896

To his Heart, bidding it have no Fear

Be you still, be you still, trembling heart;
Remember the wisdom out of the old days:
Him who trembles before the flame and the flood,
And the winds that blow through the starry ways,
Let the starry winds and the flame and the flood
Cover over and hide, for he has no part
With the lonely, majestical multitude.

1896

The Cap and Bells

The jester walked in the garden:
The garden had fallen still;
He bade his soul rise upward
And stand on her window-sill.

It rose in a straight blue garment,
When owls began to call:
It had grown wise-tongued by thinking
Of a quiet and light footfall;

But the young queen would not listen;
She rose in her pale night-gown;
She drew in the heavy casement
And pushed the latches down.

He bade his heart go to her,
When the owls called out no more;
In a red and quivering garment
It sang to her through the door.

It had grown sweet-tongued by dreaming
Of a flutter of flower-like hair;
But she took up her fan from the table
And waved it off on the air.

'I have cap and bells,' he pondered,
'I will send them to her and die';
And when the morning whitened
He left them where she went by.

She laid them upon her bosom,
Under a cloud of her hair,
And her red lips sang them a love-song
Till stars grew out of the air.

She opened her door and her window,
And the heart and the soul came through,
To her right hand came the red one,
To her left hand came the blue.

They set up a noise like crickets,
A chattering wise and sweet,
And her hair was a folded flower
And the quiet of love in her feet.

[1893] 1894

The Valley of the Black Pig

The dews drop slowly and dreams gather: unknown spears
Suddenly hurtle before my dream-awakened eyes,
And then the clash of fallen horsemen and the cries
Of unknown perishing armies beat about my ears.
We who still labour by the cromlech on the shore,
The grey cairn on the hill, when day sinks drowned in dew,
Being weary of the world's empires, bow down to you,
Master of the still stars and of the flaming door.

1896

The Lover asks Forgiveness because of his Many Moods

If this importunate heart trouble your peace
With words lighter than air,
Or hopes that in mere hoping flicker and cease;
Crumple the rose in your hair;
And cover your lips with odorous twilight and say,
'O Hearts of wind-blown flame!
O Winds, older than changing of night and day,
That murmuring and longing came
From marble cities loud with tabors of old
In dove-grey faery lands;
From battle-banners, fold upon purple fold,
Queens wrought with glimmering hands;
That saw young Niamh hover with love-lorn face
Above the wandering tide;
And lingered in the hidden desolate place
Where the last Phoenix died,
And wrapped the flames above his holy head;
And still murmur and long:
O Piteous Hearts, changing till change be dead
In a tumultuous song':

And Cumhal saw like a drifting smoke
All manner of blessed souls,
Women and children, young men with books,
And old men with croziers and stoles.

'Praise God and God's Mother,' Dathi said,
'For God and God's Mother have sent
The blessedest souls that walk in the world
To fill your heart with content.'

'And which is the blessedest,' Cumhal said,
'Where all are comely and good?
Is it these that with golden thuribles
Are singing about the wood?'

'My eyes are blinking,' Dathi said,
'With the secrets of God half blind,
But I can see where the wind goes
And follow the way of the wind;

'And blessedness goes where the wind goes,
And when it is gone we are dead;
I see the blessedest soul in the world
And he nods a drunken head.

'O blessedness comes in the night and the day
And whither the wise heart knows;
And one has seen in the redness of wine
The Incorruptible Rose,

'That drowsily drops faint leaves on him
And the sweetness of desire,
While time and the world are ebbing away
In twilights of dew and of fire.'

1897

The Secret Rose

Far-off, most secret, and inviolate Rose,
Enfold me in my hour of hours; where those
Who sought thee in the Holy Sepulchre,
Or in the wine-vat, dwell beyond the stir
And tumult of defeated dreams; and deep
Among pale eyelids, heavy with the sleep
Men have named beauty. Thy great leaves enfold
The ancient beards, the helms of ruby and gold
Of the crowned Magi; and the king whose eyes
Saw the Pierced Hands and Rood of elder rise
In Druid vapour and make the torches dim;
Till vain frenzy awoke and he died; and him
Who met Fand walking among flaming dew
By a grey shore where the wind never blew,
And lost the world and Emer for a kiss;
And him who drove the gods out of their liss,
And till a hundred morns had flowered red
Feasted, and wept the barrows of his dead;
And the proud dreaming king who flung the crown
And sorrow away, and calling bard and clown
Dwelt among wine-stained wanderers in deep woods;
And him who sold tillage, and house, and goods,
And sought through lands and islands numberless years,
Until he found, with laughter and with tears,
A woman of so shining loveliness
That men threshed corn at midnight by a tress,
A little stolen tress. I, too, await
The hour of thy great wind of love and hate.
When shall the stars be blown about the sky,
Like the sparks blown out of a smithy, and die?
Surely thine hour has come, thy great wind blows,
Far-off, most secret, and inviolate Rose?

1896

He wishes his Beloved were Dead

Were you but lying cold and dead,
And lights were paling out of the West,
You would come hither, and bend your head,
And I would lay my head on your breast;
And you would murmur tender words,
Forgiving me, because you were dead:
Nor would you rise and hasten away,
Though you have the will of the wild birds,
But know your hair was bound and wound
About the stars and moon and sun:
O would, beloved, that you lay
Under the dock-leaves in the ground,
While lights were paling one by one.

1898

He wishes for the Cloths of Heaven

Had I the heavens' embroidered cloths,
Enwrought with golden and silver light,
The blue and the dim and the dark cloths
Of night and light and the half-light,
I would spread the cloths under your feet:
But I, being poor, have only my dreams;
I have spread my dreams under your feet;
Tread softly because you tread on my dreams.

1899

He thinks of his Past Greatness when a Part of the Constellations of Heaven

I have drunk ale from the Country of the Young
And weep because I know all things now:
I have been a hazel-tree, and they hung
The Pilot Star and the Crooked Plough

Among my le[illegible] the Reeds
I became a rush
I became a man, a
Knowing one, out of mind:
May not lie on the breas[illegible]
Of the woman that he loves, that his head
O beast of the wilderness, bir[illegible] the hair
Must I endure your amorous cri[illegible]

1898

The Fiddler of Dooney

When I play on my fiddle in Dooney,
Folk dance like a wave of the sea;
My cousin is priest in Kilvarnet,
My brother in Mocharabuiee.

I passed my brother and cousin:
They read in their books of prayer;
I read in my book of songs
I bought at the Sligo fair.

When we come at the end of time
To Peter sitting in state,
He will smile on the three old spirits,
But call me first through the gate;

For the good are always the merry,
Save by an evil chance,
And the merry love the fiddle,
And the merry love to dance:

And when the folk there spy me,
They will all come up to me,
With 'Here is the fiddler of Dooney!'
And dance like a wave of the sea.

[November 1892] 1892

Upon the dancer by the dreamless wave.
Why should those lovers that no lovers miss
Dream, until God burn Nature with a kiss?
The man has found no comfort in the grave.

1891

The Dedication to a Book of Stories selected from the Irish Novelists

There was a green branch hung with many a bell
When her own people ruled this tragic Eire;
And from its murmuring greenness, calm of Faery,
A Druid kindness, on all hearers fell.

It charmed away the merchant from his guile,
And turned the farmer's memory from his cattle,
And hushed in sleep the roaring ranks of battle:
And all grew friendly for a little while.

Ah, Exiles wandering over lands and seas,
And planning, plotting always that some morrow
May set a stone upon ancestral Sorrow!
I also bear a bell-branch full of ease.

I tore it from green boughs winds tore and tossed
Until the sap of summer had grown weary!
I tore it from the barren boughs of Eire,
That country where a man can be so crossed;

Can be so battered, badgered and destroyed
That he's a loveless man: gay bells bring laughter
That shakes a mouldering cobweb from the rafter;
And yet the saddest chimes are best enjoyed.

Gay bells or sad, they bring you memories
Of half-forgotten innocent old places:
We and our bitterness have left no traces
On Munster grass and Connemara skies.

1891

THE [illegible]GE OF QUEEN MAEVE
1903

A certain poet in outlandish clothes
Gathered a crowd in some Byzantine lane,
Talked of his country and its people, sang
To some stringed instrument none there had seen,
A wall behind his back, over his head
A latticed window. His glance went up at times
As though one listened there, and his voice sank
Or let its meaning mix into the strings.

Maeve the great queen was pacing to and fro,
Between the walls covered with beaten bronze,
In her high house at Cruachan; the long hearth,
Flickering with ash and hazel, but half showed
Where the tired horse-boys lay upon the rushes,
Or on the benches underneath the walls,
In comfortable sleep; all living slept
But that great queen, who more than half the night
Had paced from door to fire and fire to door.
Though now in her old age, in her young age
She had been beautiful in that old way
That's all but gone; for the proud heart is gone,
And the fool heart of the counting-house fears all
But soft beauty and indolent desire.
She could have called over the rim of the world
Whatever woman's lover had hit her fancy,
And yet had been great-bodied and great-limbed,
Fashioned to be the mother of strong children;
And she'd had lucky eyes and a high heart,

And wisdom that caught fire like the dried flax,
At need, and made her beautiful and fierce,
Sudden and laughing.
O unquiet heart,
Why do you praise another, praising her,
As if there were no tale but your own tale
Worth knitting to a measure of sweet sound?
Have I not bid you tell of that great queen
Who has been buried some two thousand years?

When night was at its deepest, a wild goose
Cried from the porter's lodge, and with long clamour
Shook the ale-horns and shields upon their hooks;
But the horse-boys slept on, as though some power
Had filled the house with Druid heaviness;
And wondering who of the many-changing Sidhe
Had come as in the old times to counsel her,
Maeve walked, yet with slow footfall, being old,
To that small chamber by the outer gate.
The porter slept, although he sat upright
With still and stony limbs and open eyes.
Maeve waited, and when that ear-piercing noise
Broke from his parted lips and broke again,
She laid a hand on either of his shoulders,
And shook him wide awake, and bid him say
Who of the wandering many-changing ones
Had troubled his sleep. But all he had to say
Was that, the air being heavy and the dogs
More still than they had been for a good month,
He had fallen asleep, and, though he had dreamed nothing,
He could remember when he had had fine dreams.
It was before the time of the great war
Over the White-Horned Bull and the Brown Bull.

She turned away; he turned again to sleep
That no god troubled now, and, wondering
What matters were afoot among the Sidhe,
Maeve walked through that great hall, and with a sigh
Lifted the curtain of her sleeping-room,
Remembering that she too had seemed divine
To many thousand eyes, and to her own

I'd tell of that great queen
Who stood amid a silence by the thorn
Until two lovers came out of the air
With bodies made out of soft fire. The one,
About whose face birds wagged their fiery wings,
Said, 'Aengus and his sweetheart give their thanks
To Maeve and to Maeve's household, owing all
In owing them the bride-bed that gives peace.'
Then Maeve: 'O Aengus, Master of all lovers,
A thousand years ago you held high talk
With the first kings of many-pillared Cruachan.
O when will you grow weary?'
They had vanished;
But out of the dark air over her head there came
A murmur of soft words and meeting lips.

1903

Aibric. Speak lower, or they'll hear.

First Sailor. They cannot hear;
They are too busy with each other. Look!
He has stooped down and kissed her on the lips.

Second Sailor. When she finds out we have better men aboard
She may not be too sorry in the end.

First Sailor. She will be like a wild cat; for these queens
Care more about the kegs of silver and gold
And the high fame that come to them in marriage,
Than a strong body and a ready hand.

Second Sailor. There's nobody is natural but a robber,
And that is why the world totters about
Upon its bandy legs.

Aibric. Run at them now,
And overpower the crew while yet asleep!
[*The* Sailors *go out.*]

[*Voices and the clashing of swords are heard from the other ship, which cannot be seen because of the sail.*]
A Voice. Armed men have come upon us! O I am slain!

Another Voice. Wake all below!

Another Voice. Why have you broken our sleep?

First Voice. Armed men have come upon us! O I am slain!

Forgael [*who has remained at the tiller*]. There! there they come! Gull, gannet, or diver,
But with a man's head, or a fair woman's,
They hover over the masthead awhile
To wait their friends; but when their friends have come
They'll fly upon that secret way of theirs.
One – and one – a couple – five together;
And I will hear them talking in a minute.
Yes, voices! but I do not catch the words.
Now I can hear. There's one of them that says,
'How light we are, now we are changed to birds!'

Another answers, 'Maybe we shall find
Our heart's desire now that we are so light.'
And then one asks another how he died,
And says, 'A sword-blade pierced me in my sleep.'
And now they all wheel suddenly and fly
To the other side, and higher in the air.
And now a laggard with a woman's head
Comes crying, 'I have run upon the sword.
I have fled to my beloved in the air,
In the waste of the high air, that we may wander
Among the windy meadows of the dawn.'
But why are they still waiting? why are they
Circling and circling over the masthead?
What power that is more mighty than desire
To hurry to their hidden happiness
Withholds them now? Have the Ever-living Ones
A meaning in that circling overhead?
But what's the meaning? [*He cries out.*] Why do you linger there?
Why linger? Run to your desire,
Are you not happy wingèd bodies now? [*His voice sinks again.*]
Being too busy in the air and the high air,
They cannot hear my voice; but what's the meaning?

[*The* Sailors *have returned.* Dectora *is with them.*]

Forgael [*turning and seeing her*]. Why are you standing with your eyes upon me?
You are not the world's core. O no, no, no!
That cannot be the meaning of the birds.
You are not its core. My teeth are in the world,
But have not bitten yet.

Dectora. I am a queen,
And ask for satisfaction upon these
Who have slain my husband and laid hands upon me.

[*Breaking loose from the* Sailors *who are holding her.*]

Let go my hands!

Forgael. Why do you cast a shadow?

Where do you come from? Who brought you to this place?
They would not send me one that casts a shadow.

Dectora. Would that the storm that overthrew my ships,
And drowned the treasures of nine conquered nations,
And blew me hither to my lasting sorrow,
Had drowned me also. But, being yet alive,
I ask a fitting punishment for all
That raised their hands against him.

Forgael. There are some
That weigh and measure all in these waste seas –
They that have all the wisdom that's in life,
And all that prophesying images
Made of dim gold rave out in secret tombs;
They have it that the plans of kings and queens
Are dust on the moth's wing; that nothing matters
But laughter and tears – laughter, laughter, and tears;
That every man should carry his own soul
Upon his shoulders.

Dectora. You've nothing but wild words,
And I would know if you will give me vengeance.

Forgael. When she finds out I will not let her go –
When she knows that.

Dectora. What is it that you are muttering –
That you'll not let me go? I am a queen.

Forgael. Although you are more beautiful than any,
I almost long that it were possible;
But if I were to put you on that ship,
With sailors that were sworn to do your will,
And you had spread a sail for home, a wind
Would rise of a sudden, or a wave so huge,
It had washed among the stars and put them out,
And beat the bulwark of your ship on mine,
Until you stood before me on the deck –
As now.

Dectora. Does wandering in these desolate seas
And listening to the cry of wind and wave
Bring madness?

[*The* Sailors *throw* Aibric *on one side. He falls and lies upon the deck. They lift their swords to strike* Forgael, *who is about to play the harp. The stage begins to darken. The* Sailors *hesitate in fear.*]

Second Sailor. He has put a sudden darkness over the moon.

Dectora. Nine swords with handles of rhinoceros horn
To him that strikes him first!

First Sailor. I will strike him first.
[*He goes close up to* Forgael *with his sword lifted.*]
[*Shrinking back.*] He has caught the crescent moon out of the sky,
And carries it between us.

Second Sailor. Holy fire
To burn us to the marrow if we strike.

Dectora. I'll give a golden galley full of fruit,
That has the heady flavour of new wine,
To him that wounds him to the death.

First Sailor. I'll do it.
For all his spells will vanish when he dies,
Having their life in him.

Second Sailor. Though it be the moon
That he is holding up between us there,
I will strike at him.

The Others. And I! And I! And I!
[Forgael *plays the harp.*]

First Sailor [*falling into a dream suddenly*]. But you were saying there is somebody
Upon that other ship we are to wake.
You did not know what brought him to his end,
But it was sudden.

Second Sailor. You are in the right;
I had forgotten that we must go wake him.

Dectora. He has flung a Druid spell upon the air,

And set you dreaming.

Second Sailor. How can we have a wake
When we have neither brown nor yellow ale?

First Sailor. I saw a flagon of brown ale aboard her.

Third Sailor. How can we raise the keen that do not know
What name to call him by?

First Sailor. Come to his ship.
His name will come into our thoughts in a minute.
I know that he died a thousand years ago,
And has not yet been waked.

Second Sailor [*beginning to keen*]. Ohone! O! O! O!
The yew-bough has been broken into two,
And all the birds are scattered.

All the Sailors. O! O! O! O!
[*They go out keening.*]

Dectora. Protect me now, gods that my people swear by.
[Aibric *has risen from the deck where he had fallen. He has begun looking for his sword as if in a dream.*]

Aibric. Where is my sword that fell out of my hand
When I first heard the news? Ah, there it is!
[*He goes dreamily towards the sword, but* Dectora *runs at it and takes it up before he can reach it.*]

Aibric [*sleepily*]. Queen, give it me.

Dectora. No, I have need of it.

Aibric. Why do you need a sword? But you may keep it.
Now that he's dead I have no need of it,
For everything is gone.

A Sailor [*calling from the other ship*]. Come hither, Aibric,
And tell me who it is that we are waking.

Aibric [*half to* Dectora, *half to himself*]. What name had that dead king? Arthur of Britain?
No, no – not Arthur. I remember now.
It was golden-armed Iollan, and he died

Broken-hearted, having lost his queen
Through wicked spells. That is not all the tale,
For he was killed. O! O! O! O! O! O!
For golden-armed Iollan has been killed.

[*He goes out.*]

[*While he has been speaking, and through part of what follows, one hears the wailing of the* Sailors *from the other ship.* Dectora *stands with the sword lifted in front of* Forgael.]

Dectora. I will end all your magic on the instant.
[*Her voice becomes dreamy, and she lowers the sword slowly, and finally lets it fall. She spreads out her hair. She takes off her crown and lays it upon the deck.*]
This sword is to lie beside him in the grave.
It was in all his battles. I will spread my hair,
And wring my hands, and wail him bitterly,
For I have heard that he was proud and laughing,
Blue-eyed, and a quick runner on bare feet,
And that he died a thousand years ago.
O! O! O! O!

[Forgael *changes the tune.*]

But no, that is not it.
I knew him well, and while I heard him laughing
They killed him at my feet. O! O! O! O!
For golden-armed Iollan that I loved.
But what is it that made me say I loved him?
It was that harper put it in my thoughts,
But it is true. Why did they run upon him,
And beat the golden helmet with their swords?

Forgael. Do you not know me, lady? I am he
That you are weeping for.

Dectora. No, for he is dead.
O! O! O! O! for golden-armed Iollan.

Forgael. It was so given out, but I will prove
That the grave-diggers in a dreamy frenzy
Have buried nothing but my golden arms.
Listen to that low-laughing string of the moon
And you will recollect my face and voice,

For you have listened to me playing it
These thousand years.
[*He starts up, listening to the birds. The harp slips from his hands, and remains leaning against the bulwarks behind him.*]
What are the birds at there?
Why are they all a-flutter of a sudden?
What are you calling out above the mast?
If railing and reproach and mockery
Because I have awakened her to love
By magic strings, I'll make this answer to it:
Being driven on by voices and by dreams
That were clear messages from the Ever-living,
I have done right. What could I but obey?
And yet you make a clamour of reproach.

Dectora [*laughing*]. Why, it's a wonder out of reckoning
That I should keen him from the full of the moon
To the horn, and he be hale and hearty.

Forgael. How have I wronged her now that she is merry?
But no, no, no! your cry is not against me.
You know the counsels of the Ever-living,
And all that tossing of your wings is joy,
And all that murmuring's but a marriage-song;
But if it be reproach, I answer this:
There is not one among you that made love
By any other means. You call it passion,
Consideration, generosity;
But it was all deceit, and flattery
To win a woman in her own despite,
For love is war, and there is hatred in it;
And if you say that she came willingly –

Dectora. Why do you turn away and hide your face,
That I would look upon for ever?

Forgael. My grief!

Dectora. Have I not loved you for a thousand years?

Forgael. I never have been golden-armed Iollan.

Dectora. I do not understand. I know your face
Better than my own hands.

Forgael. I have deceived you
Out of all reckoning.

Dectora. Is it not true
That you were born a thousand years ago,
In islands where the children of Aengus wind
In happy dances under a windy moon,
And that you'll bring me there?

Forgael. I have deceived you;
I have deceived you utterly.

Dectora. How can that be?
Is it that though your eyes are full of love
Some other woman has a claim on you,
And I've but half?

Forgael. O no!

Dectora. And if there is,
If there be half a hundred more, what matter?
I'll never give another thought to it;
No, no, nor half a thought; but do not speak.
Women are hard and proud and stubborn-hearted,
Their heads being turned with praise and flattery;
And that is why their lovers are afraid
To tell them a plain story.

Forgael. That's not the story;
But I have done so great a wrong against you,
There is no measure that it would not burst.
I will confess it all.

Dectora. What do I care,
Now that my body has begun to dream,
And you have grown to be a burning sod
In the imagination and intellect?
If something that's most fabulous were true –
If you had taken me by magic spells,
And killed a lover or husband at my feet –
I would not let you speak, for I would know
That it was yesterday and not to-day
I loved him; I would cover up my ears,
As I am doing now. [*A pause.*] Why do you weep?

Forgael. I weep because I've nothing for your eyes
But desolate waters and a battered ship.

Dectora. O why do you not lift your eyes to mine?

Forgael. I weep – I weep because bare night's above,
And not a roof of ivory and gold.

Dectora. I would grow jealous of the ivory roof,
And strike the golden pillars with my hands.
I would that there was nothing in the world
But my beloved – that night and day had perished,
And all that is and all that is to be,
All that is not the meeting of our lips.

Forgael. You turn away. Why do you turn away?
Am I to fear the waves, or is the moon
My enemy?

Dectora. I looked upon the moon,
Longing to knead and pull it into shape
That I might lay it on your head as a crown.
But now it is your thoughts that wander away,
For you are looking at the sea. Do you not know
How great a wrong it is to let one's thought
Wander a moment when one is in love?
[*He has moved away. She follows him. He is looking out over the sea, shading his eyes.*]
Why are you looking at the sea?

Forgael. Look there!

Dectora. What is there but a troop of ash-grey birds
That fly into the west?

Forgael. But listen, listen!

Dectora. What is there but the crying of the birds?

Forgael. If you'll but listen closely to that crying
You'll hear them calling out to one another
With human voices.

Dectora. O, I can hear them now.
What are they? Unto what country do they fly?

Forgael. To unimaginable happiness.
They have been circling over our heads in the air,
But now that they have taken to the road
We have to follow, for they are our pilots;
And though they're but the colour of grey ash,
They're crying out, could you but hear their words,
'There is a country at the end of the world
Where no child's born but to outlive the moon.'
[*The* Sailors *come in with* Aibric. *They are in great excitement.*]

First Sailor. The hold is full of treasure.

Second Sailor. Full to the hatches.

First Sailor. Treasure on treasure.

Third Sailor. Boxes of precious spice.

First Sailor. Ivory images with amethyst eyes.

Third Sailor. Dragons with eyes of ruby.

First Sailor. The whole ship
Flashes as if it were a net of herrings.

Third Sailor. Let's home; I'd give some rubies to a woman.

Second Sailor. There's somebody I'd give the amethyst eyes to.

Aibric [*silencing them with a gesture*]. We would return to our own country, Forgael,
For we have found a treasure that's so great
Imagination cannot reckon it.
And having lit upon this woman there,
What more have you to look for on the seas?

Forgael. I cannot – I am going on to the end.
As for this woman, I think she is coming with me.

Aibric. The Ever-living have made you mad; but no,
It was this woman in her woman's vengeance
That drove you to it, and I fool enough
To fancy that she'd bring you home again.

'Twas you that egged him to it, for you know
That he is being driven to his death.

Dectora. That is not true, for he has promised me
An unimaginable happiness.

Aibric. And if that happiness be more than dreams,
More than the froth, the feather, the dust-whirl,
The crazy nothing that I think it is,
It shall be in the country of the dead,
If there be such a country.

Dectora. No, not there,
But in some island where the life of the world
Leaps upward, as if all the streams o' the world
Had run into one fountain.

Aibric. Speak to him.
He knows that he is taking you to death;
Speak – he will not deny it.

Dectora. Is that true?

Forgael. I do not know for certain, but I know
That I have the best of pilots.

Aibric. Shadows, illusions,
That the Shape-changers, the Ever-laughing Ones,
The Immortal Mockers have cast into his mind,
Or called before his eyes.

Dectora. O carry me
To some sure country, some familiar place.
Have we not everything that life can give
In having one another?

Forgael. How could I rest
If I refused the messengers and pilots
With all those sights and all that crying out?

Dectora. But I will cover up your eyes and ears,
That you may never hear the cry of the birds,
Or look upon them.

Forgael. Were they but lowlier
I'd do your will, but they are too high – too high.

To a Poet, who would have me Praise certain Bad Poets, Imitators of His and Mine

You say, as I have often given tongue
In praise of what another's said or sung,
'Twere politic to do the like by these;
But was there ever dog that praised his fleas?

[23–26 April 1909] 1910

The Mask

'Put off that mask of burning gold
With emerald eyes.'
'O no, my dear, you make so bold
To find if hearts be wild and wise,
And yet not cold.'

'I would but find what's there to find,
Love or deceit.'
'It was the mask engaged your mind,
And after set your heart to beat,
Not what's behind.'

'But lest you are my enemy,
I must enquire.'
'O no, my dear, let all that be;
What matter, so there is but fire
In you, in me?'

[August 1910] 1910

Upon a House shaken by the Land Agitation

How should the world be luckier if this house,
Where passion and precision have been one
Time out of mind, became too ruinous
To breed the lidless eye that loves the sun?
And the sweet laughing eagle thoughts that grow
Where wings have memory of wings, and all

That comes of the best knit to the best? Although
Mean roof-trees were the sturdier for its fall,
How should their luck run high enough to reach
The gifts that govern men, and after these
To gradual Time's last gift, a written speech
Wrought of high laughter, loveliness and ease?

[7 August 1909] 1910

At the Abbey Theatre

(Imitated from Ronsard)

Dear Craoibhin Aoibhin, look into our case.
When we are high and airy hundreds say
That if we hold that flight they'll leave the place,
While those same hundreds mock another day
Because we have made our art of common things,
So bitterly, you'd dream they longed to look
All their lives through into some drift of wings.
You've dandled them and fed them from the book
And know them to the bone; impart to us –
We'll keep the secret – a new trick to please.
Is there a bridle for this Proteus
That turns and changes like his draughty seas?
Or is there none, most popular of men,
But when they mock us, that we mock again?

[May 1911] 1912

These are the Clouds

These are the clouds about the fallen sun,
The majesty that shuts his burning eye:
The weak lay hand on what the strong has done,
Till that be tumbled that was lifted high
And discord follow upon unison,
And all things at one common level lie.

And therefore, friend, if your great race were run
And these things came, so much the more thereby
Have you made greatness your companion,
Although it be for children that you sigh:
These are the clouds about the fallen sun,
The majesty that shuts his burning eye.

[1910] 1910

At Galway Races

There where the course is,
Delight makes all of the one mind,
The riders upon the galloping horses,
The crowd that closes in behind:
We, too, had good attendance once,
Hearers and hearteners of the work;
Aye, horsemen for companions,
Before the merchant and the clerk
Breathed on the world with timid breath.
Sing on: somewhere at some new moon,
We'll learn that sleeping is not death,
Hearing the whole earth change its tune,
Its flesh being wild, and it again
Crying aloud as the racecourse is,
And we find hearteners among men
That ride upon horses.

[1908] 1909

A Friend's Illness

Sickness brought me this
Thought, in that scale of his:
Why should I be dismayed
Though flame had burned the whole
World, as it were a coal,

Now I have seen it weighed
Against a soul?

[February 1909] 1910

All Things can Tempt Me

All things can tempt me from this craft of verse:
One time it was a woman's face, or worse –
The seeming needs of my fool-driven land;
Now nothing but comes readier to the hand
Than this accustomed toil. When I was young,
I had not given a penny for a song
Did not the poet sing it with such airs
That one believed he had a sword upstairs;
Yet would be now, could I but have my wish,
Colder and dumber and deafer than a fish.

[1908] 1909

Brown Penny

I whispered, 'I am too young,'
And then, 'I am old enough';
Wherefore I threw a penny
To find out if I might love.
'Go and love, go and love, young man,
If the lady be young and fair.'
Ah, penny, brown penny, brown penny,
I am looped in the loops of her hair.

O love is the crooked thing,
There is nobody wise enough
To find out all that is in it,
For he would be thinking of love
Till the stars had run away
And the shadows eaten the moon.
Ah, penny, brown penny, brown penny,
One cannot begin it too soon.

1910

RESPONSIBILITIES

1914

'*In dreams begins responsibility.*' Old Play

'*How am I fallen from myself, for a long time now I have not seen the Prince of Chang in my dreams.*' Khoung-fou-tseu

Pardon, old fathers, if you still remain
Somewhere in ear-shot for the story's end,
Old Dublin merchant 'free of the ten and four'
Or trading out of Galway into Spain;
Old country scholar, Robert Emmet's friend,
A hundred-year-old memory to the poor;
Merchant and scholar who have left me blood
That has not passed through any huckster's loin,
Soldiers that gave, whatever die was cast:
A Butler or an Armstrong that withstood
Beside the brackish waters of the Boyne
James and his Irish when the Dutchman crossed;
Old merchant skipper that leaped overboard
After a ragged hat in Biscay Bay;
You most of all, silent and fierce old man,
Because the daily spectacle that stirred
My fancy, and set my boyish lips to say,
'Only the wasteful virtues earn the sun';
Pardon that for a barren passion's sake,
Although I have come close on forty-nine,
I have no child, I have nothing but a book,
Nothing but that to prove your blood and mine.

January 1914

[December 1913] 1914

The Grey Rock

Poets with whom I learned my trade,
Companions of the Cheshire Cheese,
Here's an old story I've re-made,
Imagining 'twould better please
Your ears than stories now in fashion,
Though you may think I waste my breath
Pretending that there can be passion
That has more life in it than death,
And though at bottling of your wine
Old wholesome Goban had no say;
The moral's yours because it's mine.

When cups went round at close of day –
Is not that how good stories run? –
The gods were sitting at the board
In their great house at Slievenamon.
They sang a drowsy song, or snored,
For all were full of wine and meat.
The smoky torches made a glare
On metal Goban'd hammered at,
On old deep silver rolling there
Or on some still unemptied cup
That he, when frenzy stirred his thews,
Had hammered out on mountain top
To hold the sacred stuff he brews
That only gods may buy of him.

Now from that juice that made them wise
All those had lifted up the dim
Imaginations of their eyes,
For one that was like woman made
Before their sleepy eyelids ran
And trembling with her passion said,
'Come out and dig for a dead man,
Who's burrowing somewhere in the ground,
And mock him to his face and then
Hollo him on with horse and hound,
For he is the worst of all dead men.'

For this Edward Fitzgerald died,
And Robert Emmet and Wolfe Tone,
All that delirium of the brave?
Romantic Ireland's dead and gone,
It's with O'Leary in the grave.

Yet could we turn the years again,
And call those exiles as they were
In all their loneliness and pain,
You'd cry, 'Some woman's yellow hair
Has maddened every mother's son':
They weighed so lightly what they gave.
But let them be, they're dead and gone,
They're with O'Leary in the grave.

[7 September 1913] 1913

To a Friend whose Work has come to Nothing

Now all the truth is out,
Be secret and take defeat
From any brazen throat,
For how can you compete,
Being honour bred, with one
Who, were it proved he lies,
Were neither shamed in his own
Nor in his neighbours' eyes?
Bred to a harder thing
Than Triumph, turn away
And like a laughing string
Whereon mad fingers play
Amid a place of stone,
Be secret and exult,
Because of all things known
That is most difficult.

[16 September 1913] 1913

Paudeen

Indignant at the fumbling wits, the obscure spite
Of our old Paudeen in his shop, I stumbled blind
Among the stones and thorn-trees, under morning light;
Until a curlew cried and in the luminous wind
A curlew answered; and suddenly thereupon I thought
That on the lonely height where all are in God's eye,
There cannot be, confusion of our sound forgot,
A single soul that lacks a sweet crystalline cry.

[16 September 1913] 1913

To a Shade

If you have revisited the town, thin Shade,
Whether to look upon your monument
(I wonder if the builder has been paid)
Or happier-thoughted when the day is spent
To drink of that salt breath out of the sea
When grey gulls flit about instead of men,
And the gaunt houses put on majesty:
Let these content you and be gone again;
For they are at their old tricks yet.
A man
Of your own passionate serving kind who had brought
In his full hands what, had they only known,
Had given their children's children loftier thought,
Sweeter emotion, working in their veins
Like gentle blood, has been driven from the place,
And insult heaped upon him for his pains,
And for his open-handedness, disgrace;
Your enemy, an old foul mouth, had set
The pack upon him.
Go, unquiet wanderer,
And gather the Glasnevin coverlet
About your head till the dust stops your ear,
The time for you to taste of that salt breath
And listen at the corners has not come;

You had enough of sorrow before death –
Away, away! You are safer in the tomb.
September 29, 1913

[29 September 1913] 1913

When Helen Lived

We have cried in our despair
That men desert,
For some trivial affair
Or noisy, insolent sport,
Beauty that we have won
From bitterest hours;
Yet we, had we walked within
Those topless towers
Where Helen walked with her boy,
Had given but as the rest
Of the men and women of Troy,
A word and a jest.

[20–29 September 1913] 1914

On those that hated *The Playboy of the Western World*, 1907

Once, when midnight smote the air,
Eunuchs ran through Hell and met
On every crowded street to stare
Upon great Juan riding by:
Even like these to rail and sweat
Staring upon his sinewy thigh.

[3 March 1909–5 April 1910] 1911

The Three Beggars

'Though to my feathers in the wet,
I have stood here from break of day,
I have not found a thing to eat,
For only rubbish comes my way.
Am I to live on lebeen-lone?'
Muttered the old crane of Gort.
'For all my pains on lebeen-lone?'

King Guaire walked amid his court
The palace-yard and river-side
And there to three old beggars said,
'You that have wandered far and wide
Can ravel out what's in my head.
Do men who least desire get most,
Or get the most who most desire?'
A beggar said, 'They get the most
Whom man or devil cannot tire,
And what could make their muscles taut
Unless desire had made them so?'
But Guaire laughed with secret thought,
'If that be true as it seems true,
One of you three is a rich man,
For he shall have a thousand pounds
Who is first asleep, if but he can
Sleep before the third noon sounds.'
And thereon, merry as a bird
With his old thoughts, King Guaire went
From river-side and palace-yard
And left them to their argument.
'And if I win,' one beggar said,
'Though I am old I shall persuade
A pretty girl to share my bed';
The second: 'I shall learn a trade';
The third: 'I'll hurry to the course
Among the other gentlemen,
And lay it all upon a horse';
The second: 'I have thought again:
A farmer has more dignity.'

What eagle look still shows,
While up from my heart's root
So great a sweetness flows
I shake from head to foot.

[January 1911] 1912

The Cold Heaven

Suddenly I saw the cold and rook-delighting heaven
That seemed as though ice burned and was but the more ice,
And thereupon imagination and heart were driven
So wild that every casual thought of that and this
Vanished, and left but memories, that should be out of season
With the hot blood of youth, of love crossed long ago;
And I took all the blame out of all sense and reason,
Until I cried and trembled and rocked to and fro,
Riddled with light. Ah! when the ghost begins to quicken,
Confusion of the death-bed over, is it sent
Out naked on the roads, as the books say, and stricken
By the injustice of the skies for punishment?

1912

That the Night Come

She lived in storm and strife,
Her soul had such desire
For what proud death may bring
That it could not endure
The common good of life,
But lived as 'twere a king
That packed his marriage day
With banneret and pennon,
Trumpet and kettledrum,
And the outrageous cannon,
To bundle time away
That the night come. 1912

An Appointment

Being out of heart with government
I took a broken root to fling
Where the proud, wayward squirrel went,
Taking delight that he could spring;
And he, with that low whinnying sound
That is like laughter, sprang again
And so to the other tree at a bound.
Nor the tame will, nor timid brain,
Nor heavy knitting of the brow
Bred that fierce tooth and cleanly limb
And threw him up to laugh on the bough;
No government appointed him.

[1907–8] 1909

The Magi

Now as at all times I can see in the mind's eye,
In their stiff, painted clothes, the pale unsatisfied ones
Appear and disappear in the blue depth of the sky
With all their ancient faces like rain-beaten stones,
And all their helms of silver hovering side by side,
And all their eyes still fixed, hoping to find once more,
Being by Calvary's turbulence unsatisfied,
The uncontrollable mystery on the bestial floor.

[20 September 1913] 1914

The Dolls

A doll in the doll-maker's house
Looks at the cradle and bawls:
'That is an insult to us.'
But the oldest of all the dolls,
Who had seen, being kept for show,
Generations of his sort,
Out-screams the whole shelf: 'Although

XI

Some burn damp faggots, others may consume
The entire combustible world in one small room
As though dried straw, and if we turn about
The bare chimney is gone black out
Because the work had finished in that flare.
Soldier, scholar, horseman, he,
As 'twere all life's epitome.
What made us dream that he could comb grey hair?

XII

I had thought, seeing how bitter is that wind
That shakes the shutter, to have brought to mind
All those that manhood tried, or childhood loved
Or boyish intellect approved,
With some appropriate commentary on each;
Until imagination brought
A fitter welcome; but a thought
Of that late death took all my heart for speech.

[14 June 1918] 1918

An Irish Airman Foresees his Death

I know that I shall meet my fate
Somewhere among the clouds above;
Those that I fight I do not hate,
Those that I guard I do not love;
My country is Kiltartan Cross,
My countrymen Kiltartan's poor,
No likely end could bring them loss
Or leave them happier than before.
Nor law, nor duty bade me fight,
Nor public men, nor cheering crowds,
A lonely impulse of delight
Drove to this tumult in the clouds;
I balanced all, brought all to mind,

The years to come seemed waste of breath,
A waste of breath the years behind
In balance with this life, this death.

[1918] 1919

Men Improve with the Years

I am worn out with dreams;
A weather-worn, marble triton
Among the streams;
And all day long I look
Upon this lady's beauty
As though I had found in a book
A pictured beauty,
Pleased to have filled the eyes
Or the discerning ears,
Delighted to be but wise,
For men improve with the years;
And yet, and yet,
Is this my dream, or the truth?
O would that we had met
When I had my burning youth!
But I grow old among dreams,
A weather-worn, marble triton
Among the streams.

[19 July 1916] 1917

The Collar-Bone of a Hare

Would I could cast a sail on the water
Where many a king has gone
And many a king's daughter,
And alight at the comely trees and the lawn,
The playing upon pipes and the dancing,
And learn that the best thing is

To change my loves while dancing
And pay but a kiss for a kiss.

I would find by the edge of that water
The collar-bone of a hare
Worn thin by the lapping of water,
And pierce it through with a gimlet and stare
At the old bitter world where they marry in churches,
And laugh over the untroubled water
At all who marry in churches,
Through the white thin bone of a hare.

[5 July 1916] 1917

Under the Round Tower

'Although I'd lie lapped up in linen
A deal I'd sweat and little earn
If I should live as live the neighbours,'
Cried the beggar, Billy Byrne;
'Stretch bones till the daylight come
On great-grandfather's battered tomb.'

Upon a grey old battered tombstone
In Glendalough beside the stream,
Where the O'Byrnes and Byrnes are buried,
He stretched his bones and fell in a dream
Of sun and moon that a good hour
Bellowed and pranced in the round tower;

Of golden king and silver lady,
Bellowing up and bellowing round,
Till toes mastered a sweet measure,
Mouth mastered a sweet sound,
Prancing round and prancing up
Until they pranced upon the top.

That golden king and that wild lady
Sang till stars began to fade,
Hands gripped in hands, toes close together,

Hair spread on the wind they made;
That lady and that golden king
Could like a brace of blackbirds sing.

'It's certain that my luck is broken,'
That rambling jailbird Billy said;
'Before nightfall I'll pick a pocket
And snug it in a feather-bed.
I cannot find the peace of home
On great-grandfather's battered tomb.'

[March 1918] 1918

Solomon to Sheba

Sang Solomon to Sheba,
And kissed her dusky face,
'All day long from mid-day
We have talked in the one place,
All day long from shadowless noon
We have gone round and round
In the narrow theme of love
Like an old horse in a pound.'

To Solomon sang Sheba,
Planted on his knees,
'If you had broached a matter
That might the learned please,
You had before the sun had thrown
Our shadows on the ground
Discovered that my thoughts, not it,
Are but a narrow pound.'

Sang Solomon to Sheba,
And kissed her Arab eyes,
'There's not a man or woman
Born under the skies
Dare match in learning with us two,
And all day long we have found

There's not a thing but love can make
The world a narrow pound.'

[1918] 1918

The Living Beauty

I bade, because the wick and oil are spent
And frozen are the channels of the blood,
My discontented heart to draw content
From beauty that is cast out of a mould
In bronze, or that in dazzling marble appears,
Appears, but when we have gone is gone again,
Being more indifferent to our solitude
Than 'twere an apparition. O heart, we are old;
The living beauty is for younger men:
We cannot pay its tribute of wild tears.

[1917] 1918

A Song

I thought no more was needed
Youth to prolong
Than dumb-bell and foil
To keep the body young.
O who could have foretold
That the heart grows old?

Though I have many words,
What woman's satisfied,
I am no longer faint
Because at her side?
O who could have foretold
That the heart grows old?

I have not lost desire
But the heart that I had;

I thought 'twould burn my body
Laid on the death-bed,
For who could have foretold
That the heart grows old?

[1915] 1918

To a Young Beauty

Dear fellow-artist, why so free
With every sort of company,
With every Jack and Jill?
Choose your companions from the best;
Who draws a bucket with the rest
Soon topples down the hill.

You may, that mirror for a school,
Be passionate, not bountiful
As common beauties may,
Who were not born to keep in trim
With old Ezekiel's cherubim
But those of Beauvarlet.

I know what wages beauty gives,
How hard a life her servant lives,
Yet praise the winters gone:
There is not a fool can call me friend,
And I may dine at journey's end
With Landor and with Donne.

[1918] 1918

To a Young Girl

My dear, my dear, I know
More than another
What makes your heart beat so;
Not even your own mother

Can know it as I know,
Who broke my heart for her
When the wild thought,
That she denies
And has forgot,
Set all her blood astir
And glittered in her eyes.

[May 1915] 1918

The Scholars

Bald heads forgetful of their sins,
Old, learned, respectable bald heads
Edit and annotate the lines
That young men, tossing on their beds,

Rhymed out in love's despair
To flatter beauty's ignorant ear.

All shuffle there; all cough in ink;
All wear the carpet with their shoes;
All think what other people think;
All know the man their neighbour knows.
Lord, what would they say
Did their Catullus walk that way?

[1914–April 1915] 1915

Tom O'Roughley

'Though logic-choppers rule the town,
And every man and maid and boy
Has marked a distant object down,
An aimless joy is a pure joy,'
Or so did Tom O'Roughley say
That saw the surges running by,
'And wisdom is a butterfly
And not a gloomy bird of prey.

'If little planned is little sinned
But little need the grave distress.
What's dying but a second wind?
How but in zig-zag wantonness
Could trumpeter Michael be so brave?'
Or something of that sort he said,
'And if my dearest friend were dead
I'd dance a measure on his grave.'

[16 February 1918] 1918

Shepherd and Goatherd

Shepherd. That cry's from the first cuckoo of the year.
I wished before it ceased.

Goatherd. Nor bird nor beast
Could make me wish for anything this day,
Being old, but that the old alone might die,
And that would be against God's Providence.
Let the young wish. But what has brought you here?
Never until this moment have we met
Where my goats browse on the scarce grass or leap
From stone to stone.

Shepherd. I am looking for strayed sheep;
Something has troubled me and in my trouble
I let them stray. I thought of rhyme alone,
For rhyme can beat a measure out of trouble
And make the daylight sweet once more; but when
I had driven every rhyme into its place
The sheep had gone from theirs.

Goatherd. I know right well
What turned so good a shepherd from his charge.

Shepherd. He that was best in every country sport
And every country craft, and of us all
Most courteous to slow age and hasty youth,
Is dead.

Goatherd. The boy that brings my griddle-cake
Brought the bare news.

Shepherd. He had thrown the crook away
And died in the great war beyond the sea.

Goatherd. He had often played his pipes among my hills,
And when he played it was their loneliness,
The exultation of their stone, that cried
Under his fingers.

Shepherd. I had it from his mother,
And his own flock was browsing at the door.

Goatherd. How does she bear her grief? There is not a
 shepherd
But grows more gentle when he speaks her name,
Remembering kindness done, and how can I,
That found when I had neither goat nor grazing
New welcome and old wisdom at her fire
Till winter blasts were gone, but speak of her
Even before his children and his wife?

Shepherd. She goes about her house erect and calm
Between the pantry and the linen-chest,
Or else at meadow or at grazing overlooks
Her labouring men, as though her darling lived,
But for her grandson now; there is no change
But such as I have seen upon her face
Watching our shepherd sports at harvest-time
When her son's turn was over.

Goatherd. Sing your song.
I too have rhymed my reveries, but youth
Is hot to show whatever it has found,
And till that's done can neither work nor wait.
Old goatherds and old goats, if in all else
Youth can excel them in accomplishment,
Are learned in waiting.

Shepherd. You cannot but have seen
That he alone had gathered up no gear,
Set carpenters to work on no wide table,

On no long bench nor lofty milking shed
As others will, when first they take possession,
But left the house as in his father's time
As though he knew himself, as it were, a cuckoo,
No settled man. And now that he is gone
There's nothing of him left but half a score
Of sorrowful, austere, sweet, lofty pipe tunes.

Goatherd. You have put the thought in rhyme.

Shepherd. I worked all day,
And when 'twas done so little had I done
That maybe 'I am sorry' in plain prose
Had sounded better to your mountain fancy.

[*He sings*]

'Like the speckled bird that steers
Thousands of leagues oversea,
And runs or a while half-flies
On his yellow legs through our meadows,
He stayed for a while; and we
Had scarcely accustomed our ears
To his speech at the break of day,
Had scarcely accustomed our eyes
To his shape at the rinsing pool
Among the evening shadows,
When he vanished from ears and eyes.
I might have wished on the day
He came, but man is a fool.'

Goatherd. You sing as always of the natural life,
And I that made like music in my youth
Hearing it now have sighed for that young man
And certain lost companions of my own.

Shepherd. They say that on your barren mountain ridge
You have measured out the road that the soul treads
When it has vanished from our natural eyes;
That you have talked with apparitions.

Goatherd. Indeed
My daily thoughts since the first stupor of youth
Have found the path my goats' feet cannot find.

Shepherd. Sing, for it may be that your thoughts have
plucked
Some medicable herb to make our grief
Less bitter.

Goatherd. They have brought me from that ridge
Seed-pods and flowers that are not all wild poppy.

[*Sings*]

'He grows younger every second
That were all his birthdays reckoned
Much too solemn seemed;
Because of what he had dreamed,
Or the ambitions that he served,
Much too solemn and reserved.
Jaunting, journeying
To his own dayspring,
He unpacks the loaded pern
Of all 'twas pain or joy to learn,
Of all that he had made.
The outrageous war shall fade;
At some old winding whitethorn root
He'll practise on the shepherd's flute,
Or on the close-cropped grass
Court his shepherd lass,
Or put his heart into some game
Till daytime, playtime seem the same;
Knowledge he shall unwind
Through victories of the mind,
Till, clambering at the cradle-side,
He dreams himself his mother's pride,
All knowledge lost in trance
Of sweeter ignorance.'

Shepherd. When I have shut these ewes and this old ram
Into the fold, we'll to the woods and there
Cut out our rhymes on strips of new-torn bark
But put no name and leave them at her door.
To know the mountain and the valley have grieved
May be a quiet thought to wife and mother,
And children when they spring up shoulder-high.

[22 February–19 March 1918] 1919

Lines Written in Dejection

When have I last looked on
The round green eyes and the long wavering bodies
Of the dark leopards of the moon?
All the wild witches, those most noble ladies,
For all their broom-sticks and their tears,
Their angry tears, are gone.
The holy centaurs of the hills are vanished;
I have nothing but the embittered sun;
Banished heroic mother moon and vanished,
And now that I have come to fifty years
I must endure the timid sun.

[1915] 1917

The Dawn

I would be ignorant as the dawn
That has looked down
On that old queen measuring a town
With the pin of a brooch,
Or on the withered men that saw
From their pedantic Babylon
The careless planets in their courses,
The stars fade out where the moon comes,
And took their tablets and did sums;
I would be ignorant as the dawn
That merely stood, rocking the glittering coach
Above the cloudy shoulders of the horses;
I would be – for no knowledge is worth a straw –
Ignorant and wanton as the dawn.

[20 June 1914] 1916

On Woman

May God be praised for woman
That gives up all her mind,
A man may find in no man
A friendship of her kind
That covers all he has brought
As with her flesh and bone,
Nor quarrels with a thought
Because it is not her own.

Though pedantry denies,
It's plain the Bible means
That Solomon grew wise
While talking with his queens,
Yet never could, although
They say he counted grass,
Count all the praises due
When Sheba was his lass,
When she the iron wrought, or
When from the smithy fire
It shuddered in the water:
Harshness of their desire
That made them stretch and yawn,
Pleasure that comes with sleep,
Shudder that made them one.
What else He give or keep
God grant me – no, not here,
For I am not so bold
To hope a thing so dear
Now I am growing old,
But when, if the tale's true,
The Pestle of the moon
That pounds up all anew
Brings me to birth again –
To find what once I had
And know what once I have known,
Until I am driven mad,
Sleep driven from my bed,
By tenderness and care,

Pity, an aching head,
Gnashing of teeth, despair;
And all because of some one
Perverse creature of chance,
And live like Solomon
That Sheba led a dance.

[25 May 1914] 1916

The Fisherman

Although I can see him still,
The freckled man who goes
To a grey place on a hill
In grey Connemara clothes
At dawn to cast his flies,
It's long since I began
To call up to the eyes
This wise and simple man.
All day I'd looked in the face
What I had hoped 'twould be
To write for my own race
And the reality;
The living men that I hate,
The dead man that I loved,
The craven man in his seat,
The insolent unreproved,
And no knave brought to book
Who has won a drunken cheer,
The witty man and his joke
Aimed at the commonest ear,
The clever man who cries
The catch-cries of the clown,
The beating down of the wise
And great Art beaten down.

Maybe a twelvemonth since
Suddenly I began,
In scorn of this audience,
Imagining a man,

And his sun-freckled face,
And grey Connemara cloth,
Climbing up to a place
Where stone is dark under froth,
And the down-turn of his wrist
When the flies drop in the stream;
A man who does not exist,
A man who is but a dream;
And cried, 'Before I am old
I shall have written him one
Poem maybe as cold
And passionate as the dawn.'

[4 June 1914] 1916

The Hawk

'Call down the hawk from the air;
Let him be hooded or caged
Till the yellow eye has grown mild,
For larder and spit are bare,
The old cook enraged,
The scullion gone wild.'

'I will not be clapped in a hood,
Nor a cage, nor alight upon wrist,
Now I have learnt to be proud
Hovering over the wood
In the broken mist
Or tumbling cloud.'

'What tumbling cloud did you cleave,
Yellow-eyed hawk of the mind,
Last evening? that I, who had sat
Dumbfounded before a knave,
Should give to my friend
A pretence of wit.'

1916

Memory

One had a lovely face,
And two or three had charm,
But charm and face were in vain
Because the mountain grass
Cannot but keep the form
Where the mountain hare has lain.

[1915–16] 1916

Her Praise

She is foremost of those that I would hear praised.
I have gone about the house, gone up and down
As a man does who has published a new book,
Or a young girl dressed out in her new gown,
And though I have turned the talk by hook or crook
Until her praise should be the uppermost theme,
A woman spoke of some new tale she had read,
A man confusedly in a half dream
As though some other name ran in his head.
She is foremost of those that I would hear praised.
I will talk no more of books or the long war
But walk by the dry thorn until I have found
Some beggar sheltering from the wind, and there
Manage the talk until her name come round.
If there be rags enough he will know her name
And be well pleased remembering it, for in the old days,
Though she had young men's praise and old men's blame,
Among the poor both old and young gave her praise.

[27 January 1915] 1916

The People

'What have I earned for all that work,' I said,
'For all that I have done at my own charge?
The daily spite of this unmannerly town,

Where who has served the most is most defamed,
The reputation of his lifetime lost
Between the night and morning. I might have lived,
And you know well how great the longing has been,
Where every day my footfall should have lit
In the green shadow of Ferrara wall;
Or climbed among the images of the past –
The unperturbed and courtly images –
Evening and morning, the steep street of Urbino
To where the duchess and her people talked
The stately midnight through until they stood
In their great window looking at the dawn;
I might have had no friend that could not mix
Courtesy and passion into one like those
That saw the wicks grow yellow in the dawn;
I might have used the one substantial right
My trade allows: chosen my company,
And chosen what scenery had pleased me best.'
Thereon my phoenix answered in reproof,
'The drunkards, pilferers of public funds,
All the dishonest crowd I had driven away,
When my luck changed and they dared meet my face,
Crawled from obscurity, and set upon me
Those I had served and some that I had fed;
Yet never have I, now nor any time,
Complained of the people.'
All I could reply
Was: 'You, that have not lived in thought but deed,
Can have the purity of a natural force,
But I, whose virtues are the definitions
Of the analytic mind, can neither close
The eye of the mind nor keep my tongue from speech.'
And yet, because my heart leaped at her words,
I was abashed, and now they come to mind
After nine years, I sink my head abashed.

[10 January 1915] 1916

His Phoenix

There is a queen in China, or maybe it's in Spain,
And birthdays and holidays such praises can be heard
Of her unblemished lineaments, a whiteness with no stain,
That she might be that sprightly girl trodden by a bird;
And there's a score of duchesses, surpassing womankind,
Or who have found a painter to make them so for pay
And smooth out stain and blemish with the elegance of his mind:
I knew a phoenix in my youth, so let them have their day.

The young men every night applaud their Gaby's laughing eye,
And Ruth St. Denis had more charm although she had poor luck;
From nineteen hundred nine or ten, Pavlova's had the cry,
And there's a player in the States who gathers up her cloak
And flings herself out of the room when Juliet would be bride
With all a woman's passion, a child's imperious way,
And there are – but no matter if there are scores beside:
I knew a phoenix in my youth, so let them have their day.

There's Margaret and Marjorie and Dorothy and Nan,
A Daphne and a Mary who live in privacy;
One's had her fill of lovers, another's had but one,
Another boasts, 'I pick and choose and have but two or three.'
If head and limb have beauty and the instep's high and light
They can spread out what sail they please for all I have to say,
Be but the breakers of men's hearts or engines of delight:
I knew a phoenix in my youth, so let them have their day.

There'll be that crowd, that barbarous crowd, through all the centuries,
And who can say but some young belle may walk and talk men wild

Who is my beauty's equal, though that my heart denies,
But not the exact likeness, the simplicity of a child,
And that proud look as though she had gazed into the
    burning sun,
And all the shapely body no tittle gone astray.
I mourn for that most lonely thing; and yet God's will be
    done:
I knew a phoenix in my youth, so let them have their day.

[January 1915] 1916

A Thought from Propertius

She might, so noble from head
To great shapely knees
The long flowing line,
Have walked to the altar
Through the holy images
At Pallas Athena's side,
Or been fit spoil for a centaur
Drunk with the unmixed wine.

1917

Broken Dreams

There is grey in your hair.
Young men no longer suddenly catch their breath
When you are passing;
But maybe some old gaffer mutters a blessing
Because it was your prayer
Recovered him upon the bed of death.
For your sole sake – that all heart's ache have known,
And given to others all heart's ache,
From meagre girlhood's putting on
Burdensome beauty – for your sole sake
Heaven has put away the stroke of her doom,
So great her portion in that peace you make
By merely walking in a room.

Your beauty can but leave among us
Vague memories, nothing but memories.
A young man when the old men are done talking
Will say to an old man, 'Tell me of that lady
The poet stubborn with his passion sang us
When age might well have chilled his blood.'

Vague memories, nothing but memories,
But in the grave all, all, shall be renewed.
The certainty that I shall see that lady
Leaning or standing or walking
In the first loveliness of womanhood,
And with the fervour of my youthful eyes,
Has set me muttering like a fool.

You are more beautiful than any one,
And yet your body had a flaw:
Your small hands were not beautiful,
And I am afraid that you will run
And paddle to the wrist
In that mysterious, always brimming lake
Where those that have obeyed the holy law
Paddle and are perfect. Leave unchanged
The hands that I have kissed,
For old sake's sake.

The last stroke of midnight dies.
All day in the one chair
From dream to dream and rhyme to rhyme I have ranged
In rambling talk with an image of air:
Vague memories, nothing but memories.

[24 October 1915] 1917

A Deep-sworn Vow

Others because you did not keep
That deep-sworn vow have been friends of mine;
Yet always when I look death in the face,

When I clamber to the heights of sleep,
Or when I grow excited with wine,
Suddenly I meet your face.

[17 October 1915] 1917

Presences

This night has been so strange that it seemed
As if the hair stood up on my head.
From going-down of the sun I have dreamed
That women laughing, or timid or wild,
In rustle of lace or silken stuff,
Climbed up my creaking stair. They had read
All I had rhymed of that monstrous thing
Returned and yet unrequited love.
They stood in the door and stood between
My great wood lectern and the fire
Till I could hear their hearts beating:
One is a harlot, and one a child
That never looked upon man with desire,
And one, it may be, a queen.

[November 1915] 1917

The Balloon of the Mind

Hands, do what you're bid:
Bring the balloon of the mind
That bellies and drags in the wind
Into its narrow shed.

1917

To a Squirrel at Kyle-na-no

Come play with me;
Why should you run
Through the shaking tree
As though I'd a gun
To strike you dead?
When all I would do
Is to scratch your head
And let you go.

[September 1912] 1917

On being asked for a War Poem

I think it better that in times like these
A poet's mouth be silent, for in truth
We have no gift to set a statesman right;
He has had enough of meddling who can please
A young girl in the indolence of her youth,
Or an old man upon a winter's night.

[6 February 1915] 1916

In Memory of Alfred Pollexfen

Five-and-twenty years have gone
Since old William Pollexfen
Laid his strong bones down in death
By his wife Elizabeth
In the grey stone tomb he made.
And after twenty years they laid
In that tomb by him and her
His son George, the astrologer;
And Masons drove from miles away
To scatter the Acacia spray
Upon a melancholy man
Who had ended where his breath began.

Many a son and daughter lies
Far from the customary skies,
The Mall and Eades's grammar school,
In London or in Liverpool;
But where is laid the sailor John
That so many lands had known,
Quiet lands or unquiet seas
Where the Indians trade or Japanese?
He never found his rest ashore,
Moping for one voyage more.
Where have they laid the sailor John?
And yesterday the youngest son,
A humorous, unambitious man,
Was buried near the astrologer,
Yesterday in the tenth year
Since he who had been contented long,
A nobody in a great throng,
Decided he must journey home,
Now that his fiftieth year had come,
And 'Mr. Alfred' be again
Upon the lips of common men
Who carried in their memory
His childhood and his family.
At all these death-beds women heard
A visionary white sea-bird
Lamenting that a man should die;
And with that cry I have raised my cry.

[August 1916] 1917

Upon a Dying Lady

I

Her Courtesy

With the old kindness, the old distinguished grace,
She lies, her lovely piteous head amid dull red hair
Propped upon pillows, rouge on the pallor of her face.
She would not have us sad because she is lying there,

And when she meets our gaze her eyes are laughter-lit,
Her speech a wicked tale that we may vie with her,
Matching our broken-hearted wit against her wit,
Thinking of saints and of Petronius Arbiter.

[January 1913] 1917

II

Certain Artists bring her Dolls and Drawings

Bring where our Beauty lies
A new modelled doll, or drawing,
With a friend's or an enemy's
Features, or maybe showing
Her features when a tress
Of dull red hair was flowing
Over some silken dress
Cut in the Turkish fashion,
Or, it may be, like a boy's.
We have given the world our passion,
We have naught for death but toys.

[January 1912] 1917

III

She turns the Dolls' Faces to the Wall

Because to-day is some religious festival
They had a priest say Mass, and even the Japanese,
Heel up and weight on toe, must face the wall
– Pedant in passion, learned in old courtesies,
Vehement and witty she had seemed –; the Venetian lady
Who had seemed to glide to some intrigue in her red shoes,
Her domino, her panniered skirt copied from Longhi;
The meditative critic; all are on their toes,

Even our Beauty with her Turkish trousers on.
Because the priest must have like every dog his day
Or keep us all awake with baying at the moon,
We and our dolls being but the world were best away.

1917

IV

The End of Day

She is playing like a child
And penance is the play,
Fantastical and wild
Because the end of day
Shows her that some one soon
Will come from the house, and say –
Though play is but half done –
'Come in and leave the play.'

1917

V

Her Race

She has not grown uncivil
As narrow natures would
And called the pleasures evil
Happier days thought good;
She knows herself a woman
No red and white of a face,
Or rank, raised from a common
Unreckonable race;
And how should her heart fail her
Or sickness break her will
With her dead brother's valour
For an example still?

1917

VI

Her Courage

When her soul flies to the predestined dancing-place
(I have no speech but symbol, the pagan speech I made
Amid the dreams of youth) let her come face to face,
Amid that first astonishment, with Grania's shade,
All but the terrors of the woodland flight forgot
That made her Diarmuid dear, and some old cardinal
Pacing with half-closed eyelids in a sunny spot
Who had murmured of Giorgione at his latest breath –
Aye, and Achilles, Timor, Babar, Barhaim, all
Who have lived in joy and laughed into the face of Death.

1917

VII

Her Friends bring her a Christmas Tree

Pardon, great enemy,
Without an angry thought
We've carried in our tree,
And here and there have bought
Till all the boughs are gay,
And she may look from the bed
On pretty things that may
Please a fantastic head.
Give her a little grace,
What if a laughing eye
Have looked into your face?
It is about to die.

[July 1914] 1917

Ego Dominus Tuus

Hic. On the grey sand beside the shallow stream
Under your old wind-beaten tower, where still
A lamp burns on beside the open book
That Michael Robartes left, you walk in the moon
And though you have passed the best of life still trace,
Enthralled by the unconquerable delusion,
Magical shapes.

Ille. By the help of an image
I call to my own opposite, summon all
That I have handled least, least looked upon.

Hic. And I would find myself and not an image.

Ille. That is our modern hope and by its light
We have lit upon the gentle, sensitive mind
And lost the old nonchalance of the hand;
Whether we have chosen chisel, pen or brush,
We are but critics, or but half create,
Timid, entangled, empty and abashed,
Lacking the countenance of our friends.

Hic. And yet
The chief imagination of Christendom,
Dante Alighieri, so utterly found himself
That he has made that hollow face of his
More plain to the mind's eye than any face
But that of Christ.

Ille. And did he find himself
Or was the hunger that had made it hollow
A hunger for the apple on the bough
Most out of reach? and is that spectral image
The man that Lapo and that Guido knew?
I think he fashioned from his opposite
An image that might have been a stony face
Staring upon a Bedouin's horse-hair roof
From doored and windowed cliff, or half upturned
Among the coarse grass and the camel-dung.
He set his chisel to the hardest stone.

Being mocked by Guido for his lecherous life,
Derided and deriding, driven out
To climb that stair and eat that bitter bread,
He found the unpersuadable justice, he found
The most exalted lady loved by a man.

Hic. Yet surely there are men who have made their art
Out of no tragic war, lovers of life,
Impulsive men that look for happiness
And sing when they have found it.

Ille. No, not sing,
For those that love the world serve it in action,
Grow rich, popular and full of influence,
And should they paint or write, still it is action:
The struggle of the fly in marmalade.
The rhetorician would deceive his neighbours,
The sentimentalist himself; while art
Is but a vision of reality.
What portion in the world can the artist have
Who has awakened from the common dream
But dissipation and despair?

Hic. And yet
No one denies to Keats love of the world;
Remember his deliberate happiness.

Ille. His art is happy, but who knows his mind?
I see a schoolboy when I think of him,
With face and nose pressed to a sweet-shop window,
For certainly he sank into his grave
His senses and his heart unsatisfied,
And made – being poor, ailing and ignorant,
Shut out from all the luxury of the world,
The coarse-bred son of a livery-stable keeper –
Luxuriant song.

Hic. Why should you leave the lamp
Burning alone beside an open book,
And trace these characters upon the sands?
A style is found by sedentary toil
And by the imitation of great masters.

Ille. Because I seek an image, not a book.
Those men that in their writings are most wise
Own nothing but their blind, stupefied hearts.
I call to the mysterious one who yet
Shall walk the wet sands by the edge of the stream
And look most like me, being indeed my double,
And prove of all imaginable things
The most unlike, being my anti-self,
And standing by these characters disclose
All that I seek; and whisper it as though
He were afraid the birds, who cry aloud
Their momentary cries before it is dawn,
Would carry it away to blasphemous men.

[5 October 1915] 1917

A Prayer on going into my House

God grant a blessing on this tower and cottage
And on my heirs, if all remain unspoiled,
No table or chair or stool not simple enough
For shepherd lads in Galilee; and grant
That I myself for portions of the year
May handle nothing and set eyes on nothing
But what the great and passionate have used
Throughout so many varying centuries
We take it for the norm; yet should I dream
Sinbad the sailor's brought a painted chest,
Or image, from beyond the Loadstone Mountain,
That dream is a norm; and should some limb of the devil
Destroy the view by cutting down an ash
That shades the road, or setting up a cottage
Planned in a government office, shorten his life,
Manacle his soul upon the Red Sea bottom.

[1918] 1918

The Phases of the Moon

An old man cocked his ear upon a bridge;
He and his friend, their faces to the South,
Had trod the uneven road. Their boots were soiled,
Their Connemara cloth worn out of shape;
They had kept a steady pace as though their beds,
Despite a dwindling and late risen moon,
Were distant still. An old man cocked his ear.

Aherne. What made that sound?

Robartes. A rat or water-hen
Splashed, or an otter slid into the stream.
We are on the bridge; that shadow is the tower,
And the light proves that he is reading still.
He has found, after the manner of his kind,
Mere images; chosen this place to live in
Because, it may be, of the candle-light
From the far tower where Milton's Platonist
Sat late, or Shelley's visionary prince:
The lonely light that Samuel Palmer engraved,
An image of mysterious wisdom won by toil;
And now he seeks in book or manuscript
What he shall never find.

Aherne. Why should not you
Who know it all ring at his door, and speak
Just truth enough to show that his whole life
Will scarcely find for him a broken crust
Of all those truths that are your daily bread;
And when you have spoken take the roads again?

Robartes. He wrote of me in that extravagant style
He had learned from Pater, and to round his tale
Said I was dead; and dead I choose to be.

Aherne. Sing me the changes of the moon once more;
True song, though speech: 'mine author sung it me.'

Robartes. Twenty-and-eight the phases of the moon,
The full and the moon's dark and all the crescents,
Twenty-and-eight, and yet but six-and-twenty

The cradles that a man must needs be rocked in;
For there's no human life at the full or the dark.
From the first crescent to the half, the dream
But summons to adventure, and the man
Is always happy like a bird or a beast;
But while the moon is rounding towards the full
He follows whatever whim's most difficult
Among whims not impossible, and though scarred,
As with the cat-o'-nine-tails of the mind,
His body moulded from within his body
Grows comelier. Eleven pass, and then
Athena takes Achilles by the hair,
Hector is in the dust, Nietzsche is born,
Because the hero's crescent is the twelfth.
And yet, twice born, twice buried, grow he must,
Before the full moon, helpless as a worm.
The thirteenth moon but sets the soul at war
In its own being, and when that war's begun
There is no muscle in the arm; and after,
Under the frenzy of the fourteenth moon,
The soul begins to tremble into stillness,
To die into the labyrinth of itself!

Aherne. Sing out the song; sing to the end, and sing
The strange reward of all that discipline.

Robartes. All thought becomes an image and the soul
Becomes a body: that body and that soul
Too perfect at the full to lie in a cradle,
Too lonely for the traffic of the world:
Body and soul cast out and cast away
Beyond the visible world.

Aherne. All dreams of the soul
End in a beautiful man's or woman's body.

Robartes. Have you not always known it?

Aherne. The song will have it
That those that we have loved got their long fingers
From death, and wounds, or on Sinai's top,
Or from some bloody whip in their own hands.

They ran from cradle to cradle till at last
Their beauty dropped out of the loneliness
Of body and soul.

Robartes. The lover's heart knows that.

Aherne. It must be that the terror in their eyes
Is memory or foreknowledge of the hour
When all is fed with light and heaven is bare.

Robartes. When the moon's full those creatures of the full
Are met on the waste hills by country men
Who shudder and hurry by: body and soul
Estranged amid the strangeness of themselves,
Caught up in contemplation, the mind's eye
Fixed upon images that once were thought,
For perfected, completed, and immovable
Images can break the solitude
Of lovely, satisfied, indifferent eyes.

And thereupon with aged, high-pitched voice
Aherne laughed, thinking of the man within,
His sleepless candle and laborious pen.

Robartes. And after that the crumbling of the moon:
The soul remembering its loneliness
Shudders in many cradles; all is changed.
It would be the world's servant, and as it serves,
Choosing whatever task's most difficult
Among tasks not impossible, it takes
Upon the body and upon the soul
The coarseness of the drudge.

Aherne. Before the full
It sought itself and afterwards the world.

Robartes. Because you are forgotten, half out of life,
And never wrote a book, your thought is clear.
Reformer, merchant, statesman, learned man,
Dutiful husband, honest wife by turn,
Cradle upon cradle, and all in flight and all

Deformed, because there is no deformity
But saves us from a dream.

Aherne. And what of those
That the last servile crescent has set free?

Robartes. Because all dark, like those that are all light,
They are cast beyond the verge, and in a cloud,
Crying to one another like the bats;
But having no desire they cannot tell
What's good or bad, or what it is to triumph
At the perfection of one's own obedience;
And yet they speak what's blown into the mind;
Deformed beyond deformity, unformed,
Insipid as the dough before it is baked,
They change their bodies at a word.

Aherne. And then?

Robartes. When all the dough has been so kneaded up
That it can take what form cook Nature fancies,
The first thin crescent is wheeled round once more.

Aherne. But the escape; the song's not finished yet.

Robartes. Hunchback and Saint and Fool are the last crescents.
The burning bow that once could shoot an arrow
Out of the up and down, the wagon-wheel
Of beauty's cruelty and wisdom's chatter –
Out of that raving tide – is drawn betwixt
Deformity of body and of mind.

Aherne. Were not our beds far off I'd ring the bell,
Stand under the rough roof-timbers of the hall
Beside the castle door, where all is stark
Austerity, a place set out for wisdom
That he will never find; I'd play a part;
He would never know me after all these years
But take me for some drunken country man;
I'd stand and mutter there until he caught
'Hunchback and Saint and Fool', and that they came
Under the three last crescents of the moon,

And then I'd stagger out. He'd crack his wits
Day after day, yet never find the meaning.

And then he laughed to think that what seemed hard
Should be so simple – a bat rose from the hazels
And circled round him with its squeaky cry,
The light in the tower window was put out.

[July 1918] 1919

The Cat and the Moon

The cat went here and there
And the moon spun round like a top,
And the nearest kin of the moon,
The creeping cat, looked up.
Black Minnaloushe stared at the moon,
For, wander and wail as he would,
The pure cold light in the sky
Troubled his animal blood.
Minnaloushe runs in the grass
Lifting his delicate feet.
Do you dance, Minnaloushe, do you dance?
When two close kindred meet,
What better than call a dance?
Maybe the moon may learn,
Tired of that courtly fashion,
A new dance turn.
Minnaloushe creeps through the grass
From moonlit place to place,
The sacred moon overhead
Has taken a new phase.
Does Minnaloushe know that his pupils
Will pass from change to change,
And that from round to crescent,
From crescent to round they range?

Minnaloushe creeps through the grass
Alone, important and wise,
And lifts to the changing moon
His changing eyes.

[1917] 1918

The Saint and the Hunchback

Hunchback. Stand up and lift your hand and bless
A man that finds great bitterness
In thinking of his lost renown.
A Roman Caesar is held down
Under this hump.

Saint. God tries each man
According to a different plan.
I shall not cease to bless because
I lay about me with the taws
That night and morning I may thrash
Greek Alexander from my flesh,
Augustus Caesar, and after these
That great rogue Alcibiades.

Hunchback. To all that in your flesh have stood
And blessed, I give my gratitude,
Honoured by all in their degrees,
But most to Alcibiades.

[1918] 1919

Two Songs of a Fool

I

A speckled cat and a tame hare
Eat at my hearthstone
And sleep there;
And both look up to me alone
For learning and defence
As I look up to Providence.

I start out of my sleep to think
Some day I may forget
Their food and drink;
Or, the house door left unshut,
The hare may run till it's found
The horn's sweet note and the tooth of the hound.

I bear a burden that might well try
Men that do all by rule,
And what can I
That am a wandering-witted fool
But pray to God that He ease
My great responsibilities?

[July–September 1918] 1919

II

I slept on my three-legged stool by the fire,
The speckled cat slept on my knee;
We never thought to enquire
Where the brown hare might be,
And whether the door were shut.
Who knows how she drank the wind
Stretched up on two legs from the mat,
Before she had settled her mind
To drum with her heel and to leap?
Had I but awakened from sleep
And called her name, she had heard,
It may be, and had not stirred,
That now, it may be, has found
The horn's sweet note and the tooth of the hound.

[July–September 1918] 1919

Another Song of a Fool

This great purple butterfly,
In the prison of my hands,
Has a learning in his eye
Not a poor fool understands.

Once he lived a schoolmaster
With a stark, denying look;
A string of scholars went in fear
Of his great birch and his great book.

Like the clangour of a bell,
Sweet and harsh, harsh and sweet,
That is how he learnt so well
To take the roses for his meat.

[Summer 1918] 1919

The Double Vision of Michael Robartes

I

On the grey rock of Cashel the mind's eye
Has called up the cold spirits that are born
When the old moon is vanished from the sky
And the new still hides her horn.

Under blank eyes and fingers never still
The particular is pounded till it is man.
When had I my own will?
O not since life began.

Constrained, arraigned, baffled, bent and unbent
By these wire-jointed jaws and limbs of wood,
Themselves obedient,
Knowing not evil and good;

Obedient to some hidden magical breath.
They do not even feel, so abstract are they,
So dead beyond our death,
Triumph that we obey.

II

On the grey rock of Cashel I suddenly saw
A Sphinx with woman breast and lion paw,
A Buddha, hand at rest,
Hand lifted up that blest;

And right between these two a girl at play
That, it may be, had danced her life away,
For now being dead it seemed
That she of dancing dreamed.

Although I saw it all in the mind's eye
There can be nothing solider till I die;
I saw by the moon's light
Now at its fifteenth night.

One lashed her tail; her eyes lit by the moon
Gazed upon all things known, all things unknown,
In triumph of intellect
With motionless head erect.

That other's moonlit eyeballs never moved,
Being fixed on all things loved, all things unloved,
Yet little peace he had,
For those that love are sad.

O little did they care who danced between,
And little she by whom her dance was seen
So she had outdanced thought.
Body perfection brought,

For what but eye and ear silence the mind
With the minute particulars of mankind?
Mind moved yet seemed to stop
As 'twere a spinning-top.

In contemplation had those three so wrought
Upon a moment, and so stretched it out
That they, time overthrown,
Were dead yet flesh and bone.

III

I knew that I had seen, had seen at last
That girl my unremembering nights hold fast
Or else my dreams that fly
If I should rub an eye,

And yet in flying fling into my meat
A crazy juice that makes the pulses beat

As though I had been undone
By Homer's Paragon

Who never gave the burning town a thought;
To such a pitch of folly I am brought,
Being caught between the pull
Of the dark moon and the full,

The commonness of thought and images
That have the frenzy of our western seas.
Thereon I made my moan,
And after kissed a stone,

And after that arranged it in a song
Seeing that I, ignorant for so long,
Had been rewarded thus
In Cormac's ruined house.

[March–April 1918] 1919

MICHAEL ROBARTES AND THE DANCER
1921

Michael Robartes and the Dancer

He. Opinion is not worth a rush;
In this altar-piece the knight,
Who grips his long spear so to push
That dragon through the fading light,
Loved the lady; and it's plain
The half-dead dragon was her thought,
That every morning rose again
And dug its claws and shrieked and fought.
Could the impossible come to pass
She would have time to turn her eyes,
Her lover thought, upon the glass
And on the instant would grow wise.

She. You mean they argued.

He. Put it so;
But bear in mind your lover's wage
Is what your looking-glass can show,
And that he will turn green with rage
At all that is not pictured there.

She. May I not put myself to college?

He. Go pluck Athena by the hair;
For what mere book can grant a knowledge
With an impassioned gravity
Appropriate to that beating breast,

That vigorous thigh, that dreaming eye?
And may the devil take the rest.

She. And must no beautiful woman be
Learned like a man?

He. Paul Veronese
And all his sacred company
Imagined bodies all their days
By the lagoon you love so much,
For proud, soft, ceremonious proof
That all must come to sight and touch;
While Michael Angelo's Sistine roof,
His 'Morning' and his 'Night' disclose
How sinew that has been pulled tight,
Or it may be loosened in repose,
Can rule by supernatural right
Yet be but sinew.

She. I have heard said
There is great danger in the body.

He. Did God in portioning wine and bread
Give man His thought or His mere body?

She. My wretched dragon is perplexed.

He. I have principles to prove me right.
It follows from this Latin text
That blest souls are not composite,
And that all beautiful women may
Live in uncomposite blessedness,
And lead us to the like – if they
Will banish every thought, unless
The lineaments that please their view
When the long looking-glass is full,
Even from the foot-sole think it too.

She. They say such different things at school.

[1918] 1920

Solomon and the Witch

And thus declared that Arab lady:
'Last night, where under the wild moon
On grassy mattress I had laid me,
Within my arms great Solomon,
I suddenly cried out in a strange tongue
Not his, not mine.'
Who understood
Whatever has been said, sighed, sung,
Howled, miau-d, barked, brayed, belled, yelled, cried, crowed,
Thereon replied: 'A cockerel
Crew from a blossoming apple bough
Three hundred years before the Fall,
And never crew again till now,
And would not now but that he thought,
Chance being at one with Choice at last,
All that the brigand apple brought
And this foul world were dead at last.
He that crowed out eternity
Thought to have crowed it in again.
For though love has a spider's eye
To find out some appropriate pain –
Aye, though all passion's in the glance –
For every nerve, and tests a lover
With cruelties of Choice and Chance;
And when at last that murder's over
Maybe the bride-bed brings despair,
For each an imagined image brings
And finds a real image there;
Yet the world ends when these two things,
Though several, are a single light,
When oil and wick are burned in one;
Therefore a blessed moon last night
Gave Sheba to her Solomon.'

'Yet the world stays.'
'If that be so,
Your cockerel found us in the wrong
Although he thought it worth a crow.
Maybe an image is too strong
Or maybe is not strong enough.'

'The night has fallen; not a sound
In the forbidden sacred grove
Unless a petal hit the ground,
Nor any human sight within it
But the crushed grass where we have lain;
And the moon is wilder every minute.
O! Solomon! let us try again.'

[1918] 1921

An Image from a Past Life

He. Never until this night have I been stirred.
The elaborate star-light throws a reflection
On the dark stream,
Till all the eddies gleam;
And thereupon there comes that scream
From terrified, invisible beast or bird:
Image of poignant recollection.

She. An image of my heart that is smitten through
Out of all likelihood, or reason,
And when at last,
Youth's bitterness being past,
I had thought that all my days were cast
Amid most lovely places; smitten as though
It had not learned its lesson.

He. Why have you laid your hands upon my eyes?
What can have suddenly alarmed you
Whereon 'twere best
My eyes should never rest?
What is there but the slowly fading west,
The river imaging the flashing skies,
All that to this moment charmed you?

She. A sweetheart from another life floats there
As though she had been forced to linger
From vague distress
Or arrogant loveliness,
Merely to loosen out a tress
Among the starry eddies of her hair
Upon the paleness of a finger.

He. But why should you grow suddenly afraid
And start – I at your shoulder –
Imagining
That any night could bring
An image up, or anything
Even to eyes that beauty had driven mad,
But images to make me fonder?

She. Now she has thrown her arms above her head;
Whether she threw them up to flout me,
Or but to find,
Now that no fingers bind,
That her hair streams upon the wind,
I do not know, that know I am afraid
Of the hovering thing night brought me.

[Summer–September 1919] 1920

Under Saturn

Do not because this day I have grown saturnine
Imagine that lost love, inseparable from my thought
Because I have no other youth, can make me pine;
For how should I forget the wisdom that you brought,
The comfort that you made? Although my wits have gone
On a fantastic ride, my horse's flanks are spurred
By childish memories of an old cross Pollexfen,
And of a Middleton, whose name you never heard,
And of a red-haired Yeats whose looks, although he died
Before my time, seem like a vivid memory.

You heard that labouring man who had served
  my people. He said
Upon the open road, near to the Sligo quay –
No, no, not said, but cried it out – 'You have come again,
And surely after twenty years it was time to come.'
I am thinking of a child's vow sworn in vain
Never to leave that valley his fathers called their home.

November 1919

[November 1919] 1920

Easter, 1916

I have met them at close of day
Coming with vivid faces
From counter or desk among grey
Eighteenth-century houses.
I have passed with a nod of the head
Or polite meaningless words,
Or have lingered awhile and said
Polite meaningless words,
And thought before I had done
Of a mocking tale or a gibe
To please a companion
Around the fire at the club,
Being certain that they and I
But lived where motley is worn:
All changed, changed utterly:
A terrible beauty is born.

That woman's days were spent
In ignorant good-will,
Her nights in argument
Until her voice grew shrill.
What voice more sweet than hers
When, young and beautiful,
She rode to harriers?
This man had kept a school

And rode our wingèd horse;
This other his helper and friend
Was coming into his force;
He might have won fame in the end,
So sensitive his nature seemed,
So daring and sweet his thought.
This other man I had dreamed
A drunken, vainglorious lout.
He had done most bitter wrong
To some who are near my heart,
Yet I number him in the song;
He, too, has resigned his part
In the casual comedy;
He, too, has been changed in his turn,
Transformed utterly:
A terrible beauty is born.

Hearts with one purpose alone
Through summer and winter seem
Enchanted to a stone
To trouble the living stream.
The horse that comes from the road,
The rider, the birds that range
From cloud to tumbling cloud,
Minute by minute they change;
A shadow of cloud on the stream
Changes minute by minute;
A horse-hoof slides on the brim,
And a horse plashes within it;
The long-legged moor-hens dive,
And hens to moor-cocks call;
Minute by minute they live:
The stone's in the midst of all.

Too long a sacrifice
Can make a stone of the heart.
O when may it suffice?
That is Heaven's part, our part

To murmur name upon name,
As a mother names her child
When sleep at last has come
On limbs that had run wild.
What is it but nightfall?
No, no, not night but death;
Was it needless death after all?
For England may keep faith
For all that is done and said.
We know their dream; enough
To know they dreamed and are dead;
And what if excess of love
Bewildered them till they died?
I write it out in a verse –
MacDonagh and MacBride
And Connolly and Pearse
Now and in time to be,
Wherever green is worn,
Are changed, changed utterly:
A terrible beauty is born.

September 25, 1916

[11 May–25 September 1916] 1917

Sixteen Dead Men

O but we talked at large before
The sixteen men were shot,
But who can talk of give and take,
What should be and what not
While those dead men are loitering there
To stir the boiling pot?

You say that we should still the land
Till Germany's overcome;
But who is there to argue that
Now Pearse is deaf and dumb?
And is their logic to outweigh
MacDonagh's bony thumb?

How could you dream they'd listen
That have an ear alone
For those new comrades they have found,
Lord Edward and Wolfe Tone,
Or meddle with our give and take
That converse bone to bone?

[17 December 1916 or 1917] 1920

The Rose Tree

'O words are lightly spoken,'
Said Pearse to Connolly,
'Maybe a breath of politic words
Has withered our Rose Tree;
Or maybe but a wind that blows
Across the bitter sea.'

'It needs to be but watered,'
James Connolly replied,
'To make the green come out again
And spread on every side,
And shake the blossom from the bud
To be the garden's pride.'

'But where can we draw water,'
Said Pearse to Connolly,
'When all the wells are parched away?
O plain as plain can be
There's nothing but our own red blood
Can make a right Rose Tree.'

[7 April 1917] 1920

On a Political Prisoner

She that but little patience knew,
From childhood on, had now so much
A grey gull lost its fear and flew

Down to her cell and there alit,
And there endured her fingers' touch
And from her fingers ate its bit.

Did she in touching that lone wing
Recall the years before her mind
Became a bitter, an abstract thing,
Her thought some popular enmity:
Blind and leader of the blind
Drinking the foul ditch where they lie?

When long ago I saw her ride
Under Ben Bulben to the meet,
The beauty of her country-side
With all youth's lonely wildness stirred,
She seemed to have grown clean and sweet
Like any rock-bred, sea-borne bird:

Sea-borne, or balanced on the air
When first it sprang out of the nest
Upon some lofty rock to stare
Upon the cloudy canopy,
While under its storm-beaten breast
Cried out the hollows of the sea.

[10–29 January 1919] 1920

The Leaders of the Crowd

They must to keep their certainty accuse
All that are different of a base intent;
Pull down established honour; hawk for news
Whatever their loose phantasy invent
And murmur it with bated breath, as though
The abounding gutter had been Helicon
Or calumny a song. How can they know
Truth flourishes where the student's lamp has shone,
And there alone, that have no solitude?
So the crowd come they care not what may come.
They have loud music, hope every day renewed
And heartier loves; that lamp is from the tomb.

[1918] 1921

Towards Break of Day

Was it the double of my dream
The woman that by me lay
Dreamed, or did we halve a dream
Under the first cold gleam of day?

I thought: 'There is a waterfall
Upon Ben Bulben side
That all my childhood counted dear;
Were I to travel far and wide
I could not find a thing so dear.'
My memories had magnified
So many times childish delight.

I would have touched it like a child
But knew my finger could but have touched
Cold stone and water. I grew wild
Even accusing Heaven because
It had set down among its laws:
Nothing that we love over-much
Is ponderable to our touch.

I dreamed towards break of day,
The cold blown spray in my nostril.
But she that beside me lay
Had watched in bitterer sleep
The marvellous stag of Arthur,
That lofty white stag, leap
From mountain steep to steep.

[December 1918–January 1919]   1920

Demon and Beast

For certain minutes at the least
That crafty demon and that loud beast
That plague me day and night
Ran out of my sight;

Though I had long perned in the gyre,
Between my hatred and desire,
I saw my freedom won
And all laugh in the sun.

The glittering eyes in a death's head
Of old Luke Wadding's portrait said
Welcome, and the Ormondes all
Nodded upon the wall,
And even Strafford smiled as though
It made him happier to know
I understood his plan.
Now that the loud beast ran
There was no portrait in the Gallery
But beckoned to sweet company,
For all men's thoughts grew clear
Being dear as mine are dear.

But soon a tear-drop started up,
For aimless joy had made me stop
Beside the little lake
To watch a white gull take
A bit of bread thrown up into the air;
Now gyring down and perning there
He splashed where an absurd
Portly green-pated bird
Shook off the water from his back;
Being no more demoniac
A stupid happy creature
Could rouse my whole nature.

Yet I am certain as can be
That every natural victory
Belongs to beast or demon,
That never yet had freeman
Right mastery of natural things,
And that mere growing old, that brings
Chilled blood, this sweetness brought;
Yet have no dearer thought
Than that I may find out a way
To make it linger half a day.

O what a sweetness strayed
Through barren Thebaid,
Or by the Mareotic sea
When that exultant Anthony
And twice a thousand more
Starved upon the shore
And withered to a bag of bones!
What had the Caesars but their thrones?

[23 November 1918] 1920

The Second Coming

Turning and turning in the widening gyre
The falcon cannot hear the falconer;
Things fall apart; the centre cannot hold;
Mere anarchy is loosed upon the world,
The blood-dimmed tide is loosed, and everywhere
The ceremony of innocence is drowned;
The best lack all conviction, while the worst
Are full of passionate intensity.

Surely some revelation is at hand;
Surely the Second Coming is at hand.
The Second Coming! Hardly are those words out
When a vast image out of *Spiritus Mundi*
Troubles my sight: somewhere in sands of the desert
A shape with lion body and the head of a man,
A gaze blank and pitiless as the sun,
Is moving its slow thighs, while all about it
Reel shadows of the indignant desert birds.
The darkness drops again; but now I know
That twenty centuries of stony sleep
Were vexed to nightmare by a rocking cradle,
And what rough beast, its hour come round at last,
Slouches towards Bethlehem to be born?

[January 1919] 1920

A Prayer for my Daughter

Once more the storm is howling, and half hid
Under this cradle-hood and coverlid
My child sleeps on. There is no obstacle
But Gregory's wood and one bare hill
Whereby the haystack- and roof-levelling wind,
Bred on the Atlantic, can be stayed;
And for an hour I have walked and prayed
Because of the great gloom that is in my mind.

I have walked and prayed for this young child an hour
And heard the sea-wind scream upon the tower,
And under the arches of the bridge, and scream
In the elms above the flooded stream;
Imagining in excited reverie
That the future years had come,
Dancing to a frenzied drum,
Out of the murderous innocence of the sea.

May she be granted beauty and yet not
Beauty to make a stranger's eye distraught,
Or hers before a looking-glass, for such,
Being made beautiful overmuch,
Consider beauty a sufficient end,
Lose natural kindness and maybe
The heart-revealing intimacy
That chooses right, and never find a friend.

Helen being chosen found life flat and dull
And later had much trouble from a fool,
While that great Queen, that rose out of the spray,
Being fatherless could have her way
Yet chose a bandy-leggèd smith for man.
It's certain that fine women eat
A crazy salad with their meat
Whereby the Horn of Plenty is undone.

In courtesy I'd have her chiefly learned;
Hearts are not had as a gift but hearts are earned
By those that are not entirely beautiful;
Yet many, that have played the fool

For beauty's very self, has charm made wise,
And many a poor man that has roved,
Loved and thought himself beloved,
From a glad kindness cannot take his eyes.

May she become a flourishing hidden tree
That all her thoughts may like the linnet be,
And have no business but dispensing round
Their magnanimities of sound,
Nor but in merriment begin a chase,
Nor but in merriment a quarrel.
O may she live like some green laurel
Rooted in one dear perpetual place.

My mind, because the minds that I have loved,
The sort of beauty that I have approved,
Prosper but little, has dried up of late,
Yet knows that to be choked with hate
May well be of all evil chances chief.
If there's no hatred in a mind
Assault and battery of the wind
Can never tear the linnet from the leaf.

An intellectual hatred is the worst,
So let her think opinions are accursed.
Have I not seen the loveliest woman born
Out of the mouth of Plenty's horn,
Because of her opinionated mind
Barter that horn and every good
By quiet natures understood
For an old bellows full of angry wind?

Considering that, all hatred driven hence,
The soul recovers radical innocence
And learns at last that it is self-delighting,
Self-appeasing, self-affrighting,
And that its own sweet will is Heaven's will;
She can, though every face should scowl
And every windy quarter howl
Or every bellows burst, be happy still.

And may her bridegroom bring her to a house
Where all's accustomed, ceremonious;
For arrogance and hatred are the wares
Peddled in the thoroughfares.
How but in custom and in ceremony
Are innocence and beauty born?
Ceremony's a name for the rich horn,
And custom for the spreading laurel tree.

June 1919

[26 February–June 1919] 1919

A Meditation in Time of War

For one throb of the artery,
While on that old grey stone I sat
Under the old wind-broken tree,
I knew that One is animate,
Mankind inanimate phantasy.

[9 November 1914] 1920

To be Carved on a Stone at Thoor Ballylee

I, the poet William Yeats,
With old mill boards and sea-green slates,
And smithy work from the Gort forge,
Restored this tower for my wife George;
And may these characters remain
When all is ruin once again.

[1918] 1921

THE TOWER
1928

Sailing to Byzantium

I

That is no country for old men. The young
In one another's arms, birds in the trees,
– Those dying generations – at their song,
The salmon-falls, the mackerel-crowded seas,
Fish, flesh, or fowl, commend all summer long
Whatever is begotten, born, and dies.
Caught in that sensual music all neglect
Monuments of unageing intellect.

II

An aged man is but a paltry thing,
A tattered coat upon a stick, unless
Soul clap its hands and sing, and louder sing
For every tatter in its mortal dress,
Nor is there singing school but studying
Monuments of its own magnificence;
And therefore I have sailed the seas and come
To the holy city of Byzantium.

III

O sages standing in God's holy fire
As in the gold mosaic of a wall,
Come from the holy fire, perne in a gyre,
And be the singing-masters of my soul.

Consume my heart away; sick with desire
And fastened to a dying animal
It knows not what it is; and gather me
Into the artifice of eternity.

IV

Once out of nature I shall never take
My bodily form from any natural thing,
But such a form as Grecian goldsmiths make
Of hammered gold and gold enamelling
To keep a drowsy Emperor awake;
Or set upon a golden bough to sing
To lords and ladies of Byzantium
Of what is past, or passing, or to come.

1927

[26 September 1926] 1927

The Tower

I

What shall I do with this absurdity –
O heart, O troubled heart – this caricature,
Decrepit age that has been tied to me
As to a dog's tail?
Never had I more
Excited, passionate, fantastical
Imagination, nor an ear and eye
That more expected the impossible –
No, not in boyhood when with rod and fly,
Or the humbler worm, I climbed Ben Bulben's back
And had the livelong summer day to spend.
It seems that I must bid the Muse go pack,
Choose Plato and Plotinus for a friend
Until imagination, ear and eye,
Can be content with argument and deal
In abstract things; or be derided by
A sort of battered kettle at the heel.

II

I pace upon the battlements and stare
On the foundations of a house, or where
Tree, like a sooty finger, starts from the earth;
And send imagination forth
Under the day's declining beam, and call
Images and memories
From ruin or from ancient trees,
For I would ask a question of them all.

Beyond that ridge lived Mrs. French, and once
When every silver candlestick or sconce
Lit up the dark mahogany and the wine,
A serving-man, that could divine
That most respected lady's every wish,
Ran and with the garden shears
Clipped an insolent farmer's ears
And brought them in a little covered dish.

Some few remembered still when I was young
A peasant girl commended by a song,
Who'd lived somewhere upon that rocky place,
And praised the colour of her face,
And had the greater joy in praising her,
Remembering that, if walked she there,
Farmers jostled at the fair
So great a glory did the song confer.

And certain men, being maddened by those rhymes,
Or else by toasting her a score of times,
Rose from the table and declared it right
To test their fancy by their sight;
But they mistook the brightness of the moon
For the prosaic light of day –
Music had driven their wits astray –
And one was drowned in the great bog of Cloone.

Strange, but the man who made the song was blind;
Yet, now I have considered it, I find
That nothing strange; the tragedy began
With Homer that was a blind man,

And Helen has all living hearts betrayed.
O may the moon and sunlight seem
One inextricable beam,
For if I triumph I must make men mad.

And I myself created Hanrahan
And drove him drunk or sober through the dawn
From somewhere in the neighbouring cottages:
Caught by an old man's juggleries
He stumbled, tumbled, fumbled to and fro
And had but broken knees for hire
And horrible splendour of desire;
I thought it all out twenty years ago:

Good fellows shuffled cards in an old bawn;
And when that ancient ruffian's turn was on
He so bewitched the cards under his thumb
That all but the one card became
A pack of hounds and not a pack of cards,
And that he changed into a hare.
Hanrahan rose in frenzy there
And followed up those baying creatures towards –

O towards I have forgotten what – enough!
I must recall a man that neither love
Nor music nor an enemy's clipped ear
Could, he was so harried, cheer;
A figure that has grown so fabulous
There's not a neighbour left to say
When he finished his dog's day:
An ancient bankrupt master of this house.

Before that ruin came, for centuries,
Rough men-at-arms, cross-gartered to the knees
Or shod in iron, climbed the narrow stairs,
And certain men-at-arms there were
Whose images, in the Great Memory stored,
Come with loud cry and panting breast
To break upon a sleeper's rest
While their great wooden dice beat on the board.

As I would question all, come all who can;
Come old, necessitous, half-mounted man;
And bring beauty's blind rambling celebrant;
The red man the juggler sent
Through God-forsaken meadows; Mrs. French,
Gifted with so fine an ear;
The man drowned in a bog's mire,
When mocking Muses chose the country wench.

Did all old men and women, rich and poor,
Who trod upon these rocks or passed this door,
Whether in public or in secret rage
As I do now against old age?
But I have found an answer in those eyes
That are impatient to be gone;
Go therefore; but leave Hanrahan,
For I need all his mighty memories.

Old lecher with a love on every wind,
Bring up out of that deep considering mind
All that you have discovered in the grave,
For it is certain that you have
Reckoned up every unforeknown, unseeing
Plunge, lured by a softening eye,
Or by a touch or a sigh,
Into the labyrinth of another's being;

Does the imagination dwell the most
Upon a woman won or woman lost?
If on the lost, admit you turned aside
From a great labyrinth out of pride,
Cowardice, some silly over-subtle thought
Or anything called conscience once;
And that if memory recur, the sun's
Under eclipse and the day blotted out.

III

It is time that I wrote my will;
I choose upstanding men
That climb the streams until
The fountain leap, and at dawn
Drop their cast at the side
Of dripping stone; I declare
They shall inherit my pride,
The pride of people that were
Bound neither to Cause nor to State,
Neither to slaves that were spat on,
Nor to the tyrants that spat,
The people of Burke and of Grattan
That gave, though free to refuse –
Pride, like that of the morn,
When the headlong light is loose,
Or that of the fabulous horn,
Or that of the sudden shower
When all streams are dry,
Or that of the hour
When the swan must fix his eye
Upon a fading gleam,
Float out upon a long
Last reach of glittering stream
And there sing his last song.
And I declare my faith:
I mock Plotinus' thought
And cry in Plato's teeth,
Death and life were not
Till man made up the whole,
Made lock, stock and barrel
Out of his bitter soul,
Aye, sun and moon and star, all,
And further add to that
That, being dead, we rise,
Dream and so create
Translunar Paradise.
I have prepared my peace
With learned Italian things

And the proud stones of Greece,
Poet's imaginings
And memories of love,
Memories of the words of women,
All those things whereof
Man makes a superhuman
Mirror-resembling dream.

As at the loophole there
The daws chatter and scream,
And drop twigs layer upon layer.
When they have mounted up,
The mother bird will rest
On their hollow top,
And so warm her wild nest.

I leave both faith and pride
To young upstanding men
Climbing the mountain side,
That under bursting dawn
They may drop a fly;
Being of that metal made
Till it was broken by
This sedentary trade.

Now shall I make my soul,
Compelling it to study
In a learned school
Till the wreck of body,
Slow decay of blood,
Testy delirium
Or dull decrepitude,
Or what worse evil come –
The death of friends, or death
Of every brilliant eye
That made a catch in the breath –
Seem but the clouds of the sky
When the horizon fades;
Or a bird's sleepy cry
Among the deepening shades.

1926

[7 October 1925] 1927

Meditations in Time of Civil War

I

Ancestral Houses

Surely among a rich man's flowering lawns,
Amid the rustle of his planted hills,
Life overflows without ambitious pains;
And rains down life until the basin spills,
And mounts more dizzy high the more it rains
As though to choose whatever shape it wills
And never stoop to a mechanical
Or servile shape, at others' beck and call.

Mere dreams, mere dreams! Yet Homer had not sung
Had he not found it certain beyond dreams
That out of life's own self-delight had sprung
The abounding glittering jet; though now it seems
As if some marvellous empty sea-shell flung
Out of the obscure dark of the rich streams,
And not a fountain, were the symbol which
Shadows the inherited glory of the rich.

Some violent bitter man, some powerful man
Called architect and artist in, that they,
Bitter and violent men, might rear in stone
The sweetness that all longed for night and day,
The gentleness none there had ever known;
But when the master's buried mice can play,
And maybe the great-grandson of that house,
For all its bronze and marble, 's but a mouse.

O what if gardens where the peacock strays
With delicate feet upon old terraces,
Or else all Juno from an urn displays
Before the indifferent garden deities;
O what if levelled lawns and gravelled ways
Where slippered Contemplation finds his ease
And Childhood a delight for every sense,
But take our greatness with our violence?

What if the glory of escutcheoned doors,
And buildings that a haughtier age designed,
The pacing to and fro on polished floors
Amid great chambers and long galleries, lined
With famous portraits of our ancestors;
What if those things the greatest of mankind
Consider most to magnify, or to bless,
But take our greatness with our bitterness?

[1921] 1923

II

My House

An ancient bridge, and a more ancient tower,
A farmhouse that is sheltered by its wall,
An acre of stony ground,
Where the symbolic rose can break in flower,
Old ragged elms, old thorns innumerable,
The sound of the rain or sound
Of every wind that blows;
The stilted water-hen
Crossing stream again
Scared by the splashing of a dozen cows;

A winding stair, a chamber arched with stone,
A grey stone fireplace with an open hearth,
A candle and written page.
Il Penseroso's Platonist toiled on
In some like chamber, shadowing forth
How the daemonic rage
Imagined everything.
Benighted travellers
From markets and from fairs
Have seen his midnight candle glimmering.

Two men have founded here. A man-at-arms
Gathered a score of horse and spent his days
In this tumultuous spot,

Where through long wars and sudden night alarms
His dwindling score and he seemed castaways
Forgetting and forgot;
And I, that after me
My bodily heirs may find,
To exalt a lonely mind,
Befitting emblems of adversity.

[1922] 1923

III

My Table

Two heavy trestles, and a board
Where Sato's gift, a changeless sword,
By pen and paper lies,
That it may moralise
My days out of their aimlessness.
A bit of an embroidered dress
Covers its wooden sheath.
Chaucer had not drawn breath
When it was forged. In Sato's house,
Curved like new moon, moon-luminous,
It lay five hundred years.
Yet if no change appears
No moon; only an aching heart
Conceives a changeless work of art.
Our learned men have urged
That when and where 'twas forged
A marvellous accomplishment,
In painting or in pottery, went
From father unto son
And through the centuries ran
And seemed unchanging like the sword.
Soul's beauty being most adored,
Men and their business took
The soul's unchanging look;
For the most rich inheritor,
Knowing that none could pass Heaven's door

That loved inferior art,
Had such an aching heart
That he, although a country's talk
For silken clothes and stately walk,
Had waking wits; it seemed
Juno's peacock screamed.

[1922] 1923

IV

My Descendants

Having inherited a vigorous mind
From my old fathers, I must nourish dreams
And leave a woman and a man behind
As vigorous of mind, and yet it seems
Life scarce can cast a fragrance on the wind,
Scarce spread a glory to the morning beams,
But the torn petals strew the garden plot;
And there's but common greenness after that.

And what if my descendants lose the flower
Through natural declension of the soul,
Through too much business with the passing hour,
Through too much play, or marriage with a fool?
May this laborious stair and this stark tower
Become a roofless ruin that the owl
May build in the cracked masonry and cry
Her desolation to the desolate sky.

The Primum Mobile that fashioned us
Has made the very owls in circles move;
And I, that count myself most prosperous,
Seeing that love and friendship are enough,
For an old neighbour's friendship chose the house
And decked and altered it for a girl's love,
And know whatever flourish and decline
These stones remain their monument and mine.

[1922] 1923

V

The Road at my Door

An affable Irregular,
A heavily-built Falstaffian man,
Comes cracking jokes of civil war
As though to die by gunshot were
The finest play under the sun.

A brown Lieutenant and his men,
Half dressed in national uniform,
Stand at my door, and I complain
Of the foul weather, hail and rain,
A pear-tree broken by the storm.

I count those feathered balls of soot
The moor-hen guides upon the stream,
To silence the envy in my thought;
And turn towards my chamber, caught
In the cold snows of a dream.

[1922] 1923

VI

The Stare's Nest by my Window

The bees build in the crevices
Of loosening masonry, and there
The mother birds bring grubs and flies.
My wall is loosening; honey-bees,
Come build in the empty house of the stare.

We are closed in, and the key is turned
On our uncertainty; somewhere
A man is killed, or a house burned,
Yet no clear fact to be discerned:
Come build in the empty house of the stare.

A barricade of stone or of wood;
Some fourteen days of civil war;
Last night they trundled down the road
That dead young soldier in his blood:
Come build in the empty house of the stare.

We had fed the heart on fantasies,
The heart's grown brutal from the fare;
More substance in our enmities
Than in our love; O honey-bees,
Come build in the empty house of the stare.

[1922] 1923

VII

I see Phantoms of Hatred and of the Heart's Fullness and of the Coming Emptiness

I climb to the tower-top and lean upon broken stone,
A mist that is like blown snow is sweeping over all,
Valley, river, and elms, under the light of a moon
That seems unlike itself, that seems unchangeable,
A glittering sword out of the east. A puff of wind
And those white glimmering fragments of the mist sweep by.
Frenzies bewilder, reveries perturb the mind;
Monstrous familiar images swim to the mind's eye.

'Vengeance upon the murderers,' the cry goes up,
'Vengeance for Jacques Molay.' In cloud-pale rags, or in lace,
The rage-driven, rage-tormented, and rage-hungry troop,
Trooper belabouring trooper, biting at arm or at face,
Plunges towards nothing, arms and fingers spreading wide
For the embrace of nothing; and I, my wits astray
Because of all that senseless tumult, all but cried
For vengeance on the murderers of Jacques Molay.

Their legs long, delicate and slender, aquamarine their eyes,
Magical unicorns bear ladies on their backs.
The ladies close their musing eyes. No prophecies,
Remembered out of Babylonian almanacs,
Have closed the ladies' eyes, their minds are but a pool
Where even longing drowns under its own excess;
Nothing but stillness can remain when hearts are full
Of their own sweetness, bodies of their loveliness.

The cloud-pale unicorns, the eyes of aquamarine,
The quivering half-closed eyelids, the rags of cloud or of lace,
Or eyes that rage has brightened, arms it has made lean,
Give place to an indifferent multitude, give place
To brazen hawks. Nor self-delighting reverie,
Nor hate of what's to come, nor pity for what's gone,
Nothing but grip of claw, and the eye's complacency,
The innumerable clanging wings that have put out the moon.

I turn away and shut the door, and on the stair
Wonder how many times I could have proved my worth
In something that all others understand or share;
But O! ambitious heart, had such a proof drawn forth
A company of friends, a conscience set at ease,
It had but made us pine the more. The abstract joy,
The half-read wisdom of daemonic images,
Suffice the ageing man as once the growing boy.

[1922] 1923

1923

Nineteen Hundred and Nineteen

I

Many ingenious lovely things are gone
That seemed sheer miracle to the multitude,
Protected from the circle of the moon
That pitches common things about. There stood

Amid the ornamental bronze and stone
An ancient image made of olive wood –
And gone are Phidias' famous ivories
And all the golden grasshoppers and bees.

We too had many pretty toys when young;
A law indifferent to blame or praise,
To bribe or threat; habits that made old wrong
Melt down, as it were wax in the sun's rays;
Public opinion ripening for so long
We thought it would outlive all future days.
O what fine thought we had because we thought
That the worst rogues and rascals had died out.

All teeth were drawn, all ancient tricks unlearned,
And a great army but a showy thing;
What matter that no cannon had been turned
Into a ploughshare? Parliament and king
Thought that unless a little powder burned
The trumpeters might burst with trumpeting
And yet it lack all glory; and perchance
The guardsmen's drowsy chargers would not prance.

Now days are dragon-ridden, the nightmare
Rides upon sleep: a drunken soldiery
Can leave the mother, murdered at her door,
To crawl in her own blood, and go scot-free;
The night can sweat with terror as before
We pieced our thoughts into philosophy,
And planned to bring the world under a rule,
Who are but weasels fighting in a hole.

He who can read the signs nor sink unmanned
Into the half-deceit of some intoxicant
From shallow wits; who knows no work can stand,
Whether health, wealth or peace of mind were spent
On master-work of intellect or hand,
No honour leave its mighty monument,
Has but one comfort left: all triumph would
But break upon his ghostly solitude.

But is there any comfort to be found?
Man is in love and loves what vanishes,
What more is there to say? That country round
None dared admit, if such a thought were his,
Incendiary or bigot could be found
To burn that stump on the Acropolis,
Or break in bits the famous ivories
Or traffic in the grasshoppers or bees.

II

When Loie Fuller's Chinese dancers enwound
A shining web, a floating ribbon of cloth,
It seemed that a dragon of air
Had fallen among dancers, had whirled them round
Or hurried them off on its own furious path;
So the Platonic Year
Whirls out new right and wrong,
Whirls in the old instead;
All men are dancers and their tread
Goes to the barbarous clangour of a gong.

III

Some moralist or mythological poet
Compares the solitary soul to a swan;
I am satisfied with that,
Satisfied if a troubled mirror show it,
Before that brief gleam of its life be gone,
An image of its state;
The wings half spread for flight,
The breast thrust out in pride
Whether to play, or to ride
Those winds that clamour of approaching night.

A man in his own secret meditation
Is lost amid the labyrinth that he has made
In art or politics;
Some Platonist affirms that in the station
Where we should cast off body and trade

The ancient habit sticks,
And that if our works could
But vanish with our breath
That were a lucky death,
For triumph can but mar our solitude.

The swan has leaped into the desolate heaven:
That image can bring wildness, bring a rage
To end all things, to end
What my laborious life imagined, even
The half-imagined, the half-written page;
O but we dreamed to mend
Whatever mischief seemed
To afflict mankind, but now
That winds of winter blow
Learn that we were crack-pated when we dreamed.

IV

We, who seven years ago
Talked of honour and of truth,
Shriek with pleasure if we show
The weasel's twist, the weasel's tooth.

V

Come let us mock at the great
That had such burdens on the mind
And toiled so hard and late
To leave some monument behind,
Nor thought of the levelling wind.

Come let us mock at the wise;
With all those calendars whereon
They fixed old aching eyes,
They never saw how seasons run,
And now but gape at the sun.

Come let us mock at the good
That fancied goodness might be gay,

And sick of solitude
Might proclaim a holiday:
Wind shrieked – and where are they?

Mock mockers after that
That would not lift a hand maybe
To help good, wise or great
To bar that foul storm out, for we
Traffic in mockery.

VI

Violence upon the roads: violence of horses;
Some few have handsome riders, are garlanded
On delicate sensitive ear or tossing mane,
But wearied running round and round in their courses
All break and vanish, and evil gathers head:
Herodias' daughters have returned again,
A sudden blast of dusty wind and after
Thunder of feet, tumult of images,
Their purpose in the labyrinth of the wind;
And should some crazy hand dare touch a daughter
All turn with amorous cries, or angry cries,
According to the wind, for all are blind.
But now wind drops, dust settles; thereupon
There lurches past, his great eyes without thought
Under the shadow of stupid straw-pale locks,
That insolent fiend Robert Artisson
To whom the love-lorn Lady Kyteler brought
Bronzed peacock feathers, red combs of her cocks.

1919

[1920–21] 1921

The Wheel

Through winter-time we call on spring,
And through the spring on summer call,
And when abounding hedges ring
Declare that winter's best of all;

And after that there's nothing good
Because the spring-time has not come –
Nor know that what disturbs our blood
Is but its longing for the tomb.

[13 September 1921] 1922

Youth and Age

Much did I rage when young,
Being by the world oppressed,
But now with flattering tongue
It speeds the parting guest.

1924

[1924] 1924

The New Faces

If you, that have grown old, were the first dead,
Neither catalpa tree nor scented lime
Should hear my living feet, nor would I tread
Where we wrought that shall break the teeth of Time.
Let the new faces play what tricks they will
In the old rooms; night can outbalance day,
Our shadows rove the garden gravel still,
The living seem more shadowy than they.

[December 1912] 1922

A Prayer for my Son

Bid a strong ghost stand at the head
That my Michael may sleep sound,
Nor cry, nor turn in the bed
Till his morning meal come round;
And may departing twilight keep
All dread afar till morning's back,

That his mother may not lack
Her fill of sleep.

Bid the ghost have sword in fist:
Some there are, for I avow
Such devilish things exist,
Who have planned his murder, for they know
Of some most haughty deed or thought
That waits upon his future days,
And would through hatred of the bays
Bring that to nought.

Though You can fashion everything
From nothing every day, and teach
The morning stars to sing,
You have lacked articulate speech
To tell Your simplest want, and known,
Wailing upon a woman's knee,
All of that worst ignominy
Of flesh and bone;

And when through all the town there ran
The servants of Your enemy,
A woman and a man,
Unless the Holy Writings lie,
Hurried through the smooth and rough
And through the fertile and waste,
Protecting, till the danger past,
With human love.

[December 1921] 1922

Two Songs from a Play

I

I saw a staring virgin stand
Where holy Dionysus died,
And tear the heart out of his side,
And lay the heart upon her hand

And bear that beating heart away;
And then did all the Muses sing
Of Magnus Annus at the spring,
As though God's death were but a play.

Another Troy must rise and set,
Another lineage feed the crow,
Another Argo's painted prow
Drive to a flashier bauble yet.
The Roman Empire stood appalled:
It dropped the reins of peace and war
When that fierce virgin and her Star
Out of the fabulous darkness called.

II

In pity for man's darkening thought
He walked that room and issued thence
In Galilean turbulence;
The Babylonian starlight brought
A fabulous, formless darkness in;
Odour of blood when Christ was slain
Made all Platonic tolerance vain
And vain all Doric discipline.

[1926] 1927

Everything that man esteems
Endures a moment or a day.
Love's pleasure drives his love away,
The painter's brush consumes his dreams;
The herald's cry, the soldier's tread
Exhaust his glory and his might:
Whatever flames upon the night
Man's own resinous heart has fed.

[1930–31] 1931

Fragments

I

Locke sank into a swoon;
The Garden died;
God took the spinning-jenny
Out of his side.

II

Where got I that truth?
Out of a medium's mouth,
Out of nothing it came,
Out of the forest loam,
Out of dark night where lay
The crowns of Nineveh.

1931

Leda and the Swan

A sudden blow: the great wings beating still
Above the staggering girl, her thighs caressed
By the dark webs, her nape caught in his bill,
He holds her helpless breast upon his breast.

How can those terrified vague fingers push
The feathered glory from her loosening thighs,
And how can body, laid in that white rush,
But feel the strange heart beating where it lies?

A shudder in the loins engenders there
The broken wall, the burning roof and tower
And Agamemnon dead.
Being so caught up,
So mastered by the brute blood of the air,
Did she put on his knowledge with his power
Before the indifferent beak could let her drop?

1923

[18 September 1923] 1924

On a Picture of a Black Centaur by Edmund Dulac

Your hooves have stamped at the black margin of the wood,
Even where horrible green parrots call and swing.
My works are all stamped down into the sultry mud.
I knew that horse-play, knew it for a murderous thing.
What wholesome sun has ripened is wholesome food to eat,
And that alone; yet I, being driven half insane
Because of some green wing, gathered old mummy wheat
In the mad abstract dark and ground it grain by grain
And after baked it slowly in an oven; but now
I bring full-flavoured wine out of a barrel found
Where seven Ephesian topers slept and never knew
When Alexander's empire passed, they slept so sound.
Stretch out your limbs and sleep a long Saturnian sleep;
I have loved you better than my soul for all my words,
And there is none so fit to keep a watch and keep
Unwearied eyes upon those horrible green birds.

[September 1920] 1922

Among School Children

I

I walk through the long schoolroom questioning;
A kind old nun in a white hood replies;
The children learn to cipher and to sing,
To study reading-books and history,
To cut and sew, be neat in everything
In the best modern way – the children's eyes
In momentary wonder stare upon
A sixty-year-old smiling public man.

II

I dream of a Ledaean body, bent
Above a sinking fire, a tale that she
Told of a harsh reproof, or trivial event
That changed some childish day to tragedy –

Told, and it seemed that our two natures blent
Into a sphere from youthful sympathy,
Or else, to alter Plato's parable,
Into the yolk and white of the one shell.

III

And thinking of that fit of grief or rage
I look upon one child or t'other there
And wonder if she stood so at that age –
For even daughters of the swan can share
Something of every paddler's heritage –
And had that colour upon cheek or hair,
And thereupon my heart is driven wild:
She stands before me as a living child.

IV

Her present image floats into the mind –
Did Quattrocento finger fashion it
Hollow of cheek as though it drank the wind
And took a mess of shadows for its meat?
And I though never of Ledaean kind
Had pretty plumage once – enough of that,
Better to smile on all that smile, and show
There is a comfortable kind of old scarecrow.

V

What youthful mother, a shape upon her lap
Honey of generation had betrayed,
And that must sleep, shriek, struggle to escape
As recollection or the drug decide,
Would think her son, did she but see that shape
With sixty or more winters on its head,
A compensation for the pang of his birth,
Or the uncertainty of his setting forth?

VI

Plato thought nature but a spume that plays
Upon a ghostly paradigm of things;

Solider Aristotle played the taws
Upon the bottom of a king of kings;
World-famous golden-thighed Pythagoras
Fingered upon a fiddle-stick or strings
What a star sang and careless Muses heard:
Old clothes upon old sticks to scare a bird.

VII

Both nuns and mothers worship images,
But those the candles light are not as those
That animate a mother's reveries,
But keep a marble or a bronze repose.
And yet they too break hearts – O Presences
That passion, piety or affection knows,
And that all heavenly glory symbolise –
O self-born mockers of man's enterprise;

VIII

Labour is blossoming or dancing where
The body is not bruised to pleasure soul,
Nor beauty born out of its own despair,
Nor blear-eyed wisdom out of midnight oil.
O chestnut tree, great-rooted blossomer,
Are you the leaf, the blossom or the bole?
O body swayed to music, O brightening glance,
How can we know the dancer from the dance?

[14 June–24 September 1926] 1927

Colonus' Praise

(From *Oedipus at Colonus*)

Chorus. Come praise Colonus' horses, and come praise
The wine-dark of the wood's intricacies,
The nightingale that deafens daylight there,
If daylight ever visit where,

Unvisited by tempest or by sun,
Immortal ladies tread the ground
Dizzy with harmonious sound,
Semele's lad a gay companion.

And yonder in the gymnasts' garden thrives
The self-sown, self-begotten shape that gives
Athenian intellect its mastery,
Even the grey-leaved olive-tree
Miracle-bred out of the living stone;
Nor accident of peace nor war
Shall wither that old marvel, for
The great grey-eyed Athena stares thereon.

Who comes into this country, and has come
Where golden crocus and narcissus bloom,
Where the Great Mother, mourning for her daughter
And beauty-drunken by the water
Glittering among grey-leaved olive-trees,
Has plucked a flower and sung her loss;
Who finds abounding Cephisus
Has found the loveliest spectacle there is.

Because this country has a pious mind
And so remembers that when all mankind
But trod the road, or splashed about the shore,
Poseidon gave it bit and oar,
Every Colonus lad or lass discourses
Of that oar and of that bit;
Summer and winter, day and night,
Of horses and horses of the sea, white horses.

[24 March 1927] 1928

Wisdom

The true faith discovered was
When painted panel, statuary,
Glass-mosaic, window-glass,
Amended what was told awry

By some peasant gospeller;
Swept the sawdust from the floor
Of that working-carpenter.
Miracle had its playtime where
In damask clothed and on a seat
Chryselephantine, cedar-boarded,
His majestic Mother sat
Stitching at a purple hoarded
That He might be nobly breeched
In starry towers of Babylon
Noah's freshet never reached.
King Abundance got Him on
Innocence; and Wisdom He.
That cognomen sounded best
Considering what wild infancy
Drove horror from His Mother's breast.

1927

The Hero, the Girl, and the Fool

The Girl. I rage at my own image in the glass
That's so unlike myself that when you praise it
It is as though you praised another, or even
Mocked me with praise of my mere opposite;
And when I wake towards morn I dread myself,
For the heart cries that what deception wins
Cruelty must keep; therefore be warned and go
If you have seen that image and not the woman.

The Hero. I have raged at my own strength because you have loved it.

The Girl. If you are no more strength than I am beauty
I had better find a convent and turn nun;
A nun at least has all men's reverence
And needs no cruelty.

The Hero. I have heard one say
That men have reverence for their holiness
And not themselves.

The Girl. Say on and say
That only God has loved us for ourselves,
But what care I that long for a man's love?

The Fool by the Roadside. When all works that have
From cradle run to grave
From grave to cradle run instead;
When thoughts that a fool
Has wound upon a spool
Are but loose thread, are but loose thread;

When cradle and spool are past
And I mere shade at last
Coagulate of stuff
Transparent like the wind,
I think that I may find
A faithful love, a faithful love.

1922

Owen Aherne and his Dancers

I

A strange thing surely that my Heart, when love had come unsought
Upon the Norman upland or in that poplar shade,
Should find no burden but itself and yet should be worn out.
It could not bear that burden and therefore it went mad.

The south wind brought it longing, and the east wind despair,
The west wind made it pitiful, and the north wind afraid.
It feared to give its love a hurt with all the tempest there;
It feared the hurt that she could give and therefore it went mad.

I can exchange opinion with any neighbouring mind,
I have as healthy flesh and blood as any rhymer's had,

But O! my Heart could bear no more when the upland caught the wind;
I ran, I ran, from my love's side because my Heart went mad.

II

The Heart behind its rib laughed out. 'You have called me mad,' it said,
'Because I made you turn away and run from that young child;
How could she mate with fifty years that was so wildly bred?
Let the cage bird and the cage bird mate and the wild bird mate in the wild.'

'You but imagine lies all day, O murderer,' I replied.
'And all those lies have but one end, poor wretches to betray;
I did not find in any cage the woman at my side.
O but her heart would break to learn my thoughts are far away.'

'Speak all your mind,' my Heart sang out, 'speak all your mind; who cares,
Now that your tongue cannot persuade the child till she mistake
Her childish gratitude for love and match your fifty years?
O let her choose a young man now and all for his wild sake.'

[24–27 October 1917] 1924

A Man Young and Old

I

First Love

Though nurtured like the sailing moon
In beauty's murderous brood,

She walked awhile and blushed awhile
And on my pathway stood
Until I thought her body bore
A heart of flesh and blood.

But since I laid a hand thereon
And found a heart of stone
I have attempted many things
And not a thing is done,
For every hand is lunatic
That travels on the moon.

She smiled and that transfigured me
And left me but a lout,
Maundering here, and maundering there,
Emptier of thought
Than the heavenly circuit of its stars
When the moon sails out.

[25 May 1926] 1927

II

Human Dignity

Like the moon her kindness is,
If kindness I may call
What has no comprehension in't,
But is the same for all
As though my sorrow were a scene
Upon a painted wall.

So like a bit of stone I lie
Under a broken tree.
I could recover if I shrieked
My heart's agony
To passing bird, but I am dumb
From human dignity.

[1926 or 1927] 1927

III

The Mermaid

A mermaid found a swimming lad,
Picked him for her own,
Pressed her body to his body,
Laughed; and plunging down
Forgot in cruel happiness
That even lovers drown.

[1926 or 1927] 1927

IV

The Death of the Hare

I have pointed out the yelling pack,
The hare leap to the wood,
And when I pass a compliment
Rejoice as lover should
At the drooping of an eye,
At the mantling of the blood.

Then suddenly my heart is wrung
By her distracted air
And I remember wildness lost
And after, swept from there,
Am set down standing in the wood
At the death of the hare.

[January 1926] 1927

V

The Empty Cup

A crazy man that found a cup,
When all but dead of thirst,
Hardly dared to wet his mouth
Imagining, moon-accursed,

Luton Sixth Form College
Learning Resources Centre

But names are nothing. What matter who it be,
So that his elements have grown so fine
The fume of muscatel
Can give his sharpened palate ecstasy
No living man can drink from the whole wine.
I have mummy truths to tell
Whereat the living mock,
Though not for sober ear,
For maybe all that hear
Should laugh and weep an hour upon the clock.

Such thought – such thought have I that hold it tight
Till meditation master all its parts,
Nothing can stay my glance
Until that glance run in the world's despite
To where the damned have howled away their hearts,
And where the blessed dance;
Such thought, that in it bound
I need no other thing,
Wound in mind's wandering
As mummies in the mummy-cloth are wound.

Oxford, Autumn 1920

[November 1920] 1921

THE WINDING STAIR AND OTHER POEMS
1933

TO EDMUND DULAC

In Memory of Eva Gore-Booth and Con Markiewicz

The light of evening, Lissadell,
Great windows open to the south,
Two girls in silk kimonos, both
Beautiful, one a gazelle.
But a raving autumn shears
Blossom from the summer's wreath;
The older is condemned to death,
Pardoned, drags out lonely years
Conspiring among the ignorant.
I know not what the younger dreams –
Some vague Utopia – and she seems,
When withered old and skeleton-gaunt,
An image of such politics.
Many a time I think to seek
One or the other out and speak
Of that old Georgian mansion, mix
Pictures of the mind, recall
That table and the talk of youth,
Two girls in silk kimonos, both
Beautiful, one a gazelle.

Dear shadows, now you know it all,
All the folly of a fight
With a common wrong or right.
The innocent and the beautiful

Have no enemy but time;
Arise and bid me strike a match
And strike another till time catch;
Should the conflagration climb,
Run till all the sages know.
We the great gazebo built,
They convicted us of guilt;
Bid me strike a match and blow.

October 1927

[September–November 1927] 1929

Death

Nor dread nor hope attend
A dying animal;
A man awaits his end
Dreading and hoping all;
Many times he died,
Many times rose again.
A great man in his pride
Confronting murderous men
Casts derision upon
Supersession of breath;
He knows death to the bone –
Man has created death.

[13 September 1927] 1929

A Dialogue of Self and Soul

I

My Soul. I summon to the winding ancient stair;
Set all your mind upon the steep ascent,
Upon the broken, crumbling battlement,
Upon the breathless starlit air,
Upon the star that marks the hidden pole;
Fix every wandering thought upon

That quarter where all thought is done:
Who can distinguish darkness from the soul?

My Self. The consecrated blade upon my knees
Is Sato's ancient blade, still as it was,
Still razor-keen, still like a looking-glass
Unspotted by the centuries;
That flowering, silken, old embroidery, torn
From some court-lady's dress and round
The wooden scabbard bound and wound,
Can, tattered, still protect, faded adorn.

My Soul. Why should the imagination of a man
Long past his prime remember things that are
Emblematical of love and war?
Think of ancestral night that can,
If but imagination scorn the earth
And intellect its wandering
To this and that and t'other thing,
Deliver from the crime of death and birth.

My Self. Montashigi, third of his family, fashioned it
Five hundred years ago, about it lie
Flowers from I know not what embroidery –
Heart's purple – and all these I set
For emblems of the day against the tower
Emblematical of the night,
And claim as by a soldier's right
A charter to commit the crime once more.

My Soul. Such fullness in that quarter overflows
And falls into the basin of the mind
That man is stricken deaf and dumb and blind,
For intellect no longer knows
Is from the *Ought*, or *Knower* from the *Known* –
That is to say, ascends to Heaven;
Only the dead can be forgiven;
But when I think of that my tongue's a stone.

II

My Self. A living man is blind and drinks his drop.
What matter if the ditches are impure?
What matter if I live it all once more?
Endure that toil of growing up;
The ignominy of boyhood; the distress
Of boyhood changing into man;
The unfinished man and his pain
Brought face to face with his own clumsiness;

The finished man among his enemies? –
How in the name of Heaven can he escape
That defiling and disfigured shape
The mirror of malicious eyes
Casts upon his eyes until at last
He thinks that shape must be his shape?
And what's the good of an escape
If honour find him in the wintry blast?

I am content to live it all again
And yet again, if it be life to pitch
Into the frog-spawn of a blind man's ditch,
A blind man battering blind men;
Or into that most fecund ditch of all,
The folly that man does
Or must suffer, if he woos
A proud woman not kindred of his soul.

I am content to follow to its source
Every event in action or in thought;
Measure the lot; forgive myself the lot!
When such as I cast out remorse
So great a sweetness flows into the breast
We must laugh and we must sing,
We are blest by everything,
Everything we look upon is blest.

[July–December 1927] 1929

Blood and the Moon

I

Blessed be this place,
More blessed still this tower;
A bloody, arrogant power
Rose out of the race
Uttering, mastering it,
Rose like these walls from these
Storm-beaten cottages –
In mockery I have set
A powerful emblem up,
And sing it rhyme upon rhyme
In mockery of a time
Half dead at the top.

II

Alexandria's was a beacon tower, and Babylon's
An image of the moving heavens, a log-book of the sun's journey and the moon's;
And Shelley had his towers, thought's crowned powers he called them once.

I declare this tower is my symbol; I declare
This winding, gyring, spiring treadmill of a stair is my ancestral stair;
That Goldsmith and the Dean, Berkeley and Burke have travelled there.

Swift beating on his breast in sibylline frenzy blind
Because the heart in his blood-sodden breast had dragged him down into mankind,
Goldsmith deliberately sipping at the honey-pot of his mind,

And haughtier-headed Burke that proved the State a tree,
That this unconquerable labyrinth of the birds, century after century,
Cast but dead leaves to mathematical equality;

And God-appointed Berkeley that proved all things a dream,
That this pragmatical, preposterous pig of a world, its farrow
    that so solid seem,
Must vanish on the instant if the mind but change its theme;

Saeva Indignatio and the labourer's hire,
The strength that gives our blood and state magnanimity of
    its own desire;
Everything that is not God consumed with intellectual fire.

III

The purity of the unclouded moon
Has flung its arrowy shaft upon the floor.
Seven centuries have passed and it is pure,
The blood of innocence has left no stain.
There, on blood-saturated ground, have stood
Soldier, assassin, executioner,
Whether for daily pittance or in blind fear
Or out of abstract hatred, and shed blood,
But could not cast a single jet thereon.
Odour of blood on the ancestral stair!
And we that have shed none must gather there
And clamour in drunken frenzy for the moon.

IV

Upon the dusty, glittering windows cling,
And seem to cling upon the moonlit skies,
Tortoiseshell butterflies, peacock butterflies,
A couple of night-moths are on the wing.
Is every modern nation like the tower,
Half dead at the top? No matter what I said,
For wisdom is the property of the dead,
A something incompatible with life; and power,
Like everything that has the stain of blood,
A property of the living; but no stain
Can come upon the visage of the moon
When it has looked in glory from a cloud.

[August 1927] 1928

Oil and Blood

In tombs of gold and lapis lazuli
Bodies of holy men and women exude
Miraculous oil, odour of violet.

But under heavy loads of trampled clay
Lie bodies of the vampires full of blood;
Their shrouds are bloody and their lips are wet.

[December 1927] 1929

Veronica's Napkin

The Heavenly Circuit; Berenice's Hair;
Tent-pole of Eden; the tent's drapery;
Symbolical glory of the earth and air!
The Father and His angelic hierarchy
That made the magnitude and glory there
Stood in the circuit of a needle's eye.

Some found a different pole, and where it stood
A pattern on a napkin dipped in blood.

[1929] 1932

Symbols

A storm-beaten old watch-tower,
A blind hermit rings the hour.

All-destroying sword-blade still
Carried by the wandering fool.

Gold-sewn silk on the sword-blade,
Beauty and fool together laid.

[October 1927] 1932

Spilt Milk

We that have done and thought,
That have thought and done,
Must ramble, and thin out
Like milk spilt on a stone.

[8 November 1930] 1932

The Nineteenth Century and After

Though the great song return no more
There's keen delight in what we have:
The rattle of pebbles on the shore
Under the receding wave.

[January–2 March 1929] 1932

Statistics

'Those Platonists are a curse,' he said,
'God's fire upon the wane,
A diagram hung there instead,
More women born than men.'

[1931] 1932

Three Movements

Shakespearean fish swam the sea, far away from land;
Romantic fish swam in nets coming to the hand;
What are all those fish that lie gasping on the strand?

[26 January 1932] 1932

The Seven Sages

The First. My great-grandfather spoke to Edmund Burke
In Grattan's house.

The Second. My great-grandfather shared
A pot-house bench with Oliver Goldsmith once.

The Third. My great-grandfather's father talked of music,
Drank tar-water with the Bishop of Cloyne.

The Fourth. But mine saw Stella once.

The Fifth. Whence came our thought?

The Sixth. From four great minds that hated Whiggery.

The Fifth. Burke was a Whig.

The Sixth. Whether they knew or not,
Goldsmith and Burke, Swift and the Bishop of Cloyne
All hated Whiggery; but what is Whiggery?
A levelling, rancorous, rational sort of mind
That never looked out of the eye of a saint
Or out of drunkard's eye.

The Seventh. All's Whiggery now,
But we old men are massed against the world.

The First. American colonies, Ireland, France and India
Harried, and Burke's great melody against it.

The Second. Oliver Goldsmith sang what he had seen,
Roads full of beggars, cattle in the fields,
But never saw the trefoil stained with blood,
The avenging leaf those fields raised up against it.

The Fourth. The tomb of Swift wears it away.

The Third. A voice
Soft as the rustle of a reed from Cloyne
That gathers volume; now a thunder-clap.

The Sixth. What schooling had these four?

The Seventh. They walked the roads
Mimicking what they heard, as children mimic;
They understood that wisdom comes of beggary.

[30 January 1931] 1932

The Crazed Moon

Crazed through much child-bearing
The moon is staggering in the sky;
Moon-struck by the despairing
Glances of her wandering eye
We grope, and grope in vain,
For children born of her pain.

Children dazed or dead!
When she in all her virginal pride
First trod on the mountain's head
What stir ran through the countryside
Where every foot obeyed her glance!
What manhood led the dance!

Fly-catchers of the moon,
Our hands are blenched, our fingers seem
But slender needles of bone;
Blenched by that malicious dream
They are spread wide that each
May rend what comes in reach.

[April 1923] 1932

Coole Park, 1929

I meditate upon a swallow's flight,
Upon an aged woman and her house,
A sycamore and lime tree lost in night
Although that western cloud is luminous,
Great works constructed there in nature's spite
For scholars and for poets after us,

Thoughts long knitted into a single thought,
A dance-like glory that those walls begot.
There Hyde before he had beaten into prose
That noble blade the Muses buckled on,
There one that ruffled in a manly pose
For all his timid heart, there that slow man,
That meditative man, John Synge, and those
Impetuous men, Shawe-Taylor and Hugh Lane,
Found pride established in humility,
A scene well set and excellent company.

They came like swallows and like swallows went,
And yet a woman's powerful character
Could keep a swallow to its first intent;
And half a dozen in formation there,
That seemed to whirl upon a compass-point,
Found certainty upon the dreaming air,
The intellectual sweetness of those lines
That cut through time or cross it withershins.

Here, traveller, scholar, poet, take your stand
When all those rooms and passages are gone,
When nettles wave upon a shapeless mound
And saplings root among the broken stone,
And dedicate – eyes bent upon the ground,
Back turned upon the brightness of the sun
And all the sensuality of the shade –
A moment's memory to that laurelled head.

[7 September 1928] 1931

Coole and Ballylee, 1931

Under my window-ledge the waters race,
Otters below and moor-hens on the top,
Run for a mile undimmed in Heaven's face
Then darkening through 'dark' Raftery's 'cellar' drop,
Run underground, rise in a rocky place
In Coole demesne, and there to finish up

Spread to a lake and drop into a hole.
What's water but the generated soul?

Upon the border of that lake's a wood
Now all dry sticks under a wintry sun,
And in a copse of beeches there I stood,
For Nature's pulled her tragic buskin on
And all the rant's a mirror of my mood:
At sudden thunder of the mounting swan
I turned about and looked where branches break
The glittering reaches of the flooded lake.

Another emblem there! That stormy white
But seems a concentration of the sky;
And, like the soul, it sails into the sight
And in the morning's gone, no man knows why;
And is so lovely that it sets to right
What knowledge or its lack had set awry,
So arrogantly pure, a child might think
It can be murdered with a spot of ink.

Sound of a stick upon the floor, a sound
From somebody that toils from chair to chair;
Beloved books that famous hands have bound,
Old marble heads, old pictures everywhere;
Great rooms where travelled men and children found
Content or joy; a last inheritor
Where none has reigned that lacked a name and fame
Or out of folly into folly came.

A spot whereon the founders lived and died
Seemed once more dear than life; ancestral trees
Or gardens rich in memory glorified
Marriages, alliances and families,
And every bride's ambition satisfied.
Where fashion or mere fantasy decrees
Man shifts about – all that great glory spent –
Like some poor Arab tribesman and his tent.

We were the last romantics – chose for theme
Traditional sanctity and loveliness;

Whatever's written in what poets name
The book of the people; whatever most can bless
The mind of man or elevate a rhyme;
But all is changed, that high horse riderless,
Though mounted in that saddle Homer rode
Where the swan drifts upon a darkening flood.

[February 1931] 1932

For Anne Gregory

'Never shall a young man,
Thrown into despair
By those great honey-coloured
Ramparts at your ear,
Love you for yourself alone
And not your yellow hair.'

'But I can get a hair-dye
And set such colour there,
Brown, or black, or carrot,
That young men in despair
May love me for myself alone
And not my yellow hair.'

'I heard an old religious man
But yesternight declare
That he had found a text to prove
That only God, my dear,
Could love you for yourself alone
And not your yellow hair.'

[September 1930] 1932

Swift's Epitaph

Swift has sailed into his rest;
Savage indignation there
Cannot lacerate his breast.
Imitate him if you dare,

World-besotted traveller; he
Served human liberty.

[1929–September 1930] 1931

At Algeciras – A Meditation upon Death

The heron-billed pale cattle-birds
That feed on some foul parasite
Of the Moroccan flocks and herds
Cross the narrow Straits to light
In the rich midnight of the garden trees
Till the dawn break upon those mingled seas.

Often at evening when a boy
Would I carry to a friend –
Hoping more substantial joy
Did an older mind commend –
Not such as are in Newton's metaphor,
But actual shells of Rosses' level shore.

Greater glory in the sun,
An evening chill upon the air,
Bid imagination run
Much on the Great Questioner;
What He can question, what if questioned I
Can with a fitting confidence reply.

November 1928

[November 1928–4 February 1929] 1929

The Choice

The intellect of man is forced to choose
Perfection of the life, or of the work,
And if it take the second must refuse
A heavenly mansion, raging in the dark.
When all that story's finished, what's the news?
In luck or out the toil has left its mark:

That old perplexity an empty purse,
Or the day's vanity, the night's remorse.

[February 1931] 1932

Mohini Chatterjee

I asked if I should pray,
But the Brahmin said,
'Pray for nothing, say
Every night in bed,
"I have been a king,
I have been a slave,
Nor is there anything,
Fool, rascal, knave,
That I have not been,
And yet upon my breast
A myriad heads have lain."'

That he might set at rest
A boy's turbulent days
Mohini Chatterjee
Spoke these, or words like these.
I add in commentary,
'Old lovers yet may have
All that time denied –
Grave is heaped on grave
That they be satisfied –
Over the blackened earth
The old troops parade,
Birth is heaped on birth
That such cannonade
May thunder time away,
Birth-hour and death-hour meet,
Or, as great sages say,
Men dance on deathless feet.'

1928

[23 January–9 February 1929] 1929

Byzantium

The unpurged images of day recede;
The Emperor's drunken soldiery are abed;
Night resonance recedes, night-walkers' song
After great cathedral gong;
A starlit or a moonlit dome disdains
All that man is,
All mere complexities,
The fury and the mire of human veins.

Before me floats an image, man or shade,
Shade more than man, more image than a shade;
For Hades' bobbin bound in mummy-cloth
May unwind the winding path;
A mouth that has no moisture and no breath
Breathless mouths may summon;
I hail the superhuman;
I call it death-in-life and life-in-death.

Miracle, bird or golden handiwork,
More miracle than bird or handiwork,
Planted on the starlit golden bough,
Can like the cocks of Hades crow,
Or, by the moon embittered, scorn aloud
In glory of changeless metal
Common bird or petal
And all complexities of mire or blood.

At midnight on the Emperor's pavement flit
Flames that no faggot feeds, nor steel has lit,
Nor storm disturbs, flames begotten of flame,
Where blood-begotten spirits come
And all complexities of fury leave,
Dying into a dance,
An agony of trance,
An agony of flame that cannot singe a sleeve.

Astraddle on the dolphin's mire and blood,
Spirit after spirit! The smithies break the flood,
The golden smithies of the Emperor!
Marbles of the dancing floor

Break bitter furies of complexity,
Those images that yet
Fresh images beget,
That dolphin-torn, that gong-tormented sea.

1930

[September 1930] 1932

The Mother of God

The three-fold terror of love; a fallen flare
Through the hollow of an ear;
Wings beating about the room;
The terror of all terrors that I bore
The Heavens in my womb.

Had I not found content among the shows
Every common woman knows,
Chimney corner, garden walk,
Or rocky cistern where we tread the clothes
And gather all the talk?

What is this flesh I purchased with my pains,
This fallen star my milk sustains,
This love that makes my heart's blood stop
Or strikes a sudden chill into my bones
And bids my hair stand up?

[3–12 September 1931] 1932

Vacillation

I

Between extremities
Man runs his course;
A brand, or flaming breath,
Comes to destroy
All those antinomies
Of day and night;

The body calls it death,
The heart remorse.
But if these be right
What is joy?

[November 1931] 1932

II

A tree there is that from its topmost bough
Is half all glittering flame and half all green
Abounding foliage moistened with the dew;
And half is half and yet is all the scene;
And half and half consume what they renew,
And he that Attis' image hangs between
That staring fury and the blind lush leaf
May know not what he knows, but knows not grief.

[1931 or 1932] 1932

III

Get all the gold and silver that you can,
Satisfy ambition, or animate
The trivial days and ram them with the sun,
And yet upon these maxims meditate:
All women dote upon an idle man
Although their children need a rich estate;
No man has ever lived that had enough
Of children's gratitude or woman's love.

No longer in Lethean foliage caught
Begin the preparation for your death
And from the fortieth winter by that thought
Test every work of intellect or faith
And everything that your own hands have wrought,
And call those works extravagance of breath

That are not suited for such men as come
Proud, open-eyed and laughing to the tomb.

[1931 or 1932] 1932

IV

My fiftieth year had come and gone,
I sat, a solitary man,
In a crowded London shop,
An open book and empty cup
On the marble table-top.

While on the shop and street I gazed
My body of a sudden blazed;
And twenty minutes more or less
It seemed, so great my happiness,
That I was blessèd and could bless.

[November 1931] 1932

V

Although the summer sunlight gild
Cloudy leafage of the sky,
Or wintry moonlight sink the field
In storm-scattered intricacy,
I cannot look thereon,
Responsibility so weighs me down.

Things said or done long years ago,
Or things I did not do or say
But thought that I might say or do,
Weigh me down, and not a day
But something is recalled,
My conscience or my vanity appalled.

[1931 or 1932] 1932

VI

A rivery field spread out below,
An odour of the new-mown hay

In his nostrils, the great lord of Chou
Cried, casting off the mountain snow,
'Let all things pass away.'

Wheels by milk-white asses drawn
Where Babylon or Nineveh
Rose; some conqueror drew rein
And cried to battle-weary men,
'Let all things pass away.'

From man's blood-sodden heart are sprung
Those branches of the night and day
Where the gaudy moon is hung.
What's the meaning of all song?
'Let all things pass away.'

[January–5 March 1932] 1932

VII

The Soul. Seek out reality, leave things that seem.
The Heart. What, be a singer born and lack a theme?
The Soul. Isaiah's coal, what more can man desire?
The Heart. Struck dumb in the simplicity of fire!
The Soul. Look on that fire, salvation walks within.
The Heart. What theme had Homer but original sin?

[3–4 January 1932] 1932

VIII

Must we part, Von Hügel, though much alike, for we
Accept the miracles of the saints and honour sanctity?
The body of Saint Teresa lies undecayed in tomb,
Bathed in miraculous oil, sweet odours from it come,
Healing from its lettered slab. Those self-same hands perchance
Eternalised the body of a modern saint that once
Had scooped out Pharaoh's mummy. I – though heart might find relief
Did I become a Christian man and choose for my belief

What seems most welcome in the tomb – play a predestined
part.
Homer is my example and his unchristened heart.
The lion and the honeycomb, what has Scripture said?
So get you gone, Von Hügel, though with blessings on your
head.

[3 January 1932] 1932

1932

Quarrel in Old Age

Where had her sweetness gone?
What fanatics invent
In this blind bitter town,
Fantasy or incident
Not worth thinking of,
Put her in a rage.
I had forgiven enough
That had forgiven old age.

All lives that has lived;
So much is certain;
Old sages were not deceived:
Somewhere beyond the curtain
Of distorting days
Lives that lonely thing
That shone before these eyes
Targeted, trod like Spring.

[November 1931] 1932

The Results of Thought

Acquaintance; companion;
One dear brilliant woman;
The best-endowed, the elect,
All by their youth undone,
All, all, by that inhuman
Bitter glory wrecked.

But I have straightened out
Ruin, wreck and wrack;
I toiled long years and at length
Came to so deep a thought
I can summon back
All their wholesome strength.

What images are these
That turn dull-eyed away,
Or shift Time's filthy load,
Straighten aged knees,
Hesitate or stay?
What heads shake or nod?

August 1931

[18–28 August 1931] 1932

Gratitude to the Unknown Instructors

What they undertook to do
They brought to pass;
All things hang like a drop of dew
Upon a blade of grass.

1932

Remorse for Intemperate Speech

I ranted to the knave and fool,
But outgrew that school,
Would transform the part,
Fit audience found, but cannot rule
My fanatic heart.

I sought my betters: though in each
Fine manners, liberal speech,
Turn hatred into sport,
Nothing said or done can reach
My fanatic heart.

Out of Ireland have we come.
Great hatred, little room,
Maimed us at the start.
I carry from my mother's womb
A fanatic heart.

August 28, 1931

[28 August 1931] 1932

Stream and Sun at Glendalough

Through intricate motions ran
Stream and gliding sun
And all my heart seemed gay:
Some stupid thing that I had done
Made my attention stray.

Repentance keeps my heart impure;
But what am I that dare
Fancy that I can
Better conduct myself or have more
Sense than a common man?

What motion of the sun or stream
Or eyelid shot the gleam
That pierced my body through?
What made me live like these that seem
Self-born, born anew?

June 1932

[23 June 1932] 1932

WORDS FOR MUSIC PERHAPS
1932

I

Crazy Jane and the Bishop

Bring me to the blasted oak
That I, midnight upon the stroke,
(*All find safety in the tomb.*)
May call down curses on his head
Because of my dear Jack that's dead.
Coxcomb was the least he said:
The solid man and the coxcomb.

Nor was he Bishop when his ban
Banished Jack the Journeyman,
(*All find safety in the tomb.*)
Nor so much as parish priest,
Yet he, an old book in his fist,
Cried that we lived like beast and beast:
The solid man and the coxcomb.

The Bishop has a skin, God knows,
Wrinkled like the foot of a goose,
(*All find safety in the tomb.*)
Nor can he hide in holy black
The heron's hunch upon his back,
But a birch-tree stood my Jack:
The solid man and the coxcomb.

Jack had my virginity,
And bids me to the oak, for he
(*All find safety in the tomb.*)
Wanders out into the night
And there is shelter under it,
But should that other come, I spit:
The solid man and the coxcomb.

[2 March 1929] 1930

II

Crazy Jane Reproved

I care not what the sailors say:
All those dreadful thunder-stones,
All that storm that blots the day
Can but show that Heaven yawns;
Great Europa played the fool
That changed a lover for a bull.
Fol de rol, fol de rol.

To round that shell's elaborate whorl,
Adorning every secret track
With the delicate mother-of-pearl,
Made the joints of Heaven crack:
So never hang your heart upon
A roaring, ranting journeyman.
Fol de rol, fol de rol.

[27 March 1929] 1930

III

Crazy Jane on the Day of Judgment

'Love is all
Unsatisfied
That cannot take the whole
Body and soul';
And that is what Jane said.

'Take the sour
If you take me,
I can scoff and lour
And scold for an hour.'
'That's certainly the case,' said he.

'Naked I lay,
The grass my bed;

Naked and hidden away,
That black day';
And that is what Jane said.

'What can be shown?
What true love be?
All could be known or shown
If Time were but gone.'
'That's certainly the case,' said he.

[October 1930] 1932

IV

Crazy Jane and Jack the Journeyman

I know, although when looks meet
I tremble to the bone,
The more I leave the door unlatched
The sooner love is gone,
For love is but a skein unwound
Between the dark and dawn.

A lonely ghost the ghost is
That to God shall come;
I – love's skein upon the ground,
My body in the tomb –
Shall leap into the light lost
In my mother's womb.

But were I left to lie alone
In an empty bed,
The skein so bound us ghost to ghost
When he turned his head
Passing on the road that night,
Mine would walk being dead.

[November 1931] 1932

V

Crazy Jane on God

That lover of a night
Came when he would,
Went in the dawning light
Whether I would or no;
Men come, men go:
All things remain in God.

Banners choke the sky;
Men-at-arms tread;
Armoured horses neigh
Where the great battle was
In the narrow pass:
All things remain in God.

Before their eyes a house
That from childhood stood
Uninhabited, ruinous,
Suddenly lit up
From door to top:
All things remain in God.

I had wild Jack for a lover;
Though like a road
That men pass over
My body makes no moan
But sings on:
All things remain in God.

[18 July 1931] 1932

VI

Crazy Jane talks with the Bishop

I met the Bishop on the road
And much said he and I.
'Those breasts are flat and fallen now,
Those veins must soon be dry;
Live in a heavenly mansion,
Not in some foul sty.'

'Fair and foul are near of kin,
And fair needs foul,' I cried.
'My friends are gone, but that's a truth
Nor grave nor bed denied,
Learned in bodily lowliness
And in the heart's pride.

'A woman can be proud and stiff
When on love intent;
But Love has pitched his mansion in
The place of excrement;
For nothing can be sole or whole
That has not been rent.'

[November 1931] 1933

VII

Crazy Jane grown old looks at the Dancers

I found that ivory image there
Dancing with her chosen youth,
But when he wound her coal-black hair
As though to strangle her, no scream
Or bodily movement did I dare,
Eyes under eyelids did so gleam:
Love is like the lion's tooth.

When she, and though some said she played
I said that she had danced heart's truth,
Drew a knife to strike him dead,
I could but leave him to his fate;
For no matter what is said
They had all that had their hate:
Love is like the lion's tooth.

Did he die or did she die?
Seemed to die or died they both?
God be with the times when I

Cared not a thraneen for what chanced
So that I had the limbs to try
Such a dance as there was danced –
Love is like the lion's tooth.

[March 1929] 1930

VIII

Girl's Song

I went out alone
To sing a song or two,
My fancy on a man,
And you know who.

Another came in sight
That on a stick relied
To hold himself upright,
I sat and cried.

And that was all my song –
When everything is told,
Saw I an old man young
Or young man old?

[29 March 1929] 1930

IX

Young Man's Song

'She will change,' I cried,
'Into a withered crone.'
The heart in my side,
That so still had lain,
In noble rage replied
And beat upon the bone:

'Uplift those eyes and throw
Those glances unafraid:

She would as bravely show
Did all the fabric fade;
No withered crone I saw
Before the world was made.'

Abashed by that report,
For the heart cannot lie,
I knelt in the dirt.
And all shall bend the knee
To my offended heart
Until it pardon me.

[1929] 1930

X

Her Anxiety

Earth in beauty dressed
Awaits returning spring.
All true love must die,
Alter at the best
Into some lesser thing.
Prove that I lie.

Such body lovers have,
Such exacting breath,
That they touch or sigh.
Every touch they give,
Love is nearer death.
Prove that I lie.

[1929] 1930

XI

His Confidence

Undying love to buy
I wrote upon
The corners of this eye
All wrongs done.

What payment were enough
For undying love?

I broke my heart in two
So hard I struck.
What matter? for I know
That out of rock,
Out of a desolate source,
Love leaps upon its course.

[1929] 1930

XII

Love's Loneliness

Old fathers, great-grandfathers,
Rise as kindred should.
If ever lover's loneliness
Came where you stood,
Pray that Heaven protect us
That protect your blood.

The mountain throws a shadow,
Thin is the moon's horn;
What did we remember
Under the ragged thorn?
Dread has followed longing,
And our hearts are torn.

[17 April 1929] 1930

XIII

Her Dream

I dreamed as in my bed I lay,
All night's fathomless wisdom come,
That I had shorn my locks away
And laid them on Love's lettered tomb:

But something bore them out of sight
In a great tumult of the air,
And after nailed upon the night
Berenice's burning hair.

[1929] 1930

XIV

His Bargain

Who talks of Plato's spindle;
What set it whirling round?
Eternity may dwindle,
Time is unwound,
Dan and Jerry Lout
Change their loves about.

However they may take it,
Before the thread began
I made, and may not break it
When the last thread has run,
A bargain with that hair
And all the windings there.

[1929] 1930

XV

Three Things

'O cruel Death, give three things back,'
Sang a bone upon the shore;
'A child found all a child can lack,
Whether of pleasure or of rest,
Upon the abundance of my breast':
A bone wave-whitened and dried in the wind.

'Three dear things that women know,'
Sang a bone upon the shore;

'A man if I but held him so
When my body was alive
Found all the pleasure that life gave':
A bone wave-whitened and dried in the wind.

'The third thing that I think of yet,'
Sang a bone upon the shore;
'Is that morning when I met
Face to face my rightful man
And did after stretch and yawn':
A bone wave-whitened and dried in the wind

[March 1929] 1929

XVI
Lullaby

Beloved, may your sleep be sound
That have found it where you fed.
What were all the world's alarms
To mighty Paris when he found
Sleep upon a golden bed
That first dawn in Helen's arms?

Sleep, beloved, such a sleep
As did that wild Tristram know
When, the potion's work being done,
Roe could run or doe could leap
Under oak and beechen bough,
Roe could leap or doe could run;

Such a sleep and sound as fell
Upon Eurotas' grassy bank
When the holy bird, that there
Accomplished his predestined will,
From the limbs of Leda sank
But not from her protecting care.

[20 or 27 March 1929] 1931

XVII

After Long Silence

Speech after long silence; it is right,
All other lovers being estranged or dead,
Unfriendly lamplight hid under its shade,
The curtains drawn upon unfriendly night,
That we descant and yet again descant
Upon the supreme theme of Art and Song:
Bodily decrepitude is wisdom; young
We loved each other and were ignorant.

[November 1929] 1932

XVIII

Mad as the Mist and Snow

Bolt and bar the shutter,
For the foul winds blow:
Our minds are at their best this night,
And I seem to know
That everything outside us is
Mad as the mist and snow.

Horace there by Homer stands,
Plato stands below,
And here is Tully's open page.
How many years ago
Were you and I unlettered lads
Mad as the mist and snow?

You ask what makes me sigh, old friend,
What makes me shudder so?
I shudder and I sigh to think
That even Cicero
And many-minded Homer were
Mad as the mist and snow.

[12 February 1929] 1932

XIX

Those Dancing Days are Gone

Come, let me sing into your ear;
Those dancing days are gone,
All that silk and satin gear;
Crouch upon a stone,
Wrapping that foul body up
In as foul a rag:
I carry the sun in a golden cup,
The moon in a silver bag.

Curse as you may I sing it through;
What matter if the knave
That the most could pleasure you,
The children that he gave,
Are somewhere sleeping like a top
Under a marble flag?
I carry the sun in a golden cup,
The moon in a silver bag.

I thought it out this very day,
Noon upon the clock,
A man may put pretence away
Who leans upon a stick,
May sing, and sing until he drop,
Whether to maid or hag:
I carry the sun in a golden cup,
The moon in a silver bag.

[8 March 1929] 1930

XX

'I Am of Ireland'

'I am of Ireland,
And the Holy Land of Ireland,
And time runs on,' cried she.

'Come out of charity,
Come dance with me in Ireland.'

One man, one man alone
In that outlandish gear,
One solitary man
Of all that rambled there
Had turned his stately head.
'That is a long way off,
And time runs on,' he said,
'And the night grows rough.'

'I am of Ireland,
And the Holy Land of Ireland,
And time runs on,' cried she.
'Come out of charity
And dance with me in Ireland.'

'The fiddlers are all thumbs,
Or the fiddle-string accursed,
The drums and the kettledrums
And the trumpets all are burst,
And the trombone,' cried he,
'The trumpet and trombone,'
And cocked a malicious eye,
'But time runs on, runs on.'

'I am of Ireland,
And the Holy Land of Ireland,
And time runs on,' cried she.
'Come out of charity
And dance with me in Ireland.'

[August 1929] 1932

XXI

The Dancer at Cruachan and Cro-Patrick

I, proclaiming that there is
Among birds or beasts or men
One that is perfect or at peace,
Danced on Cruachan's windy plain,
Upon Cro-Patrick sang aloud;
All that could run or leap or swim
Whether in wood, water or cloud,
Acclaiming, proclaiming, declaiming Him.

[August 1931] 1932

XXII

Tom the Lunatic

Sang old Tom the lunatic
That sleeps under the canopy;
'What change has put my thoughts astray
And eyes that had so keen a sight?
What has turned to smoking wick
Nature's pure unchanging light?

'Huddon and Duddon and Daniel O'Leary,
Holy Joe, the beggar-man,
Wenching, drinking, still remain
Or sing a penance on the road;
Something made these eyeballs weary
That blinked and saw them in a shroud.

'Whatever stands in field or flood
Bird, beast, fish or man,
Mare or stallion, cock or hen,
Stands in God's unchanging eye
In all the vigour of its blood;
In that faith I live or die.'

[29 June 1929–27 July 1931] 1932

XXIII

Tom at Cruachan

On Cruachan's plain slept he
That must sing in a rhyme
What most could shake his soul:
'The stallion Eternity
Mounted the mare of Time,
'Gat the foal of the world.'

[29 July 1931]

XXIV

Old Tom Again

Things out of perfection sail,
And all their swelling canvas wear,
Nor shall the self-begotten fail
Though fantastic men suppose
Building-yard and stormy shore,
Winding-sheet and swaddling-clothes.

[October 1931] 1932

XXV

The Delphic Oracle upon Plotinus

Behold that great Plotinus swim
Buffeted by such seas;
Bland Rhadamanthus beckons him,
But the Golden Race looks dim,
Salt blood blocks his eyes.

Scattered on the level grass
Or winding through the grove
Plato there and Minos pass,
There stately Pythagoras
And all the choir of Love.

August 19, 1931

[19 August 1931] 1932

A WOMAN YOUNG AND OLD
1929

I
Father and Child

She hears me strike the board and say
That she is under ban
Of all good men and women,
Being mentioned with a man
That has the worst of all bad names;
And thereupon replies
That his hair is beautiful,
Cold as the March wind his eyes.

[1926] 1929

II
Before the World was made

If I make the lashes dark
And the eyes more bright
And the lips more scarlet,
Or ask if all be right
From mirror after mirror,
No vanity's displayed:
I'm looking for the face I had
Before the world was made.

What if I look upon a man
As though on my beloved,
And my blood be cold the while
And my heart unmoved?
Why should he think me cruel
Or that he is betrayed?
I'd have him love the thing that was
Before the world was made.

[February 1928] 1929

III

A First Confession

I admit the briar
Entangled in my hair
Did not injure me;
My blenching and trembling
Nothing but dissembling,
Nothing but coquetry.

I long for truth, and yet
I cannot stay from that
My better self disowns,
For a man's attention
Brings such satisfaction
To the craving in my bones.

Brightness that I pull back
From the Zodiac,
Why those questioning eyes
That are fixed upon me?
What can they do but shun me
If empty night replies?

[June 1927] 1929

IV

Her Triumph

I did the dragon's will until you came
Because I had fancied love a casual
Improvisation, or a settled game
That followed if I let the kerchief fall:
Those deeds were best that gave the minute wings
And heavenly music if they gave it wit;
And then you stood among the dragon-rings.
I mocked, being crazy, but you mastered it
And broke the chain and set my ankles free,
Saint George or else a pagan Perseus;

And now we stare astonished at the sea,
And a miraculous strange bird shrieks at us.

[29 November 1926] 1929

V

Consolation

O but there is wisdom
In what the sages said;
But stretch that body for a while
And lay down that head
Till I have told the sages
Where man is comforted.

How could passion run so deep
Had I never thought
That the crime of being born
Blackens all our lot?
But where the crime's committed
The crime can be forgot.

[June 1927] 1929

VI

Chosen

The lot of love is chosen. I learnt that much
Struggling for an image on the track
Of the whirling Zodiac.
Scarce did he my body touch,
Scarce sank he from the west
Or found a subterranean rest
On the maternal midnight of my breast
Before I had marked him on his northern way,
And seemed to stand although in bed I lay.

I struggled with the horror of daybreak,
I chose it for my lot! If questioned on
My utmost pleasure with a man
By some new-married bride, I take
That stillness for a theme
Where his heart my heart did seem
And both adrift on the miraculous stream
Where – wrote a learned astrologer –
The Zodiac is changed into a sphere.

[February 1926] 1929

VII
Parting

He. Dear, I must be gone
While night shuts the eyes
Of the household spies;
That song announces dawn.

She. No, night's bird and love's
Bids all true lovers rest,
While his loud song reproves
The murderous stealth of day.

He. Daylight already flies
From mountain crest to crest.

She. That light is from the moon.

He. That bird . . .

She. Let him sing on,
I offer to love's play
My dark declivities.

[August 1926] 1929

VIII

Her Vision in the Wood

Dry timber under that rich foliage,
At wine-dark midnight in the sacred wood,
Too old for a man's love I stood in rage
Imagining men. Imagining that I could
A greater with a lesser pang assuage
Or but to find if withered vein ran blood,
I tore my body that its wine might cover
Whatever could recall the lip of lover.

And after that I held my fingers up,
Stared at the wine-dark nail, or dark that ran
Down every withered finger from the top;
But the dark changed to red, and torches shone,
And deafening music shook the leaves; a troop
Shouldered a litter with a wounded man,
Or smote upon the string and to the sound
Sang of the beast that gave the fatal wound.

All stately women moving to a song
With loosened hair or foreheads grief-distraught,
It seemed a Quattrocento painter's throng,
A thoughtless image of Mantegna's thought –
Why should they think that are for ever young?
Till suddenly in grief's contagion caught,
I stared upon his blood-bedabbled breast
And sang my malediction with the rest.

That thing all blood and mire, that beast-torn wreck,
Half turned and fixed a glazing eye on mine,
And, though love's bitter-sweet had all come back,
Those bodies from a picture or a coin
Nor saw my body fall nor heard it shriek,
Nor knew, drunken with singing as with wine,
That they had brought no fabulous symbol there
But my heart's victim and its torturer.

[August 1926] 1929

IX

A Last Confession

What lively lad most pleasured me
Of all that with me lay?
I answer that I gave my soul
And loved in misery,
But had great pleasure with a lad
That I loved bodily.

Flinging from his arms I laughed
To think his passion such
He fancied that I gave a soul
Did but our bodies touch,
And laughed upon his breast to think
Beast gave beast as much.

I gave what other women gave
That stepped out of their clothes,
But when this soul, its body off,
Naked to naked goes,
He it has found shall find therein
What none other knows,

And give his own and take his own
And rule in his own right;
And though it loved in misery
Close and cling so tight,
There's not a bird of day that dare
Extinguish that delight.

[June-August 1926] 1929

X

Meeting

Hidden by old age awhile
In masker's cloak and hood,

Each hating what the other loved,
Face to face we stood:
'That I have met with such,' said he,
'Bodes me little good.'

'Let others boast their fill,' said I,
'But never dare to boast
That such as I had such a man
For lover in the past;
Say that of living men I hate
Such a man the most.'

'A loony'd boast of such a love,'
He in his rage declared:
But such as he for such as me –
Could we both discard
This beggarly habiliment –
Had found a sweeter word.

[23 July-August 1926] 1929

XI

From the *Antigone*

Overcome – O bitter sweetness,
Inhabitant of the soft cheek of a girl –
The rich man and his affairs,
The fat flocks and the fields' fatness,
Mariners, rough harvesters;
Overcome Gods upon Parnassus;

Overcome the Empyrean; hurl
Heaven and Earth out of their places,
That in the same calamity
Brother and brother, friend and friend,
Family and family,
City and city may contend,
By that great glory driven wild.

Pray I will and sing I must,
And yet I weep – Oedipus' child
Descends into the loveless dust.

[15 September 1927–February 1928] 1929

PARNELL'S FUNERAL AND OTHER POEMS
1935

Parnell's Funeral

I

Under the Great Comedian's tomb the crowd.
A bundle of tempestuous cloud is blown
About the sky; where that is clear of cloud
Brightness remains; a brighter star shoots down;
What shudders run through all that animal blood?
What is this sacrifice? Can someone there
Recall the Cretan barb that pierced a star?

Rich foliage that the starlight glittered through,
A frenzied crowd, and where the branches sprang
A beautiful seated boy; a sacred bow;
A woman, and an arrow on a string;
A pierced boy, image of a star laid low.
That woman, the Great Mother imaging,
Cut out his heart. Some master of design
Stamped boy and tree upon Sicilian coin.

An age is the reversal of an age:
When strangers murdered Emmet, Fitzgerald, Tone,
We lived like men that watch a painted stage.
What matter for the scene, the scene once gone:
It had not touched our lives. But popular rage,
Hysterica passio dragged this quarry down.
None shared our guilt; nor did we play a part
Upon a painted stage when we devoured his heart.

Come, fix upon me that accusing eye.
I thirst for accusation. All that was sung,
All that was said in Ireland is a lie
Bred out of the contagion of the throng,
Saving the rhyme rats hear before they die.
Leave nothing but the nothings that belong
To this bare soul, let all men judge that can
Whether it be an animal or a man.

II

The rest I pass, one sentence I unsay.
Had de Valéra eaten Parnell's heart
No loose-lipped demagogue had won the day,
No civil rancour torn the land apart.

Had Cosgrave eaten Parnell's heart, the land's
Imagination had been satisfied,
Or lacking that, government in such hands,
O'Higgins its sole statesman had not died.

Had even O'Duffy – but I name no more –
Their school a crowd, his master solitude;
Through Jonathan Swift's dark grove he passed, and there
Plucked bitter wisdom that enriched his blood.

[1932–April 1933] 1934

Alternative Song for the Severed Head in *The King of the Great Clock Tower*

Saddle and ride, I heard a man say,
Out of Ben Bulben and Knocknarea,
What says the Clock in the Great Clock Tower?
All those tragic characters ride
But turn from Rosses' crawling tide,
The meet's upon the mountain side.
A slow low note and an iron bell.

What brought them there so far from their home,
Cuchulain that fought night long with the foam,
What says the Clock in the Great Clock Tower?
Niamh that rode on it; lad and lass
That sat so still and played at the chess?
What but heroic wantonness?
A slow low note and an iron bell.

Aleel, his Countess; Hanrahan
That seemed but a wild wenching man;
What says the Clock in the Great Clock Tower?
And all alone comes riding there
The King that could make his people stare,
Because he had feathers instead of hair.
A slow low note and an iron bell.

Tune by Arthur Duff

1934

Two Songs Rewritten for the Tune's Sake

I

My Paistin Finn is my sole desire,
And I am shrunken to skin and bone,
For all my heart has had for its hire
Is what I can whistle alone and alone.
Oro, oro!
To-morrow night I will break down the door.

What is the good of a man and he
Alone and alone, with a speckled shin?
I would that I drank with my love on my knee,
Between two barrels at the inn.
Oro, oro!
To-morrow night I will break down the door.

Alone and alone nine nights I lay
Between two bushes under the rain;

I thought to have whistled her down that way,
I whistled and whistled and whistled in vain.
Oro, oro!
To-morrow night I will break down the door.

From *The Pot of Broth*
Tune: Paistin Finn

1922; 1935

II

I would that I were an old beggar
Rolling a blind pearl eye,
For he cannot see my lady
Go gallivanting by;

A dreary, dreepy beggar
Without a friend on the earth
But a thieving rascally cur –
O a beggar blind from his birth;

Or anything else but a rhymer
Without a thing in his head
But rhymes for a beautiful lady,
He rhyming alone in his bed.

From *The Player Queen*

1922; 1935

A Prayer for Old Age

God guard me from those thoughts men think
In the mind alone;
He that sings a lasting song
Thinks in a marrow-bone;

From all that makes a wise old man
That can be praised of all;
O what am I that I should not seem
For the song's sake a fool?

I pray – for fashion's word is out
And prayer comes round again –
That I may seem, though I die old,
A foolish, passionate man.

[1934] 1934

Church and State

Here is fresh matter, poet,
Matter for old age meet;
Might of the Church and the State,
Their mobs put under their feet.
O but heart's wine shall run pure,
Mind's bread grow sweet.

That were a cowardly song,
Wander in dreams no more;
What if the Church and the State
Are the mob that howls at the door!
Wine shall run thick to the end,
Bread taste sour.

August 1934

[August 1934] 1934

SUPERNATURAL SONGS

I

Ribh at the Tomb of Baile and Aillinn

Because you have found me in the pitch-dark night
With open book you ask me what I do.
Mark and digest my tale, carry it afar
To those that never saw this tonsured head
Nor heard this voice that ninety years have cracked.

Of Baile and Aillinn you need not speak,
All know their tale, all know what leaf and twig,
What juncture of the apple and the yew,
Surmount their bones; but speak what none have heard.

The miracle that gave them such a death
Transfigured to pure substance what had once
Been bone and sinew; when such bodies join
There is no touching here, nor touching there,
Nor straining joy, but whole is joined to whole;
For the intercourse of angels is a light
Where for its moment both seem lost, consumed.

Here in the pitch-dark atmosphere above
The trembling of the apple and the yew,
Here on the anniversary of their death,
The anniversary of their first embrace,
Those lovers, purified by tragedy,
Hurry into each other's arms; these eyes,
By water, herb and solitary prayer
Made aquiline, are open to that light.
Though somewhat broken by the leaves, that light
Lies in a circle on the grass; therein
I turn the pages of my holy book.

[24 July 1934] 1934

II

Ribh denounces Patrick

An abstract Greek absurdity has crazed the man –
Recall that masculine Trinity. Man, woman, child (a
daughter or a son),
That's how all natural or supernatural stories run.

Natural and supernatural with the self-same ring are wed.
As man, as beast, as an ephemeral fly begets, Godhead begets
Godhead,
For things below are copies, the Great Smaragdine Tablet
said.

Yet all must copy copies, all increase their kind;
When the conflagration of their passion sinks, damped by
the body or the mind,
That juggling nature mounts, her coil in their embraces
twined.

The mirror-scalèd serpent is multiplicity,
But all that run in couples, on earth, in flood or air, share
God that is but three,
And could beget or bear themselves could they but love
as He.

[July 1934] 1934

III

Ribh in Ecstasy

What matter that you understood no word!
Doubtless I spoke or sang what I had heard
In broken sentences. My soul had found
All happiness in its own cause or ground.
Godhead on Godhead in sexual spasm begot
Godhead. Some shadow fell. My soul forgot
Those amorous cries that out of quiet come
And must the common round of day resume.

[1934] 1935

IV

There

There all the barrel-hoops are knit,
There all the serpent-tails are bit,
There all the gyres converge in one,
There all the planets drop in the Sun.

1935

V

Ribh considers Christian Love insufficient

Why should I seek for love or study it?
It is of God and passes human wit;
I study hatred with great diligence,
For that's a passion in my own control,
A sort of besom that can clear the soul
Of everything that is not mind or sense.

Why do I hate man, woman or event?
That is a light my jealous soul has sent.
From terror and deception freed it can
Discover impurities, can show at last
How soul may walk when all such things are past,
How soul could walk before such things began.

Then my delivered soul herself shall learn
A darker knowledge and in hatred turn
From every thought of God mankind has had.
Thought is a garment and the soul's a bride
That cannot in that trash and tinsel hide:
Hatred of God may bring the soul to God.

At stroke of midnight soul cannot endure
A bodily or mental furniture.
What can she take until her Master give!
Where can she look until He make the show!
What can she know until He bid her know!
How can she live till in her blood He live!

[1934] 1934

VI

He and She

As the moon sidles up
Must she sidle up,
As trips the scared moon
Away must she trip:

'His light had struck me blind
Dared I stop.'

She sings as the moon sings:
'I am I, am I;
The greater grows my light
The further that I fly.'
All creation shivers
With that sweet cry.

[before August 1934] 1934

VII

What Magic Drum?

He holds him from desire, all but stops his breathing lest
Primordial Motherhood forsake his limbs, the child no
longer rest,
Drinking joy as it were milk upon his breast.

Through light-obliterating garden foliage what magic drum?
Down limb and breast or down that glimmering belly move
his mouth and sinewy tongue.
What from the forest came? What beast has licked its young?

1935

VIII

Whence Had They Come?

Eternity is passion, girl or boy
Cry at the onset of their sexual joy
'For ever and for ever'; then awake
Ignorant what Dramatis Personae spake;
A passion-driven exultant man sings out
Sentences that he has never thought;
The Flagellant lashes those submissive loins
Ignorant what that dramatist enjoins,

What master made the lash. Whence had they come,
The hand and lash that beat down frigid Rome?
What sacred drama through her body heaved
When world-transforming Charlemagne was conceived?

1935

IX

The Four Ages of Man

He with body waged a fight,
But body won; it walks upright.

Then he struggled with the heart;
Innocence and peace depart.

Then he struggled with the mind;
His proud heart he left behind.

Now his wars on God begin;
At stroke of midnight God shall win.

[6 August 1934] 1934

X

Conjunctions

If Jupiter and Saturn meet,
What a crop of mummy wheat!

The sword's a cross; thereon He died:
On breast of Mars the goddess sighed.

[August 1934] 1934

XI

A Needle's Eye

All the stream that's roaring by
Came out of a needle's eye;
Things unborn, things that are gone,
From needle's eye still goad it on.

1934

XII

Meru

Civilisation is hooped together, brought
Under a rule, under the semblance of peace
By manifold illusion; but man's life is thought,
And he, despite his terror, cannot cease
Ravening through century after century,
Ravening, raging, and uprooting that he may come
Into the desolation of reality:
Egypt and Greece good-bye, and good-bye, Rome!
Hermits upon Mount Meru or Everest,
Caverned in night under the drifted snow,
Or where that snow and winter's dreadful blast
Beat down upon their naked bodies, know
That day brings round the night, that before dawn
His glory and his monuments are gone.

1934

NEW POEMS
1938

The Gyres

The gyres! the gyres! Old Rocky Face look forth;
Things thought too long can be no longer thought
For beauty dies of beauty, worth of worth,
And ancient lineaments are blotted out.
Irrational streams of blood are staining earth;
Empedocles has thrown all things about;
Hector is dead and there's a light in Troy;
We that look on but laugh in tragic joy.

What matter though numb nightmare ride on top
And blood and mire the sensitive body stain?
What matter? Heave no sigh, let no tear drop,
A greater, a more gracious time has gone;
For painted forms or boxes of make-up
In ancient tombs I sighed, but not again;
What matter? Out of Cavern comes a voice
And all it knows is that one word 'Rejoice'.

Conduct and work grow coarse, and coarse the soul,
What matter! Those that Rocky Face holds dear,
Lovers of horses and of women, shall
From marble of a broken sepulchre
Or dark betwixt the polecat and the owl,
Or any rich, dark nothing disinter
The workman, noble and saint, and all things run
On that unfashionable gyre again.

[1936–37] 1938

Lapis Lazuli

(*For Harry Clifton*)

I have heard that hysterical women say
They are sick of the palette and fiddle-bow,
Of poets that are always gay,
For everybody knows or else should know
That if nothing drastic is done
Aeroplane and Zeppelin will come out,
Pitch like King Billy bomb-balls in
Until the town lie beaten flat.

All perform their tragic play,
There struts Hamlet, there is Lear,
That's Ophelia, that Cordelia;
Yet they, should the last scene be there,
The great stage curtain about to drop,
If worthy their prominent part in the play,
Do not break up their lines to weep.
They know that Hamlet and Lear are gay;
Gaiety transfiguring all that dread.
All men have aimed at, found and lost;
Black out; Heaven blazing into the head:
Tragedy wrought to its uttermost.
Though Hamlet rambles and Lear rages,
And all the drop scenes drop at once
Upon a hundred thousand stages,
It cannot grow by an inch or an ounce.

On their own feet they came, or on shipboard,
Camel-back, horse-back, ass-back, mule-back,
Old civilisations put to the sword.
Then they and their wisdom went to rack:
No handiwork of Callimachus
Who handled marble as if it were bronze,
Made draperies that seemed to rise
When sea-wind swept the corner, stands;
His long lamp chimney shaped like the stem
Of a slender palm, stood but a day;
All things fall and are built again
And those that build them again are gay.

Two Chinamen, behind them a third,
Are carved in Lapis Lazuli,
Over them flies a long-legged bird
A symbol of longevity;
The third, doubtless a serving-man,
Carries a musical instrument.

Every discolouration of the stone,
Every accidental crack or dent
Seems a water-course or an avalanche,
Or lofty slope where it still snows
Though doubtless plum or cherry-branch
Sweetens the little half-way house
Those Chinamen climb towards, and I
Delight to imagine them seated there;
There, on the mountain and the sky,
On all the tragic scene they stare.
One asks for mournful melodies;
Accomplished fingers begin to play.
Their eyes mid many wrinkles, their eyes,
Their ancient, glittering eyes, are gay.

[July 1936] 1938

Imitated from the Japanese

A most astonishing thing
Seventy years have I lived;

(Hurrah for the flowers of Spring
For Spring is here again.)

Seventy years have I lived
No ragged beggar man,
Seventy years have I lived,
Seventy years man and boy,
And never have I danced for joy.

[December 1936] 1938

Sweet Dancer

The girl goes dancing there
On the leaf-sown, new-mown, smooth
Grass plot of the garden;
Escaped from her bitter youth,
Escaped out of her crowd,
Or out of her black cloud.
Ah dancer, ah sweet dancer!

If strange men come from the house
To lead her away do not say
That she is happy being crazy;
Lead them gently astray;
Let her finish her dance,
Let her finish her dance.
Ah dancer, ah sweet dancer!

[January 1937] 1938

The Three Bushes

An incident from the 'Historia mei Temporis' of the Abbé Michel de Bourdeille.

Said lady once to lover,
'None can rely upon
A love that lacks its proper food;
And if your love were gone
How could you sing those songs of love?
I should be blamed, young man.'
O my dear, O my dear.

'Have no lit candles in your room,'
That lovely lady said,
'That I at midnight by the clock
May creep into your bed,
For if I saw myself creep in
I think I should drop dead.'
O my dear, O my dear.

'I love a man in secret,
Dear chambermaid,' said she,
'I know that I must drop down dead
If he stop loving me,
Yet what could I but drop down dead
If I lost my chastity?'
O my dear, O my dear.

'So you must lie beside him
And let him think me there,
And maybe we are all the same
Where no candles are,
And maybe we are all the same
That strip the body bare.'
O my dear, O my dear.

But no dogs barked and midnights chimed,
And through the chime she'd say,
'That was a lucky thought of mine,
My lover looked so gay';
But heaved a sigh if the chambermaid
Looked half asleep all day.
O my dear, O my dear.

'No, not another song,' said he,
'Because my lady came
A year ago for the first time
At midnight to my room,
And I must lie between the sheets
When the clock begins to chime.'
O my dear, O my dear.

'A laughing, crying, sacred song,
A leching song,' they said.
Did ever men hear such a song?
No, but that day they did.
Did ever man ride such a race?
No, not until he rode.
O my dear, O my dear.

But when his horse had put its hoof
Into a rabbit hole

He dropped upon his head and died.
His lady saw it all
And dropped and died thereon, for she
Loved him with her soul.
O my dear, O my dear.

The chambermaid lived long, and took
Their graves into her charge,
And there two bushes planted
That when they had grown large
Seemed sprung from but a single root
So did their roses merge.
O my dear, O my dear.

When she was old and dying,
The priest came where she was;
She made a full confession.
Long looked he in her face,
And O, he was a good man
And understood her case.
O my dear, O my dear.

He bade them take and bury her
Beside her lady's man,
And set a rose-tree on her grave.
And now none living can
When they have plucked a rose there
Know where its roots began.
O my dear, O my dear.

[July 1936] 1937

The Lady's First Song

I turn round
Like a dumb beast in a show,
Neither know what I am
Nor where I go,

My language beaten
Into one name;
I am in love
And that is my shame.
What hurts the soul
My soul adores,
No better than a beast
Upon all fours.

[20 November 1936] 1938

The Lady's Second Song

What sort of man is coming
To lie between your feet?
What matter we are but women.
Wash; make your body sweet;
I have cupboards of dried fragrance,
I can strew the sheet.
The Lord have mercy upon us.

He shall love my soul as though
Body were not at all,
He shall love your body
Untroubled by the soul,
Love cram love's two divisions
Yet keep his substance whole.
The Lord have mercy upon us.

Soul must learn a love that is
Proper to my breast,
Limbs a love in common
With every noble beast.
If soul may look and body touch
Which is the more blest?
The Lord have mercy upon us.

[July 1936] 1938

The Lady's Third Song

When you and my true lover meet
And he plays tunes between your feet,
Speak no evil of the soul,
Nor think that body is the whole
For I that am his daylight lady
Know worse evil of the body;
But in honour split his love
Till either neither have enough,
That I may hear if we should kiss
A contrapuntal serpent hiss,
You, should hand explore a thigh,
All the labouring heavens sigh.

[July 1936] 1938

The Lover's Song

Bird sighs for the air,
Thought for I know not where,
For the womb the seed sighs.
Now sinks the same rest
On mind, on nest,
On straining thighs.

[November 1936] 1938

The Chambermaid's First Song

How came this ranger
Now sunk in rest,
Stranger with stranger,
On my cold breast.
What's left to sigh for,
Strange night has come;

God's love has hidden him
Out of all harm,
Pleasure has made him
Weak as a worm.

[November 1936] 1938

The Chambermaid's Second Song

From pleasure of the bed,
Dull as a worm,
His rod and its butting head
Limp as a worm,
His spirit that has fled
Blind as a worm.

[November 1936] 1938

An Acre of Grass

Picture and book remain,
An acre of green grass
For air and exercise,
Now strength of body goes;
Midnight, an old house
Where nothing stirs but a mouse.

My temptation is quiet.
Here at life's end
Neither loose imagination,
Nor the mill of the mind
Consuming its rag and bone,
Can make the truth known.

Grant me an old man's frenzy.
Myself must I remake
Till I am Timon and Lear
Or that William Blake
Who beat upon the wall
Till Truth obeyed his call;

A mind Michael Angelo knew
That can pierce the clouds
Or inspired by frenzy
Shake the dead in their shrouds;
Forgotten else by mankind
An old man's eagle mind.

[November 1936] 1938

What Then?

His chosen comrades thought at school
He must grow a famous man;
He thought the same and lived by rule,
All his twenties crammed with toil;
'What then?' sang Plato's ghost, 'what then?'

Everything he wrote was read,
After certain years he won
Sufficient money for his need,
Friends that have been friends indeed;
'What then?' sang Plato's ghost, 'what then?'

All his happier dreams came true –
A small old house, wife, daughter, son,
Grounds where plum and cabbage grew,
Poets and Wits about him drew;
'What then?' sang Plato's ghost, 'what then?'

'The work is done,' grown old he thought,
'According to my boyish plan;
Let the fools rage, I swerved in nought,
Something to perfection brought';
But louder sang that ghost 'What then?'

1937

Beautiful Lofty Things

Beautiful lofty things; O'Leary's noble head;
My father upon the Abbey stage, before him a raging crowd.
'This Land of Saints', and then as the applause died out,
'Of plaster Saints'; his beautiful mischievous head thrown back.
Standish O'Grady supporting himself between the tables
Speaking to a drunken audience high nonsensical words;
Augusta Gregory seated at her great ormolu table
Her eightieth winter approaching; 'Yesterday he threatened my life,
I told him that nightly from six to seven I sat at this table
The blinds drawn up'; Maud Gonne at Howth station waiting a train,
Pallas Athena in that straight back and arrogant head:
All the Olympians; a thing never known again.

1938

A Crazed Girl

That crazed girl improvising her music,
Her poetry, dancing upon the shore,
Her soul in division from itself
Climbing, falling she knew not where,
Hiding amid the cargo of a steamship
Her knee-cap broken, that girl I declare
A beautiful lofty thing, or a thing
Heroically lost, heroically found.

No matter what disaster occurred
She stood in desperate music wound,
Wound, wound, and she made in her triumph
Where the bales and the baskets lay
No common intelligible sound
But sang, 'O sea-starved hungry sea.'

[May 1936] 1937

To Dorothy Wellesley

Stretch towards the moonless midnight of the trees
As though that hand could reach to where they stand,
And they but famous old upholsteries
Delightful to the touch; tighten that hand
As though to draw them closer yet.
Rammed full
Of that most sensuous silence of the night
(For since the horizon's bought strange dogs are still)
Climb to your chamber full of books and wait,
No books upon the knee and no one there
But a great dane that cannot bay the moon
And now lies sunk in sleep.
What climbs the stair?
Nothing that common women ponder on
If you are worth my hope! Neither Content
Nor satisfied Conscience, but that great family
Some ancient famous authors misrepresent,
The Proud Furies each with her torch on high.

[August 1936] 1938

The Curse of Cromwell

You ask what I have found and far and wide I go,
Nothing but Cromwell's house and Cromwell's murderous crew,
The lovers and the dancers are beaten into the clay,
And the tall men and the swordsmen and the horsemen where are they?
And there is an old beggar wandering in his pride,
His fathers served their fathers before Christ was crucified.
O what of that, O what of that,
What is there left to say?

All neighbourly content and easy talk are gone,
But there's no good complaining, for money's rant is on,
He that's mounting up must on his neighbour mount
And we and all the Muses are things of no account.
They have schooling of their own but I pass their schooling by,
What can they know that we know that know the time to die?
O what of that, O what of that,
What is there left to say?

But there's another knowledge that my heart destroys
As the fox in the old fable destroyed the Spartan boy's
Because it proves that things both can and cannot be,
That the swordsmen and the ladies can still keep company,
Can pay the poet for a verse and hear the fiddle sound,
That I am still their servant though all are underground.
O what of that, O what of that,
What is there left to say?

I came on a great house in the middle of the night
Its open lighted doorway and its windows all alight,
And all my friends were there and made me welcome too;
But I woke in an old ruin that the winds howled through;
And when I pay attention I must out and walk
Among the dogs and horses that understand my talk.
O what of that, O what of that,
What is there left to say?

[November 1936–8 January 1937] 1937

Roger Casement

(*After Reading 'The Forged Casement Diaries' by Dr. Maloney*)

I say that Roger Casement
Did what he had to do,
He died upon the gallows
But that is nothing new.

Afraid they might be beaten
Before the bench of Time
They turned a trick by forgery
And blackened his good name.

A perjurer stood ready
To prove their forgery true;
They gave it out to all the world
And that is something new;

For Spring-Rice had to whisper it
Being their Ambassador,
And then the speakers got it
And writers by the score.

Come Tom and Dick, come all the troop
That cried it far and wide,
Come from the forger and his desk,
Desert the perjurer's side;

Come speak your bit in public
That some amends be made
To this most gallant gentleman
That is in quick-lime laid.

[October-November 1936] 1937

The Ghost of Roger Casement

O what has made that sudden noise?
What on the threshold stands?
It never crossed the sea because
John Bull and the sea are friends;
But this is not the old sea
Nor this the old seashore.
What gave that roar of mockery,
That roar in the sea's roar?

The ghost of Roger Casement
Is beating on the door.

John Bull has stood for Parliament,
A dog must have his day,
The country thinks no end of him
For he knows how to say
At a beanfeast or a banquet,
That all must hang their trust
Upon the British Empire,
Upon the Church of Christ.

The ghost of Roger Casement
Is beating on the door.

John Bull has gone to India
And all must pay him heed
For histories are there to prove
That none of another breed
Has had a like inheritance,
Or sucked such milk as he,
And there's no luck about a house
If it lack honesty.

The ghost of Roger Casement
Is beating on the door.

I poked about a village church
And found his family tomb
And copied out what I could read
In that religious gloom;
Found many a famous man there;
But fame and virtue rot.
Draw round, beloved and bitter men,
Draw round and raise a shout;

The ghost of Roger Casement
Is beating on the door.

[October 1936] 1938

The O'Rahilly

Sing of the O'Rahilly,
Do not deny his right;
Sing a 'the' before his name;
Allow that he, despite
All those learned historians,
Established it for good;
He wrote out that word himself,
He christened himself with blood.
How goes the weather?

Sing of the O'Rahilly
That had such little sense,
He told Pearse and Connolly
He'd gone to great expense
Keeping all the Kerry men
Out of that crazy fight;
That he might be there himself
Had travelled half the night.
How goes the weather?

'Am I such a craven that
I should not get the word
But for what some travelling man
Had heard I had not heard?'
Then on Pearse and Connolly
He fixed a bitter look,
'Because I helped to wind the clock
I come to hear it strike.'
How goes the weather?

What remains to sing about
But of the death he met
Stretched under a doorway
Somewhere off Henry Street;
They that found him found upon
The door above his head
'Here died the O'Rahilly
R.I.P.' writ in blood.
How goes the weather?

[January 1937] 1938

Come Gather Round Me Parnellites

Come gather round me Parnellites
And praise our chosen man,
Stand upright on your legs awhile,
Stand upright while you can,
For soon we lie where he is laid
And he is underground;
Come fill up all those glasses
And pass the bottle round.

And here's a cogent reason
And I have many more,
He fought the might of England
And saved the Irish poor,
Whatever good a farmer's got
He brought it all to pass;
And here's another reason,
That Parnell loved a lass.

And here's a final reason,
He was of such a kind
Every man that sings a song
Keeps Parnell in his mind
For Parnell was a proud man,
No prouder trod the ground,
And a proud man's a lovely man
So pass the bottle round.

The Bishops and the Party
That tragic story made,
A husband that had sold his wife
And after that betrayed;
But stories that live longest
Are sung above the glass,
And Parnell loved his country
And Parnell loved his lass.

[8 September 1936] 1937

The Wild Old Wicked Man

'Because I am mad about women
I am mad about the hills,'
Said that wild old wicked man
Who travels where God wills,
'Not to die on the straw at home,
Those hands to close these eyes,
That is all I ask, my dear,
From the old man in the skies.'
Day-break and a candle end.

'Kind are all your words, my dear,
Do not the rest withhold,
Who can know the year, my dear,
When an old man's blood grows cold.
I have what no young man can have
Because he loves too much.
Words I have that can pierce the heart,
But what can he do but touch?'
Day-break and a candle end.

Then said she to that wild old man,
His stout stick under his hand,
'Love to give or to withhold
Is not at my command.
I gave it all to an older man,
That old man in the skies.
Hands that are busy with His beads
Can never close those eyes.'
Day-break and a candle end.

'Go your ways, O go your ways,
I choose another mark,
Girls down on the seashore
Who understand the dark;
Bawdy talk for the fishermen,
A dance for the fisher lads;
When dark hangs upon the water
They turn down their beds.'
Day-break and a candle end.

'A young man in the dark am I
But a wild old man in the light
That can make a cat laugh, or
Can touch by mother wit
Things hid in their marrow bones
From time long passed away,
Hid from all those warty lads
That by their bodies lay.'
Day-break and a candle end.

'All men live in suffering
I know as few can know,
Whether they take the upper road
Or stay content on the low,
Rower bent in his row-boat
Or weaver bent at his loom,
Horseman erect upon horseback
Or child hid in the womb.'
Day-break and a candle end.

'That some stream of lightning
From the old man in the skies
Can burn out that suffering
No right-taught man denies.
But a coarse old man am I,
I choose the second-best,
I forget it all awhile
Upon a woman's breast.'
Day-break and a candle end.

[193[illegible]] 1938

The Great Day

Hurrah for revolution and more cannon shot;
A beggar upon horseback lashes a beggar upon foot;
Hurrah for revolution and cannon come again,
The beggars have changed places but the lash goes on.

[January 1937] 1938

Parnell

Parnell came down the road, he said to a cheering man:
'Ireland shall get her freedom and you still break stone.'

[January 1937] 1938

What Was Lost

I sing what was lost and dread what was won,
I walk in a battle fought over again,
My king a lost king, and lost soldiers my men;
Feet to the Rising and Setting may run,
They always beat on the same small stone.

[January 1937] 1938

The Spur

You think it horrible that lust and rage
Should dance attendance upon my old age;
They were not such a plague when I was young;
What else have I to spur me into song?

[7 October 1936] 1938

A Drunken Man's Praise of Sobriety

Come swish around, my pretty punk,
And keep me dancing still
That I may stay a sober man
Although I drink my fill.
Sobriety is a jewel
That I do much adore;
And therefore keep me dancing
Though drunkards lie and snore.
O mind your feet, O mind your feet,
Keep dancing like a wave,

And under every dancer
A dead man in his grave.
No ups and downs, my Pretty,
A mermaid, not a punk;
A drunkard is a dead man
And all dead men are drunk.

1938

The Pilgrim

I fasted for some forty days on bread and buttermilk
For passing round the bottle with girls in rags or silk,
In country shawl or Paris cloak, had put my wits astray,
And what's the good of women for all that they can say
Is fol de rol de rolly O.

Round Lough Derg's holy island I went upon the stones,
I prayed at all the Stations upon my marrow bones,
And there I found an old man and though I prayed all day
And that old man beside me, nothing would he say
But fol de rol de rolly O.

All know that all the dead in the world about that place are stuck
And that should mother seek her son she'd have but little luck
Because the fires of Purgatory have ate their shapes away;
I swear to God I questioned them and all they had to say
Was fol de rol de rolly O.

A great black ragged bird appeared when I was in the boat;
Some twenty feet from tip to tip had it stretched rightly out,
With flopping and with flapping it made a great display
But I never stopped to question, what could the boatman say
But fol de rol de rolly O.

Now I am in the public house and lean upon the wall,
So come in rags or come in silk, in cloak or country shawl,
And come with learned lovers or with what men you may
For I can put the whole lot down, and all I have to say
Is fol de rol de rolly O.

1937

Colonel Martin

I

The Colonel went out sailing,
He spoke with Turk and Jew,
With Christian and with Infidel
For all tongues he knew.
'O what's a wifeless man?' said he
And he came sailing home.
He rose the latch and went upstairs
And found an empty room.
The Colonel went out sailing.

II

'I kept her much in the country
And she was much alone,
And though she may be there,' he said,
'She may be in the town,
She may be all alone there
For who can say,' he said,
'I think that I shall find her
In a young man's bed.'
The Colonel went out sailing.

III

The Colonel met a pedlar,
Agreed their clothes to swop,
And bought the grandest jewelry
In a Galway shop,

Instead of thread and needle
Put jewelry in the pack,
Bound a thong about his hand,
Hitched it on his back.
The Colonel went out sailing.

IV

The Colonel knocked on the rich man's door,
'I am sorry,' said the maid,
'My mistress cannot see these things
But she is still abed,
And never have I looked upon
Jewelry so grand.'
'Take all to your mistress,'
And he laid them on her hand.
The Colonel went out sailing.

V

And he went in and she went on
And both climbed up the stair,
And O he was a clever man
For he his slippers wore,
And when they came to the top stair
He ran on ahead,
His wife he found and the rich man
In the comfort of a bed.
The Colonel went out sailing.

VI

The Judge at the Assize Court
When he heard that story told
Awarded him for damages
Three kegs of gold.
The Colonel said to Tom his man
'Harness an ass and cart,
Carry the gold about the town,
Throw it in every part.'
The Colonel went out sailing.

VII

And there at all street corners
A man with a pistol stood,
And the rich man had paid them well
To shoot the Colonel dead;
But they threw down their pistols
And all men heard them swear
That they could never shoot a man
Did all that for the poor.
The Colonel went out sailing.

VIII

'And did you keep no gold, Tom?
You had three kegs,' said he.
'I never thought of that, Sir';
'Then want before you die.'
And want he did; for my own grand-dad
Saw the story's end,
And Tom make out a living
From the sea-weed on the strand.
The Colonel went out sailing.

[10 August 1937] 1937

A Model for the Laureate

On thrones from China to Peru
All sorts of kings have sat
That men and women of all sorts
Proclaimed both good and great;
And what's the odds if such as these
For reason of the State
Should keep their lovers waiting,
Keep their lovers waiting.

Some boast of beggar-kings and kings
Of rascals black and white
That rule because a strong right arm
Puts all men in a fright,

And drunk or sober live at ease
Where none gainsay their right,
And keep their lovers waiting,
    Keep their lovers waiting.

The Muse is mute when public men
Applaud a modern throne:
Those cheers that can be bought or sold,
That office fools have run,
That waxen seal, that signature.
For things like these what decent man
Would keep his lover waiting?
    Keep his lover waiting?

[26 July 1937] 1938

The Old Stone Cross

A statesman is an easy man,
He tells his lies by rote;
A journalist makes up his lies
And takes you by the throat;
So stay at home and drink your beer
And let the neighbours vote,
    Said the man in the golden breastplate
    Under the old stone Cross.

Because this age and the next age
Engender in the ditch,
No man can know a happy man
From any passing wretch,
If Folly link with Elegance
No man knows which is which,
    Said the man in the golden breastplate
    Under the old stone Cross.

But actors lacking music
Do most excite my spleen,
They say it is more human
To shuffle, grunt and groan,

Not knowing what unearthly stuff
Rounds a mighty scene.
Said the man in the golden breastplate
Under the old stone Cross.

[April–June 1937] 1938

The Spirit Medium

Poetry, music, I have loved, and yet
Because of those new dead
That come into my soul and escape
Confusion of the bed,
Or those begotten or unbegotten
Perning in a band,
I bend my body to the spade
Or grope with a dirty hand.

Or those begotten or unbegotten.
For I would not recall
Some that being unbegotten
Are not individual,
But copy some one action,
Moulding it of dust or sand,
I bend my body to the spade
Or grope with a dirty hand.

An old ghost's thoughts are lightning,
To follow is to die;
Poetry and music I have banished,
But the stupidity
Of root, shoot, blossom or clay
Makes no demand.
I bend my body to the spade
Or grope with a dirty hand.

1938

Those Images

What if I bade you leave
The cavern of the mind?
There's better exercise
In the sunlight and wind.

I never bade you go
To Moscow or to Rome,
Renounce that drudgery,
Call the Muses home.

Seek those images
That constitute the wild,
The lion and the virgin,
The harlot and the child.

Find in middle air
An eagle on the wing,
Recognise the five
That make the Muses sing.

[on or before August 1937] 1938

The Municipal Gallery Re-visited

I

Around me the images of thirty years;
An ambush; pilgrims at the water-side;
Casement upon trial, half hidden by the bars,
Guarded; Griffith staring in hysterical pride;
Kevin O'Higgins' countenance that wears
A gentle questioning look that cannot hide
A soul incapable of remorse or rest;
A revolutionary soldier kneeling to be blessed.

II

An Abbot or Archbishop with an upraised hand
Blessing the Tricolour. 'This is not,' I say,

'The dead Ireland of my youth, but an Ireland
The poets have imagined, terrible and gay.'
Before a woman's portrait suddenly I stand;
Beautiful and gentle in her Venetian way.
I met her all but fifty years ago
For twenty minutes in some studio.

III

Heart smitten with emotion I sink down,
My heart recovering with covered eyes;
Wherever I had looked I had looked upon
My permanent or impermanent images;
Augusta Gregory's son; her sister's son,
Hugh Lane, 'onlie begetter' of all these;
Hazel Lavery living and dying, that tale
As though some ballad singer had sung it all.

IV

Mancini's portrait of Augusta Gregory,
'Greatest since Rembrandt,' according to John Synge;
A great ebullient portrait certainly;
But where is the brush that could show anything
Of all that pride and that humility,
And I am in despair that time may bring
Approved patterns of women or of men
But not that selfsame excellence again.

V

My mediaeval knees lack health until they bend,
But in that woman, in that household where
Honour had lived so long, all lacking found.
Childless I thought, 'My children may find here
Deep-rooted things,' but never foresaw its end,
And now that end has come I have not wept;
No fox can foul the lair the badger swept.

VI

(An image out of Spenser and the common tongue.)
John Synge, I and Augusta Gregory, thought

All that we did, all that we said or sang
Must come from contact with the soil, from that
Contact everything Antaeus-like grew strong.
We three alone in modern times had brought
Everything down to that sole test again,
Dream of the noble and the beggarman.

VII

And here's John Synge himself, that rooted man
'Forgetting human words,' a grave deep face.
You that would judge me do not judge alone
This book or that, come to this hallowed place
Where my friends' portraits hang and look thereon;
Ireland's history in their lineaments trace;
Think where man's glory most begins and ends
And say my glory was I had such friends.

[August–5 September 1937] 1937

Are You Content

I call on those that call me son,
Grandson, or great-grandson,
On uncles, aunts, great-uncles or great-aunts
To judge what I have done.
Have I, that put it into words,
Spoilt what old loins have sent?
Eyes spiritualised by death can judge,
I cannot, but I am not content.

He that in Sligo at Drumcliff
Set up the old stone Cross,
That red-headed rector in County Down
A good man on a horse,
Sandymount Corbets, that notable man
Old William Pollexfen,
The smuggler Middleton, Butlers far back,
Half legendary men.

Infirm and aged I might stay
In some good company,
I who have always hated work,
Smiling at the sea,
Or demonstrate in my own life
What Robert Browning meant
By an old hunter talking with Gods;
But I am not content.

1938

From ON THE BOILER
1939

Why should not Old Men be Mad?

Why should not old men be mad?
Some have known a likely lad
That had a sound fly fisher's wrist
Turn to a drunken journalist;
A girl that knew all Dante once
Live to bear children to a dunce;
A Helen of social welfare dream
Climb on a wagonette to scream.
Some think it matter of course that chance
Should starve good men and bad advance,
That if their neighbours figured plain,
As though upon a lighted screen,
No single story would they find
Of an unbroken happy mind,
A finish worthy of the start.
Young men know nothing of this sort,
Observant old men know it well;
And when they know what old books tell
And that no better can be had,
Know why an old man should be mad.

[January 1936] 1939

Crazy Jane on the Mountain

I am tired of cursing the Bishop
(Said Crazy Jane)
Nine books or nine hats
Would not make him a man.
I have found something worse
To meditate on.
A King had some beautiful cousins
But where are they gone?
Battered to death in a cellar,
And he stuck to his throne.
Last night I lay on the mountain
(Said Crazy Jane)
There in a two-horsed carriage
That on two wheels ran
Great-bladdered Emer sat,
Her violent man
Cuchulain, sat at her side,
Thereupon,
Propped upon my two knees,
I kissed a stone;
I lay stretched out in the dirt
And I cried tears down.

[July 1938] 1939

A Statesman's Holiday

I lived among great houses,
Riches drove out rank,
Base drove out the better blood,
And mind and body shrank.
No Oscar ruled the table,
But I'd a troop of friends
That knowing better talk had gone
Talked of odds and ends.
Some knew what ailed the world
But never said a thing

So I have picked a better trade
And night and morning sing:
Tall dames go walking in grass-green Avalon.

Am I a great Lord Chancellor
That slept upon the Sack?
Commanding officer that tore
The khaki from his back?
Or am I de Valéra,
Or the King of Greece,
Or the man that made the motors?
Ach, call me what you please!
Here's a Montenegrin lute
And its old sole string
Makes me sweet music
And I delight to sing:
Tall dames go walking in grass-green Avalon.

With boys and girls about him,
With any sort of clothes,
With a hat out of fashion,
With old patched shoes,
With a ragged bandit cloak,
With an eye like a hawk,
With a stiff straight back,
With a strutting turkey walk,
With a bag full of pennies,
With a monkey on a chain,
With a great cock's feather,
With an old foul tune.
Tall dames go walking in grass-green Avalon.

[April 1938] 1939

LAST POEMS
1939

Under Ben Bulben

I

Swear by what the sages spoke
Round the Mareotic Lake
That the Witch of Atlas knew,
Spoke and set the cocks a-crow.

Swear by those horsemen, by those women,
Complexion and form prove superhuman,
That pale, long-visaged company
That airs an immortality
Completeness of their passions won;
Now they ride the wintry dawn
Where Ben Bulben sets the scene.

Here's the gist of what they mean.

II

Many times man lives and dies
Between his two eternities,
That of race and that of soul,
And ancient Ireland knew it all.
Whether man dies in his bed
Or the rifle knocks him dead,
A brief parting from those dear
Is the worst man has to fear.

Though grave-diggers' toil is long,
Sharp their spades, their muscle strong,
They but thrust their buried men
Back in the human mind again.

III

You that Mitchel's prayer have heard
'Send war in our time, O Lord!'
Know that when all words are said
And a man is fighting mad,
Something drops from eyes long blind,
He completes his partial mind,
For an instant stands at ease,
Laughs aloud, his heart at peace,
Even the wisest man grows tense
With some sort of violence
Before he can accomplish fate,
Know his work or choose his mate.

IV

Poet and sculptor, do the work,
Nor let the modish painter shirk
What his great forefathers did,
Bring the soul of man to God,
Make him fill the cradles right.

Measurement began our might:
Forms a stark Egyptian thought,
Forms that gentler Phidias wrought.

Michael Angelo left a proof
On the Sistine Chapel roof,
Where but half-awakened Adam
Can disturb globe-trotting Madam
Till her bowels are in heat,
Proof that there's a purpose set
Before the secret working mind:
Profane perfection of mankind.

Quattrocento put in paint,
On backgrounds for a God or Saint,
Gardens where a soul's at ease;
Where everything that meets the eye,
Flowers and grass and cloudless sky,
Resemble forms that are, or seem,
When sleepers wake and yet still dream,
And when it's vanished still declare,
With only bed and bedstead there,
That Heavens had opened.
                                        Gyres run on;
When that greater dream had gone
Calvert and Wilson, Blake and Claude,
Prepared a rest for the people of God,
Palmer's phrase, but after that
Confusion fell upon our thought.

V

Irish poets, learn your trade,
Sing whatever is well made,
Scorn the sort now growing up
All out of shape from toe to top,
Their unremembering hearts and heads
Base-born products of base beds.
Sing the peasantry, and then
Hard-riding country gentlemen,
The holiness of monks, and after
Porter-drinkers' randy laughter;
Sing the lords and ladies gay
That were beaten into the clay
Through seven heroic centuries;
Cast your mind on other days
That we in coming days may be
Still the indomitable Irishry.

VI

Under bare Ben Bulben's head
In Drumcliff churchyard Yeats is laid,
An ancestor was rector there
Long years ago; a church stands near,

By the road an ancient Cross.
No marble, no conventional phrase,
On limestone quarried near the spot
By his command these words are cut:

Cast a cold eye
On life, on death.
Horseman, pass by!

September 4, 1938

[1938]
1939

Three Songs to the One Burden

I

The Roaring Tinker if you like,
But Mannion is my name,
And I beat up the common sort
And think it is no shame.
The common breeds the common,
A lout begets a lout,
So when I take on half a score
I knock their heads about.

From mountain to mountain ride the fierce horsemen.

All Mannions come from Manannan,
Though rich on every shore
He never lay behind four walls
He had such character,
Nor ever made an iron red
Nor soldered pot or pan;
His roaring and his ranting
Best please a wandering man.

From mountain to mountain ride the fierce horsemen.

Could Crazy Jane put off old age
And ranting time renew,
Could that old god rise up again
We'd drink a can or two,

III

Come gather round me players all:
Come praise Nineteen-Sixteen,
Those from the pit and gallery
Or from the painted scene
That fought in the Post Office
Or round the City Hall,
Praise every man that came again,
Praise every man that fell.

From mountain to mountain ride the fierce horsemen.

Who was the first man shot that day?
The player Connolly,
Close to the City Hall he died;
Carriage and voice had he;
He lacked those years that go with skill
But later might have been
A famous brilliant figure
Before the painted scene.

From mountain to mountain ride the fierce horsemen.

Some had no thought of victory
But had gone out to die
That Ireland's mind be greater,
Her heart mount up on high;
And no one knows what's yet to come
For Patrick Pearse had said
That in every generation
Must Ireland's blood be shed.

From mountain to mountain ride the fierce horsemen.

1939

The Black Tower

Say that the men of the old black tower
Though they but feed as the goatherd feeds,

And out and lay our leadership
On country and on town,
Throw likely couples into bed
And knock the others down.

From mountain to mountain ride the fierce horsemen.

II

My name is Henry Middleton,
I have a small demesne,
A small forgotten house that's set
On a storm-bitten green,
I scrub its floors and make my bed,
I cook and change my plate,
The post and garden-boy alone
Have keys to my old gate.

From mountain to mountain ride the fierce horsemen.

Though I have locked my gate on them
I pity all the young,
I know what devil's trade they learn
From those they live among,
Their drink, their pitch and toss by day,
Their robbery by night;
The wisdom of the people's gone,
How can the young go straight?

From mountain to mountain ride the fierce horsemen.

When every Sunday afternoon
On the Green Lands I walk
And wear a coat in fashion,
Memories of the talk
Of hen wives and of queer old men
Brace me and make me strong;
There's not a pilot on the perch
Knows I have lived so long.

From mountain to mountain ride the fierce horsemen.

Quattrocento put in paint,
On backgrounds for a God or Saint,
Gardens where a soul's at ease;
Where everything that meets the eye,
Flowers and grass and cloudless sky,
Resemble forms that are, or seem,
When sleepers wake and yet still dream,
And when it's vanished still declare,
With only bed and bedstead there,
That Heavens had opened.
                                        Gyres run on;
When that greater dream had gone
Calvert and Wilson, Blake and Claude,
Prepared a rest for the people of God,
Palmer's phrase, but after that
Confusion fell upon our thought.

V

Irish poets, learn your trade,
Sing whatever is well made,
Scorn the sort now growing up
All out of shape from toe to top,
Their unremembering hearts and heads
Base-born products of base beds.
Sing the peasantry, and then
Hard-riding country gentlemen,
The holiness of monks, and after
Porter-drinkers' randy laughter;
Sing the lords and ladies gay
That were beaten into the clay
Through seven heroic centuries;
Cast your mind on other days
That we in coming days may be
Still the indomitable Irishry.

VI

Under bare Ben Bulben's head
In Drumcliff churchyard Yeats is laid,
An ancestor was rector there
Long years ago; a church stands near,

By the road an ancient Cross.
No marble, no conventional phrase,
On limestone quarried near the spot
By his command these words are cut:

Cast a cold eye
On life, on death.
Horseman, pass by!

September 4, 1938

[1938]

1939

Three Songs to the One Burden

I

The Roaring Tinker if you like,
But Mannion is my name,
And I beat up the common sort
And think it is no shame.
The common breeds the common,
A lout begets a lout,
So when I take on half a score
I knock their heads about.

From mountain to mountain ride the fierce horsemen.

All Mannions come from Manannan,
Though rich on every shore
He never lay behind four walls
He had such character,
Nor ever made an iron red
Nor soldered pot or pan;
His roaring and his ranting
Best please a wandering man.

From mountain to mountain ride the fierce horsemen.

Could Crazy Jane put off old age
And ranting time renew,
Could that old god rise up again
We'd drink a can or two,

Their money spent, their wine gone sour,
Lack nothing that a soldier needs,
That all are oath-bound men;
Those banners come not in.

There in the tomb stand the dead upright,
But winds come up from the shore,
They shake when the winds roar,
Old bones upon the mountain shake.

Those banners come to bribe or threaten
Or whisper that a man's a fool
Who when his own right king's forgotten
Cares what king sets up his rule.
If he died long ago
Why do you dread us so?

There in the tomb drops the faint moonlight,
But winds come up from the shore,
They shake when the winds roar,
Old bones upon the mountain shake.

The tower's old cook that must climb and clamber
Catching small birds in the dew of the morn
When we hale men lie stretched in slumber
Swears that he hears the king's great horn.
But he's a lying hound;
Stand we on guard oath-bound!

There in the tomb the dark grows blacker,
But winds come up from the shore,
They shake when the winds roar,
Old bones upon the mountain shake.

January 21, 1939

[21 January 1939] 1939

Cuchulain Comforted

A man that had six mortal wounds, a man
Violent and famous, strode among the dead;
Eyes stared out of the branches and were gone.

Then certain Shrouds that muttered head to head
Came and were gone. He leant upon a tree
As though to meditate on wounds and blood.

A Shroud that seemed to have authority
Among those bird-like things came, and let fall
A bundle of linen. Shrouds by two and three

Came creeping up because the man was still.
And thereupon that linen-carrier said:
'Your life can grow much sweeter if you will

'Obey our ancient rule and make a shroud;
Mainly because of what we only know
The rattle of those arms makes us afraid.

'We thread the needles' eyes and all we do
All must together do.' That done, the man
Took up the nearest and began to sew.

'Now must we sing and sing the best we can
But first you must be told our character:
Convicted cowards all by kindred slain

'Or driven from home and left to die in fear.'
They sang, but had nor human tunes nor words,
Though all was done in common as before,

They had changed their throats and had the throats of birds.

January 13, 1939

[January 1939] 1939

Three Marching Songs

I

Remember all those renowned generations,
They left their bodies to fatten the wolves,
They left their homesteads to fatten the foxes,
Fled to far countries, or sheltered themselves
In cavern, crevice or hole,
Defending Ireland's soul.

Be still, be still, what can be said?
My father sang that song,
But time amends old wrong,
All that is finished, let it fade.

Remember all those renowned generations,
Remember all that have sunk in their blood,
Remember all that have died on the scaffold,
Remember all that have fled, that have stood,
Stood, took death like a tune
On an old tambourine.

Be still, be still, what can be said?
My father sang that song,
But time amends old wrong,
All that is finished, let it fade.

Fail and that history turns into rubbish,
All that great past to a trouble of fools;
Those that come after shall mock at O'Donnell,
Mock at the memory of both O'Neills,
Mock Emmet, mock Parnell,
All the renown that fell.

Be still, be still, what can be said?
My father sang that song,
But time amends old wrong,
All that is finished, let it fade.

II

The soldier takes pride in saluting his Captain,
The devotee proffers a knee to his Lord,
Some back a mare thrown from a thoroughbred,
Troy backed its Helen, Troy died and adored;
Great nations blossom above,
A slave bows down to a slave.

What marches through the mountain pass?
No, no, my son, not yet;
That is an airy spot
And no man knows what treads the grass.

We know what rascal might has defiled,
The lofty innocence that it has slain,
We were not born in the peasant's cot
Where man forgives if the belly gain.
More dread the life that we live,
How can the mind forgive?

What marches through the mountain pass?
No, no, my son, not yet;
That is an airy spot
And no man knows what treads the grass.

What if there's nothing up there at the top?
Where are the captains that govern mankind?
What tears down a tree that has nothing within it?
A blast of wind, O a marching wind,
March wind, and any old tune,
March, march, and how does it run.

What marches through the mountain pass?
No, no, my son, not yet;
That is an airy spot
And no man knows what treads the grass.

III

Grandfather sang it under the gallows,
'Hear, gentlemen, ladies, and all mankind:
Money is good and a girl might be better,
But good strong blows are delights to the mind.'
There, standing on the cart,
He sang it from his heart.

Robbers had taken his old tambourine
But he took down the moon
And rattled out a tune;
Robbers had taken his old tambourine.

'A girl I had, but she followed another,
Money I had and it went in the night,
Strong drink I had and it brought me to sorrow,
But a good strong cause and blows are delight.'

All there caught up the tune,
'On, on, my darling man.'

Robbers had taken his old tambourine
But he took down the moon
And rattled out a tune;
Robbers had taken his old tambourine.

'Money is good and a girl might be better,
No matter what happens and who takes the fall,
But a good strong cause' – the rope gave a jerk there,
No more sang he, for his throat was too small;
But he kicked before he died,
He did it out of pride.

Robbers had taken his old tambourine
But he took down the moon
And rattled out a tune;
Robbers had taken his old tambourine.

[30 November 1933–27 February 1934;
December 1938] 1934; 1939

In Tara's Halls

A man I praise that once in Tara's Halls
Said to the woman on his knees, 'Lie still,
My hundredth year is at an end. I think
That something is about to happen, I think
That the adventure of old age begins.
To many women I have said, "Lie still,"
And given everything that a woman needs,
A roof, good clothes, passion, love perhaps,
But never asked for love; should I ask that
I shall be old indeed.'
Thereon the man
Went to the Sacred House and stood between
The golden plough and harrow and spoke aloud
That all attendants and the casual crowd might hear:
'God I have loved, but should I ask return
Of God or woman the time were come to die.'

He bade, his hundred and first year at end,
Diggers and carpenters make grave and coffin,
Saw that the grave was deep, the coffin sound,
Summoned the generations of his house,
Lay in the coffin, stopped his breath and died.

[June 1938] 1939

The Statues

Pythagoras planned it. Why did the people stare?
His numbers, though they moved or seemed to move
In marble or in bronze, lacked character.
But boys and girls pale from the imagined love
Of solitary beds knew what they were,
That passion could bring character enough;
And pressed at midnight in some public place
Live lips upon a plummet-measured face.

No; greater than Pythagoras, for the men
That with a mallet or a chisel modelled these
Calculations that look but casual flesh, put down
All Asiatic vague immensities,
And not the banks of oars that swam upon
The many-headed foam at Salamis.
Europe put off that foam when Phidias
Gave women dreams and dreams their looking-glass.

One image crossed the many-headed, sat
Under the tropic shade, grew round and slow,
No Hamlet thin from eating flies, a fat
Dreamer of the Middle Ages. Empty eyeballs knew
That knowledge increases unreality, that
Mirror on mirror mirrored is all the show.
When gong and conch declare the hour to bless
Grimalkin crawls to Buddha's emptiness.

When Pearse summoned Cuchulain to his side,
What stalked through the Post Office? What intellect,
What calculation, number, measurement, replied?
We Irish, born into that ancient sect

But thrown upon this filthy modern tide
And by its formless spawning fury wrecked,
Climb to our proper dark, that we may trace
The lineaments of a plummet-measured face.

[April–June 1938] 1939

News for the Delphic Oracle

I

There all the golden codgers lay,
There the silver dew,
And the great water sighed for love
And the wind sighed too.
Man-picker Niamh leant and sighed
By Oisin on the grass;
There sighed amid his choir of love
Tall Pythagoras.
Plotinus came and looked about,
The salt flakes on his breast,
And having stretched and yawned awhile
Lay sighing like the rest.

II

Straddling each a dolphin's back
And steadied by a fin
Those Innocents re-live their death,
Their wounds open again.
The ecstatic waters laugh because
Their cries are sweet and strange,
Through their ancestral patterns dance,
And the brute dolphins plunge
Until in some cliff-sheltered bay
Where wades the choir of love
Proffering its sacred laurel crowns,
They pitch their burdens off.

III

Slim adolescence that a nymph has stripped,
Peleus on Thetis stares,
Her limbs are delicate as an eyelid,
Love has blinded him with tears;
But Thetis' belly listens.
Down the mountain walls
From where Pan's cavern is
Intolerable music falls.
Foul goat-head, brutal arm appear,
Belly, shoulder, bum,
Flash fishlike; nymphs and satyrs
Copulate in the foam.

1939

Long-legged Fly

That civilisation may not sink,
Its great battle lost,
Quiet the dog, tether the pony
To a distant post.
Our master Caesar is in the tent
Where the maps are spread,
His eyes fixed upon nothing,
A hand under his head.

Like a long-legged fly upon the stream
His mind moves upon silence.

That the topless towers be burnt
And men recall that face,
Move most gently if move you must
In this lonely place.
She thinks, part woman, three parts a child,
That nobody looks; her feet
Practise a tinker shuffle
Picked up on the street.

Like a long-legged fly upon the stream
Her mind moves upon silence.

That girls at puberty may find
The first Adam in their thought,
Shut the door of the Pope's chapel,
Keep those children out.
There on that scaffolding reclines
Michael Angelo.
With no more sound than the mice make
His hand moves to and fro.

Like a long-legged fly upon the stream
His mind moves upon silence.

[November 1937–April 1938] 1939

A Bronze Head

Here at right of the entrance this bronze head,
Human, superhuman, a bird's round eye,
Everything else withered and mummy-dead.
What great tomb-haunter sweeps the distant sky
(Something may linger there though all else die)
And finds there nothing to make its terror less
Hysterica passio of its own emptiness?

No dark tomb-haunter once; her form all full
As though with magnanimity of light
Yet a most gentle woman; who can tell
Which of her forms has shown her substance right,
Or maybe substance can be composite,
Profound McTaggart thought so, and in a breath
A mouthful hold the extreme of life and death.

But even at the starting post, all sleek and new,
I saw the wildness in her and I thought
A vision of terror that it must live through
Had shattered her soul. Propinquity had brought
Imagination to that pitch where it casts out
All that is not itself. I had grown wild
And wandered murmuring everywhere, 'My child, my
child.'

Or else I thought her supernatural;
As though a sterner eye looked through her eye
On this foul world in its decline and fall,
On gangling stocks grown great, great stocks run dry,
Ancestral pearls all pitched into a sty,
Heroic reverie mocked by clown and knave,
And wondered what was left for massacre to save.

1939

A Stick of Incense

Whence did all that fury come,
From empty tomb or Virgin womb?
Saint Joseph thought the world would melt
But liked the way his finger smelt.

1939

Hound Voice

Because we love bare hills and stunted trees
And were the last to choose the settled ground,
Its boredom of the desk or of the spade, because
So many years companioned by a hound,
Our voices carry; and though slumber bound,
Some few half wake and half renew their choice,
Give tongue, proclaim their hidden name – 'hound voice'.

The women that I picked spoke sweet and low
And yet gave tongue. 'Hound voices' were they all.
We picked each other from afar and knew
What hour of terror comes to test the soul,
And in that terror's name obeyed the call,
And understood, what none have understood,
Those images that waken in the blood.

Some day we shall get up before the dawn
And find our ancient hounds before the door,

And wide awake know that the hunt is on;
Stumbling upon the blood-dark track once more,
Then stumbling to the kill beside the shore;
Then cleaning out and bandaging of wounds,
And chants of victory amid the encircling hounds.

1938

John Kinsella's Lament for Mrs. Mary Moore

I

A bloody and a sudden end,
  Gunshot or a noose,
For death who takes what man would keep,
  Leaves what man would lose.
He might have had my sister,
  My cousins by the score,
But nothing satisfied the fool
  But my dear Mary Moore,
None other knows what pleasures man
  At table or in bed.
What shall I do for pretty girls
  Now my old bawd is dead?

II

Though stiff to strike a bargain
  Like an old Jew man,
Her bargain struck we laughed and talked
  And emptied many a can;
And O! but she had stories
  Though not for the priest's ear,
To keep the soul of man alive,
  Banish age and care,
And being old she put a skin
  On everything she said.
What shall I do for pretty girls
  Now my old bawd is dead?

III

The priests have got a book that says
  But for Adam's sin
Eden's Garden would be there
  And I there within.
No expectation fails there,
  No pleasing habit ends,
No man grows old, no girl grows cold,
  But friends walk by friends.
Who quarrels over halfpennies
  That plucks the trees for bread?
What shall I do for pretty girls
  Now my old bawd is dead?

[July 1938]   1938

High Talk

Processions that lack high stilts have nothing that catches
  the eye.
What if my great-granddad had a pair that were twenty foot
  high,
And mine were but fifteen foot, no modern stalks upon
  higher,
Some rogue of the world stole them to patch up a fence or
  a fire.

Because piebald ponies, led bears, caged lions, make but
  poor shows,
Because children demand Daddy-long-legs upon his timber
  toes,
Because women in the upper stories demand a face at the
  pane
That patching old heels they may shriek, I take to chisel and
  plane.

Malachi Stilt-Jack am I, whatever I learned has run wild,
From collar to collar, from stilt to stilt, from father to child.

All metaphor, Malachi, stilts and all. A barnacle goose
Far up in the stretches of night; night splits and the dawn breaks loose;
I, through the terrible novelty of light, stalk on, stalk on;
Those great sea-horses bare their teeth and laugh at the dawn.

[July–August 1938] 1938

The Apparitions

Because there is safety in derision
I talked about an apparition,
I took no trouble to convince,
Or seem plausible to a man of sense,
Distrustful of that popular eye
Whether it be bold or sly.
Fifteen apparitions have I seen;
The worst a coat upon a coat-hanger.

I have found nothing half so good
As my long-planned half solitude,
Where I can sit up half the night
With some friend that has the wit
Not to allow his looks to tell
When I am unintelligible.
Fifteen apparitions have I seen;
The worst a coat upon a coat-hanger.

When a man grows old his joy
Grows more deep day after day,
His empty heart is full at length
But he has need of all that strength
Because of the increasing Night
That opens her mystery and fright.
Fifteen apparitions have I seen;
The worst a coat upon a coat-hanger.

[March–April 1938] 1938

A Nativity

What woman hugs her infant there?
Another star has shot an ear.

What made the drapery glisten so?
Not a man but Delacroix.

What made the ceiling waterproof?
Landor's tarpaulin on the roof.

What brushes fly and moth aside?
Irving and his plume of pride.

What hurries out the knave and dolt?
Talma and his thunderbolt.

Why is the woman terror-struck?
Can there be mercy in that look?

[August 1936] 1938

Man and the Echo

Man

In a cleft that's christened Alt
Under broken stone I halt
At the bottom of a pit
That broad noon has never lit,
And shout a secret to the stone.
All that I have said and done,
Now that I am old and ill,
Turns into a question till
I lie awake night after night
And never get the answers right.
Did that play of mine send out
Certain men the English shot?
Did words of mine put too great strain
On that woman's reeling brain?
Could my spoken words have checked
That whereby a house lay wrecked?

And all seems evil until I
Sleepless would lie down and die.

Echo

Lie down and die.

Man

That were to shirk
The spiritual intellect's great work
And shirk it in vain. There is no release
In a bodkin or disease,
Nor can there be a work so great
As that which cleans man's dirty slate.
While man can still his body keep
Wine or love drug him to sleep,
Waking he thanks the Lord that he
Has body and its stupidity,
But body gone he sleeps no more
And till his intellect grows sure
That all's arranged in one clear view
Pursues the thoughts that I pursue,
Then stands in judgment on his soul,
And, all work done, dismisses all
Out of intellect and sight
And sinks at last into the night.

Echo

Into the night.

Man

O rocky voice
Shall we in that great night rejoice?
What do we know but that we face
One another in this place?
But hush, for I have lost the theme,
Its joy or night seem but a dream;
Up there some hawk or owl has struck
Dropping out of sky or rock,
A stricken rabbit is crying out
And its cry distracts my thought.

[July-October 1938] 1939

The Circus Animals' Desertion

I

I sought a theme and sought for it in vain,
I sought it daily for six weeks or so.
Maybe at last being but a broken man
I must be satisfied with my heart, although
Winter and summer till old age began
My circus animals were all on show,
Those stilted boys, that burnished chariot,
Lion and woman and the Lord knows what.

II

What can I but enumerate old themes,
First that sea-rider Oisin led by the nose
Through three enchanted islands, allegorical dreams,
Vain gaiety, vain battle, vain repose,
Themes of the embittered heart, or so it seems,
That might adorn old songs or courtly shows;
But what cared I that set him on to ride,
I, starved for the bosom of his fairy bride.

And then a counter-truth filled out its play,
The Countess Cathleen was the name I gave it,
She, pity-crazed, had given her soul away
But masterful Heaven had intervened to save it.
I thought my dear must her own soul destroy
So did fanaticism and hate enslave it,
And this brought forth a dream and soon enough
This dream itself had all my thought and love.

And when the Fool and Blind Man stole the bread
Cuchulain fought the ungovernable sea;
Heart mysteries there, and yet when all is said
It was the dream itself enchanted me:
Character isolated by a deed
To engross the present and dominate memory.
Players and painted stage took all my love
And not those things that they were emblems of.

III

Those masterful images because complete
Grew in pure mind but out of what began?
A mound of refuse or the sweepings of a street,
Old kettles, old bottles, and a broken can,
Old iron, old bones, old rags, that raving slut
Who keeps the till. Now that my ladder's gone
I must lie down where all the ladders start
In the foul rag and bone shop of the heart.

[November 1937–September 1938]   1939

Politics

'In our time the destiny of man presents its meanings in political terms.' – Thomas Mann

How can I, that girl standing there,
My attention fix
On Roman or on Russian
Or on Spanish politics,
Yet here's a travelled man that knows
What he talks about,
And there's a politician
That has both read and thought,
And maybe what they say is true
Of war and war's alarms,
But O that I were young again
And held her in my arms.

[23 May 1938]   1939

NOTES

THE WANDERINGS OF OISIN (1889)

This long poem was Yeats's first important success – Oscar Wilde, one of its earliest reviewers, praised its 'nobility of treatment and nobility of subject matter, delicacy of poetic instinct, and richness of imaginative resource' (*The Artist as Critic*, ed. Ellmann, p. 150). Yeats was not to become a distinguished narrative poet – he tended to rely on an abundance of cunningly contrived tropes and pictures, all presented at about the same speed, where a more economical poet, like Chaucer or William Morris, would offer swift summary gestures and a better control of pace. Kinesthetic precision, fascination with weapons, tools, and other action-helpers, sympathy for muscular strain, were all missing from Yeats's armamentarium. As Wilde noted, the reader becomes exasperated by Yeats's interest in '"out-glittering" Keats'. In addition, the characters in his narrative poems are often figments of various extreme passions, trying to escape from the confines of a human identity – for example, not one of these personages has a sense of humour. But in this poem Yeats succeeded by confining the narrative elements to a kind of frame: the hero gallops over the sea to three islands, each a flat picture, a domain of suspended animation, where the action slows to zero or mechanically repeats itself – a lyric parody of narrative. Yeats never again found a plot for a narrative poem that lent itself so well to his gifts.

The sources of the fable were mixed. The opening of the poem was based (as Yeats noted) on 'The Lay of Oisin in the Land of Youth' by Michael Comyn (Mícheál Coimín), a 'half-forgotten' Gaelic poet; the closing of the poem was based on ancient dialogues of Oisin and Patrick (*Transactions of the Ossianic Society*, 1854–63); 'The pages dealing with the three islands . . . are wholly my own, having no further root in tradition than the Irish peasant's notion that *Tir-u-au-oge* (the Country of the Young) is made up of three phantom islands' (*L* I, pp. 176–77). (Yeats knew little Gaelic and read all these poems in translation. For a learned discussion of the Gaelic sources, see James Blake's article, in *Anglo-Irish and Irish Literature* [Uppsala, 1988]: 39–48.) Comyn's lay told how Oisin and Niamh voyaged to one island, where

Oisin killed a queen-imprisoning giant; then they reached their destination, the Country of the Young, the blessed isle, where they settled down and had three children; at last Oisin grew homesick and returned to Ireland. Yeats's islands are far more gaudy, hallucinatory, and sterile; each is a plausible and specious paradise, and yet each finally famishes what it purports to satisfy, and must be rejected.

The influence of Tennyson is probably as important as that of Comyn and the old dialogues of Oisin and Patrick. Tennyson's 'The Palace of Art' (1832) showed how the artist's soul is driven mad by its desire to immure itself in a prison of beautiful images; and his 'The Voyage of Maeldune' (1880) – based on old Irish sources – told of a legendary Irish warrior who sailed to ten islands, each of which seemed to promise at first bliss and at last death. (This poem is a kind of sequel to 'The Lotos-Eaters' [1832]; the 1889 text of Yeats's poem also seems to allude to 'The Lotos-Eaters' when Niamh speaks of the 'poppy-hung house of the twilight' [*VP*, p. 8].) The Silent Isle, the Isle of Shouting, the Isle of Fruits, the Isle of Witches – each gluts some desire so thoroughly that there arises anomie, violence, or morbid torpor. Yeats's poem is similar in that each of Oisin's three islands extrapolates some normal desire – sex, aggression, sleep – into some monstrous failed dream of all-embracing fulfilment. Instead of imagining one coherent heaven, Yeats, like Tennyson, shattered his *locus amoenus* into sinister demi-paradises, reflecting the fact that human desires have no single goal: 'There are three incompatable things which man is always seeking – infinite feeling, infinite battle, infinite repose – hence the three islands' (*L* I, p. 141). For Tennyson as for Yeats, the healthiest desire seems to be the desire to wake up, to escape from fantasy: both Maeldune and Oisin end their voyages back in Ireland.

The themes and characters of *The Wanderings of Oisin* persisted in Yeats's imagination until the end of his life. The confrontation of the pagan hero and the Christian saint remained his central dialectic: the conflict between the *primary* (servile, obedient, democratic, Christian) and the *antithetical* (creative, noble, hierarchical, pagan). (All this is spelled out in *A Vision* – see Introduction XI.) Yeats's sympathies were, of course, for the *antithetical*. Oisin's denunciations of Patrick may recall Nietzsche's analysis of Christianity as a religion fit for slaves; but the young Yeats's anti-Christian rhetoric came not from Nietzsche but from his mythological sources – and from Swinburne (see the note to II 134). And yet, it is finally the antinomy that Yeats celebrates, not one side or the other.

The interminability of the dialogue between Yeats's inner Oisin and his inner Patrick is shown in a letter of 1932, summarizing his poem 'Vacillation': 'The swordsman throughout repudiates the saint, but not without vacillation. Is that perhaps the sole theme – Usheen and Patrick' (*L*, p. 798). Yeats also continued to be fascinated with the poem's construction of artificial paradises. In one of his last poems, 'News for the Delphic Oracle', Yeats lampooned

Oisin and 'Man-picker' Niamh as 'golden codgers', and deposited them on a fourth island, a preposterous and unstable heaven that falls apart as the poem proceeds. Even when he was young, Yeats feared that, in *The Wanderings of Oisin*, 'perhaps only shaddows have got them selves onto paper . . the whole poem is full of symbols – if it be full of aught but clowds' (*L* I, p. 98). But the success of the poem lies in its power to dispel shadows, to undo seductive false worlds. If, as Auden said, the purpose of poetry is 'to disenchant and disintoxicate', then *The Wanderings of Oisin* is Yeats's fullest, most comprehensive poem.

The text was substantially revised in 1895.

Epigraph: neither Tulka nor his prayer (probably invented by Yeats) has been satisfactorily identified. *The Wanderings of Oisin* may be regarded as a series of three asylums, each seeming to embody and defend a different affection – 'Vain gaiety, vain battle, vain repose', according to 'The Circus Animals' Desertion' II 4.

Dedication: Edwin J. Ellis (1848–1916) was a minor poet and artist; he collaborated with Yeats in the editing of a three-volume *Works of William Blake*, published 1893.

I 1 S. Patrick: cleric (385–465) who helped to Christianize Ireland.

I 5 Oisin: 'The poet of the Fenian cycle of legend, as Fergus was the poet of the Red Branch cycle' (*VP*, p. 796). These two cycles contain most of the ancient Irish legends; the Red Branch heroes (of which Cuchulain was the most important) supposedly flourished about two hundred years before the Fenians. The Gaelic name *Oisín* was anglicized into *Ossian*, whose adventures were retold in MacPherson's popular forgery in the eighteenth century. Yeats was pleased when an acquaintance said that his Oisin better expressed the 'mingled nobility and savagery' of the ancient heroes than MacPherson's Ossian (*L* I, p. 141).

I 13 *Caoilte*: a hero who, in 'The Secret Rose', l. 16, 'drove the gods out of their liss'; he also appears in 'The Hosting of the Sidhe', l. 3. See also I 43.

I 13 *Conan*: 'The Thersites of the Fenian cycle' (*VP*, p. 795). Thersites was the misshapen slanderer in Shakespeare's *Troilus and Cressida*. In *Diarmuid and Grania* (1901), a collaboration between Yeats and George Moore, Conan's 'bitter tongue' (I 366) calls Diarmuid a coward (II 526) and helps to provoke the hero's death.

I 13 *Finn*: Fionn Mac Cumhaill (Finn Mac Cool), Oisin's father, 'chief of the heroes of Ireland in his time' (*VP*, p. 795).

I 15 *Bran, Sceolan, Lomair*: as Finneran notes (*PNE*, p. 681), Bran and

Sceolan were cousins of Finn turned into dogs; Lomair was another dog. The same three dogs yelp in *Diarmuid and Grania* III 382–84. Yeats quoted an ancient description of Bran's markings ('Yellow feet had Bran, and red ears') in *LNI*, p. 109.

I 16 *the Firbolgs*: 'An early race who warred vainly upon the Fomorians, or Fomoroh [spirits of darkness, bestial and deformed], before the coming of the Tuath de Danaan [spirits of light, the old gods]. Certain Firbolg kings ... are supposed to be buried at Ballisodare. It is by their graves that Usheen and his companions rode' (*VP*, p. 795).

I 18 *Maeve*: 'A famous queen of the Red Branch cycle. She is rumored to be buried under the cairn [great heap of stones] on Knocknarea [a mountain overlooking Sligo]' (*VP*, p. 796); her cairn reappears at III 184. Yeats identified her with the Queen Mab of *Romeo and Juliet* I iv (*JSD*, p. 110). Maeve is the subject of *The Old Age of Queen Maeve*; and in *The Countess Cathleen* (in the 1912 revision) the poet Aleel tells of Maeve's tears at forgetting the name of a mortal who loved her (l. 301). Maeve is an important off-stage presence in Yeats's Cuchulain cycle: in *On Baile's Strand* (1904), l. 222, Cuchulain announces that he long ago drove away 'Maeve of Cruachan and the northern pirates', but she remains a menace: Cuchulain suspects her of conspiring against him (*On Baile's Strand*, l. 760); Emer tries to rouse Cuchulain from magic sleep by telling him that Maeve is attacking (*Fighting the Waves* [1929], l. 106); and, when her invasion at last takes place, Cuchulain is mortally wounded by Maeve's children and her 'latest lover' (*The Death of Cuchulain* [1939], l. 188). At l. 40 of this last play we also learn that Maeve, once pretty, has changed, and now has 'an eye in the middle of her forehead'. See also 'Red Hanrahan's Song about Ireland', l. 7, and 'The Hour Before Dawn', l. 8.

I 19–20 *dove-grey ... pearl-pale*: in 1913 Ezra Pound advised poets: 'Don't ... mop up the particular decorative vocabulary of some one or two poets whom you happen to admire. A Turkish war correspondent was recently caught red-handed babbling in his despatches of "dove-grey" hills, or else it was "pearl-pale"' (*Literary Essays*, p. 5).

I 21 *findrinny*: 'A kind of red bronze ... A kind of white bronze' (*VP*, p. 795). *White* is better Gaelic.

I 41 *Oscar's pencilled urn*: in some myths Oisin had a son named Oscar, though Yeats does not mention that his Oisin has children; see also the notes to I 43 and III 195. Yeats quoted with approval the words of Oscar 'dying the proud death of a young man' in *Ex*, pp. 22, 28. Jeffares notes (*NCP*, p. 431) that the 'pencilled urn' is taken from the end of Sir Samuel Ferguson's 'Aideen's Grave': 'A cup of bodkin pencill'd clay / Holds Oscar'. Yeats quoted some lines from Ferguson's poem in an early review (*UP* I, p. 102).

I 43 *Gabhra*: 'The great battle [AD 297] in which the power of the Fenians was broken' (*VP*, p. 795). Oisin leaves Ireland for his imaginary islands at the exact moment when his culture starts its decline. In *Diarmuid and Grania* III 400–5, Finn prophesies: 'The deaths of everyone of us and the end of the Fianna have been foretold. Many will die in a great battle, Oscar who is but a child will die in it, but I shall die long after by a spear thrust, and Diarmuid by the tusk of a boar, and Usheen will go far away, and Caoelte storm the house of the gods at Assaroe'.

I 47 *Aengus*: 'The god of youth, beauty, and poetry. He reigned in Tir-nan-Oge, the country of the young' (*VP*, p. 794); 'the old Irish god of love and poetry and ecstasy, who changed four of his kisses into birds' (*M*, p. 115); 'Aengus is the most curious of all the gods. He seems both Hermes and Dionysus. He has some part perhaps in all enthusiasm' (*L*, p. 324). In *The Old Age of Queen Maeve*, l. 85, Aengus asks Maeve's assistance in consummating his love; in *Baile and Aillinn*, l. 182, 'Aengus, the Master of Love', causes the death of the two noble lovers so that they might be happy with him, in the land of the dead; in *The King of the Great Clock Tower* (1935), l. 79, a vision of Aengus fatally incites a vulgar poet to approach a queen. Similarly in *Diarmuid and Grania* (1901) Aengus drives the boar that will kill Diarmuid (II 298, III 20); and his harp-playing conducts Diarmuid's soul away (III 423). Aengus resembles Hermes not only as psychopomp but also as trickster: in 'The Crucifixion of the Outcast', a pagan gleeman says that he learned his juggling from 'Aengus the Subtle-hearted' (*M*, p. 154). Aengus also appears in 'The Song of Wandering Aengus', 'Under the Moon', l. 8, 'The Harp of Aengus', l. 2, and *The Shadowy Waters*, ll. 42, 138, 196, and 469. He was sometimes depicted with a halo of birds – 'he had birds about his head' (*The Countess Cathleen* [from 1895 on], l. 460); 'one / About whose face birds wagged their fiery wings' (*The Old Age of Queen Maeve*, ll. 144–45); and a draft of *The Shadowy Waters* speaks of a sailor 'deafened by the birds that Angus made / Out of the kisses of his musical lips' (*DC*, p. 186).

I 47 *Edain*: 'a famous legendary queen who went away and lived among the Shee [Sidhe, the pagan gods]' (*VP*, p. 794). In *The Land of Heart's Desire* (1894), ll. 44–48, an imaginative girl sings 'How a Princess Edain ... heard / A voice singing on May Eve like this, / And followed, half awake and half asleep, / Until she came into the Land of Faery'; Edain herself sings a song about immoderate yearning in *Deirdre* (1907), ll. 121–48. Yeats wrote of the harp she wove of her own hair in *Baile and Aillinn*, l. 142, and 'The Harp of Aengus' – for her adventures as a fly, see the notes to those poems. She is also the aggressively human heroine of 'The Two Kings'. Yeats sometimes saw visions of Edain between waking and sleeping: 'once a fair woman who said she was Aedain, and both man and woman ... I noticed that once the excitement of the genital ceased, a visionary form, that of Aedain, approached'

(*Mem*, pp. 127–28); see also *VP*, p. 817.

I 48 *Niamh*: 'a beautiful woman of the Tribes of Danu [that is, a goddess], that led Oisin to the Country of the Young, as their country is called' (*VP*, p 801); 'daughter of the King / Of the Young' (*VP*, p. 5). Her ancestry in Yeats's poem, however, is less Irish pagan than English Romantic: as a seductress who enthralls a sensitive man in the coils of impoverishing fantasy she recalls Keats's Lamia and Belle Dame sans Merci; as the bringer of oblivion she recalls the spirit in Shelley's *The Triumph of Life* who effaces the mind of Rousseau; as the genius of an island of sexual languor she recalls Spenser's Phaedria and Acrasia; as the genius of a realm of perpetual sleep she recalls Tennyson's Vivien. Niamh will make a more desperate appeal to the senses in 'The Hosting of the Sidhe', l. 4; she will glimmer for a moment in the lists of fabulous creatures in 'The Lover asks Forgiveness ...', l. 13, and in 'Under the Moon', l. 12; and near the end of his life Yeats will announce that he himself was starved for Niamh's bosom ('The Circus Animals' Desertion' II 8).

I 63 *Danaan*: 'Tuath De Danaan means the Race of the Gods of Dana. Dana was the mother of all the ancient gods of Ireland. They were the powers of light and life and warmth, and did battle with the Fomoroh, or powers of night and death and cold. Robbed of offerings and honour, they have gradually dwindled in the popular imagination until they have become the Faeries' (*VP*, p. 796).

I 64 *Rhymes that rhymed on Oisin's name*: a hint that somewhere behind Yeats's text is a divine text – Yeats later wrote that great poems preexist in the *Anima Mundi* before their authors are born.

I 73 *gulph of love*: compare 'Parting', ll. 13–14: 'I offer to love's play / My dark declivities'.

I 84 *Where broken faith has never been known*: compare *The Only Jealousy of Emer* (1919), l. 282: 'Where no one speaks of broken troth'.

I 85 *the blushes of first love have never flown*: this suspension of incipience recalls Keats's 'Ode on a Grecian Urn', ll. 19–20: 'She cannot fade ... Forever wilt thou love, and she be fair!'

I 126 *Where are you*: the elegiac *ubi sunt* – compare 'Nineteen Hundred and Nineteen' V 15 and 'The Curse of Cromwell', l. 4. Also see III 195: 'What place have Caoilte and Conan, and Bran, Sceolan, Lomair?'

I 136–38 *laughter, unhuman sound ... my human sorrow*: the identification of sorrow as the defining human trait persists through the poem. At I 34 Niamh is puzzled by the sadness of the heroes; at I 241 the dancers find Oisin's songs of human joy so disturbingly melancholy that they throw his harp into a puddle; when Oisin sees a fragment of a lance (I 380–81) 'His eyes grow dim / With all the ancient sorrow of men'; and at the climax, when Oisin decides to return to Ireland, Niamh murmurs 'there moves alive in your fingers the fluttering sadness of earth' (III 124). Indeed Oisin seems to infect Niamh with his sorrow: at the beginning she is full of inhuman laughter, but by II 18–19 'the fall of tears / Troubled her song'; at II 250 she lays her weeping head on Oisin's bosom; the voyage to the third island is accompanied by Niamh's 'sliding of tears' (III 7); and finally she moans like any abandoned human girl (III 130), when Oisin departs for Ireland.

I 139–45 *a hornless deer ... a phantom hound ... a lady ... a beautiful young man*: Oisin meets these phantoms at the beginning of each sea-voyage (compare II 4 and III 3); Yeats took them directly from Comyn's lay: 'We saw also, by our sides / A hornless fawn leaping nimbly, / And a red-eared white dog, / Urging it boldly in the chase. // We beheld also, without fiction, // A young maid on a brown steed, / A golden apple in her right hand, / And she going on the top of the waves. // We saw after her, / A young rider on a white steed' (O'Looney's translation, *Transactions of the Ossianic Society* 4: 249). Yeats explained the meaning of these haunting figures: 'This hound and this deer seem plain images of the desire of the man "which is for the woman", and "the desire of the woman which is for the desire of the man", and of all desires that are as these. I have read them in this way in *The Wanderings of Oisin*, and have made my lover sigh because he has seen in their faces "the immortal desire of Immortals" [III 4] ... A solar mythologist would perhaps say that the girl with the golden apple was once the winter, or night, carrying the sun away, and the deer without horns ... darkness flying the light' (*VP*, p. 807). In the early version of *The Shadowy Waters* (1900), ll. 325–34, Dectora, peering out over the ocean, cries, 'A red-eared hound follows a hornless deer. / There! There!'; and Forgael explains that 'They lure us to the streams where the world ends' (*VP*, p. 764). (In earlier drafts the phantoms seemed slightly vicious: Forgael saw them and said, 'I am blinded by the foam of dreams' [*DC*, p. 185] – and the poet called them 'images of doom' [*DC*, p. 192], spoiling Forgael's hopes.)

Comyn's phantoms, then, are emblems of the insatiable desire that drives the universe as well as human beings. When they reappear in Yeats's later work, they become less beautiful and nonchalant, more strenuous and pained. In 'He Mourns for the Change ...', the hero himself becomes 'a hound with one red ear', relentlessly driven on a hunt until the end of time. In a discussion of the woman who obliterates Rousseau in Shelley's *The Triumph of Life*, Yeats comments that a wolf would be a better, 'more violent symbol of longing and desire' than Comyn's hound: 'his [Shelley's] wolf and deer remind me of the hound and deer that Oisin saw in the Gaelic poem chasing one another on the water ... and of a Galway tale that tells how Niamh, whose name means brightness or beauty, came to Oisin as a deer' (*EI*, p. 90). In *The King of the Great Clock Tower* (1935), ll. 10–13, the phantoms make their final, most anxious appearance: 'For there the hound that Oisin saw pursues / The hornless deer that runs in such a fright; / And there the woman clasps an apple tight / For all the clamour of a famished man'.

I 140–41 *a phantom hound / All pearly white, save one red ear*: compare the hellish dogs in *The Old Age of Queen Maeve*, ll. 117-19: 'red-eared hounds / With long white bodies ... ran at them and harried them'.

I 156 *Almhuin*: the Hill of Allen, where Finn's palace sat. Yeats recorded a journey he made to this hill in *Ex*, p. 14. In *The King's Threshold* (1904), the starving poet wakes from a vision: 'I was but now / In Almhuin, in a great high-raftered house, / With Finn and Osgar' (ll. 93–95).

I 160–62 *a trumpet-twisted shell ... Dreaming of her own melting hues*: this self-absorbed shell may be compared to the narcissistic birds of I 182–87. For Yeats's use of shells, see the note to 'The Song of the Happy Shepherd', l. 36: 'twisted, echo-harbouring shell'. For other images of nature's reflexivity, see the juvenile *The Island of Statues* I i 130–31: 'a lonely fountain sings, / And there to its own heart for ever moans'; and I ii 12: 'The whole world's sadly talking to itself' (*VP*, pp. 650, 652).

I 171 *Like sooty fingers, many a tree*: compare 'The Tower' II 3: 'Tree, like a sooty finger'.

I 176 *low laughing woodland rhyme*: compare an early draft of *The Shadowy Waters*, where a sailor wishes for a 'low laughing harp' (*DC*, p. 134).

I 183 *frozen rainbow light*: compare the deleted 'Street Dancers', l. 33: 'liquid rainbow light' (*VP*, p. 732).

I 184–85 *pondered in a soft vain mood / Upon their shadows in the tide*: a hint of the narcissism and self-infatuation of all the residents of the Island of Dancing – where all life has dwindled to a kind of water-reflection, hypnotic but unreal. For other birds bemused by their images in water, see the note to 'The Indian to His Love', l. 5. In *The Old Age of Queen Maeve*, a mortal woman remarks of the gods, 'their beauty's like a hollow dream, / Mirrored in [untroubled] streams' (ll. 88–89). Also compare Shelley's Witch of Atlas, who sees in the waters of Lake Mareotis 'all human life shadowed upon its waters in shadows that "never are erased but tremble ever" ['The Witch of Atlas' (1820) LIX 3]' (*EI*, p. 85).

I 206 *trimmed with many a crimson feather*: the birdlikeness of the dancers on the first island, and of the sleepers on the third (III 34), anticipates the many metamorphoses of man into bird in Yeats's later work – see the note to 'The Three Hermits'.

I 219 *A Druid dream of the end of days*: Yeats often attributed to the immortals a morbid preoccupation with the end of time. Compare I 246, I 425–27, and II 239.

I 241–42 *weeping over the white strings, hurled / It down*: the harp seems to stand not only for Oisin's art, but also for his whole apparatus of human feeling – after the harp's burial, Oisin is depersonalized, able to join the dim chorus of dancers.

I 249 *A house of wattles, clay*: compare 'The Lake Isle of Innisfree', l. 2: 'of clay and wattles made'.

I 252–54 *Wild flames … Like to a merry wandering rout / Of dancers*: this simile raises the possibility that the island's inhabitants are nothing more than projections of Aengus' dreams.

I 261–68 *Joy … wakes the sluggard seeds of corn … And makes the infant ferns unwrap*: Aengus' praise of joy as a force of universal generation ill comports with the seeming sterility of the Island of Dancing.

I 279 *the moon's pale twisted shell*: compare III 103: 'a moon waking white as a shell'; and 'Adam's Curse', ll. 31–32: 'A moon, worn as if it had been a shell'. The other major moon-simile in this poem is a rose (I 152, 427).

I 280 *now hearts cry that hearts are slaves*: a somewhat Blakean myth of man's fall from spontaneity into law-riddenness.

I 286 *joy is God and God is joy*: compare *The Land of Heart's Desire* (1894), l. 375: 'joy is wisdom, time an endless song'; and a deleted passage from the 1902 version of *Where There is Nothing* IV ii: 'God is joy, and will accomplish all joyful things' (*VPl*, p. 1126).

I 291 *We mocked at Time and Fate and Chance*: compare 'He mourns for the Change …', l. 9: 'Time and Birth and Change are hurrying by'; *The Countess Cathleen* (1892), l. 920: 'curses on you, Time and Fate and Change'; and *The Land of Heart's Desire*, l. 164: 'bidding Fate and Time and Change good-bye'. Shelley offers similar lists (e.g., *Prometheus Unbound* II ii 92, II iv 119).

I 329–31 *You stars … you slaves of God*: this God seems to resemble Patrick's God, or Blake's Urizen, more than the God earlier identified with joy.

I 332 *He rules you with an iron rod*: compare Tennyson, *Maud* (1855) I XVIII iv 8–9: 'A sad astrology … makes you tyrants in your iron skies'.

I 336 *Like bubbles in a frozen pond*: compare *A Vision* (1925), p. 213: 'The decadence … [that] awaits us, being democratic and *primary*, may suggest bubbles in a frozen pond – mathematical Babylonian starlight'. For the rigid Newtonian model of the heavens, see 'The Song of the Happy Shepherd', l. 28.

I 359: *The things that most of all I hate*: an echo of the lamentation of Llywarch Hen, quoted by Matthew Arnold and Yeats as a type of the Celtic (or primitive) melancholy: 'The four things I have all my life most hated fall upon me together – coughing and old age, sickness and sorrow' (*EI*, p. 183).

I 367 *broken lance*: the first two of Oisin's three adventures in unreality end with a call from some worldly object charged with emotion – see II 226. The hundred-years' dream is not quite impermeable from Ireland. Compare the trumpet call that summons Lycius from his voluptuous and unsociable dream in Keats's *Lamia* (1820) II 28.

I 400 *An old man*: the dancers of the first island imagine a surprisingly detailed picture of old age and death: an old man, an old hare (I 410), a dead kingfisher (I 422). The ordinary conditions of mortality grow increasingly visible as the film of fantasy thins and breaks. Tennyson's 'The Lotos-Eaters' similarly ends with a choral song in which those immune from suffering gloat over human misery.

I 412 *The hare ... limps along in an aged whiteness*: compare 'Ephemera', l. 15: 'A rabbit old and lame limped down the path'.

II: Yeats told Katharine Tynan that in this unusual fable – a romance of St George and the dragon, repeated as if on an endless loop of videotape – 'under disguise of symbolism I have said severel things, to which I only have the key' (*L* I, p. 98). Yeats seems never to have revealed the key, but in a corresponding passage in 'Michael Robartes and the Dancer', ll. 1–12, Yeats explained a knight's endless combat with a dragon as an allegory of a lover's struggle with his beloved's opinionated mind. If *The Wanderings of Oisin* II is also a psychomachia, a battle of the soul's internal faculties, then it may represent a struggle for self-control, always repeated because it lacks any real object to exercise itself upon.

II 36 *Dark statues*: these two statues, one abstract, astronomical, pertinent to eternity, the other as animate as a statue can be, fascinated by the minute particulars of flux, represent the will to escape from mortality and the will to participate in it – the urges that govern Oisin. They anticipate the dialectics of Yeats's later poetry – compare 'A Dialogue of Self and Soul'. The contrast between the statues follows Pater's analysis, in 'Luca della Robbia', of the contrast between the sculpture of Phidias and that of the della Robbias: the former inexpressive, permanent, monumental, the latter subtle, shaded, psychologically refined.

II 39 *stilly jet*: compare 'A cloven, dancing jet', from another poem about contrasting allegorical figments (the deleted 'Love and Death', l. 2 [*VP*, p. 680]).

II 41: In 1889 this line began, 'He seemed the watcher for a sign'.

II 42–3 *Stretched his long arm to where ... The stream churned*: compare Tennyson's description of a statue of the Lady of the Lake: 'her great and goodly arms / Stretched under all the cornice ... And drops of water fell' ('Gareth and Lynette' [1872], ll. 214–16).

II 57–58 *O sigh ... Flutter along the froth of the sea*: a version of the

Correspondent Breeze of Romantic poetry. Note that the sigh, like the wooden lance (I 367) and beech-bough (II 226) that summon Oisin, seems capable of crossing the boundary between Ireland and the islands.

II 68 *The saddest of all men*: the sweetheart of the Damsel in Distress.

II 74 *two old eagles*: the 1889 text specified that the eagles were a hundred years old, suggesting that they may represent a latent senility as Oisin wastes another hundred years of his life in dreams. Images hinting at decrepitude and decay can be found on all three islands.

II 84 *Seven Hazel Trees*: 'There was once a well overshadowed by seven sacred hazel-trees, in the midst of Ireland. A certain lady plucked their fruit, and seven rivers arose out of the well and swept her away. In my poems this well is the source of all the waters of this world, which are therefore sevenfold [as at III 52]' (*VP*, p. 796). In a note to 'He thinks of his Past Greatness . . .' Yeats wrote that 'The hazel tree was the Irish tree of Life or of Knowledge' (*VP*, p. 177). Well and hazel tree are the chief stage-props of *At the Hawk's Well* (1917).

II 87 *Aedh*: 'A God of death. All who hear his harp playing die. He was one of the two gods who appeared to Cuchoollin before his death, according to the bardic tale' (*VP*, p. 794). A less sinister Aedh was a major persona in *The Wind among the Reeds* – see the headnote to that volume. In *The Herne's Egg* (1938), Aedh is the name of the King of Tara, killed by a blow from a table-leg.

II 95–96 *no mightier soul . . . Now it is old and mouse-like*: compare the demon's speech at II 235: 'I hear my soul drop down into decay' Also compare an early draft of *The Shadowy Waters*, where a belligerent sailor complains, 'my heart turns into a trembling mouse' (*DC*, p. 135).

II 95 *Heber*: 'Heber and Heremon were the ancestors of the merely human inhabitants of Ireland' (*VP*, p. 795). Heber was, according to legend, one of the Milesians – early invaders of Ireland.

II 97 *I burst the chain: still earless, nerveless, blind*: action in fantasy can have no real consequences – the severing of the chain seems only a parody of a decisive gesture.

II 128 *Ogham*: an antique Irish alphabet.

II 128 *Manannan*: 'the sea-god . . . a son of Lir, the infinite waters' (*VP*, p. 796); he 'reigned over the country of the dead . . . the horses of Mannannan, though they could cross the land as easily as the sea, are constantly associated with waves' (*VP*, p. 808; compare *The Only Jealousy of Emer* [1919], ll. 89, 111). Manannan acts behind the scenes throughout Yeats's Cuchulain cycle: Cuchulain calls him an 'old juggler' in *The Green Helmet* (1910), l. 117; according to the 1903 version of *On Baile's Strand*, Manannan, a friend of Cuchulain's father, gave Cuchulain a cloak (*VPl*, pp. 494, 542); in early versions of *The Only Jealousy of Emer* Manannan dreams over his chessboard and judges the disputes of sea-gods (*VPl*, pp. 559, 561); Fand, the goddess who seduces Cuchulain, was Manannan's daughter, and wished to bring him to her father's undersea house (*Fighting the Waves* [1929], ll. 201–9). In 'The Book of the Great Dhoul ...' (1897), the Fenians are sent to Hell for worshiping Manannan (*VSR*, p. 186). See also 'Three Songs to the One Burden' I 10.

II 134 *milk-pale face*: that of Christ. These daringly anti-Christian lines were added in 1895. Compare the pagan narrator's admission in Swinburne's 'Hymn to Proserpine' (1866), l. 35: 'Thou hast conquered, O pale Galilean; the world has grown gray with thy breath' – a line that might describe the puny Christian Ireland of part III of this poem.

II 145–46 *shadowy face flowed into shadowy face, / Looked down on me*: compare the 'long generations of eyes' at III 40.

II 172 *noon to night gave way*: compare the juvenile *The Island of Statues* I i 158–62: 'To prove his love a knight with lance in rest / Will circle round the world upon a quest, / Until afar appear the gleaming dragon-scales: / From morn the twain until the evening pales / Will struggle' (*VP*, p. 651).

II 175–79 *many shapes ... a great eel ... A fir-tree ... a drowned dripping body*: compare 'Fergus and the Druid', ll. 32–38, where Fergus opens a bag of dreams and sees all possible identities: 'I have been many things – / A green drop ... a fir-tree ... An old slave ... / But now I have grown nothing, knowing all'. The fantastic character of the Island of Battles is made explicit by the demon's dream-shiftiness of being; and, as in 'Fergus and the Druid', there is a kind of nullity at the heart – the demon's final avatar is a sailor's drowned body. (Compare the simile of the drowned sailor at III 22.) A battle with an endlessly metamorphosing opponent recalls the legend of Proteus, who tried to evade Menelaus' clutches (according to Homer, Odyssey IV) by turning into a lion, a snake, a panther, a boar, running water, and finally a great tree. See 'At the Abbey Theatre', ll. 11–12: 'Is there a bridle for this Proteus / That turns and changes like his draughty seas?'

II 203–4 *lies / On the anvil of the world*: in an early draft of *The Shadowy Waters*, Forgael kills Dectora's harper and tells Dectora that she will soon love him; Dectora cries out, 'I lie upon the anvil of the world' (*DC*, p. 189).

II 205–6 *with thunder ... God ... speaks His angry mind*: compare 'Crazy Jane Reproved', ll. 2–4: 'All those dreadful thunder-stones ... but show that Heaven yawns'.

II 228–29: in the 1889 text, Oisin recalled, not the cries of bats, but the leaping of hares. The dancers of the first island associated a hare with mutability at I 412; but the bats may provide a better omen of the ghostliness that has overtaken all the Fenians. For other bats, see 'The Phases of the Moon', l. 137.

II 235 *I hear my soul drop down into decay*: compare Oisin's declaration at II 95–96: 'There was no mightier soul ... Now it is old and mouse-like'.

II 238–39 *the moon goad the waters ... That all be overthrown*: 'I remember rejecting, because it spoilt the simplicity, an elaborate metaphor of a breaking wave intended to prove that all life rose and fell as in my poem' (*Ex*, pp. 392–93). Fossils of this rejected metaphor abound throughout the text. The tidal pressure that threatens the island anticipates the floods that menace some of Yeats's later paradises, such as that in 'Byzantium'.

II 249 *the Island of Content*: the 1889 text called this 'the Isle of Youth' – a near-translation of Tír na nÓg, the Country of the Young, the Celtic paradise, 'the Happy Islands where the Gaelic heroes live the lives of Homer's Phaeacians' (*M*, p. 310). In Comyn's lay, Oisin reaches this land; but Yeats was careful to discriminate it from any of Oisin's destinations.

III: Yeats told Katharine Tynan that this section had 'most art', though it was less 'deep and poetic. It is not inspiration that exhausts one, but art' (*L* I, p. 98). Much of its art lies in the metrical scheme, with its haunting repetitions, its long, sinuous lines, its shadowy intricacy of rhythm. The first section is mostly in dancing tetrameter, the second section is mostly in heroic couplets, appropriate to a battle; but here Yeats tried to hypnotize the reader with an exercise in deep breathing, artful monotony – until the final stanzas, where the chant grows emphatic and war-like. It is perhaps unfortunate that Yeats's other narrative poems did not use the flexible, varied metres found here.

III 3 *those that fled, and that followed*: the 1889 text specifies 'The deer and the hound, and the lady and youth'.

III 22 *as drift from a sailor slow drowning the gleams of the world*: this simile is a kind of warning to Oisin, not to fall through the surface-tension of the watery images that constitute the three islands, lest he drown. This simile is anticipated by the demon's metamorphosis into a drowned corpse at II 179; and it is followed by similes suggesting how Oisin is sinking like a stone or foundering in dreams: 'gone like a sea-covered stone / Were the memories of the whole of my sorrow' (III 70–71); 'a long iron sleep, as a fish in the water goes dumb as a stone' (III 96); 'Like me were some galley forsaken far off' (III 117).

III 34 *The tops of their ears were feathered, their hands were the claws of birds*: see the note to I 206. Also compare 'The Old Men Admiring Themselves in the Water', l. 4: 'They had hands like claws'. In the story 'The Wisdom of the King' (1895), the hero has feathers growing from his head instead of hair – see 'Alternative Song for the Severed Head ...', l. 20.

III 39 *the owls had builded their nests in their locks*: 'Once upon a time, when herons built their nests in old men's beards ...' (*VPl*, p. 340; *EI*, p. 101).

Also compare 'Anashuya and Vijaya', l. 71, where 'unnumbered nests' are built in the hair of the gods' parents.

III 40 *generations of eyes*: the carved faces in the dome of Manannan's hall provided a similar delirium of perceivedness (II 144–46). See also III 121–22 and 205.

III 46 *a branch soft-shining with bells*: 'A legendary branch whose shaking cast all men into a gentle sleep' (*VP*, p. 794). See 'The Dedication to a Book of Stories . . .', l. 1; and 'The Harp of Aengus', l. 5.

III 51 *salt eye*: compare 'The Delphic Oracle upon Plotinus', l. 5: 'Salt blood blocks his eyes'.

III 52 *weary with passions that faded when the sevenfold seas were young*: an extrapolation of the mood of such poems as 'Ephemera'. For *sevenfold*, see the note to II 84.

III 53 *Sennachies*: story-tellers.

III 70 *The moil of my centuries filled me*: an illusory anticipation of Oisin's real aging (III 191).

III 80 *the name of the demon*: Culann, a smith. This forgetting is reversed at III 146.

III 80 *Conchubar*: the crafty king in the Red Branch (or Ulster) cycle who tricked Cuchulain, the greatest of heroes, into an oath of fealty (as told in *On Baile's Strand* [1904]); he also commanded the murder of Naoise, the young lover of the beautiful Deirdre (as told in *Deirdre* [1907]) – see the note to III 90. He also appears in 'Fergus and the Druid', l. 10, 'Cuchulain's Fight with the Sea', l. 45, and 'The Secret Rose', l. 9.

III 86 *all who are winter tales*: the Red Branch heroes mentioned below (III 86–92) 'preceded the Finian circle by about two hundred years' (*VPl*, p. 1286) – they were mythological presences even to Oisin. Yeats thought that the Fenians consciously modelled themselves on the Red Branch: 'When the Fenian militia were established in the second century they were no mere defenders of coast-line . . . They wanted to revive the kind of life lived in old days when the Chiefs of the Red Branch gathered round Cuchullin' (*UP* I, p. 164). Curiously, however, in a preface to Lady Gregory's collection of Fenian tales, Yeats wrote that in the legends of the Fenians we recognize 'an older world certainly than we find in the stories of Cuchulain, who lived . . . about the time of the birth of Christ' (*Ex*, p. 15).

III 89 *Blanaid*: 'The heroine of a beautiful and sad story told by Keating' (*VP*, p. 794). Keating's *History of Ireland* told how Blanaid, who loved Cuchulain, conspired with him to kill the warrior Curaoi, who had raped her; Curaoi's harper avenged his master by leaping off a cliff with her.

III 89 *MacNessa*: Conchubar – see III 80.

III 89 *Fergus*: 'He was the poet of the Red Branch cycle, as Oisin was of the Fenian. He was once king of all Ireland, and, as the legend is shaped by [Sir Samuel] Ferguson, gave up his throne that he might live at peace hunting in the woods' (*VP*, p. 795). See 'Fergus and the Druid'; Fergus also appears in 'To the Rose upon the Rood of Time', l. 5, 'Who Goes with Fergus?', 'The Secret Rose', l. 19, and *The Old Age of Queen Maeve*, l. 71 (where Maeve remembers that Fergus was her lover).

III 90 *Barach*: 'Barach enticed Fergus away to a feast, that the sons of Usna [Deirdre's lover Naoise and his brothers] might be killed in his absence. Fergus had made an oath never to refuse a feast from him, and so was compelled to go, though all unwillingly' (*VP*, p. 794).

III 91 *Balor*: 'The Irish Chimaera, the leader of the hosts of darkness at the great battle of good and evil, life and death, light and darkness, which was fought out on the strands of Moytura, near Sligo' (*VP*, p. 794). In *The Countess Cathleen* (from 1895 on), ll. 842–45, Balor is prominent in Aleel's vision of hell: 'The brazen door stands wide, and Balor comes / Borne in his heavy car, and demons have lifted / The age-weary eyelids from the eyes that of old / Turned gods to stone' (also compare *LNI*, p. 178, and *VSR*, p. 198). Petrifaction is something Oisin himself might well fear – compare the stone-similes cited in the note to III 22.

III 93 *the Fenians*: now Oisin starts to dream, not of mythological figures, but of his contemporaries. At the centre of Oisin's third island, dream and reality have traded places: the dream is vibrant, clamorous, human, while the 'reality' is a sodden oblivion. The dream is increasingly pregnant with mortality.

III 94 *Grania*: 'A beautiful woman, who fled with Dermot to escape from the love of aged Finn. She fled from place to place over Ireland, but at last Dermot was killed at Sligo upon the seaward point of Benbulben, and Finn won her love and brought her, leaning upon his neck, into the assembly of the Fenians, who burst into inextinguishable laughter' (*VP*, p. 795). Oisin and Grania are both characters in Yeats's and George Moore's *Diarmuid and Grania* (1901) – in that play, a Druidess shows Grania Oisin's shield, painted with 'a white deer's head', and speaks of Oisin's 'yellow hair' and 'long white hands, with fingers hard at the tips from plucking of harp strings, and they say that no woman has refused him her love' (I 171–74). In *The King's Threshold* (1904), the starving poet has a vision of 'Grania dividing salmon by a stream' (l. 98).

III 94 *sewed with her needle of bone*: tapestry was, for Yeats, a metaphor for poetic composition. He once said of *The Countess Cathleen* that it was no more 'than a piece of tapestry' (*A: DP* 10); and it is possible to take *The Wanderings of Oisin* as a tapestry, too. In the original 1892 text of *The Countess*

Kathleen, ll. 169–172, Kathleen's servant speaks of the hardness of life: 'See you where Oisin and young Niam ride / Wrapped in each other's arms, and where the Finians / Follow their hounds along the fields of tapestry, / How merry they lived once, yet men died then'. Grania's skill at sewing recalls *Diarmuid and Grania* II 325–27, where she speaks of embroidering a cloth on which 'I should have seen birds, beasts, and leaves which ever way I turned, and Diarmuid and myself wandering among them'.

III 134 *Were the winds less soft than the breath of a pigeon who sleeps on her nest*: compare Swinburne, 'Hymn to Proserpine' (1866), l. 25: 'Breasts more soft than a dove's, that tremble with tenderer breath' (from a catalogue of sensuous delights immune from Christ's spoiling).

III 135 *the sea's vague drum*: compare 'A Prayer for my Daughter', l. 15.

III 141–48: these lines replay, in reverse, the opening lines of part III – as if Oisin's horse were stepping backwards down the identical path.

III 146 *my mind made the names of the Fenians*: at III 80 Oisin started to forget names; now he remembers – indeed memory urges him on (III 152).

III 156 *grass-barnacle*: see 'High Talk', l. 11.

III 160 *Rachlin to Bera of ships*: Rathlin, an island off the north coast of Ireland; Beare Island, off the southern coast.

III 164 *a small and a feeble populace*: because Wilde objected to this line (*The Artist as Critic*, ed. Ellmann, p. 151), Yeats changed *populace* to *race*; but then he changed it back.

III 178 *my tears*: 'When Oisin is speaking with Saint Patrick of the friends and the life he has outlived, he can but cry out constantly against a religion that has no meaning for him. He laments, and the country-people have remembered his words for centuries: "I will cry my fill, but not for God, but because Finn and the Fianna are not living"' (*Ex*, p. 24; compare *EI*, pp. 183, 303).

III 179 *Crevroe or broad Knockfefin*: Crevroe (Craobh-ruadh, 'Red Branch') is the building where Conchubar and the Red Branch heroes lived. Knockfefin is unidentified, perhaps the mountain Slievenamon – see 'The Grey Rock', l. 15.

III 195 *What place have Caoilte and Conan*: one answer to this question is found in 'The Book of the Great Dhoul . . .': 'You have heard how the Fianna were sent down into Hell because they were heathens . . . but may be you have not heard that God himself, because He admired the great blows they gave, and the songs and the stories they made, put a circle of smooth green grass all round and about the place for them. They rush in their chariots on that green grass for ever and ever, making the sods fly with the hoofs of the horses; and Oscar, the biggest of them, goes before with a flail, and drives the demons from the road' (*VSR*, p. 186).

III 196 *you too are old with your memories, an old man surrounded with dreams*: this line hints at a sort of intimacy, a near-convergence of the old Christian and the old pagan. Both are beset with fantasies of a surrogate-life, an after-life.

III 197–98 *the flesh of the footsole ... Where the demons whip them*: compare 'the hair of the demons sweep your foot-soles' (*M*, p. 194).

III 198 *the burning stones of wide Hell*: 'In the older Irish books Hell is always cold, and this is probably because the Fomoroh, or evil powers, ruled over the north and the winter. Christianity adopted as far as possible the Pagan symbolism in Ireland as elsewhere, and Irish poets, when they became Christian, did not cease to speak of "the cold flagstone of Hell". The folk-tales ... make use, however, of the ordinary fire symbolism' (*VP*, pp. 795–96).

III 204 *demons be broken in pieces*: Oisin's fantasy of leading a Fenian revolt against the masters of Hell suggests that he has not yet been completely cured of his desire to live in imaginary worlds – 'How hard it was to refrain from pointing out that Oisin after old age, its illumination half accepted, half rejected, would pass in death over another sea to another island' (*Ex*, p. 393). Oisin has half accepted his fate in that he seems to want in Hell little more than what would have been available to him, had he remained in Ireland: 'feast, making converse of wars, and of old wounds, and turn to our rest' (III 212). This semi-barbarized Christian Hell is one version of Oisin's fourth island; for another, see 'News for the Delphic Oracle'.

III 222 *the chain of small stones*: the rosary – Oisin has been converted to Christianity, but here repudiates it.

CROSSWAYS (1889)

Crossways is not the title of a published volume, but a title Yeats used to denominate a section of his collected poems. It consists mostly of *The Wanderings of Oisin and Other Poems* (1889), minus the long title poem, and minus a number of poems Yeats chose to delete from his canon. ('The Ballad of Father O'Hart' and 'The Ballad of the Foxhunter' were added to *Crossways* at a later date). Though its verbal textures show a refined metrical sense, and its images and figures are carefully crafted, *Crossways* has little of the thematic concentration of the later volumes; to read it is to stroll through a Palace of Art decorated with panels of remote and exotic landscapes. As Yeats noted, 'When I first wrote I went here and there for my subjects as my reading led me, and preferred to all other countries Arcadia and India of romance, but presently I convinced myself . . . that I should never go for the scenery of a poem to any country but my own, and I think that I shall hold to that conviction to the end' (*VP*, pp. 843–44).

The personae behind these poems are often diffuse and remote, full of faint but highly saturated, gesticulated passion. The pre-Raphaelite landscapes – richly detailed and shallow – usually are more expressive and energetic than the personages who inhabit them; exhausted, frightened, or unbalanced characters seem unable to place themselves in the tense universe that surrounds them. Yeats's training as a painter is evident here; indeed these lyrics often seem to blur generic boundaries, to aspire to be paintings, or little dramas, or simply the amplified music of nature herself.

Epigraph: from Blake, *The Four Zoas* (1797) IX 653: 'And all Nations were threshed out & the stars threshd from their husks'.

Dedication: AE (from Aeon) was the pen name of George Russell (1867–1935), poet, painter, and editor. Yeats was impressed with his visionary talent, but thought that he was too much concerned with spiritual virtue, too little concerned with craft, to be a great artist. See the notes to 'To a Poet, who would have me Praise . . .' and 'A Dialogue of Self and Soul'.

The Song of the Happy Shepherd

This poem was first entitled, 'An Epilogue To "The Island of Statues" and "The Seeker,"' and captioned, '*Spoken by a Satyr, carrying a sea-shell*'; its next title was 'Song of the Last Arcadian'. The Island of Statues (1886) was a long pastoral drama about an enchantress who turned into statues those men who sought immortality, available from a certain plant on her island; when the Enchantress dies, the statues, some of them thousands of years old, return to life. 'The Song of the Happy Shepherd' is similar in mood: it affirms the value of the poetic imagination in a world that is modern, prosaic, turned to stone. Yeats was the inheritor of a long tradition of poetry as the antidote to the unnatural abstractions of history, philosophy, and science. Sir Philip Sidney, in his *Defence of Poetry* (1595), criticized the historian as the slave of fact, and praised the poet as the genius of possibility. At the turn of the nineteenth century, William Blake conceived Sir Isaac Newton as the murderer of the cosmos, the man who substituted abstract forms for the living presences of things; and John Keats said that philosophy always made life chill and charmless, that it tried to 'Unweave a rainbow' (*Lamia* II 237). In Yeats's poem, only language, and the dreamy half-images denoted by language, have any vivacity; mere action, mere ideas, are objective, dead.

1 *Arcady*: Arcadia, the valley in Greece where Pan, the goat-like god of Nature, dwelt. The death of Pan meant the end of the mythology, the end

of the world of innocent pastoral perfection; but the Happy Shepherd hopes that language can restore that world.

9 *Chronos*: the Greek word for time, sometimes identified with Cronos, the Titan leader whom the god Jupiter overthrew. Chronos' tune is cracked because history, chronological record, 'Grey Truth' (l. 4) have spoiled and sobered the world. Compare the dance of time (or of modern times) to off-key melodies in '"I am of Ireland," l. 19, and 'A Statesman's Holiday', l. 38.

12 *Rood*: cross.

19 *sudden flaming word*: in Yeats's short story 'The Tables of the Law' (1896), a mystic book teaches that 'the world only exists to be a tale in the ears of coming generations' (*M*, p. 300). Also compare the *The Island of Statues* II iii 236–37, where the dying enchantress complains, 'our lives were but two starry words / Shouted a moment 'tween the earth and sky' (*VP*, p. 675).

26 *New dreams, new dreams*: compare 'Mere dreams, mere dreams!' ('Ancestral Houses', l. 9). The modern world has corrupted dreams into vanities, and words into scientific facts (l. 32).

28 *starry men*: astronomers. Like William Blake, Yeats deplored the rigid Newtonian model of the clockwork heavens. In *The Wanderings of Oisin*, Yeats described the stars as fixed 'Like bubbles in a frozen pond' (I 336).

29 *optic glass*: Jeffares notes (*NCP*, p. 4) the source of this term in Milton, *Paradise Lost* (1674) I 287.

36 *echo-harbouring shell*: this shell acts as a sounding-box or resonator, transforming words into melody, private emotion into beauty. It is therefore a symbol of the poetic imagination. Shells are important in many of Yeats's poems (such as 'Crazy Jane Reproved' or the introductory lyric in *The Only Jealousy of Emer*), not only for their intricate beauty of design, but also as signs of sea-change, of metamorphosis into art. In *The Wanderings of Oisin*, there is a 'trumpet-twisted shell' (I 160) that dreams forever of its own beautiful colours – a suggestion of the narcissism of the artist who, like the Happy Shepherd, consults endlessly with his own imagination. An empty shell, symbolic of outer beauty and inner sterility, symbolizes a mansion in 'Ancestral Houses', l. 13.

39 *rewording*: in some printings this word reads *rewarding*.

47 *faun*: a mythical Arcadian creature, human, but with the ears, tail, and legs of a goat.

54 *My songs of old earth's dreamy youth*: compare the juvenile *Mosada* II 60–61: 'warriors whose names have sung / The world to its fierce infancy again' (*VP*, p. 698).

55 *she dreams not now*: the world, chilled by science, has lost its imagination; so the poet must take up the burden of creative utterance.

56 *poppies*: the source of opium, conducive to dreams.

The Sad Shepherd

This poem, once entitled 'Miserrimus' [Most wretched man], is a companion piece to the previous poem. Here it is not the woods of Arcady that are dead, but the poet himself: the lack of vitality is internal, not external. In neither poem is nature harmonious with man, sympathetic to his feelings. But the Happy Shepherd believed he had the power to reanimate (at least to a degree) the natural world, while the Sad Shepherd is passive, helpless before a world that is far stronger, more potently expressive than he. These two opposing models of the poet – the demigod and the victim – persist all through Yeats's career.

1 *Sorrow*: personifications of Sorrow are common in Yeats's early work. In his essay 'The Moods' (1895), Yeats said that our strong emotions – what he calls Moods – do not belong to us, but are instead messengers to us from a realm of spiritual intensities. This doctrine can lead to a certain passivity of feeling, for we feel nothing until some feeling approaches us from outside.

4 *humming sands*: compare the 'humming sea' in the previous poem, l. 35. Music lurks everywhere in the natural world.

7 *laugh on*: the stars, the sea (l. 10), and the dewdrops (l. 16), are all self-involved, unaware of the Sad Shepherd and wholly different in mood. For the theme of nature's reflexiveness, see the note to *The Wanderings of Oisin* I 160–62: 'a trumpet-twisted shell . . . Dreaming of her own melting hues'.

26 *sad dweller*: the shell. Though the shell's mood matches the shepherd's own, the magical relief for which the shepherd hoped does not come to pass. In the previous poem (l. 39), words were 'certain good'; but in this poem words are fragile, easily broken into 'inarticulate moan' (l. 27). The Happy Shepherd's confidence in art has vanished; and the Sad Shepherd's shell (his poetic imagination) is a device not for transforming his words into melody, but for fracturing his words into unintelligible syllables. In 1933 Yeats remembered his youth, when he sat 'in futile revery listening to my own mind as if to the sounds in a sea shell' (*LNI*, p. xi). And in 1937 Yeats discovered, after making a broadcast, that a radio receiver was an even better disarticulator of language than the Shepherd's shell: 'Every human sound turned into the grunt, roar or bellow of a wild beast' (*DWL*, p. 125).

The Cloak, the Boat, and the Shoes

This poem was used as the song of 'the flowers' guardian sprights' (*VP*, p. 666) at the beginning of the final scene of Yeats's long Spenserian pastoral, *The Island of Statues*; in another printing it was entitled 'Voices'. Here obsession with Sorrow leads the speakers to adorn it, to glorify it, to facilitate its passage among men.

Anashuya and Vijaya

The original title was 'Jealousy'. Yeats had no high opinion of this poem – in a 1937 radio broadcast script he wrote that it remained in his collected poems only because he had forgotten to take it out (*UP* II, p. 507). The names in the title are Hindu words meaning 'Uncomplaining' and 'Victorious', respectively. Anashuya is the name of a character in the *Sakuntalā*, a Sanskrit drama by Kālidāsa, which Yeats read in translation. This poem 'was meant to be the first scene of a play about a man loved by two women, who had the one soul between them, the one woman waking when the other slept, and knowing but daylight as the other only night' (*VP*, p. 841). The theme of the convergence of the objects of divided love is also found in Keats's *Endymion* (1818). This theme also anticipates Yeats's doctrine of the anti-self, according to which each man desires to become a person exactly opposite in character from his original self.

2 *his elbow*: Anashuya, distracted by love, has trouble concentrating on her prayers.

10 *With mingling hair*: after death, the two lovers start to dissolve into each other. In *The King of the Great Clock Tower* (1935), ll. 6–8, not only the hair, but also the whole nervous systems of two dead lovers become intermingled. A similar image is found in 'Crazy Jane and Jack the Journeyman', l. 15. Also compare the juvenile *Mosada* III 60–62: 'when death comes / My soul shall touch with his, and the two flames / Be one' (*VP*, p. 701).

14 *Brahma*: the supreme god, the creator in Hindu mythology.

26 *Kama*: 'The Indian Cupid' (*VP*, p. 72); the Hindu Eros, or god of love, popularized in English poetry in Tennyson's 'The Palace of Art' (1832), l. 115.

41 Sing you of her: the stars sympathize with and even reflect human life. Later in the poem (l. 79), a star is called 'You hunter of the fields', as if Vijaya himself had a stellar counterpart. The counterpart-theme is important in this poem, since Anashuya and Amrita constitute a single being.

43 van of wandering quiet: each lover wishes the stars to bestow quiet on the other – compare l. 81.

56 *woven woods*: the lovers live in a kind of island of quiet, isolated from the world's wretchedness. Such places are common in Yeats's early work, particularly in *The Wanderings of Oisin*.

66 *the parents of the gods*: compare 'The Blessed', l. 17, 'God's Mother'.

68 *Golden Peak*: a sacred mountain north of the Himalayas, which Yeats may have come to associate with Mount Meru – see 'Meru'.

72 *unnumbered nests*: the hair of the gigantic sleepers in *The Wanderings of*

Oisin is similarly full of birds' nests (III 39).

91 *dreams of me*: presumably the dream-Anashuya will be the real Amrita. In 'An Image from a Past Life' a woman throws her hand in front of her man's eyes because she has a nocturnal vision of a sweetheart from the man's prior life.

The Indian upon God

The premise of this poem – that every being constructs an image of God based on its own likeness – is related to a passage from Browning's dramatic monologue 'Caliban upon Setebos' (1867), where Caliban invents a Caliban-shaped image of God. Yeats's interest in this premise can be seen in a letter to Katharine Tynan, where Yeats remarked 'When I was a child ... I used often to say "what religion do the ants have?" They must have one you know' (*L* I, p. 63). The original title was 'From the Book of Kauri the Indian – / Section V. On the Nature of God'; the next title was 'Kanva, the Indian, on God'. *The Wanderings of Oisin and Other Poems* (1889) included another poem ascribed to Kanva, 'Kanva on Himself', which expresses the same sentiments found in 'Mohini Chatterjee'.

1 *the water's edge below the humid trees*: water is conspicuous in much of this poem, as if to suggest that each animal sees his water-reflection as God. In the Neoplatonic mythology important to Yeats, water is the medium for the generation of images: 'Did not the wise Porphyry think that all souls come to be born because of water, and that "even the generation of images in the mind is from water"?' (*M*, p. 80; compare *VPl*, p. 232). At the end of the poem, we climb up the scale of the four classical elements, from water to fire.

3 *moorfowl*: a species of rail. For other moor-hens and water-hens, see 'The Phases of the Moon', l. 8; 'Easter, 1916', l. 53; 'My House', l. 8; 'The Road at my Door', l. 12; and 'Coole and Ballylee, 1931', l. 2.

17 *peacock*: for other peacocks, see 'The Peacock'; 'Ancestral Houses', l. 25; 'My Table', l. 32; 'Nineteen Hundred and Nineteen' VI 18; and 'The Friends of his Youth', l. 15; peahens appear in 'The Indian to his Love', l. 3. (Some of these later peacocks signal historical change.) In 'Rosa Alchemica' (1896), tapestry images of peacocks expand until the world seems to drown in a tide of their feathers (*M*, p. 276).

19–20 He waveth all the night / His languid tail above us, lit with myriad spots of light: 'I turned to the box, and found that the peacocks of Hera spread out their tails over the sides and lid, against a background on which were wrought great stars, as though to affirm that the heavens were a part of their glory' (*M*, p. 283).

The Indian to his Love

The erotic refuge in this poem is attained by the destruction of fixed bright images; the lovers enter a disembodied state where all is subdued, faint, monotonous, hushed, a condition of murmurs and gleams appropriate to the subtlety of their emotion. Yeats quoted a version of some lines from this poem, and called it 'rather a favourite of my own' (*L* I, p. 40). The poem originally had a fifth stanza, after l. 5: 'There dreamy Time lets fall his sickle / And Life the sandals of her fleetness, / And sleek young Joy is no more fickle, / And Love is kindly and deceitless, / And life is over save the murmur and the sweetness' (*VP*, p. 77). The original title was 'An Indian Song'.

3 *The peahens dance*: Yeats was vexed by a reviewer's objection to this line: 'The Freeman reviewer is wrong about peahens they dance throughout the whole of Indian poetry' (*L* I, p. 138).

5 *Raging at his own image*: this emblem is common in Yeats's work. In a deleted poem, 'Life', Yeats spoke of 'souls that fly from their dread selves' (*VP*, p. 686); in an 1896 synopsis of *The Shadowy Waters* Forgael said that 'the supreme secret of the world' is that 'all living things ... are flying always from themselves' (*DC*, p. 196); and in a late short story Yeats wrote of an 'allegorical picture' showing 'a man whipping his shadow' (*AV*, p. 38). Such emblems came to allude to Yeats's theory that all creative effort comes from a man's struggle against himself. Compare 'The Hero, the Girl, and the Fool', l. 1: 'I rage at my own image in the glass'.

Yeats often wrote of birds preoccupied by their reflections: compare *The Wanderings of Oisin* I 180–85: 'the song-birds ... pondered in a soft vain mood / Upon their shadows in the tide'; *The King's Threshold* (1904), ll. 101–3: 'The hunger of the crane ... afraid / Of his own shadow'; and *Calvary* (1920): 'Although half-famished he'll ... stare / Upon the glittering image of a heron' (ll. 6–8; compare *LTMSB*, p. 250). In his essay on Morris Yeats remarked of an old woman's innocent praise of a naked girl, 'we listen to that joyous praise as though a bird watching its plumage in still water had begun to sing in its joy' (*EI*, pp 57–58).

15 *One with the tide*: the star's union with the tide continues the reflection theme.

18 *when we die*: just as the parrot raged against his image, so the lovers strive to rid themselves of their bodies, of the anxiety of 'unquiet lands' (l. 10).

The Falling of the Leaves

This is one of a number of early poems that, instead of constructing a refuge from mortality, simply express the exhaustion of feeling inevitable in mortal passion. Yeats used this poem to illustrate a certain kind of musicality:

'Sometimes one composes to a remembered air. I wrote and I still speak the verses that begin "Autumn is over the long leaves that love us" to some traditional air, though I could not tell that air or any other on another's lips ... When, however, the rhythm is more personal than it is in these simple verses, the tune will always be original' (*EI*, p. 21).

Ephemera

The mood is similar to that of the previous poem, except that the lover attains sufficient distance from his circumstances to see that his waning love is part of an endless reincarnative cycle of exhaustion and new passion. Yeats said that when he was young, his Muse was old (*A: BS* 7) – and like certain other lyric poets Yeats wrote his most histrionically elegiac poetry in his youth. This poem was originally subtitled 'An Autumn Idyl', and ended with a passage in which the woman described how the 'innumerable reeds' cry 'Eternity!': 'Not they are the eternal – 'tis the cry' (*VP*, p. 81).

2 *pendulous lids*: compare Balor's 'age-weary eyelids' in *The Countess Cathleen* (1892), l. 844.

9 *how old my heart!*: *old* is, other than articles and pronouns, the most frequent word in Yeats's poetic vocabulary.

15 *A rabbit old and lame*: for an old and lame hare, see *The Wanderings of Oisin* I 412. Even as late as the 1930s, Yeats was still distracted by rabbits ('Man and the Echo', l. 44).

18 *she had thrust dead leaves*: compare the juvenile *Mosada* I 20–22: 'a dying leaf ... touched my lips / With dew, as though 'twere sealing them for death'; and III 115–16: 'dead leaves, / Like happy thoughts grown sad in evil days' (*VP*, pp. 690–91, 703).

The Madness of King Goll

'Goll or Gall lived in Ireland about the third century ... O'Curry, in his "Manuscript Materials of Irish History", thus tells the tale: "Having entered the battle with extreme eagerness, his excitement soon increased to absolute frenzy, and after having performed astounding deeds of valour he fled in a state of derangement from the scene of slaughter, and never stopped until he plunged into the wild seclusion of a deep glen far up the country. This glen has ever since been called Glen-na-Gealt, or the Glen of the Lunatics, and it is even to this day believed in the south that all the lunatics of Erin would resort to this spot if they were allowed to be free"' (*VP*, p. 857). Yeats also quoted with approval the words of 'Goll, old and savage, and letting himself die of hunger in a cave because he is angry and sorry ... to the wife whose help he refuses' (*Ex*, p. 22). For Yeats's sources, see Frank Kinahan's article in *Yeats Annual* 4 (1986): 189–94.

King Goll, like most of Yeats's early heroes, wanders out of the ordinary world into a region of unearthly intensities. The anti-world of this poem is not a tranquillized dreamy place, like the refuge of 'The Indian to his Love' or the first book of *The Wanderings of Oisin*, but a condition of hyperesthesia, painful overstimulation of his perceptual nerves. Whereas Yeats was soon to stop writing about depressed Indians, the manic Goll anticipates the heroes of his later work. Indeed the great modernist Ezra Pound used this poem as a model for his study of insanity 'La Fraisne' (1908).

Title *Goll*: the name means *one-eyed* in Gaelic.

2 *Ith to Emain*: Ith is a plain in Co. Donegal; Emain, in Co. Ulster, was the capital of the kings of the Red Branch cycle, one of the great cycles of ancient Irish storytelling. A central plot element of the 1903 version of *On Baile's Strand* is Conchubar's rebuilding of Emain after its destruction in war (*VPl*, p. 460); compare *The Death of Cuchulain* (1939), l. 5. Emain is also mentioned in *Baile and Aillinn*, l. 18.

3 *Invar Amargin*: Amergin's Estuary, the mouth of the Avoca river, Co. Wicklow. Amergin was a mythical druidic poet, the presumed author of a famous transmigration spell (somewhat similar to the Druid's shape-changes in 'Fergus and the Druid') – 'the one fragment of pagan Irish philosophy come down, "the Song of Amergin", seems Asiatic' (*TPU*, p. 11).

4 *world-troubling seamen*: probably the Fomoroh, the deformed hosts of darkness in Irish mythology.

9 *Ollave*: a poet of the most learned rank (*ollamh*, in Irish). This passage first read, 'And every whispering Druid said, / Bending low his pious head, / "He brings the peaceful age of gold" ' (*VP*, p. 82).

11 *Northern cold*: 'The Fomoroh, the powers of death and darkness and cold and evil, came from the north' (*VP*, p. 796). Yeats knew a book of comparative mythology by John Rhys that stated that Cuchulain, the greatest of Irish heroes, was a kind of solar deity, whose exploits represented the triumph of day over night, or spring over winter. Goll seems, at the beginning, to be a similar solar hero.

25 *as I shouting slew*: Goll has been a peaceful, restrained king, but he starts to lose all self-control in the midst of this outpouring of violence. The poem is a parable about the perils of surrendering oneself to the expression of superhuman energies.

26 *trampled in the bubbling mire*: compare 'The Two Kings', l. 27: 'beaten into mire'.

29 *keen stars*: compare 'The Cold Heaven', l. 9: 'Riddled with light'; 'Stream

and Sun at Glendalough', ll. 12–13: 'Gleam / That pierced my body through'; and Blake's 'Mad Song' (1783): 'light doth seize my brain / With frantic pain'.

31 *I laughed aloud*: compare the juvenile 'How Ferencz Renyi Kept Silent', l. 122, where the patriot Renyi loses his sanity after watching the execution of his mother, sister, and sweetheart: 'He rushes, rolling from his lips a madman's laugh' (*VP*, p. 715).

33 *birds fluttered by*: the fluttering birds, the leaves that ceaselessly flutter throughout the poem's refrain, the flying clouds, the rolling waters, all show that Goll has become too open, too sensitive to the elemental powers around him. The original text of ll. 33–34 showed that Goll is now at the breaking point: 'And crumpled in my hands the staff / Of my long spear, with scream and laugh' (*VP*, p. 84).

40 *leopard-coloured trees*: even the trees have menace.

45 *The grey wolf knows me*: Goll's absorption into nature is almost complete – his humanity has nearly vanished. Compare 'Dhoya': 'the bats and the owls, and the brown frogs . . . [Dhoya] had made his friends' (*JSD*, p. 116).

55 *tympan*: in this case, a harp (or possibly a stringed instrument played with a bow) – the original text in fact reads 'I saw this harp all songless lie' (*VP*, p. 85). Goll has become a sort of bard, one of the ancient poets who lived in a state of uncanny sympathy with nature. See Yeats's essay 'Magic' (*EI*, p. 43).

62 *Orchil*: 'A Fomorian sorceress' (*VP*, p. 796) – Yeats conceived her as an Irish Persephone, a queen of hell. In *The Countess Cathleen* (from 1895 on), the poet Aleel has a vision of the devils: 'Orchil, her pale, beautiful head alive, / Her body shadowy as vapour drifting . . . About her is a vapoury multitude / Of women alluring devils with soft laughter . . . But all the little pink-white nails have grown / To be great talons' (ll. 864–72); in an early draft of *The Shadowy Waters* an eagle-headed Fomorian mentions 'The Passionate Orchil, & the goat horned race' (*DC*, p. 182); and in an early story Hanrahan spoke of 'the desolate land where Orchil drives the iron-horned and iron-hoofed deer' (*VSR*, p. 192). Goll is himself in a hellish state.

65–67: the meaning is perhaps clearer in the original text: 'My singing sang me fever-free' (*VP*, p. 86).

68 *ulalu*: a cry of mourning.

69 *the kind wires are torn and still*: formerly, the harp could quench Goll's inner torment (l. 66); like the Happy Shepherd's shell, the harp offered vent, expression, relief of feeling. But now, like the Sad Shepherd, Goll has reached such an unearthly pitch of fantasy that art fails to protect or to quiet him; his inhuman urgency of emotion paralyses, impoverishes, and desolates him, for he has passed the point where art can be of any use. Yeats remarked to Olivia Shakespear that 'my father painted me as King Goll, tearing the strings

out [of] a harp, being insane with youth, but looking very desirable' (*L*, p. 705). Compare the original 1892 *The Countess Kathleen*, ll. 674–75, where the pagan poet Kevin, carrying a harp with torn strings, addresses two demons: 'The crying of these strings grew burdensome, / Therefore I tore them – see – now take my soul'. In 1934 Yeats wrote that he still had Florence Farr's psaltery: 'certain strings are broken, probably nobody will play on it again' (*VPl*, p. 1009).

71 *summer's heat and winter's cold*: the seasons are now less pleasant than in the fourth stanza.

The Stolen Child

This is a poem about the seduction of a child by faeries, in the tradition of Goethe's 'Der Erlkönig'. Yeats later wrote a play on this theme, *The Land of Heart's Desire* (1894), in which the child's surrender to the faery enticement is equivalent (as in Goethe's poem) to death. The Indian lovers of 'The Indian to his Love' seek an erotic refuge from the world's sadness; the Stolen Child seeks a refuge of pure play. The faeries are like immortal children, hiding berries (l. 6), chasing bubbles (l. 21), mischievously distorting the dreams of fish (l. 34).

2 *Sleuth Wood*: on the south shore of Lough Gill, Co. Sligo – see *M*, p. 175.

11 hand in hand: compare a poem deleted from *The Wanderings of Oisin and Other Poems*, 'A Lover's Quarrel among the Fairies', ll. 1–2: 'Do not fear us, earthly maid! / We will lead you hand in hand' (*VP*, p. 726).

15 *Rosses*: a beach near Sligo. There is [at Rosses] a little point of rocks where, if anyone falls asleep, there is danger of their waking silly, the fairies having carried off their soul' (*VP*, p. 797; compare *M*, p. 88). Yeats thought that the faeries stole through underground passages at Rosses. This beach is also mentioned in 'At Algeciras . . .', l. 12, and 'Alternative Song for the Severed Head . . .', l. 5.

29 *Glen-Car*: a lake near Sligo; the name means Valley of the Monumental Stone.

34 *unquiet dreams*: such pretty mischief is common in the faeries of Yeats's juvenilia: they 'startle the naps / Of the dreaming water-fowls' in *The Island of Statues* II iii 258–59 (*VP*, p. 676); they make lambs shiver in 'A Lover's Quarrel among the Fairies', l. 7 (*VP*, p. 726); and one of them tickles the nose of a priest with a feather in 'The Priest and the Fairy', l. 30 (*VP*, p. 729).

44 *He'll hear no more*: there may be an implication that the Stolen Child has left too much behind, in abandoning the homely comfortable world of calves, kettle, and mice. This interpretation is strengthened by a letter Yeats wrote

to Katharine Tynan, 14 March 1888: 'my poetry ... is almost all a flight into fairy land, from the real world ... The chorus to the "stollen child" sums it up – That it is not the poetry of insight and knowledge but of longing and complaint – the cry of the heart against neccesity. I hope some day to alter that and write poetry of insight and knowledge' (*L* I, pp. 54–55).

Down by the Salley Gardens

Yeats wrote of this poem (originally entitled 'An Old Song Re-sung'), 'This is an attempt to reconstruct an old song from three lines imperfectly remembered by an old peasant woman' (*VP*, p. 90). Like certain similar attempts by Robert Burns, this poem has attained the status of a folksong. In 1935 Yeats wrote, 'The Free State Army march to a tune called "Down by the Salley Garden" without knowing that the march was first published with words of mine, words that are now folklore ... I want to make another attempt to unite literature and music' (*DWL*, p. 29). In a radio broadcast script of 1937, Yeats wrote, 'When I was a young man poetry had become eloquent and elaborate. Swinburne was the reigning influence and he was very eloquent. A generation came that wanted to be simple, I think I wanted that more than anybody else. I went from cottage to cottage listening to stories, to old songs; sometimes the songs were in English, sometimes they were in Gaelic – then I would get somebody to translate. Some of my best known poems were made in that way. "Down by the Salley Gardens", for instance, is an elaboration of two lines in English somebody sang to me at Ballysadare, County Sligo' (*UP* II, p. 495). As Frayne and Johnson note, Yeats's broadcast collaborator V. C. Clinton-Baddeley identified Yeats's source as an Anglo-Irish ballad, 'The Rambling Boys of Pleasure'; but according to Colin Meir's *Ballads and Songs of W. B. Yeats*, pp. 16–17, one P. J. McCall claims that he heard an 'Old country love song' called 'Down by the Sally Gardens' in 1875. Here is Meir's transcription of the first stanza of McCall's MS:

> Down by the Sally gardens my own true love and I did meet
> She passed the Sally gardens, a tripping with her snow white feet.
> She bid me take life easy just as the leaves fall from each tree;
> But I being young and foolish with my true love would not agree.

Another transcription, by Michael B. Yeats, is printed by Jeffares, *NCP*, p. 14. There is an unsentimental third stanza in which the speaker wishes he had money, liquor, and 'a fine girl on my knee'.

Joyce remembered that he sang 'Down by the Salley Gardens' at his first public concert (Joyce, *Letters* III, p. 340); and in 1904 he wrote out the text of the poem on a postcard to Nora Barnacle (*Letters* II, p. 45).

Title *Salley*: willow. In 'The Crucifixion of the Outcast' (1893), a cleric tells a pagan gleeman that his soul is 'like the wind among the salley gardens' (*M*, p. 153).

3–6: in *Where There is Nothing* (1902) III 278–79, 348–51, a version of these lines is sung by a drunken singer.

7 *as the grass grows on the weirs*: this line is quoted, and the metaphor remarkably expanded, in Pound's Canto 83.

The Meditation of the Old Fisherman

Yeats wrote, 'This poem is founded upon some things a fisherman said to me' (*VP*, p. 797). In this poem, as in 'Down by the Salley Gardens', Yeats seems to be turning away from faeryland towards common folk and usual experience. This movement continues in the following poems as well.

4 never a crack in my heart: 'I thought that for a time I could rhyme of love ... of a fisherman who had "never a crack" in his heart ... or of some cheerful fiddler, all those things that "popular poets" write of, but that I must some day ... become difficult or obscure' (*A: HC* 1).

The Ballad of Father O'Hart

Crossways, which began in Arcadia, and continued through India, faeryland, and other remote places, ends with three ballads, as the poet approaches modern Ireland and accessible metres. A certain aura of myth lingers, however. Yeats originally intended to write a story, not a poem, about Father O'Hart (*L* I, p. 57). Yeats noted, 'This ballad is founded on the story ... told by the present priest of Coloony in his interesting *History of Ballisodare and Kilvarnet*. The robbery of the lands of Father O'Hart was one of those incidents which occurred sometimes though but rarely during the penal laws. Catholics, who were forbidden to own landed property, evaded the law by giving a Protestant nominal possession of their estates' (*VP*, p. 798). Both this ballad and 'The Ballad of the Foxhunter' deal with the superior expressiveness of animals.

1 *John O'Hart*: died 1739. Yeats wrote that he lived in the 'last century, and was greatly beloved. ... No one who has held the stolen land has prospered. It has changed owners many times' (*VP*, p. 93).

2 *penal days*: from 1695 until 1727, the Irish parliament, controlled by England, passed a series of anti-Roman Catholic measures, called the Penal Laws, imposing harsh restrictions: 'no people, Lecky said at the opening of his *Ireland in the Eighteenth Century*, have undergone greater persecution, nor did that persecution altogether cease up to our own day' (*EI*, p. 519).

3 *shoneen*: upstart (*VP*, pp. 92, 797).

6 *Sleiveens*: mean fellows, or rogues (*VP*, pp. 92, 797).

13 *only*: except.

22 *keeners*: hired mourners.

27 *Coloony*: Colloney, a few miles south of Sligo.

30 *Knocknarea*: a mountain overlooking Sligo – see 'Alternative Song for the Severed Head . . .', l. 2.

31 *Knocknashee*: a round hill in Co. Sligo.

35 *Tiraragh*: a barony in Co. Sligo.

36 *Ballinafad*: a village in Co. Sligo.

37 *Inishmurray*: an island off the coast of Co. Sligo.

The Ballad of Moll Magee

This poem was based on 'a sermon preached in the chapel at Howth if I remember rightly' (*VP*, p. 843).

24 *Kinsale*: a seaport in Co. Cork.

32 *boreen*: lane.

The Ballad of the Foxhunter

This poem was 'Founded on an incident, probably itself a Tipperary tradition, in Kickham's *Knocknagow*' (*VP*, p. 798).

7 *Lollard*: a horse.

THE ROSE (1893)

Yeats's erotic fantasies, so wayward and vague in the poems of the 1880s, acquired a certain precision on that day in 1889 when he met Maud Gonne: 'she seemed a classical impersonation of the Spring, the Virgilian commendation "She walks like a goddess" made for her alone. Her complexion was luminous, like that of apple blossoms through which the light falls, and I remember her standing that first day by a great heap of such blossoms in the window' (*A: FY* 5). She was six feet tall, one of the most celebrated beauties in Ireland, and a fervent orator advocating revolution against English rule. Yeats's desperate love intrigued her, but she could not respond in kind. Yeats never mentioned her name in a poem until he wrote 'Beautiful Lofty

Things', over forty years after he met her, but the emotional tension she provoked strongly informs the poems of the 1890s.

The Rose is not the title of a published volume, but the title of a section of Yeats's collected poems, selected (except for 'Who Goes with Fergus?' and 'To Some I have Talked with by the Fire', added to *The Rose* in later printings) from *The Countess Kathleen and Various Legends and Lyrics* (1892). Yeats explained the titles of *Crossways* and *The Rose* by saying that, in the former volume, the poet has 'tried many pathways'; and in the latter volume, 'he has found, he believes, the only pathway whereon he can hope to see with his own eyes the Eternal Rose of Beauty and of Peace' (*VP*, p. 845–46). *The Rose* is perhaps the most carefully organized of all Yeats's carefully organized books of poetry, and its great sophistication of design reflects Yeats's desire for synthesis – synthesis of his love for Maud Gonne and his occult researches and his patriotic desire to isolate and liberate the Irish national spirit. In his personal life, Yeats hoped to found a mystical order, located on Castle Rock, an island in a lake near Sligo; there he and Maud Gonne and his astrologer uncle George Pollexfen would investigate spiritual reality until Blake's gates of perception were unsealed and heaven would open to them; there they would unite the radical truths of Christianity with the pagan wisdom of ancient Ireland, and restore the imaginative life in the old sacred places (*Mem*, pp. 123–34; *A: HC* 1; *LTMSB*, pp. 108, 118, 382, 387).

In his poetry, Yeats developed a vocabulary based on a single prime symbol, the Rose, which could stand for any desirable thing, and therefore could subsume a multitude of disparate objects. The Rose varies between two poles: the historical and particular Maud Gonne, and a state so ample and inclusive that it is almost a symbol of symbolism itself, an allegation of the oneness of all beautiful objects, a hypothetical apex where all upward-striving things converge. Such immense predicates are found in Romantic poetry, as in Shelley's 'Hymn to Intellectual Beauty' (1818), addressed to an abstract Beauty in which all finite beautiful things are gathered; but, as Yeats said in a 1925 note, 'the quality symbolized as The Rose differs from the Intellectual Beauty of Shelley . . . in that I have imagined it as suffering with man and not as something pursued and seen from afar' (*VP*, p. 842). By identifying this ultimate Beauty with an actual woman, Yeats achieved a flexible and economical symbolic speech. Sometimes the subject of the poem is Maud Gonne, while at other times her specific personality is lost in its own radiance. Generality and intimacy are thus combined.

In these poems, there is a complex and unsettled relationship between the natural world – full of worms, mice, and the sadness of unrequited love – and the supernatural world, where all is ecstasy. In the Rosicrucian philosophy that Yeats was studying at this time, the sensible world is only the lowest in a series of graded emanations from spiritual reality; there is a ladder connecting the low and the high. But in the Indian philosophy that Yeats studied under the Brahmin Mohini Chatterjee, the sensible world was nothing but a distraction from and impediment to the contemplation of higher truths; Chatterjee taught that 'we ourselves are nothing but a mirror and that deliverance consists in turning the mirror away [from the sensible world] so that it reflects nothing' (*TSMC*, p. 68). These two opposing models – one suggesting that spiritual truth is hidden everywhere in the objects around us, the other suggesting that (in Shelley's phrase) the deep truth is imageless – compete in Yeats's poetry. The former model rendered symbolism possible; but the latter justified the urgency of escape.

The adjustment of focus, then, between the physical world and the spiritual world continually shifts. In some poems, such as 'The Rose of the World', the physical world is transparent, easily penetrated, unable to sustain itself in front of the spiritual truth of things. But in other poems the physical world can organize itself into a fairly satisfactory expression of the spiritual world. Indeed in one poem, 'The Lake Isle of Innisfree', it even appears that the seeker can find a good approximation of the kingdom of the spirit right here on earth. Yeats was fond of quoting the occult motto attributed to Hermes Trismegistus, 'The things below are as the things above' (*EI*, p. 146). Yeats sought out those holy places – Castle Rock, Innisfree – which best seemed to mirror the shape of heaven.

Epigraph: from Augustine, *Confessions* X 27: 'Too late I have loved you, Beauty so old and so new! Too late I have loved you'. Augustine was addressing God as an indwelling Beauty that vivifies the senses with the desire to approach Him. In 1901 Yeats quoted these same Latin lines, to illustrate that the artistic life and the religious life have the same goal (*EI*, p. 207).

Dedication: for Lionel Johnson, see 'The Grey Rock', l. 62.

To the Rose upon the Rood of Time

A rood is a cross, and so the title presents the image of the Rose of Eternity crucified on the Cross of Time. This was a fundamental symbol of Rosicrucian philosophy: it denoted the point of intersection between woman (the rose) and man (the cross), the point of conjunction between the four classical elements (represented by the leaves of the rose – see *LMTSB*, p. 406) and the fifth element (spiritual quintessence), and the point of breakthrough where the strife of temporal suffering suddenly intensifies into a vision of the eternal. As Yeats wrote in 1907, 'the nobleness of the arts is in the mingling of contraries, the extremity of sorrow, the extremity of joy, perfection of personality, the perfection of its surrender, overflowing turbulent energy, and marmorean stillness; and its red rose opens at the meeting of the two beams of the cross, and at the trysting-place of mortal and immortal, time and eternity' (*EI*, p. 255). In the acting version of *The Shadowy Waters* (1911), Forgael takes the rose on the rood as an example of those after-images left behind when incandescent revelation fades:

> Yet sometimes there's a torch inside my head
> That makes all clear, but when the light is gone
> I have but images, analogies,
> The mystic bread, the sacramental wine,
> The red rose where the two shafts of the cross,
> Body and soul, waking and sleep, death, life,
> Whatever meaning ancient allegorists
> Have settled on, are mixed into one joy. (ll. 132–39)

This passage shows how little Yeats cared about the particular meanings assigned to his symbols: the rose and the cross blur into a state of infinite suggestiveness.

This poem is a microcosm of the section that it introduces, *The Rose*. In the opening lines, the poet asks his Rose-Muse to inspire him to sing of the ancient Irish myths of Cuchulain and of Fergus and the Druid; and the next two poems tell exactly these two stories. Then the poet asks for the privilege of finding 'Eternal beauty' in the midst of the natural world; this corresponds to the series of poems starting with 'The Rose of the World', in which the Rose is discovered hovering behind all the phenomena of earth. In the second stanza of 'To the Rose upon the Rood of Time', the poet reverts from eternal beauty to common life, and in the second half of this section we find several poems on homelier, more immediate topics. At the end, the poet wishes to 'Sing of old Eire'; and at the end of the section is an epilogue, 'To Ireland in the Coming Times'.

Title: in the 'Oxen of the Sun' chapter of *Ulysses*, Joyce inserts this title into a verbal squash of allusions to Blake and Dante (*A Critical and Synoptic Edition*, ed. Gabler: Episode 14, l. 291).

3 Cuchulain: the great hero of the Red Branch, the earlier of Yeats's two favourite cycles of primitive Irish mythology. See the note to 'Cuchulain's Fight with the Sea'.

5 Fergus: a king from the Red Branch cycle. See the note to 'Fergus and the Druid'.

7 silver-sandalled on the sea: the reflection of the stars in the water. As Ellmann notes (*IY*, pp. 29–34), conjunctions of the four elements, and particularly of fire and water, occur everywhere in this volume. The reflection of fire in water represents the imaging of transcendental simplicities in the material medium of the world. In Neoplatonic mythology, water is the medium for the generation of images (*M*, p. 80).

13 Ah, leave me still: Yeats first invites the Rose to come, then thrusts her away – it is difficult to find the proper distance. In 1906 Yeats feared that 'we may never see again a Shelley and a Dickens in the one body' (*EI*, p. 296) – in other words, that no writer would ever possess both accurate factual knowledge of the world and a vision of supernatural reality. In the first stanza of this poem, Yeats aspired to the visionary wisdom of Shelley; in the second stanza, to the sympathetic, cherishing realism of Dickens.

20 bright hearts: 'I do not remember what I meant by "the bright hearts", but a little later [in 'Hanrahan's Vision', *M*, p. 250] I wrote of Spirits "with mirrors in their hearts"' (*A: HC* 1).

21 a tongue men do not know: this line, and a few preceding lines, were quoted in Yeats's autobiography as an example of Yeats's fear of what he called the *Hodos Chameliontos*, the Chameleon Way – the fear that his imagination would be so bewildered by a multitude of images that it would become confused and powerless (*A: HC* 1; compare *Ex*, p. 57). In the first stanza of this poem, Yeats worried that the world's importuning would leave him blind (l. 9); and in this stanza, he worries that occult preoccupations will leave him mute. 'When I was writing ... "The Rose", I found that I was becoming unintelligible to the young. ... I have been like a traveller who, having when newly arrived in the city noticed nothing but the news of the market-place, the songs of the workmen, the great public buildings, has come after certain months to let his thoughts run upon some little carving in its niche ... or the conversation of a countryman who knows more of the "Boar without Bristles" than of the daily paper' (*VP*, p. 844).

Fergus and the Druid

The mythological basis of this poem was taken, not from an archaic source, but from Samuel Ferguson's then-recent poem 'The Abdication of Fergus MacRoy'. Fergus was always a king, but he was not a poet until Samuel Ferguson made him so – as Yeats explained, Fergus 'was the King of Uladh [Ulster], but, as the legend was shaped by Ferguson ... he gave up his throne that he might live at peace, hunting in the woods' (*UP* II, p. 161). He found the story of Fergus's abdication useful for defining the competition between the desire to be a poet and the desire to be a man of action (for further poems on this theme, see the Introductory Rhymes to *Responsibilities*, 'The Road at my Door', 'I see Phantoms ...', and 'Nineteen Hundred and Nineteen' V). For more information on Fergus, see the note to *The Wanderings of Oisin* III 89.

2 *from shape to shape*: the fairies were sometimes called Shapechangers, and human beings versed in the occult might gain similar powers. Prehistoric

poets sometimes attributed to themselves amazing distensions of being – one of the oldest Irish texts is a transmigration spell attributed to Amergin (see the note to 'The Madness of King Goll', l. 3).

5 *weasel*: in 'Nineteen Hundred and Nineteen' IV 4, the poet compares himself to a weasel.

10 *young subtle Conchubar*: the crafty High King of Ulster, who (as the next poem explains) bewitched the great hero Cuchulain into fighting the sea. In the old sources, Fergus's wife Ness tricked him into abdicating in favour of her son Conchubar; but in Ferguson's poem Fergus simply tires of rule: 'Uladh's judgment-seat to fill / I have neither wit nor will. / One is here may justly claim / Both the function and the name. // Conor is of royal blood: / Fair he is; I trust him good' (quoted by Yeats, *UP* I, p. 91). See also *The Wanderings of Oisin* III 80.

13–14 *I laid the crown / Upon his head*: for another abdicating king, see 'The Madness of King Goll'.

18–19: compare the scenery in the second stanza of 'Who Goes with Fergus?'

23 *hollow cheeks*: compare *Mosada* II 35–36, where the monk is 'hollow-cheeked / From fasting' (*VP*, p. 697); and 'Among School Children' IV 3, 'Hollow of cheek'.

27 *A king is but a foolish labourer*: compare a line Yeats was fond of quoting, from Villiers de l'Isle-Adam's symbolist play *Axël*: 'As for living, our servants can do that for us'. Fergus feels that the role of king is a mask forced upon him, and envies the solitude, the imaginative malleability of the Druid.

28 *Who wastes his blood to be another's dream*: this line originally read, 'To do and do and do and never dream' (*VP*, p. 103).

30 *wrap you round*: compare 'Cuchulain's Fight with the Sea', l. 59, 'wrap you round' – there the seductiveness of the phrase is explicit.

31 *I see my life go drifting like a river*: originally 'I see my life go dripping like a stream' (*VP*, p. 104); Bornstein (*YS*, p. 56) compares Shelley's *Alastor*, ll. 502–5: 'O stream! ... Thou imagest my life'.

32 *I have been many things*: Fergus has a vision of his prior incarnations. Yeats said in his essay 'Magic' (1901) that the boundaries of the mind were unclear, that many minds could flow into one mind (*EI*, p. 28); and here Fergus experiences a sort of transcendental shapelessness of being. Compare Erasmus, *In Praise of Folly*: Pythagoras had been philosopher, horse, even sponge, and discovered like Gryllus that man was worst.

34 *a fir-tree*: compare this to the catalogue of the Demon's metamorphoses in *The Wanderings of Oisin* II 177; and also to the similar catalogue in 'He Thinks of his Past Greatness ...', l. 6.

35–36 *An old slave ... A king*: compare 'Mohini Chatterjee', ll. 5–6: 'I have been a king, / I have been a slave'.

35 *quern*: a corn-grinder.

38 *I have grown nothing*: Fergus becomes a type of the annulled poet, lost on the *Hodos Chameliontos* (see note to the previous poem, l. 21). Finally Fergus and the Druid, mutually envious, are interdependent – the Druid represents the imagination, a formless mother of forms, while Fergus (as king) represents the perfected image, shapely and coherent. It is painful for Fergus to dissolve, just as it is impossible for the Druid to confine himself to a single shape. Instead of l. 38, the original text had the following passage, illustrating the inconsequentiality of dreams: 'The sorrows of the world bow down my head, / And in my heart the daemons and the gods / Wage an eternal battle, and I feel / The pain of wounds, the labour of the spear, / But have no share in loss or victory' (*VP*, p. 104).

In a review of Ibsen, Yeats wrote that Peer Gynt (like Fergus) had grown nothing by excess of identity: Yeats compared Peer Gynt to the alchemical elixir that 'dissolves everything into nothing ... Peer Gynt lets sheer phantasy take possession of his life, and fill him with the delusion that he is this or that personage, now a hunter, now a troll, now a merchant, now a prophet, until the true Peer Gynt is well nigh dissolved' (*UP* I, p. 344).

40 *thing*: the original word was *bag*; when Yeats changed it to the present reading, Robert Bridges urged him to return to *bag* (*LTY* I, p. 29), and Yeats replied: 'You are probably right about the word "bag". I changed it because of the urgency of someone or other who thought the word ugly for a close' (*L*, pp. 278–79).

Cuchulain's Fight with the Sea

The story of Cuchulain's unwitting murder of his son, and his combat with the waves of the sea, was, of all Irish myths, the most reverberant in Yeats's imagination. Yeats's difficulties with his own father may be related to this fascination – John Butler Yeats once smashed a glass-fronted picture over his son's head in a dispute over John Stuart Mill's philosophy (*Mem*, p. 19; *Ex*, p. 417). It is clear that Yeats feared that his father's dominant personality would overwhelm him: the Yeats-like boy in the so-called 'Island' version of the unfinished novel *The Speckled Bird* feels that disobeying his father is like disobeying God; and, further, that every thought of his, every feeling, is merely a shadow of some thought or feeling of his father's (*LTMSB*, p. 193).

The image of a hero struggling with the ocean came to represent to Yeats the highest pitch of tragic intensity. As Yeats wrote in 1917, 'The poet finds and makes his mask in disappointment, the hero in defeat. The desire that is satisfied is not a great desire, nor has the shoulder used all its might that an unbreakable gate has never strained' (*M*, p. 337).

The same story told in this poem forms the plot of Yeats's play *On Baile's Strand* (1904), one of a series of five plays on the life of Cuchulain on which Yeats worked, sporadically, for more than thirty years. In *On Baile's Strand*, however, Cuchulain's slain son is not the child of Emer (Cuchulain's wife), but of a Scottish warrior-queen named Aoife, who raised her son expressly to murder the man who conquered her. (Matthew Arnold's epic poem *Sohrab and Rustum* [1853] is based on a similar Persian legend of a father who kills his son without recognizing him.) Yeats described the character of Cuchulain in *On Baile's Strand* as follows: 'a little proud, barren and restless, as if out of sheer strength of heart ... he had put affection away ... He is probably about 40 ... a little hard, and leaves the people about him a little repelled ... self assertive yet self immolating' (*L*, p. 425). In 1938 Yeats attended a revival of *On Baile's Strand* and noted '"Cuchulain" seemed to me a heroic figure because he was creative joy separated from fear' (*L*, p. 913). Yeats mentioned Cuchulain in 'To the Rose upon the Rood of Time', l. 3, 'The Secret Rose', l. 12, and *Baile and Aillinn*, l. 73, 'the Hound of Ulad'. In the first version of 'The Secret Rose', l. 9, he made a mistaken allusion to the meaning of Cuchulain's name (Culain's Hound) by referring to 'the Hound of Cu' (*VP*, p. 169). Yeats revisited Cuchulain in some of his late poems – see 'Alternative Song for the Severed Head ...', l. 9, 'Crazy Jane on the Mountain', l. 17, 'Cuchulain Comforted', 'The Statues', l. 25, and 'The Circus Animal's Desertion' II 18.

2 *Emer*: compare 'Crazy Jane on the Mountain', l. 15: 'Great-bladdered Emer'.

2 *raddling*: dyeing with red pigment (as in *Deirdre* [1907], ll. 154, 320, and *A Full Moon in March* [1935], l. 182); and (perhaps) twisting together strands of cloth.

16 *one sweet-throated*: Cuchulain's mistress, Eithne Inguba. In the original text, the swineherd's description continued after l. 16: 'And lovelier than the moon upon the sea; / He made for her an army cease to be'. On hearing this provocation, Emer ordered her servants to beat him.

34 *horses of the sea*: a metaphor for waves, used again at ll. 81 and 84; see also 'Colonus' Praise', l. 32.

45 *Conchubar*: see the note to *The Wanderings of Oisin* III 80. In *On Baile's Strand*, Conchubar contrives to bind Cuchulain with an oath of fealty, because he sees Cuchulain's wild strength as a threat to his established political order.

59 *wrap you round*: compare 'Fergus and the Druid', l. 30.

68 *Cuchulain I*: in Yeats's original text, the son's name was Finmole.

77–78 *brood ... quietude*: the same rhyme appears in 'To Ireland in the Coming Times', ll. 15–16.

85–86: in the original text, these lines read: 'For four days warred he with the bitter tide, / And the waves flowed above him and he died' (*VP*, p. 111). The original title was 'The Death of Cuchulain'; but Yeats decided to postpone his death for a different occasion, and to reserve that title for a 1939 play on a different subject.

The Rose of the World

This poem begins a series of Rose poems, in which mutability gives way to Eternity. The mythological references in the first stanza connect this poem to the two previous ones, though Yeats is abandoning mythological narrative, for a time, in favour of a beauty higher than any described by ancient Greece or Ireland. The original title of this poem was 'Rosa Mundi'.

2 *mournful pride*: these two words chime through the whole volume – see 'The Sorrow of Love', ll. 5 and 8.

4 *Troy*: Yeats compares the Rose to Helen of Troy, for whose sake the Trojan war began, when, in the arms of her Trojan lover Paris, she abandoned her Greek husband Menelaus.

5 *Usna's children*: Naoise, and his brothers Ainle and Ardan. In the Irish story, Deirdre, espoused to the elderly king Conchubar, eloped with Naoise to Scotland, but Conchubar lured Naoise and his brothers back to Ireland by a ruse, and killed all three. 'Deirdre was the Irish Helen, and Naisi her Paris, and Concobar her Menelaus' (*VPl*, p. 389); see *Baile and Aillinn*, ll. 76, 91. Yeats takes Helen and Deirdre (and Maud Gonne) as mortal avatars of the immortal Rose.

6 *We and the labouring world are passing by*: in 1906 Yeats wrote of the poet as a fleeting, indistinct man who chases Beauty, single, distinct, and stable (*EI*, p. 271).

8: originally this was the extremely alliterative line, 'More fleeting than the sea's foam-fickle face' (*VP*, p. 118).

12 *Weary and kind*: Yeats added the third stanza, according to George Russell, after Maud Gonne returned from a mountain walk, exhausted and unusually gentle – see Jeffares, *NCP*, p. 27.

15 *wandering feet*: compare 'He gives his Beloved certain Rhymes', l. 12.

The Rose of Peace

1 *Michael*: the militant archangel, who, according to Christian tradition, guarded the gates of Eden with a flaming sword. See also 'The Happy Townland', l. 41.

16 *A peace of Heaven with Hell*: perhaps a reference to Blake's *The Marriage of Heaven and Hell* (1793), though Yeats seems less ironic than Blake. During the year when this poem was written, Yeats and Edwin Ellis published a three-volume edition of and commentary to Blake's poetry.

The Rose of Battle

The reconciliation of contraries, effected by the Rose in the previous poem, is brief. In this more typical poem Yeats expresses his conviction that the struggle of man against his fate, like the struggle of Cuchulain against the sea, will always end in defeat; there is a tragic disproportion between man's desires and the satisfactions available to him. The original title (derived from 'Ossian' 's *Cath-loda*, duan ii) was 'They went forth to the Battle, but they always fell'; this title is quoted in the *Aeolus* chapter of Joyce's *Ulysses* (*A Critical and Synoptic Edition*, ed. Gabler: Episode 7, l. 572).

2 *thought-woven sails*: compare Sorrow's boat-construction in 'The Cloak, the Boat, and the Shoes', ll. 6–10; and the cancelled opening stanza of Keats's 'Ode on Melancholy' (1819), in which the poet says that, even if you 'build a bark of dead men's bones ... Stitch shrouds together for a sail', you will not be able to find the Melancholy. There are many imaginary boats in Romantic poetry.

4 *God's bell*: the last stroke of a bell, especially a midnight bell, is Yeats's usual signal for death, the accession of eternity, as in *The King of the Great Clock Tower* (1935).

5 *a band*: in several of Yeats's works, such as 'Hanrahan's Vision' (1896), the poet meets a visionary company of spirits who teach a lesson about ultimate things.

10 him who hears love sing: the man who accepts the ordinary pleasures of domesticity does not perceive life as a continual conflict. The poet does not usually admire those who make compromises, who settle for what life offers. Compare *The Shadowy Waters*, l. 55, where the god Aengus hates those who 'keep to the one weary marriage-bed'; and *At the Hawk's Well* (1917), ll. 275–76, where a leafless tree praises the man who 'Has married and stays / By an old hearth'.

21 The sad, the lonely, the insatiable: those described in ll. 12–20.

29 *Beauty grown sad with its eternity*: Yeats noted in 1925 that the Rose

suffered with mankind. The Rose bends down to men, even as men struggle up to her. On one hand, the Rose is like the Virgin Mary, interceding for mankind's sake with God; on the other hand, the Rose is like a seductive pagan goddess who has fallen in love with a mortal – compare *The Wanderings of Oisin* I 64 and II 10.

33 *defeated in His wars*: compare 'The Four Ages of Man', l. 8: 'At stroke of midnight God shall win'.

A Faery Song

Just as Naoise and Deirdre are the tragic lovers of the Red Branch (or Ulster) cycle of Irish mythology, so Diarmuid and Grania are the tragic lovers of the later Fenian cycle (according to *VPl*, p. 1285). After helping Grania to escape from the love of the aged Finn, Diarmuid (like the Greek Adonis) was killed by a boar (as Yeats and George Moore told this story in their play of 1901, *Diarmuid and Grania*). But the original subtitle did not mention Diarmuid and Grania: 'Sung by "the Good People" over the outlaw Michael Dwyer and his bride, who had escaped into the mountains' (*VP*, p. 115). Michael Dwyer was a leader in the 1798 rebellion against England.

Caption *Cromlech*: an arrangement of prehistoric megaliths in which a lintel is placed over upright stones, as at Stonehenge in England. Yeats wrote that Irishmen refer to a cromlech as the 'Bed of Diarmuid and Grania' (*Ex*, p. 16).

The Lake Isle of Innisfree

This poem arose from the conjunction of a book and an advertising display. Yeats wrote, 'My father had read to me some passage out of *Walden*, and I planned to live some day in a cottage on a little island called Innisfree ... I thought that having conquered bodily desire and the inclination of my mind towards women and love, I should live, as Thoreau lived, seeking wisdom' (*A: R* 17); 'I had still the ambition, formed in Sligo in my teens, of living in imitation of Thoreau on Innisfree, a little island in Lough Gill, and when walking through Fleet Street [London] very homesick I heard a little tinkle of water and saw a fountain in a shop-window which balanced a little ball upon its jet, and began to remember lake water. From the sudden remembrance came my poem *Innisfree*, my first lyric with anything in its rhythm of my own music' (*A: FY* 15). In a letter to Katharine Tynan, Yeats quoted a version of the first two stanzas and cautioned that the speaker of the poem was a persona, though the feelings expressed were related to the poet's own: 'In my story [*John Sherman* IV iii] I make one of the charecters when ever he is in trouble long to go away and live alone on [Innisfree] – an old day dream of my own. Thinking over his feelings I made these verses about them' (*L* I, pp. 120–21). Many of the details from *John Sherman* recall the poem: '[Innisfree's] rocky centre, covered with many bushes, rose some forty feet above the lake. Often ... it had seemed good to dream of going away to that islet and building a wooden hut there and burning a few years out, rowing to and fro, fishing, or lying on the island slopes by day, and listening at night to the ripple of the water and the quivering of the bushes' (*JSD*, p. 92). This poem is unusual among Yeats's refuge-poems for the quantity of practical advice it offers.

Yeats quickly grew somewhat embarrassed by the remarkable success of this poem (*L*, p. 353; *TSMC*, p. 13). In 1916 Ezra Pound wrote a parody of this poem, 'The Lake Isle', which ends as follows: 'O God, O Venus, O Mercury, patron of thieves, / Lend me a little tobacco-shop, / or install me in any profession / Save this damn'd profession of writing, / where one needs one's brains all the time.' In 1938 Lily Yeats wrote, concerning some public land purchases near Innisfree: '[there] will be put up notices – this way to the "Bee glade ... anyone interfering with the bee will be severely dealt with." "The beans must not be eaten. They are the property of the Land Commission"' (*LTY* II, p. 604).

Title *Innisfree*: Yeats mentioned this island again in an uncollected poem, 'The Danaan Quicken Tree', in which the poet sails to Innisfree to eat the berries of an enchanted tree 'according to one legend, poisonous to mortals, and according to another, able to endow them with more than mortal powers' (*VP*, p. 742).

1 *arise and go*: 'I had begun to loosen rhythm as an escape from rhetoric ... but I only understood vaguely ... that I must ... use nothing but the common syntax. A couple of years later I would not have written that first line with its conventional archaism – "Arise and go" – nor the inversion in the last stanza' (*A: FY* 15).

2 *of clay and wattles*: compare *The Wanderings of Oisin* I 249: 'A house of wattles, clay'.

3 *a hive for the honey-bee*: in *John Sherman* (1891), the hero imagines a happy marital life 'in a small house with a green door and a new thatch, and a row of beehives under a hedge' (*JSD*, p. 103). For other references to bees, see 'The Stare's Nest by my Window', ll. 1–5; and 'Among School Children' V 2: 'Honey of generation'.

7 *purple glow*: Yeats explained in a radio broadcast that this referred to the reflection of heather in the water. The word *Innisfree* means *heather island.* This obscure allusion to water completes the tabulation of the four elements in ll. 6–8.

10 *lake water lapping*: in 1920 Joyce added a postscript to a long letter to Pound: 'This is a very poetical epistle. ... It should be read in the evening when the lakewater is lapping' (Joyce, *Letters* II, p. 469).

11 *pavements grey*: presumably those of London.

A Cradle Song

A draft of this poem appears in *L* I, p. 208 – 'It is supposed to be sung by a mother to her child ... The last two lines are suggested by a gaelic song'.

7 *Sailing Seven*: the visible planets – the original text read 'the old planets seven' (*VP*, p. 118.) Compare 'Under the Moon', l. 7. Some printings read 'Shining Seven' (*VP*, p. 118), as Joyce remembered at the beginning of the 'Scylla and Charybdis' chapter of *Ulysses*: 'Seven is dear to the mystic mind. The shining seven W. B. calls them' (*A Critical and Synoptic Edition*, ed. Gabler: Episode 9, l. 28).

The Pity of Love

This poem shows the flexibility of Yeats's symbolic method. In a poem like 'The Rose of the World', the object of the poet's love transcends nature; but here the object of his love has a sudden fragility, is vulnerable to all the elemental powers.

1–2 *A pity beyond all telling / Is hid in the heart of love*: in an early letter to Olivia Shakespear, Yeats wrote, 'the love that is half pity is of eternity' (*L* I, p. 468).

The Sorrow of Love

The initial premise of this poem is similar to that of the previous poem: man and his passion cannot sustain themselves before the power and splendour of the natural world. But in the second stanza the beloved appears – not herself vulnerable to nature, as in 'The Pity of Love', but instead a mediating image, connecting man to nature. After her immanence, nature is not hostile to man, but expressive of man's passion.

Yeats wrote in 1901 that he was 'not very proud of "The Sorrow of Love"' (*L*, p. 353), and he extensively revised this poem in 1925; here is the 1895 text:

> The quarrel of the sparrows in the eaves,
> The full round moon and the star-laden sky,
> And the loud song of the ever-singing leaves,
> Had hid away earth's old and weary cry.

And then you came with those red mournful lips,
And with you came the whole of the world's tears,
And all the sorrows of her labouring ships,
And all the burden of her myriad years.

And now the sparrows warring in the eaves,
The curd-pale moon, the white stars in the sky,
And the loud chaunting of the unquiet leaves,
Are shaken with earth's old and weary cry.
(*VP*, pp. 119–20)

In a diary entry of 1929, Yeats commented, 'I have felt when re-writing every poem – "The Sorrow of Love" for instance – that by assuming a self of past years, as remote from that of today as some dramatic creation, I touched a stronger passion, a greater confidence than I possess, or ever did possess' (Ellmann, *IY*, pp. 239–40). And in 1935 he added, 'I learnt that occasional prosaic words gave the impression of an active man speaking. In dream poetry, in *Kubla Khan* ... every line, every word, can carry its unanalysable, rich associations; but if we dramatise some possible singer or speaker we remember that he is moved by one thing at a time, certain words must be dull and numb. Here and there in correcting my early poems I have introduced such numbness and dullness, turned, for instance, "the curd-pale moon" into the "brilliant moon", that all might seem, as it were, remembered with indifference, except some one vivid image' (*A: DP* 15).

5 *A girl arose*: *arose* breaks down easily into *a rose*, and the girl can be identified with the Rose of other poems in this volume, and the Rose's constituents, such as Helen of Troy. See the note to 'The Rose of the World', l. 4.

7 *Odysseus*: the crafty Greek hero whose long and painful homeward journey from Troy is the subject of Homer's *Odyssey*.

8 *Priam*: the king of Troy, father of Hector and Paris and other Trojan heroes, slain by Achilles' son Neoptolemus. The Rose not only suffers with man, but seems to epitomize all human suffering.

When You are Old

This poem is based on a famous sonnet by the sixteenth-century French poet Pierre Ronsard, 'Quand vous serez bien vieille'. (Yeats also imitated a Ronsard poem in 'At the Abbey Theatre'; Pound remembered in his Cantos the labour of 'Uncle William two months on ten lines of Ronsard' [98/686; compare 80/505].) But after the first lines Yeats's poem diverges from its original: whereas Ronsard predicts that, when he becomes a boneless phantom hovering by his grave, his beloved – an old hunched woman – will regret her proud disdain of the poet's love, the gentler Yeats ascribes the failure of love, not to the woman's haughtiness, but to Love himself, who abandons the orbit of human concerns. According to Yeats's doctrine of the Moods, all powerful emotions are themselves gods, not subject to our control. A draft of this poem appears in *L* I, pp. 288–89.

2 *this book*: the text of the poem plays a role in the operation of the events described in the poem. This emphasis on the written artifact continues in 'A Dream of Death' and 'The Dedication to a Book . . .'; and in later poems such as 'Shepherd and Goatherd', l. 115, 'Presences', 'To be Carved on a Stone . . .', 'Nineteen Hundred and Nineteen' III, and 'Under Ben Bulben' VI. An ingenious variant occurs in *Baile and Aillinn*, ll. 195–96, where the medium on which the poem is written is a tablet carved from a tree described in the poem. Also compare 'The Gift of Harun Al-Rashid', l. 127, where the page of an occult text is caressed as if it were 'some dear cheek'.

5–7 *many . . . loved your beauty . . . one man loved the pilgrim soul*: the contrast between love of attributes and love of essence is treated in later poems, such as 'The Hero, the Girl, and the Fool'.

The White Birds

After Maud Gonne refused the first of Yeats's marriage proposals to her, she idly remarked – as they walked by sea-cliffs – that she would like to be a seagull, if she were a bird (Jeffares, *NCP*, p. 32). That was the inspiration of this poem, which contrasts evanescent things – foam, meteor, dew, flowers – with an imaginary paradise of immutable affection, beyond the strife and discords of human life, beyond the flickering of human passion.

Title: 'The birds of fairyland are white as snow' (*VP*, p. 799).

9 *Danaan shore*: the Tuatha de Danaan were the gods of ancient Ireland, and their shore was Tír na nÓg, the Country of the Young, the Celtic paradise. In Yeats's long poem *The Wanderings of Oisin*, the hero voyages towards Tír na nÓg, and this poem may be considered a lyric exploration of one of the themes of that narrative. Indeed the metre of this poem is similar to that of Part III of *The Wanderings of Oisin*.

A Dream of Death

The original title was 'An Epitaph'. This poem was written during Maud Gonne's recovery in France from an illness; according to Yeats, a malicious woman told him, ' "So Maud Gonne is dying in the South of France" ' (*Mem*, p. 44). It is in one respect a companion poem to 'The Sorrow of Love': in that poem the beloved managed to connect the poet to the natural world, whereas here the poet, by means of language, manages to relate the corpse of his beloved to the otherwise 'indifferent' landscape.

10 *Until I carved these words*: see 'When You are Old', l. 2.

11 thy first love: that is, the reader's first love, disparaged against the poet's first love.

The Countess Cathleen in Paradise

This was a song from the earliest version (1892) of Yeats's play *The Countess Kathleen* (ll. 808–23); it is sung by a procession of angels, carrying the heroine's corpse. (Afterward, the song was entitled 'A Dream of a Blessed Spirit'.) Cathleen sold her soul to the devil in order to feed the starving Irish peasantry; at the end of the play she dies, and the angels and devils battle in the air for possession of her soul. The extreme transcendence that Cathleen achieves here suggests that she is another incarnation of the Rose – the Rose is an over-symbol flexible and commodious enough to embrace Christian as well as pagan symbols. Indeed an angel compares Cathleen to 'the red rose by the seat of God' (l. 841 of the 1892 text).

6 *She'll not ask a haughty dress*: the original line read 'Bear the gold-embroidered dress' (*VP*, p. 124) – note the revision into simplicity.

8 *oaken press*: a clothespress, a metaphor for the coffin.

11 *footstep*: compare the 'wandering feet' of the Rose in 'The Rose of the World', l. 15.

12 *earth's old timid grace*: compare D. G. Rossetti's 'The Blessed Damozel' (1850), in which the transfigured lady retains some of her earthly graces.

15 *Heaven*: Cathleen. When Yeats revised this poem in 1927, he noted in a letter, 'It . . . is almost a poem for children . . . I like the last verse, the dancer Cathleen has become heaven itself. Is there jealousy in such dancers or did Dante find them as little so as colour is of colour?' (*L*, p. 731).

16 *Flame to flame and wing to wing*: a rhythm and an image Yeats found attractive. Compare 'To Some I have Talked with by the Fire', l. 11, 'The Everlasting Voices', l. 4, and 'He remembers Forgotten Beauty', l. 21.

Who Goes with Fergus?

Like the previous poem, this is a song from the original *The Countess Kathleen* (ll. 220–25, 232–36). It is sung by the heroine's old nurse, who tries to make her forget the ruin caused by drought and famine; after hearing it, Cathleen comments, 'My heart is longing for a deeper peace / Than Fergus found amid his brazen cars: / Would ... I could go down and dwell among the shee / In their old ever-busy honeyed land' (ll. 265–70). The old nurse evidently learned this song (ll. 173, 276) from Kevin, a young pagan poet (partly a surrogate for Yeats himself) hopelessly in love with the Christian Countess (a surrogate for Maud Gonne) – in a sense he urges himself to abandon personal affection and to turn instead to research into imaginative vision. In the revised version of *The Countess Cathleen* (1912) – from which 'Who Goes with Fergus?' was cut – the pagan poet (now renamed Aleel) urges Cathleen to flee with him to just such a honeyed land, beyond human suffering (ll. 474–80).

1 *Fergus*: see the notes to 'Fergus and the Druid'. Here Fergus seems to have taken up the bag of dreams and become a Druid magician himself.

7 *And no more turn aside*: this stanza haunts Stephen Dedalus throughout the chapters 'Telemachus', 'Proteus', and 'Circe' of Joyce's *Ulysses* (1922) – see *A Critical and Synoptic Edition*, ed. Gabler: Episode 1, ll. 239–64; Episode 3, l. 445; Episode 15, ll. 4190, 4930–42. Compare Blake's 'Introduction' to *Songs of Experience* (1794), l. 16: 'Turn away no more'.

10 *And rules the shadows of the wood*: compare the juvenile *The Island of Statues* II iii 303–4, where a petrified man awakens and asks about the god Pan: 'Doth he still dwell within the woody shade, / And rule the shadows of the eve and dawn?' (*VP*, p. 678).

11 *And the white breast of the dim sea*: the lover turns aside from his human woman only to find a huge occult female form latent in nature – compare 'dishevelled', l. 12. Yeats reused the idea of this line and its pyrrhus-spondee rhythm in *On Baile's Strand* (1904), l. 544: 'Out of the cold dark of the rich sea'.

12 *dishevelled wandering stars*: it may be relevant that *comet* comes from a Greek word meaning *hair* – a comet looked like a star trailing hair behind it. Compare 'The Rose of Peace', ll. 7–8: 'weave out of the stars / A chaplet'.

The Man who Dreamed of Faeryland

This poem examines the possibilities for fulfilment of a man's deepest wishes. In the four stanzas the usual objects of human striving – love, money, vengeance, and peaceful death – are contrasted to the joys of faeryland, a place of shivery perfection described by means of metaphors derived from the fine arts. The search for faeryland paralyses the dreamer, and spoils his enjoyment of human life.

1 *Drumahair*: a village in Co. Leitrim.

8 *a woven world-forgotten isle*: Tír na nÓg. See 'The White Birds', l. 9. The word *woven* is repeated in l. 11, and, in conjunction with *ravelled* (l. 9), suggests that the poet is describing a kind of tapestry.

13 *Lissadell*: a barony in Co. Sligo significant to Yeats. See 'In Memory of Eva Gore-Booth . . .' l. 1.

18 *lug-worm*: in each stanza a humble animal or plant tantalizes the dreamer with a glimpse of the supernatural. Yeats wrote late in life that he 'knew a man once who, seeking for an image of the Absolute, saw one persistent image, a slug, as though it were suggested to him that Being which is beyond human comprehension is mirrored in the least organised forms of life' (*AV*, p. 284).

22 *the dancer*: the irresponsibility and abundance of the dance contrasts with the prudence of l. 15.

23 *the sun and moon were in the fruit*: compare *Baile and Aillinn*, l. 176: 'apples of the sun and moon'. In alchemy, the mingling of the solar and the lunar is an image of perfection – compare 'The Tower' II 42. For paradisal abundance of fruit, see 'John Kinsella's Lament for Mrs. Mary Moore', l. 34: 'plucks the trees for bread'. The original text of ll. 22–23 read, 'A Danaan fruitage makes a shower of moons, / And as it falls awakens leafy tunes' (*VP*, p. 127).

25 *Scanavin*: in Co. Sligo.

29 *one small knot-grass*: compare the deleted conclusion of 'Ephemera': 'The innumerable reeds / I know the word they cry, "Eternity!"' (*VP*, p. 81). Also compare *The Hour-Glass* (1914), ll. 535–39: 'The sap would die out of the blades of grass / Had they a doubt. They understand it all, / Being the fingers of God's certainty, / Yet can but make their sign into the air; / But could they find their tongues they'd show it all'. Yeats also commended one of Blake's illustrations: 'Out of every . . . grass-blade comes a little creature lifting its right hand above its head' (*UP* I, p. 284). In a dream Yeats once saw an illuminated page, reading, '"The secret of the world is so simple that it could be written on a blade of grass with the juice of a berry"' (*Mem*, p. 127).

32 *ravelled*: see ll. 8–9.

35 *lover there by lover*: compare 'The Wild Swans at Coole', l. 19: 'lover by lover'.

37 *Lugnagall*: in Co. Sligo, 'the Steep Place [actually Hollow] of the Strangers' (*M*, p. 183).

45 *dreamless wave*: since faeryland is the fulfilment of all dreams, no further dreams are necessary.

47 *until God burn Nature with a kiss*: in Yeats's story 'The Untiring Ones', the faeries dance for century after century 'until God shall burn up the world with a kiss' (*M*, p. 78).

48 *no comfort*: it is ambiguous whether the dreamer is admirable for his visionary restlessness or simply a fool.

The Dedication to a Book of Stories Selected from the Irish Novelists

Title: the book of stories was *Representative Irish Tales* (1891). Yeats noted that the poem 'is a sheaf of wild oats' (*VP*, p. 129).

1 *a green branch hung with many a bell*: in Irish folk-lore, the rustling of the magic branch of Cormac lulled to sleep all who heard it; see *The Wanderings of Oisin* III 46 and *UP* II, p. 59.

20 *the saddest chimes are best enjoyed*: compare Shelley, 'To a Skylark' (1820), l. 90: 'Our sweetest songs are those that tell of saddest thought'. Also compare Yeats's juvenile 'Quatrains and Aphorisms' VII 3–4: 'Joy, in growing deeper and more deep, / Walks in the vesture of her sister Sorrow' (*VP*, p.735).

24 *Munster*: the southernmost of the four provinces of Ireland. *Connemara*: a region in Co. Galway that Yeats often associated with the virtues of sturdy peasant cloth, as in 'The Fisherman', l. 4, and 'The Phases of the Moon', l. 4.

The Lamentation of the Old Pensioner

Yeats said that this poem was the 'translation into verse of the very words of an old Wicklow peasant' (*VP*, p. 799). An account of this peasant appears in 'The Visionary' (*M*, p. 14): 'More than once also he said, waving his arm toward the mountain, "Only myself knows what happened under the thorn-tree forty years ago"; and as he said it the tears upon his face glistened in the moonlight'. Yeats received this tale second-hand from George Russell (*L* I, p. 232). In 1925 Yeats first published a stark revision; the original 1890 text follows here, for purposes of comparison:

I had a chair at every hearth,
When no one turned to see
With, 'Look at that old fellow there;
And who may he be?'
And therefore do I wander on,
And the fret is on me.

The road-side trees keep murmuring –
Ah, wherefore murmur ye
As in the old days long gone by,
Green oak and poplar tree!

> The well-known faces are all gone,
> And the fret is on me.
> (*VP*, pp. 131–32)

Fret in this version means 'doom or destiny' (*VP*, p. 799).

5 *love or politics*: the topics of stanza three and stanza two, respectively.

6 *Time transfigured*: compare 'The Gift of Harun Al-Rashid', l. 110, 'time's disfiguring'.

14 *a broken tree*: Yeats liked this arboreal metaphor – see 'The Old Men Admiring Themselves in the Water', l. 5; 'The Coming of Wisdom with Time', l. 3; 'The Road at my Door', l. 8; 'Human Dignity', l. 8; 'His Memories', l. 3': bodies broken like a thorn'; 'Crazy Jane and the Bishop', l. 1: 'blasted oak'; 'Her Vision in the Wood', l. 1: 'Dry timber'; and *Purgatory* (1939), l. 16. Also, in 'Red Hanrahan's Song about Ireland', l. 3, the poet's courage breaks like an old tree; and a 'wicked, crooked, hawthorn tree' speaks in *The King of the Great Clock Tower* (1935), l. 170. Wordsworth's 'The Thorn' (1798) offers a precedent for such images.

17 *I spit*: compare the Old Man in the Prologue to *The Death of Cuchulain* (1939), who denounces 'that old maid history. I spit!'

The Ballad of Father Gilligan

The original subtitle was 'A Legend told by the People of Castleisland, Kerry' (*VP*, p. 132). Yeats was stung by a reviewer's accusation of plagiarism, and said that he considered himself 'perfectly justified in taking a legend that belonged to ... the Irish people' (*L* I, p. 292).

25 *Mavrone*: a Gaelic exclamation meaning 'My grief'.

The Two Trees

According to Cabbalistic lore, the material world can be expressed as a series of graduated emanations from spiritual reality; these emanations are summarized in a diagram called the Sephirotic Tree: 'The "Tree of Life" is a geometrical figure made up of ten circles or spheres called Sephiroth joined by straight lines. Once men must have thought of it as like some great tree covered with its fruit and its foliage, but at some period ... touched by the mathematical genius of Arabia in all likelihood, it had lost its natural form' (*A: SB* 6). The first emanation, at the top of the tree, is pure spirit, the goal of every quest; the last emanation, at the bottom, is inert matter. Therefore the Sephirotic Tree has benign and malign aspects.

Yeats also used tree-diagrams from more orthodox religion to describe the human condition: after a friend told him of her vision of 'the Tree of Life with ever-sighing souls moving in its branches instead of sap', Yeats found 'an old Jewish book' which said: ' "The Tree, . . . is the Tree of the Knowledge of Good and Evil . . . in its branches . . . the souls and the angels have their place" ' (*EI*, pp. 44–45; compare *VP*, p. 811, and *The King's Theshold* [1904], ll. 749–50). The Tree of Life and the Tree of the Knowledge of Good and Evil (Genesis 2:9) can be identified with the two trees of this poem, both part of the general circulation of man's spiritual life. 'The kingdom that was passing was, [Blake] held, the kingdom of the Tree of Knowledge; the kingdom that was coming was the kingdom of the Tree of Life: men who ate from the Tree of Knowledge wasted their days in anger against one another . . . men who sought their food among the green leaves of the Tree of Life condemned none but . . . those who forget that even love and death and old age are imaginative art' (*EI*, p. 130). For other trees with cosmic implications, see 'He thinks of his Past Greatness . . .', ll. 3–5, 'The Rose Tree', and 'Vacillation' II 1 and VI 12.

This poem represents an extension of Yeats's development as a symbolist. In the Rose-poems near the beginning of the volume, every symbol is beautiful and good and ultimately comprehended in the Rose; what is ugly simply falls away or evaporates. But in this poem, ugliness is given a striking visual image, as if the tensions of human life could be expressed as a competition among symbols. Yeats complained that Shelley lacked 'the Vision of Evil' (*AV*, p. 144); and 'The Two Trees' is one of the first poems in which Yeats's vision of evil found a strong lyric form. In this manner he could deal with aspects of Maud Gonne's character – such as her abstract political hatred – difficult to treat in the restricted intensities of poems like 'The Rose of the World'. In 1895 Yeats wrote to Olivia Shakespear that he was delighted that she liked 'The Two Trees': 'Every influence [Yeats struck out *symbol*] has a shadow, as it were, an unballanced – the unballanced is the Kabalistic definition of evil – dublicate of itself' (*L* I, p. 463).

After publishing *A Vision*, Yeats inserted into this poem (l. 15) a reference to the gyres; thus this poem was retrospectively made the first in his canon to allude to his comprehensive philosophical system (see Introduction XI). To some extent the contraries that govern the universe can be understood to flower from the Rose. Donald R. Pearce, in 'The Systematic Rose' (*Yeats Annual* 4 [1986]: 195–200), has demonstrated how the diagrams of *A Vision* can be derived from an occult diagram of the Rose found in Yeats's 1893 notebook.

6–10 *stars . . . root . . . leafy . . . waves*: the four classical elements spring from the tree – it flowers into the universe.

13 *the Loves*: evidently Cupid-like creatures that decorate the symbolic diagram of the tree. Compare the linnets that adorn the laurel tree (a representation of Anne Yeats) in 'A Prayer for my Daughter', l. 41. Also

compare Blake, 'Song' ['Love and harmony combine'] (1783), ll. 5–6: 'Joys upon our branches sit, / Chirping loud, and singing sweet'.

15 *Gyring*: this word, pertaining to Yeats's philosophic system, was added in 1929; ll. 14–16 originally read 'Winged Loves borne on in gentle strife, / Tossing and tossing to and fro / The flaming circle of our life' (*VP*, p. 135). The gyres – a pair of interlocking, spinning cones, the apex of one touching the interior centre-point of the base of the other – were a representation of the forces that govern all things. At the extreme of one cone, human life was 'subjective' – that is, dominated by the pursuit of images of loveliness. At the extreme of the other cone, human life was 'objective' – that is, dominated by the mind's abstract analyses of reality. Joyous ignorance (l. 16) and 'unresting thought' (l. 34) are also the antithetical features of the two trees.

21 *Gaze no more in the bitter glass*: vanity depraves ideal beauty – self-consciousness is the fruit of the Tree of Knowledge. For other poems about women who regard themselves in mirrors, see 'Beggar to Beggar Cried', l. 12: 'There's a devil in the looking-glass'; 'Michael Robartes and the Dancer', ll. 10-12: 'turn her eyes ... upon the glass / And on the instant would grow wise'; 'A Prayer for my Daughter', ll. 17–19; and 'The Hero, the Girl, and the Fool', l. 1: 'I rage at my own image in the glass'. Compare also 'The mirror of malicious eyes' ('A Dialogue of Self and Soul' II 12). Yeats sometimes associated mirrors with realistic, objective art: he liked to quote Stendhal's aphorism that the novelist is a '"mirror dawdling down a lane"' (*Ex*, pp. 333, 373); and he considered that the shattering of the mind's rigid mirror was a necessary prelude to visionary revelation (*M*, p. 276). Similarly, in *The Shadowy Waters*, ll. 131–32, Forgael celebrates the fogging of the mind's mirror: 'We have fallen in the dreams the Ever-living / Breathe on the burnished mirror of the world'. Elsewhere Yeats stressed the unreality of mirror-images: for example, in *The Island of Statues* II iii 270–71: 'As figures moving mirrored in a glass, / The singing shepherds, too, have passed away' (*VP*, p. 676). This theme evolved into a consideration of the vertigo produced by mirrors, their bewildering multiplicity of images: in 'Ribh denounces Patrick', l. 10: 'The mirror-scalèd serpent is multiplicity'; and in 'The Statues', l. 22: 'Mirror on mirror mirrored is all the show'

29 *all things turn to barrenness*: in Yeats's unfinished novel *The Speckled Bird* I iv, an old tinker tells a boy that God created the world by looking at His face in a mirror; but then Satan looked in the mirror, and thereby created hell, and all ugliness and evil (*LTMSB*, p. 37–38).

34 *ravens of unresting thought*: Bloom (*Yeats*, pp. 117–18) compares Blake's 'The Human Abstract', in which 'the Raven his nest has made' in an evil tree that grows 'in the Human Brain'.

36: the original text read 'To see men's souls bartered and bought' (*VP*, p. 136) – a line that firmly connected 'The Two Trees' to Yeats's play about Maud Gonne, *The Countess Cathleen* (1892), in which owl-like demons barter for human souls.

To Some I have Talked with by the Fire

This is one of the earliest of many poems celebrating the theme of friendship. Yeats believed that the Irish myths he studied were the common property of the racial consciousness, not merely his own invention or the fruits of antiquarian research. The original subtitle was 'The Dedication of a new book of verse' – that is, *Poems* (1895).

1 *Danaan*: see 'The White Birds', l. 9.

9 *the fruit of evil and of good*: Yeats thought of the faeries as exempt from moral consequence, beyond good and evil. He often described them as soulless (e.g., *VP*, p. 676).

10 *the embattled flaming multitude*: angels. Yeats here ascends from pagan to Christian themes.

11 *wing above wing*: see 'The Countess Cathleen in Paradise', l. 16.

13 *the clashing of their sword-blades*: 'I made a certain girl see a vision of the Garden of Eden. She heard "the music of Paradise coming from the Tree of Life", and, when I told her to put her ear against the bark, that she might hear the better, found that it was made by the continuous clashing of swords' (*Ex*, p. 306; compare *EI*, p. 45 and *A: HC* 2). Similarly, in Yeats's story 'The Death of Hanrahan' (1896), the music of Heaven is 'but the continual clashing of swords' (*M*, p. 259); this same motto is also found in *Where There is Nothing* (1902) II 278, and became a central theme when that play was rewritten with Lady Gregory's help as *The Unicorn from the Stars* (1908): 'Heaven is not . . . quiet, it is not singing and making music, and all strife at an end. I have seen it, I have been there. The lover still loves, but with a greater passion, and the rider still rides, but the horse goes like the wind and leaps the ridges, and the battle goes on always, always. That is the joy of Heaven, continual battle' (III 447–54; compare III 328, 384). Yeats generally conceived spiritual reality as a state of conflict or antithesis. Also, compare the end of the *The Countess Cathleen*, in which angels in battered armour battle devils for possession of Cathleen's soul.

To Ireland in the Coming Times

The original title was 'Apologia addressed to Ireland in the coming days'. In this vigorous epilogue Yeats refutes the charge that his symbolic and artful method of composition is irrelevant to Irish political realities. He claims that politics is properly an effect of art, not a cause of it; that poetry instigates action, instead of responding to external events. This poem strives to make a convergence between patriot and poet, between Maud Gonne and the Rose, between time and eternity – between those contraries that seemed so difficult to resolve in the prefatory poem, 'To the Rose upon the Rood of Time'. Yeats insisted that the Rose had sufficient breadth of reference to include national as well as private concerns: 'The Rose is a favourite symbol with the Irish poets. It ... is used, not merely in love poems, but in addresses to Ireland' (*VP*, pp. 798-99).

This poem is an elaborate meditation on the relation between the measured and the unmeasured. Measurement is temporal and rhythmic, imagistic; the beat of the dancer's footsteps, of the emphatic tetrameter of the poem itself, produces a measured design. Measurement, proportion, is the basis of all art. But eternity is unmeasured; and the measured stresses of art spring from and return to a condition of elemental simplicity, a fruitful void. Yeats contrasted the mystic with the visionary: the mystic received such immediate intuitions of eternity that he could not be an artist; whereas the visionary perceived eternity through finite images – a less direct but more communicable experience: 'The systematic mystic is not the greatest of artists, because his imagination is too great to be bounded by a picture or a song' (*EI*, p. 150). In this sense 'To Ireland in the Coming Times' describes how apprehensions of eternity incarnate themselves in symbols.

1–2 Know that I would accounted be / True brother of a company: compare Joyce's parody of Yeats in 'The Holy Office' (1904), ll. 23–28: 'But I must not accounted be / One of that mumming company – / With him who hies him to appease / His giddy dames' frivolities / While they console him when he whinges / With gold-embroidered Celtic fringes'.

4 rann: verse.

6 the red-rose-bordered hem: in Yeats's story 'The Crucifixion of the Outcast' (1894), a pagan poet, crucified by a gang of monks, describes his vision of the 'rose-bordered dress' of an ideally beautiful woman (*M*, p, 155); and in 'The Book of the Great Dhoul ...' (1897), Hanrahan conjures up a faery goddess with 'silk stitches in the border of little embroidered roses that went round and about the edge of her robe' (*VSR*, pp. 191-92). Also compare *EI*, p. 271.

11 the measure of her flying feet: compare the 1892 version of *The Countess Kathleen*, l. 392: 'the murmur of their flying feet'; and the juvenile 'Street Dancers', ll. 1–2: 'Singing in this London street, / To the rhythm of their feet' (*VP*, p. 731).

13 Time bade all his candles flare: it is as if political troubles were only a

pretext to engage Maud Gonne's energy, a stage on which she could dance.

15–16 brood ... quietude: for this rhyme, see 'Cuchulain's Fight with the Sea', ll. 77–78.

18 Davis, Mangan, Ferguson: Irish poets. Thomas Davis (1814-45) was the guiding spirit behind the passionate 'Young Ireland' movement, urging the creation of an Irish national literature; Yeats thought him a sincere man who wrote slightly insincere verse in dull, mechanical rhythms (*A Book of Irish Verse* [1895], p. xv); but Yeats also conceded that Davis 'has influenced generations of young men' by means of his 'moral radiance', despite the defectiveness of his talent (*Mem*, p. 211; *A: DS* 23).

Clarence Mangan (1803–49) was a gloomier, more introverted poet; Yeats spoke of his 'immoral and unpractical but solitary and individual life' and considered that, even if he had 'drunk less whisky and smoked less opium ... he would have been no more than a good rhetorician' (*UP* II, pp. 34–35), despite his ample gifts.

Sir Samuel Ferguson (1810–86), 'the greatest Irish poet' (*UP* I, p. 87), wrote fluent poems on Irish mythological themes, and was an important influence on Yeats's early poetry, particularly on *The Wanderings of Oisin*. Yeats liked the 'lyric strength and panther-like speed' (*UP* I, p. 84) of Ferguson's narrative poems, and thought that he was, in 'breadth and golden severity ... like the ancients ... his spirit had sat with the old heroes of the country' (*UP* I, p. 92); Yeats praised Ferguson for bringing us 'a clear glass once more' after city-oriented poets had hidden nature behind 'the sad soliloquies of a nineteenth century egoism' (*UP* I, p. 103). In 1907 Yeats ranked the three as follows: 'It was our criticism ... that set Clarence Mangan at the head of the Young Ireland poets in the place of Davis, and put Sir Samuel Ferguson ... next in the succession' (*EI*, p. 256).

Some early reviewers reproached Yeats for immodesty in this comparison of himself to his distinguished predecessors; Yeats replied, 'I did not in the least intend the lines to claim equality of eminence ... but only community in the treatment of Irish subjects after an Irish fashion' (*L* I, p. 315).

22 only body's laid asleep: compare 'Man and the Echo', ll. 25-29.

23 elemental creatures: the four elements, pervasive throughout this volume, are here made eternal principles. There is a masque of these elemental powers in the first version of *The Countess Kathleen* (1892). Yeats wrote that 'whatever the great poets had affirmed in their finest moments was the nearest we could come to an authoritative religion, and ... their spirits of water and wind were but literal truth' (*A: R* 25). In 1928 Yeats quoted ll. 23–24, in a passage speculating on the mysterious power that could independently provide Spengler and Yeats with the same metaphor to describe Roman decadence (*AV*, p. 19).

23 unmeasured mind: compare *The Old Age of Queen Maeve*, l. 141: 'Outrun the measure'; *The Shadowy Waters*, l. 484: 'There is no measure that it would not burst'; and *Deirdre* (1907), l. 474: 'Love is an immoderate thing' (see also l. 138).

28 barter gaze for gaze: in other words, the poet must come to terms as best he can with eternity, as he tries to express the unmeasured energies in metrical form.

33 you: Ireland.

38 What measurer Time has lit above: the stars, as the original text shows: 'The mariners of night above' (*VP*, p. 139).

42 consuming ecstasy: Bornstein (*YS*, p. 59) compares Shelley's 'To Constantia, Singing' III 11: 'I am dissolved in these consuming ecstasies'.

43 No place for love or dream: the attainment of full beatitude renders vision unnecessary – the mystic supersedes the poet. Compare the dreamlessness at the end of 'The Man who Dreamed of Faeryland'.

THE WIND AMONG THE REEDS (1899)

In 1899, at the threshold of a new century, there were published two influential books, *The Wind among the Reeds* and Arthur Symons's *The Symbolist Movement in Literature*. Symons's book was the first major study in English of the French *symbolistes*, notably Verlaine, Rimbaud, and Mallarmé. Symons praised them for their prophetic intensity, for their power to reverse the usual positions of dream and reality; and he dedicated his study to his friend Yeats, who, he predicted, would inaugurate an important school of English symbolist poetry.

Yeats, in a sense, fulfilled Symons's wish, and in the very year it was uttered; for *The Wind among the Reeds* is perhaps the closest approximation (in major English poetry) to the mood and technique of French *symbolisme*. Yeats's grasp of French (and of every language other than English) was imperfect, and he relied considerably on Symons's ideas and citations; but Yeats did grasp something of the *symbolistes*' ingenuity in constructing faintly suggested half-objects or non-objects, their technique of creating an evacuated lyric space populated only by ghosts, and their mood of transcendental eeriness. In 1897 Yeats wrote a Symons-like essay 'The Autumn of the Flesh' (later retitled 'The Autumn of the Body') which claimed that poetry, having tried to embrace science, politics, and all human affairs in the generation of Tennyson and Browning, was now working towards relinquishment and intensification; the new poetry would be keener, more disembodied, than the old.

The Wind among the Reeds attempts to put these doctrines into practice. Here is the flesh's autumn, the spirit's November; all prosaic life is vanishing into ominous wisps of meaning. In an earlier poem, 'To the Rose upon the Rood of Time', Yeats felt anxious that he might 'learn to chaunt a tongue men do not know'; and in this volume he has almost attained that condition of frustration. The poems are not unintelligible, but they do not terminate in full expression. Again and again the poet speaks of the end of the world, of unimaginable things; he seems to writhe in limbo, unable to speak the unspeakable. It is noteworthy that Yeats published this book with an extremely long set of explanatory notes, as if he were conscious of the reader's difficulties and trying to make amends. But the notes do not define Yeats's discourse any more fully than the poems themselves; Yeats was working at the outermost fringes of human experience.

Another feature of many of these poems is the extremely long title. The title, like the notes, tries to do the work of stage-setting and mood-specifying; but sometimes the poem seems in danger of becoming swallowed by its title. The title refers to the poem's speaker as 'The Lover' or 'The Poet' or simply 'He' – for example, 'He mourns for the Change that has come upon him and his Beloved, and longs for the End of the World'. But originally these vacant pronouns or epithets were particular characters – an earlier title was 'Mongan mourns for the Change that has come upon him and his Beloved, and longs for the End of the World'. These original personae are significant. Of the personae Yeats used in this volume, three are predominant: Michael Robartes, Hanrahan, and Aedh (sometimes spelled *Aodh*). In the notes Yeats distinguished them as follows:

> I have used them in this book more as principles of the mind than as actual personages ... Hanrahan is the simplicity of an imagination too changeable to gather permanent possessions, or the adoration of the shepherds; and Michael Robartes is the pride of the imagination brooding upon the greatness of its possessions, or the adoration of the Magi; while Aedh is the myrrh and frankincense that the imagination offers continually before all that it loves. (*VP*, p. 803)

In other words, the three characters represent three different modes of the poetic imagination: the spendthrift imagination, casting away its images freely; the miserly imagination, hoarding its images; and the humble, unself-conscious imagination that identifies itself with its own images. Hanrahan represents a visionary inventiveness without any great craft, while Michael Robartes represents an aestheticism that dwells upon and perfects its artistic materials – each of these personae became the main character of a series of short stories, Hanrahan in six stories published in *The Secret Rose* (1897), and Michael Robartes in 'Rosa Alchemica' and its related stories (1896–97). Hanrahan is archaic ('was he not the last of that mighty line of poets which came down unbroken from ... Oisin, whose heart knew unappeased three hundred years of daemonic love?' [*VSR*, p. 198]), while Michael Robartes – magician, world traveller, reader of Blake, student of comparative mythology – represents modish trends in nineteenth-century art; but each is, in a sense, only one aspect of Yeats's own imagination. It is fitting that they should appear in *The Wind among the Reeds*, for the subject of many poems in this volume is the imagination itself, the origin and elaboration of images in the poet's mind.

But the speaker of these poems is not just 'The Poet': he is 'The Lover' as well. The later 1890s was a period of crisis in Yeats's personal life: his relation with Maud Gonne had become increasingly tangled and hopeless; and, in 1896, he had taken his first lover, a kindly married woman named Olivia Shakespear (Yeats refers to her under the pseudonym 'Diana Vernon' in *Memoirs*). Yeats carefully mixed the poems written to Maud Gonne with those written to Olivia Shakespear, in order to disguise the autobiographical element; but often the poems written to Olivia Shakespear are those which discuss the hair of the beloved. The three figments Hanrahan, Michael Robartes, and Aedh denote attitudes towards the beloved as well as attitudes towards poetry – voluble and careless, proud, or self-abasing. In some of the poems given to Aedh the self-abasement is carried to suicidal extremes (see the note to 'He gives his Beloved certain Rhymes'); and indeed, according to *The Wanderings of Oisin* II 87, Aedh was the name of a god of Death.

The Wind among the Reeds is Yeats's furthest journey into a poetry of disengagement and suggestiveness. In his later volumes Yeats repeatedly used the resources of symbolism – but he moved back towards a more worldly style and more bodily themes.

Title: this phrase appears in a prose sketch for an unwritten poem about Maud Gonne, circa 1897: 'I / hear the cry of the birds / & the cry of the deer / & I hear the wind among the / reeds, but I put my hands / over my ears for were not / they my beloved whispering to / me' (Stallworthy, *BL*, p. 3).

The Hosting of the Sidhe

The Wind among the Reeds begins with a poem (originally entitled 'The Faery Host') that summons up the frantic energies that invigorate the whole volume. In Yeats's earlier poetry the presiding deities were often faeries of the tiny, mischievous Shakespearean sort, as in 'The Stolen Child'; but here they are embittering spirits of sexual frenzy. In *The Wanderings of Oisin* Niamh was a languid and lovely temptress; but here she is a goddess of chaos. Her address to the poet is a set of audible stage-directions to his imagination, inspiring the formation of images.

In his 1930 diary, Yeats speculated that some historical eras taught that reality consisted of a plurality of beings, while other historical eras demanded a universal surrender to one God. Yeats thought that he had written good poetry only on the former theme, and cited 'The Hosting of the Sidhe' as an example (*Ex*, p. 305). Bradford (*YW*, pp. 19–28) prints early drafts of this poem.

Title *Sidhe*: the gods of Irish mythology. Yeats supposed that the word meant *wind* in Gaelic. 'They . . . let their hair stream out; and the great among them, for they have great and simple, go much upon horseback. If any one becomes too much interested in them, and sees them over much, he loses all interest in ordinary things' (*VP*, pp. 800–1).

1 *Knocknarea*: see 'The Ballad of Father O'Hart', l. 30.

2 *Clooth-na-Bare*: a faery who 'went all over the world seeking a lake deep enough to drown her faery life, of which she had grown weary, leaping from hill to lake and lake to hill . . . Clooth-na-Bare [may] sleep in peace, for [she has] known untrammelled hate and unmixed love' (*M*, p. 79); she was also a water-temptress whose enchantments turned Finn's hair white – 'The people of the waters have been in all ages beautiful and changeable and lascivious . . . for water is everywhere the signature of the fruitfulness of the body and of the fruitfulness of dreams' (*VP*, p. 802). See also 'Red Hanrahan's Song about Ireland', l. 11.

3 *Caoilte*: 'a companion of Fiann; and years after his death he appeared to a king in a forest, and was a flaming man, that he might lead him in the darkness. When the king asked him who he was, he said, "I am your candlestick"' (*VP*, p. 801). See *The Wanderings of Oisin* I 13.

4 *Niamh*: see *The Wanderings of Oisin* I 48.

6 the leaves whirl round: in 'Nineteen Hundred and Nineteen' VI, Yeats described savage visions of the Irish gods seen in a whirlwind.

The Everlasting Voices

This poem commands the divine powers to exert themselves in celestial matters only, and to stop expressing themselves in earthly cries, cries that too much agitate human beings. But the Voices seem to ignore this command: *The Wind among the Reeds* is full of nature-sounds that shriek of Apocalypse and drive the poet to distraction.

4 *Flame under flame*: see 'The Countess Cathleen in Paradise', l. 16.

The Moods

In his essay 'The Moods' (1895), Yeats said that our strongest emotions – what he called Moods – dwell outside ourselves; they are eternal messengers, inspirations from God (*EI*, p. 195; *UP* I, p. 367). This doctrine was extended in 'Rosa Alchemica' (1896), where 'the moods ... worked all great changes in the world; for just as the magician or the artist could call them when he would, so they could call out of the mind of the magician or the artist ... and ... pour themselves out into the world. In this way all great events were accomplished ... empires moved their border' (*M*, p. 285). This brief poem is a rhetorical question, suggesting that our moods are not mere whims but deities more permanent than the earth itself. Yeats quoted the complete text in his essay *Per Amica Silentia Lunae* (1917), in a passage describing the 'Condition of Fire', that condition of rest and eternal simplicity at which the soul will arrive at the end of time: 'time comes to an end, and the soul puts on the ... luminous body and contemplates all the events of its memory and every possible impulse in an eternal possession of itself in one single moment. That condition is alone animate, all the rest is fantasy, and from thence come all the passions and, some have held, the very heat of the body' (*M*, p. 357).

1–2 *Time drops in decay, / Like a candle burnt out*: compare the incantation from 'The Wisdom of the King' (1895): 'Hail and rain and thunder alone, / And red hearts we turn to grey, / Are true till Time gutter away' (*M*, p. 166); and the mad old woman's speech from 'The Death of Hanrahan' (1896): '"You and the whole race of men ... are dropping like a candle that is nearly burned out. But I laugh aloud because I am in my youth"' (*M*, p. 254); also 'He tells of the Perfect Beauty', l. 7: 'God burn time'; 'That the Night Come', l. 11: 'bundle time away'; 'In Memory of Eva Gore-Booth ...' II 7: 'strike another till time catch; and 'Mohini Chatterjee', l. 25: 'thunder time away'.

The Lover tells of the Rose in his Heart

Earlier titles included 'The Rose in my Heart' and 'Aedh tells of the Rose in his Heart' – Aedh was the self-sacrificing gift-giver among Yeats's poetical personae. This poem was written to Maud Gonne, and the 'green knoll' in l. 6 seems to allude to Yeats's schemes to study occult matters with her in some distant place. The poet struggles here to remake the universe into a bundle of images more congruous with the beauty of his beloved.

1: When Yeats was debating whether to ask Eva Gore-Booth to marry him, he thought, '"this house would never accept so penniless a suitor", and, besides, I was still deeply in love with that other [Maud Gonne] and had but just written "All Things Uncomely and Broken"' (*Mem*, p. 78).

The Host of the Air

'This poem is founded on an old Gaelic ballad that was sung and translated for me by a woman at Ballisodare in County Sligo; but in the ballad the husband found the keeners keening his wife when he got to his house' (*VP*, p. 803). During the 1890s, Yeats wrote many accounts of faery kidnappings derived from his folklore research. Brides were thought especially susceptible; and when O'Driscoll accepts food and drink from the Sidhe, he thereby, according to Irish peasant belief, puts himself into their power. Yeats tells this story in prose in 'Kidnappers' (*M*, pp. 73–74). Bradford (*YW*, pp. 29–34) prints early drafts of the poem.

Title: 'Some writers distinguish between the Sluagh Gaoith, the host of the air, and Sluagh Sidhe, the host of the Sidhe, and describe the host of the air of a peculiar malignancy.... I am inclined, however, to think that the distinction came in with Christianity and its belief about the prince of the air [a name for the devil]' (*VP*, pp. 803–4). Earlier titles included 'The Stolen Bride' and 'The Folk of the Air'.
4 *Hart Lake*: a small lake, Co. Sligo.

19–20 *red wine ... white bread*: an allusion to the Eucharist – the Sidhe offer a kind of pagan sacrament.
23 *old men playing at cards*: compare the bewitching card-player in 'The Tower' II.

40–41: between these lines there was once the following stanza: 'He knew now the folk of the air, / And his heart was blackened by dread, / And he ran to the door of his house; / Old women were keening the dead' (*VP*, p. 145).

The Fish

The original title was 'Bressel the Fisherman'; then it was called, through many printings, 'The Fisherman'. This poem may have been addressed to Maud Gonne, but its theme seems to be as much art as love: the image evades the imaginer, just as the woman evades her lover's embrace. For other seductive fish, see the note to 'The Song of Wandering Aengus'.

1–2 *Although you hide in the ebb and flow / Of the pale tide when the moon has set*: in 1914 Pound quoted these lines as a specimen of *imagisme* in Yeats's earlier work (*Literary Essays*, p. 378).

The Unappeasable Host

The original title was 'A Cradle Song', one of 'Two Poems concerning Peasant Visionaries' (the other became 'The Valley of the Black Pig'); and it appears as an 'unholy' lullaby in the 1896 story 'The Cradles of Gold' (*UP* I, pp. 415–16), where it is sung by a peasant wife seized by a fairy king in order to suckle his child. This is perhaps the windiest poem in this wind-haunted volume: not only did Yeats associate wind with the Sidhe, the old Irish gods, but he also said that wind symbolized 'the vague idealisms & impossible hopes which blow in upon us to the ruin of near & common & substantial ambitions' (*L* I, p. 380). Many of Yeats's folklore sources among the peasants spoke of the gods, or faeries, as drawing sustenance from human beings: the gods grew strong as men grew weak. In this poem it seems that human misery exhilarates the Sidhe, gives them power. For a somewhat similar lullaby by Edward Walsh, 'sung by a fairy over a child she has stolen', which Yeats quoted with approval, see *UP* I, p. 178.

1 *Danaan*: see 'The White Birds', l. 9.

3 *ger-eagle*: a bird also found in *Calvary* (1920), l. 175. In some early drafts of *The Shadowy Waters* Forgael is haunted by eagle-headed Fomorians who want to tear him with their claws; they are often called unappeasable: 'Your proud insatiate hearts are not appeased' (*DC*, p. 184).

12 *Mother Mary's feet*: the speaker of this poem is presumably a pious Catholic, but she feels that Christianity is weak compared to the pagan gods. Illuminated feet reappear in 'He gives his Beloved certain Rhymes', l. 12.

Into the Twilight

The original title was 'The Celtic Twilight' (and the poem was published at the end of *The Celtic Twilight*, 1893 [*M*, p. 141]). Whereas the previous poem described the desolation and exhaustion caused by contact with the anti-world, this poem suggests that there is hidden in the secret places of Ireland a reservoir of energy, by which men can rejuvenate themselves. The poet hopes to replace mere human emotions – love and hope – with stronger and more abiding affections, if he can align himself with superhuman forces.

2 *the nets of wrong and right*: conventional Catholic morality. Compare 'The Poet Pleads with the Elemental Powers', l. 12.

5 *Your mother Eire*: in his play *Cathleen ni Houlihan* (1902) Yeats personified Ireland as a woman, first seeming old, then young and beautiful, who calls Irishmen to sacrifice and glory.

8: 'I went to Sligo seeking to call to myself my courage once again with the lines "Into the Twilight": did not the dew shine though love decayed "Burning in fires of a slanderous tongue"?' (*Mem*, p. 68).

The Song of Wandering Aengus

The original title was 'A Mad Song'. Irish peasants sometimes called the faeries by the name of Shapechangers, and the beloved in this poem undergoes a metamorphosis from fish to woman before she dissolves entirely. (What is a metaphor in the poem 'The Fish' [fish = woman] here is turned into a narrative.) Yeats noted that the gods 'take all shapes, and those that are in the waters take often the shape of fish. A woman of Burren, in Galway, says, "There are more of them in the sea than on the land, and they sometimes try to come over the side of the boat in the form of fishes ..." At other times they are beautiful women' (*VP*, p. 806). In the unfinished novel *The Speckled Bird* I xii, Michael Herne has a vision in a boat, in which the surface of the sea seems to be torn away and a beautiful woman appears (*LTMSB*, p. 84; compare also p. 67 and *A: R* 21); and in *The Only Jealousy of Emer* (1919), the sea-goddess Fand lures Cuchulain: 'the Sidhe / Are dexterous fishers and they fish for men / With dreams upon the hook' (ll. 204–6) – these lines paraphrase a passage by Henry More, quoted in *Mem*, p. 104. This poem suggests the elusiveness of beauty, both in love and in art.

Yeats wrote, 'The poem was suggested to me by a Greek folk song; but the folk belief of Greece is very like that of Ireland' (*VP*, p. 806). (For Frayne's speculations on the identity of the Greek song, see *UP* I, p. 409.) Yeats attributed this song to another wanderer, Hanrahan, in the 1905 text of 'Hanrahan's Vision' (*VSR*, pp. 111–13).

Title *Aengus*: the name of the Celtic god of music, love, and repose – see the note to *The Wanderings of Oisin* I 47. Oliver Gogarty's nickname for Joyce was 'Wandering Aengus of the Birds', memorialized in the 'Scylla and Charybdis' chapter of *Ulysses* (*A Critical and Synoptic Edition*, ed. Gabler: Episode 9, ll. 1093, 1206; Episode 10, l. 1067).

2 *a fire was in my head*: compare another 'Mad Song', 'The Madness of King Goll', l. 28.

3 *a hazel wand*: compare the sceptre wielded by the god Aengus in *The Wanderings of Oisin* I 251. The hazel wand is the instrument of magical transformation in 'He mourns for the Change ...', l. 6, and in *Diarmuid and Grania* (1901) I 396, where a Druid hazel-stick turns a boy into an avenging boar.

8 *a little silver trout*: compare Dectora's address to her lover Forgael in *The Shadowy Waters*, ll. 609–10: 'O silver fish that my two hands have taken / Out of the running stream'. In *Diarmuid and Grania* (1901) II 306, an expediter of forbidden love (who may be the god Aengus) catches salmon for the two lovers.

14 *apple blossom*: Yeats associated Maud Gonne with apple blossoms (*A: FY* 5).

23 *The silver apples of the moon*: compare 'The Man who Dreamed of Faeryland', l. 23.

The Song of the Old Mother

Although the old mother is a figure of pathos, she seems to be beyond or beneath imagination, excluded from the raving joys and bitternesses of most of the personae in the volume.

10 *the seed of the fire*: 'the Irish phrase for the little fragment of burning turf and hot ashes which remains in the hearth from the day before' (*VP*, p. 151).

The Heart of the Woman

Although there are several female personae in this volume, this is the only poem in which the beloved woman speaks – it is a kind of feminine complement to the desperate male love poems that follow it, a hint of the possibility of requited love to balance the complicated agonies of rejection. The woman leaves first her bedroom, then her house, in order to venture into a dangerous domain of passion; she herself becomes a kind of house of love, as she uses her hair to shelter herself and her man from the storm. The hair-refuge also appears in 'He bids his Beloved be at Peace'.

The poem seems more sinister in its original context, the story 'The Rose of Shadow' (1894), in which the singer is a girl infatuated with a violent, brutal sailor, killed a year ago by the girl's decent father; by singing this song the girl evokes his ghastly spirit from a thunderstorm – her house collapses and she and her family die (*UP* I, pp. 329–32).

The Lover mourns for the Loss of Love

The original title was 'Aodh to Dectora' – the second of 'Three Songs' (with 'He hears the Cry of the Sedge' and 'He thinks of those who have Spoken Evil of his Beloved'). Aedh was the humble gift-giver among Yeats's love-personae, and the force of this poem derives from the fact that the 'gift' that the lover presents to his beautiful friend is an image of another woman. In 'The Song of Wandering Aengus' the image of the beloved is all too fleeting and elusive; here her image is all too fixed, irreplaceable. Pound praised this poem's syntax: 'a single sentence, with no word out of natural order' (Longenbach, *SC*, p. 84).

6 *saw your image was there*: as Donoghue notes, this is parallel to Yeats's account of the rupture of his relations with Olivia Shakespear: 'Then Maud Gonne wrote to me . . . would I come dine? I dined with her and my trouble increased . . . at last one morning instead of reading much love poetry, as my way was to bring the right mood round, I wrote letters. My friend [Olivia Shakespear] found my mood did not answer hers and burst into tears. "There

is someone else in your heart", she said' (*Mem*, p. 89). For a similar poem, in which Yeats apologizes to his wife for Maud's persistence in his imagination, see 'Under Saturn'.

He mourns for the Change that has come upon him and his Beloved, and longs for the End of the World

Earlier titles include 'The Desire of Man and Woman' and 'Mongan mourns from the Change . . .' (Mongan was, according to Yeats, a famous wizard who remembers past lives). This poem is a meditation on certain themes from *The Wanderings of Oisin*. In that long poem, the goddess Niamh lures Oisin, a great poet and warrior, over the sea to three enchanted islands; as they gallop over the waves on her magic horse, they pass four apparitions: a youth chasing a lady tossing an apple, and a hound with one red ear chasing a hornless deer (see the note to I 139–45). These apparitions haunted Yeats's imagination as emblems of eternal pursuit, a general paradigm of desire. (Because the lady's apple seemed symbolic of the sun, Yeats also connected the apparitions with astronomical rhythms, such as night chasing the day.)

Mongan, like the Druid of 'Fergus and the Druid', is not bound to a human shape. But, while the Druid's form was endlessly fluid and shifting, Mongan has stiffened into a single image, the likeness of a hound. He is therefore an emblem of the hopeless lover condemned to interminable pursuit of his beloved.

6 *A man with a hazel wand*: 'The man in my poem who has a hazel wand may have been Aengus, Master of Love' (*VP*, p. 807). Compare 'The Song of Wandering Aengus', l. 3.

9 *Time and Birth and Change*: compare *The Wanderings of Oisin* I 291.

10 *the Boar without bristles*: an image from Irish mythology of the darkness that will destroy the world. It is related to the bristleless boar that kills the hero Diarmuid, the Irish Adonis – see 'The Valley of the Black Pig'; *Diarmuid and Grania* (1901) I 394–413 and III 406 (the boar is a boy transformed by a hazel wand); and 'Her Vision in the Wood', l. 16. Only the end of the world can release the lover from his fruitless chase.

He bids his Beloved be at Peace

Earlier titles include 'The Shadowy Horses' (one of 'Two Love Poems', with 'The Travail of Passion'), and 'Michael Robartes bids his Beloved be at Peace'. Michael Robartes was the persona Yeats found appropriate for expressions of aestheticism and occult artifice; here he constructs a refuge from tumultuous passions. Yeats named this as a poem written to Olivia Shakespear (*Mem*, p. 86).

1 *Shadowy Horses*: in Irish folklore, the coming of winter was the season for a battle between the forces of light and of darkness. The dark warriors were called the Fomorah, and were thought to be a misshapen race that had inhabited Ireland in the earliest times. 'November, the old beginning of winter, or of the victory of the Fomor, or powers of death, and dismay, and cold, and darkness, is associated by the Irish people with the horse-shaped Púcas, who are now mischievous spirits, but were once Fomorian divinities' (*VP*, p. 808). Here, as in many poems in this volume, the poet imagines himself entering a kind of endless winter of the spirit, in which he is the victim of frightening gusts of passion.

3–6 *North ... East ... South ... West*: 'I follow much Irish and other mythology, and the magical tradition, in associating the North with night and sleep, and the East, the place of sunrise, with hope, and the South, the place of the sun when at its height, with passion and desire, and the West, the place of sunset, with fading and dreaming things' (*VP*, p. 808). For a similar attack from all four points of the compass, see 'Owen Aherne and his Dancers', ll. 5–6.

7 *Sleep, Hope, Dream, endless Desire*: inspired by the North, the East, the West, and the South, respectively.

9 *Beloved*: Olivia Shakespear.

10 *your hair*: the refuge of hair is similar to that in 'The Heart of the Woman'. See also *The Shadowy Waters*, ll. 613–14: 'Bend lower, that I may cover you with my hair, / For we will gaze upon this world no longer'. During the dance of the seductress-god Fand in *The Only Jealousy of Emer* (1919), 'she may drop her hair upon [the Ghost of Cuchulain's] head' (direction after l. 219).

He reproves the Curlew

The original title was 'O'Sullivan Rua to the Curlew', the first of two 'Windle-Straws' (the second was 'To his Heart, bidding it have no Fear'). O'Sullivan Rua – *Rua* is Gaelic for *red* – was an early version of the character Yeats later called Red Hanrahan – the most nature-attentive of his poetical personae. The sentiment of this poem is similar to that of 'The Everlasting Voices': nature-sounds are a kind of keening that embodies the poet's frustrated passion; and the poet hopes to diminish the general expressiveness of things, in order to find peace.

1 *O curlew*: in *Where There is Nothing* (1902) V 340–42, the hero hears amid nature God's voice, lamenting that the Last Judgment is still far away: 'he laments in the wind and in the reeds and in the cries of the curlews'; compare a passage deleted from *The Countess Cathleen*: 'wind cry and water cry / And curlew cry: how does the saying go / That calls them the three oldest cries in

the world?' (*VPl*, p. 89). In *The King's Threshold* (1904), the curlew's cry is also immemorial: 'Although the world be changed from worse to worse, / Amid the changeless clamour of the curlew' (ll. 887–88).

6 *the crying of wind*: compare *Baile and Aillinn*, l. 33: '*this crying in the wind*'.

He remembers Forgotten Beauty

Earlier titles include 'O'Sullivan Rua to Mary Lavell' and 'Michael Robartes remembers Forgotten Beauty'. Here is an instance of persona-switch, from the out-of-doors threadbare poet O'Sullivan Rua (Hanrahan) to the ornament-loving connoisseur Michael Robartes. This poem, with its jewelled crown, its tapestries, its statues, seems more appropriate to the aesthetical Michael Robartes; but its publication history is a useful reminder of the interchangeability of Yeats's personae. The personae are only indistinct tonalities, not elaborate characters; this is why, in the final version of *The Wind among the Reeds*, Yeats found it possible to omit their names.

In this poem of requited love – the magisterial Michael Robartes is often a more successful lover than Aedh or Mongan – the poet's imagination is loosed into an antique world of half-formed images, blurred by clouds of incense, by the moths that eat the tapestries. (As in 'The Sorrow of Love', the woman is a mediating force that connects the poet to a world.) The poet anticipates the end of time, when all images 'must fade like dew' (l. 20); but it seems that his beloved is a kind of storehouse of ancient loveliness, herself the *Anima Mundi* that will cherish beautiful things in a cloudy trance of memory.

2–3 *the loveliness / That has long faded from the world*: in the diary at the end of Joyce's *A Portrait of the Artist as a Young Man* (1916), Stephen Dedalus quotes these opening lines and comments, 'Not this. Not at all. I desire to press in my arms the loveliness which has not yet come into the world'.

21 *flame on flame, and deep on deep*: see 'The Countess Cathleen in Paradise', l. 16.

22 *Throne*: one of the orders of angels. The original text read, 'seraphs, brooding, each alone' (*VP*, p. 156).

A Poet to his Beloved

This poem was originally the second part of 'O'Sullivan the Red to Mary Lavell' – the poem now entitled 'He tells of the Perfect Beauty' was the first part. O'Sullivan the Red (that is, Hanrahan) was a prodigal, imaginatively abundant persona, and it seems that he here intends to resupply the exhausted passions of the beloved from his own huge stocks of passionate rhymes.

1–2 *I bring you ... The books of my numberless dreams*: compare 'Where My Books Go' (from *Irish Fairy Tales*, 1892):

All the words that I gather,
And all the words that I write,
Must spread out their wings untiring,
And never rest in their flight,
Till they come where your sad, sad heart is,
And sing to you in the night,
Beyond where the waters are moving,
Storm darkened or starry bright. (*VP*, p. 739)

He gives his Beloved certain Rhymes

The original title was 'Aedh gives his Beloved certain Rhymes'. This poem was also published in the 1896 story, 'The Binding of the Hair' (*UP* I, p. 393), where it is a song sung by the severed head of the poet Aodh to Queen Dectira. Yeats recollected this early story in 1934: 'A certain man swears to sing the praise of a certain woman, his head is cut off and the head sings. A poem of mine called, "He Gives His Beloved Certain Rhymes" was the song of the head. In attempting to put that story into a dance play I found that I had gone close to Salome's dance in Wilde's play' (*VPl*, p. 1010). The 'dance play' was the 1934 version of *The King of the Great Clock Tower* – a similar plot is used in *A Full Moon in March* (1935). Yeats was fond of the image of the severed head that sings, an emblem of the sexually rejected poet who attains a kind of metaphysical consummation of his love by means of art. Aedh was the self-abasing persona who identified himself with his own gifts; and a severed head is certainly a gift of self.

1 *Fasten your hair*: the women's binding of her hair and the poet's careful construction of rhyme seem to be analogous activities.

12 *but to light your passing feet*: compare 'The Rose of the World', l. 15, and 'The Unappeasable Host', l. 12.

To his Heart, bidding it have no Fear

The original title was 'Out of the Old Days', the second of two 'Windle-Straws' (the first was 'He reproves the Curlew'). This is a prayer for courage to align oneself with the elemental forces, rather than to fear them.

3–7: Yeats quoted these lines in 1907 to introduce the theme of the traditionality, the 'irreverent joy and unserviceable sorrow', of the arts (*EI*, p. 252).

The Cap and Bells

'I dreamed this story exactly as I have written it ... more a vision than a dream ... The poem has always meant a great deal to me, though, as is the way with symbolic poems, it has not always meant quite the same thing' (*VP*, p. 808). Yeats's idea of the love-poet as jester is complicated. On one hand, Yeats was aware of the humiliating role he played as Maud Gonne's perpetually rejected lover: as he wrote in later life, 'A romantic, when romanticism was in its final extravagance, I thought one woman, whether wife, mistress, or incitement to platonic love, enough for a life-time: a Parsifal, Tristram, Don Quixote, without the intellectual prepossessions that gave them solidity' (*A: DP* 14). On the other hand, the jester, with his irresponsibility, his freedom, his detachment from society, could easily be taken as an emblem of poetical power, of the liberated imagination: in 'The Queen and the Fool', Yeats wrote of 'a man who was trying to bring before his mind's eye an image of Aengus, the old Irish god of love and poetry and ecstasy, who changed four of his kisses into birds, and suddenly the image of a man with a cap and bells rushed before his mind's eye, and grew vivid and called itself "Aengus' messenger"' (*M*, p. 115). The jester could even be a figure of political power: a revolutionary magician announces (in the so-called 'De Burgh' version of the unfinished *The Speckled Bird*) that the vulgar have mistaken divine wisdom for the jingling of a jester's bells, but that one day the fool will have revenge on his mockers (*LTMSB*, p. 360).

This poem seems to mean that the beloved rejects all aspects of the poet except his art; but that, by accepting his art, she also secretly accepts the rest of his being – his full personality, in ghostly form, inheres in his poems.

One likely source is the thirteenth-century story of the Jongleur of Notre Dame – the clown who, lacking any other gift for the Virgin Mary, secretly tumbled and juggled before her statue; when he fell in a faint, exhausted, the statue stepped down from the vault of the crypt and fanned his brow with her napkin. A modern retelling of this tale is found in Auden's 'The Ballad of Barnaby' (1969).

1 *The jester walked in the garden*: Pound quoted this line twice in 'Au Jardin' (1911), a poem that recasts Yeats's jester's situation in more impudent terms.

33 *a noise like crickets*: 'the Algonquin Indians ... "could hear the shadow souls of the dead chirp like crickets"' (*UP* I, p. 286).

The Valley of the Black Pig

In 'War', Yeats described a poor Sligo woman who spoke of 'the battle of the Black Pig, which seemed to her a battle between Ireland and England, but to me an Armageddon which shall quench all things in the Ancestral

Darkness again' (*M*, p. 111). Yeats further noted that the common folk imagined this battle to be the occasion for the routing of all of Ireland's enemies – but that Yeats himself saw it as a contest in which winter will conquer summer, or death life (*VP*, pp. 808–810). This poem is central to the November mythology of this volume, its cultivation of a mood of willed passage into destruction. The poet, dwelling with the vestiges of time's beginning – cromlech and cairn – has a vision of time's end. This poem was originally one of 'Two Poems concerning Peasant Visionaries'; the other was 'The Unappeasable Host'.

Title *Black Pig*: 'the black pig is one with the bristleless boar, that killed Dearmod, in November ... The pig seems to have been originally a genius of the corn ... but as ... abhorrence took the place of reverence, pigs and boars grew into types of evil, and were described as the enemies of the very gods they once typified' (*VP*, p. 809). See also 'He mourns for the Change ...', l. 10.

3–4 *the clash ... Of unknown perishing armies*: compare 'Rosa Alchemica' (1896), where the narrator seems to hear 'the clash of unknown armies'; presently Michael Robartes predicts that there will soon come to pass 'that long-foretold battle in the Valley of the Black Pig' (*M*, p. 280–81). Later Yeats wrote, 'the countryman has need but of Swedenborg's keen ears and eagle sight to hear a noise of swords in the empty valley' (*Ex*, p. 36). Longenbach compares Joyce's poem 'I Hear an Army': 'I hear an army charging upon the land, / And the thunder of horses plunging ... They cleave the gloom of dreams' (*SC*, p. 54); Joyce noted that Yeats was fond of this poem (Joyce, *Letters* I, p. 159).

5 *cromlech*: see 'A Faery Song', caption.

6 *cairn*: a heap of stones, often a Neolithic burial site.

The Lover asks Forgiveness because of his Many Moods

Earlier titles include 'The Twilight of Peace', 'The Twilight of Forgiveness', and 'Michael Robartes asks Forgiveness because of his Many Moods'. Michael Robartes was the persona who most relished highly wrought artifice, such as the antique places mentioned in this poem. In 'The Moods' Yeats described the exterior referent of human emotions; and in this poem the beloved directly addresses these Moods, these consternating beings that fill the poet with dim, vacillating longings. As in 'He remembers Forgotten Beauty' – another Michael Robartes poem – the beloved has special intimacy with forgotten beauties. She can rehearse the ways in which the poetical imagination tests the satisfactoriness of old images as embodiments of vague desires. The lover and the beloved seem to trouble each other with the incompleteness of their emotional lives. This poem, like the other Michael Robartes poems (especially 'He bids his Beloved be at Peace') seems to look forward to some state of imagelessness, a termination of the tumult of dreams. Bradford (*YW*, pp. 35–39) prints some early drafts.

13 *Niamh*: see *The Wanderings of Oisin* I 48.
16 *Phoenix*: see 'His Phoenix', which identifies the phoenix with the beloved.

He tells of a Valley full of Lovers

An earlier title was 'Aedh tells of a Valley full of Lovers'. Aedh was the persona of extreme adulation and visionary self-abandonment. The valley full of lovers may be compared to a similar valley in the short story, 'Hanrahan's Vision' (1896).

4 *her cloud-pale eyelids . . . dream-dimmed eyes*: compare l. 1 of the next poem: 'O cloud-pale eyelids, dream-dimmed eyes'; 'The Secret Rose', l. 6: 'pale eyelids, heavy with the sleep'; and 'I see Phantoms . . .', l. 25: 'cloud-pale . . . eyes'. In an early draft of *The Shadowy Waters* Forgael gazes at Dectora's 'sad & cloud pale eyelids' (*DC*, p. 187).

He tells of the Perfect Beauty

This was originally the first part of a poem called 'O'Sullivan the Red to Mary Lavell' – its second part became 'A Poet to his Beloved'. Yeats also used the title 'Aedh tells of the Perfect Beauty'. The spirit of humility shown in the poem – the poet's effortful rhymes lose all force when put next to the beauty of the woman and the stars – seems more appropriate to the persona of Aedh. An earlier poem, 'To Ireland in the Coming Times', turns on the contrast between the measured and the unmeasured; similarly, this poem turns on the contrast between the laboured and the unlaboured. Perfect beauty is effortless; but the attempt to realize it in verse requires endless work. A later poem, 'Adam's Curse', extends the need for labour to women's beauty as well.

1 *O cloud-pale eyelids, dream-dimmed eyes*: compare l. 4 of the previous poem.
7 *God burn time*: see 'The Moods', ll. 1–2.

He hears the Cry of the Sedge

This was originally entitled 'Aodh to Dectora' – the first of 'Three Songs' (along with the poems later called 'The Lover mourns for the Loss of Love' and 'He thinks of those who have Spoken Evil of his Beloved'). Aedh (like

Mongan) is among Yeats's most cursed and desolated personae – for the theme of his beheading, see the note to 'He gives his Beloved certain Rhymes'. Yeats recorded that, for seven celibate years after the break-up of his affair with Olivia Shakespear in 1896, he lived in a condition of such extreme sexual stress that felt at times like shrieking aloud (*Mem*, p. 125). This poem is a kind of approximation to that shriek.

3 *sedge*: a plant on which Keats, in 'La Belle Dame sans Merci' (1819), owns poetical rights. This poem is somewhat similar in mood.

4 the axle: compare 'Veronica's Napkin', l. 2: 'Tent-pole'.

8 girdle of light: the heavens must be undressed before the undressing of the beloved is possible.

He thinks of those who have Spoken Evil of his Beloved

This was originally published (with the poems later called 'He hears the Cry of the Sedge' and 'The Lover mourns for the Loss of Love') as 'Aodh to Dectora' – the third of 'Three Songs'. Aedh was the persona most conscious of the act of singing, the act of giving himself to the beloved by means of verbal art. In an earlier Aedh-poem, 'He tells of the Perfect Beauty', the poet despaired of the usefulness of his art – weighed against perfect beauty, the poem was overthrown. But here the poet discovers a use for his words – weighed against human social life, the poem has devastating force. As in some earlier poems, such as 'A Dream of Death', this poem addresses itself: the text plays a role in the action the poem describes.

5 *a mouthful of air*: a phrase Yeats liked – see *The King's Threshold* (1904), l. 494; *At the Hawk's Well* (1917), l. 257; *The King of the Great Clock Tower* (1935), l. 160; *JSD*, p. 59; and *UP* I, p. 173. Here it suggests the poet's ability to create almost *ex nihilo* a weighty thing that endures for many generations – the poem is breath, inspiration, *anima*. Pound remembered this line in *Guide to Kulchur* (1938): '"I made it out of a mouthful of air" wrote Bill Yeats in his heyday. The *forma*, the immortal *concetto*, the concept, the dynamic form which is like the rose pattern driven into the dead iron-filings by the magnet' (p. 152).

The Blessed

In later life, Yeats analysed his whole poetic career as an inner dialogue between the swordsman and the saint (*L*, p. 798). That is the dialectic of *The Wanderings of Oisin*; and this poem is also a dialogue between a man of action and a holy man. But here the tension is not great, and the synthesis of worldly and otherworldly concerns seems easy. St Patrick advised Oisin that only fasting and prayers could save his soul; but the tolerant Dathi advises Cumhal that drunkenness is a fine road to blessedness. Pagan bliss and saintly wisdom here seem identical.

1 *Cumhal*: in Yeats's short story 'The Crucifixion of the Outcast', written about the same time as this poem, the hero is a pagan gleeman named Cumhal who is crucified by a gang of monks. But the name may be coincidence, for in this poem Cumhal is a king.

17 *God's Mother*: compare 'Anashuya and Vijaya', l. 66, 'the parents of the gods'.

23 *thuribles*: censers.

32 *a drunken head*: compare 'The Secret Rose', l. 4; 'The Hour before Dawn', in which a certain beer can make a man sleep for centuries; and 'A Drunken Man's Praise of Sobriety', which alleges that 'all dead men are drunk' (l. 16). In the 1927 version of *The Resurrection* (*VP*, pp. 914, 928) there is a 'Song of the Drunkard', sung by a Dionysiac orgiast; 'The drunkard with the painted eyes / Discovered thought is misery, / Now, with drum and rattle, he / Bids a drunken God arise' (ll. 195–98; 429–32). During the 1890s Yeats experimented with hashish and other artificial inductions to visionary trance.

The Secret Rose

This poem (originally entitled 'O'Sullivan Rua to the Secret Rose') is the last of Yeats's poems explicitly addressed to the Rose. It differs from its predecessors in several ways. First, the earlier Rose poems are usually short and compressed, but the visionary exuberance of 'The Secret Rose' suggests the amazing evocative power of symbols: from the leaves of the Rose story after story rises into being. Second, in the earlier volume the Rose suffered along with man, and could descend to him at any time; but now she seems to dwell at a greater distance ('Far-off, most secret, and inviolate Rose', l. 1) – she pertains less to present life than to ancient legends and to the end of the world. (*The Wind among the Reeds* imagines a more desperate and fallen world than *The Rose*.) Third, there is a feeling that the Rose is now best approached by some ceremony or rite. This poem is related to the short story 'Rosa Alchemica' (1896), in which Michael Robartes creates, after careful study of old books, a kind of ritual (combining certain elements of both 'the Holy Sepulchre / And . . . the wine-vat', ll. 3–4) in which ecstatic cultists watch the petals of a mosaic rose on the ceiling of the room turn real, fall through the air, and become pagan gods who accompany them in a dance (*M*, p. 288).

The catalogue of old legends enumerated in this poem suggests that the Rose is an asylum of forgotten beauty, a place like Oisin's Tír na nÓg in which the vision finds a refuge with the visionary – both those visionaries who admired unearthly beauty and those who were seized by it against their will.

4 *wine-vat*: compare the sacred drunkennness of 'The Blessed'. In early drafts of *The Player Queen*, the beautiful Decima hides in a wine-vat and sings (Bradford, *WPQ*, p. 37).

5 *the tumult of defeated dreams*: the Rose, like the heroine of Swinburne's 'The Garden of Proserpine' (1866), is a kind of dream attained after other dreams exhaust themselves.

6–7 *pale eyelids, heavy with the sleep / Men have named Beauty*: compare the experience of the narrator of 'Rosa Alchemica', who, when Michael Robartes induces him to a trance, sees forms with 'half-closed eyelids' before he passes into 'that Death which is Beauty herself' (*M*, p. 277). Joyce wrote in 1906, 'When I get home at 10 o'clock ... I am so tired that I can barely skim over ... a page of a novel before my eyelids are heavy with the sleep men have named etc'. (*Letters* II, p. 202).

9 *the crowned Magi; and the king*: the Magi are the wise men who followed a star to Bethlehem and gave gifts to the Christ-child (see 'The Magi'). The king is Conchubar. Conchubar, according to Yeats's note to this poem, was converted to Christianity at the end of his life, and felt such a furious desire to kill the Jews who had crucified Christ that his brains spilt out of his head, and he died (*VP*, p. 812). (For more information on Conchubar, see the note to *The Wanderings of Oisin* III 80.) The Rose synthesizes pagan and Christian mythology in its leaves.

12 *him*: Cuchulain – see the note to 'Cuchulain's Fight with the Sea'.

13 *Fand*: after Cuchulain fell into a state of 'magical weakness', the goddess Fand seduced him into the country of the gods with promises of healing, 'wine and gold and silver', and her love (*VP*, p. 813). According to the version of the story Yeats used in his play *The Only Jealousy of Emer* (1919), an insensate image of Cuchulain remained with his wife Emer, while his spirit revelled with Fand. Also see 'Under the Moon', l. 12: 'Fand, who could change to an otter or fawn'; the 1903 version of *On Baile's Strand*: 'Fand / Made all these little golden eyes' on an embroidered cloak (*VPl*, p. 511); and *Fighting the Waves* (1929), ll. 200–1: 'Fand, daughter of Manannan'.

16 *him who drove the gods out of their liss*: Caoilte – see the note to 'The Hosting of the Sidhe', l. 3. 'I have read about Caolte after the battle of Gabra, when almost all his companions were killed, driving the gods out of their Liss' (*VP*, p. 813). A *liss* is usually a haunted mound; Yeats defined it as a fort.

18 *barrows*: grave-mounds.

19 *proud dreaming king*: Fergus – see the note to 'Fergus and the Druid'. 'He married Nessa, [who] took him "captive in a single look" ... Presently, because of his great love, he gave up his throne to Conchobar, her son by another, and lived out his days feasting, and fighting, and hunting' (*VP*, p. 813).

22 *him who sold tillage*: the hero of one of Yeats's favourite folk-tales. A young man "saw a light before him on the high road. When he came as far, there was an open box on the road, and a light coming up out of it. He took up the box. There was a lock of hair in it. Presently he had to go to become the servant of a king for his living. There were eleven boys. When they were going out into the stable at ten o'clock, each of them took a light but he. ... When he went into his stable he opened the box. The light was great. It was twice as much as in the other stables" ... In the end, the young man, and not the king, marries the woman' (*VP*, pp. 813–14; compare *VSR*, p. 73). Yeats remarked that this story alters our love for a woman (*UP* I, p. 327); and he associated the woman whose hair shines at midnight with the ideal beauty of Helen of Troy (*UP* II, p. 190). To compliment Dorothy Wellesley Yeats wrote: 'I think much of the most beautiful of Chinese lanthorns, your face. I found some Irish story once of men who threshed by the light of a lock of hair, but that was a more mundane light' (*DWL*, p. 66). As the poet examines the innermost petals of the Rose, he finds that, as the outer world grows darker, the ideal becomes more luminous.

29 *stars be blown about the sky*: Bloom (*Yeats*, p. 132) compares Blake, *The Four Zoas* IX 829: 'The stars consumd like a lamp blown out'.

32: the repetition of the first line suggests closure – all is now enfolded within the Rose.

Maid Quiet

The original title was 'O'Sullivan the Red upon his Wanderings' – later publications replaced 'O'Sullivan the Red' with other names, first 'Hanrahan', then 'The Lover'. The poem once appeared in one of Yeats's Hanrahan stories, 'The Twisting of the Rope' (1892); Hanrahan, an itinerant poet, sings it on entering a farmhouse, as an impressive specimen of his art (*VSR*, pp. 199–200); later in the story a clever matron foils Hanrahan's attempt to seduce her daughter.

Title *Maid Quiet*: for other personifications of Quiet, see 'In the Seven Woods', ll. 10–11: 'Quiet ... eating her wild heart'; and *Baile and Aillinn*, l. 178: 'Quiet's wild heart'; also the juvenile 'She Who Dwelt among the Sycamores', l. 13: 'I am lone Lady Quietness' (*VP*, p. 716).

4–5: between these lines originally appeared this passage, in the apocalyptic vein of 'The Valley of the Black Pig': 'I would the pale deer had come / From Gulleon's place of pride, / And trampled the mountains away, / And drunk up the murmuring tide' (*VP*, p. 171).

7 *words that called up lightning*: the loss of Quiet seems to be accompanied by a gain in incantatory power.

The Travail of Passion

This was first published (with 'He bids his Beloved be at Peace') as one of 'Two Love Poems'. This poem is addressed to Olivia Shakespear, who is imagined as a member of a chorus of immortal passions, or Moods (compare 'The Moods'). By incarnating themselves, these Moods become subject to suffering, but also become sympathetic to man.

Title *Passion*: a pun on Christ's Passion. Compare Yeats's Wildean story about the ritual sacrifice of a poet, 'The Crucifixion of the Outcast' (1897).

5 *Kedron*: a stream near Jerusalem.

6 *We will bend down and loosen our hair*: the posture of Mary Magdalene.

The Lover pleads with his Friend for Old Friends

In the original title, the speaker was called 'The Poet'. The anticipation of the beloved's old age recalls 'When You are Old'.

1 *you*: Maud Gonne, much involved in political activity.

5 *old friends the most*: the epigraph to Pound's 'Amities' (1916).

The Lover speaks to the Hearers of his Songs in Coming Days

The original title was 'Hanrahan speaks to the Lovers of his Songs in Coming Days' – Hanrahan, 'softened with a new pity and remorse born from the fading of his powers and from the loosening of his hold upon life', sings a version of this poem in 'The Vision of O'Sullivan the Red' (1896), where it initiates the apparition of many sorts of blessed or sinful lovers (*VSR*, pp. 216–17). Here the raggedy and much-frustrated poet imagines that, because he celebrated sexual love, he will be confined after death to a purgatorial throng of ghosts similar to those he saw in his vision. The theme of the poem's preoccupation with its own effects is also found in 'A Dream of Death' and 'He thinks of those who have Spoken Evil of his Beloved'.

1 *altar-rails*: the women in church can scarcely remember their prayers,

because the seductive memory of the poet's verse blots them out. Here is the Christian-pagan dialectic of Patrick and the half-repentant Oisin in another form.

2 *songs I wove*: after singing this song, Hanrahan immediately plucked a 'frail blossom' and 'wound its stalk among the wires of his harp' (*VSR*, p. 217); from the petals of this flower spring the visionary presences.

6 *the Attorney for Lost Souls*: the Virgin Mary, as intercessor.

The Poet pleads with the Elemental Powers

Earlier titles include 'A Mystical Prayer to the Masters of the Elements, Michael, Gabriel, and Raphael' (archangels in Milton's *Paradise Lost*); a more pagan version in which the names are replaced by 'Finvara, Feacra, Caolte'; and 'Aodh pleads with the Elemental Powers'. This begins a series of poems on astronomical themes: many of the earlier poems in this volume spoke of the confounding of the stars at the end of time, and the volume approaches its own end with a more detailed look at stellar processes. The self-sacrificing Aedh, the beheaded poet who disperses himself in the text of his poems, is an appropriately apocalyptic persona.

The theme of this poem is the removal of the Rose from human ken – the Rose, that suffered along with man in the previous volume, that was 'Far-off, most secret, and inviolate' in 'The Secret Rose', now seems to have ascended to a wholly inaccessible realm. (The abstraction of the Rose may be related biographically to the impossibility of wooing Maud Gonne.) The constellations lament her absence, but are powerless to act – only the powers that are underneath, above, or beyond the material world have jurisdiction over the Rose. In 1898 Yeats wrote an essay, 'The Autumn of the Flesh', that announced a school of keener, more disembodied poetry; and this poem is typical of that school, in that it strives to disembody the Rose from any natural form – to keep her symbolic in the largest, most indefinite manner.

1 *The Powers whose name and shape no living creature knows*: compare the 'elemental powers' of 'To Ireland in the Coming Times', l. 23 – another poem in which the relation of measured to unmeasured, or of shaped to shapeless, is important.

2 *the Immortal Rose*: 'The Rose has been for many centuries a symbol of spiritual love and supreme beauty ... once a symbol of the sun, – itself a principal symbol of divine nature, and the symbolic heart of things. ... Because the Rose, the flower sacred to the Virgin Mary ... is the western Flower of Life, I have imagined it growing upon the Tree of Life' (*VP*, p. 811).

3 *the Seven Lights*: Ursa Major (also referred to in 'He thinks of his Past Greatness . . .', l. 4, and *The Player Queen* [1922] I 298, II 460, 531).

4 *The Polar Dragon*: the constellation Draco. 'I have made the Seven Lights . . . lament for the theft of the Rose, and I have made the Dragon . . . the guardian of the Rose, because these constellations move about the pole of the heavens, the ancient Tree of Life' (*VP*, p. 812). As Ellmann notes, the cover of Yeats's book *The Secret Rose* depicts a serpent entwined about the Tree of Life (*IY*, p. 78). Dragons recur in 'Michael Robartes and the Dancer', l. 4, and 'Her Triumph', l. 1 – in both cases associated with feminine wilfulness. Also compare *The Shadowy Waters*, l. 598, where the rope that holds Forgael's ship to earth is called a 'Dragon'; and the coils of the 'mirror-scalèd serpent' in 'Ribh Denounces Patrick', l. 10.

5 *His heavy rings uncoiled*: the verse movement, with its alternation of long and short lines, may attempt to imitate this.

9 *Encircle*: compare the imperative *enfold* in 'The Secret Rose', l. 2 – another poem in which transcendent meaning nestles inviolably in the centre of things.

12 *The nets of day and night*: compare 'Into the Twilight', l. 2.

15: this line originally read 'Or as the changing spears flung by the golden stars' (*VP*, p. 156) – closely following a line in Blake's 'The Tyger' (1794).

17 *let a gentle silence*: yet another prayer for the winds to still themselves in this wind-blown volume. The Rose seems to live in the eye of the storm.

18 *her footsteps*: compare 'The Rose of the World', l. 15, and 'He gives his Beloved certain Rhymes', l. 12.

He wishes his Beloved were Dead

The original title was 'Aodh to Dectora'. In an early short story, 'The Binding of the Hair', Aedh's severed head sang to his beloved; here the beloved herself would be more valuable to the poet dead than alive. As in the previous poem, there is a movement towards detachment, disembodiment, the flesh's autumn – the drama of the poet's love intensifies as it grows morbid, immaterial. For the superiority of the dead beautiful woman to all other subjects for poetry, see Poe's essay 'The Philosophy of Composition' (1846), a work important to Baudelaire and to the tradition of French Symbolism.

9–10 *your hair was bound and wound / About the stars and moon and sun*: the image of the woman's hair intertwined through the heavens may be seen as the ultimate extension of the sheltering-hair theme of 'The Heart of the Woman' and 'The Travail of Passion'. Yeats once mentioned 'a venerated book of the Cabala where the beard of God winds in and out among the stars, its hairs all numbered' (*AV*, p. 23); this may suggest that the form of the beloved is a kind of symbolical diagram of the universe itself, as in 'The Two Trees'. Similar majesty is attributed to hair in 'His Bargain', ll. 10–11 – the beloved's hair is stronger than the threads of Necessity. It is possible, however, that the binding of her hair around the stars may mean that she is, despite all efforts, still connected to the natural world, still impeded from moving into complete ideality. At the end of *The Shadowy Waters*, a work similar in theme, Dectora's lover severs a rope to symbolize their souls' perfect detachment from nature.

He wishes for the Cloths of Heaven

The original title was 'Aedh wishes for the Cloths of Heaven'. Here the reticent Aedh – more concerned with his gifts than with himself – imagines himself as a kind of cosmic Sir Walter Raleigh. The poem's chief technical interest lies in that it has no rhymes, only repetitions of end-words.

1 *heavens' embroidered cloths, / Enwrought with golden and silver light*: the heavens are also seen as artwork in a song added to *The Countess Cathleen* in 1895: 'covered the door of the infinite fold / With the pale stars and the wandering moon' (ll. 676–77).

8 *you tread on my dreams*: the beloved seems to grow wrapped, sheltered in the poet's fantasy – another kind of encircling or enfolding, as in 'The Secret Rose' or 'The Poet pleads with the Elemental Powers'. Compare Pound's Cantos: 'the problem after any revolution is what to do with / your gunmen / as old Billyum found out in Oireland / in the Senate, Bedad! or before then / Your gunmen tread on moi drreams' (80/496).

He thinks of his Past Greatness when a Part of the Constellations of Heaven

In the original title the subject was not 'He' but 'Mongan'. The persona of Mongan appears in only two poems – this and 'He mourns for the Change ...' – but these are unusually important poems. When Yeats codified his esoteric beliefs in *A Vision* (1925), he spoke of the ultimate component of human identity as the *daimon*, that part of a man that survives from one reincarnative state to the next; and the Mongan poems constitute Yeats's first attempt to define the tragedy of the *daimon* as it passes, unappeasable, through all its thousands of inflections of being. In *A Vision* Yeats described how a painfully knotted love relation could persist for centuries, even though the actors might be husband and wife in one generation, mother and son in the next, and so forth. Similarly Mongan feels that, despite his amazing plasticity of being, there is one thing that he cannot be, that he cannot experience; and this solitary interdiction to his fantasy blights all his lives.

1 *I have drunk ale from the Country of the Young*: in 'The Cradles of Gold' (1896), a faery king demands silence so that he 'might meditate upon the wisdom that Mongan raved out after he had drunk from the seven vats of wine!' (*UP* I, p. 416). For the theme of drinking and blessedness, see 'The Blessed'. '"The Country of the Young" is a name in Celtic poetry for the country of the gods and of the happy dead' (*VP*, p. 177) – see 'The White Birds', l. 9, and 'Sailing to Byzantium', l. 1.

2 *I know all things now*: Yeats defined the persona of Mongan as a wizard who remembers past lives.

3 *a hazel-tree*: 'the Irish tree of Life or of Knowledge, and in Ireland it was doubtless, as elsewhere, the tree of the heavens' (*VP*, p. 177); compare the shape-changing hazel-wand in 'He mourns for the Change . . .', l. 6.

4: 'The Crooked Plough and the Pilot Star are translations of the Gaelic names of the Plough [Ursa Major] and the Pole Star' (*VP*, p. 177). Compare the tree on which the moon hangs, 'Vacillation' VI 13, and the first tree in 'The Two Trees'. The pole-star also appears in 'A Dialogue of Self and Soul' I 5. For references to Ursa Major, see 'The Poet pleads with the Elemental Powers', l. 3.

6 *I became a rush*: compare the fir-tree, one of the avatars of the dream-malleable Fergus in 'Fergus and the Druid', l. 34.

12 *Must I endure your amorous cries?*: compare the torturing nature-noises in 'The Everlasting Voices', 'He reproves the Curlew', and 'He hears the Cry of the Sedge'. In the original text of ll. 11–12 the nature-noises expressed the speaker's own emotion: 'Although the rushes and the fowl of the air / Cry of his love with their piteous cries' (*VP*, p. 177).

The Fiddler of Dooney

After all the tormented poems of this volume, disguised, deflected, and perpetuated in difficult symbolic forms, Yeats ends this collection with a sweet, folk-like ballad – many of Yeats's sequences end with a similar movement towards impersonal simplicity.

Title *Dooney*: 'The places mentioned in the poem are all in County Sligo. Dooney Rock is a great rock on the edge of Loch Gill. I had been to many picnics there and in gratitude called my fiddler by its name' (*UP* II, p. 496).

3 *Kilvarnet*: a township.

4 *Mocharabuiee*: a plain on the outskirts of Co. Sligo.

12 *call me first through the gate*: another reconciliation of singer and saint. The merry fiddler takes precedence in heaven over his pious relatives – the grasshopper triumphs over the ant.

THE OLD AGE OF QUEEN MAEVE (1903)

Yeats was fond of stories like this, in which the living assist in the affairs of supernatural beings. Aengus and the other Irish gods seem to be bound by mysterious constraints – the fences and walls built by men can symbolize thresholds that the gods themselves may not pass (see ll. 91–99). Aengus is too shadowy and attenuated, despite his divinity, to work out his own fate – he seeks out both a porter (l. 37) and Ailell (l. 73) to give him a voice; and he seeks out Maeve and her grandchildren to release certain hidden powers in the earth, that he may consummate his love. To an extent, this poem is, like Yeats's last narrative poem, 'The Gift of Harun Al-Rashid', a tale of mediumship: spirits search for human bodies in order to utter themselves, to embody their will.

1–8: Yeats added these lines in 1933. By providing a frame in which this poem is sung to an audience at Byzantium, Yeats seems to push the narration back into an aesthetical antiquity. This distancing is opposed by the apostrophes to the poet's heart (ll. 30–35) and to Maud Gonne (ll. 130–41), which give an impression of intimacy and personableness – though both introduction and apostrophes serve to dramatize the poet's presence. Yeats liked costumed minstrels: 'The reciter must be made exciting and wonderful in himself, apart from what he has to tell, and that is more difficult than it was in the Middle Ages ... I can think of nothing better than ... to give the story-teller a definite fictitious personality and find for him an appropriate costume' (*Ex*, p. 216).

9 *Maeve*: see the note to *The Wanderings of Oisin* I 18.

11 *Cruachan*: in Co. Roscommon, the site of Maeve's palace, named after her mother Cruacha.

31 *another*: Maud Gonne, also 'beautiful and fierce' (l. 29). Yeats's first poems on Maud Gonne's aging, such as 'The Folly of Being Comforted', were written at about this time.

36–37 *a wild goose / Cried from the porter's lodge*: compare the Old Beggar who falls into a trance and brays like a donkey in *The Player Queen* (1922) I 330.

41 *Sidhe*: the old gods of Ireland. Yeats thought that the word *sidhe* meant wind – see l. 125.

57–58 *the great war / Over the White-Horned Bull and the Brown Bull*: see *Baile and Aillinn*, ll. 14–15.

69 *Ailell*: when Yeats rewrote *The Countess Cathleen*, he changed the poet-hero's name from Kevin to Aleel, in honour of Maeve's husband; Aleel tells the Countess how Maeve wept because she forgot her human lover's name (l. 301).

71 *Fergus*: see *The Wanderings of Oisin* III 89.

77 *Magh Ai*: a plain surrounding Cruachan.

85 *Aengus*: see *The Wanderings of Oisin* I 47.

88–89 *their beauty's like a hollow dream, / Mirrored in streams*: for the water-reflection theme, see *The Wanderings of Oisin* I 184–85. Also compare *Baile and Aillinn*, l. 172, 'nothing troubles the great streams' (of paradise).

92 *Maines*: according to Lady Gregory's *Cuchulain of Muirthemne*, the Maines were Maeve's children by Ailell – compare 'The Hour Before Dawn', l. 8. The children of the Maines were therefore Maeve's grandchildren (l. 109).

93 *Bual*: one of the Sidhe. Earlier printings give this name as *Anbual*.

117–18 *red-eared hounds / With long white bodies*: compare *The Wanderings of Oisin* I 140–41.

132 *you've not her wandering heart*: Yeats did not wish to attribute Maeve's promiscuity to Maud Gonne – 'Maeve had three in an hour, they say' (*The Death of Cuchulain* [1939], l. 200).

134–35 *there is no high story about queens / In any ancient book but tells of you*: compare *Baile and Aillinn*, l. 202: 'You [Maud Gonne] are more high of heart than she [Deirdre]'. In a draft written around 1897 as a subject for a poem about Maud Gonne, Yeats wrote, 'I put away all the romances. / How care I now of queens / & of noble women, whose / very dust is full of sorrow, / are they not all but my / beloved whispering to me' (Stallworthy, *BL*, p. 3). Also compare 'The Circus Animals' Desertion' II 9–16, where Yeats explains how *The Countess Cathleen* treats Maud Gonne.

141 *Outrun the measure*: the poet's feeling overflows the boundaries of the poem's metre. Compare 'To Ireland in the Coming Times', l. 25: '*unmeasured mind*'.

143–44 *two lovers came out of the air / With bodies made out of soft fire*: compare 'Ribh at the Tomb of Baile and Aillinn', ll. 15–16: 'the intercourse of angels is a light / Where . . . both seem lost, consumed'. *The Dreaming of the Bones* (1919) offers a parody of this plot: the ghosts of Diarmuid and Dervorgilla, quivering with unexpressed love, beg a young man to forgive them so that they may embrace: but he refuses, and they must stay apart.

BAILE AND AILLINN (1903)

Yeats's principal source for this tale was Lady Gregory's *Cuchulain of Muirthemne* (1902); according to her chapter 'Battle of Rosnaree', 'a strange, wild-looking man' approached Baile, 'coming . . . as fast as a hawk that darts from a cliff', and told him that his beloved Aillinn was dead; and Baile dropped dead; then the same strange man appeared to Aillinn, far away, and told her that Baile was dead; and Aillinn dropped dead. The mysterious herald explained only that 'it was foretold by Druids that were friendly to them that they would not come together in their lifetime, but that after their death they would meet, and be happy for ever after' (p. 231). Yeats identified Lady Gregory's fatal messenger as the god Aengus, who wished to provide for the two lovers an erotic refuge in the land of the dead. This poem resembles *The Wanderings of Oisin* in that satisfaction for human desires exists only in a superhuman realm; but *Baile and Aillinn* makes the deathliness of such satisfaction more explicit. This poem also resembles *The Shadowy Waters* – one version of which was complete by 1900 – in that it posits a kind of *Liebestod* as the terminal experience of man; but what is grand opera in *The Shadowy Waters* is here a kind of dance, a deft consummation of love through symbols and images. In 1932 Yeats wrote an occult sequel to this poem, 'Ribh at the Tomb of Baile and Aillinn'.

In the italicized sections (as in the italicized sections of 'The Grey Rock') the poet attempts to relate the archaic tale to contemporary life. As in such lyrics as 'To the Rose upon the Rood of Time', the poet understands that the gooseflesh of divine love tends to spoil, to trivialize human enjoyment (ll. 95–96, 205–7); and yet he wishes to cherish such satisfactions as life can provide (ll. 38–40).

1 I hardly hear the curlew cry: compare Buck Mulligan's obscene song in the 'Scylla and Charybdis' chapter of Joyce's *Ulysses*, beginning '*I hardly hear the purlieu cry*' (*A Critical and Synoptic Edition*, ed. Gabler: Episode 9, l. 1143).

4 Ulad: Ulster.

4 Buan: a local Ulster goddess. Compare the 1903 version of *On Baile's Strand*: 'The heavy inlaid brooch / That Buan hammered' (*VPl*, p. 511).

5 honey mouth: 'because he was so sweet-spoken . . . they called him Baile of the Honey-Mouth' (*CM*, p. 231).

7 Lugaid: father of Aillinn, and son of a King of Munster.

14–15 *the long wars for the White Horn / And the Brown Bull*: 'What the "long wars for the White Horn and the Brown Bull" were . . . I shall not explain. The reader will find all that he need know about them, and about the story of Baile and Aillinn itself, in Lady Gregory's "Cuchulain of Muirthemne", the most important book that has come out of Ireland in my time' (*VP*, p. 188). In the chapter 'The Two Bulls' Lady Gregory told of the heroic fight between a White-horned bull and a Brown bull, champions of Connaught and Ulster respectively – the Brown killed the White-horned (pp. 208–9); the war over possession of the Brown bull is told in the earlier chapter 'The War for the Bull of Cuailgne'.

18 *Emain*: see 'The Madness of King Goll', l. 2.

21 *Muirthemne*: a plain, Cuchulain's birthplace.

33 this crying in the wind: compare 'He reproves the Curlew', l. 6: 'the crying of wind'. A curlew cries in l. 1 of this poem.

35 Kate or Nan: compare Blake, 'To The Accuser who is The God of This World', l. 4: 'Kate into Nan'.

40 A child's laughter, a woman's kiss: compare 'Vacillation' III 8: 'children's gratitude or woman's love'. This is a common theme in Yeats's narrative poems: in *The Shadowy Waters*, ll. 124-25, the world's deceitful message is 'You will have all you have wished for when you have earned / Land for your children'; in 'The Two Kings', l. 121, Edain claims that women are best satisfied by giving 'Happiness to children and to men'; and in 'The Gift of Harun Al-Rashid', ll. 101–2, the Caliph says that 'mouth to mouth / Is a man's mockery of the changeless soul'.

73 *the Hound of Ulad*: Cuchulain, whose name means Hound of Culain.

76 *the harper's daughter and her friend*: Deirdre (daughter of Cuchulain's reciter) and her lover Naoise.

79 *betrayed*: see the notes to *The Wanderings of Oisin* III 89-90. Cuchulain's tears show that the tragedy of Deirdre and Naoise has mythological force even to their contemporaries.

91 Deirdre: although Yeats often alluded to the story of Deirdre and Naoise – see *The Wanderings of Oisin* III 90 and 'The Rose of the World', l. 5 – he mentioned her name in his non-dramatic poetry only here and at l. 97. She is the subject of the play *Deirdre* (1907); in *On Baile's Strand* (1903 version), she is called 'that high-headed even-walking queen' (*VPl*, p. 492).

98 being lovely was so wise: compare l. 201, and also 'Michael Robartes and the Dancer', l. 12, where a woman is advised to look at her beauty in a mirror and thence 'grow wise'.

108–10 *As though their music were enough / To make the savage heart of love / Grow gentle*: 'love itself would [not] be more than an animal hunger but for the poet' (*EI*, p. 158).

111–12: in the early printings, these lines read, 'And leather-coated men with slings / Who peered about on every side' (*VP*, p. 193).

117 *Ogham*: an ancient Irish alphabet.

118 Rury's seed: Baile 'was of the race of Rudraige' (*CM*, p. 231). Finneran notes (*PNE*, p. 686) that this pedigree was ascribed to Red Branch heroes other than Cuchulain.

122 *clip and clip*: compare *The King of the Great Clock Tower* (1935), ll. 131–32, also on the theme of supernatural sex: 'Clip and lip and long for more, / Mortal men our abstracts are'.

123: *the Great Plain*: ' "The Great Plain" is the Land of the Dead and of the Happy; it is called also "The Land of the Living Heart", and many beautiful names besides' (*VP*, p. 188).

130 *the Hill Seat of Leighin*: a fort, seat of the kings of Leinster.

135–36 *Two swans ... Linked by a gold chain*: 'when Baile and Aillinn take the shape of swans linked with a golden chain, they take the shape that other enchanted lovers took before them in the old stories' (*VP*, p. 188). Yeats told one of these 'old stories' in 'Away': in his account of the Only Jealousy of Emer, Yeats wrote that Cuchulain saw 'two birds, bound one to the other with a chain of gold', whose song caused a magical stupor among the warriors; Cuchulain threw his spear at them, wounded one, and fell into an uncanny sleep (*UP* II, p. 280). Yeats also used similarly chained birds as emblems of pure, inter-involved love in 'The Withering of the Boughs', ll. 17–21.

141–42 *the harp-strings / That Edain, Midhir's wife, had wove*: 'Midhir was a king of the Sidhe, or people of faery, and Etain his wife, when driven away by a jealous woman, took refuge once upon a time with Aengus in a house of glass, and there I have imagined her weaving harp-strings out of Aengus' hair. I have brought the harp-strings into ['The Harp of Aengus', from] "The Shadowy Waters", where I interpret the myth in my own way' (*VP*, p. 188). For Edain, see also *The Wanderings of Oisin* I 47.

144 *What shall I call them?*: some of the following metaphors for the dead lovers (suggesting intimacy, concealment, vanishing) recall Shelley's similes for the skylark in 'To a Skylark' (1820).

161–65 *Gorias, / And Findrias and Falias, / And ... Murias ... Cauldron and spear and stone and sword*: 'four mysterious cities where the Tuatha De Danaan, the divine race, came to Ireland, cities of learning out of sight of the world, where they found their four talismans, the spear, the stone, the cauldron, and the sword' (*VP*, p. 188). Murias also appeared in the first printing of 'The Grey Rock': 'old stringed instruments, hung there / By the ancient holy hands that brought them / From murmuring Murias' (*VP*, p. 271). The four talismans were central to Yeats's and Maud Gonne's occultism of the 1890s: 'the old gods and heroes took their places gradually in a symbolic fabric that had for its centre the four talismans ... which related themselves in my mind with the suits of the Tarot' (*Mem*, p. 125). The four talismans are important in Yeats's Hanrahan stories (in texts published after 1903 – see *M*, pp. 220–21, 259); and in a passage from 'The Adoration of the Magi' (1897), deleted after 1914, the talismans are associated with the resurgence of pagan values after the end of the Christian era (*VSR*, p. 170). The stone is traditionally identified with the Stone of Scone, associated with the coronation of Scottish kings and now kept in Westminster Abbey, London.

168 *some huge watcher*: 'men are only able to fashion into beautiful speech the most delicate emotions of the soul ... when they are certain that the soul will not die with the body and that the gates of peace are wide and that the watchers are at their places upon the wall' (*UP* II, p. 131). Also compare *The Shadowy Waters*, l. 320: 'lasting watchers, that outlive the moon'; and in the Acting Version of *The Shadowy Waters* (1911), ll. 43–44, a sailor explains that man-headed birds 'are sent by the lasting watchers to lead men away from this world' (*VPl*, p. 319). Some of the entities in Yeats's later verse, such as the Chinamen in 'Lapis Lazuli', seem to play a role similar to that of watcher.

171 *where earth withers away*: compare 'The Withering of the Boughs' – as spirit grows strong, matter grows weak. Also compare *The Old Age of Queen Maeve*, ll. 85–86.

172 *Though nothing troubles the great streams*: compare *The Old Age of Queen Maeve*, l. 89.

175 *fruit that is of precious stone*: compare 'The Harp of Aengus', ll. 5–6: '*apples made / Of opal and ruby*'. T. Sturge Moore denounced this and the following line as 'the most loathsome upholstery that was ever invented to cushion poetry with' (*TSMC*, p. 10).

176 *apples of the sun and moon*: compare 'The Man who Dreamed of Faeryland', l. 23: 'the sun and moon were in the fruit'.

178 *Quiet's wild heart*: compare 'In the Seven Woods', ll. 10–11: 'Quiet ... eating her wild heart'.

182 *birds of Aengus*: 'The birds that flutter over the head of Aengus are four birds that he made out of his kisses' (*VP*, p. 188) – see *The Wanderings of Oisin* I 47.

188–90 *A yew tree where his body lay; / But a wild apple hid the grass ... where hers was*: 'an apple-tree grew out of her grave, and a yew tree out of Baile's grave' (*CM*, p. 232). Compare 'Ribh at the Tomb of Baile and Aillinn', l. 8: 'juncture of the apple and the yew'. By making the trees twine together in the later poem, Yeats recalled the legend of Tristram and Iseult.

195–96 *They wrote on tablets of thin board, / Made of the apple and the yew*: compare the first version of *The Shadowy Waters* (1900), ll. 28–29: 'tales / That druids write on yew and apple wood' (*VP*, p. 748); and 'Shepherd and Goatherd', l. 115: 'Cut out our rhymes on strips of new-torn bark'. Ultimate love seems to be not only poetry's best theme, but its publication-medium as well. For other examples of the encroachment of text upon theme, see 'When You are Old'. Nature (the noises of rush and bird, ll. 31 and 198) and poetic art alike transmit the story of ideal love.

200–5 I am not afraid of her . . . But I'd have bird and rush forget / Those other two: the poet does not think that Deirdre provides unbeatable competition to Maud Gonne; but the story of Baile and Aillinn disturbs his peace of mind, for nothing known to the modern world matches their consummation in bliss.

202 you are more high of heart than she: compare *The Old Age of Queen Maeve*, ll. 134–35: 'there is no high story about queens / In any ancient book but tells of you [Maud Gonne]'.

IN THE SEVEN WOODS (1904)

Yeats wrote little lyric poetry in the first decade of the twentieth century: most of his energies went into organizing the Abbey Theatre and writing plays for it; and his personal life became somewhat more settled after Maud Gonne's marriage in 1903. *In the Seven Woods* originally comprised the narrative poems *The Old Age of Queen Maeve* and *Baile and Aillinn*, the play *On Baile's Strand*, and all but four of the following poems ('Old Memory' and 'Never Give all the Heart' were added to this section in 1906, 'The Ragged Wood' and 'O Do Not Love Too Long' in 1908). The poems of *In the Seven Woods* are mostly less intense but clearer in focus than those of the previous volume. Yeats does not manipulate a tangle of strangled mythological personae, but instead tends to speak (particularly in 'Adam's Curse') in an agreeably humane and contemporary voice. Faeryland is still a constant theme, but the world to which it is an alternative makes its presence felt more strongly. Also, the aristocratic ideal represented by Lady Gregory, Yeats's fellow researcher into folklore – an ideal of high manners and of selfless devotion to a code of service – begins to embody itself in his poetry. His metres begin to evolve during this period from the slow, congested subtleties of his earlier style to sparer, more determined and rapid rhythms, with high contrast between stressed and unstressed syllables.

In the Seven Woods

The apocalyptic prophecy at the end of this poem follows the model of many poems in *The Wind among the Reeds*, but the poet's receptivity to immediate nature-experience and the political indignation introduce new themes in Yeats's poetry. This is the first of Yeats's poems in which the poet is obviously a man who reads the newspaper.

Title *the Seven Woods*: in Coole Park, the seat of Lady Gregory's family – celebrated in the Introductory Lines to *The Shadowy Waters*.

6 *Tara uprooted*: prehistorical burial site and supposed seat of the ancient Irish kings – uprooted because of recent excavations. See also 'The Two Kings', l. 2, and 'In Tara's Halls'.

6 *new commonness*: Queen Victoria's dissolute son became King Edward VII in 1901. Yeats predicted this in an essay of 1900 in which he derided Irishmen who would soon be thronging to see 'an elderly man ... who has used his example and his influence to make the love of man and woman seem a light and vulgar thing' (*UP* II, p. 212).

8 *paper flowers*: coronation decorations in Dublin.

10–11 *Quiet ... eating her wild heart*: compare *Baile and Aillinn*, l. 178: 'Quiet's wild heart'. See also 'Maid Quiet'. Here she is a figure of tense repose and wayward happiness – for the theme of aimless joy, see 'Tom O'Roughley', l. 4.

12 *that Great Archer*: the constellation Sagittarius. An arrow is also significant in the next poem. For another celestial archer, see 'Parnell's Funeral', l. 10.

14 *Pairc-na-Lee*: one of the Seven Woods – see the Introductory Lines to *The Shadowy Waters*, l. 7.

The Arrow

In some earlier poems (such as 'When You are Old' and 'The Lover pleads with his Friend ...'), Yeats had hinted that Maud Gonne's beauty would be subject to decay. But this is the first poem in which such alterations are actually observed – for later poems on this theme, see especially 'The Folly of Being Comforted', 'Peace', 'Fallen Majesty', 'Broken Dreams', 'Among School Children', and 'A Bronze Head'. In the earlier series of Rose poems, Maud Gonne was identified with Beauty itself, only provisionally brought down to earth in human form; but here she is more profoundly incarnate, subject to time. The arrow that cuts the poet arises from the contrast between her old beauty and her present, 'kinder' beauty.

Title *Arrow*: compare another poem addressed to Maud, 'No Second Troy', l. 8: 'beauty like a tightened bow'.

5–6: these lines originally read: 'Blossom pale, she pulled down the pale blossom / At the moth hour and hid it in her bosom' (*VP*, p. 199); Yeats noted the revised version in his journal for 9 November 1909 (*Mem*, p. 236).

Yeats quoted this to show how 'All is but faint to me beside a moment when she passed before a window, dressed in white, and rearranged a spray of flowers in a vase. Twelve years afterwards I put that impression into verse' (*Mem*, p. 42).

6 *an apple blossom*: Yeats first saw Maud during apple-blossom season – see *A: FY* 5 and *Mem*, p. 236. 'I found I could call dreams by my symbols ... I would go to sleep, say with a spray of apple blossoms on my pillow. Sometimes ... I had gone to sleep with the endeavour to send my soul to that of Maud Gonne' (*Mem*, p. 128).

The Folly of Being Comforted

In this poem Yeats seems to be cultivating his obsession with Maud Gonne, as if his poetic inspiration were dependent on his hopeless affection.

1 *One that is ever kind*: possibly Lady Gregory.

2 *Your well-belovèd*: Maud Gonne.

4 *easier to be wise*: that is, not to be dazzled by her beauty.

6 *Heart cries*: in the early printings, the poet addresses his heart; in the later printings (from 1922 on), the heart addresses the poet (compare the Heart's direct discourse in such later poems as 'Owen Aherne and his Dancers').

Old Memory

This poem was written after Maud Gonne's marriage in February 1903 to Captain John MacBride, a man whom Yeats did not respect. When Yeats heard the news of her marriage, he felt as if he had been struck by lightning – and this despair made him write that his relation with her had 'come to naught' (l. 8).

1 *O thought, fly to her*: an extremely tentative and indirect mode of address, suitable for estranged lovers: the poet does not speak to the beloved, but dispatches a half-formed telepathic thought that he later partly withdraws.

6 *but half yours*: the poet claims that he contributed to the strength and presence of his beloved; man and woman are inextricably involved in one another's being. The counter-theme – that the beloved contributes to the poet's achievement – appears in a later poem, 'Against Unworthy Praise', l. 6: 'So did she your strength renew'. Yeats recorded a double vision of Maud Gonne as a hollow statue, and of himself as the flames playing within the statue's head – a remarkable image of the oneness of poet and beloved (*Mem*, p. 134).

A still further evolution of the theme of Maud Gonne's vicariousness occurred in a passage where Yeats discussed how 'A nation in crisis becomes like a single mind ... through "telepathic contact" at some depth below that of normal consciousness': 'I was sedentary and thoughtful; but Maud Gonne was not sedentary, and I noticed that before some great event she did not think but became exceedingly superstitious. Are not such as she aware, at moments of great crisis, of some power beyond their own minds ... ?' (*A: SB* 4). And Yeats went on to end this description of Maud with a relevant quotation from *The Only Jealousy of Emer* (1919), ll. 7–14: 'How many centuries spent / The sedentary soul / In toil of measurement / Beyond eagle or mole, / Beyond hearing and seeing, / Or Archimedes' guess, / To raise into being / That loveliness?'

12 *children*: compare 'Against Unworthy Praise', l. 20, where Yeats referred to Maud as 'Half lion, half child'.

Never Give all the Heart

Jeffares notes (*NCP*, p. 77) that this lyric is similar to Blake's fragment 'Never pain to tell thy Love'.

6–7 *everything that's lovely is / But a brief, dreamy, kind delight*: compare 'Two Songs from a Play', ll. 25–26: 'Everything that man esteems / Endures a moment or a day'.

10 *the play*: this poem turns on the contrast between men who surrender themselves to a woman, and women who surrender themselves to a play – that is, to delicate courtship, intrigue, and coquetry. The need for playfulness in love, the need for eloquence above complete sincerity, reflects Yeats's concern with the theatre, and anticipates the doctrine of the Mask that he elaborated at the end of this decade.

12 *deaf and dumb and blind*: compare 'The Withering of the Boughs', l. 20, 'All Things can Tempt me', l. 10, and 'Reconcilation', l. 3.

The Withering of the Boughs

The premise of this poem is explained in 'The Queen and the Fool': 'There is a war between the living and the dead, and the Irish stories keep harping on it. They will have it that when the potatoes or the wheat or any other of the fruits of the earth decay, they ripen in Faery, and that our dreams lose their wisdom when the sap rises in the trees, and that our dreams can make the trees wither, and that one hears the bleating of the lambs of Faery in November ...' (*M*, p. 116; compare *Ex*, p. 40). Restated in other words, this sentence became a sacred doctrine to be explicated in the play *The Hour-*

Glass (prose version, 1903): 'Where is that passage I am to explain to my pupils to-day? Here it is, and the book says that it was written by a beggar on the walls of Babylon: "There are two living countries, the one visible and the one invisible; and when it is winter with us it is summer in that country, and when the November winds are up among us it is lambing-time there."' (ll. 1–8; compare *AV*, p. 210). Later the Wise Man adds that his 'mother used to say something of the kind. She would say that when our bodies sleep our souls awake, and that whatever withers here ripens yonder' (ll. 138–41).

Faeryland is an anti-world, 180 degrees out of phase with ours; and because it is the locus of all dreams and legends, our dreams grow rich and elaborate, beautiful, only at the expense of natural vitality. Similarly, in *Baile and Aillinn*, l. 171, 'the earth withers away' as the dead lovers approach ultimate bliss; and in *The Dreaming of the Bones* (1919), the dreams of dead spirits 'darken our sun ... Our luck is withered away, / And wheat in the wheat-ear withered' (ll. 297, 300–1). This reciprocity became a fundamental principle in the esoteric doctrines of *A Vision*, and in the first book of this mystical treatise Yeats summarized a story based on exactly the same premise as this poem: 'Flaubert ... talked much of writing a story called "La Spirale". He died before he began it ... It would have described a man whose dreams during sleep grew in magnificence as his life grew more and more unlucky, the wreck of some love affair coinciding with his marriage to a dream princess' (*AV*, p. 70; compare *DWL*, p. 26).

4 *there is no place to my mind*: Faeryland provides the place that is absent in the natural world.

6 *lonely Echtge*: Slieve Echtge, a mountain in Co. Galway. Echtge was also the name of a faery princess encountered by Hanrahan in Yeats's story 'Red Hanrahan' (1903). Hanrahan found her asleep at night, in a house lit by sunlight from within; his failure to ask about her led to a curse that beggared his wits and ruined his life. The original title of this poem was 'Echtge of Streams'.

12 *Danaan*: see 'The White Birds', l. 9.

13: this line reads (perhaps as a misprint) in *CP* (1933), 'Wind and unwind dancing when the light grows cool'. A draft of 'Byzantium' mentioned 'a certain square where tall flames wind and unwind' (Stallworthy, *BL*, p. 123).

17–18 *swans fly round / Coupled with golden chains*: in the story of Cuchulain and Fand, as told in an ancient text, *The Book of the Dun Cow*, Cuchulain throws his spear at two swans so coupled, and injures the wing of one; this causes him to fall into a mysterious trance (*UP* II, p. 280; compare *VP*, p. 812). In Yeats's *Baile and Aillinn*, ll. 136–37, an old man sees two similarly chained swans, apparitions of the lovers.

20 *so deaf and so blind*: compare 'Never Give all the Heart', l. 12.

22 *I know*: the poet's desolate 'knowing' contrasts with the happy wisdom of paradise in ll. 20–21.

Adam's Curse

This poem is based on a conversation among Yeats, Maud Gonne, and her sister Kathleen Pilcher – Maud Gonne recorded an account of the same conversation in *A Servant of the Queen*, pp. 328–30. Like 'Easter, 1916' and certain other fine poems, its theme is the process whereby random casual life attains, at a great cost, dignity and permanent form. Yeats's first assumption seems that expressed in his poem 'He tells of the Perfect Beauty': the poet labours endlessly while beauty is unlabouring, effortless. But Kathleen Pilcher corrects this: a woman's beauty requires equal labour – to be the model for the artist is as expensive as to be an artist.

Title: 'Unto the woman [God] said, I will greatly multiply thy sorrow and thy conception; in sorrow thou shalt bring forth children ... and unto Adam he said ... In the sweat of thy face shalt thou eat bread, till thou return unto the ground' (Genesis 3:16–19).

2 *that beautiful mild woman*: Kathleen Pilcher.

3 *you*: Maud Gonne.

5 *if it does not seem a moment's thought*: Yeats was learning about the Renaissance ideals of noble courtesy described in Castiglione's *The Courtier*. This book recommended *sprezzatura* or elegant disdain – the mastery that dismisses its own effort. See Salvadori, *Yeats and Castiglione*.

19 *they do not talk of it at school*: compare 'Michael Robartes and the Dancer', l. 52: 'They say such different things at school'.

20 *we must labour to be beautiful*: 'is not beauty, even as lasting love, one of the most difficult of the arts?' (*EI*, p. 270). Compare 'To a Young Beauty', ll. 13–14: 'I know what wages beauty gives, / How hard a life her servant lives'; 'The Phases of the Moon', ll. 65–71; and the stanza from *The Only Jealousy of Emer* quoted in the note to 'Old Memory', l. 6.

31 *The moon, worn as if it had been a shell*: compare *The Wanderings of Oisin* I 280: 'the moon's pale twisted shell'.

38 *weary-hearted*: to maintain the discipline of love, or of beauty, or of poetry, exhausts the natural self – just as fantasy exhausts nature in 'The Withering of the Boughs'. According to the doctrine of the Mask, developed around 1909, every elaboration of a studied and disciplined self tends to impoverish one's natural being.

Red Hanrahan's Song about Ireland

This was first published (with many differences of detail) in a story (1894) eventually called 'Hanrahan and Cathleen, the Daughter of Houlihan', in which a vision of Cathleen troubles a brief period of domestic tranquillity in the poet's life. Cathleen ni Houlihan was a traditional personification of Ireland – Yeats also used her in his play *Cathleen ni Houlihan* (1902), in which she was played by Maud Gonne. In this poem, the condition of the human soul is perceived as distorted, anxious, and bloated, accurately reflected in ugly, violent nature-images; but a supernatural ideal, latent in man, allows concentration, intensity, refinement, and purification. This poem is partly based on Clarence Mangan's translation of an old Gaelic poem, 'Caitilín Ní Uallacháin', by a peasant-poet whose name is anglicized as William Heffernan – see Ole Munch-Pedersen's article in *Orbis Litterarum* (1981) 36, 155–72; Pound had earlier noted the connection between Mangan's poem and Yeats's (*Literary Essays*, p. 285).

1 *Cummen Strand*: on the south shore of the Sligo estuary.

2 *a bitter black wind that blows from the left hand*: Munch-Pedersen (see headnote) points out that in Medieval Ireland the winds were ascribed colours, and the north wind was considered black; also, in Old Irish the words for *north* and *left* are identical (pp. 163–65).

6 *Knocknarea*: see 'The Ballad of Father O'Hart', l. 30.

7 *Maeve*: a mythological queen, whose burial site was said to be the cairn on top of Knocknarea. See *The Wanderings of Oisin* I 18.

11 *Clooth-na-Bare*: see 'The Hosting of the Sidhe', l. 2. It is uncertain whether Yeats meant a lake, or (incorrectly) a mountain.

The Old Men Admiring Themselves in the Water

This poem is based on a system of reflections, in which copies keep degrading from the originals: the distortions inflicted on beautiful things by the passing of time are like the caricatures produced by water-reflections and poetic similes. Compare *Where There is Nothing* (1902) V 283–85: 'We have learned too much, our minds are like troubled waters – we get nothing but broken images'. In 1914 Pound used this poem to illustrate how Yeats 'has driven out the inversion and written with prose directness' (*Literary Essays*, p. 379).

4 *They had hands like claws*: compare *The Wanderings of Oisin* III 34 – the sleeping old giants whose 'hands were the claws of birds'.

4–5 *their knees / Were twisted like the old thorn-trees*: for other bodies like broken trees, see the note to 'The Lamentation of the Old Pensioner', l. 14.

Under the Moon

Often in Yeats's poetry ancient legends, dreams of superhuman beauty and emotional intensity, are used to escape from the lax and compromised present world; but in this poem such legends are seen not as a refuge from mortality, but as a too-potent expression of its pangs. In earlier poems, such as 'He reproves the Curlew', the poet finds the expressiveness of nature-sounds intolerable; in this poem he finds the expressiveness of old legends similarly burdensome. This psychological approach to mythology, this rejection of the charm of myths, anticipates the attitude of such late poems as 'The Circus Animals' Desertion'. See also the draft beginning 'I put away all the romances', in the notes to *The Old Age of Queen Maeve*, ll. 134–35.

1 *Brycelinde*: the Breton forest in which Vivien charmed Merlin into a perpetual stupor.

2 *Avalon*: the Blessed Isle to which the dying King Arthur is borne away by weeping queens – see 'A Statesman's Holiday', l. 13.

2 *Joyous Isle*: where Lancelot, recovered from madness, lived with Elaine, according to John Rhys.

4 *Ulad*: Ulster.

4 *Naoise*: see 'The Rose of the World', l. 5.

6 *Land-under-Wave*: the Celtic undersea paradise. See *The Countess Cathleen* (from 1912 on), ll. 518–19: 'There have been women that bid men to rob / Crowns from the Country-under-Wave'; *On Baile's Strand* (1904), ll. 590–91: 'Nine queens out of the Country-under-Wave / Have woven it with the fleeces of the sea'; and *The Only Jealousy of Emer* (1919), l. 202, where the seductress Fand 'has hurried from the Country-under-Wave'.

7 *Seven old sisters*: perhaps the visible planets (compare 'A Cradle Song', l. 7) or Ursa Major (compare 'The Poet pleads with the Elemental Powers . . .', l. 3).

8 *Land-of-the-Tower*: unidentified; conceivably related to the 'tower of glass', in which Aengus kept Edain, in 'The Harp of Aengus', l. 2.

8 *Aengus*: see *The Wanderings of Oisin* I 47.

9 *Wood-of-Wonders*: according to Sheila O'Sullivan (in *Heritage: Essays and Studies*, ed. Almqvist *et al.*, p. 267), this is the Forest of Wonders from Douglas Hyde's 'Adventures of the Children of the King of Norway', where a queen walks in a procession bearing the golden bier of a wondrous ox, wounded by the hero Cod.

11 *Branwen*: the daughter of Llŷr, and the sister of Manannan (both sea-gods) in the Celtic collection of mythology the *Mabinogion*.

11 *Guinevere*: King Arthur's unfaithful queen.

12 *Niamh*: see *The Wanderings of Oisin* I 48.

12 *Laban and Fand*: for Fand, see 'The Secret Rose', l. 13. Laban was Fand's sister, wife of Manannan.

13 *the wood-woman*: in 'The Adventures of the Children of the King of Norway' (see l. 9), Cod meets a wood-woman whose lover had been changed into a blue-eyed hawk.

14 *dun*: fort.

20 *a burden*: the burden of this incoherent assemblage of noble suffering women may be related to the sorrows of Maud Gonne's career.

The Ragged Wood

Like the previous poem, this is a rejection of mythology: instead of searching for an ideal paradigm of love in some remote source, the poet wishes to depopulate the world of lovers – all of them, even the most celestial, less perfect than he and his beloved. The original title was 'The Hollow Wood'. In the 1905 text of 'The Twisting of the Rope', Hanrahan sings a version of this poem instead of 'The Happy Townland' (*VSR*, p. 99). A draft of this poem is printed in *Mem*, pp. 241–42.

3 *they have but looked upon their images*: the deer feel that even water-reflections of themselves intrude on the privacy of their love.

4 *Would none had ever loved but you and I!*: compare *Deirdre* (1907), ll. 147–48, where the Musicians stop singing of the marvellous love of a legendary queen – a mere intrusion to the modern lovers: 'What is all our praise to them / That have one another's eyes?'

6 *queen-woman*: a goddess of the moon, such as Artemis.

O Do Not Love Too Long

As in 'Never Give all the Heart', the lover feels that excessive sincerity and constancy are likely to be boring, lacking in drama or charm.

3–4 *out of fashion / Like an old song*: the poet is replaced by his poems, both stale and trite. Compare 'Men Improve with the Years', l. 2, in which the poet calls himself 'A weather-worn, marble triton'.

6–7 *Neither could have known / Their own thought from the other's*: for the psychic unity of Yeats and Maud Gonne, see the note to 'Old Memory', l. 6.

9 *she changed*: perhaps an allusion to Maud Gonne's marriage.

The Players ask for a Blessing on the Psalteries and on Themselves

The original title was 'Prayer to the Seven Archangels to bless the Seven Notes' (*L*, p. 373). Yeats was far from musical – indeed all but tone-deaf – but this poem, like 'Adam's Curse', reflects Yeats's growing preoccupation with craftsmanship, with the artist's workshop as the proper theme of art. This poem may be compared with the final stanza of Dryden's 'Alexander's Feast' (1697), in which the poet remarks of St Cecilia, 'She drew an Angel down'.

Title *Psalteries*: ancient stringed instruments. Arnold Dolmetsch built a reconstruction of a psaltery for the actress Florence Farr, who chanted some of Yeats's poems to its accompaniment in public performances. Sample notations of these chants appear in *EI*, pp. 17, 23–27.

1 *bless the hands that play*: compare 'To a Friend ...', l. 12: 'mad fingers play'; and 'Lapis Lazuli', l. 54: 'Accomplished fingers begin to play'.

4 *lay the shrilly trumpet down*: compare the trumpet to be blown by the archangel Michael in 'The Happy Townland', l. 41. Yeats advocated a style of poetry that was subtle and monotonous in rhythm (*EI*, p. 159) – the laying down of the rhetorical trumpet in favour of the quiet psaltery reflects a desire for a less blatant art. Also compare the hushing of loud music at the end of *The King's Threshold* (1904).

6 *Over the ramparts*: in 'The Book of the Great Dhoul ...' (1897), a faery goddess tells Hanrahan how 'high and merry notes ... rose beyond the highest ramparts of heaven' (*VSR*, p. 192).

14 *Three in One*: the Trinity.

The Happy Townland

This poem may be read as a sophisticated imitation of naive constructions of heaven. In his 1908 revision of two of the Hanrahan stories, 'The Twisting of the Rope' (1892) and 'Hanrahan's Vision' (1896), Yeats spliced in passages from this poem, as if it approximated the simplicity of folksong. (Indeed in 'The Twisting of the Rope' we are told that the decrepit, wandering poet Hanrahan originally heard this song, or composed it, in Gaelic [*M*, p. 229].) Jeffares notes (*NCP*, p. 89) that in a 1932 radio talk, Yeats remarked that this poem symbolized the striving after an impossible ideal.

Title: 'In Paradise, in that happy townland, I have seen the shining people ... not one of them was at work. All that they did was but the overflowing of their idleness, and their days were a dance bred of the secret frenzy of their hearts, or a battle where the sword made a sound that was like laughter'

(*The Unicorn from the Stars* [1908] II 410–17; compare *Where There is Nothing* [1902] III 178–79, which adds a mock-heaven for capitalists: 'heaven as it should be, the saints with spades and hammers in their hands'). Yeats once entitled the poem 'The Rider from the North / From the play of The Country of the Young'.

1–4: in 'The Twisting of the Rope' these lines read: 'O Death's old bony finger / Will never find us there / In the high hollow townland / Where love's to give and to spare' (*M*, p. 229). This sustains the pretence that the poem is derived from Gaelic – compare an adaptation by Yeats of an actual Gaelic text, 'Love Song / From the Gaelic' (1888), ll. 8–9: 'And death, oh my fair one, will never come near / In the bosom afar of the fragrant wood' (*VP*, p. 717; *UP* I, p. 153; *EI*, p. 179).

7–8 *Rivers are running over / With red beer and brown beer*: one of Yeats's favourite Gaelic poems, Midhir's wooing song to Edain, ran: 'Ireland is beautiful, but not so beautiful as the Great Plain I call you to. The beer of Ireland is heady, but the beer of the Great Plain is much more heady. How marvellous is the country I am speaking of: Youth does not grow old there; streams of warm blood flow there, sometimes meed, sometimes wine' (*UP* II, p. 206; *VP*, p. 805; *Ex*, p. 23). Also compare l. 2 of the song 'I was going the road one day', a kind of appendix to *The Hour-Glass*: 'O the brown and the yellow beer!' (*VPl*, p. 644).

14 the world's bane: Grace Jameson (*Mysticism in AE and Yeats*, p. 162 – cited in Jeffares, *NCP*, p. 84) compares Blake's affirmation in 'The Grey Monk', ll. 13-16 (from which the lyric in *Jerusalem* 52 was derived): 'God ... told me the writing I wrote should prove / The Bane of all that on earth I lovd'. Also, Yeats liked the following story: 'The child William Blake said to somebody who had told him of a fine city, that he thought no city fine that had not walls of gold and silver. It may be that poetry is the utterance of desires that we can only satisfy in dreams' (*UP* II, p. 190). Earth grows pale and ugly in contrast to the ideal – indeed the construction of the ideal sucks the life out of the earth, according to 'The Withering of the Boughs'.

16 The moon plucked at my rein: nature tries to detain the poet on his journey to supernature.

25–26 *all that are killed in battle / Awaken to life again*: compare the demon that awakens from death every fourth day in *The Wanderings of Oisin* II 214; and the old tales that 'tell of a time when nothing had consequences, when even if you were killed, if only you had a good heart, somebody would bring you to life again with the touch of a rod' (*M*, p. 125).

41 *Michael will unhook his trumpet*: according to Yeats, Michael, not Gabriel, is the angel that 'calls the body to resurrection' (*EI*, pp. 316, 404); compare a line deleted from *The Countess Cathleen*: 'There is no medicine but Michael's

trump' (*VPl*, p. 79). It is typical of the playfulness, the casual impudence, of the happy townland that Michael uses the trumpet of the Last Judgment as a summons to supper. Michael also appears in 'The Rose of Peace', l. 1.

45 *Gabriel will come from the water*: 'Gabriel is angel of the Moon in the Cabala and might ... command the waters at a pinch' (*A: HC* 6).

51 *asleep*: the rhythms of dancing, fighting, and sleeping are those of the three islands in *The Wanderings of Oisin*.

THE SHADOWY WATERS (1906)

As Bradford has noted (*WPQ*, p. 3), much of Yeats's creative life was consumed by the struggle to write three intractable works: *The Shadowy Waters* (1900, 1906, 1911), *The Player Queen* (1922), and *A Vision* (1925, 1937). Yeats was never fully satisfied with any of them – and it is unlikely that many readers regard them as his three finest compositions. Yet of Yeats's works, they may be the ones most crucial to an understanding of his peculiar genius. They are also among Yeats's most original acts of mythopoeia. The plot of *The Shadowy Waters*, as Yeats mentioned in a note, has 'no definite old story for its foundation, but was woven to a very great extent out of certain visionary experiences' (*VP*, p. 817). 'Visionary experiences' is no mere figure of speech: Yeats wrote that Aengus and Edain had 'so completely become a part of my own thought that in 1897, when I was still working on an early version of *The Shadowy Waters*, I saw one night with my bodily eyes, as it seemed, two beautiful persons, who would, I believe, have answered to their names' (*VP*, p. 817).

The Shadowy Waters is an attempt to write pure theatre, in the sense of pure poetry – that is, an attempt to eliminate from the dramatic experience every prosaic element, to present spiritual essence liberated from material considerations. It is (except for a few rude cries by the sailors) in every way anti-realistic: instead of credible characters, full of convincingly awkward gestures and halting speech, instead of actions similar to those we observe in our common lives, Yeats provides us with tenuous figments of extreme desire, speaking the most ornate verse, and gesticulating faintly in their private twilight. Indeed Yeats called *The Shadowy Waters* 'more a ritual than a human story. It is deliberately without human characters'; and he asked for stage-scenery that would 'lose the persons in the general picture' (*L*, p. 425). Almost the only action in the play is the severing of the rope that connects the two lovers to the mortal world; indeed nothing else could happen, for the play is little more than a dramatization of its own disengagement from human life.

The textual history is complicated. In 1900 Yeats first published *The Shadowy Waters* as a poem of 431 lines, similar in plot to the present text, but far more encrusted with mythological allusions. The desired effect was 'grave ecstasy' (*L*, pp. 280, 322). (AE responded to the hieratic quality of this version by writing to Yeats, 'I feel that a nineteenth century person in this hideous world ought not to read it until he has cast aside his modern clothes and put on an ancient robe, and found out somewhere an old hall in a castle ... to read it in' [*LTY* I, p. 75].) Yeats wrote the present text (1906) in order to make the poem more stage-worthy: 'I am at work on *The Shadowy Waters*, changing it greatly, getting rid of needless symbols, making the people answer each other, and making the groundwork simple and intelligible' (*L*, p. 453). But Yeats was still not satisfied – what he had called his 'best verse' (*L*, p. 320) nevertheless seemed to him 'the worst thing I ever did dramatically' (*L*, p. 459); and he made an Acting Version (1907, 1911), written partly in prose, in a final attempt to extort a watchable play out of his poem. In 1906 he wrote, 'the whole of our literature as well as our drama has grown effeminate through the over development of the picture-making faculty. The great thing in literature, above all in drama, is rhythm and movement' (*L*, p. 466). But in *The Shadowy Waters* the picture swallows everything – as Yeats himself admitted. No exertion could compel the picture to move, to dance; though the static image has its impressiveness.

And yet, from another perspective this poem aspires less to be a picture than to be music. *The Shadowy Waters* is one of several *fin-de-siècle* plays that attempt to find a non-singing equivalent to Wagner's music-drama *Tristan und Isolde* (1865), where the highest love-rapture is attained in death; the most notable of these is Villiers de l'Isle-Adam's 1890 play *Axël* (in which the lovers commit suicide by drinking poison, rather than allow their love to fall from its high pitch back to common life). Like Tristan and Isolde, Forgael and Dectora are natural enemies (l. 337) compelled by forces beyond themselves to an intolerable love-intensity; the rough loyal Aibric (l. 364) resembles Wagner's Kurwenal; and passions are wholly governed by musical modulations (l. 423). Yeats had little of the musical knowledge or sensitivity of the French symbolist playwrights, but he knew a good many strategies for etherealizing a text, for evacuating it of common denotation. The words are scarcely words at all, but surrogate music; the images point to something beyond images: 'Yet sometimes there's a torch inside my head / That makes all clear, but when the light is gone / I have but images, analogies' (the Acting Version of *The Shadowy Waters*, ll. 132–34 [*VPL*, p. 323]). Arthur Symons's essay on Wagner helped Yeats to rewrite *The Shadowy Waters*, as he told Symons (*L*, p. 460); Yeats wanted the costumes for *The Shadowy Waters* to suggest mythical antiquity, 'Wagner's period more or less' (*TSMC*, p. 7) – though he specified that there should be no winged helmets (*DC*, p. 191); and the text remains a kind of opera of speech. In 1916 Ezra Pound was to write an imitation Noh-play, *Tristan*, inspired by a performance of Wagner's opera – see *Plays Modelled on the Noh (1916)*, ed. Donald C. Gallup.

For a study of the MS drafts, see Michael J Sidnell, George P. Mayhew, and David R. Clark, *Druid Craft: The Writing of 'The Shadowy Waters'*. In the 1890s Yeats wrote several drafts in which the central theme was Forgael's spiritual narcissism – the poet compared Forgael to 'a man living in a tower made of polished black stones which each reflect his face' (*DC*, p. 193); and Yeats contemplated an ending in which Forgael perishes alone, scorning Dectora because she is only a vain repetition of himself: 'Your eyes are but my eyes, your voice is but my voice' – and then Forgael orders the eagle-headed Fomorians who menace his ship to 'Take her & tare her in pieces / For she too is but my self' (*DC*, p. 73).

Dedication: for Lady Gregory, see Introduction IX and 'Beautiful Lofty Things', l. 7.

[Introductory Lines]

This poem extends the dedication to Lady Gregory into a graceful celebration of her estate, Coole Park. *The Shadowy Waters* proper suggests that the End of the World can be reached only on the farthest ocean-voyage (l. 100) – but here it seems that it can be found in one's own back-yard (ll. 30–35). Eden seems to be only an intensification of Coole Park. As T. S. Eliot wrote in 'Little Gidding' (1942), 'There are other places / Which are also at the world's end, some at the sea jaws ... But this is the nearest'.

1 the seven woods: see 'In the Seven Woods'.

2 Shan-walla: 'Old Wall', or perhaps 'Old Road'.

4 Kyle-dortha ... Kyle-na-no: 'Dark Wood' and 'The Wood of the Nuts'.

7 Pairc-na-lee: 'The Field of the Calves'. See 'In the Seven Woods', l. 14.

9 Pairc-na-carraig: 'The Field of the Rock'.

11 Pairc-na-tarav: 'The Field of the Bulls'.

13 Inchy Wood: probably 'The Wood of the Water-meadows'.

15 Biddy Early: a peasant visionary famous around Galway for her fairy gifts. Much of Yeats's 'Ireland Bewitched' is a summary of lore about her, gathered by Lady Gregory (*UP* II, p. 171). See also *The Pot of Broth* (1904), ll. 345–46: 'I'll be as rich as Biddy Early before I die!'; and *M*, p. 22.

25–26 a chattering tongue / Heavy like stone: see 'A Dialogue of Self and Soul' I 40: 'my tongue's a stone'.

30 Is Eden far away, or do you hide: Yeats once dreamed of an illuminated page, reading, '"The rivers of Eden are in the midst of our rivers"' (*Mem*, p. 127); and Yeats knew an old countrywoman who said of the Celtic paradise, '"Tir ná nOg is not far from any of us"' (*EI*, p. 420 – Yeats went on to

quote a stanza from the end of Shelley's 'The Sensitive Plant').

The Harp of Aengus (1900)

It is fitting that *The Shadowy Waters* should begin with a hymn to the harp, for the harp is in some ways the liveliest character in the poem – the agent of metamorphosis and transfiguration, burning with light, capable of playing itself without a human hand. These lines were originally a speech by Forgael in the 1900 version of *The Shadowy Waters*, ll. 296–309.

1 Edain: see *The Wanderings of Oisin* I 47.

1 Midhir: see *Baile and Aillinn*, l. 142.

2 Aengus: see *The Wanderings of Oisin* I 47.

2 tower of glass: Aengus kept Edain, transformed into a fly, in a house of glass – see the note to *Baile and Aillinn*, ll. 141-42. Compare *The Shadowy Waters*, ll. 47–50: 'Aengus . . . carried Edain off . . . And hid her among fruits of jewel-stone / And in a tower of glass'; in a passage deleted from *Deirdre* (1907), Naoise boasts that he would not flinch even if 'Aengus from his glassy tower' came to warn him (*VPl*, p. 357). Yeats once lampooned Catholic missionary-work in India by calling the Church 'a sort of diabolical Aengus carrying not a glass house for Etain . . . but a whole convent, altar lights, vegetarian kitchen and all' (*L*, p. 469). In an unused prologue to *The Shadowy Waters*, a juggler keeps both Aengus and Edain in a glass bottle around his neck (Ellmann, *IV*, p. 314).

5 sleepy boughs: compare the bell-branch of *The Wanderings of Oisin* III 46.

5–6 apples made / Of opal and ruby and pale chrysolite: compare *The Shadowy Waters*, l. 49, 'fruits of jewel-stone', and l. 214, 'charmèd apples made of chrysoprase'; and *Baile and Aillinn*, l. 175, 'fruit that is of precious stone'. Compare also the eerie spring landscape in 'The Heart of the Spring': 'The roses . . . were like glowing rubies, and the lilies had the dull lustre of pearl' (*M*, p. 175).

7–8 wove seven strings . . . out of his long hair: compare Eliot, *The Waste Land* (1922), ll. 378–79: 'A woman drew her long black hair out tight / And fiddled whisper music'.

10 Midhir's wife: named Fuamnach – Aengus killed her for casting this spell on Edain.

10 changed her to a fly: compare the early version of *The Shadowy Waters* (1900), ll. 209–210: 'Aengus . . . awaits / Till his Edaine, no longer a golden fly' (*VP*, p. 757). This fly-metamorphosis may be another sign of the incorporealizing power of love – compare *The Shadowy Waters*, l. 283. For Edain's rebirth in human shape, see the headnote to 'The Two Kings'.

The Shadowy Waters

Stage directions: in the earlier printings, they continued with a description of the colours of the set, predominantly dark green and blue, accented with 'a little copper colour here and there' (*VP*, p. 221); Dectora was also dressed in 'pale green, with copper ornaments' (*VP*, p. 234).

23–24 *a bird / Like a grey gull on the breast of each*: these are the 'man-headed birds' 'With human voices' of ll. 99, 204, 245, 435, and 522. For the soul's tendency to change into bird's shape, see the note to 'The Three Hermits'.

26 *strange cries*: Yeats wrote of a pre-dawn sea voyage taken in adolescence, 'I had wanted the birds' cries for the poem that became fifteen years afterwards "The Shadowy Waters"' (*A: R* 17).

42 *Aengus and Edain*: see *The Wanderings of Oisin* I 47. 'I took the Aengus and Edain of *The Shadowy Waters* from poor translations of the various Aengus stories, which, new translated by Lady Gregory, make up so much of what is most beautiful in both her books [*Cuchulain of Muirthemne* and *Gods and Fighting Men*]. They had, however, so completely become a part of my own thought that in 1897, when I was still working on an early version of *The Shadowy Waters*, I saw one night with my bodily eyes, as it seemed, two beautiful persons, who would, I believe, have answered to their names' (*VP*, p. 817).

49 *fruits of jewel-stone*: see 'The Harp of Aengus', ll. 5–6.

50 *a tower of glass*: see 'The Harp of Aengus', l. 2.

55 *keep to the one weary marriage-bed*: for Yeats's scorn of the domestic life, see 'The Rose of Battle', l. 10. As in the romance of Tristram and Iseult, this poem exalts adulterous passion over wedded bliss.

56 *net*: a recurring symbol of irresistible fate – see ll. 323, 329, 352, 360, 536, and 615. It is often associated with the harp, and at the end also with Dectora's hair, as if the two lovers were at once seized in a divine fish-net, tangled in harp-strings, and clutched by a woman's hair.

91 *flying towards their peace*: Forgael's unworldliness is shown by the fact that he steers, not by the stars (l. 61) but by these death-vectors.

100–4: Yeats quoted these lines in a letter to Florence Farr, and said that they summarized the play's 'one single idea' (*L*, p. 454).

116: in earlier printings, Aibric noted here that 'I've nothing to complain of but heartburn, / And that is cured by a boiled liquorice root' (*VP*, p. 227). When revising the play, Yeats wrote to John Quinn that he had 'very joyfully got "creaking shoes" [see l. 128] and "liquorice-root" into what had been a very abstract passage' (*L*, p. 462).

121 *Where I am rid of life*: AE, after consulting with Yeats, wrote to Sean

O'Faolain, 'His hero was a world wanderer trying to *escape from himself*. He surprises a galley in the waters. There is a beautiful woman there. He thinks through love he can escape from himself. He casts a magical spell on Dectora. Then in the original version he found the love created by a spell was an empty echo, a shadow of himself, and he unrolled the spell seeking alone for the world of the immortals' (Ellmann, *YMM*, p. 78).

124–25 *You will have all you have wished for when you have earned / Land for your children*: compare *Baile and Aillinn*, ll. 39–40: '*all this life can give us is / A child's laughter*'.

131–33 *the dreams the Ever-living / Breathe on the burnished mirror of the world / And then smooth out*: compare ll. 188–89: 'Could we but mix ourselves into a dream, / Not in its image on the mirror!' In *A Vision*, Yeats wrote: 'The man [an artist such as Rembrandt or Synge] wipes his breath from the window-pane, and laughs in his delight at all the varied scene'; 'A Robinson Crusoe who died upon his island ... would continue to look through a window-pane upon which he had breathed' (pp. 165, 228). All these metaphors (perhaps related to Wordsworth's difficulty in seeing the river-bed through his own reflection in the water – *The Prelude* [1805] IV 252–61) contrast the objective gaze (the sharp image seen through the window or reflected in the mirror) with the image-formation of dreams, subjective and vague. For the theme of mirrors, see 'The Two Trees', l. 21.

148–50 *The bed of love ... Is no more than a wine-cup*: compare 'The Empty Cup'.

152 *there is no other way*: compare ll. 454–55: 'not one among you that made love / By any other means'. Forgael continually struggles against the limitations of human (and even superhuman) love.

158–59 *It's not a dream, / But the reality*: Arthur Symons, in *The Symbolist Movement in Literature* (1899), defined symbolism as a reversal of dream and reality. See also ll. 177–89.

198 *face to face*: compare 'Upon a Dying Lady' VI 3, and I Corinthians 13:12: 'For now we see through a glass, darkly; but then face to face'.

202–3 *None but the dead ... Can know that ecstasy*: 'ecstasy is a kind of death. The dying Lionel [in Shelley's *Rosalind and Helen*, ll. 1123–24] hears the song of the nightingale, and cries ... "those who die / Awake in a world of ecstasy"' (*EI*, pp. 71-72).

212 *the world's core*: the centre of the earth. Later Forgael sees Dectora (ll. 277–80) and says, 'You are not the world's core ... My teeth are in the world, / But have not bitten yet' – suggesting that the world is a tempting fruit, like that Eve offered to Adam.

214 *charmèd apples made of chrysoprase*: see 'The Harp of Aengus', ll. 5–6.

237–38 *There's nobody is natural but a robber, / And that is why the world totters*: 'the earth's a thief ... all that you meet are thieves' (Shakespeare, *Timon of Athens* IV iii 445–49).

265 *why are they still waiting?*: the birds seem to linger because they are fascinated by the spectacle of Forgael and Dectora – here the birds act as a stage-audience, later they become stage-directors (l. 527).

280 *Dectora*: some of the poems in *The Wind among the Reeds* were originally entitled 'Aodh to Dectora' – there, as here, she represented the feminine ultimate. Also compare Dectira, the heroine of Yeats's story 'The Binding of the Hair' (1896, reprinted in *UP* I, pp. 390–93) – she was a queen to whom the severed head of the poet Aodh sang a worshipful song.

283 *Why do you cast a shadow?*: Forgael is seeking a dematerialized love; according to the Acting Version, ll. 44–45, he thirsts after 'some place of shining women that cast no shadow' (*VPl*, p. 319). Compare the end of *The Island of Statues* (1885), where the ideal beloved loses her shadow, as an emblem of her passage into sheer spirituality (*VP*, p. 679; see also *L* I, p. 98). Hugo von Hofmannsthal's libretto to Strauss's *Die Frau ohne Schatten* (1919) is the finest modern treatment of the theme of shadowlessness.

320 *watchers*: see *Baile and Aillinn*, l. 168.

320 *outlive the moon*: compare l. 531.

340 *One moment has no might*: the causal chain is broken, anticipating the rope-severing at the play's end. See also ll. 392 and 493.

345 *kiss for kiss*: compare *On Baile's Strand* (1904), l. 421, where demon-women give a lost man 'kiss for kiss'.

366: to the stage directions following this line, the earlier printings add, 'The harp begins to give out a faint light. The scene has become so dark that the only light is from the harp' (*VP*, p. 239).

370 *He has caught the crescent moon out of the sky*: moon and harp are further identified at l. 432: 'that low-laughing string of the moon'. Also compare ll. 509–11: 'I looked upon the moon, / Longing to ... lay it on your head as a crown'. For other unusual uses of the moon, see 'Vacillation' VI 13.

404 *Arthur of Britain*: see 'Towards Break of Day', l. 23.

406 *golden-armed Iollan*: Finneran notes (*Review* 7 [1985]: 187) that Yeats's source for 'golden-armed Iollan' was Douglas Hyde's 'Adventures of the Children of the King of Norway' (see the note to 'Under the Moon', l. 9); there Iollan woos a sea-princess and, under a harper's spell, falls into a murderous trance. The epithet *golden-armed* may be compared to *golden-thighed*, Yeats's description of Pythagoras in 'Among School Children' VI 5; compare also the golden breastplate in 'The Old Stone Cross'.

417–19 *he died a thousand years ago ... But no ... I knew him well*: these confusions of chronology illustrate the loss of sequence predicted by Forgael at l. 340 – time has been deranged by an infusion of eternity.

430–31 *the grave-diggers ... Have buried nothing but my golden arms*: compare 'Under Ben Bulben' II 9.

454–55 *made love / By any other means*: compare ll. 151–52: 'All that ever loved / Have loved that way – there is no other way'.

459 *love is war, and there is hatred in it*: compare *On Baile's Strand* (1904), ll. 332–38: 'I have never known love but as a kiss / In the mid-battle ... A brief forgiveness between opposites / That have been hatreds'. For more on this theme, see the notes to 'Crazy Jane Grown Old ...'

484 *There is no measure that it would not burst*: for the theme of the measured vs. the unmeasured, see 'To Ireland in the Coming Times', l. 25.

499–500 *I weep because bare night's above, / And not a roof of ivory and gold*: the world of experience cannot be reconstructed into the imagination's paradise – that can be found only at the world's end (l. 530).

536 *a net of herrings*: At the end of *A Vision* (1925), Yeats compared his whole system of thought to 'a good net for a herring fisher' (p. 251).

540–41 *We have found a treasure that's so great / Imagination cannot reckon it*: the ship seems to represent Art, itself formal and measured, but a vehicle useful for carrying the soul towards the infinite and unmeasured.

555 *the dust-whirl*: compare 'Nineteen Hundred and Nineteen' VI 6, where another dust-whirl conjures up vain images.

567 *the Immortal Mockers*: compare 'Among School Children' VII 8: 'self-born mockers of man's enterprise'.

574 *I will cover up your eyes and ears*: compare Odysseus' stratagem for saving his sailors from the Sirens' song.

582 *When we have put their changeless images on*: compare *The Player Queen* (1922) II 479–80: 'Man is nothing till he is united to an image'.

598 *Dragon*: Dectora seems to have borrowed this metaphor from the 'Dragons with eyes of ruby' that the sailors found in the ship's hold (l. 535) – it is as if the ship were an aesthetic quarry, a treasure-chest of tropes. For other dragons, see 'The Poet pleads with the Elemental Powers', l. 4.

608–10 *O flower ... O bird ... O morning star*: this series of apostrophes recalls the fifth stanza of Raftery's hymn to Mary Hynes (*M*, p. 24). Such wealth of images also recalls the practice of Shelley; and indeed Yeats mentioned that the morning star was Shelley's most important symbol (*EI*, p. 88).

609 *silver fish*: compare 'The Song of Wandering Aengus', l. 8.

613–14 *Bend lower, that I may cover you with my hair, / For we will gaze upon this world no longer*: Frayne compares Yeats's citation of a passage from Villiers de l'Isle-Adam's symbolist play *Axël* (1890), in which a 'strange, Medusa-like' woman addresses the man with whom she will commit suicide: '"... Oh, to veil you with my hair, where you will breathe the spirit of dead roses"' (*UP* I, p. 324). Also compare 'He bids his Beloved be at Peace', ll. 9–10: 'Beloved, let ... your hair fall over my breast'.

615: just before Forgael's final speech, the Acting Version inserts a stage direction: *The harp begins to burn as with fire* (*VPl*, p. 339). Yeats went to great trouble to ensure that the stage-carpenter produced a suitable prop, less a harp than a psaltery 'where the strings could be slits covered with glass or gelatine on the surface of ... a semi-transparent box.... There is no reason for objecting to a mechanical effect when it represents some material thing, becomes a symbol, a player, as it were.... a symbol of something incapable of direct expression, something that is superhuman' (*VPl*, pp. 341–42). An Abbey Theatre programme note interprets that the 'flaming up of the harp may mean the coming of a more supernatural passion, when Dectora accepts the death-desiring destiny. Yet in one sense ... this destiny is not death; for she, the living will, accompanies Forgael, the mind, through the gates of the unknown world. Perhaps it is a mystical interpretation of the resurrection of the body' (Ellmann, *IY*, p. 81).

617–19 *that old harp awakens of itself ... dreams, / That have had dreams for father*: the harp and the dreams are alike self-awakening, self-begetting – Yeats's typical sign for the passage into a higher reality (see 'A Prayer for my Daughter', ll. 67–68). Yeats's summary of the poem's action ends: 'Forgael and the woman drifted on alone following the birds, awaiting death and what comes after, or some mysterious transformation of the flesh, an embodiment of every lover's dream' (*VPl*, p. 340).

From THE GREEN HELMET AND OTHER POEMS (1910)

The themes of *In the Seven Woods*, such as the praise of the classic splendour of Maud Gonne and the scrutiny of the technique of verse-construction, continue here, but this volume is still more public and contemporary – the debonair poet appears at the university, the theatre, a fine old country house, the racetrack; he is so comfortably famous that he can afford to ridicule his imitators in a witty epigram. Although some of the poems in this volume are intimate and soulful in the old manner, in other poems the poet is rather detached and aloof, a spectator rather than a participant.

The title of the volume comes from the play with which the poems were published: *The Green Helmet*, the second play in Yeats's Cuchulain cycle, told the story of an eerie giant who offers to let others cut off his head if, afterwards, he may cut off theirs; eventually Cuchulain offers his own head to the sword, but the giant instead gives him a helmet because Cuchulain took his fancy: 'I choose the laughing lip / That shall not turn from laughing, whatever rise or fall; / The heart that grows no bitterer although betrayed by all; / The hand that loves to scatter; the life like a gambler's throw' (ll. 278–81). The rough, rollicking fourteen-syllable verse, the cultivated archaism (a similar story appears in the Middle English *Sir Gawain and the Green Knight*), the mythological characters, all make the play seem different from the sophisticated, neoclassical poems printed with it; and yet both play and poems recommend a heady nonchalance as the best approach to life.

Most of the poems in this section were originally grouped into two large sequences.

NICOLAS FLAMEL AND HIS WIFE PERNELLA

The first eight poems in *The Green Helmet and Other Poems* were published under the general title 'Raymond Lully and his wife Pernella'; an erratum-slip corrected this: 'AN ERROR By a slip of the pen when I was writing out the heading for the first group of poems, I put Raymond Lully's name in the room of the later Alchemist, Nicolas Flamel' (*VP*, p. 253). Yeats had been interested in old alchemists for some time: in 'Rosa Alchemica' (1896), the narrator owns a set of alchemical apparatus that 'once belonged to Raymond Lully'; he looks at the stars and 'it seemed to my troubled fancy that all those little points of light filling the sky were the furnaces of innumerable divine alchemists, who labour continually, turning lead into gold, weariness into ecstasy, bodies into souls, the darkness into God' (*M*, pp. 269–70); later he consults the works 'of Lully, who transformed himself into the likeness of a red cock; of Flamel, who with his wife Pernella achieved the elixir many hundreds of years ago, and is fabled to live still in Arabia among the Dervishes' (*M*, p. 282). And in *The Speckled Bird* III ii, a character based on MacGregor Mathers claims that magic is superior to the fine arts – that King Arthur's knights are nothing when compared to Flamel and Lully, the great masters who attained all human wisdom and made death itself their servant (*LTMSB*, p. 153). Lully and Flamel, then, suggest the search for immortality through transmutation of shape.

This sequence (extending from 'His Dream' to 'Against Unworthy Praise') chiefly treats Yeats's blighted relationship with Maud Gonne, who had married John MacBride in 1903; the general title insinuates, however, that spiritually – alchemically – she is Yeats's own wife, though flesh and society refuse to confirm this occult truth. In a draft (around 1897) for an unwritten lyric about Maud Gonne, Yeats wrote, 'I play at / marriage – I play / with images of the life / you will not give to me o / my cruel one' (Ellmann, *YMM*, p. 163; Stallworthy, *BL*, p. 3); and the personae of Nicolas Flamel and his wife may be part of this playing at marriage. Yeats remembered that, when he and Maud Gonne were initiated into the Hermetic Society of London, 'I began to form plans of our lives devoted to mystic truth, and spoke to her of Nicholas Flamel and his wife, Pernella' (*Mem*, p. 49).

His Dream

'A few days ago I dreamed that I was steering a very gay and elaborate ship upon some narrow water with many people upon its banks, and that there was a figure upon a bed in the middle of the ship. The people were pointing to the figure and questioning, and in my dream I sang verses which faded as I awoke, all but this fragmentary thought, "We call it, it has such dignity of limb, by the sweet name of Death"' (*VP*, p. 253). This poem suggests that the poet (like the alchemist) plays at the threshold between life and death; the poet may be a kind of reverse Charon – his art is a vehicle introducing death into life. It is also possible that the dreamer's attempt to hush the crowd is related to the poet's uneasiness about glorifying death in his work. Directions for interpreting this poem are suggested by Yeats's interpretation of a dream in which he saw an infernal ape eating jewels (*M*, p. 100); by his account of a dream in which 'a steam barge, and a bus were going side by side' (*Mem*, p. 238); and by a juvenile poem, 'The Phantom Ship', in which a fishing-village sees a ghost-ship on which appear 'All the drowned that ever were drowned from that village by the sea' (*VP*, p. 719). (A draft of this poem can be found in *Mem*, pp. 231–32.)

9: the first printing read, 'And fishes, bubbling to the brim' (*VP*, p. 254) – the fishes' cry is reminiscent of the singing fishes in 'The Man who Dreamed of Faeryland', l. 6.

13 *my finger on my lip*: compare the juvenile 'Street Dancers', ll. 18–19: 'hush! On every lip / Lies a chilly finger tip' (*VP*, p. 732).

14 *What could I but take up the song?*: compare the poet's surrender to mass hysteria in 'I see Phantoms . . .', ll. 14-16.

17–18 *Crying amid the glittering sea . . . ecstatic breath*: compare 'News for the Delphic Oracle' II 5–6: 'The ecstatic waters laugh because / Their cries'.

A Woman Homer Sung

This poem turns on the contrast between the splendour of Maud Gonne's presence and the shadows or images of that presence that can be produced in literature. (An early draft of this poem can be found in *Mem*, pp. 244–45.)

Title *Homer*: Greek poet probably of the eighth century BC. For other references, see 'The Tower' II 36: 'Homer that was a blind man'; 'Coole and Ballylee, 1931', l. 47: 'that saddle Homer rode'; 'Vacillation' VII 6: 'What theme had Homer but original sin?' and VIII 10: 'Homer is my example'; and 'Mad as the Mist and Snow', which attributes wild passion to Homer.

7 *an indifferent eye*: the poet is jealous of other admirers of his beloved, yet indignant at those indifferent to her.

11 *To such a pitch my thought*: compare 'The Double Vision of Michael Robartes' III 10: 'To such a pitch of folly I am brought'.

13–14 *He shadowed in a glass / What thing her body was*: see I Corinthians 13:12 – 'now we see through a glass, darkly; but then face to face'. Yeats sometimes thought of his poetry as a kind of verbal reconstruction of a woman's body – indeed, at the end of 'The Gift of Harun Al-Rashid', Yeats remarked of his whole system of thought, 'all those gyres and cubes and midnight things / Are but a new expression of her body'. It is noteworthy that Yeats did not describe the beloved's body – we learn nothing of the colour of her eyes or the shape of her chin – but instead imitated its inner tension, the magnificence of its effect.

18 *As 'twere upon a cloud*: she is like a Homeric goddess. Compare Yeats's description of the young Maud Gonne: 'she seemed a classical impersonation of the Spring, the Virgilian commendation "She walks like a goddess" made for her alone' (*A: FY* 5).

Words

The theme of this poem is found in a passage in Yeats's 1909 journal: 'Today the thought came to me that [Maud Gonne] never really understands my plans, or nature, or ideas. Then came the thought, what matter? How much of the best I have done and still do is but the attempt to explain myself to her? If she understood, I should lack a reason for writing' (*Mem*, pp. 141–42; drafts of 'Words' follow). It is as if Yeats felt that he was forced to give his best efforts to make himself explicit because he had to strain against Maud Gonne's inviolable incomprehension of his work. This may be one of the difficulties discussed in 'The Fascination of What's Difficult'. The original title was 'The Consolation'.

2 *My darling cannot understand*: compare 'Human Dignity', ll. 2-3, where the poet speaks of the beloved's kindness: 'If kindness I may call / What has no comprehension in't'; and 'Ribh in Ecstasy', l. 1: 'What matter that you understood no word!' In a 'subject' (circa 1897) for an unwritten poem about Maud Gonne, Yeats wrote, 'O my beloved what were verse to me / If you were not then to listen / & yet all my verses are little to you. / Your eyes set

upon far magnificence / Upon impossible heroism / Have made you blind' (Stallworthy, *BL*, p. 4).

4 *this blind bitter land*: compare 'To a Wealthy Man ...', l. 7: 'the blind and ignorant town'; and 'Quarrel in Old Age', l. 3: 'this blind bitter town'. According to Jeffares (*NCP*, p. 87), Maud Gonne complained because Yeats's art was insufficiently propagandistic.

12 *And words obey my call*: compare 'An Acre of Grass', l. 18: 'Till Truth obeyed his call'.

15–16 *I might have thrown poor words away / And been content to live*: compare 'The Choice', ll. 1–2: 'The intellect of man is forced to choose / Perfection of the life, or of the work'; also 'A Dialogue of Self and Soul' II 17: 'content to live'. The idea that words are a substitute for human relations can be found in the Introductory Rhymes to *Responsibilities*, l. 21.

No Second Troy

The theme of this poem is the contrast between the stress of Maud Gonne's splendour and the laxness and cowardice of the modern age – no easy relation between them is possible. Yeats may have been fond of this poem, for he copied it into his journal as the epigraph (*Mem*, p. 137).

2 *of late*: but not now – for Maud Gonne withdrew from political activity after her marriage failed in 1905.

3 *most violent ways*: not an exaggeration. Maud Gonne served as a link between the revolutionary Irish Republican Brotherhood and French intelligence; and she plotted with a Boer agent in Brussels to smuggle bombs on to British warships bound for Africa during the Boer War.

7 *simple as a fire*: compare 'Vacillation' VII 4: 'the simplicity of fire'.

8–12: in his review of *Responsibilities*, Pound quoted these lines to illustrate the 'new note' in Yeats's poetry (*Literary Essays*, p. 379).

8 *beauty like a tightened bow*: compare 'The Arrow', l. 1, and the vision of the archer who shoots an arrow beyond the earth, discussed in the note to 'Parnell's Funeral' I 10.

9 *not natural in an age like this*: her beauty ought to have unfolded into a conflagration, in the manner of Helen of Troy, but in the present age all her potential energy is balked and unrealized.

12 *Was there another Troy for her to burn?*: this question is answered by the title. In the so-called 'Leroy' version of the unfinished *The Speckled Bird*, the hero contrasts ancient times, when warriors died gladly for those whom poets praised, and a city was burned for Helen, with modern times, when

beauty appeals only to a few, and the masses prefer a coarse prettiness (*LTMSB*, p. 238).

Reconciliation

This poem records Yeats's responses after he learned, in the course of a public lecture in 1903, of Maud Gonne's marriage. The poem turns on the contrast between direct, authentic expression of emotion ('our laughing, weeping fit', l. 9) and oblique and evasive expression of emotion ('a song about kings, / Helmets, and swords', ll. 5–6). Here Yeats analyses his decision to write plays on old Irish mythological topics as a wilful escape from the asperities of his own life – *The Green Helmet*, the play that gave the title to this volume, is a fine example of a play full of kings and helmets and swords. This poem is part of a sequence of anti-mythological meditations including 'Under the Moon', 'A Coat', and 'The Circus Animals' Desertion'. (Drafts of this poem are printed in *Mem*, pp. 172–74, 259.)

1 *Some may have blamed you*: this is the epigraph to Pound's 'The Fault of It' (1911), another poem that announces a change of subject matter.

3 *deafened ... blind*: compare 'Never Give all the Heart', l. 12.

6–7 *Helmets, and swords, and half-forgotten things / That were like memories of you*: compare 'The Circus Animals' Desertion' II 23–24: 'Players and painted stage took all my love / And not those things that they were emblems of'. Also compare the notion that Yeats's body of work was secretly derived from the beloved's body, discussed in the note to 'A Woman Homer Sung', ll. 13–14.

8 *We'll out*: that is, we'll show ourselves – the poet contrasts his present self-exposure, his honesty, with his past deviousness. Compare 'A Coat', ll. 9–10: 'there's more enterprise / In walking naked'.

10 *pit*: grave, with a pun on theatre pit. An early draft read, 'we / Will tumble crown and helmet in the sea' (*Mem*, p. 172).

12 *chilled me to the bone*: the poet's emotional nakedness can be warmed only by the genuine contact he has so long avoided, dissembled.

King and No King

A King and No King is the title of a play by Beaumont and Fletcher (1611), about a ranting, histrionic king who incestuously desires to marry his sister. But it turns out that the king is in fact a foster-child, unrelated to his 'sister', so a happy ending is available. In this poem Yeats contrasts the Jacobean romance with his own plight, where no happy end seems possible. As in the previous poem, old legends seem inadequate and misleading, oversimple and oversweet, when compared to the bitter complexities of real emotional life. (A draft of this poem appears in *Mem*, p. 236.)

1 *'Would it were anything but merely voice!'*: as Ellmann notes (*IY*, p. 252), a misquotation of *A King and No King* IV iv 126. The whole of King Arbaces' crucial speech to his sister is as follows: 'I have lived / To conquer men, and now am overthrown / Only by words, brother and sister. Where / Have those words dwelling? I will find 'em out, / And utterly destroy 'em; but they are / Not to be grasped: let 'em be men or beasts, / And I will cut 'em from the earth; or towns, / And I will raze 'em, and then blow 'em up: / Let 'em be seas, and I will drink 'em off, / And yet have unquenched fire left in my breast; / Let 'em be anything but merely voice'. The mysterious, intangible power of words to control destiny is a common theme in Yeats's work.

6 *somehow that I have forgot*: compare 'The Tower' II 57: 'I have forgotten what – enough'.

9 *that pledge*: Maud Gonne may have sworn at some point that she would never marry – see 'A Deep-sworn Vow'; or Yeats may have interpreted the intimate episode that terminates his suppressed autobiography (*Mem*, p. 134) as the moral equivalent of a ceremony wedding him and her.

11 *your faith*: Maud Gonne converted to Roman Catholicism in 1897.

12 *blinding light beyond the grave*: compare 'The Cold Heaven', l. 9: 'Riddled with light'.

15 *The habitual content of each with each*: the poet posits an imaginary life with his beloved, what would have come to pass if Beaumont and Fletcher had written the script of their lives.

Peace

This poem was written during a visit to Maud Gonne's house at Calvados, in Brittany. It argues that she is a fitter subject for art now that she is older – in youth her life was too stormy to allow her to project a coherent image of herself. For the theme of Maud Gonne's aging, see 'The Arrow'. (A draft of this poem is printed in *Mem*, pp. 245–46.)

3 *a hero's wage*: Maud Gonne's estranged husband, John MacBride, was a hero during the Boer War – but Yeats may write with some irony here.

9 *sweetness amid strength*: Yeats was fond of the biblical passage, 'Out of the strong came forth sweetness' (Judges 14) – see 'Ancestral Houses', ll. 19–20, and the note to 'Vacillation' VIII 13. Maud Gonne's beauty lies at the intersection of contraries, as in the Rose poems, such as 'To the Rose upon the Rood of Time'; compare also 'Against Unworthy Praise', l. 20.

10 *peace*: compare 'Against Unworthy Praise', l. 20; and 'Broken Dreams', ll. 12–13: 'that peace you make / By merely walking in a room'.

Against Unworthy Praise

Many of the poems in this volume concern, explicitly or implicitly, the loss of proper critical standards in modern times; this is one reason for Yeats's frequent appeal to Homer and classical Greece for a norm of excellence. Here the poet denies to his age the responsibility of either praise or blame. (A draft of this poem appears in *Mem*, p. 246.)

2 *knave nor dolt*: compare 'The Fascination of What's Difficult', l. 10: 'knave and dolt'.

4 *for a woman's sake*: compare the theme of 'Words'.

6 *So did she your strength renew*: Yeats regarded Maud Gonne as the Muse and secret cause of his work – and to some extent he thought the converse, that he inspired her, according to 'Old Memory', l. 6.

11 *you*: his heart.

12 *a haughtier text*: the poet wishes to take to heart his beloved's indifference to praise or blame – her standard of taste is the real one, not that of the masses.

16 *slander, ingratitude*: Jeffares notes (*NCP*, p. 90) that an audience at the Abbey Theatre hissed Maud Gonne in 1905, after her separation from her husband became known; this precipitated a long withdrawal from public life.

20 *Half lion, half child, is at peace*: as in 'Peace', l. 9, Maud Gonne is seen as a tense union of contraries. Yeats often mentioned Maud Gonne's child-like simplicity of demeanour, as in 'His Phoenix', l. 28 ('the simplicity of a child'), or 'Old Memory', l. 12 ('children that have strayed'); and he used similar language in describing Helen of Troy in 'Long-Legged Fly', l. 15 ('part woman, three parts a child'). Indeed much of the fascination of her character seemed to originate in the combination of the child with the lion. Yeats commented on her strange combination of inward gentleness and outward violence (*Mem*, p. 124); and his imagination was haunted by fractured images of these traits, as if Maud Gonne could not maintain herself as a coherent woman – her internal tension was too great. In 'Presences', the poet broods on his 'Returned yet unrequited love' (l. 8) until he has a vision of three presences: 'One is a harlot, and one a child . . . And one, it may be, a queen' (ll. 12, 14). And in a late poem, 'Those Images', the poet advises his Muses to 'Seek those images / That constitute the wild, / The lion and the virgin, / The harlot and the child' (ll. 9–12).

MOMENTARY THOUGHTS

Under this general title were grouped the remaining poems in *The Green Helmet and Other Poems* (1910), except 'On hearing that the Students ...' and 'At the Abbey Theatre' (both of which were added in the 1912 reprinting of this collection). The poems in this sequence tend to respond less to private love-affair than to external circumstances – to the vexations of Yeats's career as poet and man-of-letters, or to social or political matters.

The Fascination of What's Difficult

Yeats was not one to shirk difficult tasks – he would spend hours, particularly when he was young, to perfect a single line of verse (as described in 'Adam's Curse', ll. 4–14); and, according to his esoteric system, it was the highest calling of a man of his sort to follow 'whatever whim's most difficult / Among whims not impossible' ('The Phases of the Moon', ll. 40–41). Indeed much of his life was spent in various exercises to give precision and discipline to his imagination, and to embody his received images in complex and demanding metrical schemes. But, as poems such as 'Reconciliation' show, he was starting to find that the genres, the personae, the style he had laboriously created to express himself were all beginning to impede him as much as to express him; he felt ensnarled in mythologies, in his own verse-techniques. In this poem he announces his intention to write in a freer, more flexible style, more responsive to human urgencies – in a few years, in 'A Coat', he will even claim that he has divested his style of all impediments. (A draft of this poem appears in *Mem*, pp. 242–43; and a note discussing the poem's theme and rhymes in *Mem*, p. 229.)

1–4: Yeats quoted these lines to illustrate that 'true Unity of Being, where all the nature murmurs in response if but a single note be touched' is almost impossible 'without a Unity of Culture in class or people that is no longer possible at all' (*A: SB* 2).

4 *our colt*: Pegasus, the winged horse beloved of the Muses after he raised the fountain of Hippocrene on Mt Helicon with a blow from his hoof. The joke of using Pegasus – always a symbol for lofty, free-wheeling imagination – for lowly purposes is an old one; as Jeffares notes (*NCP*, p. 90), Yeats may have heard it from Sturge Moore, who said that Swift used Pegasus as a carthorse. Yeats thought of Pegasus as essentially irresponsible and untamable – he wrote that there was only one beast that Adam forgot to name: it 'permits us to call it Pegasus, but it does not answer to that or any name' (*Mem*, p. 244). (It may be noted that the name Pegasus does not appear in this poem or in any other of Yeats's.) Other allusions to Pegasus appear in 'Under Saturn', l. 6 ('my horse's flanks are spurred'), in 'Easter, 1916', l. 25 (where Patrick Pearse 'rode a wingèd horse'), and in 'Coole and Ballylee,

1931', l. 46 ('That high horse riderless'). For a related beast of inspiration – earthier, less aerial – see the centaur of 'Lines Written in Dejection', l. 7.

8 *My curse on plays*: the drama, as a collaborative art form, seemed especially compromised, constrained, and troublesome – see 'Reconciliation'.

10 *knave and dolt*: compare 'Against Unworthy Praise', l. 2.

13 *pull out the bolt*: Yeats refuses to exert further conscious control over his imagination – it must subsequently respond to exterior forces. This wish anticipates Yeats's surrender, eight years later, to his wife's trances of automatic writing, and other strategies of self-liberation.

A Drinking Song

This song was written for Lady Gregory's *Mirandolina* (1910), an adaptation of a Goldoni comedy; it was to be sung by an innkeeper flirting with a woman-hating captain. It bears some structural and thematic resemblance to a much later poem, 'The Lover's Song'. (A draft may be found in *Mem*, p. 260.)

1–2 *Wine comes in at the mouth / And love comes in at the eye*: Yeats quoted these lines in 1936, and noted, 'I have found, being no intellectual, that even in old age eye & mouth are still there' (*DWL*, p. 117).

The Coming of Wisdom with Time

This poem is one of many Yeats wrote on the bleak consolations of old age. It turns on the contrast between blatant self-expression, self-publicity, and reticent self-knowledge – a theme similar to that of 'All Things can Tempt Me'. The original title was 'Youth and Age'. (For a draft of this poem, see *Mem*, pp. 196–97.)

2 *lying days*: multiplicity seems illusory, unity real. In 1928 Yeats was to debate the 'antinomy between *the one* and *the many*'; T. Sturge Moore took the position that *the one* was a mere verbal construct, while Yeats presumably took the opposite position (*TSMC*, p. 130). Compare 'Ribh denounces Patrick', l. 10: 'The mirror-scalèd serpent is multiplicity'.

3 *I swayed my leaves*: for the comparison of man and tree, see 'The Lamentation of the Old Pensioner', l. 20.

4 *Now I may wither into truth*: the poet devolves from his leaves to his root, from the many to the one. Compare Yeats's statement, 'to die into the truth is still to die' (*AV*, p. 271). Pound commented, 'Yeats burbles when he talks of "withering into the truth". You *wither* into non-curiosity' (*Selected Prose*, p. 76).

On hearing that the Students of our New University have joined the Agitation against Immoral Literature

The 'new university' was the Royal [later, National] University of Ireland, founded 1908, the successor institution to the Catholic University, founded 1854 – Joyce's alma mater. The fear that mankind was evolving towards increasing timidity and small-mindedness was one of Yeats's long-standing preoccupations. (A draft of this poem may be found in *Mem*, p. 264.)

2 *to give themselves for wage*: to prostitute themselves. Compare 'wench Wisdom', *AV*, p. 32; and a passage from an unfinished poem of 1929 identifying the bride of Reason: 'the slut's in bed / Truth is her name' (Ellmann, *IY*, p. 37).

4 *reckless middle-age*: in so far as Yeats himself is among those reckless in middle age, this poem shows one of his earliest hints of the persona of the Wild Old Wicked Man.

To a Poet, who would have me Praise certain Bad Poets, Imitators of His and Mine

The original title was 'To AE [George Russell], who wants me [to] praise some of his poets, imitators of my own'. (Drafts of this poem appear in *Mem*, pp. 221–22.)

The Mask

Much of Yeats's intellectual energies from about 1909 to 1925 went into his formulation and elaboration of the doctrine of the Mask – the self fabricated around the natural man by conscious artifice. In his early meditations, recorded in his 1909 journal, Yeats found, wherever he looked, that people wore masks, and that these masks offered the joy of imaginative self-liberation, a kind of superior child's play:

> I think that all happiness depends on the energy to assume the mask of some other self; that all joyous or creative life is a re-birth as something not oneself, something which has no memory and is created in a moment and perpetually renewed. We put on a grotesque or solemn painted face to hide us from the terrors of judgment, invent an imaginative Saturnalia where one forgets reality, a game like that of a child, where one loses the infinite pain of self-realisation. Perhaps all the sins and energies of the world are but its flight from an infinite blinding beam. (*A: DS* 6; *Mem*, p. 191)

A man cannot be judged, cannot be defined and dismissed, if he cannot be located in the first place; and the Mask permits an endless dissembling of identity – 'He will play with all masks' (*A: E* 23; *Mem*, p. 152). A face might be vulgar, disfigured; but a Mask was distinguished, shapely, 'the only escape from ... the money changers' (*Mem*, p. 139). (In his later doctrine, as recorded in 'Ego Dominus Tuus' and *A Vision*, Yeats came to think that the Mask could be either a vehicle of self-realization, or an escape from self-realization, depending on the type of man; and he came to think that each man had a unique Mask, instead of the immense assortment from the costume-maker's shop that he discussed in his earlier writings.)

Love presented an important test-case for the doctrine of the Mask, for it multiplied by two the number of participants in the love-affair: he, she, his mask, her mask. One benign application of Mask-theory could be observed when lovers played roles in order to help one another realize their noblest selves:

> It seems to me that true love is a discipline ... Each [lover] divines the secret self of the other, and refusing to believe in the mere daily self, creates a mirror where the lover or the beloved sees an image to copy in daily life; for love also creates the Mask. (*A: E* 7; *Mem*, pp. 144–45)

Thus lovers can improve one another's being by a complex rite of inter-imitation: he wears the mask of her best self, and she of his; so the live faces under the masks find a continual model for self-reshaping, face-lifting.

But the poem 'The Mask' describes a more sinister situation. Here the man is not a wise fellow who divines the best self of his beloved, and helps her to realize it in daily life; he is instead deceived and anxious, blind to all but the narrowest spectrum of his beloved. Here the woman is not a sympathetic, loving soul, but a Salomé who has carefully shielded herself in artifice, and allows no one a glimpse within. Here the mask is not a felicitous ideal but a dazzling screen.

In *The Green Helmet and Other Poems* (1910), 'The Mask' was entitled 'A Lyric from an Unpublished Play'. The play was *The Player Queen* (1922), in which the opening stanza of this poem appears at II 223–28. There the poet-hero's wife boasts of her cruel treatment of the poet, how she refuses him every solace but teases him with her icy beauty – how he might go to prison for her sake, but find her all the more beautiful. 'Because I am a devil I have his every thought,' she says, just before reciting 'The Mask'. But she does not know that the woman to whom she boasts, a comfortable middle-aged person, is in fact the poet's mistress. This scene recapitulates some of the emotional drama of Yeats's relation with Maud Gonne and Olivia Shakespear. (A draft of this poem appears in *Mem*, pp. 258–59; for its history in the play, see *WPQ*, pp. 30, 46.) See also 'A Song from *The Player Queen*'.

1 *Put off that mask*: the man speaks the first two lines of each stanza, the woman the last three.

10 *Not what's behind*: compare 'The Hero, the Girl, and the Fool', ll. 1–2: 'I rage at my own image in the glass / That's so unlike myself'.

11 *lest you are my enemy*: Yeats once wrote, paraphrasing Blake, that 'it may be that "sexual love" ... is "founded on spiritual hate"' (*M*, p. 336; see 'Crazy Jane Grown Old ...'). Also compare 'Before the World was made', l. 13, 'Why should he think me cruel' – a poem about a much less drastic sort of make-up.

Upon a House shaken by the Land Agitation

The house was Lady Gregory's estate, Coole Park; the land agitation occurred when a court ordered reductions in rent. (A prose draft and a poetic draft of this poem appear in *Mem*, pp. 225–26.) Yeats feared that Coole Park's magnificence would be strangled from lack of income: 'This house has enriched my soul out of measure, because here life moves without restraint through spacious forms. Here there has been no compelled labour, no poverty-thwarted impulse' (*Mem*, p. 226).

3 *became too ruinous*: this is the first of several prophecies Yeats made of the destruction of Coole Park; see also 'Coole Park, 1929', ll. 26–27: 'When all those rooms and passages are gone, / When nettles wave upon a shapeless mound'. In 1932 Coole Park was indeed demolished, for no good reason, as Yeats was to remember in 'Man and the Echo', ll. 15–16: 'Could my spoken words have checked / That whereby a house lay wrecked?' Yeats regarded his play *Purgatory* (1939) as the tragedy of the destruction of a house.

4 *the lidless eye that loves the sun*: eagles were once thought to be able to stare directly into the sun. Compare 'To a Wealthy Man ...', l. 32: 'Look up in the sun's eye'; 'His Phoenix', l. 29: 'that proud look as though she had gazed into the burning sun'; and *Calvary* (1920), l. 177: 'one-eyed day can meet his [the ger-eagle's] stare'. In old age Yeats wrote that 'I have never been able to read without tears a passage in *Sigurd the Volsung* describing how the new-born child lay in the bed and looked "straight on the sun"' (*VPl*, p. 570; *Ex*, p. 375). And in early drafts of *The Player Queen* Decima claims to be descended from eagles, and veils her eyes so that the lightning in her gaze does not dazzle the populace (Bradford, *WPQ*, p. 57).

8 *Mean roof-trees*: a metonymy for the cottages whose dwellers farmed the grand estates, such as Coole Park.

10 *govern men*: Lady Gregory's husband William had been governor of Ceylon.

11 *a written speech*: a style equal to that of Lady Gregory's works.

At the Abbey Theatre

Yeats's relations with the audiences at the Abbey Theatre were never easy – he had had a number of occasions to revile them in public, such as the riots touched off at the opening of Synge's *The Playboy of the Western World* in 1907. In this poem Yeats compares the attempt to create a standard of taste in the theatre audience to the attempt to impose shape upon a completely shapeless thing. (A draft of this poem appears in *Mem*, p. 261.)

Caption *Ronsard*: French poet (1524–85), leader of the circle known as *la Pléiade* – itself a group that tried to restore classical standards of taste. The poem imitated here is 'Tyard, on me blasmoit, à mon commencement'. Yeats used another Ronsard poem as the model for 'When You are Old'.

1 *Craoibhin Aoibhin*: Gaelic for 'pleasant little branch', the pseudonym of Dr Douglas Hyde (1860–1949), poet, Gaelic scholar, and statesman, a man whom Yeats much admired, though Yeats thought he had ruined his literary genius from too much concern with worldly affairs and from a lack of self-criticism. In his autobiography Yeats discussed Hyde's limitations and quoted some lines from this poem (*A: IP* 6). Compare 'Coole Park, 1929', ll. 9–10: 'Hyde before he had beaten into prose / That noble blade the Muses buckled on'.

8 *You've dandled them*: perhaps a reference to Hyde's translations of ancient texts into English – Hyde diligently tried to create an Irish national culture.

10 *a new trick to please*: actually Yeats was not certain that the Abbey Theatre should become too popular: 'I would sooner our theatre failed through the indifference or hostility of our audiences than gained an immense popularity by any loss of freedom' (*Ex*, p. 117).

11 *Proteus*: the Old Man of the Sea in Greek mythology, who could assume any shape Yeats here imagined himself in the position of his own character Oisin, fighting a monster that kept altering its form (*The Wanderings of Oisin* II 176–80). Yeats also compared to Proteus the spirits who become the *dramatis personae* of our dreams (*Ex*, p. 57). For Yeats's fascination with shape-changing sorcerers, see 'Fergus and the Druid'. In the same section of his autobiography where he wrote of Hyde, Yeats called Ireland (and himself) 'soft wax' (*A: IP* 1, 3).

These are the Clouds

A draft of this elegy can be found in *Mem*, pp. 259–60.

1–2: some of the vocabulary of these lines is repeated in 'Fallen Majesty' (title and l. 8).

2 *burning eye*: compare *The Unicorn from the Stars* (1908) II 363–64: 'all life will become like a flame of fire, like a burning eye'.

7 *friend*: Lady Gregory.

10 *for children that you sigh*: that is, her sigh is not for selfish reasons but because her descendants may not enjoy what is to be destroyed.

At Galway Races

This poem was written at Coole Park, Lady Gregory's estate in Co. Galway. Like 'At the Abbey Theatre', the poem is concerned with the relation of poet to audience: the poet envies the horse-riders for their immediate rapport with the spectator, and he dreams of reestablishing the old unity of poet and hearer. (This attempt to create, or synthesize, a proper audience for his poetry led Yeats to write 'The Fisherman' and the fifth part of his epitaph, 'Under Ben Bulben'.) Yeats often lamented that the poet and the man of action seemed wholly severed from one another – here he wishes to recreate that prehistoric link.

3 *The riders upon the galloping horses*: note the imitative rhythm.

5 *We*: poets.

8 *the merchant and the clerk*: this anticipates the savage anti-clerk poems such as 'Paudeen'.

9 *Breathed on the world with timid breath*: compare Swinburne, 'Hymn to Proserpine' (1866), l. 35: 'Thou hast conquered, O pale Galilean; the world has grown gray with thy breath'.

A Friend's Illness

This poem bears some formal resemblance to 'The Moods' – both are rhetorical questions posed in seven short lines. (A draft of this poem appears in *Mem*, p. 162.)

Title *A Friend's*: Lady Gregory's. 'This morning I got a letter telling me of Lady Gregory's illness.... She has been to me mother, friend, sister and brother' (*Mem*, pp. 160–61).

2 *that scale of his*: the poet seems to personify Sickness (like Justice) as the holder of a balance, in which true values can be properly judged – see the word *weighed*, l. 6.

All Things can Tempt Me

Yeats wrote little lyrical verse during 1904–10, when he managed the Abbey

Theatre. It is noteworthy that the things enumerated as hindrances to verse-writing are also the themes of many of Yeats's poems – what disable and what enable are peculiarly the same. Another treatment of the theme of withdrawal – more serious than this impudently exasperated poem – can be found in 'The Coming of Wisdom with Time'. The original title was 'Distraction'.

3 *fool-driven land*: in 1926 a hostile senator quoted the first three lines of this poem during a session of the senate; Yeats replied, 'when I talked of this "fool-driven land" ... I meant that it was fool-driven in ... poetry and the theatre' – not necessarily politics (*SSY*, pp. 128, 132).

8 *one believed he had a sword upstairs*: the poet used to believe that poets should resemble heroes – men of action taking part in public affairs. But now, he says, he believes that the poet must retreat from public affairs, be cold and dumb and deaf (l. 10). To find the proper middle ground between solitude and public clamouring was an important issue for Yeats in these years, just as, in the 1890s, he vexed himself in finding a proper middle ground between commonplace life and spiritual transcendence – see 'To the Rose upon the Rood of Time'.

10 *Colder and dumber and deafer than a fish*: compare 'Never Give all the Heart', l. 12; and *At the Hawk's Well* (1917), ll. 64–65: 'To-day you are as stupid as a fish ... less lively and as dumb'.

Brown Penny

Here is another example of a poem that concludes a volume in a spirit of wise simplicity and smiling ease. Its original title was 'The Young Man's Song'.

8 *I am looped in the loops of her hair*: compare the hair-traps of several of the poems in *The Wind among the Reeds*, such as 'He bids his Beloved be at Peace.'

9–14: Finneran prints a version of these lines that Yeats sent to Scribner's around 1937 for a proposed edition of his work: 'And the penny sang up in my face, / "There is nobody wise enough / To find out all that is in it, / For he would be thinking of love / That is looped in the loops of her hair, / Till the loops of time had run"' (*PNE*, p. 98).

9–10 *O love is the crooked thing, / There is nobody wise enough*: compare Yeats's statement that love 'needs so much wisdom that the love of Solomon and Sheba must have lasted' (*A: E* 7)

RESPONSIBILITIES (1914)

This volume begins with a well known epigraph, '*In dreams begins responsibility*'. It is possible to read this epigraph as a capsule summary of Yeats's evolution as a poet between the 1880s and World War I: for Yeats began his career as a dreamer of mythologies and moved increasingly to a sort of art that shouldered the burden of public affairs. When he was young, Yeats defined his art by all that it excluded, and he saw the poetry of the great Victorians as compromised by the public themes it discussed – as he wrote in a review of a book by Arthur Symons:

> It seems to me the poetry which found its greatest expression in Tennyson and Browning pushed its limits as far as possible, tried to absorb into itself the science and philosophy and morality of its time, and to speak through the mouths of as many as might be of the great persons of history; and that there has been a revolt . . . and that poetry has been for two generations slowly contracting its limits and becoming more and more purely personal and lyrical in spirit. (*UP* II, pp. 39–40; compare *EI*, p. 190)

Responsibilities offers the counter-theme to this doctrine, a new spirit of inclusiveness and historical interest. This volume comprises poems about the première of Synge's *The Playboy of the Western World*, about the ghost of the politician Charles Parnell, and about a legal dispute over the location of some Impressionist paintings. But Yeats might still properly claim that his responsibility began in his dreams, for, as he studies the social scene, he judges what he sees by the standards of perfection and felt splendour that he had been elaborating in his speech of symbols during his whole career. To some extent the form of the volume is dictated by the famous epigraph: at the beginning there are a number of poems about responsibility (such as the Introductory Rhymes and 'To a Wealthy Man . . .'), and afterwards come a number of poems about sleep, wishes, and dreams ('The Three Beggars', 'The Hour before Dawn'), about vision and inspiration ('The Magi', 'A Coat', the Closing Rhymes). Responsibility thus reveals its origin in dreams.

Responsibilities shows a considerable preoccupation with the irresponsible – with incompetent politicians, venal rich men, bad poets, philistines; and also with beggars, children, and others who are too simple and lowly to be responsible. In *A Vision*, Yeats set out a model of the responsible man:

> . . . a code of personal conduct . . . being formed from social and historical tradition, remains always concrete in the mind. All is sacrificed to this code; moral strength reaches its climax. . . . There is great humility – 'she died every day she lived' – and pride as great, pride in the code's acceptance, an impersonal pride, as though one were to sign oneself 'servant of servants'. . . . The code . . . is obeyed in pain – can there be mercy in a rigid

> code? – the man is flooded with the joy of self-surrender; and flooded with mercy – what self can there be in self-surrender? – for those over whom the code can have no rights, children and the nameless multitude. Unmerciful to those who serve and to himself, merciful in contemplating those who are served, he never wearies of forgiveness. (*AV*, p. 169–70)

Yeats was thinking of Lady Gregory when he wrote this passage, and she is a continual example of responsibility throughout this volume. This description of responsibility also helps to explain the peculiar mixture of derision and forgiveness, arrogance and self-sacrifice, found among these poems. For later references to the theme of responsibility, see 'Vacillation' V 6.

The number of narrative poems in this volume is unusually large. Some of them, particularly 'The Grey Rock' and 'The Hour before Dawn', strive to establish a strong relation between an ancient story and modern life. In T. S. Eliot's famous *Dial* magazine review of Joyce's *Ulysses* (1922), Eliot noted that other authors would find attractive Joyce's method of manipulating a parallel between antiquity and contemporaneous life. Eliot was thinking chiefly of his own *The Waste Land* (1922); but Yeats had already tried a similar sort of counterpoint in 'The Grey Rock' and his play *The Dreaming of the Bones* (1919).

First Epigraph *Old Play*: the ascription seems to be a ruse – Yeats evidently wrote this pentameter line himself. In an uncollected poem of 1892, 'Wisdom and Dreams' (printed in the note to 'On Woman', l. 30), Yeats wrote that all wisdom originates in dreams.

Second Epigraph *Khoung-fou-tseu*: Confucius, in a French transliteration (from Pauthier's version). The epigraph is from the *Analects* VII v. In 1950 Pound translated this section, 'He said: deep my decadence, I haven't for a long time got back to seeing the Duke of Chou in my dreams' (*Confucius*, p. 219).

[Introductory Rhymes]

This poem was provoked by George Moore's attack on Yeats in *Hail and Farewell* III: Moore said that Yeats's ancestry did not justify his remark that he should have been the Duke of Ormonde (who was distantly related to Yeats) nor did his life of regular meals justify his self-sacrifice to art (see also the Closing Rhymes). But even without Moore's remark, Yeats felt a considerable need to justify his sedentary, aesthetical, unheroic way of life – see 'All Things can Tempt Me', l. 8, 'Under Saturn', l. 16, 'The Road at my Door', l. 13, 'I see Phantoms . . .', l. 35, and especially 'Are You Content', l. 6. It is likely that Yeats would have preferred more aristocratic, less mercantile ancestors than those he in fact had, but in this poem he does his best to uphold them as fierce paradigms of conduct. (Yeats was also touchy about the family's English origin, and tried to distance the family from England as far as possible: 'The family of Yeats, never more than small gentry, arrived, if I can trust the only man among us who may have seen the family tree before it was burnt by Canadian Indians, "about the time of Henry VII"' [*VPl*, p. 959].)

3 Old Dublin merchant: probably Benjamin Yeats (1750–95), a wholesale linen merchant, the poet's great-great-grandfather.

3 'free of ten and four': in a note Yeats explains this as an error – 'Irish merchants exempted from certain duties by the Irish Parliament were, unless memory deceives me again, "free of the eight and six"' (*VP*, p. 818). Yeats's memory did deceive him again, for (according to Finneran [*PNE*, p 605] and Jeffares [*NCP*, p. 100]) Benjamin Yeats – who, as a wholesaler, did not have to pay import duties – was free of the six and ten per cent tax at the Customs House, Dublin, from 1783–94 (ten per cent on wine and tobacco, six per cent on all other goods).

5 Old country scholar: John Yeats (1774–1846), the poet's great-grandfather. At Trinity College he won the Berkeley Medal for his work in Greek, and was appointed Rector of Drumcliff, near Sligo, by the Church of Ireland in 1805. He 'had been Robert Emmett's friend and was suspected and imprisoned though but for a few hours' (*A: R* 3). He is also mentioned in 'Are You Content', l. 9, and 'Under Ben Bulben' VI 3: 'An ancestor was rector there'.

5 Robert Emmet: the great Irish patriot (1718–1803), who led the 1803 revolt against England and was executed – see also 'September 1913', l. 21, 'Parnell's Funeral' I 18, and 'Three Marching Songs' I 25.

11 the Boyne: the river in Ireland where the Protestant William of Orange (the Dutchman, l. 12) defeated James II and his Irish Catholic forces on 12 July 1690 – the battle that established Protestant hegemony in Northern Ireland. This passage had to be rewritten, for Yeats once thought mistakenly that his Butler ancestors had fought on the side of the Englishman James II, not the Dutchman William of Orange – see Jeffares, *NCP*, p. 101.

13 Old merchant skipper: William Middleton (1770–1832), the poet's maternal great-grandfather, a ship-owner and merchant. He is mentioned in 'Under Saturn', l. 8, and 'Are You Content', l. 15: 'The smuggler Middleton'.

15 silent and fierce old man: William Pollexfen (1811–92), the poet's maternal grandfather. Yeats associated him with King Lear, and, as a boy, Yeats feared and admired him: 'He had won the freedom of some Spanish city, for saving life perhaps, but was so silent that his wife never knew it till he was near eighty ... He had great physical strength ... He owned many sailing ships ... I once saw him hunt a party of men with a horsewhip' (*A: R* 1). His death

is mentioned in 'In Memory of Alfred Pollexfen', l. 2; in 'Are You Content', l. 13, he is called 'that notable man'.

18 'Only the wasteful virtues earn the sun': in *The King's Threshold* (1904), the poet-hero tells the king that poets establish all values – the value of gold, even the value of courage: no man would join the king's army 'had not / Our heady craft commended the wasteful virtues' (ll. 526–27); elsewhere Yeats attributed the 'high wasteful virtues' to the Celtic influence (*Ex*, p. 27).

19–20 Pardon that for a barren passion's sake, / Although I have come close on forty-nine: the passion was barren because of Maud Gonne's lack of response. T. S. Eliot, in his essay 'Yeats' (1940), discussed this 'violent and terrible epistle' as an example of Yeats's growing ability 'to speak as a particular man' while speaking for all mankind; Eliot cited these two 'great lines' and commented: 'The naming of his age in the poem is significant. More than half a lifetime to arrive at this freedom of speech. It is a triumph' (*On Poetry and Poets*, p. 300). Eliot imitated something of this particularity in *East Coker* V (1940). Yeats also named his age in 'Lines Written in Dejection', l. 10: 'I have come to fifty years'; in 'Among School Children' I 8: 'A sixty-year-old smiling public man'; in 'Owen Aherne and his Dancers' II 3: 'How could she mate with fifty years'; and possibly in 'Imitated from the Japanese', l. 5: 'Seventy years have I lived'.

21 I have no child: compare Conchubar's speech to Cuchulain in *On Baile's Strand* (1904), ll. 276–77: 'I have heard you cry, aye, in your very sleep, / "I have no son", and with such bitterness'. Also compare 'The Municipal Gallery Re-visited' V 4–5: 'Childless I thought, "My children may find here / Deep-rooted things."'

21 I have nothing but a book: the idea of a text as a surrogate for a human relation can be found in 'Words', l. 15.

The Grey Rock

This poem is addressed to the poets of the Rhymers' Club, particularly to Lionel Johnson and Ernest Dowson. Yeats had been one of the founders of the Rhymers' Club in 1891 – a group consisting mostly of young poets willing to sacrifice their lives to their art; the club revered Rossetti and Pater, and thought that life should be ceremonious, art elaborate, and women vague, beautiful, and sybilline. But the club's two most talented members (other than Yeats) led such dissipated lives that the club had exhausted most of its stock of congeniality even before Dowson's death in 1900 and Johnson's in 1902.

Yeats introduces his story to his old comrades by saying, '*The moral's yours because it's mine*' (l. 11) – and indeed the moral of the tale is pointed at Dowson and Johnson, as well as at himself. The story takes place in the year 1014; just before the battle of Clontarf, Aoife offered two hundred years of life to her lover if he would stay out of the battle; but he refused, and died. In Yeats's version, the lover fights in the battle first with a charm that renders him invisible, invulnerable, and then, fatally, as a mere man; afterwards Aoife raves with grief, and the gods give her a drink that makes her forget his existence. (For Yeats's early exposure to this tale, see *L* I, p. 370.) Therefore the narrative concerns the wretchedness that comes to pass when a man tries to become like a god, and when a goddess becomes too intimate with a man: the proper state of a man is death; the proper state of a god is oblivion. Yeats thought of the Rhymers (especially Johnson) as men whose lives had been wrecked by their vision of supernatural splendour, and who wasted away or unbrained themselves with alcohol because death and oblivion are the likely outcome of too much research into ultimate things.

As Longenbach notes (*SC*, p. 101), Pound wrote, '*The Grey Rock* is, I admit, obscure, but it outweighs this by a curious nobility, a nobility which is ... the very core of Mr Yeats' production.... It is as obscure, at least, as *Sordello*, but I can not close without registering my admiration for it all the same' (*Literary Essays*, pp. 379, 381).

Title *Grey Rock*: the home of the legendary Aoife, in Co. Clare – compare 'Aoibheal of the Grey Rock' (*M*, p. 152; also *Ex*, p. 8).

2 the Cheshire Cheese: a London chophouse, where the Rhymers' Club met.

7–8 passion / That has more life in it than death: an allusion to the self-destructiveness and obsession with death found in some of the Rhymers.

10 Goban: 'Forges and smiths have always been magical in Ireland . . the old romances are loud with the doings of Goibnui, the god of the smiths, who is remembered in folktale as the Mason Goban, for he works in stone as in metal' (*UP* II, p. 103; see also *M*, p. 66). According to Douglas Hyde, Goibnui's skill at weapon-work helped the Tuatha de Danaan to defeat the Fomorians, the spirits of darkness. He brewed an ale that gave immortality. See 'The Hour before Dawn', l. 50.

15 *Slievenamon*: Gaelic for 'The Mountain of the Women', Co. Tipperary, the headquarters of a king of the Danaan.

29 *one that was like woman*: Aoife. She seems a member of the faery class called the '*Leanhaun Shee* (fairy mistress) ... the Gaelic Muse, for she gives inspiration to those she persecutes ... a malignant phantom' (*Fairy and Folk Tales*, p. 76). Presumably she differs from the warrior-queen Aoife who conspired to kill Cuchulain in *On Baile's Strand* (1904). As a malevolent muse Aoife seems similar to the title character in Lionel Johnson's most famous poem, 'The Dark Angel': 'Through thee, the gracious Muses turn / To

Furies, O mine Enemy! / And all the things of beauty burn / With flames of evil ecstasy. // Because of thee, the land of dreams / Becomes a gathering places of fears'. Yeats quoted these lines as an example of how Johnson's Catholicism 'deepened despair and multiplied temptation' (*A: TG* 9).

32 *a dead man*: Aoife's lover.

41 a woman: Maud Gonne.

47 some poor lout: John MacBride, whom Yeats later called 'a drunken, vainglorious lout' ('Easter, 1916', l. 32); this marriage was one of many examples of self-destructive behaviour in this poem.

54 wine or women: compare Dowson's well-known lines from 'The Villanelle of the Poet's Road': 'Unto us they belong / Us the bitter and gay, / Wine and women and song'. Yeats quoted these lines as proof that 'Dowson's poetry is sad, as he himself seemed, and pictures his life of temptation and defeat' (*A: TG* 8; compare *EI*, p. 492, and *OBMV*, p. x).

62 Dowson and Johnson: 'Two members of the [Rhymers'] Club are vivid in my memory: Ernest Dowson [1867–1900], timid, silent, a little melancholy, lax in body, vague in attitude; Lionel Johnson [1867–1902], determined, erect, his few words dogmatic, almost a dwarf but beautifully made, his features cut in ivory' (*EI*, p. 491). Johnson was a scholarly drunkard who, though tormented by lust (as the poem 'The Dark Angel' records), was found at his autopsy never to have become sexually mature (*A: TG* 8). Dowson was a drunkard who (as Ezra Pound said in *Hugh Selwyn Mauberley* VII) 'found harlots cheaper than hotels'. Yeats used them as examples of poets who wasted their lives because their imaginations were focused beyond earthly life. Yeats dedicated *The Rose* to Johnson, and elegized him in 'In Memory of Major Robert Gregory' III; both poets are remembered in 'Ego Dominus Tuus', ll. 49–51.

65 *The Danish troop was driven out*: Brian Boru, the Irish king, drove the Danes from Ireland in AD 1014, at the Battle of Clontarf. In 1910 Yeats intended to write a poem 'about the man who left Aoibhinn of Craiglea to die at Clontarf and put in it all the bitter feeling one has sometimes about Ireland' (*Mem*, p. 241).

71 *Murrough*: Brian Boru's son.

92 *But there it's gone*: a mortal's renunciation of godlike powers is a turning-point in several of Yeats's narrative poems: see *The Wanderings of Oisin* III 125, and the end of 'The Two Kings'.

98 *two hundred years*: compare the three hundred years that Oisin spends with Niamh in *The Wanderings of Oisin*.

122 *No more remembering*: the emotions of Yeats's gods are either unusually permanent or unusually fleeting. The human national loyalties of Murrough

and of Aoife's lover seem all the more precious by contrast to the distasteful oblivion of Aoife. Compare *The Countess Cathleen* (from 1912 on), ll. 293–318, in which the poet Aleel condemns the mindless gods who forget the adoration of their human lovers; and *Fighting the Waves* (1929), ll. 234–35: 'once [Cuchulain] lands in Manannan's house, he will be as the gods who remember nothing'. The parallels between Aoife and Maud Gonne also suggest that a faithful lover ought not to be forgotten.

125 rock-born . . . foot: Maud Gonne's. Compare l. 88, 'Rock-nurtured Aoife'.

127 I am in no good repute: as Jeffares notes (*NCP*, p. 105), the Irish Republican Brotherhood disapproved of Yeats's acceptance in 1910 of a pension from the British government. Yeats's relations with Irish institutions were uneasy ever since the supposed anti-Catholicism of *The Countess Cathleen* in 1899, and the Abbey Theatre's productions gave continuing offence to many.

The Two Kings

When assembling his *Collected Poems* (1933), Yeats severed this poem from *Responsibilities* and placed it in a separate section of narrative poems; but that arrangement was principally a publisher's convenience. This poem terminates a series of long poems derived from confused Irish lore about Aengus and Edain, the parents of Niamh, the heroine of *The Wanderings of Oisin*. (For more information about Aengus and Edain, see *The Wanderings of Oisin* I 47.) In *Baile and Aillinn* and *The Shadowy Waters*, Aengus and Edain inspire dreams of unearthly love-consummation, as if desire could be satisfied only on some isle of the blest, or in the grave. But this poem experiments with a more humane counter-truth: the temptation to supernatural love should be resisted, because the fact of mortality itself intensifies love – what is doubly brief is doubly sweet (ll. 206–7). This rejection of divine in favour of human ethics resembles that of 'The Grey Rock'.

Edain, the heroine, was originally a mortal woman who was lured away by Midhir, one of the gods. She was turned into a fly by Midhir's jealous wife, and Aengus kept her in a house of glass (see 'The Harp of Aengus'); after a very long time she was swallowed and reincarnated in human form ('betrayed into a cradle', 'The Two Kings', l. 169); then she married the human King Eochaid, and Midhir again tried to lure her. 'The old Gaelic literature is full of the appeals of the [gods] to mortals whom they would bring into their country; but the song of Midher to the beautiful Etain, the wife of the king who was called Echaid the ploughman, is the type of all. "O beautiful woman, come with me to the marvellous land where one listens to a sweet music . . . Youth does not grow old there. Streams with warm flood flow there; sometimes mead, sometimes wine [as in Yeats's 'The Happy Townland', l. 8]" '

(*VP*, p. 805). This seduction-song worked in the original myth, and Edain and Midhir turned into birds and flew away; but Yeats reversed the ending, and made her stubbornly human, carnal. Man defeats god, just as Eochaid conquers the supernatural stag at the beginning of the poem.

In his review of *Responsibilities*, Pound wrote that 'it is impossible to take any interest in a poem like *The Two Kings* – one might as well read the *Idylls* of [Tennyson]' (*Literary Essays*, p. 379). Yeats's father took violent exception to this: '*The Two Kings* is immortal because of its *intensity* and *concentration* ... and concentration and intensity are not Tennysonian.... In *The Two Kings* there is another quality often sought by Tennyson, but never attained, and that is *splendor of imagination*, a *liberating splendor*, cold as sunrise' (*LTY* I, p. 289; see also p. 301).

The poem originally opened with a conversation between Eochaid and his shield-bearer, lamenting those fallen in the war.

2 *Tara*: see 'In the Seven Woods', l. 6.

6 *a stag*: a transformation of Midhir, the king of the Sidhe (one of the Two Kings of the title). Compare the 'marvellous stag' of 'Towards Break of Day', l. 23.

19 *unicorn*: a fanciful image for Eochaid, 'horned' with his sword. But this whole scene recalls the Tapster's speech in *The Player Queen* (1922) I 185–88, telling how a boy shot a pistol at a unicorn, only to see it vanish, just as the stag does at l. 38 of the present poem. For other unicorns, see 'I see Phantoms ...', l. 18.

27 *beaten into mire*: compare 'The Madness of King Goll', l. 26, 'trampled in the bubbling mire'.

30 *hoof and horn that had sucked in their speed*: the gods can absorb surrounding energies – compare ll. 159–60: 'my craft / Sucked up the passion out of him'.

31 *elaborate wilderness of the air*: compare 'Nineteen Hundred and Nineteen' VI 9: 'labyrinth of the wind'.

45 *King Eochaid ran*: in the first printing this read 'King Eochaid gazed', and continued as follows: 'And then, as terror-stricken as a child / Who has seen a garden image or twisted tree / In the half light, and runs to its own door / Its terror growing wilder at every foot-fall, / He ran' (*VP*, p. 279). Eochaid's childlikeness reappears at l. 192.

51 *Nor door, nor mouth, nor slipper made a noise*: as a parable about enforced and unnatural silence, 'The Two Kings' bears some relation to Tennyson's 'Geraint and Enid' (1859). Later, Ardan fears that if he speaks he will explode (l. 100); but Edain replies that even evil is better than soul-destroying muteness (l. 104). The court's uncanny stillness is at last broken by bellowings and shoutings (ll. 214–16).

65 *Some passion had made her stone*: the petrifying power of extreme passion, inspired by the gods, is an important theme. Edain's stoniness is a kind of contagion from her brother-in-law Ardan, who says, 'There are things / That make the heart akin to the dumb stone' (ll. 93–94). The fatality of such an image becomes explicit by the references to tombstones at ll. 106 and 179. Divine passion is here associated with paralysis, reticence, rigor mortis; human passion with fluency, expressiveness, warmth. In Yeats's early pastoral, *The Island of Statues*, those who fail in their quest for a supernatural flower turn literally to stone.

71–72 *one / Who is self-accused*: Edain herself.

83 *Ogham*: an ancient Irish alphabet.

94 *the heart akin to the dumb stone*: compare 'Easter, 1916', ll. 41–43: 'Hearts . . . enchanted to a stone'.

113 *Loughlan*: Scandinavian. In *Diarmuid and Grania* (1901) II 50–51, Ireland is invaded: 'The men of Lochland have dragged up 70 galleys on to the beach'.

120–21 *we give . . . Happiness to children and to men*: compare *Baile and Aillinn*, ll. 39–40: '*all this life can give us is / A child's laughter, a woman's kiss*'.

124 *You . . . could work the cure*: that is, Edain's sexual favour would cure Ardan. But it is not Ardan who speaks, but the god Midhir, who has possessed his body. After an agony of indecision, Edain agrees to sleep with her brother-in-law at l. 137.

129 *mound's*: *wound's*, according to some of the earlier texts.

148–49 *a man / Who had unnatural majesty*: Midhir.

167 *Danced in the whirling foam and in the dust*: see 'Nineteen Hundred and Nineteen' VI 6.

181 *Pleasure itself can bring no weariness*: compare 'Among School Children' VIII 2: 'body is not bruised to pleasure soul'.

183 *wandering dance*: for the authority of this reading (over *whirling dance*), see *EYP*, pp. 31–32.

186 *How should I love*: compare 'Dhoya' (1891), where a goddess says, 'I have left [the gods] for thee, Dhoya, for they cannot love. Only the changing, and moody, and angry, and weary can love' (*JSD*, p. 120).

189 *pass away*: compare 'Vacillation' VI 5: 'Let all things pass away'.

194–95 *her nest . . . Above a windy precipice*: this precarious habitation contrasts with another aerial house, the 'sudden palaces in the still air' (l. 180) built by the gods.

198 *This human life blotted from memory*: a somewhat similar oblivion is attributed to the gods themselves in 'The Grey Rock', l. 122.

To a Wealthy Man who promised a Second Subscription to the Dublin Municipal Gallery if it were proved the People wanted Pictures

The philanthropist Sir Hugh Lane (1875–1915), the nephew of Lady Gregory, amassed an important collection of French Impressionist paintings (for other references to Lane, see 'Coole Park, 1929', l. 14, and 'The Municipal Gallery Re-visited' III 6). He decided to donate this collection to the Dublin Municipal Gallery, but only if the Dublin Corporation would build an art gallery over the River Liffey. Otherwise he threatened to give them to London, where esteem of art seemed greater. This poem is addressed to an 'imaginary' correspondent (*L*, p. 573 – the same letter suggests that Yeats might have had Lord Ardilaun in mind) who might be persuaded to supplement Sir Hugh's bounty by donating money, but only if the common people themselves would contribute part. Yeats believed that standards of taste could be imposed only from above, and that to ask the mob to cooperate in the improvement of culture was foolish. Yeats considered it the duty of the Dublin authorities to behave like the great Renaissance dukes whose patronage of art was governed by bold judgments of merit, not by public opinion polls; but 'To a Wealthy Man ...' anticipates the rejection that Lane's proposal indeed was to suffer. In writing this poem, Yeats strove for a diction of casual magniloquence – Yeats wished not only to call for models of excellence, but to be one himself.

This poem had an unusual sequel: in his will Sir Hugh stipulated that his great collection should go to London; but in an unwitnessed codicil, written just before his departure for America on the *Lusitania* in 1915, he specified Dublin instead as the destination of his paintings; and the *Lusitania* was indeed, as he feared, sunk by a German submarine. Yeats was to go to endless trouble – lobbying, letter-writing, and so forth – to ensure that Sir Hugh's legally invalid last wish was obeyed. Yeats even tried to persuade Lane's ghost to give the location of a signed codicil (*MAV* I, pp. 75, 93).

Title: the original title was 'The Gift / To a friend who promises a bigger subscription than his first to the Dublin Municipal Gallery if the amount collected proves that there is a considerable "popular demand" for the pictures'.

2 *Paudeen*: a member of the crowd – a coarse diminutive of *Patrick*.

7 *the blind and ignorant town*: see 'Words', l. 4, 'this blind bitter land'.

9 *Duke Ercole*: Ercole d'Este (1431–1505), the Duke of Ferrara described as a patron of the arts in Castiglione's *The Courtier*. Yeats had visited Ferrara in 1907.

12 *Plautus*: early Roman playwright (*c.* 254–184 BC). Duke Ercole patronized the Renaissance revival of interest in the classics.

14 *Guidobaldo*: Guidobaldo di Montefeltro (1472–1508), the Duke of Urbino.

17 *Urbino*: an Italian city, like Ferrara a model of Renaissance magnificence and unity of achievement. Yeats aspired to become an aristocrat of art, comparable to the nobles at Urbino: 'Every day I notice some new analogy between the long-established life of the well-born and the artist's life. We come from the permanent things and create them, and instead of old blood we have old emotions and we carry in our heads always that form of society aristocracies create now and again for some brief moment at Urbino or Versailles' (*A: E* 25; *Mem*, p. 156). See 'The People', l. 12.

19 *the shepherd's will*: when Yeats came to classify the Masks of the various poets, he assigned as his own Mask the figure of a shepherd, and he compared this dream-identity of Arcadian simplicity to a passage in *The Courtier* – 'of what else did [Cardinal] Bembo think when he cried, "Would that I were a shepherd that I might look daily down upon Urbino"?' (*AV*, p. 109; compare *A: BS* 9). Yeats was careful to distinguish the fantasy-shepherd – a sophisticated dream of rustic ease – from the real shepherd, clumsy and illiterate. In 'Fallen Majesty', l. 3, Yeats spoke of himself, 'Like some last courtier at a gypsy camping-place'.

20 *Cosimo*: Cosimo de' Medici (1384–1464), one of the great patrons of Florence. His rejection by the public – he was briefly banished in 1433 – made him comparable to Sir Hugh Lane. '[Lane] was the most generous of men. A famous artist said of him that he had raised the profession of a picture dealer into the magnificence of the Medici' (*SSY*, p. 123).

23 *Michelozzo*: an architect (1396–1472), a pupil of Brunelleschi, who accompanied Cosimo into exile.

25–26 *turbulent Italy should draw / Delight in Art whose end is peace*: Yeats often conceived art as a violent man's construction of peace, or a bitter man's construction of sweetness ('Ancestral Houses', ll. 19–20, and 'The Gift of Harun Al-Rashid', ll. 47-48). Compare also 'Peace', l. 9 ('sweetness amid strength'), the allusion to Samson's riddle in 'Vacillation' VIII 11, and the Proud Furies that climb the elegant old house's staircase in 'To Dorothy Wellesley', l. 16.

26–28 *peace . . . Greece*: this telling rhyme recurs in 'The Tower' III 37–39.

32 *Look up in the sun's eye*: see 'Upon a House shaken . . .', l. 4.

36 *an eagle's nest*: compare the jackdaw's nest in 'The Tower' III 52, also a metaphor for civilization.

September 1913

This poem, like 'To a Wealthy Man . . .' and 'Paudeen', begins with the image of unpleasant money-handlers – all three poems pertain to the Lane controversy (see the note to 'To a Wealthy Man ...'). The previous poem shows what can happen when a culture accepts the discipline of a paradigm of conduct; this poem shows the chaos and ill-breeding that results when a culture refuses such a discipline. Ireland does not lack models of propriety – O'Leary, Fitzgerald, Emmet, Tone – but it lacks the will to imitate them. In his review of *Responsibilities*, Pound wrote that this poem 'is no better than Red Hanrahan's song about Ireland, but it is harder' (*Literary Essays*, p. 379).

Title: the original title was 'Romance in Ireland / (On reading much of the correspondence against the Art Gallery)'.

1 *you*: the cash register and the prayers suggest that Yeats is addressing the Catholic shopkeeping class, indicted as more likely to save money than souls (l. 6).

7: '"Romantic Ireland's dead and gone" sounds old-fashioned now [July 1916]. It seemed true in 1913, but I did not foresee [the Easter Rebellion of] 1916' (*VP*, p. 820). For *Romantic*, compare 'Three Movements', l. 2: 'Romantic fish'; and 'Coole and Ballylee, 1931', l. 41: 'We were the last romantics'.

8 *O'Leary*: John O'Leary (1830–1907), the Fenian leader, imprisoned for years, whom Yeats admired deeply – indeed Yeats lived with him for a time. Yeats called him 'the handsomest old man I had ever seen' and spoke of his 'moral genius': 'Sometimes he would say things that would have sounded well in some heroic Elizabethan play. It became my delight to rouse him to these outbursts ... Once when I was defending an Irish politician who had made a great outcry because he was treated as a common felon, by showing that he did it for the cause's sake, he said, "There are things that a man must not do to save a nation"' (*A:R* 28). Note that the word *save* is crucial both in O'Leary's sentence and in this poem (ll. 6, 14). O'Leary's life, 'Romantic', even Elizabethan, is contrasted with the meaninglessness and formlessness of modern Irish life. O'Leary will reappear as the first of the 'Beautiful Lofty Things'. Compare also *EI*, p. 246, and *UP* II, pp. 35–37.

14 *what, God help us, could they save?*: compare 'A Bronze Head', l. 28: 'what was left for massacre to save'.

17 *the wild geese*: Irishmen who served in armies in continental Europe after the passage in 1691 of the Penal Laws, harshly restricting the freedom of conduct of Catholic Irishmen.

20 *Edward Fitzgerald*: Irish patriot (1763–98), a Member of Parliament from Athy, who died in Wolfe Tone's uprising of 1798. Compare 'Sixteen Dead Men', l. 16: 'Lord Edward and Wolfe Tone'; and 'Parnell's Funeral' I 18.

21 *Emmet*: see the Introductory Rhymes, l. 5.

21 *Wolfe Tone*: Irish patriot (1763–98) who led French forces to Ireland in 1798 in order to overthrow British hegemony; he probably committed

suicide in prison after his capture by the British. He is mentioned in 'Parnell's Funeral' I 18. Yeats's play *Cathleen ni Houlihan* (1902) is set during this uprising.

28–29 *You'd cry, 'Some woman's yellow hair / Has maddened every mother's son'*: the bloodless rabble, beholding the fervour of the old patriots, would find a banal explanation for it.

To a Friend whose Work has come to Nothing

'Lady Gregory in her Life of Sir Hugh Lane assumes that the poem which begins "Now all the truth is out" was addressed to him. It was not; it was addressed to herself' (*VP*, p. 819). The work that came to nothing was her strenuous effort to persuade the Dublin government to build a picture gallery (see 'To a Wealthy Man ...'). This poem, like the following, recommends complete withdrawal into solitary imagination, after the exasperations of public life – this is one solution to the conflict between private and public interests.

5 *one*: probably William Martin Murphy, a newspaper owner who opposed the picture gallery. As Jeffares notes, Murphy wrote, 'I would rather see in the city of Dublin one block of sanitary houses at low rents replacing a reeking slum than all the pictures Corot and Degas ever painted' (*NCP*, p. 113). See 'To a Shade', l. 17.

9–10 *Bred to a harder thing / Than Triumph*: compare 'Nineteen Hundred and Nineteen' III 20: 'triumph can but mar our solitude'.

11 *like a laughing string*: in many Romantic poems, such as Coleridge's 'The Eolian Harp' (1796), the artist is compared to the string of a musical instrument, vibrating in response to an unknown agent.

12–13 *Whereon mad fingers play / Amid a place of stone*: compare 'The Players ask for a Blessing ...', l. 1: 'bless the hands that play'; 'Shepherd and Goatherd', ll. 25–26: 'The exultation of their stone, that cried / Under his fingers'; 'Lapis Lazuli', l. 54, 'Accomplished fingers begin to play'; and *The Dreaming of the Bones* (1919), ll. 298–99: 'Those crazy fingers play / A wandering airy music'. Yeats thought that the range of expression was greatest on small, stringed instruments: he contrasted the heavy, mechanical, impersonal sound of the piano with the nimbleness of the guitar: 'The little instrument is quite light, and the player can move freely and express a joy that is not of the fingers and the mind only but of the whole being' (*EI*, p. 269). Frayne compares this poem to a passage in an early review: 'Man is like a musical instrument of many strings, of which only a few are sounded by the narrow interests of his daily life ... Heroic poetry is a phantom finger swept over all the strings ... those of wonder and pity, of fear and joy' (*UP* I, p. 84).

14–16 *Be secret and exult, / Because of all things known / That is most difficult*: Yeats quoted a version of these lines in a letter to Margot Ruddock, to illustrate the motto 'Never be swept away into anything; live in self-possession, wisdom' (*ASD*, p. 21). Also compare 'The Phases of the Moon', l. 40: 'whatever whim's most difficult'.

Paudeen

This poem may suggest why Yeats, who had a talent for satire, did not often use it: in a sudden enlargement of vision, the poet abandons his rancour for a kind of ecstasy. The desolate landscape and the ruined inhabitants give way to a further evacuation – in the phrase that Yeats used as the title of a story (and, in slightly different form, of a play), 'Where there is Nothing, there is God'.

1–2 *fumbling ... stumbled*: compare 'The Hour before Dawn', ll. 3, 16: 'Stumbled ... fumbled'; 'The Tower' II 45: 'He stumbled, tumbled, fumbled to and fro'; also 'September 1913', l. 2.

7 *confusion of our sound forgot*: compare 'The Cold Heaven', l. 10: 'Confusion of the death-bed over'.

8 *A single soul that lacks a sweet crystalline cry*: Yeats often wrote of a mysterious voice that told him that every human soul is precious, because each satisfies a different need of God's (*The Countess Cathleen*, ll. 386–91; *M*, pp. 68, 348; *Mem*, p. 126; *A: SB* 6; *LTMSB*, p. 75). Even Paudeen can attain a divine self-possession. Many of Yeats's works end with a wordless cry that suggests the soul's transcendence of the body – see 'The Three Hermits' and the story 'The Heart of the Spring' (*M*, p. 176).

To a Shade

This poem is addressed to Charles Stewart Parnell (1846–91), the greatest Irish politician of his time. He led the Irish delegation to Parliament, and seemed capable of organizing Ireland's independence – for a time Parnell held the balance of power, and he managed in 1886 to convert Prime Minister Gladstone to the cause of Home Rule for Ireland; but his affair with Kitty O'Shea, a married woman, was exposed, and many devout Roman Catholics turned against the Protestant adulterer. Yeats admired his iron self-control, his resolution, and his political creativity – see *AV*, pp. 121–24. In the year of Parnell's death Yeats wrote a poem about him ('Mourn – And Then

Onward!', *VP*, pp. 737–38), never reprinted:

Ye on the broad high mountains of old Eri,
Mourn all the night and day,
The man is gone who guided ye, unweary,
Through the long bitter way.

Ye by the waves that close in our sad nation,
Be full of sudden fears,
The man is gone who from his lonely station
Has moulded the hard years.

Mourn ye on grass-green plains of Eri fated,
For closed in darkness now
Is he who laboured on, derided, hated,
And made the tyrant bow.

Mourn – and then onward, there is no returning
He guides ye from the tomb;
His memory now is a tall pillar, burning
Before us in the gloom!

At the end of this early poem, the spirit of Parnell is like the pillar of fire that led the Israelites out of the wilderness (Exodus 13:21); but at the end of 'To a Shade', the people seem to prefer the wilderness to Canaan. As in 'September 1913', a model of disciplined purpose is readily available to the Irish, but is rejected. Yeats wrote again of Parnell in 'Parnell's Funeral', in 'Three Marching Songs' I 25, in 'Come Gather Round Me Parnellites', and in 'Parnell'. Around 1893 Yeats wrote an unpublished poem, 'The Watch-Fire' (printed by Edward O'Shea, *Poetry*, Jan. 1980), addressed to Mother Eri and evidently a tribute to Parnell – even feebler than 'Mourn – And Then Onward!'

2 *your monument*: on O'Connell Street, Dublin. Compare 'The Three Monuments', l. 2.

9 *A man*: Sir Hugh Lane. See 'To a Wealthy Man . . .'.

11 *what*: Lane's collection of French Impressionist paintings.

17 *Your enemy*: probably William Martin Murphy, who owned two newspapers opposed to Parnell. See 'To a Friend . . .', l. 5.

18 *The pack*: Yeats was fond of quoting a statement that Goethe told Eckermann, '"the Irish seem to me like a pack of hounds, always dragging down some noble stag"' (*A: TG* 10). See also 'Parnell's Funeral' I 22: '*Hysterica passio* dragged this quarry [Parnell] down'.

19 *Glasnevin*: the cemetery where Parnell is buried.

20 *dust stops your ear*: compare the posthumous 'Reprisals', l. 23, addressed to the ghost of Robert Gregory: 'close your ears with dust' (*VP*, p. 791).

24 *Away, away!*: the spirit of Parnell might be reincarnated, at least metaphorically, but the disillusioned poet seems to fear that the age might persecute him once again.

When Helen Lived

The source of this poem was a diary entry from 1909: 'I dreamed this thought two nights ago: "Why should we complain if men ill-treat our Muses, when all that they gave to Helen while she still lived was a song and a jest?"' (*A: DS* 31). Many of the poems in this volume, particularly 'To a Wealthy Man. . .', strive to enforce a firm division between the aristocracy of talent and the tasteless rabble. But there is a countermovement, consisting of several poems that strive to abolish such distinctions. In 'Paudeen' and, to some extent, in the Closing Rhymes, a spirit of magnanimity and forgiveness overcomes all hatred; here, the poet can imagine himself as wretched a philistine as any Paudeen, no better than another man. In a later poem, 'Nineteen Hundred and Nineteen' V, Yeats also includes himself among the objects of his mockery.

At a peacock dinner organized by Pound, several poets honoured W. S. Blunt by presenting him with a reliquary containing the MSS of their poems – this poem was Yeats's contribution (see W. T. Going's article in *Journal of Modern Literature* 1 [1971]).

Title *Helen*: allusions to Helen of Troy (but not her name) appeared earlier in 'The Rose of Battle', 'The Sorrow of Love', and 'No Second Troy'. For other references to Helen, see 'The Double Vision of Michael Robartes' III 8, 'A Prayer for my Daughter', l. 25, 'The Tower' II 37, 'A Man Young and Old' VI 13 and X3, 'Lullaby', l. 6, 'Why should not Old Men be Mad?', l. 7, 'Three Marching Songs' II 4, and 'Long-legged Fly', l. 12. In *The Player Queen* II 423-29 an actor tells of a play, *The Fall of Troy*, in which he played Agamemnon and 'reproached Helen for all the misery she had wrought'.

8 *topless towers*: compare Marlowe, *Dr Faustus* (1588) V i 94-95: 'Was this the face that lancht a thousand shippes? / And burnt the toplesse Towres of *Ilium*?' Yeats also used the phrase in 'Long-legged Fly', l. 11; and in the so-called 'De Burgh' version of the unfinished *The Speckled Bird* the infatuated hero completes Marlowe's quotation by telling his beloved that it is her face that launches all his ships (*LTMSB*, p. 382).

On those that hated *The Playboy of the Western World*, 1907

J. M. Synge's *The Playboy of the Western World* concerns a young Irishman, Christy Mahon, who claims to have murdered his father and is the more admired by the townsmen the more he embellishes his story; but then his father appears, and the young man finds that he must kill him in earnest if he is to keep up his self-respect. There is a happy ending. It was first performed in 1907 by the Abbey Theatre, and led to a kind of riot. It 'roused the populace to fury. We played it under police protection, seventy police in the theatre the last night, and five hundred ... keeping order in the streets outside. It is never played before any Irish audience for the first time without something or other being flung at the players' (*A:IDM*). Some spectators brought tin trumpets to drown out the play (*Ex*, p. 226); Arthur Griffith attacked Synge in his newspaper, on the grounds that literature ought to be subservient to politics.

This poem is a moralized description of a painting by Charles Ricketts. Yeats wrote in his diary that suppressed hungers grow morbid ('sexual abstinence ... reacts ... on the imagination, so that we get at last that strange eunuch-like tone and temper'[*A: E* 42]) – and here he imagines the populace that reviled Synge as a gang of eunuchs, envious of and spiteful against the creative energy that can never be theirs. There may be a parallel between the eunuchs' reception of Don Juan and the reception of Christy Mahon in Synge's play. For a later poem about Synge, see 'In Memory of Major Robert Gregory' IV 1.

2 *Eunuchs*: 'the political class in Ireland ... have suffered through the cultivation of hatred as the one energy of their movement, a deprivation which is the intellectual equivalent to [castration] ... They contemplate all creative power as the eunuchs contemplate Don Juan as he passes through Hell on the white horse' (*A: E* 41; *Mem*, p. 176). Compare the marrowless bones of the middle class in 'September 1913', l. 5. For other eunuchs, see 'Vacillation' II.

The Three Beggars

This is the first of a sequence of poems about beggars – after dismissing the urban middle class and lamenting the absence of aristocracy in the first part of this volume, Yeats turns towards the rural lower class, towards careless simplicity – hermits, drunkards, children, and loose women. Yeats's beggars are usually figures of large, inconsequent, easily distracted imagination, like the poet Hanrahan whom Yeats invented in the 1890s (see the note to *The Wind among the Reeds*). The beggars of the 1910s are sometimes more haggard, mindless, and brutal than their predecessors in Yeats's work; but precisely because their lives are so spare, stark, harsh, bleak, they seem on the brink of wisdom. Paul Ruttledge in Yeats's play *Where There is Nothing* (1902) said that he was 'plucking off the rags and tatters of the world' (IV 423) – and when the world shrinks and falls apart, there is a compensating increase in vision.

This poem can be read as a parable recommending self-surrender and indifference, just as self-dispossession leads to enlightenment in 'Paudeen', and as the sleeper is called the only blessed man in 'The Hour before Dawn', l. 104. There may also be an artistic corollary: the imagination is best rewarded by images when it sinks into a passive state of trance, instead of labouring fretfully – compare 'The Fascination of What's Difficult'.

5 lebeen-lone: minnows, or what minnows eat.

6 the old crane of Gort: Gort is a town in Co. Galway. In Yeats's play *Calvary* (1920), a heron's fishing is counterpointed with the action of the play.

8 *Guaire*: a generous king of Connacht, d. AD 663. He appears in the play *The King's Threshold* (1904), where he also shows a certain inclination towards psychological experiment.

13–14 *Do men who least desire get most, / Or get the most who most desire?*: in Carlyle's *Sartor Resartus* (1831), Teufelsdröckh says that a man can better increase his fraction of happiness by lowering the denominator than by raising the numerator. Although this poem seems to advocate decreasing one's desires, Yeats in other works seems most to respect the man with the most strenuous desires. The beggars' desires, however, are commonplace.

24 *Sleep*: to strain and struggle after sleep is a particularly futile action – a desire not to have desires.

68 If but I do not seem to care: compare Castiglione's doctrine of *sprezzatura*, the noble dismissal of one's own labour in mastering a discipline – here parodied.

The Three Hermits

Yeats wrote that this was 'my first poem which is comedy or tragi-comedy' (*L*, p. 577). It is a parable on the vanity of abstract speculation about the hereafter. The first two beggars bicker and debate about reincarnation; but the third simply sings wordlessly, 'like a bird'. The first two bind themselves to this world by their speech; the last frees himself from it by his song. In 'Paudeen', Yeats wrote of how the soul, once divested of the body, uttered a 'sweet crystalline cry' (l. 8); and the third hermit of this poem is at the threshold of this passage into the superhuman. As 'The White Birds' might suggest, Yeats's imagination was always haunted by an image of a man who turns into a bird as he passes into a higher state: in *The Wanderings of Oisin*, the dancers of the first island have feathers sewn on their cloaks (I 206), while the sleepers of the third island have bird-claws instead of hands (III 34); in *The Shadowy Waters*, ll. 23–24, the sailors see 'a bird / Like a grey gull on the breast of each' corpse floating on the waves; in 'Under the Round Tower', a king and a queen, emblematical of sun and moon, whirl up to the top of a tower and sing 'like a brace of blackbirds' (l. 24); in 'Sailing to Byzantium' the poet says that he will choose the form of a golden bird (IV 6) when he enters the 'artifice of eternity'; in *The King of the Great Clock Tower* (1935), ll. 2–3, a musician sings of paradise, 'There every lover is a happy rogue; / And should he speak, it is the speech of birds'; in 'Cuchulain Comforted', the spirits that greet the newly dead hero first speak, then change 'their throats and had the throats of birds' (l. 25); and in *The Death of Cuchulain* (1939), the hero's severed head turns into a black parallelogram, and a few faint bird's notes are heard: 'There floats out there / The shape that I shall take when I am dead, / My soul's first shape, a soft feathery shape' (ll. 177–79). It is always possible that the highest relevation will be the least verbal, the most inarticulate – though Yeats also feared the disintegration of meaning, as in 'The Sad Shepherd', l. 27, and 'To the Rose upon the Rood of Time', l. 21.

7 *bird*: the full stop after this word follows the editions before *CP* (1933), which ends the line with a colon (misleading in that it implies that the speaker of ll. 8–12 is the third hermit).

12 *Fall asleep when I should pray*: in *At the Hawk's Well* (1917), an Old Man, waiting for the appearance of the waters of immortality at a dry well, falls asleep whenever those waters appear (l. 138).

32 *Sang unnoticed like a bird*: compare the old holy man in 'The Pilgrim', ll. 9–10: 'And that old man beside me, nothing would he say / But fol de rol de rolly O'.

Beggar to Beggar Cried

According to Hone (*WBY*, p. 301), Lady Gregory advised Yeats to marry for the sake of his peace of mind, after a wretched incident in 1910, when Mabel Dickinson sent Yeats a telegram falsely saying that she was pregnant by him. In this poem, the vision of a moderate, cosily respectable life – spent with a wife who is neither too pretty nor too rich – seems as fanatical, discordant, and unreal as the wildest dream of paradise. Yeats thought such a marriage would violate the law of his being.

3 frenzy-struck: as in 'The Three Beggars', strenuous desires lead to frantic unhappiness.

4 *make my soul*: see 'The Tower' III 61.

6 *the devil in my shoes*: in 'The Twisting of the Rope' (1892), Hanrahan speaks of the 'devil in the soles of my feet' (*VSR*, p. 199).

10 *She need not be too comely*: Yeats expressed a similar wish for his daughter in 'A Prayer for my Daughter', l. 17.

12 *a devil in a looking-glass*: see 'The Two Trees', l. 21.

20 *the barnacle-geese*: a goose's honk is perhaps the right ending to the beggar's scheme. For other barnacle-geese, see 'High Talk', l. 11.

Running to Paradise

In a radio broadcast script of 1934, Yeats read 'The Fiddler of Dooney', and, to link that poem to this, said, 'Years later I tried to return to this early style in "Running to Paradise". Some Gaelic book tells of a man running at full speed, who, when asked where he is running, answers "to Paradise". I think you will notice the difference in style. The poem is more thoughtful, more packed with little pictures' (*UP* II, p. 497).

This poem gives a strong impression of speed: the beggar runs so quickly that he becomes a kind of blur, casting everything away, while his slower acquaintances accumulate a family, servants, money; his only friend is the wind that rushes him on. Yeats similarly associated velocity and a kind of nirvana in 'In Memory of Major Robert Gregory', where Gregory consumes all his energy in one great flare (XI 5), and in *Ex*, p. 398, where Yeats speaks of the soul hurrying through its many incarnations in order to escape from the circuit of life and death.

1 *Windy Gap*: in his unfinished novel *The Speckled Bird* Yeats mentioned a valley among the hills to the south of Galway Bay, called in Irish Gleann-na-Gae and in English Windy Gap (*LTMSB*, p. 241).

4 *all that I need do is wish*: ideal dispossession correlates with a mysterious satisfaction of one's needs – the beggar seems more than halfway to Paradise.

7 And there the king *is* but as the beggar: in the King James Bible, words added to the English text by the translators, such as forms of the verb *to be*, are italicized. Yeats does the same to impart a biblical sententiousness to his refrain.

9 *skelping*: beating.

18 *many a darling wit's grown dull*: in 'Why should not Old Men be Mad?', ll. 5–6, Yeats wrote, 'A girl that knew all Dante once / Live to bear children to a dunce'.

19 *a bare heel*: 'I could ink my socks, that they might not show through my shoes, with a most haughty mind' (*A: FY* 15).

20 *an old sock full*: of money. The beggar feels himself happily out of the circuit of wealth and poverty.

The Hour before Dawn

The beggar in the previous poem was running to Paradise; the sleeper in this poem has found a more relaxing way to make time accelerate into eternity. Yeats was fond of the image of the sleeper who sleeps through centuries – such a person's dreams formed a connective tissue from the mythological origins of things to the present day to the Last Judgment. The sleeper could be almost a human equivalent of the Anima Mundi, the great storehouse of images common to all men. Compare the world-weary giant sleepers in *The Wanderings of Oisin* III; and 'On a Picture of a Black Centaur by Edmund Dulac', ll. 11–12: 'seven Ephesian topers slept and never knew / When Alexander's empire passed'.

1: this line originally read, 'A one-legged, one-armed, one-eyed man' (*VP*, p. 302).

4 *Cruachan*: Maeve's supposed headquarters in Co. Roscommon, the old capital of Connaught – see also 'The Dancer at Cruachan and Cro-Patrick' and 'Tom at Cruachan'.

8 *Maeve*: see *The Wanderings of Oisin* I 18.

8 *nine Maines*: Maeve's sons by Ailell – see *The Old Age of Queen Maeve*, l. 92.

25 *Hell Mouth*: the Cave of Cruachan, a legendary entrance to the underworld.

29 *a tub of beer*: compare 'The Blessed', ll. 31–32: 'I see the blessedest soul in the world / And he nods a drunken head'.

50 *Goban*: see 'The Grey Rock', l. 10.

94 *If time were suppler in the joint*: time, like the one-legged wanderer, is an old cripple.

98 *all life longs for the Last Day*: compare 'The Wheel', ll. 7-8: 'what disturbs our blood / Is but its longing for the tomb'.

100 *Michael's trumpet*: see 'The Happy Townland', l. 41.

103 *nothing but God left*: compare the title of Yeats's story, 'Where there is Nothing, there is God'; and 'Blood and the Moon' II 18: 'Everything that is not God consumed with intellectual fire'.

106 *wait Him in a drunken sleep*: like 'The Three Beggars', this poem seems to advocate passivity over action: the sleeper is immune to the pummelling that he receives (l. 113).

A Song from *The Player Queen*

Yeats laboured on his apocalyptic farce *The Player Queen* through many drafts over a span of many years – from 1907 to 1922. The plot concerns a company of strolling players who visit a court ruled by a weak, unworldly, pious queen, a representative of the Christian era; eventually the leading woman of the company, Decima – a fierce and promiscuous, beautiful woman – puts on the mask of the queen and rules in her place, in order to appease a revolutionary mob. This dénouement prophesies the haughty, heroic, anti-Christian age that, in Yeats's opinion, would arise after AD 2000 (see 'The Second Coming').

Decima sings the song printed here (minus the first stanza); it was presumably written by her drunkard husband Septimus, the company's lead actor and poet. She interrupts the song, after the third stanza, to comment: 'It is the song of the mad singing daughter of a harlot. The only song she had. Her father was a drunken sailor waiting for the full tide, and yet she thought her mother had foretold that she would marry a prince and become a great queen' (II 113–17). After completing the song, Decima remarks, 'The moment ago as I lay here I thought I could play a queen's part, a great queen's part'. Then Nona, Septimus' mistress, replies, 'You play a queen's part? You that were born in a ditch between two towns and wrapped in a sheet that was stolen from a hedge' (II 126–131). The song, then, symbolizes the origin of a new, anti-Christian dispensation, born of a harlot instead of a virgin. For the history of Yeats's insertion of the song into the play, see Bradford, *WPQ*, pp. 264–65. For other songs used in *The Player Queen*, see 'The Mask', 'A Thought from Propertius', and 'Two Songs Rewritten for the Tune's Sake' II.

9–10: Decima sings these lines again near the end of *The Player Queen* (II 711–12), when all kneel to her, accept her as Queen.

11–12: in the first publication of *The Player Queen*, Decima sings these lines again immediately before the curtain line (*VPl*, p. 759).

15 *a flake of the yellow foam*: this descent of seagull-semen parodies the dove's descent to the Virgin Mary.

The Realists

The theme of this poem is that realism depresses the will to live, whereas romanticism rejuvenates it. This poem may be compared to 'Three Movements'.

5 *Sea-nymphs*: compare 'News for the Delphic Oracle' III 1.

I. The Witch

This poem, like the previous one, contrasts the goals of materialistic, 'realistic' society – goals that depress and enervate – with dreams of ideal fulfilment. (Drafts of this poem appear in *Mem*, pp. 265–66.)

1 *Toil and grow rich*: compare 'Vacillation' III 1: 'Get all the gold and silver that you can'.

3 *witch*: as Jeffares notes (*NCP*, p. 120), Yeats originally wrote 'bitch'.

II. The Peacock

There are several poems in the volume, including 'Running to Paradise' and 'The Witch', that recommend dispossession; but this poem most explicitly shows the advantages that dispossession brings to the artist. The more depopulated and barren the landscape, the more conducive it is to vision. Indeed the material world finally dwindles so much that the artist himself is absent, reduced to a gay ghost elaborating his fantasy on an empty space. As Yeats wrote in 1917, 'I shall find the dark grow luminous, the void fruitful when I understand I have nothing' (*M*, p. 332).

The peacock was a bird that had long interested Yeats – see 'The Indian upon God', l. 17 – but (as Kenner has noticed, in *A Colder Eye*, pp. 54–55), the immediate source for this poem was probably Pennell's *Life of Whistler*: Whistler made a proposal, never executed, for a ten-foot-high peacock design for the Boston Library, and recommended dispossession to the artist, a diet of bread and cheese.

2–3 *has made a great peacock / With the pride of his eye*: Ezra Pound, in Canto 83, has left a remarkable account of Yeats's composition of these lines – Pound lived with Yeats in Sussex during the winter of 1913–14: 'so that I recalled the noise in the chimney / as it were the wind in the chimney / but was in reality Uncle William / downstairs composing / that had made a great Peeeeacock / in the proide ov his oiye / had made a great peeeeeecock in the . . . / made a great peacock/ in the proide of his oyyee // proide ov his oy-ee / as indeed he had, and perdurable // a great peacock aere perennius . . . at Stone Cottage in Sussex by the waste moor' (83/534). In Pound's description, Yeats himself sounds spooky, like the gay ghost of l. 10.

5 *Three Rock*: a mountain overlooking Dublin.

The Mountain Tomb

The Rosicrucian order was founded, according to their lore, in 1484 by a Father Rosenkreuz, or Rosicrux, or Rosicross (see 'To the Rose upon the

Rood of Time'). In this poem Yeats imagines Father Rosicross, undecayed in his tomb, as a kind of Antichrist who ought to reawaken to inaugurate a new age, in which drinking, dancing, and kissing will be virtues instead of vices (see 'A Song from *The Player Queen*' and 'The Second Coming'). The dance-ritual that attempts to invoke him is reminiscent of that in the story 'Rosa Alchemica' (1896).

4 *Father Rosicross is in the tomb*: in 1895, Yeats identified Father Rosicross with the imagination, and said that he had been entombed by the spirit of criticism (*EI*, p. 196); and in the same year he wrote the uncollected 'A Song of the Rosy Cross', which begins 'He who measures gain and loss, / When he gave to thee the Rose, / Gave to me alone the Cross' (*VP*, p. 744).

6 *room*: the comma after this word follows early editions, not *CP* (1933).

I. To a Child Dancing in the Wind

The child was Iseult Gonne (1895–1954), Maud Gonne's illegitimate daughter – see Introduction IX. Yeats became fond of Iseult – for his unhappy wooing of her, see 'Men Improve with the Years', 'The Living Beauty', 'To a Young Girl', and 'Owen Aherne and his Dancers'; and for a witty celebration of her beauty, combined with sage advice for her education, see 'To a Young Beauty' and 'Michael Robartes and the Dancer'.

1 *Dance there upon the shore*: 'I remember a beautiful young girl [Iseult Gonne] singing at the edge of the sea in Normandy words and music of her own composition. She thought herself alone, stood barefooted between sea and sand; sang with lifted head of the civilisations that there had come and gone, ending every verse with the cry: "O Lord, let something remain"' (*AV*, p. 220).

8 *Love lost as soon as won*: perhaps an allusion to the rapid failure of her mother's marriage.

11–12 *What need have you to dread / The monstrous crying of wind?*: the child, like the beggars in the previous poems, is carefree, outside the circuit of mankind's confusions. As in the first stanza of 'The Sorrow of Love', nature has not yet been put into relation with mankind – the sound of the wind is, to a child, inexpressive of human suffering.

II. Two Years Later

Like the previous poem, this Song of Experience depicts an innocent girl from a fallen perspective – the poet feels that he cannot instruct her, because he and she share no common language. In a later poem addressed to Iseult

Gonne, 'Owen Aherne and his Dancers', Yeats contrasts her wildness with his tameness (II 4); here he contrasts her insouciance with his batteredness.

2 *eyes should be more learn'd*: in another poem addressed to Iseult, 'Michael Robartes and the Dancer', Yeats smilingly argues against the education of women.

12 *a barbarous tongue*: compare 'Her Courage', l. 2: 'I have no speech but symbol, the pagan speech I made'.

A Memory of Youth

The initial premise of this poem, addressed to Maud Gonne, is that their love has decayed into wisdom (l. 2), into abstract verbal praise (l. 9) – the expression of love seems itself to estrange the poet from the love he expresses. But the sudden shock of moonlight revivifies the emotion that poet and beloved felt in youth – an unforeseen vision accomplishes what the best-contrived words cannot. In 'The Fascination of What's Difficult' and 'The Three Beggars', Yeats suggested that improvisation and spontaneity yielded better results than intentional design; and here he extends this doctrine to love-relations.

Title: originally 'Love and the Bird'.

1 *a play*: the poet, and perhaps the beloved, feel themselves part of a drama, in which the presence or absence of the moon is pathetic, ominous, symbolic.

6–7: these lines originally read, 'And she seemed happy as a king, / Love's moon was withering away' (*VP*, p. 313).

20 *a most ridiculous little bird*: the poet retains the perspective of wisdom just long enough to call the bird ridiculous, before he abandons himself to the surge of emotion. Compare a passage deleted from *The Only Jealousy of Emer*: 'frail bird heard and seen / In the incredible clear light love cast' (*VPl*, p. 559). Bird-cries often stand for exultant feeling in Yeats's work, especially in 'Solomon and the Witch', l. 9, where an orgasmic cockerel crows, and in 'Her Triumph', l. 12, where a woman's surrender to her love culminates with the line, 'a miraculous strange bird shrieks at us'. The transcendental cries of disembodied souls at the end of 'Paudeen' and the bird-like singing in 'The Three Hermits' are also relevant.

19–21 *Love . . . Tore from the clouds his marvellous moon*: originally 'love . . . Threw up in the air his marvellous moon' (*VP*, p. 314). At the end of 'When You are Old', another personification of Love 'hid his face amid a crowd of stars'; here a less reticent, more theatrical version of Love exposes himself for all to see. A third personification of Love appears in 'His Confidence', l. 12 – another poem on the theme of the transformation of despair into love.

The thrilling apparition of the moon is compared to the favour of the beloved in 'First Love', l. 18.

Fallen Majesty

The theme of this poem is the contrast between Maud Gonne's past and present selves – for other poems about her aging, see 'The Arrow'.

2 *even old men's eyes grew dim*: Yeats once compared the celebrated peasant beauty Mary Hynes to Helen of Troy, and wrote of the old men who had known her, 'though they can be hard, they grow gentle as the old men of Troy grew gentle when Helen passed by on the walls' (*M*, p. 28). For a poem on the old men of Troy, see 'When Helen Lived'.

2 *this hand alone*: for other insistences on the poet's uniqueness, see 'When You are Old', l. 7, and 'Old Memory', l. 6.

3 *Like some last courtier at a gypsy camping-place*: for the relation of courtiers to rustics, see 'To a Wealthy Man ...', l. 20. For the theme of Yeats as survivor, see 'Coole and Ballylee, 1931', l. 41: 'We were the last romantics' (contrasted with Arab nomads).

5 *a heart that laughter has made sweet*: for the tenderizing effect of age on Maud Gonne, see 'Peace', ll. 10–11.

8 *a burning cloud*: the words *fallen*, *majesty*, *burning*, and *clouds* all appear in 'These are the Clouds', ll. 1–2.

Friends

At the beginning of this volume, Yeats celebrated his fellow poets from the days of the Rhymers' Club; towards the end of the volume, Yeats celebrates the women who shaped his personal life. For Yeats's women, see Introduction IX.

4 *One*: Olivia Shakespear (1867–1938). Yeats spoke of himself and Olivia as likes, and of himself and Maud Gonne as complementary unlikes (*Mem*, pp. 86, 124).

10 *one*: Lady Gregory – see 'Beautiful Lofty Things', l. 7. Yeats attributed to her influence his change from morbid introspection to high purposefulness.

13 *What none can have and thrive*: compare *On Baile's Strand* (1904), l. 400: 'The women none can kiss and thrive'.

16 *Labouring in ecstasy*: compare 'To a Friend whose Work has come to Nothing', l. 14: 'Be secret and exult'.

17 *her*: Maud Gonne.

27 *So great a sweetness flows*: compare 'A Dialogue of Self and Soul' II 29: 'So great a sweetness flows'.

The Cold Heaven

According to *A Vision*, the soul after death moves towards oblivion of its past life through a number of stages: one of these stages is called the *Dreaming Back*, in which 'the *Spirit* is compelled to live over and over again the events that had most moved it ... They occur in the order of their intensity or luminosity, the most intense first, and the painful are commonly the more intense' (*AV*, p. 226). When Yeats wrote this poem, he had not yet formulated this doctrine; but this poem seems to be a premonition during life of the dead soul's agony in reliving its memories. Another poem in which the poet seems to anticipate the feelings of his ghost is 'All Souls' Night'.

7 *I took all the blame*: compare 'Vacillation' V.

9 *Riddled with light*: see the note to 'The Madness of King Goll', l. 29; also 'King and No King', l. 12: 'the blinding light beyond the grave'.

10 *Confusion of the death-bed over*: compare 'Paudeen', l. 7, 'confusion of our sound forgot'. 'Paudeen', like this poem, ends in a region of naked souls.

That the Night Come

A persistent theme in Yeats's work in the 1910s is the soul's hastening of its extinction – see the notes to 'Running to Paradise' and to 'The Hour before Dawn'. The concept of an all-consuming, pan-intensive moment – at once orgasm and battle-triumph – eventually evolved into what Yeats was to call 'tragic joy' ('The Gyres', l. 8).

1 *She*: Maud Gonne.

10–11 *And the outrageous cannon, / To bundle time away*: compare 'Mohini Chatterjee', ll. 24–25: 'That such cannonade / May thunder time away'; also 'The Moods', ll. 1–2.

An Appointment

The original title was 'On a Recent Government Appointment in Ireland'. This is one of Yeats's first poems on a public theme: Yeats was upset that Lord Aberdeen and Mr Birrell had neglected to appoint Sir Hugh Lane (see 'To a Wealthy Man ...') as curator of the National Gallery of Ireland. Yeats here contrasts the thoughtless excellence of the natural order with the deliberate bunglings found among men. Yeats also wrote in 1909 an epigram on Birrel's behaviour: 'He thinks to set his world aright / And be no longer parasite / Now that he's master of the trick / That turns a flea into a tick' (*Mem*, p. 231); Birrell had told Yeats that 'writers are parasites' (*Mem*, p. 146).

3 *squirrel*: rhymes with *Birrell*.

The Magi

This and 'The Dolls' (written on the same day) were originally published as companion poems, with Roman numerals I and II before their respective titles. As Yeats explained in his note to 'The Dolls', the theme of these two poems is that 'all thought among us is frozen into "something other than human life" ... I looked up one day into the blue of the sky, and suddenly imagined, as if lost in the blue of the sky, stiff figures in procession. I remembered that they were the habitual image suggested by blue sky' (*VP*, p.820). (As in 'The Peacock', the imagination is especially adept at summoning images when the background is empty.) In 1898 Yeats recorded a somewhat similar vision: 'I closed my eyes a moment ago, and a company of people in blue robes swept by me in a blinding light ... [I] recognised one of the company by his square, black, curling beard ... he seemed too perfected a soul for any knowledge that cannot be spoken in symbol or metaphor' (*EI*, pp. 151–52).

In *A Vision*, begun in 1917, Yeats was to describe how, behind each historical age, there hovered an age opposite in character, waiting for the opportunity to realize itself; and in this poem he imagines a tableau of Magi who seem to contradict, to deny the validity of, the whole Christian era. Themselves pure artifice (like the dolls of the next poem), they seem disgusted with the disorder and corruption of the organic – in this way they are images of 'something other than human life', something that finds human life insufficient. (Yeats borrowed the quoted phrase from Blake's *Public Address*, p. 18 [*Complete Poetry and Prose*, ed. Erdman (1982), p. 580]: 'Princes appear to me to be Fools Houses of Commons & Houses of Lords appear to me to be fools they seem to me to be something Else besides Human Life' [compare *Ex*, p. 149, *DWL*, p. 143].) There is a later poem, 'Wisdom', that deals with a similar contrast, between elaborate Christian art-works and the squalid facts told in the Gospels.

'The Magi' is a kind of Christian companion piece to Ezra Pound's 'The Return' (1912), a poem that imagines the old Greek gods as exhausted images lingering on the threshold of vision: 'See, they return, one, and by one, / With fear, as half-awakened; / As if the snow should hesitate / And murmur in the wind, / and half turn back; / These were the "Wing'd-with-Awe", / Inviolable'. Yeats quoted Pound's poem in *AV*, p. 29 and *OBMV*, p. xxvi.

Title *Magi*: the three wise men who followed the star to Bethlehem and gave gifts to the infant Jesus (Matthew 2:1–11) – see 'The Secret Rose', l. 9. The story 'The Adoration of the Magi' (1897) describes three old Irishmen who, by attending the deathbed of a Parisian prostitute, become the Magi of a new pagan era. In 1898 Yeats used the Magi to describe the disembodied and distinguished personages in *Axël*: 'persons from whom has fallen all even of personal characteristic except a thirst for that hour when all things shall pass away like a cloud, and a pride like that of the Magi following their star' (*EI*, p. 190). In the unfinished novel *The Speckled Bird* II i, an occultist (partly based on MacGregor Mathers) likes to take out a battered theatrical crown and an ermine coat, and to pretend that he is one of the Magi (*LTMSB*, p. 119; see also pp. 197, 398).

1–5 As Longenbach notes (*SC*, p. 32), Pound quoted these lines as an example of *imagisme*, and found in them a 'quality of hard light', contrasting with 'glamourlets and mists and fogs' of the 1890s (*Literary Essays*, p. 380).

7 *Being by Calvary's turbulence unsatisfied*: in Yeats's play *The Resurrection* (1931), the Hebrew looks out at Calvary (where Christ was crucified) and concludes that Jesus 'was nothing more than a man' (l. 109) – he feels that Christ's disciples are but 'dogs who have lost their master' (l. 65). Similarly the Magi of this poem are disappointed that a god would compromise his authority by dying, and hope for the birth of a starker, more potent deity.

8 *The uncontrollable mystery on the bestial floor*: Yeats quoted this line to illustrate the spasm of energy that occurs when a new god is born to undo the settled work of the previous age: 'the old realisation of an objective moral law is changed into a subconscious turbulent instinct. The world of rigid custom and law is broken up by "the uncontrollable mystery upon the bestial floor"' (*AV*, p. 105).

The Dolls

Yeats wrote that the theme of this poem was that 'all thought among us is frozen into "something other than human life"' – see the note to the previous poem. 'The Magi' concerned an artifice that seeks nature, 'The Dolls' concerns an artifice that rejects it. Yeats was haunted for much of life by the conflict between man's organic nature and man's possibility of abstracting himself into an image, a work of art – as in 'Sailing to Byzantium', where the poet dreams of casting his body aside and becoming a golden bird. In a related poem, 'Byzantium', Yeats imagined a similar golden bird that would 'scorn aloud . . . all complexities of mire or blood' (ll. 21, 24); and 'The Dolls' shows an earlier version of this theme, for the dolls scream that the doll-maker's baby is a disgraceful thing, ugly, dirty, and undignified.

For another poem about dolls, see 'Certain Artists bring her Dolls and

Drawings'. Also, in 'The Double Vision of Michael Robartes' I, Yeats uses the image of a puppet that fashions other puppets to show how human life can subside into purely mechanical function, a world of automata.

20 *an accident*: the doll-maker's wife claims that her pregnancy was unplanned. As in 'The Magi', organic life is random and spontaneous, whereas doll-making is a refined craft. But as 'The Fascination of What's Difficult' and 'A Coat' show, Yeats was not necessarily in favour of the frozen and inhuman.

A Coat

This poem ends the short sequence that began with 'The Magi', and shows explicitly that Yeats rejects what is ' "other than human life" ' – this poem announces directly that Yeats prefers the raw to the cooked. This poem also ends the main part of the volume, and seems to announce that subsequent volumes will be different in style and theme. 'A Coat' may be compared with a passage in *Reveries over Childhood and Youth*, written not long after the poem: 'when I had finished *The Wanderings of Oisin*, dissatisfied with its yellow and its dull green, with all that overcharged colour inherited from the romantic movement, I deliberately reshaped my style, deliberately sought out an impression as of cold light and tumbling clouds' (*A: R* 17). Though this passage may refer to an earlier shift in style, it uses a similar metaphor of divestment. (In 1901 Yeats wrote of ridding his poetry of 'reds and yellows ... by making my rhythms faint and nervous and filling my images with a certain coldness, a certain wintry wildness' [*EI*, p. 5].)

When Yeats quoted Pound's 'The Return' in *AV*, p. 29 (see the note to 'The Magi'), he remembered that Pound wrote the poem only in order to announce 'a change in style' – and that is one of Yeats's purposes in publishing the final poems in *Responsibilities*. Pound himself hailed 'A Coat' as a confirmation of his theories about a 'new note' in Yeats's poetry, corresponding to a change from a minor to a major musical key – 'one has felt his work becoming gaunter, seeking greater hardness of outline': 'The verses, *A Coat*, should satisfy those who have complained of Mr Yeats' four and forty followers, that they would "rather read their Yeats in the original" [i.e., Yeats's Gaelic sources]' (*Literary Essays*, pp. 379–80).

But the reader should remember that Yeats, far from removing his embroidery of old mythologies once and for all, made a career out of taking off his coat – in 'Reconciliation', in 'The Fascination of What's Difficult', in 'A Coat', in 'On a Picture of a Black Centaur ...', and in 'The Circus Animals' Desertion'.

3 *Out of old mythologies*: Jeffares notes (*NCP*, p. 127) that the manuscript specifies 'Dragons and Gods and moons'.

5 *the fools*: compare 'To a Poet, who would have me Praise certain Bad Poets ...'.

10 *walking naked*: compare Pound's 'Salutation the Second' (1913): 'Go, little naked and impudent songs'; and 'Further Instructions' (1913): 'But you, newest song of the lot ... I will get you a green coat out of China / With dragons worked upon it'. The device of commanding one's own song to perform itself is typical of Pound. For a more metaphysical nakedness, see 'Ribh considers Christian Love insufficient', ll. 16–17: 'Thought is a garment and the soul's a bride / That cannot in that trash and tinsel hide'.

[Closing Rhymes]

The original title was 'Notoriety / (*Suggested by a recent magazine article*)'. The article was by Yeats's former collaborator, George Moore – see the Introductory Rhymes – and its sting helped induce Yeats to a desire to return to private life. In the Introductory Rhymes, Yeats asked his ancestors to pardon him for leading the inactive and ungallant life of a poet; here, Yeats finds justification for retreating from the world of action, so contaminated by stupidity and ill-breeding. In 'A Coat', Yeats undressed himself from Irish mythology; in this poem he divests himself of public themes as well. The poet proves his mettle and spites his detractors by a dazzling feat of craft: this poem is one long, intricately suspended sentence.

1 that reed-throated whisperer: poetic inspiration, so quiet that it needs a country retreat in order to be heard. In a quatrain written in his 1909 diary, but 'Made long ago', Yeats described George Moore's own Muse – a honker, not a whisperer: 'Moore once had visits from the Muse / But fearing that she would refuse / An ancient lecher took to geese / He now gets novels at his ease' (*Mem*, p. 182).

3 a clear articulation in the air: Yeats refers to publicly audible and intelligible poetry – as in 'To a Wealthy Man ...', a poem in which the Muse was less a whisperer than a loudspeaker.

4 inwardly: in *A Vision*, Yeats describes how a group of disembodied spirits called Communicators came to him in 1917, saying 'We have come to give you metaphors for poetry' (p. 8). These intimate Communicators, discovered in his wife's automatic writing, seem to be elaborations of the inward whisperers of this poem.

4–5 surmise companions / Beyond the fling of the dull ass's hoof: that is, the poet looks for noble comrades (such as Lady Gregory) immune to the slanders of the low-bred.

6 Ben Jonson's phrase: Jonson (1572–1637) wrote of the dull ass's hoof in

'An Ode to Himself' and in the Epilogue to *The Poetaster* (1601) Compare 'The Municipal Gallery Re-visited' VI 1: 'An image out of Spenser'.

7 Kyle-na-no: 'The Wood of Nuts', one of the seven woods at Coole Park – see 'In the Seven Woods', and 'To a Squirrel at Kyle-na-no'.

7 that ancient roof: Coole Park.

9 I can forgive: for another poem in this volume on the theme of forgiveness, see 'Paudeen'.

14 a post that passing dogs defile: a phrase from Erasmus, according to Yeats's 1930 Diary (*Ex*, p. 330). Yeats's poem prefers the company of Jonson and Erasmus, just as the poet preferred the company of Lady Gregory.

THE WILD SWANS AT COOLE (1919)

This is perhaps the most heterogeneous volume of Yeats's career. The decade of the 1910s was for Yeats (as for Pound and for Eliot, much younger men) the most tumultuous of his career – he evolved rapidly in forming and codifying his philosophy, in experimenting with new verse techniques, and in arranging his personal affairs.

The turning-point of Yeats's life occurred in the autumn of 1917. Maud Gonne's estranged husband, John MacBride, had been executed by the British in 1916 as a conspirator in the Easter rebellion, and so she was free to marry. Yeats therefore proposed to her; was rejected; proposed to her daughter Iseult, then twenty-two years old; was rejected. Then he proposed to a fellow-student of the occult, Georgie Hyde-Lees, a young woman of 'barbarous beauty'; and she at last accepted him. (For Yeats's women, see Introduction IX.)

Just after Yeats's marriage, his new bride thought that she would play a trick on him: she would counterfeit a bout of automatic writing – that is, script produced during a mediumistic trance, sometimes spelt continuously over the page without word breaks. But, to her astonishment, she found that she could actually do it:

> On the afternoon of October 24th 1917, four days after my marriage, my wife surprised me by attempting automatic writing. What came in disjointed sentences, in almost illegible writing, was so exciting, sometimes so profound, that I persuaded her to give an hour or two day after day to the unknown writer, and after some half-dozen such hours offered to spend what remained of life explaining and piecing together those scattered sentences. 'No', was the answer, 'we have come to give you metaphors for poetry'. The unknown writer took his theme at first from my just published

> *Per Amica Silentia Lunae*. I had made a distinction between the perfection that is from a man's combat with himself and that which is from a combat with circumstance, and upon this simple distinction he built up an elaborate classification of men ... (*AV*, pp. 8–9)

Yeats spent several years struggling with these communications, mostly derived from two helpful dead men, Dionertes and Thomas, who spoke through his wife, first in automatic writing, later orally in a trance. Yeats's wife had been thoroughly imbued with his ideas, and was perhaps better acquainted with classical philosophy than he; and so Yeats fought to make sense of a garbled, dreamlike synthesis of his own ideas with those of better thinkers, seemingly presented as objective truths from the world beyond the grave. It is fitting that, in *The Wild Swans at Coole*, Yeats sometimes uses the persona of Solomon, gifted with divine wisdom and clarity; and that he speaks of his wife as Sheba. But often the battle with the unintelligible, the dramatizing of ignorance, are more compelling in these poems than the sense of attained lucidity.

The coherence of this volume is threatened by its mixture of love poems to different women, funeral elegies, and investigations into the inner workings of the imagination – some written before the great moment in October 1917, some after. Indeed *The Wild Swans at Coole* was published twice, in 1917 and 1919: in the 1919 version Yeats added many poems, including those on Robert Gregory's death, and some verse expositions of his new philosophy (such as 'The Phases of the Moon'), further threatening the cohesiveness of the book. It took Yeats some years before the doctrines he found in his wife's automatic writing (eventually codified into *A Vision* – see Introduction XI) were fully assimilated into his poetic practice – before the lunar dynamic of the philosophy, in which one element waxes as its counter-element wanes, turned into the internal dynamic of the verse movement. And yet the expository poems, discursive and tendentious though they may be, nonetheless are full of awe and mystery, as the poet gropes towards the construing of images and propositions that are beyond his complete grasp.

The Wild Swans at Coole derives its title from a poem about the presence and absence of swans – and commingled themes of absence and presence keep arising through the volume: absence of dead friends, presence of fulfilled love; absence of full comprehension, presence of hair-raising suggestions of truth. Yeats continually evokes images in which exaltation and depression combine into a kind of wonder.

When Yeats was a young man, he devoted himself to the perfection of tight, closed lyrics; but now, in his early fifties, he seems more flexible, more open – open to spiritual revelation from dubious sources, open to new themes, new personae, new verse techniques. Not only does he experiment with the mask of Solomon, but he even writes a kind of dramatic monologue spoken by a contemporary persona, wearing an aviator's helmet ('An Irish Airman Foresees his Death'). And in 'Broken Dreams' he verges, for almost the only time in his career, on something like free verse; yet this modernity is counterpointed by other poems that resurrect the most archaic verse forms, such as the pastoral elegy in 'Shepherd and Goatherd'. Not all of these experiments proved useful; but many features of his later volumes are extensions or consolidations of discoveries made in *The Wild Swans at Coole*.

The Wild Swans at Coole

Swans are important in several of Yeats's romantic or elegiac poems: in *Baile and Aillinn*, ll. 136–37 (and 'The Withering of the Boughs', l. 17), two lovers metamorphose into swans; in 'The Tower' III 20 the poet sings his swan-song; in 'Nineteen Hundred and Nineteen' III, a swan symbolizes the human soul; in 'Coole and Ballylee, 1931', l. 17, the poet sees a swan and exclaims, 'Another emblem there!' – but an emblem of nothing in particular. In this poem, too, there is a vague, tantalizing intimacy between the poet and the swans, as if the swans represent human souls or human feelings liberated from mere flesh; 'They're but an image on a lake', wrote Yeats in an early draft (Bradford, *YW*, p. 50). The swan of Shelley's *Alastor* (1815) may partly anticipate Yeats's: 'A swan was there, / Beside a sluggish stream among the reeds. / It rose as he approached, and with strong wings / Scaling the upward sky, bent its bright course' (ll. 275–78); the poet goes on to lament that, while the swan has his home and mate, 'what am I that I should linger here . . . ?'

In the first printing, the stanzas were published in the order 1, 2, 5, 3, 4.

3 *water*: as in Yeats's earlier poems, water is the medium for the generation of images – see 'The Indian upon God'.

4 *Mirrors*: the poem is governed by a structure of mirrorings. Compare 'Coole and Ballylee, 1931', ll. 13–14: 'And all the rant's a mirror of my mood: / At sudden thunder of the mounting swan'.

7 *The nineteenth autumn*: Yeats first visited Coole Park in 1897, when he began his folklore researches with Lady Gregory and tried to sever himself from Maud Gonne.

8 *my count*: compare a line from a draft of 'A Prayer for my Daughter': 'Where every year I have counted swans' (Stallworthy, *BL*, p. 41).

11 *great broken rings*: compare the falcon's wheeling in 'The Second Coming', l. 1.

15 *All's changed*: compare 'Easter, 1916', l. 15: 'All changed, changed utterly'; and 'Coole and Ballylee, 1931', l. 46: 'all is changed'.

19 *lover by lover*: compare the chain-linked swans of *Baile and Aillinn*, ll. 136–

37; and 'The Man who Dreamed of Faeryland', l. 35: 'lover there by lover'. Also compare the Acting Version of *The Shadowy Waters*, ll. 181–82, where Forgael sees man-headed and woman-headed birds wheeling above him: 'friend's run by friend; / They've gone to their beloved ones in the air' (*VPl*, p. 325).

22 *Their hearts have not grown old*: compare 'The Living Beauty', l. 8: 'O heart, we are old'; and 'A Song', l. 6: '*the heart grows old*'; and many early poems about the exhaustion of passion, such as 'Ephemera'.

30 *they have flown away*: compare *Calvary* (1920), ll. 180–83: 'But where have last year's cygnets gone? / The lake is empty; why do they fling / White wing out beside white wing? / What can a swan need but a swan?' Jeffares believes (*NCP*, p. 131) that Yeats wrote 'The Wild Swans at Coole' in a state of despair over his inability to summon much feeling over Maud Gonne's last rejection of his proposal of marriage. The loss of feeling corresponds to the coming absence of the swans: the swans resemble the Moods, those exterior passions that inspire mankind or fail to do so according to divine caprice. Beauty and passion will exist, but will no longer have any relation to the poet. (For another poem about loss of feeling, see 'Demon and Beast'.) Herbert J. Levine (in *ELH* 48: 413) notes that Yeats associated Maud Gonne with a swan as early as 1897: 'You only know that it is / of you I sing when I tell / of the swan in the water' (Ellmann, *YMM*, p. 161); Levine regards Yeats's swan-lyrics as stages in his exorcism of Maud Gonne.

In Memory of Major Robert Gregory

Lady Gregory's only son, Robert Gregory (1881–1918), died fighting in Italy on 23 January 1918. A man notable for the versatility of his gifts, Robert Gregory had, like Yeats, received formal training as an artist (at the Slade School, London); and, unlike Yeats, he had taken his regular education at the best schools (Harrow and New College, Oxford). Yeats's first tribute after his death was a prose appreciation:

> I have known no man accomplished in so many ways as Major Robert Gregory, who was killed in action a couple of weeks ago and buried by his fellow-airmen in the beautiful cemetery at Padua. His very accomplishment hid from many his genius. He had so many sides: painter, classical scholar, scholar in painting and in modern literature, boxer, horseman, airman – he had the Military Cross and the Légion d'Honneur – that some among his friends were not sure what his work would be. To me he will always remain a great painter in the immaturity of his youth, he himself the personification of handsome youth. I first came to understand his genius when, still almost a boy, he designed costumes and scenery for the Abbey Theatre. (*UP* II, pp. 429–30)

Yeats thought of Robert Gregory as a Renaissance man; and twice he wrote elegies for him in Renaissance verse-forms, first the pastoral elegy 'Shepherd and Goatherd', then the present poem, written in a metre borrowed from a poem by Abraham Cowley. (Gregory also inspired 'An Irish Airman Foresees His Death' and the suppressed 'Reprisals'; a painting of him is mentioned in 'The Municipal Gallery Re-visited' III 5.) If Robert Gregory seemed a model of human perfection, a personification of youth and talent and largeness of being, Yeats celebrated him in poems that tried to embody something of the antique splendour that seemed incarnate in him.

I 1 *our house*: Thoor Ballylee, an ancient Norman tower in Co. Galway (not far from Lady Gregory's estate at Coole Park) that Yeats bought in 1917.

I 5 *winding stair*: all the rooms in Thoor Ballylee are accessible from a single long staircase in the interior. In many later poems, such as 'A Dialogue of Self and Soul', this stair symbolizes the soul's ascent towards wisdom.

I 6 *Discoverers of forgotten truth*: Yeats liked to write elegies about occultists whose thoughts during life were fixed upon the soul's condition after death, or about those whose work somehow represented a retreat from the usual conditions of human life – such men are found in stanzas III-V and in 'All Souls' Night'.

III 1 *Lionel Johnson*: see 'The Grey Rock', l. 62. The poet approaches Robert Gregory indirectly, through Johnson, Synge, and Pollexfen. Each seems to possess some fraction of Robert Gregory's gifts, though that fraction may have evolved in a distorted form – Robert Gregory seems to be a composite of all the illustrious dead.

III 2 *loved his learning better than mankind*: when Yeats worried that Johnson was becoming too far separated from men and women 'he replied, "In my library I have all the knowledge of the world that I need"' (*A: TG* 6).

III 3 *much falling*: Yeats knew a false rumour that Johnson, an alcoholic, had died from falling off a barstool. A line from Johnson's 'Mystic and Cavalier' is also relevant: 'Go from me: I am one of those, who fall' (quoted by Yeats in *A: IP* 7). Compare Pound, *Hugh Selwyn Mauberley* (1919) VII: 'Told me how Johnson (Lionel) died / By falling from a high stool in a pub'.

III 4 *Brooded upon sanctity*: 'after a certain number of glasses, [he] would become more ascetic, more contemptuous of all that we call human life.... I can remember his saying with energy, "I wish those people who deny the eternity of punishment could realise their unspeakable vulgarity" ... "I believe in nothing but the Holy Roman Catholic Church" ... his friends believed ... that he would shortly enter a monastery' (*A: IP* 7; compare *Ex*, p. 276).

III 5 *all his Greek and Latin learning*: not only was Johnson learned, but also a personification of classical culture: 'He had the delicate strong features of a certain filleted head of a Greek athlete in the British Museum, an archaistic Graeco-Roman copy' (*A: IP* 7).

III 6 *the horn*: compare Michael's trumpet, 'The Happy Townland', l. 41 – in the same stanza another archangel uses a drinking-horn to get drunk.

III 8 *measureless*: see 'To Ireland in the Coming Times' – another poem dependent on the contrast between discourse (measurement, balance, metre, learning, patterns of argument) and eternity.

IV 1 *John Synge*: the controversial playwright (1871–1909), who worked with Yeats at the Abbey Theatre. Yeats thought of Synge as a melancholy, complicated aesthete who had attained greatness by submitting his genius to the discipline of the simple peasant life he found in the Aran Islands; a sick, timid, courteous man whose art was boisterous, rousing. In *A Vision*, Yeats took Synge and Rembrandt as the exemplars of the passive artist, filled with pity, who accurately records the humble life around him. Yeats further celebrated Synge in his diary *The Death of Synge*, and in 'Coole Park, 1929', l. 13, and 'The Municipal Gallery Re-visited' IV 2 and VII 1–2.

Although Yeats wrote an epigram about the riot that attended Synge's most famous play ('On those that hated *The Playboy of the Western World*, 1907'), Yeats found Synge's most memorable work to be the third act of his unfinished play *Deirdre of the Sorrows*; in 'The Tragic Theatre', Yeats used the moment when Deirdre 'touched with compassionate fingers him that had killed her lover' as a perfect example of 'that tragic ecstasy which is the best that art – perhaps that life – can give' (*EI*, p. 239). Robert Gregory had designed stage decorations for Synge's *Deirdre*, and in this elegy Yeats treated Gregory's life, like that of Synge, as a kind of tragic theatre.

IV 2 *that dying chose the living world*: Johnson turned away from life, Synge towards it, but both reached the world's end.

IV 6 *a most desolate stony place*: the Aran Islands, off Ireland's western coast, the most primitive remaining Gaelic culture – 'When he found that wild island he became happy for the first time' (*A: IDM*). Compare the Ceylon of 'All Souls' Night', l. 46, to which the dying Florence Farr retreats.

V 1 *George Pollexfen*: Yeats's mother's brother (1839–1910), an astrologer, with whom Yeats conducted occult research. He also appears in 'In Memory of Alfred Pollexfen', l. 8.

V 3 *horsemanship*: Pollexfen had been 'the best rider in Connaught' (*A: R* 17). This trait will be assimilated into the portrait of Robert Gregory in stanza VIII.

V 5 *solid*: in 1897 Yeats called Pollexfen 'a genius of regularity' who 'reduces my habits into order as a mangle does clothes' (*L*, p. 286). He was also solid in that he used barbells to maintain a trim figure in old age (*A: HC* 2).

V 6 *as the outrageous stars incline*: like MacGregor Mathers in 'All Souls'

Night' – almost a twin poem to this elegy – Pollexfen searched for a supernatural determinant of natural events.

V 7 *opposition, square and trine*: these astrological terms refer to the angles between two heavenly bodies with respect to the earth: 180, 90, and 120 degrees respectively.

V 8 *sluggish*: Pollexfen was a hypochondriac who saw the worst in any situation (*A: R* 17).

VI 4 *some old picture-book*: compare the premise of 'The Municipal Gallery Re-visited'.

VI 7 *our Sidney*: Sir Philip Sidney (1554–86), the great Elizabethan poet, scholar, and warrior who died fighting in Holland. In his ease and range of accomplishment, and in his early death, Robert Gregory resembled him – just as Yeats resembled Edmund Spenser, who wrote his noble elegy 'Astrophel' as a tribute to Sidney.

VIII: this stanza was added at the request of Gregory's widow.

VIII 1 *Galway*: the county in western Ireland in which Thoor Ballylee and Lady Gregory's Coole Park (and all the places named in this stanza) are located.

VIII 2 *Roxborough*: Lady Gregory's childhood home.

IX 1 *a great painter*: Yeats thought Robert Gregory's paintings insufficiently detailed, but praised them for their 'grave distinction' of imagination and for their quality of subjective reverie. Yeats considered his paintings of the Clare coast 'with its cloud shadows upon blue-grey stony hills' among the finest of contemporary landscapes, and compared their mood to that of Blake's woodcuts and of Wordsworth's 'Resolution and Independence' (*UP* II, p. 430; compare *EI*, p. 209).

X 1 *What other could so well have counselled us*: it is as if Thoor Ballylee, and perhaps the world, have been left not quite finished, for the lack of Robert Gregory's informing genius.

XI 1–2 *others may consume / The entire combustible world*: in earlier poems Yeats had meditated much on the theme of the soul's quickening to its end – see 'Running to Paradise' and 'That the Night Come'. In a poem written in the same year as this elegy, 'The Phases of the Moon', l. 107, Yeats puzzled over the means for escaping from the whole circuit of life and death and rebirth; and a self-consuming blaze of genius, like Robert Gregory's, seemed a possible answer: 'escape may be for individuals alone who know how to exhaust their possible lives, to set, as it were, the hands of the clock racing' (*Ex*, p. 398). (Similarly, in *The Unicorn from the Stars* [1908] III 113–14 a beggar predicts that the dying hero 'will go through Purgatory as quick as lightning through a thorn-bush'.) But elsewhere Yeats suggested that genius would be better advised to husband its resources than to explode: 'Dowson or Johnson ... had what I still lacked, conscious deliberate craft ... They had taught me that violent energy, which is like a fire of straw, consumes in a few minutes the nervous vitality, and is useless in the arts. Our fire must burn slowly' (*A: TG* 10).

XII 8 *took all my heart for speech*: previously the poet mentioned the heartening force of Robert Gregory's paintings (IX 5); but in the end the poet's heart fails him, as if Gregory's flare of being had used up the materials of Yeats's life as well.

An Irish Airman Foresees his Death

The Irish airman was Robert Gregory – see the note to the previous poem. Yeats thought that Robert Gregory, whose paintings were full of subjective moodiness, had welcomed military service because the life of common action helped him to flee from his solitary world of reverie: 'Major Gregory [said] ... that the months since he joined the Army had been the happiest of his life. I think they brought him peace of mind, an escape from that shrinking ... before the growing absorption of his dream, the loneliness of his dream, as from his constant struggle to resist those other gifts that brought him ease and friendship. Leading his squadron in France or in Italy, mind and hand were at one, will and desire' (*UP* II, p. 431). But in this poem his military mission seems less an escape from solitude than the epitome of it.

In a sequel, 'Reprisals', written in 1921 but suppressed (until 1948) for fear of offending the Gregory family, Yeats imagined Robert Gregory's ghost declining from ecstasy into bitterness:

Some nineteen German planes, they say,
You had brought down before you died.
We called it a good death. Today
Can ghost or man be satisfied?
Although your last exciting year
Outweighed all other years, you said,
Though battle joy may be so dear
A memory, even to the dead,
It chases other thought away,
Yet rise from your Italian tomb,
Flit to Kiltartan cross and stay
Till certain second thoughts have come
Upon the cause you served, that we
Imagined such a fine affair:
Half-drunk or whole-mad soldiery
Are murdering your tenants there.
Men that revere your father yet

Are shot at on the open plain.
Where may new-married women sit
And suckle children now? Armed men
May murder them in passing by
Nor law nor parliament take heed.
Then close your ears with dust and lie
Among the other cheated dead.
(*VP*, p. 791)

'Reprisals' is to Robert Gregory's death what 'To a Shade' is to Parnell's death: a plea to a ghost to avoid the taint of mankind, to return to the tomb. Several points of comparison may be noted between 'Reprisals' and 'Nineteen Hundred and Nineteen' I.

3 *Those that I fight*: the Germans, in Italy.

4 *Those that I guard*: the English, in whose army he fought. The rhetoric of these two lines is echoed in 'I see Phantoms . . .', l. 30: 'Nor hate of what's to come, nor pity for what's gone'.

5 *Kiltartan Cross*: crossroads near Coole Park, Lady Gregory's estate in Co. Galway. In *The Cat and the Moon* (1926), l. 19, a beggar fears that he will drown in the Kiltartan River.

11 *A lonely impulse of delight*: the poet, speaking in Robert Gregory's voice, rejects all public purpose in favour of the moment of self-combustion described in 'In Memory of Major Robert Gregory' XI. This line offers an early example of the emotion that Yeats was to call tragic joy – the union of the highest self-surrender and the highest self-perfection (see 'The Gyres', l. 8).

13 *I balanced all*: the poem is a series of balances: enemies and friends (ll. 3–4), loss and gain (ll. 7–8), the past and the future (ll. 14–15) are juxtaposed and dismissed. The speaker of this poem is notable for his *sprezzatura*, the aristocratic scorn of life that Yeats learned from Castiglione's *The Courtier*.

Men Improve with the Years

This poem concerns Yeats's infatuation with Iseult Gonne, then twenty-one years old – see the note to 'To a Child Dancing in the Wind'. The theme of the man who turns into a statue has many resonances among Yeats's works. Most of Yeats's statues are godlike prototypes designed to inspire men, as in the poem 'The Statues'. But the worn triton of this poem is different: it is reminiscent of those surrogate-images of men left behind by supernatural kidnappers in such plays as *The Land of Heart's Desire* (1894), or *The Only Jealousy of Emer* (1919), ll. 86–87, where Cuchulain returns from the ocean in a semi-animate state – as Emer says, 'An image has been put in his place, / A sea-borne log bewitched into his likeness'. Yeats collected many folktales about faeries who stole men and left behind either a few bits of trash or a zombie image; and once Yeats himself awoke from sleep hearing mysterious words coming out of his mouth: ' "We make an image of him who sleeps, and it is not him who sleeps but it is like him who sleeps, and we call it Emmanuel" ' (*Mem*, p. 126; compare *M*, p. 366 and *AV*, p. 233) – as if Yeats felt some power stiffening him into an icon of himself (see Introduction X). Compare also *The Island of Statues* I iii 70–80, where an Arcadian hunter plucks the wrong flower and turns to stone (*VP*, pp. 657–58).

This ironically titled poem contrasts with the previous poems: Robert Gregory burned up in a great conflagration of self; but here the poet decays into numb old age.

2 *A weather-worn, marble triton*: compare Donne, 'Twicknam garden', ll. 15–18: 'Love let mee / Some senslesse peece of this place bee; / Make me a mandrake, so I may groane here, / Or a stone fountaine weeping out my yeare'. (Yeats mentioned Donne in 'To a Young Beauty', l. 18.) Also compare 'O Do Not Love Too Long', ll. 3–4, where the poet 'grew to be out of fashion / Like an old song'; and 'Sailing to Byzantium' II 1–2: 'An aged man is but a paltry thing, / A tattered coat upon a stick'. Something of the drama of this poem is repeated in 'Among School Children' III-IV (contrasting a beautiful child and a scarecrow).

7 *A pictured beauty*: the lover and the beloved are both aestheticized: instead of a man embracing a woman, we have a statue contemplating a picture. (In a related poem, 'The Living Beauty', l. 5, the poet asks himself to be content with an indifferent beauty that seems made of bronze or marble.) Compare Browning's 'The Statue and the Bust' (1855), where two lovers, too timid to commit adultery, dwindle after their deaths into two mutually regarding statues.

13 *Is this my dream, or the truth?*: compare 'The Double Vision of Michael Robartes' III 2–3 for a similar sentiment.

14–15 *O would that we had met / When I had my burning youth!*: compare 'Politics', ll. 11–12: 'But O that I were young again / And held her in my arms'.

The Collar-Bone of a Hare

Many of Yeats's visions of paradise are like slightly threadbare tapestries: the more closely he inspects the scene, the more he see holes in the fabric. In the early *The Wanderings of Oisin*, for example, the fantasy of sexual heaven grows ever thinner and more elaborate, until the common world of suffering and strife is visible beneath it; and in the late 'News for the Delphic Oracle', the Isles of the Blessed finally collapse from cumulative unreality. Much the same effect is found in this poem, a kind of Song of Innocence that self-deflates into a Song of Experience.

12 *pierce it through with a gimlet and stare*: in one of Yeats's stories, the members of a family dig futilely for faery gold, knowing that in 'the dim kingdom' there is more love and dancing and treasure than there is on earth: 'A peasant of the neighbourhood once saw the treasure. He found the shin-bone of a hare lying on the grass. He took it up; there was a hole in it; he looked through the hole, and saw the gold heaped up under the ground' (*M*, p. 87). This x-ray vision is similar to the disenchanting lens provided by the hare's collar-bone in this poem. Also compare *LTMSB*, p. 250.

13 *the old bitter world where they marry in churches*: possibly a rebuttal to Lady Gregory's wish that Yeats would marry.

Under the Round Tower

This poem is, among other things, a clandestine celebration of Yeats's marriage, then six months old. It is one of the first poems to arise from the automatic script produced by his wife (see Introduction XI). On 20 March 1918 Yeats's wife wrote in trance: 'The medium must meditate on the image of a shuttle spiral and funnell'; and the Control further specified that the tower was a symbol of 'abundant flowing life' (*MAV* I, p. 240). This poem was written quickly in obedience to the command.

Title *The Round Tower*: a long thin tower in a graveyard in Glendalough, built to repel Scandinavian invaders; but Yeats's own (square) tower, Thoor Ballylee (see 'In Memory of Major Robert Gregory' I 1) was not far from his mind.

6 *great-grandfather's battered tomb*: the tomb of Billy Byrne, a local hero in Wolfe Tone's rebellion, hanged in 1798, much remembered in Glendalough.

8 *Glendalough*: a valley in Co. Wicklow, where St Kevin (d. 618) founded a monastery. See also 'Stream and Sun at Glendalough'.

13 *golden king and silver lady*: representations of the sun and the moon, dancing together in a tightly interlocked cosmic pattern; also representations of Yeats and his wife, ascending out of the commonplace world into the ecstasies of occult wisdom. At a great enough height all symbols converge; as Yeats's fictitious poet Hanrahan told his lass, after a wild dance: 'The sun and the moon are the man and the girl, they are my life and your life, they are travelling and ever travelling through the skies ... God made them ... that they might go through the world, up and down, like the two best dancers' (*M*, pp. 227–28). Compare also the man in 'Those Dancing Days are Gone',

who carries '*the sun in a golden cup, / The moon in a silver bag*'; and 'He and She', in which sun and moon are personified as man and woman.

15 *a sweet measure*: the fixed whirl of their ascent suggests sexual congress, but also the paths traced by the gyres – the interpenetrating cones that govern all motion in time and space according to the automatic script (see Introduction XI).

21–24: these lines are quoted in *AV*, p. 270, to indicate the intricate design of historical antithesis, the dance-like balance of 'Ionic elegance' and 'Doric rigour' around 500 BC; also see *AV* (1925), p. 182.

24 *like a brace of blackbirds sing*: for the theme of men about to turn into birds, see 'The Three Hermits'.

25 *my luck is broken*: as in 'The Withering of the Boughs', supernatural splendour is linked to natural poverty – as one increases, the other decreases. Billy Byrne's ambition is strictly earthbound, according to l. 1, and he understands an exalted vision as an omen of bad luck.

Solomon to Sheba

Like the previous poem, Yeats wrote this as a secret epithalamium on his own marriage. In many of his earlier poems, such as 'The Folly of Being Comforted' and 'Men Improve with the Years', Yeats dwelt on the antithesis between love and wisdom; but here he suggests that they are one. In 'She turns the Dolls' Faces to the Wall', l. 4, a doll is described as 'Pedant in passion'; and passion is itself the scholarship valued in this poem. The persona of Solomon, at once wise man and lover, was convenient for this theme – the story of his relation to Sheba is told in I Kings 10. Other poems on Solomon include 'On Woman' and 'Solomon and the Witch'. Yeats referred to Solomon and Sheba in many different contexts: in the 1927 version of *The Resurrection*, l. 121, a character says that Judas mistook Christ for Solomon (*VP*, p. 910); and in MS drafts of *The Player Queen*, Decima asked Septimus to write a play starring her as Sheba (Bradford, *WPQ*, pp. 43, 48), and once sang a quatrain about Sheba: 'Had Solomon such joy of Sheba / Under the shade of the palm by the still marble? / O upon me, poor wretch that I am, / Should Sheba have gazed with envy' (*WPQ*, p. 280). In 1923 Yeats wrote a quatrain about Mrs Yeats, disguised as Sheba: 'The Queen of Sheba's busy / King Solomon is mute / Because a busy woman / Is a savage brute' (*Mem*, p. 274). In the so-called 'De Burgh' version of the unfinished *The Speckled Bird*, there is a story about a crazy French poet, in love with the Queen of Sheba, who hanged himself with a piece of string which he believed to be her garter (*LTMSB*, p. 289).

In 1909 Yeats wrote in his diary, 'It seems to me that true love is a discipline, and it needs so much wisdom that the love of Solomon and Sheba must have lasted ... Each divines the secret self of the other, and refusing to believe in the mere daily self, creates a mirror where the lover or the beloved sees an image to copy in daily life; for love also creates the Mask' (*A: E* 7; *Mem*, pp. 144–45). The noble masks of Solomon and Sheba may be just such ideal selves, posited by Yeats and his wife for mutual improvement. (For a more demonic poem about the masks of lovers, see 'The Mask'.) In listening to the voices of dead spirits coming from his wife's mouth (see Introduction XI), in struggling to interpret half-familiar, half-incomprehensible texts produced during his wife's trances, Yeats must have felt that his marriage was a drama played by strange masks, dramatis personae from beyond the grave.

15–16 *my thoughts, not it, / Are but a narrow pound*: the modest Sheba declares that her learning is limited – but it is clear that it is she who brings Solomon to wisdom (as in 'On Woman', ll. 11-12).

23–24 *love can make / The world a narrow pound*: love's amplitude renders all other knowledge narrow by comparison; as in 'When You are Old', love is larger than the compass of earth. Compare the 'contracted' world of Donne, 'The Sunne Rising', ll. 29–30: 'Shine here to us, and thou art every where; / This bed thy center is, these walls, thy spheare'.

The Living Beauty

In the summer of 1917, at Maud Gonne's home at Calvados in Normandy, Yeats proposed marriage to her daughter Iseult (see 'To a Child Dancing in the Wind'). She refused, but the indifference attributed to her in l. 7 is not entirely just – for later that year she wept for shame at her selfishness in not wanting Yeats to marry Georgie Hyde-Lees (Hone, *WBY*, p. 306). The position of this poem about age and frigidity, directly after the exhilarated 'Solomon and Sheba', suggests the complexity of Yeats's emotions during the wild year 1917–18.

1 *wick and oil*: compare 'Solomon and the Witch', l. 30: 'When oil and wick are burned in one'.

2 *frozen are the channels of the blood*: compare 'Broken Dreams', l. 19: 'age might well have chilled his blood'; and 'Demon and Beast', l. 39: 'Chilled blood'.

3 *My discontented heart*: compare 'The Tower' I.

5 *In bronze, or that in dazzling marble appears*: compare 'Men Improve with the Years', l. 7, in which a statue admires a book illustration. Late in life,

Yeats wrote that his early devotion to Maud Gonne 'might as well have been offered to an image in a milliner's window, or to a statue in a museum' (*A: DP* 6). The drama of a man who is forced against his will to choose aesthetic images instead of living flesh is reminiscent of the argument of 'Sailing to Byzantium'.

8 *O heart, we are old*: compare 'The Wild Swans at Coole', l. 22.

A Song

Like the previous poem, this song concerns the loss of affect in old age – though, whereas 'The Living Beauty' treats the theme with tense resignation, here the poet describes the subterfuges, the artificial efforts to maintain a sexual identity.

3 *dumb-bell and foil*: Ezra Pound taught Yeats to fence: 'I sometimes fence for half an hour at the day's end' (*M*, p. 337).

6 the heart grows old: compare 'The Wild Swans at Coole', l. 22.

To a Young Beauty

1 *fellow-artist*: Iseult Gonne – see 'To a Child Dancing in the Wind'.

2 *every sort of company*: Iseult Gonne's Bohemian friends – compare 'The Leaders of the Crowd', where Yeats frowns on Con Markiewicz's friends.

3 *Jack and Jill*: compare the song of the severed head in *A Full Moon in March* (1935), l. 166: 'I sing a song of Jack and Jill'.

7 *that mirror for a school*: compare another poem of advice to Iseult, 'Michael Robartes and the Dancer', in which the lady is asked to turn her eyes 'upon the glass / And on the instant would grow wise' (ll. 11–12).

11 *Ezekiel's cherubim*: many-eyed angels, described in Ezekiel 10. Ezekiel was the most hallucinatorily imaginative of the Old Testament prophets – Blake was much indebted to Ezekiel's imagery. Yeats suggests that Iseult was meant to be a vision of celestial rapture.

12 *Beauvarlet*: Jacques Beauvarlet (1731–93), an unimaginative French painter.

13 *what wages beauty gives*: compare 'Adam's Curse', l. 20: 'We must labour to be beautiful'; and 'Michael Robartes and the Dancer', ll. 14–15: 'your lover's wage / Is what your looking-glass can show'.

16 *not a fool can call me friend*: in Yeats's last radio broadcast script, he said of his childhood education, 'though ... I was near the bottom of the class, my friends were at the top, for then, as now, I hated fools' (*UP* II, p. 506).

18 *Landor*: Walter Savage Landor (1775–1864), a poet noted for the classical austerity of his verse. In Yeats's classification of human types, Landor appeared in the same category as Dante, Shelley – and Yeats himself: 'The most violent of men, [Landor] uses his intellect to disengage a visionary image of perfect sanity ... seen always in the most serene and classic art imaginable' (*AV*, pp. 144–45). Yeats also described Landor as surviving 'loving and hating, ridiculous and unconquered, into extreme old age, all lost but the favour of his Muses' (*M*, p. 342). W. F. Stead wrote to Yeats an anecdote of Landor's love of his garden: 'One evening the dinner was a failure. Landor in a rage hurled his cook out of the window, and then exclaimed in horror: "Good God, I forgot the violets"' (*LTY* II, p. 434). This sort of persona – the Wild Old Wicked Man – became more and more useful as Yeats grew old; and indeed Landor reappears near the end of Yeats's career to assist in the violent theatre of 'A Nativity' (l. 6). Longenbach notes (*SC*, pp. 188–89) that the desire to dine at journey's end with Landor may have been an echo of a passage from one of Landor's *Imaginary Conversations*, between 'Archdeacon Hare and Walter Landor': 'I shall dine late; but the dining-room will be well lighted, the guests few and select'.

18 *Donne*: John Donne (1571–1631), the 'metaphysical' poet. Yeats's interest in him predated T. S. Eliot's great Donne revival in the 1920s. When Grierson's edition of Donne's poetry appeared, Yeats wrote a letter thanking him: 'the more precise and learned [Donne's] thought the greater the beauty, the passion ... His pedantry and his obscenity ... but make me the more certain that ... [he] has seen God' (*L*, p. 570). Note the union of thought and passion in the last clause: Yeats, like Eliot, esteemed Donne for his power to pass easily between thinking and feeling, mind and body; 'Donne could be as metaphysical as he pleased, and yet never seemed unhuman or hysterical as Shelley often does, because he could be as physical as he pleased' (*A: TG* 13). In 1906 Yeats published a brief essay called 'The Thinking of the Body' deprecating abstract cerebration, 'which stirs the brain only', in favour of thoughts that rush out 'to the edges of our flesh' (*EI*, p. 292) – and the locus classicus of this theme in English poetry is a passage in Donne's 'Second Anniversarie' (1621), ll. 244–46: 'her pure and eloquent blood / Spoke in her cheekes, and so distinckly wrought / That one might almost say, her bodie thought'. The thinking-body theme is present in such poems as 'Solomon to Sheba', with its union of love and wisdom; also see 'On Woman', 'The Hawk', 'Michael Robartes and the Dancer', 'The Gift of Harun Al-Rashid', ll. 62–63 ('poet's thought / That springs from body and in body falls'), and 'A Prayer for Old Age', ll. 3–4 ('He that sings a lasting song / Thinks in a marrow-bone'). Yeats mentioned Donne again in *The Words upon the Window-Pane* (1934), ll. 103–4, where a student opines that 'Stella' was a better poet than Swift himself; her verse reminds him 'of a seventeenth-century poet, Donne or Crashaw'.

To a Young Girl

Iseult Gonne (see 'To a Child Dancing in the Wind') proposed marriage to Yeats in 1915, when she was twenty years old; Yeats rejected this playful proposal by claiming (as Jeffares notes in *Yeats: Man and Poet*, p. 190) there was too much Mars in her horoscope. But this frivolity soon led to a serious passion on his part.

4 *your own mother*: Maud Gonne.

9 *forgot*: the poet remembers, and affirms a continuity of passion between two generations.

The Scholars

For many years Yeats elaborated a notion that the best thinking was done with the body and not with the brain – see the note to 'To a Young Beauty', l. 18. His dislike of disembodied thought is most directly stated in this poem; but in three other poems in this volume there appear forms of the word *pedantry* ('The Dawn', l. 6; 'On Woman', l. 9; 'She turns the Dolls' Faces to the Wall', l. 4). Yeats's dislike of scholars began much earlier – in one juvenile poem, 'The Fairy Pedant' (*VP*, p. 707), a fairy wastes away from counting, measuring, mice and flowers; in another, 'A Legend' (*VP*, p. 725), a grey professor denounces the shallowness of God's mind; the story 'The Old Men of the Twilight' (1895) describes a grumpy and contentious band of prosodists whom St Patrick turned into herons (*M*, p. 194); in 1899 Yeats wrote that 'An academic class is always a little dead and deadening' (*UP* II, p. 150); and in 1900 he wrote of that 'Death whose most manifest expression in this country is Trinity College' (*UP* II, p. 243). One opposite of the anaemic scholar is the dancer, as 'Among School Children' VIII makes clear, with its antithesis between 'blear-eyed wisdom' burning 'midnight oil' and the dancer whose knowledge is incarnate in her body; another opposite of the scholar is the fool (see the next poem). Yeats's final wisdom on this theme was: 'Man can embody truth but he cannot know it' (*L*, p. 922).

This poem was the opening selection in Pound's *Catholic Anthology*. In 1912, Pound had suggested a way to approach Catullus superior to the scholars' way: 'I would much rather lie on what is left of Catullus' parlour floor and speculate the azure beneath it and the hills off to Salo and Riva with their forgotten gods moving unhindered amongst them, than discuss any processes and theories of art whatsoever' (*Literary Essays*, p. 9). In his essay 'Making, Knowing and Judging', W. H. Auden quoted this poem, commenting: 'Ignoring the obvious libel – that all dons are bald and respectable – the sentiments are still nonsense. Edit indeed; Thank God they do. If it had not been for scholars working themselves blind copying and collating manuscripts, how many poems would be unavailable, including those of Catullus . . . ?' (*The Dyer's Hand*, p. 43).

1 *Bald heads*: compare Yeats's denunciation of Bertrand Russell in 1927–28: a 'peaky-nosed, bald-pated, pink-eyed harridan'; 'what more can you expect from a man who has been entirely bald during the whole course of his life'; 'his person is contorted, and all of him an outward expression of essential vacuity and disorder' (*TSMC*, pp. 114, 124, 126).

10 *All know the man their neighbour knows*: Jeffares reports (*NCP*, p. 144) that this line originally read 'And only sin, when no one knows', and that, according to Yeats's wife, the poem softened when Yeats was away from Pound's influence. Pound's own hatred of philology is memorably stated in Canto 14.

12 *Catullus*: Roman poet (84–54 BC), notable for erotic desperation. Compare 'Mad as the Mist and Snow', ll. 16–18: 'even Cicero / And many-minded Homer were / *Mad as the mist and snow*'.

Tom O'Roughley

The recommendations of this imaginary character include illogic, recklessness, inconstancy, and irresponsibility – in this sense Tom O'Roughley belongs to the large class of Yeats's beggars and fools. He is the antithesis of the scholars in the previous poem, and shows something of Yeats's increasing fascination with the spontaneous carnality of human life. (For a related persona, see 'Two Songs of a Fool'.) The aggressive advocacy of innocence expressed in this poem has a somewhat Blakean quality; and Yeats noted that Blake 'said once that he preferred to any man of intellect a happy thoughtless person . . . It followed, I suppose, from his praise of life – "all that lives is holy" – and from his dislike of abstract things' (*A: E* 26; *Mem*, p. 158; compare *Ex*, p. 43).

Title: Tom is a generic name for fools (as in 'Tom the Lunatic'); 'There is one seaboard district known as Roughley, where the men are never known to shave or trim their wild red beards, and where there is a fight ever on foot' (*M*, p. 95).

1 *logic-choppers*: Yeats deplored those materialists who substitute 'for the old humanity with its unique irreplaceable individuals something that can be chopped and measured like a piece of cheese' (*Ex*, p. 436); also compare Yeats's aphorism, 'Descartes, Locke, and Newton took away the world and gave us its excrement instead' (*Ex*, p. 325).

4 *An aimless joy is a pure joy*: Yeats quoted this line as an illustration that joy depends on the man who feels, not on the external object (*EI*, p. 408). There are many echoes in Yeats's poetry of the phrase *aimless joy*, and of the doctrine that the best happiness is unpremeditated: see 'In the Seven Woods', ll. 10–11: 'Quiet / Wanders laughing'; 'The Fascination of What's Difficult', l. 3: 'Spontaneous joy'; 'Demon and Beast', l. 22: 'aimless joy'; and the sudden blazing of the poet's body in a London coffee-shop in 'Vacillation' IV. To an extent the 'tragic joy' of the later poetry ('The Gyres', l. 8) differs from 'aimless joy' in that it assumes the burden of human suffering; personages like Tom O'Roughley lack the inertia of character necessary for such a feeling. And yet Yeats did find a certain aimlessness in tragic joy: 'will, or energy, is greatest in tragedy ... "will or energy is eternal delight", and when its limit is reached it may become a pure, aimless joy, though the man, the shade, still mourns his lost object' (*Ex*, p. 449).

7–8 *And wisdom is a butterfly / And not a gloomy bird of prey*: Yeats often scribbled these favourite lines in copy-books (*TSMC*, p. 132); and he quoted them in a note to 'Meditations in Time of Civil War': 'I have a ring with a hawk and a butterfly upon it, to symbolize the straight road of logic, and so of mechanism, and the crooked road of intuition' (*VP*, p. 827). Compare also 'The Hawk' and 'Another Song of a Fool', l. 1.

11 *What's dying but a second wind?*: reincarnation suggests that human life is not direct and linear, pointed towards a single goal (compare l. 3), but erratic and vaguely cyclical.

12 *zig-zag wantonness*: Yeats wrote that each man is conducted to the moments of crisis that define his being along a 'zigzag' path (*M*, p 361).

13 *trumpeter Michael*: see 'The Happy Townland', l. 41.

Shepherd and Goatherd

This was the first-written of the remarkable trilogy in this volume on the death of Robert Gregory – see 'In Memory of Major Robert Gregory'. 'In Memory of Major Robert Gregory' treats his death from the point of view of the bereaved Yeats, mourning him along with other dead friends. 'An Irish Airman Foresees his Death' treats his death from the point of view of Robert Gregory himself, in the spectral dramatic monologue of a soul at a moment of peak intensity, passing beyond the human. This poem is, technically, almost exactly opposite to 'An Irish Airman Foresees his Death': instead of contemporaneity of action and immediacy of speech, 'Shepherd and Goatherd' is set in a pastoral never-never land, where anonymous rustics grieve at the death of a blank ideality. Yeats thought that his own Mask, or

Anti-self, was a kind of shepherd (see the note to 'To a Wealthy Man ...', l. 19); and so in this poem he abstracts the drama of his grief for Robert Gregory to an oversimple domain of masks, a toy world where bereavement can be studied in its purest form.

Here Robert Gregory is no longer a painter or a horseman or a boxer or a dashing aviator looking down at the world with faint scorn; he is simply a soul moving towards oblivion, quickly losing human identity. The Communicators who spoke through the automatic script (see Introduction XI) told Yeats about the *Daimon*, the fundamental component of human identity that passes undisturbed through a man's thousand reincarnations; and it may be said that the subject of this poem is Robert Gregory's Daimon, his naked essence. The pastoral, the most conventional of literary genres, well befits such an abstraction.

Yeats wrote that this poem was 'modelled on what Virgil wrote for some friend of his and on what Spenser wrote of Sidney ['Astrophel']' (*L*, pp. 647–48). The poem's original title was 'The Sad Shepherd' – a title used for a very early poem in *Crossways*.

2 *I wished*: compare l. 73: 'I might have wished'.

15 *The sheep had gone from theirs*: as the poem grows measured, the sheep grow unmeasured – interior control of emotion correlates with exterior disorder. For the theme of measure, see 'To Ireland in the Coming Times'.

22 *the great war beyond the sea*: in Spenser's 'Astrophel' (1595), the hero went 'To seek abroad, of daunger nought y'drad ... his own fame' (ll. 87–88) – Sidney died fighting in a British war in Holland.

24–25 *when he played it was their loneliness, / The exultation of their stone, that cried*: Robert Gregory was a painter, not a piper, but Yeats praised him in similar terms, describing his moody landscapes of 'blue-grey stony hills', and speaking of the 'loneliness of his dream' (*UP* II, pp. 430–31). Compare 'To a Friend whose Work ...', ll. 13–14: 'Amid a place of stone, / Be secret and exult' (written to Robert Gregory's mother); and 'An Irish Airman Foresees his Death', l. 11: 'A lonely impulse of delight'.

31 *When I had neither goat nor grazing*: Lady Gregory lent money to Yeats so that he could give up journalism.

32 *old wisdom*: Lady Gregory and Yeats investigated Irish folklore together.

34 *his children*: see 'For Anne Gregory', written to Robert Gregory's daughter.

50 *Set carpenters to work on no wide table*: Robert Gregory was not immersed in domestic life or bound to the world – he was dispossessed from the beginning. Like the subjects of other elegies by Yeats, he had, even in life, something of the aspect of a disembodied spirit. Compare 'To be Carved on a Stone at Thoor Ballylee', in which Yeats makes exactly the furnishing-arrangements that Robert Gregory neglected.

54 *cuckoo*: see l. 1. The cuckoo does not build a nest, but uses another bird's.

62 *the speckled bird*: this was the title of an unfinished novel on which Yeats worked around 1902. The title of the novel alludes to a passage in Jeremiah concerning the owl, despised by all other birds; but here Yeats means a migratory bird, not an owl. For another poem in which the soul is compared to a migratory bird, see 'At Algeciras – A Meditation upon Death'; a related comparison appears in 'Coole Park, 1929', l. 17.

73 *wished*: see l. 2.

75 *the natural life*: the Shepherd's song, just concluded, is a kind of pastoral digest of the themes to be used in 'In Memory of Major Robert Gregory'; the Goatherd's song will be a supernatural sequel to it.

78 *certain lost companions*: compare 'In Memory of Major Robert Gregory' III, IV, V.

83 *stupor of youth*: see 'Man and the Echo', l. 28: 'Body and its stupidity'.

88 *not all wild poppy*: that is, genuine revelation and consolation, not just an anaesthesia.

89 *He grows younger every second*: 'After death a lunar man ... grows always closer to objective experience, which in the spiritual world is wisdom, while a solar man mounts gradually to the most extreme subjective experience possible to him. In the spiritual world subjectivity is innocence' (*VPl*, pp. 777 – Yeats went on to quote ll. 89–112 of this poem). In other words, some men perfect themselves after death by growing ever older and wiser, others by growing ever younger and more innocent. Yeats refined these esoteric doctrines when writing *A Vision*: the Control told him on 11 Nov. 1917 that dead spirits 'dream backwards remember ... When they reach the prenatal they [can] ... go forward' (*MAV* I, pp. 28–29). In this doctrine the Control may have been influenced by Swedenborg – Yeats wrote of 'Swedenborg's muscular angels that move "towards the day-spring of their youth"' (*TSMC*, p. 114; *EI*, p. 495). Yeats concluded that the soul of each dead man has two components, moving through time in reverse directions: 'the *Celestial Body* is said to age as the *Passionate Body* grows young ... see Blake's *Mental Traveller*' (*AV*, p. 189).

Yeats's imagination often dwelt on the strategies of self-purification by the dead, and the Goatherd's song in this poem describes one of Yeats's more attractive visions of Purgatory. Yeats was able to imagine himself, like the Robert Gregory of this poem, rewinding the spool of his life, and in Robert Gregory's own venue: 'the woods at Coole ... are so much ... knitted to my thought, that when I am dead they will have, I am persuaded, my longest visit. When we are dead ... we live our lives backward .. treading the paths that we have trodden, growing young again, even childish again, till some attain an innocence that is ... the human intellect's crowning achievement'

(*A: SB* 6). Other souls suspended between death and life rejuvenate themselves similarly – see *The Only Jealousy of Emer* (1919), l. 209: 'The dead move ever towards a dreamless youth'; and *Ex*, p. 366: 'the unpurified dead ... examine their past ... tracing events to their source, and as they take the form their thought suggests, seem to live backward through time'.

There is some poetic precedence for this doctrine: see D. G. Rossetti's *House of Life* 58 1: 'to grow old in Heaven is to grow young' (quoted by Yeats, *Ex*, p. 39); and Shelley's soul-boat that 'sails against the current from age to youth, from youth to infancy, and so to the pre-natal condition "peopled by shapes too bright to see" [*Prometheus Unbound* II v 108]' (*EI*, p. 419).

Several other poems suggest Yeats's fascination with the childlikeness of the dying or the dead, the smiling innocence latent in experience. In 'Upon a Dying Lady', Mabel Beardsley's doll collection seems to grow more animate as she herself weakens; in 'Easter, 1916', the poet is struck by the silliness of the pre-revolutionary lives of the executed rebels; and in 'News for the Delphic Oracle' – a poem organized by a backward movement from old age to youth – the Innocents slaughtered by Herod cavort ecstatically in the waves.

97 *pern*: spool, in Irish dialect. In 'The Hero, the Girl, and the Fool', l. 20, the Fool speaks of human life as a spool to be rewound 'From grave to cradle'. In the automatic script of 19 March 1918, Yeats asked whether human life took place '[be]tween two funnels', and the Control said the funnel 'moves up & down – no, the whole like a top' (*MAV* I, p. 238).

100 *the outrageous war shall fade*: compare the theme of the oblivion of the gods, 'The Grey Rock', l. 122.

103 *close-cropped grass*: 'smooth grass' was one component of 'the peaceful Swedenborgian heaven' inherited by Blake (*Ex*, p. 44).

112 *sweeter ignorance*: compare 'Among School Children' V 4.

115 *Cut out our rhymes on strips of new-torn bark*: compare *The Island of Statues* II i 8–9: 'thy name / He carved on trees' (*VP*, p. 659); and *Baile and Aillinn*, l. 195: 'They wrote on tablets of thin board'. The text of the poem is a thematic element in it, as in 'When You are Old', l. 2.

116 *put no name*: this elegy anonymizes all its actors – the elegist seems to move towards oblivion at almost the same speed as the elegized.

117 *the mountain and the valley*: the home of goats and of sheep, respectively.

Lines Written in Dejection

The title of this poem recalls Shelley's 'Stanzas written in Dejection' (1818), in which dejection reaches such a level that it flattens the poet's whole system of emotional response – 'now despair itself is mild' (l. 28). But still more relevant is Coleridge's 'Dejection: An Ode' (1802), a poem about the loss of poetic power caused by the mind's withering into abstraction. The elderly speaker of 'Men Improve with the Years' was too decayed to attract the attention of a young woman; the elderly speaker of this poem is too decayed to attract the favour of the Muse. This is one of many poems Yeats wrote about the failure of imagination – see 'The Fascination of What's Difficult', 'The Tower' I, and 'The Circus Animals' Desertion'. The poem is remarkable for its irresolute pulse and irregular metre, as if the dejected poet had difficulty in finding force of utterance. (For early drafts of this poem, see *Mem*, p. 134, and Bradford, *YW*, p. 6.)

3 *leopards of the moon*: the full moon symbolizes the light of imagination. For the feline quality of the moon, see 'The Cat and the Moon'.

6 *Their angry tears, are gone*: for another poem about the loss of feeling in old age, see 'Demon and Beast'.

7 *centaurs*: Yeats once wrote, 'All art should be a Centaur finding in the popular lore its back and strong legs' (*A: FY* 22). Ezra Pound was also attracted to this image – in 'Tenzone' (1913), he wondered whether the public would flee from his poems 'As a timorous wench from a centaur'. Yeats wrote of centaurs again in 'A Thought from Propertius' and 'On a Picture of a Black Centaur ...'; also compare the Pegasus of 'The Fascination of What's Difficult', l. 4.

8 *the embittered sun*: the sun symbolizes the prosaic light of common life – see 'The Tower' II 30. In two of the first automatic scripts (5–6 Nov. 1917), the Control warned Yeats, 'Sun in moon sanity of feeling and thinking ... Too much moon ... so you must invoke sun very forcibly' (*MAV* I, pp. 8, 12) – as if Yeats were too *antithetical*, lunar, for his own good.

10 *fifty years*: see the Introductory Rhymes to *Responsibilities*, l. 20, for other mentions of Yeats's age.

The Dawn

The persona of Solomon, in 'Solomon to Sheba' and 'On Woman', combines the masks of sage and lover; but many of the personae in this volume – such as the marble triton of 'Men Improve with the Years', the Goatherd of 'Shepherd and Goatherd', and the exhausted poet of 'Lines Written in Dejection' – are inconsolable and decrepit old men. The Goatherd's song, however, with its description of a counterclockwise life – old age rejuvenating into the 'sweeter ignorance' of a baby (l. 112) – anticipates the movement from bleak wisdom to higher ignorance and imaginativeness found in this poem. The figure of the sage yields, incompletely, to the lover, the fisherman, and the fool, in a number of poems in the second half of this volume.

3 *that old queen measuring a town*: Emain, daughter of Hugh Roe, wished to rule after her father's death, so she killed one of his brothers and married another; she forced the defeated man's sons to build a palace on a site she measured with a pin (see Jeffares, *NCP*, p. 151). Like Blake, Yeats contrasted measurement and astronomy – activities of the abstract or predatory intellect – with a more imaginative response to the world.

6 *pedantic Babylon*: when Yeats came to develop his theory of history, he described cycles of 500 or 1000 or 2000 years, during which *subjective* ages (governed by imagination and the desire for beauty) alternated with *objective* ages (governed by intellect and the desire for truth). When Yeats tried to conceive the objective age that preceded Homer's Greece, he could see only 'Babylonian mathematical starlight' (*AV*, p. 268). (Note that the symbolic values of night and day are roughly reversed from those of the previous poem.) For the theme of pedantry, see 'The Scholars'. For other references (mostly astronomical) to Babylon, see *The Hour-Glass* (1914), ll. 369–70: 'the Babylonian moon / Blots all away' (and l. 65: 'a beggar wrote it upon the walls of Babylon'); 'I see Phantoms ...', l. 20: 'Babylonian almanacs'; 'Two Songs from a Play' II 4: 'The Babylonian starlight'; 'Wisdom,' l. 14: 'starry towers of Babylon'; 'Blood and the Moon' II 1–2: 'Babylon's / An image of the moving heavens'; and 'Vacillation' VI 7. Babylon could also suggest sumptuousness instead of astronomy, as in a passage from Francis Thompson's 'The Heart' quoted by Yeats: 'all man's Babylon's strive but to impart / The grandeurs of his Babylonian heart' (*EI*, p. 159); and in early drafts of *The Player Queen* Yeats thought of having Decima (wearing a golden veil) star in a play called *The Queen of Babylon* (Bradford, *WPQ*, pp. 76–83).

7 *careless planets*: they seem to resist formulations of their orbits – like the 'ignorant dawn'.

8 *The stars fade out when the moon comes*: compare 'First Love', ll. 16–18.

9 *tablets and ... sums*: compare the calendars of 'Nineteen Hundred and Nineteen' V 7, the star-charts of 'Blood and the Moon' II 2, and the diagram of 'Statistics', l. 3.

11 *That merely stood*: this phrase originally read, 'Yet did but look' (*VP*, p. 344). The sun, stars, and planets keep looking down, indifferently or contemptuously, at the 'wise' people who attempt to chart or calculate them.

11 *the glittering coach*: probably that of Apollo, whose chariot pulled the sun across the sky. The intrusion of mythology suggests the presence of creative imagination.

14 *Ignorant and wanton as the dawn*: compare 'The Fisherman', ll. 39–40: 'cold / And passionate as the dawn'. In a description of Gainsborough's paintings, Yeats wrote, 'In frail women's faces the soul awakes – all its prepossessions, the accumulated learning of centuries swept away – and looks

out upon us wise and foolish like the dawn' (*AV*, pp. 297–98). And in 1935 Yeats wrote, 'When I come to write of poetry I seem . . . completely ignorant. I wrote once "I would be ignorant as the dawn" but now I want to explain and cannot' (*DWL*, p. 4). In 'Lines Written in Dejection' Yeats felt himself contaminated by knowledge; here he hopes to regain a higher innocence.

On Woman

For the persona of Solomon, see 'Solomon to Sheba', a poem written to Yeats's wife. As Jeffares notes (*NCP*, p. 153), this poem, written four years earlier, had nothing to do with Yeats's wife; it was addressed to Maud Gonne. In certain early poems, such as 'The Sorrow of Love', a beautiful woman serves to connect the poet with the natural world; in this poem, a beautiful woman serves to replenish the male abstract intellect with a truer wisdom founded on sexual energy. In this way she offers a solution to the desiccation of faculty found in 'Lines Written in Dejection'. For a prose draft of this poem, see Bradford, *YW*, p. 6

6 *flesh and bone*: for the superiority of the thinking body to the thinking brain, see 'To a Young Beauty', l. 18. Compare 'The People', l. 30, also addressed to Maud Gonne: 'You, that have not lived in thought but deed'.

7 *Nor quarrels with a thought*: the beautiful woman seems to embody man's thought, not to dispute it. This idea is found in J. S. Mill's once widely read essay *The Subjection of Women* (1869): 'A woman seldom runs wild after an abstraction . . . Women's thoughts are thus . . . useful in giving reality to those of thinking men'. Donoghue compares Yeats's reminiscence of Arthur Symons: 'he could listen as a woman listens, never meeting one's thought as a man does with a rival thought, but taking up what one said and changing, giving it as it were flesh and bone' (*Mem*, p. 87). Also compare the unfinished novel *The Speckled Bird* I vii, where the hero's father offers a similar, but less flattering, assessment of a character partly based on Maud Gonne: her conversation merely repeats the things that others speak of, and yet others are so charmed by the reflected images of their own thoughts that they credit her with originality of mind (*LTMSB*, pp. 55–56).

9 *pedantry*: for this theme, see 'The Scholars'.

11–12 *Solomon grew wise / While talking with his queens*: compare 'Against Unworthy Praise', l. 6, in which Yeats credited Maud Gonne as the renewer of his strength.

21 *stretch and yawn*: Yeats's usual periphrasis for sexual languor – see 'Three Things', l. 17, for other references.

25 *no, not here*: the modest, aging poet hopes for Sheba's revelation of the flesh only in the next life. But (according to Mrs Yeats) Yeats did in fact

sleep with Maud Gonne, in 1907–8, when she was separated from her husband and living in Normandy, and Yeats may have alluded to this in two deeply disguised passages – the other is 'His Memories', l. 18.

30 *The Pestle of the moon*: compare 'The Phases of the Moon', l. 116: 'cook Nature'; and 'The Double Vision of Michael Robartes' I 6. A similar metaphor occurs in l. 4 of a remarkable uncollected poem, 'Wisdom and Dreams' (1892), which anticipates Solomon's unity of wisdom and imagination – indeed the first stanza might have served as the epigraph to *A Vision*: 'I pray that I ever be weaving / An intellectual tune, / But weaving it out of threads / From the distaff of the moon. // Wisdom and dreams are one, / For dreams are the flowers ablow, / And Wisdom the fruit of the garden: / God planted him long ago' (*VP*, p. 743).

36 *Sleep driven from my bed*: compare 'The Empty Cup', l. 10: 'my sleep is gone'.

39 *Gnashing of teeth, despair*: the poet invites all passion to recur, despite attendant pain – compare 'A Dialogue of Self and Soul' II 24.

41 *chance*: see 'Solomon and the Witch', l. 14.

The Fisherman

This poem carefully synthesizes an imaginary fisherman to act as an ideal audience for Yeats's poems. This theme shows Yeats's strong desire to investigate and to control every aspect of the poetic act – from the disciplined invention of images to the poem's reception by the reader. In a 1934 broadcast script Yeats offered an account of the poem's composition: 'I had met much unreasonable opposition. To overcome it I had to make my thoughts modern. Modern thought is not simple; I became argumentative, passionate, bitter; when I was very bitter I used to say to myself, "I do not write for these people who attack everything that I value ... I am writing for a man I have never seen". I built up in my mind the picture of a man who lived in the country where I had lived, who fished in mountain streams where I had fished; I said to myself, "I do not know whether he is born yet, but born or unborn it is for him I write"' (*UP* II, p. 498). Yeats was himself a skilled fisherman.

The image of a mythic fisherman appears in an early poem, 'The Song of Wandering Aengus'. The final decay of the fisherman occurs in a late poem, 'Why should not Old Men be Mad?', ll. 3–4, where the poet saw a likely lad 'That had a sound fly-fisher's wrist / Turn to a drunken journalist'.

4 *Connemara*: see 'The Dedication to a Book of Stories ...', l. 24. Yeats was disappointed to learn that Connemara cloth – rough tweed – was made in Scotland (*A: SB* 4).

5 *cast his flies*: Yeats considered the tranquillizing effect of fly-casting in a passage from the so-called 'De Burgh' version of the unfinished *The Speckled Bird*, comparing the boy who puts his will to sleep by casting a fly, to the saint-like man, sitting under the Buddha's tree, who has extinguished all of life's desires (*LTMSB*, p. 360).

11 *To write for my own race*: compare 'At Galway Races', where the poet yearned for an audience of horsemen, as in ancient times.

13–14 *The living men that I hate, / The dead man that I loved*: compare 'An Irish Airman Foresees his Death', ll. 3–4. Yeats wrote that 'the common condition of our life is hatred' (*M*, p. 365).

31–34: these lines are closely imitated in 'The Tower' III 3–6.

35 *A man who does not exist*: Longenbach (*SC*, p. 154) compares a passage from 'The Non-Existence of Ireland', where Pound wrote that because of the Irish people's rejection of Joyce, Synge, and Lane, Ireland 'ceased, quite simply, to exist' (*New Age* 16 [25 Feb. 1915]: 452).

39–40 *cold / And passionate as the dawn*: compare 'The Dawn', l. 14: 'Ignorant and wanton as the dawn'. Near the end of his life, Yeats wrote, concerning tragedy, 'imagination must dance, must be carried beyond feeling into the aboriginal ice. Is ice the correct word? I once boasted, copying the phrase from a letter of my father's, that I would write a poem "cold and passionate as the dawn"' (*EI*, p. 523).

The Hawk

In his autobiography, Yeats advocated 'Unity of Being' – that condition in which a man's faculties were so harmoniously arranged that (as Yeats's father put it) the soul was like 'a musical instrument so strung that if we touch a string all the strings murmur faintly' (*A: FY* 22). In the same chapter, Yeats wrote that 'the enemy of this unity was abstraction, meaning by abstraction not the distinction but the isolation of occupation, or class or faculty', and he went on to quote the first stanza of the present poem. Its theme, then, is the mind's haughty desire to isolate itself from the rest of the human sensibility, causing a general friction and cramp within the poet. (For the related theme of the thinking body, see 'To a Young Beauty', l. 18.) The hawk often symbolized the abstract intelligence: 'I have a ring with a hawk and a butterfly upon it, to symbolize the straight road of logic, and so of mechanism, and the crooked road of intuition' (*VP*, p. 827); see also 'Tom O'Roughley', l. 8.

4 *larder and spit are bare*: the intellect's disengagement has left the poet impoverished.

5 *The old cook*: compare 'The Black Tower', l. 21.

12 *tumbling cloud*: compare 'An Irish Airman Foresees his Death', l. 12.

14 *Yellow-eyed hawk of the mind*: compare 'An Acre of Grass', l. 24: 'eagle mind'. A 'blue-eyed hawk' appears in 'Under the Moon', l. 13.

18 *A pretence of wit*: the poet can command only the semblance of wit, because the actual faculty is elsewhere. For other flighty and undependable faculties, see 'The Balloon of the Mind' and the Pegasus of 'The Fascination of What's Difficult'.

Memory

1 *a lovely face*: perhaps that of Olivia Shakespear.

4 *the mountain grass*: an emblem of the persistence of memory, retaining the form imprinted on it. Compare 'Solomon and the Witch', l. 42: 'the crushed grass where we have lain'.

6 *the mountain hare*: perhaps Maud Gonne; or Iseult Gonne, leporine in Yeats's imagination in 'The Death of the Hare'.

Her Praise

The original title of this poem was 'The Thorn Tree', a title that emphasized that (as in such earlier poems as 'Paudeen') destitution and evacuation constituted the right landscape for visionary wisdom. The metre of this poem is unusual, a kind of hendecasyllabics in which a sixth stressed syllable is sometimes thrust against one of the normal pentameter stresses; this may imitate the Homeric metre proper to the classical beauty of Maud Gonne.

7–8 *A woman* ... *A man*: Longenbach notes that, while Yeats was writing this poem at Stone Cottage, 'Neither Dorothy nor Ezra Pound would listen to his praise of Maud Gonne' (*SC*, p. 149).

14 *Manage the talk*: as in 'The Fisherman', the poet tries to exert control by constructing an ideally receptive audience.

15 *he will know her name*: Donoghue compares Yeats's reminiscence: 'I became gradually aware of many charities – old women or old men past work were always seeking her out' (*Mem*, p. 61).

17 *old men's blame*: an allusion to the disparagement of Helen by the old men of Troy in the *Iliad* – see 'No Second Troy'.

The People

In the previous poem, Yeats summoned a chorus of praise for Maud Gonne; and in this and the next several poems, that praise becomes more particular and her image grows sharper or more obsessive. This poem (originally entitled 'The Phoenix') begins, like 'Her Praise', with a rejection of urban life and public affairs; but here the poet's sympathy broadens, under the influence of his beloved's magnanimity, and he comes to judge his nostalgia for distant times and places, his cultivation of antique courtliness, as a failure of spirit.

This poem is related to an unpublished quatrain (1909) written in response to Maud Gonne's marriage in 1903 to John MacBride: 'My dear is angry that of late / I cry all base blood down / As though she had not taught me hate / By kisses to a clown' (*Mem*, p. 145).

3 *this unmannerly town*: Dublin.

6 *Between the night and morning*: this line is quoted in Ezra Pound's 'Villanelle: The Psychological Hour' (1915). It first appeared in *The Golden Helmet* (1908): 'a man's good name drifts away between night and morning' (*VPl*, p. 423); compare *The Green Helmet* (1910), l. 18.

9 *Ferrara*: see 'To a Wealthy Man . . .', l. 9. In *The Dreaming of the Bones* (1919), the hero suggests that, if Diarmuid and Dervorgilla had not betrayed Ireland to the English, the city of Galway would have lain 'Amid its gables and its battlements / Like any old admired Italian town' (ll. 253–54).

12 *Urbino*: see 'To a Wealthy Man . . .', l. 17.

13 *the Duchess*: Elisabetta Gonzaga (1471–1526), who talked with her friends until dawn about the fitness of women for divine love, according to Castiglione's *The Courtier*. 'Art . . . approved before all men those that talked or wrestled or tilted under the walls of Urbino, or sat in those great window-seats discussing all things, with love ever in their thought, when the wise Duchess ordered all' (*EI*, pp. 292–93).

25 *my luck changed*: Maud Gonne became less popular after her separation from John MacBride in 1905.

28–29 *never have I . . . complained of the people*: 'the one thing Plutarch thought one should never complain of is the people' (*TSMC*, p. 13).

30 *You, that have not lived in thought but deed*: for the theme of the superior integration of women's faculties, see 'On Woman', l. 6.

34 *The eye of the mind*: the poet's intellectual detachment, his escapism, is shown by his predilection for Urbino and Ferrara; he might better confront contemporary Dublin.

His Phoenix

The tripping gait of this patter-song – Yeats's closest approximation to operetta – contrasts strongly with the severity or sobriety of the poems that precede and follow it in this sequence addressed to Maud Gonne. In this poem Yeats multiplies false or partial images of feminine dignity, elegance, talent, grace, and sexiness, only to dismiss them in favour of his own beloved.

Title *Phoenix*: a legendary bird, the unique member of its species, periodically immolated and reborn; Shakespeare used it in 'The Phoenix and the Turtle' (1601) as an emblem of eternal love. Compare 'The Lover asks Forgiveness . . .', l. 16; in a draft of *The Player Queen* Septimus compared Decima to a phoenix (Bradford, *WPQ*, p. 378).

4 *that sprightly girl trodden by a bird*: Leda – see 'Leda and the Swan'.

9 *Gaby*: Gaby Deslys (1884–1920), a French dancer and actress.

10 *Ruth St. Denis*: American dancer (1879–1968), one of the founders of modern dance.

11 *Pavlova*: the famous Russian ballerina (1885–1931), also mentioned in Pound's 'The Garret' (1913).

12 *a player*: Julia Marlowe (1866–1950). Yeats saw her in 1903-4.

17–18 *Margaret and Marjorie and Dorothy and Nan, / A Daphne and a Mary*: Ezra Pound's girlfriends, according to Ellmann (*ED*, p. 73). Pound married Dorothy Shakespear, daughter of Yeats's former mistress Olivia, in 1914.

28 *not the exact likeness*: 'A lover will admit a greater beauty than that of his mistress but not its like' (*AV*, p. 275).

28 *the simplicity of a child*: compare l. 14, and see 'Against Unworthy Praise', l. 20, 'Half lion, half child'.

29 *gazed into the burning sun*: see 'Upon a House shaken . . .', l. 4.

A Thought from Propertius

Ezra Pound may have introduced Yeats to the Roman elegist Sextus Propertius (*c*. 50–16 BC) – in a few years Pound published his remarkable imitation *Homage to Sextus Propertius* (1919). The passage here adapted is from Elegy II ii. Yeats considered, but rejected, this as a song in *The Player Queen*, to be sung by a gloating Decima as a sample of Septimus' poems of homage to herself (Bradford, *WPQ*, pp. 279–80).

1 *She*: Maud Gonne.

6 *Pallas Athena*: the Greek goddess of wisdom. See 'The Phases of the Moon', l. 47; 'Michael Robartes and the Dancer', l. 19; 'Nineteen Hundred and

Nineteen' I 6; 'Two Songs from a Play' I 1; 'Colonus' Praise', l. 16; and 'Beautiful Lofty Things', ll. 10-11: 'Maud Gonne at Howth station waiting a train, / Pallas Athena in that straight back and arrogant head'.

7 *centaur*: see 'Lines Written in Dejection', l. 7. As in 'The Two Trees' and 'A Bronze Head', Yeats can construct opposing versions of Maud Gonne – here she attains an apotheosis into high wisdom or violent bodily passion.

Broken Dreams

Most of Yeats's poems addressed to Maud Gonne celebrate her unearthly perfection; but, from 'The Two Trees' onward, there has been a countertheme, a construction of a distorted or broken image of her. This experimental poem tries to behold the two aspects of the woman – one ideally beautiful, the other deformed or violent, old – at the same time; but the effort seems to lead to a kind of headache of incoherent images. The metre is one of Yeats's nearest approaches to free verse: he strives for the effect of artless intimacy of diction, and also for the effect of formless periods (barely held together by vague rhymes) that imitate the muttering and rambling of an old man's thought.

1 *grey in your hair*: for Maud Gonne's aging, see 'The Folly of Being Comforted'.

4 *some old gaffer mutters a blessing*: see 'Her Praise', l. 15.

12 *that peace*: compare 'Peace'.

19 *chilled his blood*: see 'The Living Beauty', l. 2.

22 *I shall see that lady*: a similar thought appears in 'Quarrel in Old Age', ll. 9–16.

26 *muttering like a fool*: compare 'First Love', ll. 14–15: 'a lout, / Maundering here'.

28 *your body had a flaw*: this contradicts 'His Phoenix', l. 30: 'all the shapely body no tittle gone astray'. In the system of *A Vision* (not yet begun) Yeats assigned to Maud Gonne the lunar phase 16, just after the full moon – a phase in which ideal beauty started to fall asunder, grow compromised and hysterical. According to the system, no human incarnation of phase 15, complete beauty, is possible.

29 *Your small hands were not beautiful*: compare Yeats's judgment of certain visionary paintings where 'some little irrelevance of line ... may indeed put us at our ease' (*EI*, p. 244). Also compare 'The Phases of the Moon', ll. 66-67: 'those that we love got their long fingers / From death, and wounds'.

32 *always brimming lake*: this lake, like the stream that made all of Achilles invulnerable except his heel, seems to exclude one part of the beloved's body

33 *those that have obeyed the holy law*: the poet accuses the beloved of transgression, perhaps against both her vow to the poet – see the next poem – and her political destiny. The misshapenness of her hands is a sign of moral failure, yet still makes her endearingly human.

36 *sake's*: most other editions print the apostrophe after the *s* – but the singular form seems better, because the poem twice refers to *sole sake*, and for the reasons given by Finneran in *EYP*, p. 42.

37 *The last stroke of midnight dies*: compare 'The Four Ages of Man', l. 8.

39–40 *rhyme to rhyme . . . In rambling talk*: Yeats seems to conceive this poem as partly verse and partly prose; compare 'The Phases of the Moon', l. 30: 'True song, though speech'.

40 *an image of air*: see 'An Image from a Past Life', l. 7.

A Deep-sworn Vow

Although Maud Gonne told Yeats that she had 'a horror and terror of physical love' (*Mem*, p. 134) and could never marry him, Yeats considered that she had made a vow of sacred relationship to him, and that she had promised never to marry another. 'No, she could not marry – there were reasons – she would never marry; but in words that had no conventional ring she asked for my friendship' (*Mem*, p. 46). Compare 'King and No King', l. 9.

2 *friends*: that is, lovers.

Presences

Elaborate dream-processions of beautiful legendary women are not uncommon in Yeats's earlier works, such as 'Under the Moon' or the story 'Hanrahan's Vision' (1896). In this poem Yeats evokes a somewhat similar vision of female images – but in a much more direct and contemporary landscape.

2 *the hair stood up*: compare 'The Mother of God', l. 15: 'bids my hair stand up'. For more hair-raising, see *A: HC* 9 and *A: TG* 11, *Ex*, p. 302, *The Unicorn from the Stars* II 397, *Sophocles' Oedipus at Colonus*, l. 1355, *The Words upon the Window-Pane*, l. 239, and *The Herne's Egg* IV 171.

6 *Climbed up my creaking stair*: compare the male ghosts in 'The Tower' II 67 that 'climbed the narrow stairs'.

6 *They had read*: as in certain early poems, such as 'When You are Old', the text of Yeats's poetry plays a role in the poem.

12 *harlot*: perhaps a reference to Mabel Dickinson, who had announced (falsely) that Yeats had made her pregnant (Hone, *WBY*, p. 301). But it may be that harlot, child, and queen are all aspects of Maud Gonne.

12 *child*: perhaps Iseult Gonne.

14 *queen*: probably Maud Gonne. In 'Against Unworthy Praise', l. 20, Yeats called Maud Gonne 'Half lion, half child'; and in this poem it is possible that Maud's various constituents are divided into separate women. A similar sequence is assembled in a late poem, 'Those Images', ll. 11–12: 'The lion and the virgin, / The harlot and the child'.

The Balloon of the Mind

The theme of this quatrain is similar to that of 'The Hawk': the difficulty of coping with the intellect's airy disengagement from common life. Compare Yeats's recollection of his school days: 'My thoughts were a great excitement, but when I tried to do anything with them, it was like trying to pack a balloon into a shed in a high wind' (*A: R* 6).

To a Squirrel at Kyle-na-no

Kyle-na-no is one of the seven woods at Coole Park – see the Closing Rhymes to *Responsibilities*, l. 7.

On being asked for a War Poem

According to Jeffares (*NCP*, p. 160), this poem was once called 'To a friend who has asked me to sign his manifesto to the neutral nations'; another title was 'A Reason for Keeping Silent'. Yeats sent a version of it to Henry James and commented that he would keep near 'the seven sleepers of Ephesus [see 'On a Picture of a Black Centaur . . .', l. 11], hoping to catch their comfortable snores till bloody frivolity is over' (*L*, p. 600). The publication of the poem inspired an angry letter from Yeats's friend John Quinn: 'those five or six lines were quite unworthy of you and the occasion . . . I do not believe in divorce between letters and life or art and war' (Alan Himber, *The Letters of John Quinn to William Butler Yeats*, p. 192).

The poem 'Politics' – the last poem in Yeats's last volume of verse – is a more ribald restatement of this theme. In another late poem, 'Lapis Lazuli', Yeats mocks the 'hysterical women' (l. 1) who think that the threats of war make impossible the enjoyment of poetry.

3 *no gift to set a statesman right*: whether poets should have political power was an issue that concerned Yeats. In his play *The King's Threshold* (1904), for example, a poet starved himself before the king's threshold because he was denied his ancient political privileges.

In Memory of Alfred Pollexfen

This is a much lighter and swifter poem than any of Yeats's other funeral elegies. The other elegies concern meditative, disciplined, otherworldly people of great talent and energy – Lionel Johnson, J. M. Synge, Robert Gregory, Florence Farr, MacGregor Mathers, and so forth. But Alfred Pollexfen (1854-1916), the youngest of Yeats's maternal uncles, was a normal, ungifted, unassuming businessman, of no particular character or profile; Yeats's father even called him a mental simpleton. The running, almost galloping rhythms of this poem suggest that his death is no great tragedy – all flesh is grass. Others may be transfigured into fiery presences in the after life; but for Alfred Pollexfen the grave seems to hold nothing but a dim absorption into family memories.

2 *William Pollexfen*: Alfred's father. See the Introductory Rhymes to *Responsibilities*, l. 15.

4 *Elizabeth*: a 'gentle and patient woman' (1819–92), as Yeats described her (*A: R* 1), in marked contrast to her violent husband.

8 *George*: see 'In Memory of Major Robert Gregory' V 1. He was a Mason (*L*, p. 553) and a hypochondriac.

15 *The Mall and Eades's grammar school*: a street and a school in Sligo.

17 *John*: Alfred's brother, John Pollexfen (1845–1900). Jeffares notes (*NCP*, p. 162) that J. B. Yeats wrote to his son that a sailor's self-control compelled him to form a personality, and he used John Pollexfen as an example (*LS*, p. 224).

23 *Where have they laid the sailor John?*: in Liverpool.

25 *A humorous, unambitious man*: Alfred. Brother George was not humorous; brother John was not unambitious. As in 'In Memory of Major Robert Gregory', Yeats approaches the prime elegiac subject by means of other dead men who express aspects of his being – here by contradiction.

30 *Decided he would journey home*: in 1910 Alfred returned from Liverpool to Sligo, in order to replace George in the family firm.

37 *A visionary white sea-bird*: 'my sister awoke dreaming that she held a wingless sea-bird in her arms . . . for a sea-bird is the omen that announces the death or danger of a Pollexfen' (*A: R* 1).

39 *with that cry I have raised my cry*: the poet, like Alfred Pollexfen, seems at last to be reintegrated into his family.

Upon a Dying Lady

The lady was Mabel Beardsley (1871–1916), dying painfully of cancer. She was the wife of an actor and the sister of the famous artist Aubrey Beardsley, whose elegantly grotesque and sinuously sinister line drawings illustrated many poems and stories in the 1890s – often decadent and erotic texts, such as Wilde's *Salomé*. She herself had a large collection of dolls. Dolls, stylized sexuality, actors' masks – these were her family themes, and these are the themes of Yeats's poems about her. In an earlier poem, 'The Dolls', Yeats imagined the enmity felt by a gang of rowdy puppets towards the doll-maker's actual baby. Here Yeats seems to imagine death as a kind of passage from the world of men to the world of dolls to the artifice of eternity.

As in other elegies, Yeats praises the person who most closely resembles a ghost while still alive. In 1917 Yeats wrote that the newly dead 'are still but living in their memories, harmonies, symbols, and patterns, as though all were being refashioned by an artist, and they are moved by emotions ... like those of children dancing in a ring' (*M*, p. 356); and 'even the most wise dead can but arrange their memories as we arrange pieces upon a chessboard' (*M*, p. 359). Mabel Beardsley is, in a sense, already a wise dead woman, whose world has shrunk into toys, game-pieces to be arranged for her private amusement. Like the dead Robert Gregory in 'Shepherd and Goatherd', l. 89, she is growing younger, entering a phase of high childishness. Yeats was impressed by her 'pathetic gaiety', her capacity to make jokes about going to heaven (*L*, pp. 573–75); and the eerie combination of childlike playfulness and unflinching confrontation of pain, gives this poem its peculiar savour. She attributed to her brother Aubrey a 'passion for reality', and seemed to possess such a passion herself. Here Yeats anticipates the doctrine of tragic gaiety, elaborated in his later work (see 'The Gyres', l. 8).

I. Her Courtesy

2 *dull red hair*: Pound commented, 'Mabel's red head was a fine sight / worthy his [Yeats's] minstrelsy' (Canto 80/507). As Longenbach notes, Pound initially disliked the 'stale riming' of these poems (*SC*, p. 158).

3 *rouge on the pallor*: she herself is slightly doll-like. Compare V 6, 'red and white of a face'.

8 *Petronius Arbiter*: the first-century AD companion of the emperor Nero, known as the Arbiter of Elegances, supposed to be the author of the *Satyr-*

icon – the opposite of a saint. Petronius is mentioned in *The Player Queen* (1922) as someone who died telling 'witty, scandalous tales' (II 403–4); and in 1905 Yeats wrote that the *Satyricon* 'satirises, or perhaps one should say celebrates, Roman decadence' (*Ex*, p. 195).

II. Certain Artists bring her Dolls and Drawings

These dolls were costumed like the characters in Aubrey Beardsley's drawings; they were made by the artists Charles Ricketts and Edmund Dulac.

11 *naught for death but toys*: compare 'Nineteen Hundred and Nineteen' I 9: 'We too had many pretty toys'; and 'All Souls' Night', l. 59, where Florence Emery's dead soul can 'Forget its broken toys'.

III. She turns the Dolls' Faces to the Wall

2 *Mass*: the Beardsleys were Roman Catholics. There is a kind of struggle in this section between two arrays of symbols: the religious drama of the Eucharist and the profane drama of the doll-play.

4 *Pedant in passion*: compare the passion-pedantry of 'Solomon to Sheba'. The female dolls seem to express partial aspects of Mabel Beardsley's being – they play roles similar to those of Lionel Johnson, Synge, and George Pollexfen in 'In Memory of Major Robert Gregory'.

7 *Longhi*: Pietro Longhi (1702–62), Venetian genre painter.

12 *We and our dolls being but the world were best away*: the suppression of the world anticipates the state of the soul in purgatory.

IV. The End of Day

5 *some one*: Death.

V. Her Race

5 *woman*: *CP* (1933) introduces a comma after this word, but (since there is an implied *that* after *woman*) the earlier reading seems better.

11 *dead brother's valour*: Aubrey Beardsley (1872–98) died of tuberculosis aged twenty-six – 'In Beardsley I found that noble courage that seems to me ... the greatest of human faculties' (*Mem*, p. 92). Yeats thought of him as a kind of saint beset by tormenting visions: 'I see in his fat women and shadowy, pathetic girls, his horrible children, half child, half embryo, in all the lascivious

monstrous imagery of the privately published designs, the phantasms that from the beginning have defied the scourge and the hair shirt'. On his deathbed Beardsley 'made two or three charming and blasphemous designs', examples of 'his recognition that historical Christianity had dwindled to a box of toys, and that it might be amusing to empty the whole box on to the counterpane'. Yeats and Ezra Pound were both fond of quoting Beardsley's maxim, 'Beauty is so difficult' (*A: TG* 16).

VI. Her Courage

In this poem Yeats imagines Mabel Beardsley in the midst of an extremely complex heaven, populated with pagan heroes, barbarian conquerors, and even a Christian cardinal – but all are sensualists, people who delight in life. (A similar hodge-podge of an afterlife will occur in 'News for the Delphic Oracle'.) In the earlier poems in this sequence, Mabel Beardsley had to make choices – between the Mass and the dolls, between the world and the relinquishing of the world; but now it appears that heaven can embrace all contraries. Heaven is a kind of superior doll-house.

2 *I have no speech but symbol, the pagan speech*: Yeats's symbol-speech, full of determined visual images, is itself a sort of doll-play. Compare 'Two Years Later', l. 12: 'I speak a barbarous tongue'.

3 *face to face*: compare *The Shadowy Waters*, l. 198, and I Corinthians 13:12: 'Now we see through a glass, darkly; but then face to face'.

4–6 *Grania ... Diarmuid*: see 'A Faery Song', Caption.

8 *Giorgione*: Venetian painter (*c.* 1478–1510). Walter Pater, in 'The School of Giorgione', praised him for his sensuous compositions, and was inspired to make his famous remark, '*All art constantly aspires towards the condition of music*' (*The Renaissance* [1893], ed. Hill, p. 106). Yeats had reproductions of Giorgione and other painters in his room at Coole, and remarked of them, 'Here everywhere is the expression of desire ... All display bodies to please an amorous woman's eyes or the eyes of a great King. The martyrs and saints even must show the capacity for all they have renounced' (*A: DS* 4).

9 *Achilles*: the sullen, impetuous Greek hero in the *Iliad*, also mentioned in 'The Phases of the Moon', l. 45, and alluded to in 'News for the Delphic Oracle' III 5.

9 *Timor*: the warlord (*c.* 1336–1405) whose hordes swept across Asia and menaced Europe, also called Tamburlain.

9 *Babar*: the founder (1480–1530) of the Mogul dynasty in India, noted for lavishness and cruelty.

9 *Barhaim*: a hunter mentioned in FitzGerald's *Rubáiyát* (1859).

10 *laughed into the face of Death*: compare VII 10-11, and 'Vacillation' III 16, 'laughing to the tomb'. In 'Vacillation' VI some great conquerers exclaim, 'Let all things pass away'.

VII. Her Friends bring her a Christmas Tree

The Christmas tree of this poem may glitter with some of the eeriness of a tree described in *A Vision*: 'Certain London Spiritualists for some years past have decked out a Christmas tree with presents that have each the names of some dead child upon it, and sitting in the dark on Christmas night they hear the voice of some grown-up person, who seems to take the presents from the tree, and the clamorous voices of the children as they are distributed. Yet the presents still hang there and are given next day to an hospital' (p. 221).

1 *great enemy*: Death.

7 *pretty things*: the ornaments are reminiscent of the dolls in the earlier poems.

Ego Dominus Tuus

From his earliest poems on, Yeats was preoccupied with the construction of an anti-world, a faeryland in which every desire was gratified, an artificial domain related to the ordinary world as presence is to absence. In this poem Yeats tries to illustrate how a human identity can be constructed according to the same principle: since one's ordinary self is cramped, partial, incompetent, one should strive towards an anti-self, the exact reverse of the self with which one was born. Around 1909 Yeats conceived the doctrine of the Mask (see 'The Mask' and 'Solomon to Sheba'), and noted that the exchanging of masks permitted a multiplication of being, a liberation from the usual constraints of self, an access of power. The anti-self described in this poem is an attempt to create an ideal Mask – not a succession of various faces but a single self-image valid for any occasion, at once particular, precisely incised, and universal, containing every human faculty.

In this theory we see how Yeats's thinking was dominated by the notion of complementariness: he manufactured a setting for his poetry in the fashion of a Venn diagram, by taking the Universe minus earth; he manufactured a persona by taking the Universe minus himself. Similarly, in his description in *A Vision* of the loss of private identity of the dead soul, its journey into complete beatitude, Yeats wrote that the soul must relive a mirror-image of its life, in which every good deed is replaced by an evil one, and vice versa; only by adding a complement of its life to itself can the soul attain complete fullness, sphericality of being (*AV*, p. 231). And similarly, Yeats's method when writing a funeral elegy, such as 'In Memory of Major Robert Gregory', was to add up fragmentary souls until the total is sufficient to represent a full soul. According to the doctrine of the Anti-self, each of us has a kind of guardian angel, a photographic negative of oneself, who can be summoned to furnish an uncanny intensity and repletion of identity.

Also in 1909 Yeats began to attend séances in which he talked with a sixteenth-century Moorish travel-writer named Leo Africanus, whom Yeats grew partly to accept as real: 'He was no secondary personality ... but the person he claimed to be. He was drawn to me because in life he had been all undoubting impulse, all that his name and Africa might suggest ... I was doubting, conscientious and timid'. Leo Africanus asked Yeats to address letters to him, expressing his doubts about Leo's authenticity, and then to reply to those letters as if Leo were speaking: 'He would control me in that reply so that it would be really from him' (*Yeats Annual* 1 [1982]: 13). In this strange manner Yeats conducted his dialogue with his anti-self. (For more on secondary personalities – twiformed, short-lived beings begotten by spirits upon mediums – see 'Let images of basalt ...', quoted in the headnote to 'The Statues'; and *LTMSB*, p. 124.)

The title 'Ego Dominus Tuus' ('I am your lord') is derived from Dante's *La vita nuova*; as Yeats explains in his essay *Per Amica Silentia Lunae* (1917) – the first half of which is a commentary on this poem – a poet's visions are not his own, but derived from some shivery and alien agency:

> That which comes as complete, as minutely organised, as are those elaborate, brightly lighted buildings and sceneries appearing in a moment, as I lie between sleep and waking, must come from above me and beyond me. At times I remember that place in Dante where he sees in his chamber the 'Lord of Terrible Aspect', and how, seeming 'to rejoice inwardly that it was a marvel to see, speaking, he said many things among the which I could understand but few, and of these this: ego dominus tuus ...' (*M*, pp. 325–26)

The origin of the power lies beyond the poet, sheltered in an intimate and disturbing angel, the anti-self. 'Ego Dominus Tuus' is written in dialogue form, appropriate to its dialectic. The names *Hic* and *Ille* are simply Latin for *This one* and *That one*; but, because *Ille* is clearly Yeats's spokesman, Ezra Pound once declared (remembering the author's first name) that the characters ought to be named *Hic* and *Willie* (Ellmann, *YMM*, p. 201).

In a sense this dialogue-poem offers both a model and a theory for such important experimental plays as *At the Hawk's Well* (1917) and *The Only Jealousy of Emer* (1919), in which the hero wrestles with an immortal phantom of power. At about the same time that Yeats wrote 'Ego Dominus Tuus', he also wrote a prose dialogue, 'The Poet and the Actress', in which a poet (similar to Ille) tries to persuade a reluctant actress (somewhat similar to Hic) to wear a mask, on the grounds that a theatre of masks is appropriate to the interior soul-drama supplanting the 'realism' of Ibsen and his followers. Yeats never published this dialogue, and was uneasy about 'Ego Dominus Tuus' as well: in *A Vision* (1925), p. xii, he said, 'I can now ... find the simplicity I have sought in vain. I need no longer write poems like "The Phases of the Moon" nor "Ego Dominus Tuus."'

2 *your old wind-beaten tower*: since Yeats lived in a wind-beaten tower beside a shallow stream, the identification of Ille with Yeats is reinforced.

1–7 *On the grey sand ... trace ... Magical shapes*: when Yeats came to write *A Vision*, he imagined its diagrams of the universe-controlling forces as traced in sand – see 'The Gift of Harun Al-Rashid', l. 156. Bornstein (*YS*, p. 91) compares Shelley's *The Revolt of Islam* VII xxxii: 'And on the sand would I make signs ... Clear, elemental shapes, whose smallest change / A subtler language within language wrought' (quoted by Yeats, *EI*, p. 78).

4 *Michael Robartes*: a personification of the imagination's self-esteem, its rejoicing in its own power – see the headnote to *The Wind among the Reeds*. In certain short stories written around 1897, Yeats thought of Robartes as a tutor in occult wisdom and an instructor in occult ceremony.

7 *by the help of an image*: compare the dolls that give precision to Mabel Beardsley's fantasies in the previous poems.

9 *handled least, least looked upon*: compare 'A Prayer on going into my House', l. 6: 'handle nothing and set eyes on nothing'. For more hand-eye imagery, see the note to 'Towards Break of Day', and 'Another Song of a Fool', ll. 2–3.

12 *gentle, sensitive mind*: 'our culture, with its doctrine of sincerity and self-realisation, made us gentle and passive ... the Middle Ages and the Renaissance were right to found theirs upon the imitation of Christ or of some classic hero' (*M*, p. 333); 'We have been gradually approaching this art [of Day Lewis and MacNeice] through that cult of sincerity, that refusal to multiply personality which is characteristic of our time' (*OBMV*, p. xxxvi). Hic believes that character is formed, not by the difficult struggle towards a mask, but by passive self-examination, the sifting of personal feelings and impressions. Yeats defined one sort of passivity in art by the inability to create a persona.

15 *We are but critics*: unlike Wilde, who regarded criticism as the highest form of art, Yeats conceived the literary critic as a kind of mortician, embalming the imagination – see 'The Body of Father Christian Rosencrux' (*EI*, p. 196).

19 *Dante Alighieri*: Italian poet (1265–1321), author of *The Divine Comedy*.

23 *the hunger that had made it hollow*: the self is emptied by the stress of the

drive to find the anti-self. Compare Maud Gonne's face, 'Hollow of cheek as though it drank the wind' ('Among School Children', l. 27), and Hamlet 'thin from eating flies' ('The Statues', l. 19). Hollow cheeks also are attributed to such starvers as the Druid in 'Fergus and the Druid', l. 23, and Ebremar in the juvenile *Mosada* II 35 (*VP*, p. 697).

25 *Most out of reach*: compare 'The Phases of the Moon', l. 40: 'He follows whatever whim's most difficult'.

26 *Lapo and ... Guido*: *Lapo* is perhaps Lapo Gianni, prominent in Rossetti's introduction to his translation of *La vita nuova*; *Guido* is Guido Cavalcanti (1230–1300), Italian poet – Rossetti called him 'the one whom Dante has styled his "first friend"' (*Works* II, p. 5). Pound admired Guido and translated many of his poems.

29 *a Bedouin's horse-hair roof*: compare 'Coole and Ballylee, 1931', l. 40: 'some poor Arab tribesman and his tent'.

30 *doored and windowed cliff*: possibly Yeats was thinking of the ancient city of Petra in Jordan.

33 *mocked by Guido for his lecherous life*: 'Guido Cavalcanti, as Rossetti translates him, finds "too much baseness" in his friend: ... "But now I dare not, for thy abject life, / Make manifest that I approve thy rhymes"' (*M*, p. 330).

37 *The most exalted lady*: Beatrice. For Yeats one expression of the quest for a Mask is the quest for an ideal beloved: 'I think of life as a struggle with the Daimon who would ever set us to the hardest work among those not impossible ... I even wonder if there may not be some secret communion, some whispering in the dark between Daimon and sweetheart' (*M*, p. 336).

45 *The struggle of the fly in marmalade*: according to Yeats, Verlaine said that he knew Paris '"too well" and "lived in it like a fly in a pot of marmalade"' (*A: TG* 18); compare also 'a spider smothered in its own web' (*Ex*, p. 403).

46 *The rhetorician would deceive his neighbours*: the rhetorician and the sentimentalist are artists of action, aiming for worldly effect. Yeats often denounced the rhetorician: 'what is rhetoric but the will trying to do the work of the imagination?' (*EI*, p. 215); 'We make out of the quarrel with others, rhetoric, but of the quarrel with ourselves, poetry' (*M*, p. 331); and there is a passage in the unfinished *The Speckled Bird* discussing pictorial rhetoric – the nearest thing to an artistic gift possible to those whose gift is for action (*LTMSB*, p. 270). Yeats traced the classification of poets into rhetoricians and seers to Hallam's essay on Tennyson (*UP* II, pp. 130–31).

48 *a vision of reality*: true art is not a manipulation of emotions or opinions – one's own, or another man's – but a struggle towards the not-self, the anti-self. Compare 'reality itself is found ... in ... the Ghostly Self' (*AV*, p. 22);

'the desolation of reality' ('Meru', l. 7); and 'we perish into reality' (*The Hour-Glass* [1903 prose version], l. 468 [*VPl*, p. 634]).

49–62: Yeats quoted these lines to illustrate the powers of the Gatekeepers, those eerie agents who control the dramatic shape of history, who 'contrived Dante's banishment, and snatched away his Beatrice, and thrust Villon into the arms of harlots . . . that Dante and Villon might through passion become conjoint to their buried selves' (*A: HC* 9).

49 *the artist*: Yeats was thinking of Lionel Johnson and Ernest Dowson: 'Johnson and Dowson, friends of my youth, were dissipated men, the one a drunkard, the other a drunkard and mad about women, and yet they had the gravity of men who had found life out and were awakening from the dream . . . The other self, the anti-self . . . comes but to those who are no longer deceived, whose passion is reality' (*M*, p. 331). For Johnson and Dowson, see 'The Grey Rock', l. 62.

52 *Keats*: according to the schema of *A Vision*, John Keats (1795–1821) is the preeminent visionary poet, standing at Phase 14, just on the brink of the incandescent revelation given by the full moon. In the automatic script of 24 Jan. 1918, Thomas (the Control) – perhaps remembering 'Ego Dominus Tuus' – told Yeats that Keats 'loved or sought the material good of world' (*MAV* I, p. 164).

56 *nose pressed to a sweet-shop window*: in some of Keats's famous odes, the poet is unable to participate in the world of luxury and keen sensation that he imagines.

61 *coarse-bred son*: Keats's contemporaries ridiculed him as a member of the Cockney school of poetry – but to Yeats his low origins only heightened his inner tension-level, his genius.

65 *sedentary toil*: in 'The Tower' poetry is called 'this sedentary trade' (III 60).

67 *I seek an image, not a book*: Ille insists that the origin of poetry lies not in the servile imitation of previous poems but outside of natural experience. By means of the anti-self the poet can become his own Muse: to impose shape and discipline on oneself – to make a kind of idol stamped with one's own features (l. 28) – is preliminary to the imposition of verbal shape on a poem. In the automatic script of 21 Dec. 1917, Yeats tried to use the end of this poem to clarify the meaning of Thomas's discourse on Genius (*MAV* I, p. 78). And in a draft of *The Player Queen*, the poet Septimus identifies genius with the anti-self: 'nobody finds their genius till they have found some role, some image, some pose that liberates something within them or beyond them that had else been dumb and numb' (Bradford, *WPQ*, p. 317).

76 *whisper it*: for another command to keep esoteric things secret, see 'The

Gift of Harun Al-Rashid', ll. 33–34. Also compare the Closing Rhymes of *Responsibilities*, l. 1.

A Prayer on going into my House

As in some of his other prayers, such as 'A Prayer for my Son' and 'At Algeciras – a Meditation upon Death', Yeats tended to revert to an almost Christian kneel when he wished to postulate a prayable deity. As he wrote in 'A Prayer for Old Age', ll. 9–10, 'fashion's word is out / And prayer comes round again'.

1 this tower: Thoor Ballylee – see 'In Memory of Major Robert Gregory', l. 1.

2 *my heirs*: see 'My Descendants'.

3 *table or chair or stool*: as Jeffares notes (*NCP*, p. 172), Yeats commissioned local craftsmen to make such items from local elms.

6 *handle nothing and set eyes on nothing*: compare 'Ego Dominus Tuus', l. 9: 'handled least, least looked upon'.

7 *what the great and passionate have used*: compare 'My Table', ll. 15–21.

10 *Sinbad*: as Henn notes (*LT*, p. 263), Yeats knew Dulac's illustrated edition of the *Arabian Nights*; on Sinbad's sixth voyage his ship was destroyed by a magnetic mountain. Also compare: 'Am I not Sinbad thrown upon the rocks & weary of the sea?' (*L* I, p. xl).

12 *That dream is a norm*: in a 1924 footnote to his essay 'The Celtic Element in Literature' – in the midst of a discussion of traditional European mythologies – Yeats wrote, 'I should have added ... that the supernatural may at any moment create new myths' (*EI*, p. 185).

16 *Manacle his soul upon the Red Sea bottom*: in 'A Letter to Michael's Schoolmaster', Yeats wrote, 'If ... my son comes from school a smatterer like his father, may your soul lie chained on the Red Sea bottom' (*Ex*, p. 321; compare p. 56).

The Phases of the Moon

After wrestling for some months with the difficult doctrines educed from his wife's automatic script – see Introduction XI – Yeats wrote this summarizing poem. Whereas the point of view of *A Vision* is that of a tenacious man of no particular brilliance of mind wrestling with advanced, intractable ideas, the point of view of this poem is that of his supernatural instructors, effortlessly wise, derisive of Yeats's dim-witted misunderstandings. It pleased Yeats to suppose that the doctrines of *A Vision* could be compressed to a point of transcendental simplicity; 'The Phases of the Moon' is half a statement of these terse truths, half an apology for the cloudiness, the obscurity, of any attempt to render these truths intelligible. Yeats hinted that *A Vision* was only a stylized reconstruction of human life, and the pleasure of studying it was akin to that of cubist art (*AV*, p. 25); similarly the pleasure of reading this poem is like that of an animated cartoon in which a welter of human shapes take form from clay, whirl about in a frantic circle, and at last subside into clay again. Yeats was diffident about 'The Phases of the Moon', and even wrote to Pound (on 15 July 1918) that it should probably be published only because 'Without it "The Double Vision [of Michael Robartes]" is too obscure' (*MAV* II, p. 19).

The speakers of this dialogue, Michael Robartes and Owen Aherne, were personae of long standing in Yeats's imagination – see the headnote to *The Wind among the Reeds*. In an 'Introduction by Owen Aherne' to the 1925 *A Vision* (deleted from the 1937 edition), Aherne explains how Michael Robartes, despite his long enmity with Mr Yeats, decided to share with the poet the mysterious wisdom he had brought back from Arabia, the diagrams of lunar motion he had seen traced in the sand by the feet of dancers. Aherne is a kind of Roman Catholic, austere and ceremonious, heretical in that he believes in the reincarnation of the soul. Robartes is a kind of high priest of imagination, eager to find expression of the supernatural in rituals, designs, artifices; indeed in the short story 'Rosa Alchemica' (1896) Robartes leads a hypnotic rite – petals seem to fall from a rose painted on the ceiling, and gods assume human bodies. (It is likely that Aherne was partly based on Lionel Johnson, Robartes on MacGregor Mathers – for Mathers, see 'All Souls' Night', l. 61.) Yeats wrote the 'Introduction by Owen Aherne' in order to provide a Christian counterbalance to his own, and Robartes', preference for paganism, aristocracy, creativity: Aherne embodies an ethic of self-suppression and obedience.

'The Phases of the Moon', then, could have been as dialectical as 'Ego Dominus Tuus', a true dialogue between a character representing the values of the full moon (Robartes) and one representing the values of the new moon (Aherne). But instead Aherne was demoted to a Glaucon or an Adeimantus, capable of little more than murmuring agreement with the all-wise Robartes. Pirandello, a playwright whom Yeats mentioned in the 1925 *A Vision*, wrote of Six Characters in Search of an Author; here we have two characters who have learned to dispense with an author, indeed to mock him, as if the creative process could be more immediate in his absence.

4 Connemara cloth: see 'The Fisherman', l. 4. Yeats's Fisherman, a synthetic and ideal audience for his poems, wore the same fabric as those who come to bring Yeats (or to withhold from him) material for poetry.

8 *water-hen*: see 'The Indian upon God', l. 3

10 *the tower*: Thoor Ballylee, where Yeats lived – see 'In Memory of Major Robert Gregory', I 1.

15 *Milton's Platonist*: from Milton's 'Il Penseroso' (1631): 'Or let my Lamp at midnight hour, / Be seen in some high lonely Tow'r, / Where I may oft outwatch the *Bear*, / With thrice great *Hermes*, or unsphere / The spirit of *Plato*' (ll. 85–89). Compare 'My House', l. 14: '*Il Penseroso*'s Platonist'; and the curse on Platonists in 'Statistics', l. 1. For references to Plato, see 'The Tower' I 12. Yeats places himself in the tradition of Milton (1608–74) and Shelley (1792–1822) because they were the authors of two of the most detailed cosmographies (in *Paradise Lost* and *Prometheus Unbound*) in previous English poetry.

16 *Shelley's visionary prince*: an allusion to Shelley's fragment *Prince Athanase* (1817), where the prematurely gray-haired prince contemplates 'apart from men, as in a lonely tower' (l. 33); fishermen at night see his lamp gleaming from a turret (l. 189). In 1906 Yeats referred to the motive power of 'that solitary light burning in the tower of Prince Athanase' (*EI*, p. 294). Like Milton's pensive one, Prince Athanase was a Platonist: 'Plato's words of light ... lingered like moonlight' (ll. 224–25). Yeats also remembered Shelley's towers in 'Blood and the Moon' II 3.

17 *Samuel Palmer*: one of Blake's most fervent disciples (1805-81), who engraved a moody woodcut illustrating the tower in 'Il Penseroso': 'I commit my emotions to shepherds, herdsmen, camel-drivers, learned men, Milton's or Shelley's Platonist, that tower Palmer drew' (*EI*, p. 522). See also 'Under Ben Bulben' IV 28.

19 *he seeks in book*: the derogation of book-research follows that in 'Ego Dominus Tuus', l. 67. Robartes perhaps implies that wisdom is incarnate in Robartes and Aherne, not reduced to mere abstract formula. See l. 97.

27 *Pater*: Walter Pater (1839–94), Oxonian critic, whose stately and ornate, and yet sensuous, teasing prose influenced Oscar Wilde and many other writers. Pater's prose 'taught us to walk upon a rope, tightly stretched through serene air, and we were left to keep our feet upon a swaying rope in a storm' (*A: TG* 5). Yeats also commented on Pater's 'golden sentences, laden as with sleepy sunlight' (*LNI*, p. 137). Yeats sometimes thought Pater too serene, too languid – 'Surely the ideal of culture expressed by Pater can only create feminine souls' (*Mem*, p. 159). Yeats's *OBMV* begins with Pater's sentence on the Mona Lisa, arranged as poetry; remembering this haunting sentence, Yeats asked, 'did Pater foreshadow a poetry, a philosophy, where the individual is nothing, the flux of *The Cantos* of Ezra Pound ... human experience no longer shut into brief lives ...?' (*OBMV*, p. xxx).

28 *Said I was dead*: at the end of 'Rosa Alchemica' (1896), the narrator describes Robartes' death at the hands of a mob inflamed by his un-Christian

religious activities. In *A Vision* (1925), Robartes tells Aherne, '"You will remember the village riot which Yeats exaggerated in 'Rosa Alchemica'"' (p. xvii).

30 *'mine author sung it me'*: Yeats used the same phrase in *EI*, p. 340, and *DWL*, p. 26.

35 *For there's no human life at the full or the dark*: Yeats quoted this line to illustrate why the Renaissance could attain only an approximation of complete beauty (*A: TG* 3).

36 *From the first crescent to the half*: Phases 2 to 8, the quarter of the reincarnative cycle when the inchoate soul gradually grows self-aware, disengages itself from the natural world, starts to systematize its knowledge.

39 *while the moon is rounding towards the full*: Phases 9 to 14, the quarter in which the soul gains painful mastery over the world; in Phase 13 (e.g., Baudelaire) and Phase 14 (e.g., Keats) the objects of fantasy and desire are far more vivid than the objects of the natural senses.

40 *whatever whim's most difficult*: the anti-self or Mask – see 'Ego Dominus Tuus'. Also compare 'To a Friend ...', ll. 15-16: 'of all things known / That is most difficult'; and *M*, p. 336.

42 *the cat-o'-nine-tails of the mind*: imagery of self-whipping is frequent at this period: see l. 68, and 'The Saint and the Hunchback', l. 8. In Yeats's last short story, Michael Robartes reports an allegorical picture of 'a man whipping his shadow' (*AV* [1937], p. 38). It is an emblem of the tortured intimacy of man and Mask. In this passage the body grows more beautiful as the soul realizes a more precise image of bodily splendour, flogs away all ugliness. Compare *The Only Jealousy of Emer* (1919), ll. 1–28.

44 *Eleven pass*: in an unpublished MS connected with *A Vision*, Robartes says that in Phase 11 'one discovers now a Pantheistic image of man little more precise than my own legs when I study them through the water where I am bathing and now the reason[ed] conviction of Spinoza' (*CEAV [1925]*, Notes, p. 18). Yeats thought of Spinoza as a kind of mystic who tried to organize his insights into mathematical propositions. The desire to systematize the human body and mind is starting to appear.

45 *Athena takes Achilles by the hair*: see *Iliad* XXII 330; *The Resurrection* (1931), ll. 225–27: 'When the goddess came to Achilles in the battle she did not interfere with his soul, she took him by his yellow hair'; and *A Vision* (1925), p. 215: 'The supreme experience, Plotinus' ecstasy, ecstasy of the Saint, will recede ... and men may be long content with those more trivial benedictions as when Athena took Achilles by his yellow hair'. For Achilles, see 'Her Courage', l. 9. Athena's own hair will be plucked in 'Michael Robartes and the Dancer', l. 19; she appeared as a more decorous goddess of wisdom in 'A Thought from Propertius', l. 6.

46 *Hector*: the great Trojan hero dragged in the dust behind his slayer Achilles' chariot – see also 'The Gyres', l. 7.

46 *Nietzsche*: Friedrich Nietzsche (1844–1900), German philosopher. Yeats placed him in Phase 12 as the model of the Hero, whose triumphant Will to Power (in the anti-self) is accomplished at the expense of every physical and mental sanity in the ordinary self – 'Like all before Phase 15 the man is overwhelmed with the thought of his own weakness and knows of no strength but that of Image and *Mask*' (*AV*, p. 129).

49 *helpless as a worm*: compare 'The Chambermaid's First Song', l. 10: 'Weak as a worm'.

50–51 *the soul at war / In its own being*: after conquering the world and dismissing it, the soul sets its energies against itself. See the note to 'Ego Dominus Tuus', l. 46.

55 *labyrinth of itself*: compare 'The Tower' II 96, 'the labyrinth of another's being'.

58 *All thought becomes an image*: according to *A Vision*, at the full moon the faculties of mind and imagination coalesce: the soul beholds nothing except detached and perfect images. See also l. 80.

67 *Sinai's top*: Moses received the Commandments on Mt Sinai. 'Perhaps Moses when he descended the mountain-side ... had cut Tables and *Mask* out of the one rock' (*AV*, p. 124).

68 *bloody whip*: see l. 42.

74 *all is fed with light and heaven is bare*: compare 'First Love', ll. 16–18.

79 *Caught up in contemplation*: the imaginer and the imagined alike are among the eerie creatures of the full moon. As at ll. 20, 85, and 129, it seems that the human poet has little role to play in the drama of high aesthetics.

87 *the crumbling of the moon*: the third quarter, Phases 16–22, and the fourth quarter, Phases 23–28. The third quarter is the lunar season when the high fantasy achieved at the full moon starts to break down, to become compromised by worldly facts. The transfigured images contemplated at Phase 15 start to grow less vivid, and the suppressed background of commonplace objects starts to become visible again. Poets start to fall in love with real women instead of ravishing goddesses; history starts to replace mythology, and the photograph conquers the painting. During the fourth quarter the soul increasingly drowns itself in the objective world, surrenders its integrity to some external system – these are the phases of scientists, moralists, etiquette experts, and the writers of scholarly glosses.

90 *the world's servant*: 'The *primary* is that which serves, the *antithetical* is that which creates' (*AV*, p. 85).

91 *whatever task's most difficult*: compare l. 40, 'whatever whim's most diffi-

cult'. In the ascent to Phase 15, the soul was governed by its own desires; on the other side, the soul submits to some external authority.

96–97 *Because you ... never wrote a book, your thought is clear*: Hugh Kenner compares (*Yeats: An Annual of Critical and Textual Studies* 3 [1985]: 173) a passage from Yeats's 1909 diary: 'Neither Christ nor Buddha nor Socrates wrote a book, for to do that is to exchange life for a logical process' (*A: E* 1; *Mem*, p. 139); and also the end of Coleridge's *Biographia Literaria* XI, quoting Herder: 'With the greatest possible solicitude avoid authorship ... he, who sends away through the pen and press every thought ... will become a mere journeyman of the printing-office, a *compositor*'.

101–2 *no deformity / But saves us from a dream*: 'The world begins to long for the arbitrary and accidental, for the grotesque, the repulsive and the terrible, that it may be cured of desire' (*AV*, p. 295).

103 *the last servile crescent*: Phase 28, that of the Fool, where the soul 'is but a straw blown by the wind' (*AV*, p. 182).

108–9 *to triumph / At the perfection of one's obedience*: compare 'The Double Vision of Michael Robartes' I 16: 'Triumph that we obey'.

112 *Insipid as the dough*: at Phase 1, 'Mind has become indifferent to good and evil, to truth and falsehood; body has become undifferentiated, dough-like' (*AV*, p. 183).

115 *cook Nature*: the fourth quarter ends in the soul's dissolution in God; but when the soul is reborn again at Phase 2, in the first quarter, it finds itself dissolved in Nature, and needs to discover a human shape.

117 *the escape*: Yeats's system permits an escape from the cycles of generation, called the Thirteenth Cone – though nowhere (except perhaps in 'All Souls' Night', ll. 54–60) did Yeats invest any great effort of imagination in describing it. In the following lines Robartes suggests that at Phase 1 the lucky soul might slip off the cycle and enter this nirvana. 'Neither between death and birth nor between birth and death can the soul find more than momentary happiness; its object is to pass rapidly round its circle and find freedom from that circle' (*AV*, p. 236).

118 *Hunchback and Saint*: Phases 26 and 27, respectively. See 'The Saint and the Hunchback'.

119–20 *The burning bow that once could shoot an arrow / Out of the up and down*: the arrow represents the soul's escape from the gravitational pull of the reincarnative cycles. Yeats once had a vision of 'a marvellous naked woman shooting an arrow at a star'; when he asked a 'soror of my Order' what this meant, she told him that it signified the straight path of the intellect out of 'winding nature' (*Mem*, p. 100, 103–4) – see also *M*, p. 340, 'Parnell's Funeral' I 8, and 'The Gift of Harun Al-Rashid', ll. 142–43: 'Those terrible implacable straight lines / Drawn through the wandering vegetative dream'. Bloom (*Yeats*, p. 259) compares the arrow from Albion's bow shot through the heavens in Blake's *Jerusalem* 98:3, heralding the final regeneration of the human race.

121 *beauty's cruelty and wisdom's chatter*: the *antithetical* and the *primary*, respectively, in their most maddening aspects.

123 *Deformity of body and of mind*: the first quarter and the fourth quarter, respectively. Yeats quoted this line and some preceding words to describe the climax of *The Cat and the Moon*, where a lame beggar is blessed and starts to dance (*VPl*, p. 805).

128 *I'd play a part*: Aherne imagines himself as a persona in Yeats's imagination – but soon withdraws into uncommunicative transcendence.

136–37 he laughed to think that what seemed hard / Should be so simple: compare *The Hour-Glass* (1914), ll. 501–4: 'Strange that I should be blind to the great secret, / And that so simple a man might ... laugh and cry, because it was so simple'.

137 a bat rose: a literalizing of the simile of l. 106, where the soul at Phase 1 is compared to a bat – indeed the 'natural' landscape of the whole poem seems populated with supernatural images. For other bats, see *The Wanderings of Oisin* II 229, where a bat-cry summons Oisin away from the second island; and *The Resurrection* (1931), ll. 231–32: 'in their faces a high keen joy like the cry of a bat'.

The Cat and the Moon

The final poems in *The Wild Swans at Coole* attempt to relate the abstract entities posited in 'The Phases of the Moon' to common life. It is as if Robartes and Aherne had delivered a challenge to the poet burning the midnight oil in his lonely tower – in the following poems Yeats tried to show that the most abstruse and difficult parts of the Great Wheel exert power over the particulars of man's existence.

'The Cat and the Moon' is the lyric that opens and closes Yeats's play of the same name, written in 1917 but not published until 1926. The play concerns a blind man who carries a lame saint on his back – emblems of self and anti-self, or of body and soul, as reciprocal and coordinated as the cat and the moon:

> I wrote a little poem where a cat is disturbed by the moon, and in the changing pupils of its eyes seems to repeat the movement of the moon's changes, and allowed myself as I wrote to think of the cat as the normal

> man and of the moon as the opposite he seeks perpetually, or as having any meaning I have conferred upon the moon elsewhere. Doubtless, too, when the lame man takes the saint upon his back, the normal man has become one with his opposite . . . (*VPl*, p. 807; *Ex*, pp. 402–3)

The poem can also be interpreted as an exposition of the tidal pressure exercised upon unconscious human life by the moon's changes of phase. Yeats associated his wife with a cat, as he explained in his account of how her dreams sometimes interfered with the transmission of the automatic script: 'she dreamed she was a cat lapping milk or a cat curled up asleep and therefore dumb. The cat returned night after night, and once when I tried to drive it away by making the sound one makes when playing at being a dog to amuse a child, she awoke trembling' (*AV*, p. 10). Yeats also suggested at the end of 'The Gift of Harun Al-Rashid' that *A Vision* was nothing more than an expression of his wife's body. The shift of the pupils of the cat's eyes, then, can be seen as an anticipation of Mrs Yeats's trance-sensitivity to the lunar forces that dictated *A Vision* – though the cat here is male.

1–4, 17–28: Yeats quoted these lines to illustrate his thesis that national Unity of Culture is impossible in our age, except for 'some small circle of men and women . . . till the moon bring round its century' (*A: TG* 3).

1–2 *The cat went here and there / And the moon spun round like a top*: compare 'He and She', ll. 1–2: 'As the moon sidles up / Must she sidle up'.

2 *the nearest kin of the moon*: compare 'Lines Written in Dejection', l. 3: 'the dark leopards of the moon'. In 1910 Yeats used lunar kinship as a metaphor for general aesthetic receptiveness: 'poets . . . ladies who delight in Ricard's portraits or Debussy's music, all those whose senses feel instantly every change in our mother the moon' (*EI*, p. 238).

5 *Minnaloushe*: Iseult Gonne's Persian cat – see *M*, p. 319.

6 *wander and wail*: the cat's random motion, as it comes under the moon's control, turns into a 'dance' (l. 11).

11 *do you dance?*: Henn has compared (*LT*, p. 187) a passage from *John Sherman* II iv: 'a little black cat was leaping after its shadow. "Ah! . . . it would be a good thing to be a little black cat. To leap about in the moonlight . . ."' (*JSD*, p. 69).

14 *Maybe the moon may learn*: it seems that the cat can influence the moon, as well as vice versa.

22–24: compare 'Easter, 1916', ll. 46–48.

The Saint and the Hunchback

The Saint and the Hunchback are the emblems of two of the last three phases (26 and 27 – the Fool is Phase 28) of the Great Wheel, the soul's reincarnative cycle, in which each incarnation corresponds to a day of the lunar month. During these phases the soul loses all identity, all peculiarity, and vanishes into objectivity – the cold, rigid state where only things are real, and dreams and fantasies do not exist. In *A Vision* Yeats explained that the Hunchback, or Multiple Man, was only a lump of clay or dough (see 'The Phases of the Moon', l. 112) in which every personality was latent, but none could be realized. In this dialogue-poem, the Hunchback is wretched because some heroic self cannot be fully manifested; the Saint is wretched because a heroic self cannot be fully suppressed.

1 *lift your hand and bless*: compare 'The Double Vision of Michael Robartes' II 4: 'Hand lifted up that blest'.

4 *A Roman Caesar is held down*: the Hunchback's 'deformity may be of any kind, great or little, for it is but symbolised in the hump that thwarts what seems the ambition of a Caesar or of an Achilles' (*AV*, p. 177). In a 1910 draft of *The Player Queen*, Decima, boasting of her skill at acting lofty parts, said, 'There are a hundred queens inside my ribs'; a little later we hear of 'kings that cried "I am great Alexander / Or Caesar come again"' (Bradford, *WPQ*, pp. 205, 208).

5 *God tries each man*: compare 'Two Songs of a Fool' I 13–14.

8 *taws*: compare 'The Phases of the Moon', ll. 42 and 68; also 'Among School Children' VI 3, where Aristotle thrashes Alexander the Great with taws. Yeats sometimes imagined the Hunchback also engaged in violent self-purgation: in a table of emblems, Yeats listed for Phase 26, 'Hunchback fighting his shadow on ground with sword which bleeds' (*MAV* II, p. 401) The Hunchback, like the Saint, must at all costs expunge his *Mask*.

10 *Greek Alexander from my flesh*: Alexander the Great (356–323 BC), conqueror of the known world. Yeats wrote of the Saint: 'If he possess intellect he will use it but to serve perception and renunciation. His joy is to be nothing, to do nothing, to think nothing' (*AV*, p. 180). The hunchback's fate, by contrast, is to be everything.

11 *Augustus Caesar*: Roman emperor (63 BC–AD 14). The Saint 'scourges in his body the Roman and Christian conquerors: Alexander and Caesar are famished in his cell' (*M*, p. 338). Compare 'Demon and Beast', l. 50: 'What had the Caesars but their thrones?' – a line written from a Saint's perspective

12 *Alcibiades*: friend of Socrates, celebrated for beauty, bravery, and cleverness (450–404 BC). The ugly hunchback is fascinated by beauty.

Two Songs of a Fool

Yeats had previously spoken in the voice of the fool, for example in 'Tom O'Roughley'; but here he gave unusual precision to the persona by suggesting the whole progress of masks through the final quarter of the Great Wheel – from wise man to saint to fool, illustrating the soul's steady loss of control over the ascendant power of the objective world. The fool of these poems is a caricature of the wise man, perplexed by his responsibilities, anxious not to betray the small trusts assigned him.

I 1 *A speckled cat and a tame hare*: the cat is associated with Georgie Yeats (see 'The Cat and the Moon'), and the hare with Iseult Gonne (see 'The Death of a Hare').

I 13 *I bear a burden that might well try*: compare 'The Saint and the Hunchback', l. 5.

I 18 *My great responsibilities*: compare the motto of *Responsibilities*: 'In dreams begins responsibility'.

II 2 *cat slept on my knee*: compare 'Solomon to Sheba', ll. 9–10: 'Sheba, / Planted on his knees'.

II 6 *she drank the wind*: compare 'Among School Children' IV 3: 'Hollow of cheek as though it drank the wind' (referring to Maud Gonne).

Another Song of a Fool

This poem develops the theme of the end of the play *The Hour-Glass* (1914), where the Wise Man dies and a white butterfly comes out of his mouth; the Fool takes the butterfly in his hands and puts it in a golden casket, which an Angel carries to paradise. The butterfly is an old symbol for the soul; Yeats specifically associated butterflies with a joyous escape from pedantic learning: 'wisdom is a butterfly / And not a gloomy bird of prey' ('Tom O'Roughley', ll. 7–8). In the context of *A Vision*, the soul of the schoolmaster – the learned man – passes over the cusp between Phase 28 and Phase 1, and turns natural and random, ignorant. The fool is simply a more highly evolved version of the wise man, further along the Great Wheel; 'he would know all wisdom if he could know anything' (*AV*, p. 182; compare *The Hour-Glass*, ll. 570, 629). For a diagram of this poem's imagery sketched by Mrs Yeats, see the note to 'The Double Vision of Michael Robartes'.

2–3 *hands . . . eye*: see the note to 'Towards Break of Day', and 'Ego Dominus Tuus', l. 9.

5 *Once he lived a schoolmaster*: Yeats perhaps remembered Blake's picture, 'The Ghost of a Flea', which shows the flea as a muscular, scaly, humanoid

figure, carrying the eyepiece of a microscope. The schoolmaster once inflicted discipline; now he is himself a victim, in 'prison' (l. 2).

9–12: Yeats quoted these lines to illustrate how the talented, exuberant, undisciplined, but bitter young Irish writers of the early 1890s 'might yet lie ... nearest the honeyed comb' (*A: IP* 3).

12 *take the roses for his meat*: compare Marvell's 'The Nymph complaining for the death of her Faun' (1681), l. 83: 'Upon the Roses it would feed'; and also 'Among School Children' IV 4: 'took a mess of shadows for its meat'.

The Double Vision of Michael Robartes

This poem represents the extreme bound of Yeats's attempts to imagine the unimaginable – not until the poem 'Byzantium' did Yeats again go to such unearthly verges. The first of Michael Robartes' visions is of the objectivity of Phase 1, the dark of the moon, the state where the human soul contracts to zero, the zone of sheer thingliness. The second vision is of the subjectivity of Phase 15, the full moon, a condition of intolerable splendour, in which the outer world has effaced itself into a velvet backdrop against which distinct images preen, images so supercharged with meaning that they mean almost nothing at all.

Each vision is also an allegory of the artistic process. The first vision shows how the *primary* imagination operates: it is an automaton, a puppet that keeps generating more puppets in an endless mechanical multiplication of the inhuman. Yeats thought that this procedure was typical of twentieth-century art: in a passage from a document preliminary to *A Vision*, Yeats had Michael Robartes speak of 'Mr Pound, not transfigured but transfixed contemplat[ing] the race ... till hatred turns the flesh to wood and the nerves to wire' (*MAV* II, p. 28). In *A Vision* Yeats wrote that in modern art 'the intellect turns upon itself': 'Mr Ezra Pound, Mr Eliot, Mr Joyce, Signor Pirandello ... either eliminate from metaphor the poet's phantasy ... or ... break up the logical processes of thought by flooding them with associated ideas or words that seem to drift into the mind by chance' (*AV* [1925], p. 211). The randomness and the rigidity of modern art are both part of a movement to depersonalize, to move towards complete objectivity.

The second vision shows how the *antithetical* imagination operates. At Phase 1 all was apathy and numbness of mind; but here are the images that propose to gratify the intensest desires of body and intellect. The supernatural quality of these images is indicated by a language of paradox and oxymoron: the imagination has travelled to a domain where the categories of stillness and motion, death and life, are no longer valid. It is possible to educe some significance from the images, but they are so lofty, elated, self-referential, that they scarcely gesture towards the lower world where words have common meanings. Indeed the sequence of dancer, sphinx, and Buddha has a certain defiant arbitrariness: Yeats even wrote that 'I should have put Christ instead of Buddha' (*AV* [1937], p. 208), but it little troubled him to leave the wrong God in the poem. Yeats's description of the difficulties of Italian Renaissance painters in embodying ultimate beauty could serve as a gloss on part II of this poem: 'Because the 15th Phase can never find direct human expression, being a supernatural incarnation, it impressed upon work and thought an element of strain and artifice, a desire to combine elements which may be incompatible, or which suggest by their combination something supernatural' (*AV*, p. 292).

The personal significance of this poem, and of 'Another Song of a Fool' and of 'Towards Break of Day', is shown in the automatic script of 7 Jan. 1919, when Mrs Yeats drew a diagram (signed 'Thomas', the Control) of the ruined chapel at Cashel and the hill on which it rests, surrounded by images, some of which Yeats used in this complex of poems: an eye, a book, a hand holding a rod, a Maltese cross depending from a bird, and perhaps a butterfly. Mrs Yeats evidently drew this sketch without lifting her hand from the paper, and possibly the lines connecting all these images suggest the intimacy between the senses (eye and hand) and their objects. (This sketch is reproduced in *MAV* II, p. 199.) When asked the meaning of this drawing, Thomas explained: 'You are empty – drained dry – the true moment for vision – a new influx must come this time from the past – you are drained dry from looking into the future . . . so go to the past – A historical and spiritual past – the church the castle on the hill . . . Cormac' (*MAV* II, p. 200). The final poems in *The Wild Swans at Coole* (and indeed the volume as a whole) seem to depend greatly upon the juxtaposition of visual emblems; when Yeats asked T. Sturge Moore to design the book cover, he mentioned these motifs: 'a torch, a candle in waves, a hawk, a phoenix, a moon, a butterfly, a hunchback' (*TSMC*, p. 33).

It should be noted that much of the poem's effect comes from its metre. It is a Horatian Ode, a metre with a most distinguished history in English prosody, from Milton's translation of Horace's Ode I v, to Marvell's 'An Horatian Ode upon Cromwel's return from Ireland', to Collins' 'Ode to Evening', to Auden's 'The Horatians'.

I 1 *Cashel*: site of the ruins of an ancient chapel (Co. Tipperary) restored by Cormac MacCarthy in the early 12th century – 'no congregation has climbed to the Rock of Cashel since the stout Church of Ireland bishop took the lead roof from the Gothic church to save his legs' (*Ex*, pp. 266–67). Yeats once retold D. R. McAnally's story of a young man, mourning his drowned sweetheart, and communing till old age with the ghosts on the rocks of Cashel (*LNI*, p. 202).

I 6 *pounded*: compare 'On Woman', l. 30: 'The Pestle of the moon'; also 'The

Phases of the Moon', l. 115: 'cook Nature'.

I 7 *When had I my own will?*: Michael Robartes participates imaginatively in the involuntary obedience typical of Phase 1.

I 9–12: these lines are quoted in *AV* (1925), p. 213, to illustrate the decadent adoration of physical force found at the end of a millennium. With a similar intent ll. 9–16 are quoted in 'A People's Theatre' to suggest the condition of the human race if it fell 'under some tyranny that would cease to be a tyranny, so perfect our acquiescence' (*Ex*, p. 259).

I 10 *wire-jointed jaws and limbs of wood*: see 'The Dolls' for the theme of puppets. In *The Herne's Egg* (1938) II 209, the priestess Attracta, summoned by her god, is called 'A doll upon a wire'.

I 16 *Triumph that we obey*: compare 'The Phases of the Moon', ll. 108–9: 'to triumph / At the perfection of one's own obedience'.

II 2–3 *A Sphinx* ... *A Buddha*: these two creatures flank the dancer who symbolizes Phase 15 – the Sphinx stands for Phases 12–14, and the Buddha for Phases 16–18. In *A Vision*, Yeats wrote of certain astrological correspondences to the Great Wheel: Phases 16–18 are associated with the conjunction of the planets Mars and Venus, Phases 12–14 with the conjunction of Jupiter and Saturn: 'These two conjunctions . . are certainly ... the outward-looking mind, love and its lure, contrasted with introspective knowledge of the mind's self-begotten unity, an intellectual excitement. They stand, so to speak, like heraldic supporters guarding the mystery of the fifteenth phase. In certain lines written years ago in the first excitement of discovery I compared one to the Sphinx and one to Buddha' (*AV* [1937], pp. 207–8; see also the poem 'Conjunctions').

As the soul approaches Phase 15, its universe narrows and intensifies until it comprises only a few objects of uncanny brilliance. The Buddha is an emblem of desire (seeking fulfilment outside itself), and the Sphinx is an emblem of intellect (seeking fulfilment inside itself); and thus it seems that the soul at Phase 15 stares at a landscape so depopulated that it contains nothing but the soul's own faculties resolved into images. At Phase 15 desire and intellect – *Will* and *Creative Mind* in Yeats's technical language – are fully united; therefore, in some still weirder landscape, still closer to perfection, the Sphinx and the Buddha will become one hybrid being.

In 'The Philosophy of Shelley's Poetry' (1900), Yeats wrote that the tower and the cave were obsessive elements in Shelley's landscapes because they suggested 'a contrast between the mind looking outward upon men and things and the mind looking inward upon itself' (*EI*, p. 87). Yeats placed Shelley in the same lunar niche as himself, Phase 17; and in this poem he seems to repeat Shelley's symbolic scheme under different, more exotic, figures. The Sphinx may have been partly suggested by Wilde's poem 'The Sphinx'

(1894), where a sphinx – who copulates with monstrous Egyptian gods – embodies the highest aesthetic and sexual tension; in later life Yeats remembered Hegel's use of Oedipus solving the sphinx's riddle as an allegory of mankind's self-deliverance from bondage to nature (*EI*, p. 466).

Buddha appears again in Yeats's work in 'The Statues', l. 24; see also the note to 'Under Ben Bulben' I 1, and a passage from the so-called 'De Burgh' version of the unfinished *The Speckled Bird*, which uses the image of the inactive Buddha, sitting under a tree, to illustrate the principle that doing things always destroys the power of thinking (*LTMSB*, pp. 359–60). Buddha plays little role in the historical scheme of *A Vision* as published, but Yeats once thought of using Buddha as an *antithetical* forerunner of the *primary* Christ (*MAV* II, p. 34). Yeats again paired Buddha and Sphinx in an essay on Japanese theatre: 'It is even possible that being is only possessed completely by the dead, and that it is some knowledge of this that makes us gaze with so much emotion upon the face of the Sphinx or of Buddha' (*EI*, p. 226).

II 4 *Hand lifted up that blest*: compare 'The Saint and the Hunchback', l. 1: 'lift your hand and bless'.

II 5 *a girl at play*: this dancer represents Phase 15 because she has superseded all the divisions of human life – she is a Thinking Body (see 'To a Young Beauty', l. 18).

II 9–20: these lines are quoted in *AV*, p. 208.

II 25–26 *what but eye and ear silence the mind / With the minute particulars of mankind?*: the phrase 'minute particulars' is from Blake ('every Minute Particular is Holy', *Jerusalem* 69:42, and elsewhere), as is the idea that the organs of sense ('eye and ear') clog, impede the superior vision of the inner eye. Yeats also associated the phrase *minute particulars* with Blake's one-time mentor Swedenborg, in whose 'earth-resembling' afterlife 'the "most minute particulars which enter the memory remain there and are never obliterated"' (*Ex*, p. 35).

II 27–28 *Mind moved yet seemed to stop / As 'twere a spinning-top*: these lines are quoted in *AV* (1925), p. 238, to illustrate the state of *Beatitude* reached by the soul after death, where 'an extreme activity is indistinguishable from an equal passivity'. Also see 'The Cat and the Moon', ll. 1–2. T. S. Eliot's image of 'the still point of the turning world' ('Burnt Norton' II and elsewhere) similarly attempts to describe the supernatural through the meeting of the extremes of motion and stasis.

II 1–3 *I knew that I had seen ... Or else my dreams*: compare 'Men Improve with the Years', l. 13: 'Is this my dream, or the truth?'; and Keats, 'Ode to a Nightingale' (1819), l. 79: 'Was it a vision, or a waking dream?' Also compare 'Under Ben Bulben' IV 26: 'When sleepers wake and yet still dream'.

III 5 *fling into my meat*: in 'The Thinking of the Body' Yeats wrote of paintings that make our thought 'rush out to the edges of our flesh' (*EI*, p. 292). Just as Michael Robartes turned into an automaton during his first vision (I 7), so the Thinking Body of the dancer energizes his body here – compare 'Michael Robartes and the Dancer', l. 47.

III 6 *A crazy juice*: compare 'A Prayer for my Daughter', l. 35: 'A crazy salad'.

III 8 *Homer's Paragon*: Helen of Troy, called a paragon in Marlowe's *Dr Faustus* V i 31.

III 10 *pitch of folly*: compare 'A Woman Homer Sung', l. 11.

III 13: the syntax is difficult. 'The commonness of thought' is parallel to 'the dark moon'; 'images' is parallel to 'the full' (III 12).

III 16 *kissed a stone*: in 'Crazy Jane on the Mountain', ll. 19–20, Crazy Jane sees a vision of Cuchulain and Emer, then 'Propped upon my two knees, / I kissed a stone'. Possibly this is a gesture by which the dreamer reorients himself in normal reality.

MICHAEL ROBARTES AND THE DANCER (1921)

The theme of the poem that gives the title to this volume is education – the superiority of the discipline of the body, of the whole self, to the schooling of the mind alone. This theme is pursued in several more poems: the contrast between abstract mental hatred and physical grace ('On a Political Prisoner', 'A Prayer for my Daughter'); or the contrast between the aged and disengaged poet, freed at last from bodily passion, and the fauna of nature ('Demon and Beast'). In many ways Yeats attempts to see the body as the vehicle of true wisdom; even the historical process of *A Vision* has little meaning unless a rough beast (in 'The Second Coming') can be found to embody it.

A feature of this book is the poet's unusual candour about his relation to his wife (in poems such as 'Under Saturn'), and his unusual specificity about politics. In certain earlier poems, such as 'To a Wealthy Man ...' and 'Paudeen', Yeats discussed local politics and urban situations. But there he wrote chiefly to disparage them against the background of antiquity; in this volume Yeats attempts to write sympathetically of contemporary events, and to use the doctrines of *A Vision* to see a design in modern history, to show how political actions are governed by forces beyond the ordinary world. In 1932 Yeats, reviewing the evolution of modern Irish literature, noted with some displeasure that 'a school of satire' had become dominant: 'we might ... have founded a school that could have substituted, as only a literature without satirical or realistic prepossessions could, positive desires for the negative passion of a national movement' (*VPl*, p. 572). Here the satirist becomes, guardedly, a panegyrist.

Michael Robartes and the Dancer

The Dancer in this poem was based on Iseult Gonne. Michael Robartes was originally an unworldly persona associated with the imagination's pride in its images (see the headnote to *The Wind among the Reeds*), then a code name for the instructors who presented Yeats with supernatural revelation (see 'The Phases of the Moon' and Introduction XI), and at last simply an emphatic and self-confident disguise of Yeats himself. The argument against female education that Robartes advances is playfully meant (and the Dancer's responses, as at l. 41, are as witty as his own) – but in the context of the rest of the volume, in which vehement, dragonish women like Con Markiewicz ruin themselves by pursuing abstract ideals, it seems likely that the poet was partly serious in discouraging a beautiful woman from attending college, from losing physical suppleness and grace. As Elizabeth Cullingford notes (*Yeats Annual* 4 [1986]: 32), Yeats had nothing but scorn for the woman who has abandoned the artistic discipline of beauty – for the 'woman of New York or Paris who has renounced her rouge pot to lose her figure and grow coarse of skin' (*AV* [1925], p. 213). Many of these themes reappear in a later poem on the subject of education, 'Among School Children'.

1 *Opinion is not worth a rush*: compare 'A Prayer for my Daughter', l. 58: 'let her think opinions are accursed'.

2 *the knight*: St George, a common theme in Renaissance art.

4 *That dragon*: compare *The Wanderings of Oisin* II, in which Oisin fights a demon every fourth day for a hundred years; also 'The Poet pleads with the Elemental Powers', l. 4: 'The Polar Dragon'; and 'Her Triumph', l. 1: 'I did the dragon's will until you came'.

6 *The half-dead dragon was her thought*: in many poems, beginning with 'The Two Trees', Yeats discussed the uglifying power of abstract thought, vs. the sanctity of bodily self-possession. For another metaphor of thought, see 'Ribh considers Christian Love insufficient', ll. 16–17: 'Thought is a garment and the soul's a bride / That cannot in that trash and tinsel hide'. For another dragon in a woman's mind, see *Deirdre* (1907), ll. 163–65: 'Myself wars on myself, for I myself – / That do my husband's will, yet fear to do it – / Grow dragonish to myself'.

10–12 *She would have time to turn her eyes . . . upon the glass / And on the instant would grow wise*: compare *Baile and Aillinn*, l. 98, '*Who being lovely was so wise*'. For the theme of the wisdom of the Thinking Body, see 'To a Young Beauty', l. 18, and *EI*, p. 292. Though he once wrote of 'the heroic discipline of the looking-glass' (*EI*, p. 270), Yeats usually discouraged women from looking in mirrors – see 'The Two Trees', l. 21, and 'A Prayer for my Daughter', l. 19; also compare 'The Hero, the Girl, and the Fool', l. 1: 'I rage at my own image in the glass'.

16–17 *he will turn green with rage / At all that is not pictured there*: that is, the lover will dismiss the importance of a woman's every accomplishment not directly visible on her body – this is also the meaning of l. 24, and of the parable of the knight and the dragon.

19 *Athena*: the Greek goddess of wisdom – see 'A Thought from Propertius', l. 6.

26 *Paul Veronese*: Paolo Veronese (1528–88), a painter active in Venice (the 'lagoon' of l. 29), notable for his sensuous and appetizing scenes.

32 *Michael Angelo*: official great genius of the Italian Renaissance (1475–1564), who painted scenes from the Old Testament on the roof of the Sistine Chapel of the Vatican in Rome. Many of the figures have thick torsos, with muscular tension visible in contorted limbs – this carnal forthrightness led Yeats to take these paintings as proof of the body's majesty. See also 'An Acre of Grass', l. 19, 'Under Ben Bulben' IV 9, and 'Long-legged Fly', l. 26.

33 *His 'Morning' and his 'Night'*: sculptures in the Medici Chapel in Florence, which Yeats visited in 1907.

40 *His thought or His mere body?*: the Eucharist, in which Christ's body is given to the communicants – the final proof that Incarnation is the source of revelation. Compare *EI*, p. 235: 'the Deity gives us ... not His thoughts or His convictions but His flesh and blood'.

41 *My wretched dragon*: that is, my thought, or mind – see l. 6.

43 *this Latin text*: a parody of Michael Robartes' appeals to obscure sacred documents – as in *AV* (1925), p. xix. Compare 'For Anne Gregory', l. 15.

44 *composite*: divided into body and soul. Compare 'A Bronze Head', l. 12.

47 *lead us to the like*: as in 'The Double Vision of Michael Robartes' III 5, the spectacle of profound embodiedness inspires a similar condition in the spectator.

52 *They say such different things at school*: compare 'Adam's Curse', l. 19: 'they do not talk of it at school'.

Solomon and the Witch

For the persona of Solomon, in whom wisdom is combined with bodily vigour, see 'Solomon to Sheba'. The present poem explains Mrs Yeats's mediumistic powers as an expression of ideal sexual passion – just as 'The Gift of Harun Al-Rashid', l. 185, explains the magical designs of *A Vision* as an expression of Mrs Yeats's body.

1 *that Arab lady*: the Queen of Sheba – Georgie Yeats.

6 *Who understood*: the persona of Solomon, the universal interpreter, contrasts

strongly with the ignorant 'Yeats' of such poems as 'The Phases of the Moon'.

9 *A cockerel*: Yeats's poetry is full of bird's cries – see 'A Memory of Youth', l. 19. The crowing of this cock signifies the shriek of orgasm, and the soul's sudden shock of receptivity to something beyond life, and also the end of the world. (According to 'The Moods', all grand passion comes from some supernatural source.) For another eerie cock, even more difficult to please, see 'Byzantium', l. 20. In 'An Image from a Past Life', l. 5, a bird's or beasts's scream signals the approach of a sweetheart from a former incarnation; in 'My Table', l. 32, Juno's peacock screams to announce the end of an era; and in 'Under Ben Bulben' I 4, the sages' speech sets 'the cocks a-crow'. In all these instances a bird's cry heralds historical or personal upheaval. For other transcendental cock-a-doodle-doos, marking divisions between epochs, see 'The Adoration of the Magi' (1897), where an old man, announcing the end of the Christian era, suddenly crows like a rooster (*M*, pp. 311–12); the early drafts of *The Player Queen*, where a beggar crows like a cock whenever the kingdom's ruler dies (Bradford, *WPQ*, p. 39); and an essay on Berkeley, where Yeats wrote of 'the morning cock-crow of our Hellenistic age' (*EI*, p. 407). Less spectacular cock-crows can be found in the juvenile *Mosada* II 29 (a song about Peter's denial of Christ [*VP*, p. 697]) and in *The Dreaming of the Bones* (1919), ll. 105, 308, where a cock's crow will dispel the spectres of night.

14 *Chance being one with Choice at last*: *Chance* is what you get; *Choice* is what you want. On earth they never coincide – the world never offers a man the exact object of his desire. In a note to *Calvary* (1920), Yeats reported that Michael Robartes said, '"Kusta ben Luki has taught us to divide all things into Chance and Choice ... In God alone, indeed, can they be united, yet each be perfect"' (*VPl*, p. 790). In the automatic script of 26 Nov. 1919, the spirit Ameritus said that the Beatific Vision is achieved when there is 'neither choice nor chance'; Yeats took this to mean 'when chance & choice are one' (*MAV* II, p. 363). Compare also 'On Woman', l. 41; 'All Souls' Night', l. 58: 'Being both Chance and Choice'; and 'Chosen', l. 1: 'The lot of love is chosen'. This antithesis appeared already in Yeats's juvenilia: in *The Island of Statues* I iii 38–39, Almintor wonders whether 'Mayhap 'twere better that aside I throw / All choice, and give to chance for guiding chance' (*VP*, p. 656); and Chance wins the chess-game in 'Time and the Witch Vivien', l. 60 (*VP*, p. 722).

15 *the brigand apple*: the fruit of the tree of knowledge of good and evil, in Eden.

19 *love has a spider's eye*: as Henn notes (*LT*, p. 57), the source of this is Donne's 'Twicknam garden', ll. 6–7: 'The spider love, which transubstantiates all, / And can convert Manna to gall'. Yeats also may allude to this poem in 'Men Improve with the Years', l. 2.

24 *when at last that murder's over*: compare 'Crazy Jane Grown Old . . .', in which the sexual act is imagined as an act of double murder.

26–27 *each an imagined image brings / And finds a real image*: this seems to paraphrase the situation in Keats's 'The Eve of St Agnes' (1819) XXXIV.

28 *Yet the world ends*: since the world's existence, according to *A Vision*, depends on the antinomy of objectivity (Chance) and subjectivity (Choice), the world ends when those two collapse into one. Compare *A Vision*, p. 52, where Robartes says, '"The marriage bed is the symbol of the solved antinomy, and were more than symbol could a man there lose and keep his identity."'

30 *oil and wick*: compare 'The Living Beauty', l. 1: 'wick and oil'.

42 *the crushed grass where we have lain*: compare 'Memory'.

An Image from a Past Life

In the previous poem Yeats posited, and seemed almost to attain, a perfect sexual passion where each lover found his ideal of love in the other's arms. In this poem, however, the imaginary woman and the real one diverge sharply. Yeats's long note to this poem begins with a 'letter' by Michael Robartes describing the Arabian seer Kusta-ben-Luki:

> 'He saw occasionally during sleep a woman's face and later on found in a Persian painting a face resembling, though not identical with the dream-face, which was he considered that of a woman loved in another life. Presently he met & loved a beautiful woman whose face also resembled, without being identical, that of his dream. Later on he made a long journey to purchase the painting which was, he said, the better likeness, and found on his return that his mistress had left him in a fit of jealousy'. (*VP*, p. 821)

Michael Robartes went on to describe how (contrary to psychoanalytic theory) 'no concrete dream-image is ever from our memory', and Yeats commented that he found this true, for people he knew were always represented in his dreams by a 'stool or a chair' or some other remote object. In another 'letter' Robartes taught:

> 'No lover, no husband has ever met in dreams the true image of wife or mistress. She who has perhaps filled his whole life with joy or disquiet cannot enter there. Her image can fill every moment of his waking life but only its counterfeit comes to him in sleep; . . . these counterfeits . . . are the forms of those whom he has loved in some past earthly life, chosen from *Spiritus Mundi* by the subconscious will, and through them, for they are not always hollow shades, the dead at whiles outface a living rival'. They are the forms of Over Shadowers as they are called. (*VP*, p. 822)

Yeats at last mentioned his poem as a presentation of an obsessive Over Shadower, 'continually perplexing and frustrating natural instinct':

> When I wrote An Image from a Past Life, I had merely begun my study of the various papers upon the subject, but I do not think I misstated Robartes' thought in permitting the woman and not the man to see the Over Shadower ... No mind's contents are necessarily shut off from another, and in moments of excitement images pass from one mind to another with extraordinary ease ... (*VP*, p. 823)

(For more information about the Over Shadower, see *MAV* II, p. 316.) In the context of the following poem, 'Under Saturn', it is tempting to see 'An Image from a Past Life' as a description of a phantom Maud Gonne interposing herself between Yeats and his wife. Maud Gonne was, of course, alive when the poem was written; but Yeats thought that his soul and hers had played out many dramas together in previous incarnations.

As F. F. Farag notes (*W. B. Yeats 1865–1939 Centenary Essays*, ed. Maxwell and Bushrui, p. 43), a poem by Tagore, beginning with the words, 'In the dusky path of a dream I went to seek the love who was mine in a former life', was one of Yeats's sources – Yeats was to include Tagore's poem in *OBMV*.

5 *that scream*: compare the cockerel's crowing in 'Solomon and the Witch', l. 9.

7 *Image of poignant recollection*: compare 'Broken Dreams', l. 40: 'rambling talk with an image of air' (addressed to Maud Gonne).

14 *It had not learned its lesson*: that is, that 'He' had loved other women.

15 *Why have you laid your hands upon my eyes?*: compare *The Only Jealousy of Emer* (1919), ll. 251–53: 'my memories / Weigh down my hands, abash my eyes'.

27 *starry eddies of her hair*: compare 'He wishes his Beloved were Dead', ll. 9–10: 'your hair was bound and wound / About the stars'.

40 *her hair streams upon the wind*: the Sidhe, the pagan gods of old Ireland, 'are almost always said to wear no covering upon their heads, and to let their hair stream out' (*VP*, p. 800).

Under Saturn

This poem is an apology to Georgie Yeats for a gloomy mood – the poet is afraid that she will impute it to his brooding over Maud Gonne.

Title: the influence of the planet Saturn was thought to produce a cold, sluggish, leaden sensibility.

4 *the wisdom*: the automatic script preliminary to *A Vision*.

6 *my horse*: Pegasus – see 'The Fascination of What's Difficult', l. 4.

7–8 *an old cross Pollexfen ... a Middleton*: William Pollexfen and William Middleton – see the Introductory Rhymes to *Responsibilities*, ll. 15 and 13.

9 *a red-haired Yeats*: Rev. William Butler Yeats (1806–62), the poet's grandfather.

12 *Sligo*: town in northwest Ireland, the old home of the Yeats family, where the poet spent some summers in childhood.

Easter, 1916

This poem was inspired by the execution of fifteen leaders of the Easter Rebellion of 24 April 1916, when some 700 members of the Irish Republican Brotherhood occupied the centre of Dublin and proclaimed the founding of an Irish state no longer under the dominion of the British crown. British soldiers quickly moved in; after five days the uprising collapsed, and its leaders were court-martialled and, in some cases, shot. On 11 May 1916 Yeats wrote to Lady Gregory that he was trying to write a poem on the men executed: ' "terrible beauty has been born again" ... I had no idea that any public event could so deeply move me – and I am very despondent about the future. At the moment I feel that all the work of years has been overturned, all the bringing together of classes, all the freeing of Irish literature and criticism from politics' (*L*, p. 613).

The poem turns on the mutation of comedy into tragedy. Yeats described the differences between the two genres as follows: 'tragedy must always be a drowning and breaking of the dykes that separate man from man, and ... it is upon these dykes comedy keeps house'; and he quoted a phrase of Congreve's to define ' "humour" itself – the foundation of comedy – as a "singular and unavoidable way of doing anything peculiar to one man only" ' (*EI*, p. 241). The rebels of 'Easter, 1916' are comedians, full of idiosyncrasy, of 'character', until the rebellion begins: then, under a kind of historical pressure, coal fuses into diamond, and the rebels grow impersonal, universal, outside the flux of nature, no more individual than stones or tombstones. In his portraits of the rebels, Yeats shows how attractive youth, a somewhat lax sweetness of disposition, a comic boastfulness, can be altered by extreme tension into self-resignation, self-oblivion. (For more on the theme of tragedy, see 'The Gyres', l. 8.)

1 *them*: the rebels.

14 *where motley is worn*: Frayne compares a passage in a early review: 'this faithfulness to things tragic and bitter ... the Celt has above all others. Those

who have it, alone are worthy of great causes. Those who have it not, have in them some vein of hopeless levity, the harlequins of the earth' (*UP* I, p. 87).

15 *All changed, changed utterly*: compare 'The Wild Swans at Coole', l. 15: 'All's changed'.

16 *A terrible beauty is born*: Elizabeth Cullingford (*Yeats Annual* 4 [1986]: 39) compares Shelley's 'On the Medusa ...' (1819) V 1–6: 'the temptestuous loveliness of terror .. all the beauty and the terror there' – a poem on the petrifying power of grace. Pater remembered these lines when he wrote of the 'interfusion of the extremes of beauty and terror' in Leonardo's mind when he painted the *Medusa* (*The Renaissance* [1893], ed. Hill, p. 82). Shelley, Pater, and Yeats all posited a collapse of Burke's distinction between the sublime and the beautiful. Also compare Eliot, 'Gerontion' (1920): 'To lose beauty in terror'.

17 *That woman*: Con Markiewicz (1868–1927), née Gore-Booth, whom Yeats had known since 1894 (*L*, p. 239). She was active in the Rebellion, but her death sentence was commuted. Her beauty and poise in former years are celebrated in 'On a Political Prisoner' and 'In Memory of Eva Gore-Booth and Con Markiewicz'.

20 *Until her voice grew shrill*: 'her voice became shrill and high, but [in the 1890s] it was low and soft' (*Mem*, p. 78).

24 *This man had kept a school*: Patrick Pearse (1879–1916), the chief of the Rebellion and Commandant-General of the Provisional Government; his surrender to the British at the Dublin Post Office ended the Rebellion. He had founded a boys' school and was active in the movement to promote the Gaelic language. Pearse also appears in 'Sixteen Dead Men', l. 10, 'The Rose Tree', l. 2, 'The O'Rahilly', l. 12, 'Three Songs to the Same Burden' III 24, 'The Statues', l. 25, and *The Death of Cuchulain* (1939), l. 215. According to Pound, Yeats 'has said for years that Pearse was half-cracked and that he wouldn't be happy until he was hanged. He seemed to think Pearse had Emmet mania, same as some other lunatics think they are Napoleon or God' (Longenbach, *SC*, p. 256).

25 *our wingèd horse*: Pegasus – see 'The Fascination of What's Difficult', l. 4. Pearse wrote poetry.

26 *This other*: Thomas MacDonagh (1876–1916), an English teacher at University College, Dublin, and author of a play performed at the Abbey Theatre. In 1909 Yeats described him as a man of 'distinguished feeling', 'crushed by the mechanical logic and commonplace eloquence' of Ireland (*A: E* 44). He also appears in 'Sixteen Dead Men', l. 12.

31 *This other*: John MacBride, whom Maud Gonne had married in 1903 – compare 'The Grey Rock', l. 47: '*some poor lout*'. The marriage was unhappy,

and they separated in 1905.

34 *some*: Maud and Iseult Gonne.

43 *Enchanted to a stone*: compare 'The Two Kings', l. 94: 'the heart akin to the dumb stone'; and 'First Love', l. 8: 'a heart of stone'.

44 *trouble the living stream*: Yeats once wrote of an obsessive vision of a woman shooting at a star, an image that 'stood still, as it were, in the midst of the stream of my daily thought, so little did it resemble it' (*Mem*, p. 104).

53 *moor-hens*: see 'The Indian upon God', l. 3.

60–62: Yeats quoted these lines, and commented that, when he wrote them, he was thinking of an old Irish politician who composed a ballad of no literary merit; the ballad lamented that 'new poets and new movements should have taken something of their sacredness away' from Tone, Emmet, Roe – the great old names of the Irish heroes who fought England a hundred years ago (*A: TG* 5).

62 *As a mother names her child*: according to 'Shepherd and Goatherd', l. 89, the dead live their lives backwards until they become children again – here too death exerts some simplifying power.

66 *No, no, not night but death*: now the poet reasserts the terrible truth, after the beautiful simile of the mother and child – the poem is governed, as its refrain suggests, by rhythms of terror and beauty.

68 *England may keep faith*: the Home Rule Bill, granting Ireland a measure of independence, was passed by Parliament in 1913, then suspended in 1914 when the Great War began. Yeats considered that the rebellion might have been easily averted by more skilful English politicians (*L*, p. 613). It was always thought likely that the suspension would some day be lifted.

72–73 *excess of love / Bewildered*: Cullingford (*Yeats Annual* 4 [1986]: 37) notes that this recalls Shelley's *Alastor* (1816), ll. 181–82: 'sickened with excess / Of love'.

76 *Connolly*: James Connolly (1870–1916), a trade union leader and military commander of the uprising. He also appears in 'The Rose Tree', l. 2, 'The O'Rahilly', l. 12, and *The Death of Cuchulain*, l. 215.

Sixteen Dead Men

Just as 'Easter, 1916' described the pressure that turned Pearse and MacDonagh from sensitive educators and artists into revolutionaries, so the present poem describes the pressure that the ghosts of Pearse and MacDonagh can exert upon political controversies. The endless jabber of politicians, the art of compromise, the counsel of moderation, vanish before the focused intensity of the martyrs' call to action. The poem is based on the opposition between talk (ll. 1, 3, 9) and bone (ll. 12, 18): in death Pearse and Connolly are stripped to the essential – their message cuts to the quick. The metre of the poem is emphatic, marching, ballad-like – a call to popular action, as the poet himself stirs 'the boiling pot' (l. 6).

Title *Sixteen*: the fifteen rebel leaders executed by the British in 1916, plus Roger Casement – see 'Roger Casement'.

10 *Pearse*: see 'Easter, 1916', l. 24.

12 *MacDonagh's bony thumb*: see 'Easter, 1916', l. 26. Like a butcher who puts his thumb on the scales, the dead MacDonagh prevents a deliberate consideration of the issues for and against action against the British.

16 *Lord Edward and Wolfe Tone*: see 'September 1913', ll. 20-21, and also the passage cited in the note to 'Easter, 1916', ll. 60–62.

The Rose Tree

This poem can be seen as a specimen of the 'bone to bone' conversations of the heroic dead, as described in the last line of the previous poem.

1 *words are lightly spoken*: this continues the deprecation of political talk begun in the previous poem.

4 *our Rose Tree*: Irish culture, or a free Ireland. The Rose, Yeats's master-symbol, always had an Irish nationalistic component – see 'To Ireland in the Coming Times'. Jeffares quotes a ballad, 'Ireland's Liberty Tree' (*NCP*, p. 194), which may be a source for this poem.

17 *red blood*: as Jeffares notes (*NCP*, p. 194), Pearse once wrote, 'Bloodshed is a cleansing and a sanctifying thing' – see also 'Three Songs to the Same Burden' III 24–26; and *The Dreaming of the Bones* (1919), ll. 88–89, where a 1916 rebel speaks of 'fields / That have grown red from drinking blood like mine'. In occult lore, a blood pool can be a medium to invoke, excite, and vivify the spirits of the dead (*Ex*, p. 366–67); and in this poem the blood of martyrs becomes a kind of medium for the growth of Irish culture. For another tree fed on blood, see 'Vacillation' VI 11.

On a Political Prisoner

The political prisoner was Con Markiewicz – see 'Easter, 1916', l. 17. The reader may note that Yeats's account of her degeneration from ideal image to 'a bitter, an abstract thing' (l. 9) recalls the poet's descriptions of Maud Gonne – and indeed Yeats wrote to his wife, concerning this poem, 'I'm writing one on Con to avoid writing one on Maud. All of them in prison . . .'

(Jeffares, *NCP*, p. 195); and Yeats wrote to Pound, 'When Madame Gonne quarreled with me I felt it necessary to denounce Madame Markiewicz' (*MAV* II, p. 202). In fact it seems that Yeats regarded Con Markiewicz as a kind of miniature surrogate for Maud Gonne: 'She surprised me now at our first meeting by some small physical resemblance to Maud Gonne, through so much shorter and smaller, and by a very exact resemblance in voice' (*Mem*, p. 78).

The relation between the Countess Markiewicz and the gull is complex: since the poet compares her, as she formerly was, to a gull (l. 18), it is as if a lost, detached simile flies down to the prisoner, to remind her of the grace and simplicity that she no longer possesses.

3 *A grey gull lost its fear*: compare the wild animals that lose their fear of the mad king in 'The Madness of King Goll', ll. 45-47. A gull takes a bit of bread from the poet himself in 'Demon and Beast', l. 25. Gulls often suggest enchantment in Yeats's work: in *Deirdre* (1907), Lugaid Redstripe's wife 'had a seamew's body half the year' (l. 181), and in *The Player Queen* (1922), the heroine's father seems to be a seamew (II 119).

11–12 *Blind ... Drinking the foul ditch*: compare 'A Dialogue of Self and Soul' II 19: 'a blind man's ditch'.

13 *I saw her ride*: she was famous for her horsemanship.

14 *Ben Bulben*: a high promontory overlooking the Sligo estuary, dear to Yeats from childhood – see also 'Towards Break of Day', l. 6, 'The Tower' I 9, 'Alternative Song for the Severed Head ...', l. 2, and 'Under Ben Bulben'.

24 *the hollows of the sea*: the sea partly signifies tumultuous historical process, as is explicit in 'A Prayer for my Daughter', l. 16. The gull soared above the sea; but now, broken and fallen, the prisoner is engrossed in it. Compare the sea-bird of *Calvary* (1920), l. 173, flying 'Under a great wave's hollowing crest'.

The Leaders of the Crowd

The previous poems, such as 'Sixteen Dead Men', show Yeats's distaste for popular rhetoric; and in 'On a Political Prisoner' Yeats accused Con Markiewicz of submitting to 'some popular enmity' (l. 10). The present poem develops Yeats's objections to the populus and its opinions. The admirable man forms his own convictions; the weak, *primary* man succumbs to mass thought and mass feeling, is most pleased when most like everyone else.

2 *base intent*: Donoghue compares Yeats's wish for the founding of 'a new *Nation*, forbidding ... all personal attacks and all arguments that assume a

base motive in opponents' (*Mem*, p. 186).

6 *gutter*: 'In a battle like Ireland's which is one of poverty against wealth, we must prove our sincerity by making ourselves unpopular to wealth. We must accept the baptism of the gutter' (*A: DP* 9).

6 *Helicon*: a Greek mountain sacred to the Muses; the fountain of Hippocrene spurted from it when Pegasus struck it with his hoof.

8 *the student's lamp*: compare 'Ego Dominus Tuus', l. 3, and 'The Phases of the Moon', l. 11.

9–10 *solitude . . . crowd*: compare 'Parnell's Funeral' II 10: 'Their school a crowd, his master solitude'. Yeats often wrote of the visionary's need for solitude: for instance, he deplored Shelley's urge to write pamphlets and to change the world (*AV*, p. 143). Also see 'Long-legged Fly', where the poet claims that all great deeds come from solitary self-communion.

11 *loud music*: Yeats deprecated the '"vitality" . . . the energy . . . which is under the command of our common moments, sings, laughs, chatters, or looks its busy thoughts' (*EI*, p. 244).

12 *that lamp is from the tomb*: compare 'The Mountain Tomb', ll. 10–12: 'The everlasting taper lights the gloom . . . Our Father Rosicross sleeps in his tomb'.

Towards Break of Day

The explanation of the premise of this poem is found in a section of *A Vision* (1925), pp. 173–74, called 'Complementary Dreams':

> When two people meditate upon the one theme, who have established a supersensual link, they will invariably in my experience, no matter how many miles apart, see pass before the mind's eye complementary images, images that complete one another. One for instance may see a boat upon a still sea full of tumultuous people, and the other a boat full of motionless people upon a tumultuous sea. . . . One, for instance, will receive from a dream figure a ripe apple, another an unripe; one a lighted and one an unlighted candle, and so on. . . . I put an experience of this kind into ['Towards Break of Day'].

The complementary relationship of certain dreams is the same as that between self and anti-self (see 'Ego Dominus Tuus') – another example of the tendency of Yeats's imagination to run towards wholes. In the automatic script for 7 Jan. 1919, Thomas explains that the origin of complementary dreaming is not the memory: 'in nervous states you are more closely linked psychically – the nightmare of one runs along this link creates a shock to the other & then reacts [perhaps *then reacts* should read *the wire acts*] on the dreamer'; during the same session Mrs Yeats wrote 'Hand & eye / waterfall & stag . . . touch – desire to grasp / eye – desire to see / possessive hand – desiring eye' (*MAV* II, pp. 201–2). This is a summary of the imagery of the present poem, in which the hand fails to possess the object of touch – the waterfall – in the man's dream, and the eye fails to follow the object it desires to see – the stag – in the woman's dream. For more on hand-eye imagery, see the note to 'Ego Dominus Tuus', l. 9: 'handled least, least looked upon'.

Complementary dreams figure importantly in Yeats's work, partly because they represented a certain intimacy with the sharer – two dreamers embracing in the *Anima Mundi*, the world's storehouse of images. For another poem based on a complementary dream with Mrs Yeats, see 'The Double Vision of Michael Robartes'. Indeed Yeats thought of *A Vision* itself as a kind of dream shared by him and his wife – 'Two contemplating passions chose one theme / Through sheer bewilderment' ('The Gift of Harun Al-Rashid', ll. 117–18). Yeats's suppressed autobiography ends with an account of a complementary dream he shared with Maud Gonne, concerning flames that shot through the interior of a hollow statue (*Mem*, p. 134); and the third book of Yeats's unfinished novel *The Speckled Bird* ends with a complementary dream about the resurrection of Christ, shared by two characters who are versions of Yeats and Maud Gonne (*LTMSB*, pp. 165–66).

But complementary dreams intrigued Yeats philosophically as well as emotionally. In *On the Boiler* Yeats recounted some complementary dreams: 'My wife dreamt of a cat, daughter and nurse [dreamt of] a rat and a mouse between them. Events in time come upon us head-on like waves, each wave in some main character the opposite of its predecessor. But there are other events that lie side by side in space, complements one of another' (*Ex*, p. 449). Thus complementary dreams seemed proof that reality was founded upon antithesis, not upon cause-and-effect.

1–4: these lines are quoted in *AV* (1925), p. 174. The question asks whether the two dreams repeat each other, or complement each other.

6 *Ben Bulben*: see 'On a Political Prisoner', l. 14.

13 *knew my finger could but have touched*: compare 'To Dorothy Wellesley', l. 2: 'As though that hand could reach'.

23 *The marvellous stag of Arthur*: mentioned in Malory's *Morte d'Arthur* and in the Welsh collection of tales, *The Mabinogion*; in one episode a stag chased by hounds appears at Arthur's and Guinevere's marriage feast. In 'Miraculous Creatures' Yeats wrote of the Enchanted Woods, containing creatures 'of the race of the white stag that flits in and out of the tales of Arthur' (*M*, p. 65). In the unfinished *The Speckled Bird* II iv, the hero – who read the *Morte d'Arthur* as a boy – devises for his magical rituals a diagram of a stylized forest where Arthur's knights were to hunt symbolical creatures (*LTMSB*,

p. 134; see also p. 153). And in the automatic script for 24 Dec. 1918, Thomas spoke of 'The stag the will of the wisp the lure' – which Yeats equated with the Stag of Arthur in his wife's dream (*MAV* II, p. 191; see also p. 209). The crucial word here is *will-of-the-wisp*: the dream of the stag, like the dream of the waterfall, shows the elusiveness of the object of desire – even husband and wife are imponderable to each other's touch, incapable of being fully grasped. Yeats also mentioned King Arthur in *The Shadowy Waters*, l. 404, and in the juvenile *The Island of Statues* II iii 296 (*VP*, p. 678); and another marvellous stag, a transformation of the god Midhir, appears in 'The Two Kings', l. 6. In Ezra Pound's 'The White Stag' (1909), Arthur's stag becomes an emblem of the pursuit of fame.

Demon and Beast

In 1914 Yeats enumerated the traditional masks of the lyric poet as 'lover or saint, sage or sensualist, or mere mocker of all life' (*A: R* 24). Of these masks, the lover and the sage were most congenial to Yeats; but in this poem he tries to put on the unusual mask of the saint. According to the mathematics of *A Vision*, the man of Phase 17 – Yeats's phase of the moon – derives his *Body of Fate* (the sum of events destined to befall him) from Phase 27, the saint's phase. *A Vision* denominates this *Body of Fate* as *Loss* (p. 141). Here the poet attempts to come to terms with loss: loss of feeling, loss of passion, loss of receptivity to the world. This poem corresponds to 'Lines Written in Dejection' as mania corresponds to depression; and this poem is an important precursor of 'Sailing to Byzantium', in that its theme is the attempt to find compensation for the loss of the physical body.

2 *That crafty demon and that loud beast*: as l. 6 shows, the demon stands for hatred, the beast for desire – especially sexual desire. The situation is similar to that depicted on an allegorical emblem in *A Vision*: 'a man torn in two by an eagle and some sort of wild beast' (p. 38). This poem celebrates the liberation that comes when old age rids a man of attraction to and revulsion from the objects of the senses.

5 *perned in the gyre*: *perned* is Yeats's private word for *spun*, deriving from *pern*, meaning *spool* – there was a pern-mill in Sligo when Yeats was a boy (*A: R* 2). For *gyre*, see 'The Two Trees', l. 15.

7 *my freedom won*: this experience offers a foretaste of the soul's escape from the cycle of birth and death, described in 'The Phases of the Moon', ll. 119–23.

10 *Luke Wadding*: an Irish Franciscan monk (1588–1657), who founded a college in Rome; his portrait, by Ribera, hangs in the National Gallery in Dublin. The portraits in the gallery show the honourable dead, who seem to

invite the poet to participate in their abstraction from common life; they serve a function similar to that of the mosaic saints in 'Sailing to Byzantium'.

11 *Ormondes*: members of this family, to whom Yeats was related, were also portrayed in the National Gallery.

13 *Strafford*: the first Earl of Strafford (1593–1641) advised King Charles I and served as Ireland's Lord Deputy. His portrait is attributed to the school of Van Dyck.

22 *aimless joy*: see 'Tom O'Roughley', l. 4: 'An aimless joy is a pure joy'. Tom O'Roughley is a kind of holy fool; and in this stanza Yeats seems to be moving from the persona of the saint to that of the fool – the short step from Phase 27 to Phase 28. See 'The Phases of the Moon', l. 118.

23 *the little lake*: according to Jeffares (*NCP*, p. 200), this lake is in St Stephen's Green, Dublin, near Maud Gonne's house, where Yeats and his wife were staying.

24 *gull*: see 'On a Political Prisoner', l. 3.

28 *green-pated bird*: a duck. Because the poet is rid of the beast that attaches him to the world, he can participate in the superhuman emotions of the dead; because the poet is rid of the demon that inspires hatred of the world, he can participate in the subhuman emotions of the duck.

38–39 *mere growing old ... this sweetness brought*: this benediction contrasts with the rage against old age in 'The Tower' II 83.

39 *Chilled blood*: 'I become more conservative and do not know whether that is because my thoughts are deeper or my blood more chill' (*L*, p. 604). Also compare 'Broken Dreams', l. 19: 'age might well have chilled his blood'. In T. S. Eliot's 'Little Gidding' II (1942), a ghost – roughly identifiable as the ghost of Yeats – tells the poet of the 'gifts reserved for age', one of which is 'the cold friction of expiring sense'.

44 *Thebaid*: the Egyptian desert in the vicinity of Thebes. Yeats always associated this region with Christian ascetics who had forsaken the world in order to induce themselves to ecstasy. To describe the change from the Greek to the Christian sensibility, Yeats wrote: 'God is now conceived of as something outside man and man's handiwork, and it follows that it must be idolatry to worship that which Phidias and Scopas made, and seeing that He is a Father in Heaven, that Heaven will be found presently in the Thebaid, where the world is changed into a featureless dust and can be run through the fingers' (*AV*, pp. 273–74). This sentence, in a sense, recapitulates the movement of the poem, from the portrait gallery to a region beyond art.

Elsewhere Yeats associated the Thebaid with Lionel Johnson: '"Yeats", he has said to me, "you need ten years in a library, but I have need of ten years in the wilderness". When he said "Wilderness" I am certain, however, that he thought of some historical, some bookish desert, the Thebaid, or the lands about the Mareotic sea' (*A: TG* 6). Since the austere Johnson (according to Yeats) was found at his autopsy to be a man who never reached sexual maturity, the association of Johnson and the Thebaid suggests an important under-theme in the poem, the male climacteric. For other telling references to the Thebaid, see *Ex*, p. 301, and *EI*, p. 405.

45 *the Mareotic sea*: Lake Mareotis, near Alexandria, Egypt. Compare 'Under Ben Bulben' I 2–3: 'the Mareotic Lake / That the Witch of Atlas knew'. In Shelley's 'The Witch of Atlas' (1820), the beautiful witch sees in the waters of Lake Mareotis 'all human life shadowed upon its waters in shadows that "never are erased but tremble ever" ['The Witch of Atlas' LIX 3]' (*EI*, p. 85). She beheld ultimate reality, the Forms of things reflected in (or refracted through) the waters that symbolize earthly existence.

46 *Anthony*: St Anthony of Egypt, a fourth-century saint who lived in a delirium of vision – his fantasies inspired artists as diverse as Hieronymus Bosch and Gustave Flaubert (*La tentation de Saint-Antoine*). 'These are those who must seek no image of desire . . . St. Simon Stylites upon his pillar, St. Anthony in his cavern, all whose preoccupation is to seem nothing; to hollow their hearts till they are void and without form' (*A: IP* 14). Also see *Ex*, p. 301.

48 *Starved*: in the unfinished novel *The Speckled Bird* I iv, a sensitive boy inculcates hallucinations by fasting (*LTMSB*, pp. 37–40; compare pp. 68, 126); and Yeats recorded that, when young, he hoped to rid his poetry of bad influences 'by eating little and sleeping upon a board' (*EI*, p. 5). In 'The Heart of the Spring' (1893) an old man fasts in order to become an immortal god (*M*, p. 171). Compare also *Where There is Nothing* IV ii 25, 112, and V 172, where the hero starves himself into ecstasy; *The King's Threshold* (1904), l. 19, where the poet starves himself to win a position from the king; *The King of the Great Clock Tower* (1935), l. 78, where the vulgar poet fasts nine days and sees a vision of Aengus; and the juvenile poem *Mosada* II 20–21: 'A saint of Munster, when much fasting, saw / This vision' (*VP*, p. 696). The last of Yeats's fasters is found in 'The Pilgrim', l. 1.

49 *a bag of bones*: compare the speech of the girl in *The King's Threshold*, who notes that the hunger-striking poet has become 'a bag of bones' (l. 450).

50 *the Caesars*: according to Yeats's historical mythology, Caesar and Christ were opposites – the *primary* Christ came to supplant the *antithetical* Caesar; indeed Yeats called Christ the anti-self of the whole classical world (*M*, p. 337). Yeats further remarked, 'The typical men of the classical age . . . lived public lives, pursuing curiosities of appetite, and so found in Christianity, with its Thebaid and its Mareotic Sea the needed curb' (*A: TG* 9).

The Second Coming

According to orthodox Christianity, the faithful live in expectation that, after a Second Coming, Christ will establish on earth a kingdom of sanctity and bliss. The purpose of the present poem is to subvert that happy hope: the poet predicts that, at the end of the millennium, there will arise not Christ but Christ's opposite, a savage god whose reign will establish a system of behaviour antithetical to that recommended by Christ. At the end of the previous poem, demon and beast – the poet's personal passions and hatreds – ran away, left the poet evacuated and content; in this poem the beast reappears, as a monster to reinvigorate not just the poet but the whole world.

In his long note to this poem, Yeats described the system of the gyres: how all the progress of the human soul and the progress of history can be analysed mathematically as the movement of two interlocking spinning cones, the apex of one screwing into the centre of the base of the other. All movement, then, consists of a simultaneous diminishing of one cone and an expanding of the other (see Introduction XI). In our age the *primary* cone, the cone of the Christian era, objective and self-effacing, has expanded almost to its maximum extent. But as it has enlarged, it has weakened, lost its fervour; and at the turning point of the gyres, a new god, the Antichrist of l. 21, will be born at the narrow point of the *antithetical* cone, and will inaugurate a subjective age, violent, arrogant, hierarchical, polytheistic, aesthetic, and immoral: 'All our scientific, democratic, fact-accumulating, heterogeneous civilization belongs to the outward gyre and prepares not the continuance of itself but the revelation as in a lightning flash, though in a flash that will not strike only in one place, and will for a time be constantly repeated, of the civilization that must slowly take its place' (*VP*, p. 825).

Like Blake in *The Marriage of Heaven and Hell* (1793), Yeats prophesied a transvaluation of the values of good and evil; like Blake in 'The Mental Traveller', Yeats thought that such transvaluations occurred in tightly-organized cycles of diminishment and augmentation. These historical patterns may seem abstract, but 'The Second Coming' was written in direct response to the Great War of 1914–18; in fact an early draft of its opening lines read, 'The gyres grow wider and more wide / The hawk can no more hear the falconer / The germans to Russia to the place' (Stallworthy, *BL*, p. 17).

But 'The Second Coming' is not only a poem about history; it is also a poem about the process of image-making. Indeed it is almost a versification of Yeats's story of an occult experiment in imagination conducted by MacGregor Mathers on Yeats and other researchers:

> He gave me a cardboard symbol and I closed my eyes. Sight came slowly . . . there rose before me mental images that I could not control: a desert and black Titan raising himself up by his two hands from the middle of a heap of ancient ruins. Mathers explained that I had seen a being of the

> order of Salamanders because he had shown me their symbol, but it was not necessary even to show the symbol, it would have been sufficient that he imagined it.... [I discovered] that for a considerable minority ... the visible world would completely vanish, and that world, summoned by the symbol, take its place. (*A: FY* 20; compare *Mem*, p. 27)

In the year 2000 a new world will be summoned into being by the mass imagination of the human race.

The poem's metre – blank verse – is unusual in English lyric poetry, although there were some distinguished precedents, such as Tennyson's 'Tears, Idle Tears'. Yeats's earliest sketches show that he intended to write it in rhyme; and indeed the first four lines almost fall into rhymed couplets. The abandonment of this half-suggested rhyme scheme in the subsequent lines may imitate the disintegration of civilization discussed in them.

Title *The Second Coming*: Yeats wrote in 1926, 'I do not believe in it [the Second Coming] – at least not in its Christian form' (*UP* II, p. 464).

1–8: Yeats quoted these lines to illustrate the sentence 'I did not foresee, not having the courage of my own thought: the growing murderousness of the world' (*A: FY* 22).

2 *the falcon*: this bird seems to inscribe in air the shape of the historical gyre spiralling outwards to its furthest bound. In the automatic script for 17 April 1918 Yeats asked Thomas, 'Is not world as spiral ascends getting farther from reality' (*MAV* II, p. 13). A passage from a 1910 draft of *The Player Queen* anticipates this image – the Chancellor is anticipating the ruin that will come to the state if the Queen retires to convent or martyrdom: 'Come, your Majesty, I am like a falconer that bears upon the wrist a hawk that struggles to lose itself in the heavens, and all I understand is to keep the jesses tight; yet it may be, before the day end, some murderer's hand may cut them' (Bradford, *WPQ*, p. 200). For other birds that trace significant aerial patterns, see 'The Wild Swans at Coole', l. 11: 'wheeling in great broken rings'; 'My Descendants', ll. 17–18: 'The Primum Mobile that fashioned us / Has made the very owls in circles move'; and 'Coole Park, 1929', l. 21, where the swallows 'seemed to whirl upon a compass-point'.

4 *Mere anarchy*: according to *A Vision*, anarchy and the adoration of violence are characteristic of the end of a historical era (*AV*, p. 272). Compare 'From the *Antigone*', ll. 7–8: 'hurl / Heaven and Earth out of their places'.

6 *The ceremony of innocence*: compare 'A Prayer for my Daughter', ll. 77–78: 'How but in custom and in ceremony / Are innocence and beauty born?'; and 'Three Marching Songs' II 12: 'The lofty innocence ... slain'. In 1936 Yeats told Ethel Mannin to 'look up a poem called *The Second Coming*. It ... foretold what is happening.... every nerve trembles with horror at what is happening in Europe, "the ceremony of innocence is drowned" ' (*L*, p. 851).

7–8 *The best lack all conviction, while the worst / Are full of passionate intensity*: compare 'Why should not Old Men be Mad?', ll. 9–10: 'chance / Should starve good men and bad advance'; and 'A Statesman's Holiday', ll. 9–10: 'Some knew what ailed the world / But never said a thing'. Swift expressed a similar thought in a passage quoted by Yeats: '"those who engage in the pursuits of malice and revenge are much more sedulous than such as would prevent them"' (*Ex*, p. 357). Henn notes (*LT*, p. 144) a related passage in Shelley's *Prometheus Unbound* I 625–26: 'The good want power ... The powerful goodness want'.

12 Spiritus Mundi: another name for the *Anima Mundi* or World's Soul, the treasure-house of images not invented by man but given to him from beyond. 'I think of *Anima Mundi* as a great pool or garden where [a series of related images] moves through its allotted growth like a great water-plant or fragrantly branches in the air' (*M*, p. 352).

14 *A shape with lion body and the head of a man*: a sphinx – in the automatic script for 2 June 1918, Yeats asked, referring to the initiator of the cycle that will replace the Christian cycle, 'Can we call it the Sphynx' (*MAV* II, p. 39). Perhaps the two most important precursors of this image are the murderous sphinx of the Oedipus legend, who asked the famous riddle whose answer is *Man*; and the sexually obsessive, feline and aesthetic sphinx of Wilde's poem 'The Sphinx' (1894), the concubine of Egyptian gods. In 'A Packet for Ezra Pound', Yeats takes Oedipus as the opposite of Christ (*AV*, p. 27); and the sphinx's bloodiness and sexiness make it also appropriate as the contrary of the pale, abstract Christ. See also 'The Double Vision of Michael Robartes' II 2.

17 *desert birds*: in *Calvary* (1920), l. 28, 'great desert birds' pick bones bare.

19 *twenty centuries of stony sleep*: the whole Christian era. Yeats sometimes thought of Christianity as stony (see 'Demon and Beast', ll. 44–45), sometimes as sleepy (as in *The Countess Cathleen* (1892), ll. 496–97: 'The passionate, proud heart – that all the angels ... would rock to sleep'). Also compare 'On a Picture of a Black Centaur ...', l. 13: 'sleep a long Saturnian sleep'. The phrase 'stony sleep' is taken (as Bloom notes, *Yeats*, p. 319) from Blake's *The [First] Book of Urizen* (1794) 6:7–8: 'But Urizen laid in a stony sleep / Unorganiz'd, rent from Eternity'.

21 *what rough beast*: in a summary of his career as a poet, Yeats wrote that around 1904 'I began to imagine, as always at my left side just out of the range of the sight, a brazen winged beast that I associated with laughing, ecstatic destruction' (*Ex*, p. 393). Similarly Yeats predicted the end of the refined, almost disembodied *fin-de-siècle* art that he loved: 'After Stephane Mallarmé, after Paul Verlaine, after Gustave Moreau ... after our own verse ... what more is possible? After us the Savage God' (*A: TG* 20). Also compare

The King's Threshold (1904), ll. 849–50: 'He needs no help that joy has lifted up / Like some miraculous beast out of Ezekiel'. Closely related (in Yeats's taxonomy) to the rough beast are the unicorns that prance, inspire, trample grapes, copulate with queens and prostitutes, and cause general havoc in *Where There is Nothing* (1902) IV ii 175 (compare also II 304–5, 378–79 on the 'wild beast . . . Laughter, the mightiest of the enemies of God', with 'a face smoky from the eternal fires, and wings of brass'), *The Unicorn from the Stars* I 309, 502, II 43, 370, and 487, *The Player Queen* (1922) I 238 and II 383, and the 1925 version of 'The Adoration of the Magi' (*M*, p. 312). See also 'What Magic Drum?', l. 6: 'What beast has licked its young?'

22 *Slouches towards Bethlehem to be born*: 'the next civilisation may be born, not from a virgin's womb, nor a tomb without a body, not from a void, but of our own rich experience' (*Ex*, p. 437). Yeats liked to describe the origin of an antithetical civilization as a sensual thrashing, a spasm of horror – see 'The Magi', l. 8: 'The uncontrollable mystery on the bestial floor'; and 'Leda and the Swan'.

A Prayer for my Daughter

'The Second Coming' foresees a future that, for all the horror of its approach, will offer a civilization superior to that in which the poet lives; 'A Prayer for my Daughter' laments the loss of some attractive features of past ages. 'The Second Coming' ends with the birth of a monster that embodies the energies of a new age; 'A Prayer for my Daughter' begins with the birth of an untremendous baby who will shatter no worlds (although Yeats may have entertained some notion of becoming the father of a god – when his wife was pregnant, in 1918, he wrote in a notebook, 'For the first time a[n automatic] script suggesting that our child would be in some way *an avatar*' [*MAV* II, pp. 130, 134]). Here the poet hopes that she will not become troublingly beautiful (l. 17), that she will possess such moderate and civil virtues as courtesy (l. 37). In the lunar scheme of *A Vision*, Yeats resided in Phase 17, two steps after the Full Moon, the maximum intensity of vision; in the later Phases, there was a continual compromise with commonplace reality: 'Goethe [in Phase 18] did not . . . marry his cook, but he certainly did not marry the woman he had desired, and his grief at her death showed that, unlike Phase 16 or Phase 17, which forget their broken toys, he could love what disillusionment gave' (*AV*, p. 146–47).

The wish for a well-mannered, humane daughter instead of a harrowingly attractive one suggests that Yeats was himself somewhat disillusioned by the over-intense, the too-shivery. Such visions as that recorded in 'The Second Coming' would give good reason for a desire to find a lower tension-level of existence; and the behaviour of amazing women, such as Maud Gonne – estranged from mankind and liable to craziness – did not provide a model for a girl to follow. Anne Yeats, the poet's first child, was born on 26 February 1919 – her father was then fifty-three years old.

1 *Once more the storm is howling, and half hid / Under this cradle-hood*: the combination of storm and cradle appeared in 'The Unappeasable Host'. Coleridge's 'Frost at Midnight' (1798) also begins with a juxtaposition of the weather and a 'cradled infant'. The early drafts show that Yeats conceived a metaphorical storm ('a popular tempest') before the real one (Stallworthy, *BL*, p. 29).

4 *Gregory's wood*: Thoor Ballylee, the Yeatses' home, was near Coole Park, Lady Gregory's estate.

5 *roof-levelling wind*: compare 'Nineteen Hundred and Nineteen' V 5: 'the levelling wind'.

15 *a frenzied drum*: compare *The Wanderings of Oisin* III 135, 'the sea's vague drum'; also 'What Magic Drum?', l. 4. In *The Hour-Glass* (1914), ll. 108–9, the Wise Man trembles to think that 'Reason is growing dim; / A moment more and Frenzy will beat his drum'.

16 *the murderous innocence of the sea*: perhaps the sea – the force of historical process – is innocent because it is impersonal, superhuman, not petty, spiteful, or divided against itself.

17–18 *not / Beauty to make a stranger's eye distraught*: compare 'Beggar to Beggar Cried', l. 10: 'She need not be too comely'.

19 *Or hers before a looking-glass*: this volume begins with the opposite request – a beautiful woman is asked to look in a looking-glass and grow wise ('Michael Robartes and the Dancer', ll. 10–12). This reversal is a measure of distance travelled from the ideal to the worldly.

24, 25, 29 *chooses . . . chosen . . . chose*: the role of choice in human relationships is discussed in 'Solomon and the Witch', l. 14: 'Chance being at one with Choice at last'. *Chance* also appears in the present poem, at l. 53.

26 *later had much trouble from a fool*: *later* suggests that the fool Yeats meant was not Menelaus, the husband of Helen of Troy, but Paris, the Trojan prince who abducted her. Yeats was also thinking of John MacBride, the boisterous husband of Maud Gonne – see also l. 36.

27 *that great Queen*: Aphrodite, the Greek goddess of sexual love, born from sea-water.

28 *fatherless*: perhaps a sly suggestion that only a father's wise counsel prevents a daughter from going astray.

29 *bandy-leggèd smith*: Hephaestos, the lame armour-maker of the gods, cuckolded husband of Aphrodite.

31 *a crazy salad*: too-beautiful women find either that they are helpless victims, or that their most grotesque wishes are granted. Compare 'The Double Vision of Michael Robartes' III 6: 'A crazy juice'. Also compare: 'the deification of the moment, that . . . turned the world into fruit-salad' (*L*, p. 782).

32 *the Horn of Plenty*: a horn perpetually abounding with fruit, a gift to Zeus from a motherly goat – compare 'The Tower' III 16. Its shape may suggest the gyre-form of the historical process, breaking asunder in the present age – see 'The Second Coming', l. 1.

33 *courtesy*: an idea that Yeats associated with strength, nonchalance, and self-discipline – he cited with approval the '"recklessness" Castiglione [see the note to 'To a Wealthy Man . . .', l. 9] thought necessary in good manners' (*EI*, p. 256). Compare 'Her Courtesy'.

37–38, 40 *beauty's very self . . . a poor man . . . a glad kindness*: Maud Gonne, Yeats, and Georgie Yeats, respectively. As Hone notes, Yeats once wrote to Lady Gregory, 'My wife is a perfect wife, kind, wise, and unselfish' (*WBY*, p. 307).

41 *a flourishing hidden tree*: compare 'The Two Trees', in which Maud Gonne is likened, first to a flourishing tree, then to a blighted tree.

42 *a linnet*: a songbird celebrated by Wordsworth and other poets. Compare the circling Loves in 'The Two Trees', l. 13; and the lone gull that comes to Con Markiewicz' hand in 'On a Political Prisoner', l. 3.

46 *but in merriment a quarrel*: playfulness is the recommended virtue, as opposed to Maud Gonne's vehemence.

51 *Prosper but little*: Maud Gonne and Con Markiewicz had recently spent some time in prison.

56 *never tear the linnet from the leaf*: the gull that descended to Con Markiewicz (see the note to l. 42) perhaps represented an abstract kind of thinking, detached from the person; the linnet represents thought embodied in the person.

58 *opinions are accursed*: Donoghue compares a journal entry: 'Women . . . give all to an opinion as if it were some terrible stone doll . . . At last the opinion is so much identified with their nature that it seems a part of their flesh becomes stone and passes out of life' (*A: DS* 7; *Mem*, p. 192); also compare 'Michael Robartes and the Dancer', l. 1: 'Opinion is not worth a rush'.

59 *the loveliest woman*: Maud Gonne.

64 *wind*: compare 'Among School Children' IV 3.

67–68 *self-delighting, / Self-appeasing, self-affrighting*: when hatred vanishes, the soul is not defined by things outside itself, such as its enmities; like the Horn of Plenty and the laurel tree, the soul becomes perpetually abundant with its own treasures. This rhetoric of autonomic reflexivity grows increasingly important in Yeats's poetry: e.g. 'Monuments of its own magnificence' ('Sailing to Byzantium' II 6); 'life's own self-delight' ('Ancestral Houses', l. 11); 'self-delighting reverie' ('I see Phantoms . . .', l. 29); 'self-born mockers' ('Among School Children' VII 8); 'The self-sown, self-begotten shape' (the olive tree in 'Colonus' Praise', l. 10); 'Self-born, high-born, and solitary truths' ('The Gift of Harun Al-Rashid', l. 141); 'sink into its own delight' (Florence Farr's soul in 'All Souls' Night', l. 60); 'Flames begotten of flame' ('Byzantium', l. 27); 'Self-born, born anew' ('Stream and Sun at Glendalough', l. 15); 'Nor shall the self-begotten fail' ('Old Tom Again', l. 3); 'Godhead begets Godhead' ('Ribh denounces Patrick', l. 5 – see also 'Ribh in Ecstasy', ll. 3–6, and *The Herne's Egg* [1938] VI 164); and '"O sea-starved, hungry sea"' ('A Crazed Girl', l. 14). Yeats's first important use of this construction was the climax to *The Shadowy Waters*, ll. 617–19: 'that old harp awakens of itself . . . dreams, / That have had dreams for father, live in us'.

This rhetoric of self-involvement and self-enclosure, this constitution of a private universe, is the sign of extreme transcendence; indeed it is officially sanctioned in the discussion of Phase 15 spirits in *A Vision*: 'They suffer from the terror of solitude, and can only free themselves from terror by becoming entirely *antithetical* and so self-sufficing' (*AV* [1925], p. 241). In his description of the soul's journey after death, Yeats wrote that, after attaining *Beatitude*, the soul becomes 'self-shaping, self-moving, plastic to itself' (*AV* [1937], p. 233). The origin of Yeats's fascination with this rhetoric may come from Plato's *Phaedrus*: 'All soul is immortal; for that which is ever in motion is immortal. But that which while imparting motion is itself moved by something else can cease to be in motion, and therefore can cease to live; it is that which moves itself that never intermits its motion . . . this self-mover is the source and first principle of motion for all other things that are moved. . . . precisely that is the essence and definition of soul, to wit self-motion' (245C-E). This passage immediately precedes Plato's famous figure of the soul as a chariot drawn by a black horse and a white horse, a figure that helped Yeats to define the *primary* and *antithetical* tendencies that govern *A Vision* (*MAV* I, pp. 10–11). Yeats alluded to Plato's self-moving soul: 'the soul, self-moving and self-teaching' (*M*, p. 368); 'the spirit which is, according to the old definition, "that which moves itself"' (*L*, p. 472); 'What's dearth and death and sickness to the soul / That knows no virtue but itself?' (*The Hour-Glass* [1914], ll. 281–82).

Much of the purpose of 'A Prayer for my Daughter' is to embed the child in a richly articulated social world, to make no prayers for unusual glory of self; nevertheless, in this stanza, Yeats impresses on her something of the weird splendour of his highest apparitions, such as the dancer in 'The Double Vision of Michael Robartes' II.

73–80: this concluding stanza was an afterthought; the early drafts end with three stanzas imagining Anne Yeats at the age of twenty-five, strolling at Coole Park by places dear to her dead father:

> Daughter if you be happy & yet grown –
> Say when you are five & twenty – walk alone
> Through Coole Domain & visit for my sake
> The stony edges of the lake,
> Where every year I have counted swans, & cry
> That all is well till all that's there
> Spring sounding on to the still air
> And all is sound between the lake & sky
>
> Then where what light beach foliage can let through
> Falls green on ground the ivy has made blue
> Cry out that all is well but cry it not
> Too loud for that is a still spot
> And after to the garden on that side
> Where the Katalpa's grow & call
> Until an echo in the wall
> Above Maecenas' image has replied.
>
> What matters it if you be overheard
> By gardener, labourer or herd
> They must that have strong eye-sight meet my shade
> When the evening light's begun to fade
> Amid the scenery it has held most dear
> Till many a winter has gone by.
> No common man will mock the cry
> Nor think that being dead I cannot hear.
> (Stallworthy, *BL*, pp. 41–42)

The reference to Maecenas (the patron of Virgil and Horace) is explained by Lady Gregory: at the end of one of Coole's gravel paths was a 'colossal marble bust of Maecenas' (*Coole* [1931], p. 39). Yeats once wrote of 'the woods at Coole', 'when I am dead they will have ... my longest visit' (*A:SB* 6).

77–80: when Yeats was arguing in the Senate that the custom of judges' wigs should be abolished, an opponent quoted these lines to refute Yeats (*SSY*, p. 129).

80 *custom for the spreading laurel tree*: this leisurely and poised conclusion – the symbols themselves ramify like a tree – is deliberately antique in feeling. For similarly old-fashioned concretions of abstract things, see 'Ancestral Houses', l. 30: 'slippered Contemplation finds his ease'; and 'To Dorothy Wellesley', ll. 13–14: 'Neither Content / Nor satisfied Conscience'.

A Meditation in Time of War

This poem is an extreme development of the doctrine of 'The Moods', that our actions and passions are not our own but the vicarious motions of unearthly forces – see also 'Whence Had They Come?' Yeats thought of modern warfare as the mechanical havoc of mechanical men (see 'I see Phantoms . . .', l. 32); and this may partly account for the loss of animateness at the end of this war-meditation.

1 *one throb of the artery*: derived from a favourite line of Blake's: 'Every Time less than a pulsation of the artery / Is equal in its period & value to Six Thousand Years. / For in this Period the Poet's Work is Done' (*Milton* 28 [30]:62 ff). Yeats quoted this passage directly (*UP* II, p. 199, and *EI*, pp. 135, 172), and indirectly: 'We perceive in a pulsation of the artery, and after slowly decline' (*M*, p. 361); see also *AV*, p. 24, and 'Hanrahan's Vision' (1896): 'the gateway of Eternity had opened and closed in a pulsation of the heart' (*VSR*, p. 220; compare *M*, p. 252). Compare 'The Double Vision of Michael Robartes' III 6: 'A crazy juice that makes the pulses beat'.

4 *One is animate*: compare 'A Voice': 'One day I was walking over a bit of marshy ground . . . when I felt, all of a sudden, and only for a second, an emotion which I said to myself was the root of Christian mysticism. There had swept over me a sense of weakness, of dependence on a great personal Being' (*M*, p. 68; compare *A: SB* 6).

5 *Mankind inanimate phantasy*: compare Yeats's description of eternal self-possession at the end of time: 'That condition is alone animate, all the rest is fantasy' (*M*, p. 357).

To Be Carved on a Stone at Thoor Ballylee

This volume begins with a stylized and playful conversation between an ideal poet and an ideal woman; and it ends with a decisive statement by a homeowner and his wife, both identified by name. Yeats quoted a draft of this poem in a letter, in which he described how he and his wife 'had bought the whole contents of an old mill – great beams and three-inch planks, and old paving stones; and the local carpenter and mason and blacksmith are at work for us. On a great stone beside the front door will be inscribed these lines ...' (*L*, p. 651). The poem's text is a theme of the poem itself: its inscribing on the rock is an act of physical construction comparable to (and competing with) the rebuilding of the tower itself – for other examples of thematic texts, see 'When You are Old', l. 2.

4 *Restored this tower*: what Robert Gregory neglected to do in 'Shepherd and Goatherd', l. 50: 'Set carpenters to work on no wide table'.

4 *my wife George*: née Hyde-Lees (1892–1968).

5–6 *may these characters remain / When all is ruin once again*: compare 'My Descendants', l. 24: 'These stones remain their monument and mine'.

THE TOWER (1928)

In 1922 Yeats was appointed a senator of the new-born free state of Ireland; in 1923 he won the Nobel Prize. His celebrity and public presence were far greater than before; but instead of becoming a Venerable Old Poet, 'honoured and empty-witted' (such was Yeats's description of Wordsworth – *M*, p. 342), Yeats wrote poetry that drew its energy from a sustained attack on himself and on the age that revered him. The image that the smiling public man constructed, the poet laboured to tear down.

But the persona of the public man, visiting schools (in 'Among School Children'), talking with soldiers ('The Road at my Door'), and versifying his senate speeches ('The Tower' III 6-13), is not the only persona found in this volume. The sage is equally common, and equally ironical. Many of these poems are written by the author of *A Vision*, the Platonist labouring in his tower to construe difficult texts dictated from beyond the grave, 'the half-read wisdom of daemonic images' ('I see Phantoms ...', l. 39). In *A Vision* (1925), this persona is usually quite serious – he is the medium through whom ecstatic wisdom is transmitted to mankind. But in Yeats's poetry, starting as early as 'The Phases of the Moon' (1918), the Platonist is often derided for his pretension and futility, as if he were less a conductor of wisdom than a resistor to it. Ezra Pound wrote much of his greatest poetry on the theme of his inadequacy as a poet, from 'Near Perigord' to Canto 81 and beyond. Yeats was not quite so dependent for inspiration on his anxiety about lack of inspiration, but self-mockery, both of the senator and of the sage, provides much of the tension of this great volume. The poet contemplates his defective wisdom, his aging, impotent body, and his aging, impotent historical era, and grows potent from the sad spectacle.

The structure of *The Tower* is congruent to the structure of *A Vision* (1925). The first book of *A Vision* describes the Great Wheel, the progress of the soul through the twenty-eight incarnations of the lunar month; similarly the opening poems in *The Tower* trace the progress of Yeats's soul, from

Ireland to Byzantium, from rural simplicity to the brink of the grave, from his comfortable home to a landscape desolated by war. The third book of *A Vision* describes the historical gyre, offers a map of the events of the last 4000 years arranged in great cyclical heaves, each initiated by the birth of a god; and in the middle of *The Tower* there appear poems on historical themes: the chaos of the first world war in 'Nineteen Hundred and Nineteen', a summary incantation of the gyres in 'Two Songs from a Play', and the spasmodic birth-processes of a new age in 'Leda and the Swan'. The fourth and final book of *A Vision* describes the journey of the soul after death, its passage from reenactments of its past life to blessed oblivion; and the last poem in *The Tower*, 'All Souls' Night', presents the ghosts of Yeats's friends, and prepares the poet for his own assimilation to their company. Indeed 'All Souls' Night' is also printed on the final pages of *A Vision* – thus it is the common epilogue to *A Vision* and *The Tower*.

Sailing to Byzantium

From his earliest work on, Yeats dreamed of a world exempt from the usual sadnesses of life – a domain of greater appetites more greatly gratified. Byzantium became the most lavishly imagined and the most famous of these anti-worlds. In *A Vision* Yeats wrote of Justinian's construction of the cathedral of Hagia Sophia (AD 560) as one of history's closest approximations to the ahistorical beauty of the full moon, Phase 15 of the gyre:

> Byzantium ... substituted for formal Roman magnificence, with its glorification of physical power, an architecture that suggests the Sacred City in the Apocalypse of St. John. I think if I could be given a month of Antiquity and leave to spend it where I chose, I would spend it in Byzantium ... I think I could find in some little wine-shop some philosophical worker in mosaic who could answer all my questions, the supernatural descending nearer to him than to Plotinus even, for the pride of his delicate skill would make [religious truths] show as a lovely flexible presence like that of a perfect human body. (*AV*, p. 279)

The characteristics of Byzantium, then, are: (1) an almost complete dematerialization, as if the city were the pleasure dome in Coleridge's 'Kubla Khan' (1797), manufactured out of air and shadowed on water – in fact a draft of 'Sailing to Byzantium' mentioned 'St Sophia's sacred dome ... Mirrored in water' (Stallworthy, *BL*, p. 95); (2) a deliberate destruction of the boundary between life and art – men are translated into mosaic, while symbols have the presence of 'a perfect human body'; (3) anonymity – art is the cooperative effect of a community of workers and thinkers; the oblivion and beatitude of dead souls were realized there on earth. Byzantium is an abstraction from life, and Byzantine art is notable for its abstract character, as Owen Aherne says in a passage (later deleted) from the 1908 version of 'The Tables of the Law': 'the Byzantine style ... moves me because these tall, emaciated angels and saints seem to have less relation to the world about us than to an abstract pattern of flowing lines, that suggest an imagination absorbed in the contemplation of Eternity' (*VSR*, p. 154; compare *EI*, pp. 243, 257).

Yet, for all its seductiveness, Byzantium is finally forced to confess its inadequacy. There is a covert allusion in the poem's first line to *Tír na nÓg*, the paradise for which Oisin searches in *The Wanderings of Oisin*; and in that early poem, as in so many later ones, paradise at last famishes the appetites that it promises to glut. All representations of the supernatural must contain some grotesquerie, a straining for effect, a juxtaposition of incompatible elements, as Yeats himself noted (*AV*, p. 292); but the poet's metamorphosis into a golden bird, at the end of this poem, may suggest a certain laborious triviality as well as an eerie splendour, as if life in Byzantium were at last shown as a superior sort of folly.

I 1 *That is no country for old men*: the following details suggest that the country is Ireland, famous for salmon-streams; but the line also contains a pun on *Tír na nÓg*, literally *the Country of the Young*, the Celtic name for paradise. Yeats at one time thought that this first line should read: 'Old men should quit a country where the young' – see Finneran, *EYP*, p. 120. In the early drafts Yeats intended further to contrast the old and the young by juxtaposing the 'old gods' of pagan Ireland with the infant Christ, 'a smiling child upon his mother's knees' (*BL*, p. 91).

I 1–2 *The young / In one another's arms*: that the implicit subject of the whole poem is sex – Yeats's feeling that a post-sexual man has no place in the normal world – is suggested by an early prose draft of the poem: 'For many loves have I taken off my clothes / for some I threw them off in haste, for some slowly & indifferently ... but now I will take off my body' (*BL*, p. 89). Yeats used this same idea in 'A Last Confession', ll. 13-16.

II 2 *A tattered coat upon a stick*: age renders the old man fleshless, a caricature of a man. Compare 'Among School Children' IV 8, 'a comfortable kind of old scarecrow', and VI 8, 'Old clothes upon old sticks to scare a bird'; also the 'weather-worn, marble triton' into which the aging poet turns in 'Men Improve with the Years', l. 2; also the '*coat upon a coat-hanger*', the most sinister apparition in 'The Apparitions'. Pound's Propertius exclaimed to his mistress, 'I am hung here, a scarecrow for lovers' (*Homage to Sextus Propertius* XI [1917]).

II 3 *Soul clap its hands*: according to *A Vision*, p. 168, impersonal and impartial artists, such as Rembrandt and Synge, 'look on and clap their hands' at the spectacle of the objective world.

II 6 *Monuments of its own magnificence*: for the theme of self-referentiality, see 'A Prayer for my Daughter', ll. 67–68.

II 7 *I have sailed the seas*: Yeats liked to begin poems by sailing forth – compare 'Swift's Epitaph', l. 1: 'Swift has sailed into his rest'; 'Old Tom Again', l. 1: 'Things out of perfection sail'; 'The Delphic Oracle upon Plotinus', l. 1: 'Behold that great Plotinus swim'; and 'Colonel Martin' I 1: 'The Colonel went out sailing'. Originally the poem had a much stronger emphasis on sailing, as a draft of its second stanza shows: 'After a dozen storms to come / I therefore voyage towards Byzantium / Among these sun browned friendly mariners / Another dozen days & we shall come / Among the waves to where the noise of oars / Under the shadow of its marble stairs' (*BL*, p. 93).

III 1–2 *O sages standing ... As in the gold mosaic*: Yeats was evidently thinking of the mosaic procession of martyrs in the church of Sant' Apollinare Nuovo in Ravenna, Italy (the capital of the western Roman Empire during the century when Justinian ruled in Constantinople) which he visited in 1907. (In 'Rosa Alchemica' [1896], the narrator sees a figured corridor 'not less beautiful than the mosaic in the Baptistery at Ravenna' [*M*, p. 287].) Yeats also saw Byzantine mosaics in Sicily in 1925.

In a letter to Olivia Shakespear, Yeats reported that a medium unconsciously directed him to associate the sages of this poem with two of Blake's pictures, 'Dante entering the Holy Fire' and 'The serpent attacking Vanni Fucci': 'I found [in *Inferno* 24:97] that at the serpent's sting Vanni Fucci is burnt to ashes and then recreated from the ashes and that this symbolizes "the temporal Fire" ... Certainly we suck always at the eternal dugs. How well too it puts my own mood between spiritual excitement, and the sexual torture and the knowledge that they are somehow inseparable!' (*L*, p. 731).

III 3 *perne in a gyre*: spin in a spiral – see 'Demon and Beast', l. 5. The poet asks the sages, immune from decay, to reenter the world of process long enough to seize him away to their realm.

III 5 *Consume my heart away*: in *A Vision* (1925), Yeats wrote: 'In our system ... it is a cardinal principle that anything separated from its opposite ... "consumes itself away"' (p. 134; compare *A: IP* 12). Here the poet prays for an escape from the antitheses that govern the world by means of a declension into art.

III 8 *the artifice of eternity*: in the story 'The Tables of the Law' (1896), Yeats wrote that 'terror and content, birth and death, love and hatred ... are but instruments for that supreme art which is to win us from life and gather us into eternity like doves into their dove-cots' (*M*, pp. 300–1).

IV 2 *My bodily form*: according to *A Vision* (1937) III, the visible forms of dead souls are extremely plastic, susceptible to imaginative pressure.

IV 3–4 *such a form . . . of hammered gold*: 'I have read somewhere that in the Emperor's palace at Byzantium was a tree made of gold and silver, and artificial birds that sang' (*VP*, p. 825). This species of embodied disembodiment may have been suggested by Hans Christian Andersen's fairy-tale 'The Nightingale', which tells of a song-contest in the Chinese court between a mechanical bird and a real one. The mechanical bird gains the greater applause, but later, when the emperor seems to be dying, only the real nightingale can revive his spirits. This stanza firmly asserts that art can offer a body superior to mere flesh; but Andersen's parable may hint that the poet's sympathies were more on the side of nature than may first appear. Another sign of the faint ludicrousness of the golden bird is found in *The King's Threshold* (1904), ll. 576–79, where the pagan poet-hero derides the Christian god as a tame bird that 'has learned to sing quite softly / Because loud singing would disturb the King, / Who is sitting drowsily among his friends / After the table has been cleared'. (For the theme of the soul's transfiguration into a bird-shape, see the note to 'The Three Hermits'.) Auden commented, 'When Yeats assures me, in a stanza of the utmost magnificence, that after death he wants to become a mechanical bird, I feel that he is telling what my nanny would have called "A story"' (*The Dyer's Hand*, p. 281).

IV 8 *what is past, or passing, or to come*: the poet, fastened to the temporal world, dreams of eternity; the bird, twittering in eternity, sings of time, history. This ending seems to foreshadow a return to nature, perhaps a rebirth of the poet's soul.

The Tower

As in 'Sailing to Byzantium', the poet here struggles to translate himself into a being immune from the ravages of old age. But instead of mutating into an unnatural artifice – a golden bird – the poet finds that his natural self, battered and feeble as it is, can be so transfigured by the imagination that no ascent out of common life is needed. The face and the mask almost coincide – here Yeats bequeathes himself to posterity as a kind of cultural artifact.

The structure of the poem is unusual for Yeats. The first part, written in stately undivided quatrains, sets up an antithesis between imaginative vigour and bodily weakness, and suggests that poetry is an undignified, unsuitable occupation for an old man. It seems that imagination cannot justify life, give purpose, inform experience; only philosophy can. The second part, written in a *canzone*-like stanza form, is a series of almost random anecdotes about victims, each an expression of some aspect of Yeats's predicament. Here there is no antithesis between imagination and weakness – in fact the imagination gains its strength from the man's incompetence, wretchedness, destitution, and frustration. Old age, then, far from disqualifying the poet, enhances his power; and the imagination, not abstract reason, is the faculty that turns poverty into plenty, that sustains the young, the old, and the dead. The third part, written in emphatic trimeter, moves from fierce incantation, a hymn to the universal creative power of man, to a valediction, a disengagement of the creator from his work, a bequest of civilization from a poet who had contributed to its glory.

The use of symbols in this and subsequent poems differs from Yeats's previous practice. In his early work, he depended on symbols with a predetermined, transcendental meaning, such as the Rose; but his later symbols, such as the tower, are not so much donors of meaning as receivers of it. The poem illustrates the process by which ordinary, opaque objects become luminous, permeable, significant.

Title *The Tower*: Thoor Ballylee, home of the Yeatses – see 'In Memory of Major Robert Gregory', I 1. In 1927 Yeats wrote, 'I like to think of that building as a permanent symbol of my work plainly visible to the passer-by' (*TSMC*, p. 114).

I: the prose draft reads, 'What shall I do with this absurd toy which they have given me, this grotesque rattle? O heart, O nerves, you are as vigourous as ever. You still hunger for the whole world, and they have given you this toy' (Bradford, *YW*, p. 4).

I 2 *O heart*: an organ important in Yeats's later work. In 'Sailing to Byzantium' III 5 ('Consume my heart away') he tried to get rid of it; but in 'The Circus Animals' Desertion' I 4 ('I must be satisfied with my heart') he took it as the locus of all poetic themes.

I 4–6 *Never had I more / Excited, passionate ... Imagination*: Yeats quoted with approval a letter written by the aged Blake, in which he called himself '"an old man, feeble and tottering, but not in the spirit and life, not in the real man, the imagination, which liveth for ever. In that I am stronger and stronger as this foolish body decays"' (*EI*, p. 138; *LNI*, p. 94).

I 8 *with rod and fly*: in *The Prelude* (1850) I 485, Wordsworth described the enchantment of 'rod and line'.

I 9 *Ben Bulben*: see 'On a Political Prisoner', l. 14.

I 11 *bid the Muse go pack*: the Muses were the nine daughters of Mnemosyne (Memory), the inspirers of the various arts. Yeats often thought of them as fickle, irresponsible, and sexy: 'Muses resemble women who creep out at night and give themselves to unknown sailors and return to talk of Chinese porcelain' (*AV*, p. 24). The Muses reappear later in the poem to select an attractive girl as their favourite (II 88). Compare 'Two Songs from a Play' I 6: 'then did all the Muses sing'; 'Among School Children' VI 7: 'careless Muses'; 'A Model for the Laureate', l. 17: 'The Muse is mute'; 'Those

Images', l. 8: 'Call the Muses home'; see also 'The Fascination of What's Difficult', l. 4.

I 12 *Choose Plato and Plotinus for a friend*: compare Sir Thomas Wyatt, 'Ffarewell, Love, and all thy lawes for ever' (1557): 'Senec and Plato call me from thy lore'. Something of the drama of this passage is also found in 'The Living Beauty', where Yeats instructed his heart to love a statue, not a real woman. Yeats thought of the two Greek philosophers as opponents of the flesh and as lovers of bloodless abstraction; he noted that 'the most beautiful of [Plotinus'] *Enneads* [was] "The Impassivity of the Dis-Embodied"' (*AV*, p. 232). The philosopher Plato (*c.* 429–347 BC) will reappear in 'Two Songs from a Play' II 7, 'Among School Children' II 7 and VI 1, 'His Bargain', l. 1, 'Mad as the Mist and Snow', l. 8, 'The Delphic Oracle upon Plotinus', l. 8 – and Plato's ghost haunts the refrain of 'What Then?' (Yeats previously had compared himself to a Platonist in 'The Phases of the Moon', l. 15.) The Neoplatonic philosopher Plotinus (AD 205–270) will return as a heroic swimmer, seeking the Isles of the Blest, in 'The Delphic Oracle upon Plotinus' and 'News for the Delphic Oracle' I 9.

I 14–15 *deal / In abstract things*: compare the source of the poet's dejection in 'Lines Written in Dejection'.

II 3 *Tree, like a sooty finger*: compare *The Wanderings of Oisin* I 171: 'Like sooty fingers, many a tree'.

II 9 *Beyond that ridge*: the four anecdotes are associated with places progressively nearer to Yeats's tower: compare II 19 ('upon that rocky place'), II 43 ('somewhere in the neighbouring cottages'), and II 64 ('this house').

II 9 *Mrs. French*: as Yeats's note explains, Mrs French was a grandee described by Sir Jonah Barrington, a local historian. She represents the eighteenth-century Anglo-Ireland of Swift and Burke, a settled, thorough culture that tolerated no assaults to its dignity. Her wish, even if unspoken, is instantly gratified; the personages in the following stanzas, much less wealthy, will have more vehement desires, and – since they lack serving-men with ready shears – will have to use imagination to gratify themselves.

II 15 *an insolent farmer*: one Dennis Bodkin.

II 18 *A peasant girl*: Mary Hynes (d. 1840?), a famous local beauty, described in Yeats's '"Dust Hath Closed Helen's Eye"' (*M*, p. 22).

II 18 *commended by a song*: the song was written by Anthony Raftery (*c.* 1784–1835), a blind wandering Gaelic poet, whose name is mentioned in 'Coole and Ballylee, 1931', l. 4. He addressed Mary Hynes 'O star of light and O sun in harvest, / O amber hair'; a later stanza reads, in translation, 'There is sweet air on the side of the hill / When you are looking down upon Ballylee; / When you are walking in the valley picking nuts and blackberries, / There is music of the birds in it and music of the Sidhe' (*M*, p. 24–25). Yeats conceived Raftery as a poet nearly without craft – 'chanting fine verses, and playing badly on his fiddle' (*EI*, p. 212) – immediately, urgently responsive to the world around him: '"He was the greatest poet in Ireland, and he'd make a song about that bush if he chanced to stand under it. There was a bush he stood under from the rain, and he made verses praising it, and then when the water came through he made verses dispraising it"' (*M*, p. 23). Yeats further noted that Mary Hynes and Raftery were turning into 'perfect symbols of the sorrow of beauty and of the magnificence and penury of dreams' (*M*, p. 30). The whole of 'The Tower' is governed, in a sense, by dream-rhythms of magnificence and penury, glory and bankruptcy.

In 1906 Yeats recorded a visit he had made some years before to Raftery's grave: a priest blessed a new headstone and Raftery's poetry was read in his memory; Yeats was moved by 'its *naïveté* – that is to say, its way of looking at the world as if it were but an hour old' (*Ex*, p. 203). In Yeats's unfinished novel *The Speckled Bird* I xiv, an old tinker points out Raftery's bush, and remembers Mary Hynes; as the tinker and the young hero stroll by the ruins of Mary Hynes' house, the hero sings Raftery's song about her, and the tinker suspects that he must have a sweetheart of his own (*LTMSB*, pp. 109–10). And in his Nobel Prize address, Yeats quoted the first stanza of Raftery's song about Mary Hynes, and recommended Raftery's intimacy with reality (*A: IDM*).

II 25 *certain men*: '"There was a lot of men up beyond Kilbecanty one night sitting together drinking, and talking of her, and one of them got up and set out to go to Ballylee and see her; but Cloone Bog was open then, and when he came to it he fell into the water, and they found him dead there in the morning"' (*M*, p. 26).

II 29 *they mistook the brightness of the moon*: the moonshine represents the glamour of imagination – under its spell, illusion is indistinguishable from reality. Compare II 38–39: 'O may the moon and sunlight seem / One inextricable beam'.

II 30 *the prosaic light of day*: compare 'Lines Written in Dejection', l. 11: 'the timid sun'. In 'The Tower' – a poem of sunset – sunlight is often mingled, confused, or fading: compare II 5 ('day's declining beam'), II 103–4 ('the sun's / Under eclipse'), III 21 ('a fading gleam') and III 73 ('the horizon fades').

II 32 *one was drowned*: compare 'The Secrets of the Old', ll. 5-6: 'what had drowned a lover once / Sounds like an old song'.

II 33 *Strange, but the man who made the song was blind*: 'In primitive times the blind man became a poet . . . because he had to be driven out of activities all his nature cried for, before he could be contented with the praise of life. And often it is Villon or Verlaine, with impediments plain to all, who sings of life with the ancient simplicity' (*EI*, pp. 277–78). Out of life's penury comes the magnificence of dreams.

II 36 *Homer*: for other references, see 'A Woman Homer Sung'.

II 38–39 *O may the moon and sunlight seem / One inextricable beam*: 'To lunar influence belong all thoughts and emotions that were created by the community, by the common people, by nobody knows who, and to the sun all that came from the high disciplined or individual kingly mind. I myself imagine a marriage of the sun and moon in the arts' (*Ex*, p. 24).

II 40 *if I triumph I must make men mad*: the poet prays for Raftery's sort of poetic power, prehistoric or Druidical in intensity, capable of direct imaginative influence: 'Instead of learning their craft with paper and a pen they [early poets] may have sat for hours imagining themselves to be stocks and stones and beasts of the wood, till the images were so vivid that the passers-by became but a part of the imagination of the dreamer, and wept or laughed or ran away as he would have them' (*EI*, p. 43).

II 41 *I myself created Hanrahan*: an imaginary poet, chief character in six short stories included in *The Secret Rose* (1897) and in 'Red Hanrahan' (1903); also mentioned in 'Alternative Song for the Severed Head ...', ll. 15–16. Hanrahan was originally an itinerant schoolmaster; but his life was blighted by contact with a faery queen, and he became a half-mad rhapsodic poet, a seer of visionary women, a failed seducer of real women, and a great curser of old age.

II 44 *an old man*: the 'ancient ruffian' of l. 50.

II 45 *stumbled, tumbled, fumbled*: compare 'Paudeen', ll. 1–2: 'fumbling ... stumbled'.

II 46 *broken knees*: compare 'A Crazed Girl', l. 6, 'Her knee-cap broken'.

II 49 *old bawn*: a bawn is a ringed mound; but Yeats's original story took place in a barn (*M*, p. 213).

II 50 *ancient ruffian*: a weird old conjurer who bewitched a pack of playing cards in 'Red Hanrahan' (1903). The tale is derived from Irish folklore, summarized in Yeats's 'Ireland Bewitched' (*UP* II, p. 169).

II 57 *towards I have forgotten what*: Hanrahan followed those baying creatures towards a splendid house lit from within by sunlight, even though it was night outside; there he found a pale, inhumanly beautiful woman, weary and little animate, sitting on a throne; her four attendant crones expected Hanrahan to ask the queen who she was, and what she was waiting for, but Hanrahan was tongue-tied, cowardly, and the crones derided him and took away his wits forever (*M*, pp. 218–22). It is implied that Echtge, the faery queen, was waiting for Hanrahan's love. This is a parable of the dangers of trespassing in a too-elevated realm of imagination: the poet's earthly life is blasted. (See 'To the Rose upon the Rood of Time', ll. 13 and 21.) In 1905 Yeats disparaged the world-transcendence in the Hanrahan stories: 'my Red Hanrahan, who should have trodden the same roads with myself, [went] into some undiscoverable country' (*EI*, pp. 298–99). Also compare 'King and No King', l. 6, 'somehow that I have forgot'.

II 58 *a man*: a former owner of Thoor Ballylee during the early nineteenth century – Yeats's note to the poem adds, 'According to one legend he could only leave the Castle upon a Sunday because of his creditors, and according to another he hid in the secret passage' (*VP*, p. 825). The four anecdotes of 'The Tower' II progress from Mrs French, whose whims were so easily gratified that she needed no imagination or art, to this bankrupt tower-dweller, whose needs were so extreme that no imagination or art could suffice to satisfy them. Artists like Raftery and Hanrahan built great edifices of dreams because poverty compelled them; but there exists a level of poverty where dreams themselves fail.

II 67 *climbed the narrow stairs*: compare 'Presences', l. 6, where phantom women 'Climbed up my creaking stair'.

II 68 *certain men-at-arms*: 'The ghosts have been seen at their game of dice in what is now my bedroom' (*VP*, p. 825). The tower, like all symbols, is somewhat animate; and in this stanza the tower's own soul or *genius loci* seems to embody itself in these fierce, coarse revenants of soldiers once quartered there. Yeats's imagination, as it works up its rage against old age, is best satisfied by such ugly, turbulent, urgent images as these.

II 69 *the Great Memory*: the *Anima Mundi*, the universal treasure-house of symbols and images, in which our finite memories all take part. See 'The Second Coming', l. 12, and *M*, pp. 343–66. Yeats labours throughout the poem to force the aperture of memory as wide as possible: compare 'Images and memories' (II 6), 'Some few remembered' (II 17), 'I have forgotten what' (II 57), 'I need all his mighty memories' (II 88), 'if memory recur' (II 103), 'memories of love, / Memories of the words of women' (III 41–42).

II 72 *dice*: compare the dice with which Roman soldiers gamble for Christ's cloak in *Calvary* (1920), ll. 146–68.

II 72 *beat on the board*: compare the refrain of 'The Ghost of Roger Casement': '*The ghost of Roger Casement / Is beating on the door*'.

II 74 *half-mounted man*: the tower's previous owner, from II 58.

II 75 *blind rambling celebrant*: Raftery.

II 76 *the red man*: Hanrahan.

II 80 *the country wench*: Mary Hynes, evidently not wholly chaste: 'She "had seen too much of the world"; but these old men and women, when they tell of her, blame another and not her, and though they can be hard, they grow gentle as the old men of Troy grew gentle when Helen passed by on the walls' (*M*, p. 28).

II 81–84 *Did all old men and women ... rage / As I do now against old age?*: the poem's central question. After rambling through local legends, the poet now reverts to his personal fate, the 'battered kettle' (I 16) of his own body.

II 87 *Go therefore; but leave Hanrahan*: of the convocation of phantoms summoned to provide wisdom about old age, all but Hanrahan can be dismissed. The cultural unanimity that guided Mrs French is impossible in the troubled modern age; the magical art of Raftery is difficult except among pre-literate peoples. But Yeats was neither a squirearch nor an antique bard, and so he had to look to some more intimate, harassed, and diminished model. In part I Yeats asked whether he must 'Choose Plato and Plotinus for a friend' (I 12); but instead he chose Hanrahan, the body's squalor and not the mind's abstraction. It is typical of Yeats (as in the case of Michael Robartes) to choose his mentors from the cast of his own creations.

II 93–94 *Reckoned up every unforeknown, unseeing / Plunge*: according to *A Vision*, one of the stages of the soul's journey after death is called the *Dreaming Back*: there the soul relives the events of its life 'in the order of their intensity or luminosity' (p. 226) in order to exhaust pleasure and pain, its whole natural life. According to *Per Amica Silentia Lunae*, 'even the most wise dead can but arrange their memories as we arrange pieces upon a chessboard' (*M*, p. 359). Here Yeats imagines the dead Hanrahan dreaming back, arranging memories of his haphazard sexual contacts into some formal order. For Yeats the imagination is often sexual in origin, aesthetic and rigorous in tendency.

II 96 *labyrinth*: this word often suggested to Yeats an unintelligible and unearthly, but beautiful and engrossing, complexity. Compare 'Against Unworthy Praise', l. 13: 'The labyrinth of her days' (referring to Maud Gonne); 'The Phases of the Moon', ll. 54–55: 'The soul begins . . . / To die into the labyrinth of itself!'; 'Nineteen Hundred and Nineteen' III 11–12: 'A man . . . / Is lost amid the labyrinth that he has made' (and VI 9: 'labyrinth of the wind'); 'Blood and the Moon' II 11: 'labyrinth of the birds' (i.e., the state); and the essay 'The Tragic Theatre', where the lover chooses 'that beauty which seems unearthly because the individual woman is lost amid the labyrinth of its lines' (*EI*, pp. 244–45).

II 97–98 *Does the imagination dwell the most / Upon a woman won or woman lost?*: according to *A Vision*, the destiny of a man belonging to Yeats's own lunar phase is Loss (p. 141); and both Hanrahan and Yeats were poets whose imaginations were dominated and empowered by a woman lost – the faery queen Echtge or Maud Gonne. There is a stage in the soul's progress after death called the *Phantasmagoria*, in which all 'the objects of hope may be completed, for only that which is completed can be known and dismissed. . . .

The *Phantasmagoria* completes not only life but imagination' (*AV*, p. 230). It is possible that Yeats here conceives the dead Hanrahan as moving through this stage.

II 101–2 *some silly over-subtle thought / Or anything called conscience once*: compare another passage on the world-transforming power of remorse, 'Vacillation' V 11–12: 'But something is recalled, / My conscience or my vanity appalled'.

II 103–4 *the sun's / Under eclipse*: this light-extinguishing obsession recalls the blind Raftery (II 33) – imagination both begins in blindness and ends in it.

III 2–6, 54–57: these lines are closely based on 'The Fisherman', ll. 31–34, written in the same metre: 'Climbing up to a place / Where stone is dark under froth, / And the down-turn of his wrist / When the flies drop in the stream'. In the earlier poem Yeats synthesized an ideal (but non-existent) audience for his poems; and here he keeps similar control over the creative act, by bequeathing his pride in Irish (and all Western) culture to a character of his own devising.

III 9–11 *Bound neither to Cause nor to State, / Neither to slaves ... Nor to the tyrants*: this is the lofty, disdainful rhetoric of 'An Irish Airman Foresees his Death'.

III 12 *The people of Burke and of Grattan*: Edmund Burke (1729-97), political scientist, parliamentary orator, and author of a treatise on the sublime and the beautiful (see 'Blood and the Moon' II 6, 10 and 'The Seven Sages', l. 1); Henry Grattan (1746-1820), Protestant Member of Parliament for Dublin who supported the rights of the Catholic population. Though the young Yeats denounced Grattan as a rhetorician who 'charmed [the] ears and darkened [the] understandings' (*L* I, p. 371), the mature Yeats respected him: Grattan appears favourably in 'The Seven Sages', l. 2; and Yeats noted in his 1930 diary that Grattan's body should be moved to Ireland (*Ex*, p. 296). Compare Yeats's senate speech advocating divorce: 'We are the people of Burke; we are the people of Grattan .... We have created the most of the modern literature of this country. We have created the best of its political intelligence' (*SSY*, p. 99). Also: 'If you had asked an ancient Spartan what made Sparta Sparta, he would have answered, the Laws of Lycurgus [; similarly we] look back ... to Grattan and to Mitchel' (*EI*, p. 248). Grattan is mentioned in *The Words upon the Window-Pane* (1934), l. 66. Yeats at one time thought of including 'John Synge' with Grattan in 'The Tower' III (*YW*, p. 98).

III 16 *the fabulous horn*: the Horn of Plenty – see 'A Prayer for my Daughter', l. 32.

III 20 *the swan*: a bird Yeats associated with the poignancy of age and absence – see 'The Wild Swans at Coole'.

III 23 *Last reach of glittering stream*: compare 'Coole and Ballylee, 1931', l. 16, 'The glittering reaches' (also a setting for swans). Also compare T. Sturge Moore's 'The Dying Swan', ll. 11–12: 'thy last living reach / Of river'; in his note to 'The Tower', Yeats quoted this poem in full, and accused himself of unconsciously echoing it (*VP*, p. 826; compare *EI*, p. 496).

III 24 *his last song*: the swan was reputed to sing only in the moments before its death. In *The King's Threshold* (1904), ll. 896–98, Yeats attributed a prophetic power to the swan-song – a pupil laments over the corpse of his dead poet-mentor, 'Long-throated swans upon the waves of time, / Sing loudly, for beyond the wall of the world / That race may hear our music and awake'. In 1936 Yeats wrote, 'I am physically but not mentally weak. At last I shall, I think, sing the heroic song I have longed for – perhaps my swan song' (*DWL*, p. 74).

III 26–27 *I mock Plotinus' thought / And cry in Plato's teeth*: the dismal possibility that Plato and Plotinus might have to remain as Yeats's only friends (I 12) is at last repudiated: Yeats affirms the value of imagination, not shadowy abstractions. 'The Tower' moves from Platonic ideality to more and more tangible, sweaty, and thorough embodiments of human creative energy. In Yeats's note to the poem, however, he claimed that he had erred in saying that Plotinus divorced reality from the human imagination, and quoted a passage where Plotinus wrote, '"soul is the author of all living things … whatever is nourished by earth and sea … the divine stars in the sky; it is the maker of the sun; itself formed and ordered this vast heaven"' (*VP*, p. 826). Indeed 'The Tower' III 28–32 could be regarded as a paraphrase of this passage. Compare also the curse on Platonists in 'Statistics', l. 1.

III 28–29 *Death and life were not / Till man made up the whole*: compare 'Death', l. 12: 'Man has created death'. Yeats attributed to the Druids the belief that mankind created the world (*LTMSB*, p. 154; *Ex*, p. 24); and in a letter refuting the existence of an external world, Yeats wrote, 'In so far therefore as Time and Space are deduced from our sense-data we are the creators of Time and Space' (*TSMC*, p. 82). Elsewhere Yeats wrote that 'I have read in a fabulous book that Adam had but to imagine a bird, and it was born into life, and that he created all things out of himself by nothing more important than an unflagging fancy' (*Ex*, p. 20).

III 30–31 *lock, stock, and barrel / Out of his bitter soul*: the culmination of the theme of the magnificence and penury of dreams: the universe itself, and all of paradise, are beheld as the creative acts of an impoverished and victimized mankind. For the theme of the creative power of bitterness, see 'Ancestral Houses', ll. 17–21; 'My House', ll. 16–17: 'the daemonic rage / Imagined everything'; and 'Vacillation' VI 11–12: 'From man's blood-sodden heart are sprung/Those branches of the night and day'. In the early drafts Yeats strongly identified mankind with God – Jehovah or Christ: 'I mock at Greek and Jew / Why could no Rabbi say / That Eternal Man / rested the seventh day'; 'Men on the third day rise ... Dream and so create / A second Paradise' (*YW*, pp. 84, 88).

III 37–39 *peace ... Greece*: this rhyme can be found in 'To a Wealthy Man ...', ll. 25–29, a passage similar in theme and structure.

III 40–41 *imaginings / And memories*: an echo of II 6, 'Images and memories'.

III 44–45 *Man makes a superhuman / Mirror-resembling dream*: Western art, architecture, philosophy, and poetry together constitute a vast image of mankind – just as, on a smaller scale, this poem constitutes an image of the poet.

III 47–48 *The daws ... drop twigs layer upon layer*: the building of a nest, like the building of a civilization, is the act of an entire race. 'The dead living in their memories are ... the source of all that we call instinct ... it is the dream martens that, all unknowing, are master-masons to the living martens building about church windows their elaborate nests' (*M*, p. 359; also *EI*, p. 414). Compare 'The Gift of Harun Al-Rashid', ll. 26–28: 'the truth / That ... can give birds wit'. In Yeats's last short story, a woman spends her life teaching a cuckoo how to build a nest – presumably to prepare for the hatching of the next historical era (*AV*, p. 49). Compare also 'The Stare's Nest by My Window'.

III 53 *faith and pride*: declared at III 25 and III 7.

III 60 *This sedentary trade*: compare 'Ego Dominus Tuus', l. 65: 'A style is found by sedentary toil'; and 'Hound Voice', l. 3: 'boredom of the desk'.

III 61–75: these lines were added to the poem after the rest was finished, perhaps in 1926 (*YW*, p. 101).

III 61 *make my soul*: compose my soul in anticipation of death. Compare 'Beggar to Beggar Cried', l. 4: 'make my soul before my pate is bare'; also several short stories – in one, a tinker visited by Death cries, ' "I'll ... make me sowl an Hail Marys" ' (*UP* I, p. 315; compare *LTMSB*, p. 349); in another, an old smuggler bends over his rosary and has 'no thought for anything but for the making of his soul' (*M*, p. 191); in a third, Owen Aherne declares that ' "Swift made a soul for the gentlemen of this city by hating his neighbour as himself" ' (*M*, p. 301). In an unused broadcast script, Yeats wrote that 'Sailing to Byzantium' recorded thoughts on 'the state of my soul, for it is right for an old man to make his soul' (Jeffares, *NCP*, p. 213); and in an essay on Blake Yeats noted that 'we are agreed that we "make our souls" out of some one of the great poets' (*EI*, p. 111), not out of listening to sermons. Yeats even expressed a hope that his Blake edition would 'help good people "to make their souls"' (*L* I, p. 256).

III 63 *a learned school*: compare the 'singing school' of 'Sailing to Byzantium' II 5. It may seem that Plato and Plotinus, so furiously rejected at III 26–27, have now been re-invited as tutors; but even as Yeats extricates himself from physical suffering and the natural world, his values are those of earth and the body.

III 72 *but the clouds of the sky*: just as dead souls compose their memories into formal patterns – see the note to II 93–94 – so the aged poet can attain deliverance, anaesthesia, by a process of detachment and artful arrangement.

III 74 *a bird's sleepy cry*: perhaps in this cry there can be heard elements both of the swan song (III 24) and the mother daw's chatter (III 47).

Meditations in Time of Civil War

In 'The Tower', Yeats tried to erect from a loose heap of local lore a tightly designed structure of wisdom. In this series of poems, he tries, with little success, to make sense of equally intimate, but more random and violent events – in 1922 some soldiers of de Valéra's Irish Republican Army, fighting against Nationalist troops loyal to the Irish Free State (created by the British partition of Ireland in December 1921, ratified by the Irish parliament in January 1922), took the war right to Yeats's doorstep: 'Last night I heard two explosions at 4 a.m. [blowing up two local bridges] . . . A motor has just passed with a National soldier and a coffin up on end . . . The National army is in control here and the people are with them but the Irregulars come out at night' (*TSMC*, p. 46); 'Before they were finished the Republicans blew up our "ancient bridge" [II 1] one midnight. They forbade us to leave the house, but were otherwise polite, even saying at last "Good-night, thank you", as though we had given them the bridge' (*VP*, p. 827).

As in 'The Tower', Yeats struggles to see his whole neighbourhood as a field of symbols, where everything is precious, significant – no ordinary flower blossoms by his door, only the 'symbolic rose' (II 4) – but in this sequence the meaningfulness of objects is threatened by a pervasive chaos. The persona of 'The Tower' was an elderly poet trying to recapture his flagging imaginative energies; but here the persona is the sage, the Platonist burning midnight oil, the author of the historical myth of *A Vision* paralysed and disabled by historical events too spastic, mechanical, destructive, and inconsequential to be assimilated into smooth historical mythology.

The poems in this series offer a number of experiments in achieving a home despite the catastrophe of historical chance. The sequence is arranged to begin with the most impersonal and distant habitation; the following poems discuss increasingly private, tender, and nearby places and things; and the final poems – most intimate of all – present Yeats's dreams, hopes, and fantasies.

I. Ancestral Houses

This poem, written before the start of the Civil War, shows an antique and ceremonious civilization, evidently forever lost.

3–4 *Life overflows ... And rains down life until the basin spills*: compare 'A Dialogue of Self and Soul' I 33–34: 'Such fullness ... overflows / And falls into the basin'.

7–8 *mechanical / Or servile*: characteristic of the present age – for more machines, see the note to VII 32. According to *A Vision*, the present age is at the end of the *primary* gyre, all its creative energy spent, servile and weak yet adoring physical violence (p. 272).

11 *life's own self-delight*: for the theme of reflexivity, see the note to 'A Prayer for my Daughter', ll. 67–68.

12 *the abounding glittering jet*: like the Horn of Plenty in 'A Prayer for my Daughter' (l. 32), the fountain is an important symbol of effortless, ever-self-renewing abundance. Compare 'The Gift of Harun Al-Rashid', ll. 89–90: 'youth's very fountain, / Being all brimmed with life'. Yeats likened both art and national culture to a fountain: 'Art bids us touch and taste and hear and see the world, and shrinks from ... every abstract thing, from all that is of the brain only, from all that is not a fountain jetting from the entire hopes, memories, and sensations of the body' (*EI*, pp. 292–93); 'The greater part of [a nation's] creative life ... should be the jet of a fountain that falls into the basin where it rose' (*UP* II, p. 442). There is also direct evidence of the inspiring quality of the fountain: 'The Lake Isle of Innisfree' came to Yeats when he saw 'a fountain in a shop-window which balanced a little ball upon its jet' (*A: FY* 15).

13 *some marvellous empty sea-shell*: a counter-symbol to the fountain – the life within the shell is dead, and only the gorgeous outside remains. For other sea-shells, see 'The Song of the Happy Shepherd', l. 36.

19–20 *Bitter and violent men, might rear in stone / The sweetness that all longed for*: compare 'The Gift of Harun Al-Rashid', ll. 47–48: 'violent great hearts can lose / Their bitterness and find the honeycomb'. Yeats often derived sweetness from bitterness and violence – see 'To a Wealthy Man ...', ll. 25–26. The theme recurs in this sequence at III 13-14.

23–24 *the great-grandson ...'s but a mouse*: the theme of degeneration recurs, in a more personal and painful manner, at IV 9.

25 *gardens where the peacock strays*: evidently the gardens at Lady Ottoline Morrell's estate at Garsington, near Oxford. The peacock is sacred to Juno (I 27), and later in the sequence a peacock's cry will announce the emergence of a new historical era (III 32). For other peacocks, see 'The Indian upon God', l. 17.

30 *slippered Contemplation finds his ease*: an allusion to Milton to match the age of the 'ancestral houses': 'And add to these retired Leisure, / That in trim Gardens takes his pleasure; / But first, and chiefest, with thee bring ... The Cherub Contemplation' ('Il Penseroso' [1631], ll. 49–51, 54). 'Il Penseroso' reappears at II 14. For other old-fashioned personifications, see 'A Prayer for my Daughter', ll. 79–80.

II. My House

This poem hints at a convergence of two styles of solitude, rage, and desperation – one active, one contemplative: that of the Norman soldier who founded Thoor Ballylee, and that of Yeats, trying to rehearse in his own mind the violence of imagination that created the world.

8 *water-hen*: see 'The Indian upon God', l. 3.

13 *a candle*: in 1922 Yeats wrote, remembering recent horrors and those of the Anglo-Irish War: 'the Black and Tans [fighting against the IRA] dragged two young men tied alive to a lorry by their heels, till their bodies were rent in pieces ... There is no longer a virtuous nation and the best of us live by candle light' (*L*, pp. 690–91).

14 Il Penseroso's *Platonist*: see 'The Phases of the Moon', l. 15: 'Milton's Platonist'.

16–17 *How the daemonic rage / Imagined everything*: compare 'The Tower' III 28–32, and a deleted line of 'The Circus Animals' Desertion': 'Cannon the god and father of mankind' (Bradford, *YW*, p. 163).

20–21: between these lines the original text had a fourth stanza: 'The river rises, and it sinks again; / One hears the rumble of it far below / Under its rocky hole. / What Median, Persian, Babylonian, / In reverie, or in vision, saw / Symbols of the soul, / Mind from mind has caught: / The subterranean streams, / Tower where a candle gleams, / A suffering passion and a labouring thought?' (*VP*, p. 420). This stanza provided themes for the opening of 'Coole and Ballylee, 1931'.

21 *A man-at-arms*: a member of the de Burgo family. In one draft of the unfinished *The Speckled Bird*, Yeats used the name *De Burgh*, or *De Burgo*, to represent the family modelled on his own; for a fanciful history of the De Burgos, see *LTMSB*, pp. 242, 307.

24 *long wars and sudden night alarms*: seemingly parallel to Yeats's situation during the Civil War.

28 *My bodily heirs*: compare IV 3 and 'A Prayer on Going into my House', l. 2.

30 *Befitting emblems of adversity*: for self-conscious emblem-making, compare 'A Dialogue of Self and Soul' I 28–29: 'all these I set / For emblems of the day against the tower'; and 'Blood and the Moon' I 8–9: 'I have set / A powerful emblem up'.

III. My Table

This poem explores one of those 'emblems of adversity' mentioned in the last line of the previous poem: Sato's sword becomes a focus of meditation. The poet hopes that the sword's decisiveness and immutability may inspire him with a sense of purpose, an assurance that incoherent life may culminate in the perfection of art; but in the end the sword leads him back to the ache of changeable human life. Yeats later remarked that the sword was 'my symbol of life' (*L*, p. 729); and in 'Coole Park, 1929', ll. 9–10, it is also a symbol of art: 'Hyde . . . had beaten into prose / That noble blade the Muses buckled on' – as if the sword were the incisive tool that probed reality, that cut it into its fundamental divisions.

2 *Sato's gift*: Yeats received this sword in Portland, Oregon, from an admirer of his poetry. 'A rather wonderful thing happened . . . A very distinguished looking Japanese came to see us. . . . He had something in his hand wrapped up in embroidered silk . . . He untied the silk cord that bound it and brought out a sword which had been for 500 years in his family. It had been made 550 years ago' (*L*, p. 662). This sword and the silk embroidery reappear as 'emblems of the day' in 'A Dialogue of Self and Soul' I 9–32; and a draft of 'Under Ben Bulben' III mentioning Sato's sword (*VR*, p. 156) is quoted in the note to that section. Compare also 'Symbols', l. 5, and *Ex*, p. 320.

8 *Chaucer had not drawn breath*: poor arithmetic – the poet was born around 1343.

10 *Curved like new moon*: the sword, like the lunar month in *A Vision*, seems to be a diagram, an embodiment of a system of change. This simile will be reversed at VII 3–5.

13–14 *only an aching heart / Conceives a changeless work of art*: a summary of the controlling principle of 'Ancestral Houses' (see I 17–20). This aphorism begins a cycle of freezes and thaws: first the aching heart, then the changeless work of art; then (as in 'Sailing to Byzantium') human life starts to imitate the changelessness of art (III 24); at last change reenters the static system, and the heart aches again (III 28).

17–20 *A marvellous accomplishment ... through the centuries ran*: compare 'A Prayer on Going into My House', ll. 7–8: 'what the great and passionate have used / Throughout so many varying centuries'.

32 *Juno's peacock screamed*: the traditionalist is startled out of complacency by a shriek that announces historical upheaval: 'A civilisation is a struggle to keep self-control ... The loss of control over thought comes towards the end; first a sinking in upon the moral being, then the last surrender, the irrational cry, revelation – the scream of Juno's peacock' (*AV*, p. 268). In the story 'The Adoration of the Magi' (1897) the coming of the Antichrist is announced when an old man suddenly 'crowed like a cock, till the room seemed to shake with the crowing' (*M*, p. 311); and in *The Player Queen* (1922), an old beggar who brays like a donkey similarly heralds a new age. For other peacocks, see I 25 and 'The Indian upon God', l. 17. For other, sexier bird-shrieks, see 'Solomon and the Witch', l. 9.

IV. My Descendants

In the previous poems Yeats was able to find significance in the things around him – the tower, the sword – but no refuge from the world's violence; indeed all his symbols seemed to symbolize only further ruin. In this poem (a kind of sequel to the Introductory Rhymes to *Responsibilities*) Yeats speculates on the fact that his children enjoy no immunity from destruction; but even though his family and the tower itself may decay, enough will remain to provide a monument to his own labour. The meaning of a symbol, it seems, can outlast its physical integrity.

3 *a woman and a man*: Anne Butler Yeats (b. 1919) and Michael Butler Yeats (b. 1921) – the 'bodily heirs' of II 28.

12 *marriage with a fool*: compare 'Why should not Old Men be Mad?', ll. 5–6: 'A girl that knew all Dante once / Live to bear children to a dunce'. Yeats wrote a treatise on eugenics, *On the Boiler* (*Ex*, pp. 405–453), relevant to this poem; and *Purgatory* (1939) describes the ruin of a great house from a poor marriage.

13–14 *May ... this stark tower / Become a roofless ruin*: this curse on his own dwelling shows how strongly the poet wants to keep a symbolic correspondence between the house and its owner – unlike the disparity emblematized by the empty sea-shell in 'Ancestral Houses' (I 13–16). By VI 4 ('My wall is loosening'), the tower's collapse seems to be coming to pass – compare the 'Falling towers' in Eliot's *The Waste Land*, l. 374 (both Eliot's and Yeats's towers may be related to a design on the Tarot card-pack). Also compare the prophecy of Coole Park's ruin in 'Coole Park, 1929', ll. 26–28.

18 *the very owls in circles move*: the motion of the birds imitates the whirl of the gyres that control history – see 'The Second Coming', ll. 1–2.

20 *an old neighbour*: Lady Gregory, whose estate at Coole Park was near Thoor Ballylee.

22 *a girl*: Georgie Yeats.

24 *These stones remain their monument and mine*: compare 'To be Carved on a Stone at Thoor Ballylee', ll. 5–6: 'may these characters remain / When all is ruin once again'.

V. The Road at my Door

In the first four poems in this sequence, Yeats's dreams and fantasies were solidly embodied in the things and places around him. But in the final three poems, they start to detach themselves from the physical world. This poem is the turning point: the war seems to have become intolerably close, and the poet needs to take refuge in evasion.

1 *An affable Irregular*: a member of the Irish Republican Army – the Civil War began when the IRA opposed the signing of the Anglo-Irish treaty (December 1921).

2 *Falstaffian man*: Falstaff was the fat, emphatic, witty, lustful, boastful, loud-roaring knight in Shakespeare's *1 and 2 Henry IV* and *The Merry Wives of Windsor*.

5 *The finest play*: as the reference to Falstaff suggests, the Civil War is seen as a kind of theatre – compare 'Two Songs from a Play', l. 8: 'As though God's death were but a play'.

6 *A brown Lieutenant*: a member of the National Army, loyal to England's version of an independent Ireland.

10 *A pear-tree broken by the storm*: for other broken trees, see 'The Lamentation of the Old Pensioner', l. 14.

12 *The moor-hen*: see 'The Indian upon God', l. 3.

13 *To silence the envy*: the old theme of the contemplative man's envy for the active man – see the note to 'Fergus and the Druid'.

15 *the cold snows of a dream*: as in 'My Table', this poem has a rhythm of freezing and thawing – but here life freezes, not into triumphant art, but into a state of paralysis and sterility. The poet is becoming increasingly disgusted with his own dreaminess – his dreams seem to have lost the creative power found in 'My House'. The metaphor 'snows of a dream' will be literalized at VII 2. For another passage on snowy dreams, see *The Herne's Egg* (1938) II 62–67.

VI. The Stare's Nest by my Window

Yeats explained that he wrote these lines after hearing explosions and seeing coffins driven past his house, at a time when no news of the war's progress could be got: 'One felt an overmastering desire not to grow unhappy or embittered, not to lose all sense of the beauty of nature. A stare (our West of Ireland name for a starling) had built a hole beside my window and I made these verses out of the feeling of the moment . . . Presently a strange thing happened. I began to smell honey in places where honey could not be' (*A: Notes*). Here the poet tries to use the logic of cyclical history to coerce some hope from the mere fact of ruin: if winter comes, can spring be far behind? Like Sato's sword (III 2), the honey-bees are easy to moralize, to make emblematic.

Title *Stare*: in the first printing the bird was a jay.

1 *The bees*: see 'The Lake Isle of Innisfree', l. 3.

4 *My wall is loosening*: the collapse of the tower, proposed at IV 13–14, seems to be happening.

5 *the empty house*: compare the 'empty sea-shell' (I 13).

6 *We are closed in, and the key is turned*: compare T. S. Eliot, *The Waste Land* (1922), ll. 412–13: 'I have heard the key / Turn in the door once and turn once only'.

14 *that dead young soldier in his blood*: compare 'Nineteen Hundred and Nineteen' I 28, 'crawl in her own blood'.

16–17 *We had fed the heart on fantasies, / The heart's grown brutal*: this preference for deliberate unreality is the exact counterpart of the cannibalism and annihilation of the war itself (VII 11–14) – there is objectless fantasy on one hand, objectless violence on the other.

18–19 *More substance in our enmities / Than in our love*: compare 'The Second Coming', ll. 7–8: 'The best lack all conviction, while the worst / Are full of passionate intensity'. The reference to *substance* calls attention to the growing insubstantiality infecting the whole sequence of poems.

VII. I see Phantoms of Hatred and of the Heart's Fullness and of the Coming Emptiness

In Shakespeare's *Antony and Cleopatra*, Antony sees images in cloud – a bear, a lion, a citadel, a mountain – and then watches as 'That which is now a horse . . . the rack dislimbs, and makes it indistinct, / As water is in water' (IV xiv 9–11). In this poem Yeats too beholds cloud-images take shape and dissolve in vivid incoherencies. This is the sort of imagination that Yeats called *Hodos Chameliontos*, the road of unintelligible images (see the note to 'Fergus and the Druid', l. 38). Instead of symbols securely founded on sensuous reality – the sword of III, the stare's nest of V – an exciting but groundless phantasmagoria troubles and sickens the poet's mind.

In 'The Tables of the Law' (1896), Owen Aherne – 'half monk, half soldier of fortune' – was described as a man who 'must needs turn action into dreaming, and dreaming into action' (*M*, p. 294); but the Yeats of this poem has no such integrity of being – his dreams no longer culminate in acts, nor do his acts lead to further dreams. In I and III the act and the dream exhibited a complex synergy, but here the whole antithesis between action and contemplation seems to be, not a healthy contrary, but a negation.

2 *blown snow*: see V 15.

3–5 *a moon ... A glittering sword*: see III 10.

5–6 *A puff of wind / And those white glittering fragments of the mist sweep by*: this resembles a passage in 'Hanrahan's Vision' (1896), a story about images that form out of mist: 'the mist rose of a sudden and hid them [beautiful lovers], and then a light gust of wind blew them away ... and covered Hanrahan ... with a white wing of cloud' (*M*, p. 250).

10 *Vengeance for Jacques Molay*: 'A cry for vengeance because of the murder of the Grand Master of the Templars [burned at the stake in 1314] seems to me fit symbol for those who labour for hatred, and so for sterility in various kinds. It is said to have been incorporated in the ritual of certain Masonic societies of the eighteenth century, and to have fed class hatred' (*VP*, p. 827). Browning's 'The Heretic's Tragedy' (1855) is about Molay's immolation. As Elizabeth Cullingford has shown (*ELH* 50 [1983]: 763–89), Yeats associated the Knights Templar with the French Revolution and with Bolshevism – all movements tending towards mob control.

13–14 *Plunges towards nothing, arms and fingers spreading wide / For the embrace of nothing*: compare 'The Crazed Moon', ll. 17–18: 'spread wide that each / May rend'; and the quatrain on nothingness cited in the note to 'The Gyres', l. 22. This will to annihilation is contrasted with the purposive, productive violence of former times (I 17–21).

14–16 *I ... all but cried / For vengeance*: for the poet's absorption into hysteria, see 'His Dream', l. 14.

18 *Magical unicorns*: as Henn notes (*LT*, p. 255), Yeats is describing a painting by Gustave Moreau, *Ladies and Unicorns*, a print of which decorated a room of Thoor Ballylee – see the note to 'The Lover's Song'. Usually – as in *The Unicorn from the Stars* (1908) and *The Player Queen* (1922) – Yeats's unicorns have something of the significance of the rough beast of 'The Second Coming', l. 21 – the avatars of a vehement, unholy, *antithetical* civilization, come to prance, to trample our world to pieces (see the note to that line). But these

too-pretty, virginal unicorns seem to retain only a vestige of their power to transform history. It may be relevant that in 'The Adoration of the Magi' (1897; 1925), the last word of the dying harlot who gives birth to the unicorn of the New Dispensation is 'the name of a symbolist painter' (*M*, p. 314). Yeats also referred to unicorns in *On Baile's Strand* (1904), l. 417, and in *Deirdre* (1907), l. 91. Outside of the plays, unicorns appear in Yeats's poetry only in this poem and in 'The Two Kings', l. 19.

20 *Babylonian almanacs*: these almanacs, like the mechanical warfare of VII 30–31, belong to a *primary*, objective era – see 'The Dawn', l. 6.

21 *a pool*: the fountain of I 12 suggested spurting abundance; this pool, by contrast, may suggest that the beautiful images of the stanza are simply films, water-reflections. Yeats suggested this antithesis in a 1902 letter to Joyce: 'Remember what Dr Johnson said about somebody "let us wait until we find out whether he is a fountain or a cistern"' (Joyce, *Letters* II, p. 13).

22 *longing drowns under its own excess*: compare *Deirdre* (1907), l. 244: 'love drowns in its own flood'.

25 *cloud-pale ... eyes*: compare 'He tells of a Valley ...', l. 4: 'cloud-pale eyelids'.

29 *brazen hawks*: 'I suppose that I must have put hawks into the fourth stanza because I have a ring with a hawk and a butterfly upon it, to symbolize the straight road of logic, and so of mechanism, and the crooked road of intuition: "For wisdom is a butterfly and not a gloomy bird of prey" [see 'Tom O'Roughley', ll. 7–8]' (*VP*, p. 827).

29 *self-delighting reverie*: the condition of the ladies and the unicorns of the previous stanza – for the theme of self-delight, see 'A Prayer for my Daughter', ll. 67–68.

30 *Nor hate of what's to come, nor pity for what's gone*: in 'The Double Vision of Michael Robartes' – another poem based on the extreme contrast of ugly and lovely images – the misshapening puppets 'do not even feel' (I 14); similarly, the aerial warriors of this poem have reached a state of objectivity beyond affect. The rhetoric of this line oddly recalls 'An Irish Airman Foresees his Death', ll. 3–4: 'Those that I fight I do not hate, / Those that I guard I do not love'.

34 *I could have proved my worth*: as in the Introductory Rhymes to *Responsibilities*, Yeats wishes that he could have been a fighter, a man of action.

38 *It had but made us pine the more*: contentment is impossible, because the man of action and the man of contemplation envy each other – as in 'Fergus and the Druid'.

39 *The half-read wisdom*: compare 'Nineteen Hundred and Nineteen' III 25, 'the half-written page'. The sage feels self-derision because of the blurriness

and impotence of his understanding – as in 'The Phases of the Moon', ll. 20 and 136.

40 *Suffice the ageing man as once the growing boy*: the 'growing boy' seems to echo Wordsworth's 'Ode: Intimations of Immortality . . .', ll. 68–69: 'Shades of the prison-house begin to close / Upon the growing Boy'. Also compare 'The Gift of Harun Al-Rashid', ll. 173–74: 'that midnight voice / That is to age what milk is to a child'.

Nineteen Hundred and Nineteen

Each of the first four poems in this volume offers a definition of the relation between art and life. In 'Sailing to Byzantium', art and life are antithetical, as distant from one another as Byzantium from Ireland. In 'The Tower', art is seen not as a refuge from life but as an expression of it. In 'Meditations in Time of Civil War', art is still expressive of life's violence and bitterness, but that violence, that bitterness, threaten to overwhelm any attempt at order or stability. In 'Nineteen Hundred and Nineteen', art fails – it can offer neither refuge nor insight nor adornment. It should be noted that this remarkable sequence of four poems at the beginning of *The Tower* was written in reverse order: 'Sailing to Byzantium', with its fervour, its numbness, its slightly eccentric composure, was the last written; yet its placement in the book makes the reader feel that all its mosaic saints and golden birds are being sucked into the whirlpool of 'Nineteen Hundred and Nineteen'. In this poem of iconoclasm, art is shattered and the artist mocked. There is a kind of appetite for chaos – 'A bunch of martyrs (1916) were the bomb and we are living in the explosion' (*L*, p. 690).

The poem was first published as 'Thoughts upon the Present State of the World' (and dated 'May, 1921'). The retitling and redating may reflect Yeats's sense of the importance of 1919, the year in which Ireland's war of independence took on a new ferocity; the rebel Irish Republican Army was opposed by the Black and Tans, consisting chiefly of British soldiers demobilized from the Great War (the Civil War was to begin in December 1921, when England created the Irish Free State but retained Northern Ireland, thereby internalizing the Anglo-Irish War described in this poem). Yeats wrote to Olivia Shakespear on 9 April 1921 that these poems 'are not philosophical but simple and passionate, a lamentation over lost peace and lost hope. My own philosophy does not make brighter the prospect' (*L*, p. 668).

I 3–4: these lines read in one draft: 'Changeless and deathless; above the murdering moon / Above the insolence of the sun' (Bradford, *YW*, p. 65).

I 6 *An ancient image made of olive wood*: an image of Athena carved of olive wood was kept in the Erechtheum, on the Acropolis of Athens. The olive tree was sacred in Athens: when Poseidon and Athena competed for the patronage of Attica, Poseidon created a salt spring on the Acropolis, while Athena caused an olive tree to grow. Compare I 46, 'that stump on the Acropolis', and 'Colonus' Praise', ll. 12–13: 'the grey-leaved olive-tree / Miracle-bred out of the living stone'.

I 7 *Phidias*: the great sculptor of the fifth century BC, who built a monumental statue of Athena in the Parthenon. Compare 'Under Ben Bulben' IV 8, 'gentler Phidias'; and 'The Statues', ll. 15–16: 'Phidias / Gave women dreams and dreams their looking-glass'. In *A Vision* Yeats takes Phidias as example of an artist working at maximum imaginative synthesis: 'in Phidias Ionic and Doric influence unite – one remembers Titian – and all is transformed by the full moon, and all abounds and flows' (p. 270).

I 8 *golden grasshoppers*: Thucydides wrote that Athenian women fastened their hair with golden brooches in the shape of grasshoppers (see Finneran, *PNE*, p. 650). For another passage on the general destruction of art, see 'Lapis Lazuli', ll. 29–32.

I 9 *pretty toys*: this epithet, along with 'showy thing' (I 18), recalls Yeats's dismissals of his own art in 'Reconciliation' and 'The Circus Animals' Desertion' (originally entitled 'Tragic Toys') – but here it is a civilization that is dismissed, not a career. For other toys, see 'Certain Artists bring her Dolls and Drawings', l. 11.

I 19–20 *cannon ... ploughshare*: see Isaiah 2:4.

I 21–23 *unless a little powder burned ... it lack all glory*: 'Love would be nothing if it lacked / Thunder' (Bradford, *WPQ*, p. 210).

I 25 *days are dragon-ridden*: this describes the atrocities in the Anglo-Irish War, after World War I. The dragon reappears at II 3.

I 25–26 *the nightmare / Rides upon sleep*: compare 'The Gyres', l. 9: 'numb nightmare ride on top'.

I 26 *drunken soldiery*: compare 'Byzantium', l. 2, and the posthumous 'Reprisals', l. 15: 'Half-drunk or whole-mad soldiery' (*VP*, p. 791).

I 27 *the mother, murdered in her blood*: Lady Gregory wrote in her journal that Eileen Quinn, a young mother of three, was 'shot dead ... with her child in her arms' by Black and Tan soldiers shooting from a passing lorry (5 November 1920).

I 29 *as before*: a hint of the cyclical rhythms to be described in part II. Yeats wrote in *A Vision* that 'A civilisation is a struggle to keep self-control' (p. 268) – a struggle that regularly fails.

I 32 *weasels*: see IV 4.

I 33 *read the signs*: as in many poems in this volume, the poet continually struggles to construe and interpret ominous, nearly illegible signs – see III 25.

I 39–40 *all triumph would / But break upon his ghostly solitude*: a kind of refrain – see III 20, 'triumph can but mar our solitude'. Yeats first stated this doctrine in *The King's Threshold* (1904), ll. 893–903, where the dead poet-hero's pupils quarrel over funeral-decorum: the Youngest Pupil wants trumpets to sound and swans to sing, while the Oldest Pupil wants silence or the most muted sounds: 'You wrong his greatness speaking so of triumph ... nor song nor trumpet-blast / Can call up races ... To mend the wrong and mar the solitude'. Yeats often seems to echo the end of *The King's Threshold* in *The Tower*, as if his life recalled the tragedy of that self-starving early hero.

According to *A Vision*, the dead soul labours to purify itself of all achievement, all memory, in order to prepare for *Beatitude*; this is why a consciousness of triumph impedes the poet in this poem from his work of self-disengagement.

I 42 *vanishes*: the poem continually tries to confront evanescence – see III 18 and VI 5. Compare 'Two Songs from a Play' II 9–10: 'Everything that man esteems / Endures a moment'.

I 43 *What more is there to say?*: compare the refrain of 'The Curse of Cromwell': '*What is there left to say?*'

I 46 *that stump*: Athena's olive tree – see I 6. Herodotus claimed that, after the Persians burned the Acropolis, the sacred olive grew a cubit in one day.

II 1 *Loie Fuller*: American dancer (1862–1928), famous at the Folies Bergères in Paris, where she used sticks to whirl glittering lengths of cloth. Her veils inspired Debussy's *Voiles* (*Preludes* I 2). Frank Kermode notes (in *Partisan Review* 28 [1961]: 70) that Fuller's dancing represented 'a kind of spatial equivalent of Music'.

II 3 *a dragon of air*: the metaphor of the 'dragon-ridden' days (I 25) is literalized into this surprisingly beautiful image, an instant of aesthetic relief amid the poem's general bewilderment. But the only lasting art is that of change itself, of the passing of time. This 'half-imagined' poem (II 25) is governed by the whirlwind, by provisional images that half-constitute themselves out of air, such as this dragon and Robert Artisson (VI 16).

II 6 *the Platonic Year*: the most inclusive of all cycles, the period during which the constellations make a full circuit of the zodiac – Yeats quoted Taylor's speculation that it lasted 36,000 years (*AV*, p. 248). Compare 'Two Songs from a Play' I 7.

II 7–8 *Whirls out new right and wrong, / Whirls in the old instead*: a parody of Tennyson's *In Memoriam A.H.H.* (1850) CVI: 'Ring out the old, ring in the new, / Ring, happy bells, across the snow: / The year is going, let him go; / Ring out the false, ring in the true'. Also compare 'Three Marching Songs' I 9, '*time amends old wrong*'.

II 9 *All men are dancers*: compare 'Mohini Chatterjee', l. 28: 'Men dance on deathless feet'.

II 10 *gong*: see 'Byzantium', l. 4.

III 1–2 *Some ... poet / Compares the solitary soul to a swan*: Shelley has been suggested: 'My soul is an enchanted Boat / Which, like a sleeping swan, doth float' (*Prometheus Unbound* II v 72–73); see also *Alastor*, l. 275. But Yeats's swans are usually much more desperate (as in this poem and 'The Tower' III) or violent (as in 'Leda and the Swan'). In Browning's Shelleyan poem *Pauline* (1833), ll. 102–11, the poet compares his soul, choking in solitude, to a swan trapped in a dark cave. Yeats associated swans with absence in 'The Wild Swans at Coole'; and in the present poem too he uses the swan as an emblem of departure, absence, willed vanishing. In 'Coole and Ballylee, 1931', l. 19, Yeats would extend the metaphor of soul as swan.

III 3 *I am satisfied with that*: the sufficiency of emblems and images is discussed in 'I see Phantoms ...', l. 40.

III 4 *a troubled mirror*: the swan, studying its image on the rippling surface of historical change, is another of the many jejune or poorly constituted images in this poem. In 1937 Yeats wrote to Dorothy Wellesley: 'I begin to see things double – doubled in history, world history, personal history ... Perhaps there is a theme for poetry in this "double swan and shadow"' (*DWL*, p. 135).

III 12 *labyrinth*: see 'The Tower' II 96.

III 17–18 *if our works could / But vanish with our breath*: instead of lamenting that 'Man ... loves what vanishes' (I 42), the poet here finds virtue in the fact of vanishing – all the self-construction, the nest-building of 'The Tower' III is here deliberately demolished.

III 20 *triumph can but mar our solitude*: see I 39–40.

III 22–23 *a rage / To end all things*: compare 'Ribh considers Christian Love insufficient', ll. 3–5: 'hatred ... A sort of besom that can clear the soul'.

III 23–25 *to end ... The half-imagined, the half-written page*: the poet is sick of his own vision – his imagination can terminate in no fixed or satisfying image. The poet seems ready to destroy the text of this very poem – for other poems in which the poem's text is a theme, see 'When You are Old', l. 2. Compare 'I see Phantoms ...', l. 39, where the poet wanly embraces his 'half-read wisdom'; and also 'Parnell's Funeral' I 28, where the poet discusses poetry as a mode of extermination, 'the rhyme rats hear before they die'.

IV 4 *the weasel's tooth*: the self-undressing of part III reaches a kind of climax – the poet strips himself of pretence and dreams until he turns into a weasel (compare I 32). In 'A Dialogue of Self and Soul' Yeats asks how a man could escape 'That defiling and disfigured shape / The mirror of malicious eyes / Casts upon his eyes until at last / He thinks that shape must be his shape?' (II 11–14). Here the poet, staring at his own image in the 'troubled mirror' (III 4) of society, sees not a swan but a puny, vicious animal. Compare 'Fergus and the Druid', l. 5, where the Druid assumes a weasel's shape; and 'Parnell's Funeral' I 32, where Yeats asks men to judge his own soul, 'Whether it be an animal or a man'. Also note John O'May's 1910 letter to Yeats, describing the Malay magic in which a boy is hypnotized and turned 'into a musang – a kind of civet-cat': 'his companions rush off, imitating the clucking of fowls ... The subject starts up and pursues, and it goes ill with any whom he catches, for he bites and tears as a musang tears the body of a fowl. He uses only nails and teeth' (*LTY* I, p. 232).

V 5 *the levelling wind*: compare 'A Prayer for my Daughter', l. 5: 'roof-levelling wind'.

V 7–9 *those calendars ... how seasons run*: the contrast between chart and reality recalls the 'diagram' of 'Statistics', l. 3, and the star-calculations of 'The Dawn', l. 9; compare also the opposition between Catullus and the bald and feeble classicists in 'The Scholars'.

V 15 *where are they?*: *ubi sunt* – see *The Wanderings of Oisin* I 126.

V 16 *Mock mockers*: as at III 30 and IV 4, the poem's fury recoils on the poet himself – the desire for annihilation easily turns into a desire for self-annihilation.

V 17 *would not lift a hand*: the poet envies the man of action – see the note to 'Fergus and the Druid'.

VI 1 *violence of horses*: 'The country people see at times certain apparitions whom they name now "fallen angels", now "ancient inhabitants of the country", and describe as riding at whiles "with flowers upon the heads of the horses". I have assumed in the sixth poem that these horsemen, now that the times worsen, give way to worse.... Are not those who travel in the whirling dust also in the Platonic Year [see II 6]?' (*VP*, p. 433).

VI 4–5 *wearied running round and round in their courses / All break and vanish*: the cyclical course of the horsemen is reminiscent of the historical gyre described in II 6–8; but now there is a breakdown of the orderly process – compare 'The Second Coming', ll. 1–2.

VI 6 *Herodias' daughters*: 'Sidhe is ... Gaelic for wind, and certainly the Sidhe [the pagan gods of ancient Ireland] have much to do with the wind.

They journey in whirling winds, the winds that were called the dance of the daughters of Herodias in the Middle Ages, Herodias doubtless taking the place of some old goddess. When the country people see the leaves whirling on the road they bless themselves, because they believe the Sidhe to be passing by' (*VP*, p. 800 – compare also *UP* II, p. 69). In *The Shadowy Waters*, l. 555, Aibric similarly uses a 'dust-whirl' to symbolize the craziness of empty dreams; in the 1903 version of *On Baile's Strand* the Fool says of the sea-goddess Boann, 'Nobody knows how lecherous these goddesses are. I see her in every kind of shape but oftener than not she's in the wind and cries "give a kiss and put your arms about me"' (*VPl*, p. 458); and in 'The Two Kings', l. 167, a god remembers how the gods 'Danced in the whirling foam and in the dust'. When Yeats rewrote a ballad by Dorothy Wellesley, he added a line in which a Dame, anticipating her death, says, 'I am but a whirl of wind'; Yeats commented, 'remember that the dead move in a whirl of wind in, I think, all folk lore' (*DWL*, pp. 97, 95).

According to Mark 6: 19–29, Herodias was the wife of King Herod; her daughter's dance led to the execution of John the Baptist, who had denounced Herodias' marriage as incestuous – sexual perversion will reappear a few lines later in the case of Robert Artisson. In early drafts of *The Player Queen*, the heroine desired to act the part of Herodias on stage (*WPQ*, pp. 48, 202, 245). Edward Hirsch (in *Irish Renaissance Annual* III [1982]: 71–92) notes that Yeats's immediate source was Arthur Symons's 'The Dance of the Daughters of Herodias' (1899); Yeats quoted from Symons's translation of Mallarmé's 'Hérodiade' in *A: TG* 11.

VI 9 *labyrinth of the wind*: compare 'The Two Kings', l. 31: 'elaborate wilderness of the air'.

VI 14 *There lurches past*: compare 'The Second Coming', where a sphinx-Antichrist 'Slouches towards Bethlehem to be born' (l. 22) – both these poems conjure a terminal image of historical terror, but here the image is wholly depraved.

VI 16 *Robert Artisson*: 'My last symbol, Robert Artisson, was an evil spirit much run after in Kilkenny at the start of the fourteenth century' (*VP*, p. 433).

VI 17 *Lady Kyteler*: Dame Alice Kyteler, a fourteenth-century witch said to have poisoned three husbands and to have summoned an incubus, Robin son of Art, who came to her in the shapes of a Negro, a cat, and a hairy black dog (see Jeffares, *NCP*, pp. 235-36). Yeats seems to suggest that historical depravity and chaos are explicitly willed by mankind in order to gratify an appetite for the loathsome. W. H. Auden would later speak of the imagination's 'promiscuous fornication with her own images' (*For the Time Being*, *CP*, p. 300) – a good description (in the light of III 22–25) of what is happening in this poem.

VI 18 *peacock*: a bird that Yeats associated with millennial change – see 'The Indian upon God', l. 17.

The Wheel

This poem is an adaptation of a passage from 'The Tables of the Law' (1896): 'Leonardo da Vinci ... has this noble sentence: "The hope and desire of returning home to one's former state is like the moth's desire for the light; and the man who with constant longing awaits each new month and new year, deeming that the things he longs for are ever too late in coming, does not perceive that he is longing for his own destruction"' (*M*, pp. 301–2; compare *Mem*, p. 88). In 'The Phases of the Moon', Yeats discussed the possibility of escape from the reincarnative cycle, 'the wagon-wheel / Of beauty's cruelty and wisdom's chatter' (ll. 120–21); here he asserts that every dissatisfaction with the seasons is a longing to escape from the cycle of the year.

7–8 *what disturbs our blood / Is but its longing for the tomb*: compare *Deirdre* (1907), ll. 484–85: 'love-longing is but drouth / For the things come after death'; 'The Hour before Dawn', l. 98: 'all life longs for the Last Day'; 'From *Oedipus at Colonus*', l. 3: 'Delight becomes death-longing'.

The New Faces

A draft of this poem appears in *Mem*, p. 267.

1 *you*: Lady Gregory.

8 *The living seem more shadowy than they*: according to Symons's *The Symbolist Movement in Literature*, symbolism understands dreams to be real, and the phenomenal world to be unreal. Such reversals of reality between ghosts and men are common in Yeats's work: in 'Rosa Alchemica' (1896), Robartes announces 'There is Lear ... and he laughs because you thought yourself an existence who are but a shadow, and him a shadow who is an eternal god' (*M*, p. 275); in *The Death of Synge*, Yeats wrote that 'It was as though we and the things about us died away from him and not he from us' (*A: DS* 17); and in *The King of the Great Clock Tower* (1935), a severed head sings, 'Mortal men our abstracts are' (l. 132).

A Prayer for my Son

Michael Yeats was born on 22 August 1921. By counterpointing the birth of Yeats's son with the birth of Christ, this poem begins a sequence of poems on the theme of births that initiate historical change. As in 'A Prayer on going into my House', Yeats found the Christian God easier to hypothesize as an object for prayer than any pagan or occult deity.

1 *Bid a strong ghost*: Senator Michael Yeats remembered that, as a schoolchild, other children teased him by calling out 'Bid a strong ghost' or simply 'B.A.S.G.'

6 *All dread afar*: 'In order to keep myself from nightmare, I had formed the habit of imagining four watch-dogs, one at each corner of my room' (*A: HC* 5). In 'Rosa Alchemica' (1896), the mystic order believes that 'if you powerfully imagined a hound at your bedside it would keep watch there until you woke, and drive away all but the mightiest demons, but that if your imagination was weakly, the hound would be weakly also, and the demons prevail, and the hound soon die' (*M*, pp. 284–85).

11 *Such devilish things*: when spirits narrated the truths of *A Vision* through his wife's trances, a hostile class of spirits (called Frustrators) would sometimes confuse the transmission: 'A little after my son's birth I came home to confront my wife with the statement "Michael is ill". A smell of burnt feathers had announced what she and the doctor had hidden ... I was told that henceforth the Frustrators would attack my health and that of my children ... I felt before I could recover self-control the mediaeval helpless horror at witchcraft' (*AV*, p. 16).

17 *You*: Christ.

18–19 *teach / The morning stars to sing*: see Job 38:4–7: 'Where wast thou ... When the morning stars sang together, and all the songs of God shouted for joy?' Compare *The King's Threshold* (1904), ll. 716–17: 'The stars had come so near me that I caught / Their singing'; and 'Among School Children' VI 7: 'What a star sang'.

20 *You have lacked articulate speech*: compare T. S. Eliot, 'Gerontion' (1919), l. 18: 'The word within a word, unable to speak a word'.

22 *Wailing upon a woman's knee*: compare Christ's 'wild infancy' in 'Wisdom', l. 19; also 'The Magi', l. 8.

23–24 *ignominy / Of flesh and bone*: compare 'A Dialogue of Self and Soul' II 5: 'ignominy of boyhood'.

26 *Your enemy*: Herod, whose slaughter of the Innocents is remembered in 'News for the Delphic Oracle' II 3. Compare *The Cat and the Moon* (1926), ll. 244–45: 'Would you be as bad as Caesar and as Herod ...?'

32 *human love*: as the poem concludes, the poet seems to dismiss the mythological apparatus of guardian angels and ghosts in favour of the attention of human parents. The mystery of the Incarnation requires a descent into the most ordinary life.

Two Songs from a Play

The first song opens, and the second song closes, *The Resurrection* (1927; 1931), a play about the mystery of the Incarnation. A Greek and a Hebrew argue, just after the Crucifixion, about the divinity of Christ. The Greek claims that Christ was too divine to possess a human body: 'No god has ever been buried; no god has ever suffered. Christ only seemed to be born, only seemed to eat, seemed to sleep, seemed to walk, seemed to die' (ll. 97–100). The Hebrew takes the contrary position: 'He was nothing more than a man, the best man who ever lived' (ll. 109–10). But a Syrian rushes in to announce that Christ has risen from the tomb; and at last the figure of Christ enters – the Greek hesitantly touches it, expecting that his hand will slide right through an unreal image, but instead screams, 'The heart of a phantom is beating!' (ll. 392–93). The songs, like the play as a whole, depend on the shock of discovering a heart – a human, suffering heart – at the centre of the supernatural drama of historical change. A similar heart-shock occurs in 'Leda and the Swan', l. 8, when Leda feels Zeus' heart beating against her breast.

The second stanza of the second song was not written until about 1931 – after the publication of *The Tower* in 1928.

I 1 *a staring virgin*: Athena – see 'A Thought from Propertius', l. 6.

I 2 *Dionysus*: the Greek god of drunkenness and ecstasy, son of Zeus; according to some legends, after his mother Astraea bore him, he was torn apart by Titans ('The great hands of those Titans / Tore limb from limb' – *The Resurrection*, ll. 214–15), but Zeus swallowed his heart and reconceived him through the mortal woman Semele, who died at the sight at Zeus' unfeigned glory. The dismemberment and rebirth of Dionysus recall the mythologies (described at length in Frazer's *The Golden Bough*) in which the passage from winter to spring was attributed to the rejuvenation of a god; but here the poet witnesses a divine drama, not of seasonal change, but of millennial change. Dionysus also appears in 'Colonus' Praise', l. 8; and in the 1927 version of *The Resurrection*, ll. 177–78, the Egyptian describes how revellers eat a live kid, 'And all the while they keep crying out upon the God Dionysus whose flesh they eat and whose blood they drink' (*VPl*, p. 912).

I 3 *tear the heart out of his side*: compare 'Parnell's Funeral' I 14: 'Cut out his heart'; and *A Full Moon in March* (1935), ll. 172–76: 'Jack had a hollow heart, for Jill ... Had hung his heart beyond the hill, / A-twinkle in the sky'.

I 6–7: this couplet is quoted in *A Vision*, p. 254, to suggest the mystery of the spring equinox, when Caesar was assassinated and Christ crucified; it is also quoted in the Introduction to *The Resurrection* (*Ex*, p. 394), to hint that the Communicators that brought to Yeats the wisdom of *A Vision* were his Muses.

I 6 *Muses*: see 'The Tower' I 11.

I 7 *Magnus Annus*: the Great Year of classical philosophy, equal to thousands of our years – see 'Nineteen Hundred and Nineteen' II 6.

I 8 *As though God's death were but a play*: to the Muses the drama of history is comedy, to mankind tragedy – the Muses resemble the gods of Lucretius' *De Rerum Natura* III 18–22, who take aesthetic delight at the spectacle of human suffering. Indeed Yeats thought of *A Vision* itself as a kind of *Commedia dell' Arte* (*AV*, p. 84). Compare 'Vacillation' VIII 9: 'play a predestined part'; 'Parnell's Funeral' I 22–23: 'nor did we play a part / Upon a painted stage when we devoured his heart'; and 'Whence Had They Come?', l. 4: 'Ignorant what Dramatis Personae spake'.

I 9–12 *Another Troy* ... *Another Argo*: these lines paraphrase a passage in Virgil's fourth eclogue, prophesying the return of the Golden Age – a passage taken by the Church fathers as a prophecy of Christ's coming. Shelley adapted the same passage, in a metre similar to Yeats's, in *Hellas* (1821), ll. 1060–1101 ('A loftier Argo cleaves the main ... Another Athens shall arise'). In *The Resurrection*, ll. 319–21, the Syrian repeats what the audience has already heard in this opening song: 'What matter if it [Christ's resurrection] contradicts all human knowledge? – another Argo seek another fleece, another Troy is sacked'. This chant had earlier precedents in Yeats's work: in the 1897 version of 'The Adoration of the Magi', the voice of Hermes, speaking through an old man (fond of reading Virgil) says that 'the old things shall be again, and another Argo shall carry heroes over the deep, and another Achilles beleaguer another Troy' (*VSR*, p. 169). Also compare 'Samhain: 1904': 'has not Virgil ... foretold that other Argonauts shall row between cliff and cliff, and other fair-haired Achaeans sack another Troy?' (*Ex*, p. 150); and 'Discoveries' (1906): 'Civilisation, too, will not that also destroy where it has loved, until it shall bring the simple and natural things again, and a new Argo with all the gilding on her bows sail out to find another Fleece?' (*EI*, p. 290).

I 15 *that fierce virgin and her Star*: the Virgin Mary and Christ, conceived here (as in 'The Mother of God', ll. 1–2) as a star fallen to earth. But (as Ellmann notes, *IY*, p. 260) there are rich correspondences with other virgins and other stars: the constellation Virgo (the sidereal version of Astraea, the presiding goddess of the Golden Age imagined in Virgil's fourth eclogue) contains Spica, one of the sky's brightest stars; and Athena, the 'staring virgin' of I 1, cradles Dionysus' heart as if it were the star of a new dispensation. (A song in *The Resurrection*, l. 199, refers to Dionysus as 'Astrea's holy child'.) By means of such repeated image-patterns history folds into congruent periods, becomes a cycle. Compare the goddess of 'Parnell's Funeral' I 12, who shoots a star with an arrow.

II 1 *In pity*: according to Yeats, Christ's chief emotion was pity – cool, abstract, objective: 'We say of Him because His sacrifice was voluntary that He was love itself, and yet that part of Him which made Christendom was not love but pity ... for the common lot, man's death, seeing that He raised Lazarus, sickness, seeing that He healed many, sin, seeing that He died' (*AV*, p. 275)

II 2 *He*: Christ.

II 4 *Babylonian starlight*: see 'The Dawn', l. 6.

II 5 *fabulous, formless darkness*: Yeats prophesied that at the end of the present millennium, the modern age would 'plunge as Rome did in the fourth century according to some philosopher of that day into "a fabulous, formless darkness"' (*Ex*, p. 377). Also compare *A Vision*: 'The world became Christian, "that fabulous formless darkness" as it seemed to a philosopher of the fourth century, blotted out "every beautiful thing"' (p. 278). According to Dodds, Eunapius was the philosopher who conceived the Church as '"a fabulous and formless darkness mastering the loveliness of the world"' – see *CEAV (1925)*, notes, p. 52.

II 8 *vain all Doric discipline*: 'A civilisation is a struggle to keep self-control' (*AV*, p. 268).

II 9–10 *Everything that man esteems / Endures a moment*: compare 'Never Give all the Heart', ll. 6–7: 'everything that's lovely is / But a brief ... delight'; and 'Nineteen Hundred and Nineteen' I 42: 'Man is in love and loves what vanishes'.

II 11 *Love's pleasure drives his love away*: compare 'Her Anxiety', ll. 10–11: 'Every touch they give, / Love is nearer death'; and 'Crazy Jane and Jack the Journeyman', ll. 3–4: 'The more I leave the door unlatched / The sooner love is gone'. In an early novella, the hero, contemplating marriage, remarks on 'the decree which compels every step we take in life to be a death in the imagination' (*JSD*, p. 68); and in Yeats's last short story, Robartes says, '"Exhausted by the cry that it can never end, my love ends"' (*AV*, p. 40). In 1929 Yeats wrote that 'Sexual desire dies because every touch consumes the Myth' (*TSMC*, p. 154).

II 12 *The painter's brush consumes his dreams*: 'Our love letters wear out our love; no school of painting outlasts its founders, every stroke of the brush exhausts the impulse, pre-Raphaelitism had some twenty years; impressionism thirty perhaps. Why should we believe that religion can never bring about its antithesis?' (*A: TG* 9); 'all the old systematic idealisms are dead and are forced to death by sheer mathematics. The world is like the schools of painting which exhaust any technical method in a few years' (*L*, p. 666); 'Just when some school of painting has become popular, reproductions in every print-shop window, millionaires outbidding one another, everybody's affection stirred, painters wear out their nerves establishing something else' (*Ex*, p. 430).

II 16 *Man's own resinous heart*: the logic of the previous stanzas attributes great events to a divine pageant; but in this stanza the poet's gaze contracts, refocuses – it is man's heart, not Dionysus', that consumes itself for glory.

Fragments

In the midst of several serious poems of Annunciation, Yeats inserted (in the 1933 *Collected Poems*) this mock-theogony, in which John Locke plays the role of Madonna or Leda, the mother of a perverse mechanical cosmos. This premise may derive from Blake, who addressed Satan as 'Newtons Pantocrator weaving the Woof of Locke / To Mortals thy Mills seem every thing' (*Milton* 4: 11–12). Like Blake, Yeats conceived Newton and Locke as materialists and objectivists – men who killed the universe by depriving it of its sanctity: 'Descartes, Locke, and Newton took away the world and gave us its excrement instead' (*Ex*, p. 325; compare *VPl*, p. 574).

Locke's division of the sensible world into primary qualities (such as mass and shape) and secondary qualities (such as colour) angered Yeats: 'I can see in a sort of nightmare vision the "primary qualities" torn from the side of Locke ... some obscure person somewhere inventing the spinning-jenny' (*Ex*, pp. 358–59; Yeats went on to quote ll. 1–4 of this poem). It is as if Locke gave birth to the thingliness of the world. Yeats also wrote: 'of all these [sterile abstractions] the most comprehensive, the most useful, was invented by Locke when he separated the primary and secondary qualities; and from that day to this the conception of a physical world without colour, sound, taste, tangibility ... has remained the assumption of science ... It worked, and the mechanical inventions of the next age ... worked even better' (*EI*, pp. 400–1).

Yeats anticipated a New Dispensation that would overcome Locke's inane vision of reality, as shown in an untitled, uncollected poem in which a battery of symbols advances menacingly upon the narrow world of science and materialistic philosophy:

> Move upon Newton's town,
> The town of Hobbes and of Locke,
> Pine, spruce, come down
> Cliff, ravine, rock:
> What can disturb the corn?
> What makes it shudder and bend?
> The rose brings her thorn,
> The Absolute walks behind.
> (*VPl*, p. 570; *Ex*, p. 377)

Yeats commented on these lines: 'Such thoughts, come from the waste places and the begging bowl, are our sole protection from that doctrine imagined in towns separated by rigidity from torrent and foliage, which benumbs daring and makes art photographic' (*VPl*, p. 574).

I 1 *Locke*: John Locke (1632–1704), empirical philosopher.

I 3 *spinning-jenny*: an early machine for spinning thread, in which several spindles were run from one wheel. Because *jenny* sounds like a girl's name (it was named after the inventor's wife), Yeats can treat the machine as a parody of Eve. A passage from *Where There is Nothing* (1902) describes Newton as a mock Eve: 'I am among those who think that sin and death came into the world the day Newton eat the apple ... I know you are going to tell me he only saw it fall. Never mind, it is all the same thing' (I 427–32). In a related vein, Yeats wrote of the good social movements 'content to be the midwife of Nature and not a juggling mechanist who would substitute an automaton for her living child' (*Ex*, pp. 277–78).

I 4 *Out of his side*: compare Genesis 2:21–22: 'And the Lord God caused a deep sleep to fall upon Adam, and he slept: and he took one of his ribs ... And the rib ... made he a woman'.

II 1–6: Yeats quoted these lines to illustrate the process by which spirits from beyond the grave brought him the system described in *A Vision* (*Ex*, p. 394).

II 3 *Out of nothing*: compare 'The Gyres', l. 22: 'any rich, dark nothing'.

II 6 *Nineveh*: an ancient Assyrian city. Compare 'Vacillation' VI 7: 'Babylon or Nineveh'. Nineveh had some prestige in Victorian poetry: 'This [outward movement of symbols] is maybe what Arthur O'Shaughnessy [in 'Ode', l. 19] meant when he made his poets say they had built Nineveh with their sighing; and I am certainly never sure, when I hear of some war, or of some religious excitement ... that it has not all happened because of something that a boy piped in Thessaly' (*EI*, p. 158; see also *Ex*, p. 337). An uncollected quatrain of 1934 mentions Nineveh in the context of Vico's cyclical history: 'Decline of day, / A leaf drifts down; / O dark leaf clay / On Nineveh's crown!' (*VPl*, p. 806; *Ex*, p. 401).

Leda and the Swan

Yeats's note explains that this study of mythological brutality began with a meditation on contemporary politics: 'I wrote Leda and the Swan because the editor [AE] of a political review asked me for a poem. I thought, "After the individualist, demagogic movement, founded by Hobbes and popularized by the Encyclopaedists and the French Revolution, we have a soil so exhausted that it cannot grow that crop again for centuries". Then I thought, "Nothing is now possible but some movement from above preceded by some violent annunciation". My fancy began to play with Leda and the Swan for metaphor, and I began this poem; but as I wrote, bird and lady took such possession of the scene that all politics went out of it, and my friend tells me that his "conservative readers would misunderstand the poem"' (*VP*, p. 828). In an interview, Yeats continued this line of political analysis: 'Everything seems to show that the centrifugal movement which began with the Encyclopedists and produced the French Revolution ... has worked itself out to the end. Now we are at the beginning of a new centripetal movement [towards Mussolini and authoritarian government]' (*UP* II, p. 434).

'Fragments' showed the exhausted soil of which Yeats's note speaks, the impoverished and impoverishing idea-world of empiricist philosophy and democratic politics; 'Leda and the Swan' offers a vivid metaphor for the terror of the *antithetical* age soon to be born. According to *A Vision*, 2000 BC (the year at which the swan came to Leda to inaugurate the heroic age) and AD 2000 rhyme with each other; and so it is to be expected that this poem bears many similarities to 'The Second Coming'. Indeed there is a sense in which both poems depict beast-rapes of Yeats's imagination by a vehement overwhelming image. The sexual frenzy, the emphatic jagged diction of the sonnet's opening, were unprecedented in Yeats's poetry. In *Pansies* (1929), D. H. Lawrence published a sequence of poems on the Leda theme: 'the vast white bird / furrows our featherless women / with unknown shocks / and stamps his black marsh-feet on their white and marshy flesh' ('Swan', *Complete Poems*, p. 436).

Drafts of this sonnet appear in *Mem*, pp. 272–75, under the title 'Annunciation'. The whole poem is quoted to introduce the chapter in *A Vision* on historical process, 'Dove or Swan' (p. 267). A comprehensive review of Yeats's sources in mythology, poetry, sculpture, and painting (perhaps the most important was Michelangelo's image of Leda and the swan, a copy of which Yeats kept by his desk as he wrote the poem) appears in Ian Fletcher's *W. B. Yeats and his Contemporaries*, pp. 220–51.

Title *Leda and the Swan*: Zeus took the form of a swan in order to rape the mortal girl Leda; she presently laid three eggs: 'two eggs [had] already hatched ... Castor and Clytaemnestra [the wife of Agamemnon, the Greek leader during the Trojan War] broke the one shell, Helen [of Troy] and Pollux the other' (*AV*, p. 51); the third hung 'in a Spartan temple, strung up to the roof as a holy relic' (*AV*, p. 268). In the 1927 version of *The Resurrection*, ll. 274–75, a character hears an eyewitness account of this Spartan temple, and exclaims, 'An egg of Leda, did you say? And unhatched? What frustrated destiny!' (*VPl*, p. 918). But Yeats, in his last short story, invented a sequel in which this destiny was no longer frustrated: Michael Robartes and his friends come into possession of the third egg – 'the size of a swan's egg ...

Hyacinthine blue' (*AV*, p. 51) – and prepare to hatch it; this will lead to the return of the heroic age. For other references to Leda, see 'His Phoenix', l. 4: 'that sprightly girl trodden by a bird'; 'Among School Children' II 1: 'Ledaean body' (referring to Maud Gonne); and 'Lullaby', ll. 13–18, where Leda is oddly solicitous of her rapist's comfort. In a passage added to 'The Adoration of the Magi' in 1925, a mysterious voice prophesies the transformation of the world: 'another Leda would open her knees to the swan, another Achilles beleaguer Troy' (*M*, p. 310). In *The Player Queen* (1922) a actress, flirting with actors dressed as animals, sings, 'Shall I fancy beast or fowl? / Queen Pasiphae chose a bull, / While a passion for a swan / Made Queen Leda stretch and yawn' (II 360–63). And in *The Herne's Egg* (1938) a king claims that virgins invent divine ravishers to appease frustrated sexual desire: 'Ovid had a literal mind, / And though he sang it neither knew / What lonely lust dragged down the gold / That crept on Danae's lap, nor knew / What rose against the moony feathers / When Leda lay upon the grass' (II 68–73).

1–4: in the first printing these lines read, 'A rush, a sudden wheel, and hovering still / The bird descends, and her frail thighs are pressed / By the webbed toes, and that all-powerful bill / Has laid her helpless face upon his breast' (*VP*, p. 441).

3 *webs ... bill*: compare Attracta's song in *The Herne's Egg* about her intercourse with a divine heron: 'When beak and claw their work begin / Shall horror stir in the roots of my hair?' (IV 170–71).

5 *vague fingers*: Leda was a popular subject for painting in the Renaissance – this phrase may refer to a blur representing the rapid movement of Leda's hand as well as to her hesitancy of resistance against an irresistible force. (The next poem in this volume is explicitly about a picture of a mythological animal.) Compare 'vague wing' (*The Dreaming of the Bones*, l. 111).

6 *thighs*: this edition follows *AV*, p. 267, in putting a comma, instead of a question mark, after this word.

8 *strange heart beating*: as in *The Resurrection* (see the note to 'Two Songs from a Play'), the heartbeat manifests the god's full descent to earth.

10 *The broken wall*: the destruction of Troy was one consequence of Zeus' insemination.

13 *Did she put on his knowledge with his power*: compare 'The Gift of Harun Al-Rashid', l. 169: 'I must buy knowledge with my peace'; and 'Ribh considers Christian Love insufficient', l. 23: 'What can she know until He bid her know!' Mankind's incompetence at comprehending historical revelation is a common theme in Yeats's work: 'I see Phantoms ...' also ends with a man's difficulty in construing 'The half-read wisdom of daemonic images' (l. 39).

On a Picture of a Black Centaur by Edmund Dulac

In Yeats's unfinished novel *The Speckled Bird* I v, the young artist-hero meditates on a painting of the Madonna until, delirious from fasting and from imagining, he conjures up in a mirror a three-dimensional world of significant images, images that move (*LTMSB*, p. 42). This poem celebrates a more playful transference of one's identity into the world of a painting. The poet lets us into his workshop of symbols (here described as a kind of kitchen, l. 9) in order to apologize for his occult and laboured method of poem-production. The centaur seems to represent a spontaneous, improvisatory, vitally physical and kinetic kind of art (see 'Lines Written in Dejection', l. 7); the parrots seem to represent mimetic art – the slavish art that copies reality instead of creating it. Yeats's poetry has evidently been too recondite and recherché, abstruse, to please the centaur; but now the poet announces that he has turned to a richer, more direct style, likely to gratify the centaur's *antithetical* taste. This poem, then, may be seen as a sequel to 'The Fascination of What's Difficult' – another poem centred on an inspirational beast. For other poems that announce a change in poetic style, see 'A Coat'.

Yeats's friend Edmund Dulac (1882–1953) designed some of the masks and sets for productions of Yeats's plays, composed musical settings for some of his poems, and also made a pseudo-medieval woodcut illustration of 'Giraldus', the imaginary author of the wisdom contained in *A Vision* (reproduced in *AV*, p. 39); he was the dedicatee of *The Winding Stair and Other Poems*. Although Dulac's picture ('The good Chiron taught his pupils how to play upon the harp', an illustration for Hawthorne's *Tanglewood Tales*, 1918) may have been the initial inspiration, Yeats owed some of the details to another picture of a centaur, made by Cecil Salkeld as an illustration to a rough draft of this very poem – see Hone, *WBY*, pp. 326–28.

6–7 *driven half insane / Because of some green wing*: perhaps a reference to Yeats's many polemics against imitative or 'realistic' art, especially in the theatre.

7 *mummy wheat*: wheat found in Egyptian tombs, able to sprout after thousands of years. Compare 'Conjunctions', l. 2; and Tennyson's 'To Professor Jebb, with the Following Poem', ll. 5–6: 'here the torpid mummy wheat / Of Egypt bore a grain as sweet' (referring to Tennyson's publication of a poem on old themes from Greek mythology). Mummies also appear in 'All Souls' Night', ll. 14, 86, and 100, and 'Byzantium', l. 11.

8 *the mad abstract dark*: the secret oracles behind *A Vision* – compare 'Fragments' II 1–5: 'Where got I that truth? ... Out of dark night'. Yeats often worried about the excessive abstraction of *A Vision*: 'My imagination was ... haunted by figures that, muttering "The great systems", held out to

me the sun-dried skeletons of birds' (*AV*, p. 214).

10 *full-flavoured wine*: a species of poetry less philosophical and arid, more enjoyable, than that emblematized by the 'mummy wheat' – wine, not bread.

10 *out of a barrel*: in *Where There is Nothing* (1902) V 143–53, the rapt hero compares his intoxicating revelation to a drink from a barrel rolled 'out of a cellar that is under the earth ... It was made in a good still, the barley was grown in a field that's down under the earth'.

11 *seven Ephesian topers*: legendary Christian martyrs of the third century AD, shut up in a cave; two centuries later the cave was reopened, and they were found to be asleep, not dead. In 1915 Yeats wrote to Henry James that he intended to write no more poetry on the Great War and would 'keep the neighbourhood of the seven sleepers of Ephesus, hoping to catch their comfortable snores till bloody frivolity is over' (*L*, p. 600). Compare also the interminable sleeper in 'The Hour before Dawn'.

12 *When Alexander's empire passed*: an anachronism, for the empire of Alexander the Great (356–323 BC) broke up soon after his death. Alexander reappears in 'Among School Children' VI 4 and 'The Saint and the Hunchback', l. 10.

13 *sleep a long Saturnian sleep*: Saturn presided over the Golden Age, and Virgil prophesied that Saturn's reign would come again – see 'Two Songs from a Play' I 9–12. The poet expects the centaur to sleep until the restoration of the *antithetical* age – heroic, sensuous, frisky – appropriate to it. Indeed Dulac's picture seems to constitute the centaur in a state of suspended animation, waiting to spring to life. The poem compresses immense spans of time – while writing it, Yeats told Salkeld, '"eternity is not a long time but a *short* time ... Eternity is in the glitter on the beetle's wing"' (*WBY*, p. 327). Compare 'The Second Coming', l. 19: 'twenty centuries of stony sleep'.

14 *I have loved you better than my soul*: in 'The Book of the Great Dhoul ...' (1892), a faery goddess tells Hanrahan, '"You have always loved me better than your own soul"' (*VSR*, p. 192).

Among School Children

Preceding poems in this volume dealt with conception ('Leda and the Swan') and birth ('A Prayer for my Son'). Here the poet arrives at the theme of childhood; at the end of *The Tower* there come old age ('A Man Young and Old') and death ('All Souls' Night'). The theme of this poem is education: in February 1926 Yeats visited St Otteran's School, established according to Montessori principles – in a report to the Irish Senate on the condition of schools, Yeats praised the method for its aptness to an agricultural nation (see *SSY*, p. 111; Torchiana, in *In Excited Reverie*, pp. 123ff; and – for a favourable report on a visit to a convent school made twenty years earlier –

EI, p. 262). But in the poem he regards St Otteran's School with colder eyes: as in an earlier poem about education, 'Michael Robartes and the Dancer', Yeats here concludes that education should be a dance, not ciphering or reading or sewing or another sort of labour. The poet rejects any sort of education (such as that associated with Plato's academy) that excludes any part of existence; instead he finds that life gains purpose, gains meaning, only by moving towards ever-greater wholeness and largeness.

Yeats wrote a note shortly after his school-visit: 'Topic for poem. School children, and the thought that life will waste them, perhaps that no possible life can fulfill their own dreams or even their teacher's hope. Bring in the old thought that life prepares for what never happens' (Bradford, *YW*, p. 4). (Compare the end of Yeats's *Reveries over Childhood and Youth*: 'all life weighed in the scales of my own life seems to me a preparation for something that never happens' [*A: R* 33; also *Mem*, pp. 230, 233]; and the refrain of 'What Then?': '"*What then?*" *sang Plato's ghost*'. An early draft of *At the Hawk's Well* [1917] ends with a similar statement of the accursedness of man's life.)

I 8 *A sixty-year-old smiling public man*: the self-conscious poet is aware of the disengaged, arbitrary roles he plays, the appearances he presents (compare IV 8) – he has lost the integrity of being that is celebrated at II 8 and VIII 1–8. For mentions of his age, see the Introductory Rhymes to *Responsibilities*, l. 20.

II 1 *a Ledaean body*: Maud Gonne's. In the context of 'Leda and the Swan', this epithet at once applauds her as the mother of a heroic age and suggests how history has deformed her life (see IV 3).

II 5–6 *our two natures blent / Into a sphere*: at the end of his suppressed autobiography, Yeats described their complementary nature: 'My outer nature was passive – but for her I should never perhaps have left my desk – but I knew my spiritual nature was passionate, even violent. In her all this was reversed, for it was her spirit only that was gentle and passive and full of charming fantasy' (*Mem*, p. 124; compare pp. 128–34). Compare 'Summer and Spring', l. 6: 'we'd halved a soul'.

II 7 *Plato's parable*: in Plato's *Symposium*, the Greek comic playwright Aristophanes describes how people used to be two-headed, four-armed, four-legged, bisexual; but Zeus severed these man-spheres into separate men and women, just as a hair cleaves a cooked egg. Stephen Winnett has transcribed a passage from a 1917 draft of *The Only Jealousy of Emer* on the same theme, in which Fand tells Cuchulain that she can offer him completion of self: 'Have you not heard that man before his birth / Is two in one: the yoke & white of the egg / And that one half is born in wretchedness / While the other half remains amid the Sidhe' (David R. Clark, '*That Black Day*', p. 10). For Plato, see 'The Tower' I 12. For other agglomerations of a man and a woman into a sphere, see 'Ribh at the Tomb of Baile and Aillinn', l. 14; and the Hindu creation myth in *TPU*, p. 119, in which the 'first Person ... was as big as man and wife together; He divided himself into two, husband and wife were born'.

II 8 *yolk and white of the one shell*: Donald Torchiana notes that in 1919 Maud Gonne designed a book-illustration showing two swans squeezed into a tight sphere (*In Excited Reverie*, p. 139).

III 4–5 *daughters of the swan ... every paddler's heritage*: the 'Ledaean body' (II 1) has reminded the poet of Hans Christian Andersen's fable of the ugly duckling. Children are eggs that can hatch into any adult shape – even Maud Gonne's.

IV 2 *Quattrocento*: fifteenth century – see also 'Her Vision in the Wood', l. 19, and 'Under Ben Bulben' IV 17. In one draft Yeats wrote 'Da Vinci'.

IV 3 *Hollow of cheek as though it drank the wind*: compare 'Two Songs of a Fool' II 6: 'she drank the wind' (referring to a hare, emblematic of Iseult Gonne); 'A Prayer for my Daughter', l. 64: 'an old bellows full of angry wind' (referring to Maud Gonne); and 'In Memory of Eva Gore-Booth ...' I 12: 'skeleton-gaunt'. Yeats once wrote of certain bad men 'who fed the gaping mouths with the east wind until they had destroyed all taste for better food' (*UP* I, p. 307; *L* I, p. 370; compare also *L*, p. 591). For more hollow cheeks, see 'Fergus and the Druid', l. 23.

IV 4 *shadows for its meat*: compare 'Another Song of a Fool', l. 12: 'roses for his meat'; and 'The Statues', l. 19: 'Hamlet thin from eating flies'.

IV 6 *pretty plumage*: compare 'The Gift of Harun Al-Rashid', l. 178: 'All my fine feathers would be plucked away'.

IV 8 *old scarecrow*: for another scarecrow – also an image of the disembodiment inflicted by old age – see 'Sailing to Byzantium' II 2. The scarecrow recurs here at VI 8.

V: Bradford (*YW*, pp. 9, 11) prints a draft of this stanza, and Yeats's note to himself: 'I think of my grandfather and grandmother, to whom I was so much, and as I look in the glass, as I look at old age coming, I wonder if they would [have] thought it worth the bother ... I think of my father and mother ... What have I that they value, what would have seemed sufficient at the moment? My thoughts would have seemed superstition to the one and to the other a denial of God'. Also compare *At the Hawk's Well* (1917), a play about the search for waters that render a man immortal: 'A mother that saw her son / Doubled over a speckled shin, / Cross-grained with ninety years, / Would cry, "How little worth / Were all my hopes and fears / And the hard pain of his birth!"' (ll. 11–16).

V 2 *Honey of generation*: 'I have taken the "honey of generation" from

Porphyry's essay on "The Cave of the Nymphs"' (*VP*, p. 828). Porphyry was a Neoplatonic philosopher; he wrote a famous essay on Homer's Cave of the Nymphs, showing it as an allegory of the unborn soul's descent – the sexual pleasure of the parents acted as a kind of honey, luring the child's soul into incarnation (see *EI*, p. 83).

V 2 *betrayed*: 'The sorrow of death ... is not so bitter as the sorrow of birth, and had our ears the subtlety we could listen amid the joy of lovers and the pleasure that comes with sleep to the wailing of the spirit betrayed into a cradle' (*Ex*, pp. 48-49).

V 4 *recollection or the drug*: the newborn baby's recollection of his beatitude before birth, that makes him miserable about his present estate; or the drug – the 'honey of generation' – that causes the baby to forget. Yeats found 'no warrant in Porphyry for considering [the honey] the "drug" that destroys the "recollection" of pre-natal freedom' (*VP*, p. 828). Compare 'Vacillation' III 9: 'Lethean foliage'.

VI: Yeats quoted a draft of this stanza in a letter to Olivia Shakespeare: 'Here is a fragment of my last curse upon old age. It means that even the greatest men are owls, scarecrows, by the time their fame has come' (*L*, p. 719).

VI 1 *Plato thought nature but a spume*: Plato (see 'The Tower' I 12) taught that the physical world, mutable and corruptible, was only a humble shadow, an undignified copy of a world of ideal Forms.

VI 3 *Solider Aristotle*: Plato's pupil Aristotle (384–322 BC) gave a little more dignity to the physical world, by teaching that reality was form ingredient in matter. An early draft of this stanza stressed Aristotle's talent for category: 'Aristotle was / The first who had a place for everything' (Donald Pearce, *Yeats Eliot Review* 7 [1982]: 61).

VI 4 *a king of kings*: Alexander the Great (see 'On a Picture of a Black Centaur ...', l. 12). 'Aristotle, remember, was Alexander's tutor, hence the taws (form of birch)' (*L*, p. 719).

VI 5 *golden-thighed Pythagoras*: Pythagoras (*c.* 582–507 BC) was said to have discovered the fact that musical pitches can be described mathematically as ratios of vibrating lengths of string; he also developed a doctrine of metempsychosis, teaching that the soul perpetually migrated from one body to the next. Like Plato's and Aristotle's, his investigations into reality took him (according to Yeats) too far from the hard facts of bodily life. The epithet *golden-thighed* was applied to Pythagoras in classical times; compare 'golden-armed Iollan' (*The Shadowy Waters*, l. 406), and the tranvestite singer with gilded finger-nails in *The Resurrection* (1931), l. 193. Pythagoras reappears in 'The Delphic Oracle upon Plotinus', l. 9, 'The Statues', ll. 1 and 9, and in 'News for the Delphic Oracle', l. 8; and in *A Full Moon in March* (1935), ll. 16–18, a singer sings of love's excrementitiousness: '*Crown of gold or dung of swine.* // Should old Pythagoras fall in love / Little may he boast thereof'.

VI 7 *What a star sang*: see 'A Prayer for my Son', l. 19.

VI 7 *careless Muses*: see 'The Tower' I 11.

VI 8 *Old clothes upon old sticks*: no inquiry into ultimate changeless reality can compensate for the decay of the philosophers' bodies. For other scarecrows, see 'Sailing to Byzantium' II 2.

VII 1 *worship*: in stanza VI, the poet asked whether human purpose might be found in the objects of intellectual speculation; here he asks whether purpose might be found in objects of affection. In the terms of *A Vision*, stanza VI concerns *creative mind*, stanza VII *will*.

VII 5 *they too break hearts*: the nun's heart is broken by her veneration of an icon, just as the mother's heart is broken by her love for her child. Compare 'The Friends of His Youth', where old Madge nurses a stone at her breast and 'Thinks that the stone's a child' (l. 12).

VII 5–6 *O Presences / That passion, piety or affection knows*: the beloved (compare II 8), the icon, and the child, respectively. The Presences addressed by the poet include all objects of human affect.

VII 8 *self-born mockers*: in *The Shadowy Waters*, l. 567, the gods are called 'Immortal Mockers'. For *self-born*, see 'A Prayer for my Daughter', ll. 67–68.

VIII 1 *Labour is blossoming or dancing*: in the previous stanzas, all the things that could complete human life or endow it with meaning continually evade man's grasp; but in this final stanza the poet suggests that there is another perspective than that of the sad mutable world – a perspective that reveals the unity of man and what he loves, what he thinks, what he works on (compare 'Quarrel in Old Age', ll. 12–16).

VIII 2 *The body is not bruised to pleasure soul*: compare 'The Two Kings', ll. 179–83: 'where we build / Our sudden palaces in the still air / Pleasure itself can bring no weariness, / Nor can time waste the cheek, nor is there foot / That has grown weary of the wandering dance'.

VIII 4 *Nor blear-eyed wisdom out of midnight oil*: compare 'The Living Beauty', l. 1: 'wick and oil are spent'; and the image of the Platonist toiling at his 'midnight candle' in 'My House', l. 20. According to 'Two Songs from a Play' II 11–16 a man is consumed by his labour; but here the poet describes a labour that endlessly refreshes.

VIII 6 *Are you the leaf, the blossom, or the bole?*: the chestnut tree is an indivisible whole – a metaphor for the human being who attains Unity of Being. Donald R. Pearce compares these lines to a speech in which Yeats urged school teachers to teach religion as 'a part of history and of life itself, a part, as it were, of the foliage of Burke's tree' (*SSY*, pp. 19, 173; *UP* II,

p. 459). For Burke's figure of the state as tree, see 'Blood and the Moon' II 10.

VIII 8 *How can we know the dancer from the dance?*: in this poem about education, the poet understands *knowing* as *making discriminations*; but the kind of education he values is not analysis, but synthesis. In the dance, the artist and the artifact are one; there is no distinction to be *known*. In *The Player Queen* (1922) the poet-hero announces, 'Man is nothing till he is united to an image' (II 478–79); and Yeats's personal quest for union with an image led him to such extreme measures as the vision of his soul as a golden bird in 'Sailing to Byzantium' IV. This dance is a more secular and feasible mode of transfiguration. Yeats's art was, of course, not the dance but poetry; and he sometimes postulated a magical identity between himself and his poems – for instance, in a quatrain about rewriting his works (1908), Yeats wrote, 'It is myself that I remake' (*VP*, p. 778). In other words: how can we know the poet from the poem? (This is exactly opposite to the mood of 'Nineteen Hundred and Nineteen' III, where Yeats felt lost in the labyrinth of his own works and hoped to be severed from them.)

Yeats conceived human life as wretchedly corruptible, human faculties as wretchedly divided and self-impeding; but he often teased himself with a vision of personal wholeness and liberty. At the end of *A Vision* (1937), Yeats wrote of the '*thirteenth sphere* or cycle which is in every man and called by every man his freedom' (p. 302); and elsewhere he referred to the *thirteenth sphere* – the sphere into which all the gyres resolve themselves – as a 'great dancer ... conscious of his or her own life and of the dance' (*AV*, p. 240). This poem celebrates the moment of blessed introspection when a man sees his own integrity, the dance-figure traced by his total effort.

Colonus' Praise

This poem is a translation of Paul Masqueray's French translation of a chorus from Sophocles' *Oedipus at Colonus*; Yeats's version of the whole play was produced by the Abbey Theatre in 1927. Here the chorus urges reverence for a sacred region, a region that Yeats associated with Ireland: 'when I prepared "Oedipus at Colonus" for the Abbey stage I saw that the wood of the Furies in the opening scene was any Irish haunted wood' (*VPl*, p. 899). This chorus (ll. 648–79 of Yeats's translation) is uttered immediately after Theseus has offered his protection to the aged, beggarly, blind Oedipus; earlier the Chorus had condemned Oedipus as an intruder and desecrator. Yeats once wrote of Oedipus as a kind of Antichrist, the patron of an *antithetical* era: 'Oedipus ... passed with Theseus to the wood's heart until amidst the sound of thunder earth opened, "riven by love" [l. 1518 of Yeats's version], and he sank down soul and body into the earth. I would have him balance Christ who ... went into the abstract sky soul and body' (*AV*, p. 27). Oedipus is one of Yeats's models for the tragedy of old age – see 'A Man Young and Old' XI and *A Woman Young and Old* XI.

1 *Colonus' horses*: Colonus (north of Athens) was sacred to Poseidon, who furnished mankind with horses – see l. 28.

2 *wine-dark*: the famous Homeric epithet for the sea. Compare 'Her Vision in the Wood', l. 2: 'wine-dark midnight' – in a context also suggestive of Dionysiac ritual.

8 *Semele's lad*: Dionysus – see 'Two Songs from a Play' I 2.

9 *the gymnast's garden*: the Academy, where Plato was to establish his school.

10 *self-sown, self-begotten shape*: see 'A Prayer for my Daughter', ll. 67–68.

11, 16 *intellect its mastery ... grey-eyed Athena stares thereon*: compare 'The Double Vision of Michael Robartes' II 15, 17: 'triumph of intellect ... eyeballs never moved'. The contrast in the earlier poem between the Buddha (emblematic of desire) and the sphinx (emblematic of intellect) is repeated here in the contrast between Dionysus and Athena. Yeats noted that 'The Greeks painted the eyes of marbles statues and made out of enamel or glass or precious stones those of their bronze statues' (*AV*, pp. 275–76). For Athena, see 'A Thought from Propertius', l. 6.

12 *olive-tree*: see 'Nineteen Hundred and Nineteen' I 6. Athena provided the Academy with an olive-tree after she caused the first one to grow from the Acropolis.

19 *the Great Mother, mourning for her daughter*: Demeter, the goddess of grain, mourned for her daughter Persephone, who spent the winter months in the underworld, as Hades' wife.

23 *Cephisus*: a local river.

28 *Poseidon*: the god of the sea.

32 *horses of the sea*: see 'Cuchulain's Fight with the Sea', l. 34, and 'High Talk', l. 14: 'Those great sea-horses bare their teeth'.

Wisdom

This poem turns on the contrast between the squalor of Christ's real origin and the magnificence of the art that embellished and glorified him. A similar insistence on the humble and spasmodic aspect of the Incarnation is found in 'The Magi' and 'A Prayer for my Son'.

1 *The true faith*: perhaps ironic.

5 *some peasant gospeller*: Matthew, Mark, Luke, or John.

6 *Swept the sawdust from the floor*: Yeats may have been imagining a sentimental modern painting of Christ's simple childhood: 'Whenever we or our forefathers have been most Christian – not the Christ of Byzantine mosaic but the soft, domesticated Christ of the painter's brush ... we have been haunted by those [*antithetical*] faces dark with mystery' (*Ex*, p. 434).

14 *Babylon*: the *primary* civilization, stark and star-struck, that preceded the *antithetical* Greek civilization founded by Leda – see 'The Dawn,' l. 6.

15 *Noah's freshet*: a playfully dismissive term for the Deluge. Like the mosaics in 'Sailing to Byzantium' III, the images of Christ's splendour are immune from contamination by earthly things.

16–17 *King Abundance ... Innocence ... Wisdom*: God the Father, the Virgin, and Christ. These allegorizing epithets may suggest the efforts of the Church Fathers to add philosophical prestige to the story of the Gospels. Yeats was impressed by the disembodied character of early church art: Byzantine mosaics 'displayed a Christ with face of pitiless intellect, or a pinched, flat-breasted virgin holding a child like a wooden doll' (*UP* II, p. 478).

19 *wild infancy*: compare 'A Prayer for my Son', l. 22. Christ's Wisdom – his abstract godhead – comports poorly with not-very-awesome babyhood.

20 *horror from His Mother's breast*: compare 'The Mother of God', ll. 4–5: 'The terror of all terrors that I bore / The Heavens in my womb'.

The Hero, the Girl, and the Fool

During the 1920s Yeats often pondered the quality of a man's engagement with his works: is a man one with his deeds (as 'Among School Children' suggests), or is a man finally isolated from his own accomplishment (as 'Nineteen Hundred and Nineteen' III suggests)? This poem poses the still more disturbing possibility that a human being is ultimately unrelated to his attributes, even to his character – just as the soul, according to *A Vision*, is a shorn, impredicable thing, moving through incarnations of beauty and ugliness, strength and weakness, wisdom and folly.

This poem was published in 1922 (under the title 'Cuchulain the Girl and the Fool'), and in the 1928 *The Tower*; later Yeats omitted all but ll. 18–29, published as 'The Fool by the Roadside'.

1 *I rage at my own image in the glass*: compare 'The Indian to his Love', ll. 4–5: 'A parrot ... Raging at his own image'. For the theme of women gazing into mirrors, see 'The Two Trees', l. 21. Yeats remarked of Maud Gonne, 'she hated her own beauty, not its effect upon others, but its image in the mirror. Beauty is from the antithetical self, and a woman can scarce but hate it, for not only does it demand a painful daily service, but it calls for the denial or the dissolution of the self' (*A: SB* 4).

9 *I have raged at my own strength because you have loved it*: compare *The Green Helmet* (1910), ll. 225–31, where Emer boasts that she is distinguished, not because of her husband Cuchulain's deeds, but because of his being: 'Himself on the wind / Is the gift that he gives'. Also compare 'The Gift of Harun Al-Rashid', ll. 112–14, where the seer asks why his young wife loves him: 'was it love of me, or was it love / Of the stark mystery that has dazed my sight . . . ?'

16 *only God has loved us for ourselves*: compare 'For Anne Gregory', ll. 16–18: 'only God . . . Could love you for yourself alone / And not your yellow hair'.

18–29: Yeats used these lines as the epigraph for the last book of *A Vision* (1925), 'The Gates of Pluto', describing the soul's journey after death.

20 *From grave to cradle run*: for the doctrine that the soul after death relives its life backward, see 'Shepherd and Goatherd', l. 89.

23 *loose thread*: in *The Hour-Glass* (1914), the pupils sing of how an angel stole the Fool's wits away: 'And now they are but a rag / On the moon's horn' (ll. 331–32). Yeats also wrote of 'a voice of lamentation out of the Golden Age. It told me that we are imperfect, incomplete . . . like a bundle of cords knotted together and flung into a corner' (*M*, p. 104). Also compare 'Crazy Jane and Jack the Journeyman', l. 5: 'a skein unwound'.

26–27 *Coagulate of stuff / Transparent like the wind*: the Fool, according to *A Vision*, p. 182, belongs to the last phase of the lunar month, when personality has attenuated to a mere wisp, 'a straw blown by the wind'.

29 *A faithful love*: only a man without qualities – such as the Fool – can be confident that he is not loved because of his qualities. Compare 'Crazy Jane on the Day of Judgment', when a madwoman suggests that true love could exist 'If Time were but gone' (l. 19).

Owen Aherne and his Dancers

This poem, written a few days after Yeats's marriage, attempts to define some of the internal conflicts Yeats felt about Iseult Gonne. In September 1917, she refused Yeats's marriage proposal; soon thereafter he married Georgie Hyde-Lees (see Introduction IX). Although this poem was written much earlier than most of the poems in this volume, its personification of the Heart concords well with such poems as 'The Tower', which begins with the poet's apostrophe to his heart; and its autobiographical character helps to introduce the stylized autobiography of the next sequence of poems, 'A Man Young and Old'.

Part I was originally entitled 'The Lover Speaks', Part II 'The Heart

Replies'. On 29 Oct. 1917, Yeats wrote to Lady Gregory that he would send them to her: 'the misery produced two poems ... they are among the best I have done' (*L*, pp. 633–34). Yeats's gloom was dispelled by a reassuring message from one of his wife's first trances.

Title: in 'The Tables of the Law' (1896) Owen Aherne was an austere Roman Catholic, '"a spoilt priest"' (*VSR*, p. 150) haunted by a vision of the Last Judgment and convinced of his damnation – perhaps partly based on the poet Lionel Johnson. Yeats may have chosen this persona because of the severity of the poet's judgment against himself; and also because, like the eunuch-like Johnson, Yeats felt that sexual interest was inappropriate for him. The title also suggests that the poem is a companion piece to 'Michael Robartes and the Dancer', another poem about Iseult Gonne, but ascribed to a far more confident, impudent, and sexy persona.

I 2 *Norman*: Iseult and Maud Gonne lived at Calvados, in Normandy.

I 5–6 *south ... east ... west ... north wind*: for the moods that Yeats associated with these winds, see 'He bids his Beloved be at Peace', ll. 2–7. Here the poet's heart seems engorged, riddled with emotion.

I 10 *healthy flesh and blood*: compare 'The Tower' III 58.

I 11 *upland caught the wind*: compare 'To a Child Dancing in the Wind', l. 12 (another poem addressed to Iseult Gonne).

II 3 *fifty years*: for mentions of Yeats's age, see the Introductory Rhymes to *Responsibilities*, l. 20.

II 3 *so wildly bred*: compare 'The Death of the Hare', l. 9: 'wildness lost' (also concerning Iseult Gonne).

II 7 *the woman at my side*: Georgie Hyde-Lees. A fuller exploration of the romantic quadrilateral of Yeats, his wife, and Maud and Iseult Gonne is found in *The Only Jealousy of Emer* (1919). As Yeats wrote to Lady Gregory, during the same week that he wrote this poem, 'I have betrayed three people' (*L*, p. 633).

A Man Young and Old

These poems (excluding 'From *Oedipus at Colonus*', not added to *The Tower* until 1933) were originally grouped under the titles 'More Songs of an Old Countryman' (VI-VIII, X of the present sequence), 'Four Songs from the Young Countryman' (I-IV), and 'Two Songs from the Old Countryman' (V, IX). They constitute a spare and terse autobiography, simplified into the story of everyman. The continual permutation of a few elements – moon, stone, thorn, shriek – suggests that life has stiffened into a few stark detachable images, rearranged from one poem to the next to provide metaphors and stage-props. These elements are familiar from Yeats's earlier poems (as in 'He mourns for the Change …', l. 3: 'I have been in the Path of Stones and the Wood of Thorns'); but here is a reduction, almost to absurdity, of the symbolist method – Yeats's closest approximation to the fierce economy of a Beckett play.

I. First Love

3 *She*: Maud Gonne. In the schema of *A Vision*, Yeats placed her at Phase 16, only one night after the full moon – thus permitting this poem's likening of the woman to the moon. A similar comparison reappears at II 1: 'Like the moon her kindness is'.

7–12: a draft of this stanza is cited in a letter to Olivia Shakespear (*L*, p. 720).

8 *a heart of stone*: the stone represents the woman's lunar remoteness from earthly life, and also suggests the quality of the poet's own concentrated obsession – compare 'Easter, 1916', l. 43: 'Enchanted to a stone'. Stones appear so frequently that 'A Man Young and Old' could almost be described as a pebble-arrangement: II 7, 'So like a bit of stone I lie'; VII 6 and 12, 'Thinks that the stone's a child'; X 11, 'Being all alone I'd nurse a stone'.

13 *that transfigured me*: compare 'The Lamentation of the Old Pensioner', l. 6: 'Ere Time transfigured me' (a similarly ambiguous shape-change).

14–15 *a lout / Maundering*: compare 'Broken Dreams', l. 26: 'muttering like a fool'.

16–17 *Emptier of thought / Than the heavenly circuit of its stars*: compare *The Hour-Glass* (1914), ll. 366–70: 'my mind has been swept bare. … the Babylonian moon / Blots all away'; and 'The Dawn', l. 8: 'The stars fade out where the moon comes'. There is a parallel passage in *A Woman Young and Old*, at the end of 'A First Confession'.

18 *When the moon sails out*: the paralysing dazzle of the moon is also associated with love's fascination in 'A Memory of Youth', ll. 19–21: 'Love … Tore from the clouds his marvellous moon'.

II. Human Dignity

3 *What has no comprehension in't*: compare 'Words', l. 2: 'My darling cannot understand' – also about Yeats's difficulties in explaining himself to Maud Gonne.

4 *is the same for all*: Yeats distinguished love from pity, in that 'we love only that which is unique', while pity is an undiscriminating sympathy for man's

'common lot' (*AV*, p. 275). In 'The Circus Animals' Desertion' II 11 the poet calls Maud Gonne 'pity-crazed'.

5–6 *a scene / Upon a painted wall*: under the woman's objective, pitying gaze, the poet feels himself turning into a spectacle. Many passages in this sequence suggest such a theatrical depersonalization of human life – compare VI 2: 'Being but holy shows'; and the Greek chorus in XI.

7 *a bit of stone*: see I 8.

8 *a broken tree*: this telling piece of scenery recurs at VIII 1 and 12, and becomes an explicit simile for the aging body at VI 3 ('bodies broken like a thorn') and VI 11. For similar references, see 'The Lamentation of the Old Pensioner', l. 14.

9 *I could recover if I shrieked*: in his suppressed autobiography, Yeats described the seven-year period after the break-up in 1896 of his affair with Olivia Shakespear as follows: 'I was tortured by sexual desire and disappointed love. Often as I walked in the woods at Coole it would have been a relief to have screamed aloud ... I was never before or since so miserable' (*Mem*, p. 125). Shrieks recur in this sequence at VI 18 (a shriek of orgasm) and at VII 15 and 20 (a shriek of pride); compare also the 'peacock cry' of X 8. In one sense 'A Man Young and Old' is a series of extorted shrieks quickly stifled. For a more pleasant shriek, see 'Solomon and the Witch', l. 9.

11 *I am dumb*: compare IX 7: 'Margery is stricken dumb'; and 'A Dialogue of Self and Soul' I 40: 'my tongue's a stone'.

III. The Mermaid

1 *A mermaid*: Olivia Shakespear – see Introduction IX. This poem may recall various Irish tales of sea-goddesses who lure heroes, such as that told in *The Only Jealousy of Emer*. Yeats again mentioned a mermaid in 'A Drunken Man's Praise of Sobriety', l. 14.

IV. The Death of the Hare

When an anthologist asked Yeats about the meaning of this poem, he declined other than to write, 'You can say that the poem means that the lover may, while loving, feel sympathy with his beloved's dread of captivity' (*L*, pp. 840–41).

2 *The hare*: Iseult Gonne – also disguised as a hare in 'Two Songs of a Fool' I 1 and II 4.

9 *wildness lost*: compare 'Owen Aherne and his Dancers' II 3: 'wildly bred' (also concerning Iseult Gonne).

12 *the death of the hare*: that is, Iseult Gonne's marriage to Francis Stuart, of whom Yeats disapproved: 'A girl that knew all Dante once / Live to bear children to a dunce' ('Why should not Old Men be Mad?', ll. 5–6).

V. The Empty Cup

Yeats quoted a draft of this poem in a letter to Olivia Shakespear (whom the poem concerns): 'I came upon two early photographs of you yesterday ... Who ever had a like profile? – a profile from a Sicilian coin. One looks back to one's youth as to [a] cup that a mad man dying of thirst left half tasted. I wonder if you feel like that' (*L*, p. 721). A few months earlier, Yeats had written to her, 'One never tires of life and at the last must die of thirst with the cup at one's lip' (*L*, p. 711). In a note added in 1924 to an early essay on Blake, Yeats thought 'how I must have wasted the keenness of my youthful senses' (*EI*, p. 145). Compare also *The Shadowy Waters*, ll. 148-51: 'The bed of love ... Is no more than a wine-cup in the tasting, / And as soon finished'.

6 *his beating heart would burst*: compare the sensation of drowning in 'The Mermaid', l. 6.

7 *October last*: Yeats and Olivia Shakespear met again in October, 1926.

10 *my sleep is gone*: compare 'On Woman', l. 36: 'Sleep driven from my bed'.

VI. His Memories

2 *but holy shows*: see II 5–6.

3 *bodies broken like a thorn*: see II 8.

5 *Hector*: son of King Priam, Hector was the greatest Trojan hero in the Iliad – slain by the Greek warrior Achilles. These archaizing references prepare for the chorus from *Oedipus at Colonus* in XI.

13 *The first of all the tribe*: Helen of Troy – also mentioned at X 3. Possibly Yeats was thinking of the occasion in 1907–8 when he slept with Maud Gonne – see 'On Woman', l. 25.

18 '*Strike me if I shriek*': see II 9. For an orgasmic shriek in *A Woman Young and Old*, see 'Her Triumph', l. 12: 'a miraculous strange bird shrieks at us'.

VII. The Friends of His Youth

6 *stone*: see I 8.

12 *Thinks that the stone's a child*: old age tends to petrify both the adorer and the object of adoration. For other poems on the relation between a child and

a dead image, see 'The Dolls' and 'Among School Children' VII. Note that the poet will assume Madge's role – 'I'd nurse a stone' (X 11).

15 *Shrieks, 'I am King of the Peacocks'*: for the shriek, see II 9; for peacocks, see 'The Indian upon God', l. 17. Note that the poet will assume Peter's 'peacock cry' (X 8).

VIII. Summer and Spring

1 *old thorn-tree*: see II 8.

6 *we'd halved a soul*: compare 'Among School Children' II 5–6: 'our two natures blent / Into a sphere'.

IX. The Secrets of the Old

According to *A Vision* III, the dead are compelled 'to trace every passionate event to its cause until all are related and understood, turned into knowledge' (p. 226) – and in this poem the old seem to anticipate this stage of the soul's progress.

5 *what had drowned a lover once*: compare 'The Tower' II 32, where a crazed admirer of Mary Hynes 'was drowned in the great bog'.

6 *like an old song*: compare 'O Do Not Love Too Long', ll. 3–4: 'out of fashion / Like an old song'.

7 *stricken dumb*: compare II 11.

X. His Wildness

1 *sail*: a rich word in this volume – compare the 'sailing moon' of I 1 and the title 'Sailing to Byzantium'. The poet seems to wish to be transfigured into a lunar image.

3 *Paris' love*: Helen of Troy, abducted by the Trojan hero Paris – see VI 13.

4 *so straight a back*: compare 'Beautiful Lofty Things', ll. 10–11: 'Maud Gonne . . . waiting a train, / Pallas Athena in that straight back'.

8–11 *I'd have a peacock cry . . . I'd nurse a stone*: the poet imagines himself assimilating the traits of Peter (VII 15) and Madge (VII 6). The personages in this sequence seem almost interchangeable, as if old age withered away all peculiarity, reduced all men to a single caricature – like the scarecrow of 'Sailing to Byzantium' II 2 and 'Among School Children' IV 8 and VI 8.

XI. From *Oedipus at Colonus*

During 1926–27, Yeats made a version of Sophocles' *Oedipus at Colonus* – see 'Colonus' Praise'. The stoic wisdom of this chorus (ll. 1147–58 of Yeats's version) serves here to dismiss the life rehearsed in spasmodic flashes in the previous ten poems. As in 'Nineteen Hundred and Nineteen' III, it seems that memories, even of delight, only impede the soul's journey to oblivion.

10 *Never to have lived is best*: compare Yeats's translation of *King Oedipus*, ll. 1191–92: 'Call no man fortunate that is not dead. / The dead are free from pain'. In *The Birth of Tragedy* (1872), chapter 3, Nietzsche declared that the folktale of the Silenus offered the ground of all Greek wisdom: 'There is an ancient story that King Midas hunted in the forest a long time for the wise *Silenus*, the companion of Dionysus, without capturing him. When Silenus at last fell into his hands, the king asked what was the best and most desirable of all things for man. [At length the Silenus answered] "What is best of all is beyond your reach forever: not to be born, not to *be*, to be *nothing*. But the second best for you – is quickly to die."' Compare also *The Words upon the Window-Pane* (1934), which ends when the ghost of Swift (echoing Job) speaks through a medium's mouth 'Perish the day on which I was born!' (l. 554).

12 *The second best's a gay goodnight*: in a letter to Olivia Shakespear, Yeats remarked of this line (quoted along with the previous two stanzas) that it 'is very bad Grecian but very good Elizabethan and so it must stay' (*L*, p. 723). Compare 'The Wild Old Wicked Man', ll. 60–62: 'I choose the second-best ... a woman's breast' (instead of choosing fast death).

The Three Monuments

Yeats paraphrased the sentiments of this poem in his famous speech (11 June 1925) urging the Irish Senate to permit divorce, in which he pointed out that the public monuments of Dublin encouraged a spirit of sexual tolerance:

> I am thinking of O'Connell, Parnell, and Nelson.... It was said about O'Connell, in his own day, that you could not throw a stick over a workhouse [for the unemployed] wall without hitting one of his children, but he believed in the indissolubility of marriage, and when he died his heart was very properly preserved in Rome.... We had a good deal of trouble about Parnell when he married a woman who became thereby Mrs. Parnell.... The [Protestant] Bishop of Meath would not, like his predecessors in Ireland eighty years ago, have given Nelson a pillar. He would have preferred to give him a gallows, because Nelson should have been either hanged or transported. I think ... we have in our midst three very salutary objects of meditation which may, perhaps, make us a little

> more tolerant. . . . I do not think that the memories of these great men of genius were swept away by their sexual immoralities. (*SSY*, pp. 97–98, 102)

Yeats's point is that the mask of dignity and rectitude achieved by these statesman and embodied in the public monuments is a kind of anti-self – behind the stone image is all manner of irresponsibility and sexual licence. This theme is related to that of 'Ancestral Houses', in which greatness stems from violence and bitterness.

3 *One among the birds*: a pillar commemorating Admiral Horatio Nelson (1758–1805), the British hero whose victory at Trafalgar broke the power of Napoleon's navy; a noted adulterer. This pillar was higher than the two flanking monuments on O'Connell street.

4 *A stumpier on either hand*: statues of Charles Parnell (see 'To a Shade'); and of Daniel O'Connell (1775–1847), Irish leader who helped emancipate the Catholic population but who later resisted progressive causes. O'Connell is called 'the Great Comedian' in 'Parnell's Funeral' I 1.

11 *pride bring in impurity*: the dialectic of pride and purity recurs in 'Blood and the Moon', another poem about distinguished Irishmen.

The Gift of Harun Al-Rashid

When Yeats assembled his *Collected Poems*, he removed this poem from *The Tower* and placed it at the end of the volume, with other narrative poems; but *The Tower* seems to provide a more fitting context. 'The Gift of Harun Al-Rashid' and 'All Souls' Night' both initiate the reader into the mysteries of *A Vision*; indeed this poem rehearses Yeats's own initation into those mysteries, for it is a veiled account of the poet's marriage, late in life, to an attractive young woman, and of the trances through which his wife conveyed the ruling structures of the universe. Yeats liked to deflect the most intimate matters on to the most preposterous fictions: 'as my wife was unwilling that her share should be known, and I to seem sole author, I had invented an unnatural story of an Arabian traveller which I must amend and find a place for some day because I was fool enough to write half a dozen poems that are unintelligible without it' (*AV* [1937], p. 19). This is one such poem; and indeed it was itself included in the text of *A Vision* (1925), pp. 121–27.

Yeats claimed in 1924 that the poem was derived from a letter by Owen Aherne:

> 'After the murder for an unknown reason of Jaffer . . . Harun-al-Rashid seemed as though a great weight had fallen from him, and in the rejoicing of the moment, a rejoicing that seemed to Jaffer's friends a disguise for his

remorse, he brought a new bride into the house. Wishing to confer an equal happiness upon his friend, he chose a young bride for Kusta-ben-Luka. According to one tradition of the desert, she had, to the great surprise of her friends, fallen in love with the elderly philosopher, but according to another, Harun bought her from a passing merchant. Kusta, a Christian like the Caliph's own physician, had planned, one version of the story says, to end his days in a monastery at Nisibis, while another story has it that he was deep in a violent love-affair that he had arranged for himself. The only thing upon which there is general agreement is that he was warned by a dream to accept the gift of the Caliph, and that his wife, a few days after the marriage, began to talk in her sleep, and that she told him all those things which he had searched for vainly all his life in the great library of the Caliph, and in the conversation of wise men. One curious detail has come down to us in Bedouin tradition. When awake she was a merry girl with no more interest in matters of the kind than other girls of her age, and Kusta, the apple of whose eye she had become, fearing that it would make her think his love but self-interest, never told her that she talked to him in her sleep. Michael Robartes frequently heard Bedouins quoting this as proof of Kusta-ben-Luka's extraordinary wisdom ... Even in the other world Kusta's bride is supposed to remain in ignorance of her share in founding the religion of the Judwalis [Diagrammatists, according to *AV*, p. 41], and for this reason young girls who think themselves wise are ordered by their fathers and mothers to wear little amulets on which her name has been written. All these contradictory stories seem to be a confused recollection of the contents of a little old book, lost many years ago with Kusta-ben-Luka's larger book ... This little book was discovered, according to tradition, by some Judwali scholar or saint between the pages of a Greek book which had once been in the Caliph's library. The story of the discovery may however be the invention of a much later age ...'

In my poem I have greatly elaborated this bare narrative. (*VP*, pp. 828–29)

It is possible to dismiss this note as fatuous or heavily coy, but it serves to enforce the indeterminacy and arbitrariness of the sources of spiritual revelation, of poetic composition. The Caliph may have been joyous, or he may have been remorseful; Kusta may have planned a life of celibacy or violent lust; ignorance is the condition of the next world, we are told, as well as of our own. *A Vision*, it is suggested, is but an invention based on a confused memory of a little book that doubtfully reflected the contents of a larger book – all authority vanishes into a reverberating abyss. The poem, like much of Yeats's poetry, attempts to verbalize what is beyond the range of words:

As I write I find myself looking for words that do not exist to express what can be expressed accurately in geometrical lines – three times this morning

> I had given up in despair [did] I not remember that this task has been laid upon me by those who cannot speak being dead & who if I fail may never find another interpreter. Kusta ben Luka himself once so learned & so eloquent could now, lacking me but twitter like a swallow. (*MAV* II, p. 408)

Yeats made 'The Gift of Harun Al-Rashid' an obvious piece of costume-play in order to suggest the sense of entering into a supernatural theatre that he felt at the events of the first days of his marriage; and perhaps to suggest something of the general fictitiousness of human life. The supernatural Communicators told Yeats, 'we have come to give you metaphors for poetry' (*AV*, p. 8); and in this poem Yeats found, or was given, metaphors for the whole process of the descent of revelation, and for his wife, and for himself.

Title *Harun Al-Rashid*: an actual Caliph (766–809); but Yeats knew him less from history than from tall tales: 'We know Harun a[l] Rashid through the *Arabian Nights* alone, and there he is the greatest of all traditional images of generosity and magnanimity. In one beautiful story he finds that a young girl of his harem loves a certain young man, and though he himself loves that girl he sets her free and arranges her marriage' (*Ex*, p 448); 'when ... Harun Al-Rashid looked at the singer Heart's Miracle, and on the instant loved her, he covered her head with a little silk veil to show that her beauty "had already retreated into the mystery of our faith" ... the Caliph [saw a beauty that] was its own sanctity, and it was this ... sanctity ... that created romance' (*AV*, p. 286). 'The Gift of Harun Al-Rashid' is itself a romance about the relation between beauty and sanctity. Some commentators interpret the Harun Al-Rashid of this poem as God; but it can be argued that he is Kusta's supernatural counterpart, *daimon* or anti-self (see l. 98), mysteriously ordering the events of his life, and enacting on a high plane the same marriage that Kusta makes on earth.

1 *Kusta Ben Luka*: according to Finneran (*PNE*, p. 689), a doctor and translator (d. *c*. 913). Yeats himself noted the anachronism: '"The Gift of Harun Al-Rashid" seems to have got the dates wrong, for according to the story Robartes told [Owen Aherne], the Founder of the Judwali Sect, Kusta ben Luka, was a young or youngish man when Harun al-Rashid died. However, poetic licence may still exist' (*AV*, p. 54).

6 *banners*: 'The banners of the Abbasid Caliphs were black as an act of mourning for those who had fallen in battle at the establishment of the Dynasty' (*VP*, p. 829). See also l. 188: 'A woman's beauty is a storm-tossed banner'.

12 *Sappho*: the great poetess (b. *c*. 612 BC), noted for erotic lyrics, of which only some fragments have survived.

13–14 *a boy's / Love-lorn, indifferent hands*: 'I print [one of my poems] and never hear about it again, until I find the book years after with a page dog-eared by some young man, or marked by some young girl with a violet, and ... I am a little ashamed' (*A: BS* 2).

16 *Parmenides*: pre-Socratic philosopher (b. *c.* 514 BC). 'I do not think it too great a poetical licence to describe Kusta as hesitating between the Poems of Sappho and the Treatise of Parmenides as hiding places. Gibbon says the poems of Sappho were extant in the twelfth century, and it does not seem impossible that a great philosophical work, of which we possess only fragments, may have found its way into an Arab library of the eighth century. Certainly there are passages of Parmenides, that for instance numbered 130 by Burkitt, and still more in his immediate predecessors, which Kusta would have recognized as his own thought. This from Heraclitus for instance: "Mortals are Immortals and Immortals are Mortals, the one living the others' death and dying the others' life" [compare *AV*, p. 68]' (*VP*, p. 829). As Finneran notes (*PNE*, pp. 689–90), Yeats marked Parmenides' fragment 130 in his copy of Burnet's *Early Greek Philosophy*: 'The narrower circles are filled with unmixed fire, and those surrounding them with night, and in the midst of these rushes their portion of fire. In the midst of these circles is the divinity that directs the course of all things; for she rules over all painful birth and all begetting, driving the female to the embrace of the male, and the male to that of the female. First of all the gods she contrived Eros'.

The hesitation between Sappho and Parmenides suggests the dialectic of beauty and sanctity, or of the erotic and the spiritual – although, as Yeats's note hints, Parmenides' thought itself had an erotic component. Parmenides was an opponent of Heraclitus: whereas Heraclitus believed that the world came into being through the strife of the elements, Parmenides believed that the world was an indivisible unity. The Treatise of Parmenides, then, provides a brief glimpse of the Sphere that lies on the other side of the 'gyres and cubes and midnight things' (l. 184) that, according to Kusta's wife, constitute the world. The Parmenidean theme is found in Kusta's taste for the 'Unchanging' (l. 96).

26–28 *the truth / That ... can give birds wit*: 'The dead living in their memories are ... the source of all that we call instinct ... it is the dream martens that, all unknowing, are master-masons to the living martens building ... their elaborate nests' (*M*, p. 359). Compare 'The Tower' III 47–48.

30 *speak but fantasy*: in part, a confession of the poem's fantastical character – compare the 'impossible history' of ll. 108–9.

32 *Jaffer*: for Yeats's sources for Jaffer's execution, see Stallworthy, *BL*, pp. 63–64.

33–34: for another image of the desire for extreme secrecy, see the end of 'Ego Dominus Tuus'.

44 *goldfish in the pool*: compare 'gold-fish swimming in a bowl' ('All Souls' Night', l. 40) – an image of heaven. In 1927 Yeats wrote from Seville that he looked forward 'to some weeks of the gardens of the Alcazar, dropping crumbs to some equally old and dignified goldfish' (*TSMC*, p. 115).

47–48 *violent great hearts can lose / Their bitterness and find the honeycomb*: compare 'Ancestral Houses', ll. 19–20: 'Bitter and violent men, might rear in stone / The sweetness that all longed for'. For *honeycomb*, see 'Vacillation' VIII 11.

50 *Change the bride with spring*: compare l. 75: 'love has seasons'.

62–63 *poet's thought / That springs from body and in body falls*: compare ll. 66–67: 'our souls / Are nearer to the surface of the body'. For the theme of the Thinking Body, see 'To a Young Beauty', l. 18.

66 *mimicry*: that is, the poet's thought, like the hunter's eye, retains the spontaneity of youth through continual interchange with physical life; but the hunter's eye retains only a practised semblance of youth, whereas the poet's thought is really young (in the first publication, this sentence began, at l. 62, 'An artist's thought' and ended 'Can be no mimicry' [*VP*, pp. 463–64]).

71 *my lantern*: that is, my body. Kusta argues for the divisibility of soul and body.

78 *the Byzantine faith*: Christianity.

80 *when I choose a bride I choose for ever*: 'I thought one woman, whether wife, mistress, or incitement to platonic love, enough for a life-time' (*A: DP* 14).

86 *those old crabbed mysteries*: Georgie Hyde-Lees was a student of the occult before she met Yeats.

89–90 *youth's very fountain, / Being all brimmed with life*: a metaphor derived from the 'pure jet' of l. 64. Compare 'Ancestral Houses', l. 12: 'abounding glittering jet'.

94 *Itself and not some other soul*: the supernatural determinants of human identity are the subject of Book I of *A Vision*.

101–2 *mouth to mouth / Is a man's mockery of the changeless soul*: see *Baile and Aillinn*, ll. 39–40: '*all that life can give us is / A child's laughter, a woman's kiss*'.

110 *time's disfiguring*: compare 'The Lamentation of the Old Pensioner', l. 6: 'Time transfigured me'.

112–13 *was it love of me, or was it love / Of the stark mystery*: the counter-anxiety appears at ll. 170–71: 'What if she ... Dream that I love her only for the voice'. Yeats often wondered whether love was directed at a man or at his attributes – see 'The Hero, the Girl, and the Fool', l. 9: 'I have raged at my own strength because you have loved it'.

115–16 *did the torchlight of the mystery / Pick out my features*: to Kusta's wife, the object of occult research and the object of her human love are strangely equivalent – just as Kusta finds the supernatural diagrams an expression of his wife's body (l. 185). This convergence of spiritual truth and psychoanalytic insight is partly explained by ll. 91–94. Note also the tactile confusion between sacred texts and Kusta's cheek (ll. 125–27) – Yeats sometimes hinted that *A Vision* itself was nothing but the image of his own face multiplied as 'in a room full of mirrors' (*AV*, p. 214). The text is not only autobiography, but a magical image of the poet's body.

125: the first printing contained here a passage stressing the wife's susceptibility: 'She moved her limbs confusedly as though / Hands upon either shoulder made her move' (*VP*, p. 466).

126–27 *As if that writing ... Were some dear cheek*: for other poems in which a text is a thematic element, see the note to 'When You are Old', l. 2.

141 *Self-born*: Yeats's usual epithet for the supernatural – see 'A Prayer for my Daughter', ll. 67–68.

142–43 *Those terrible implacable straight lines / Drawn through the wandering vegetative dream*: the occult diagrams suggest how a transcendental intellect can carve up the incoherent profusion of nature. See the note to 'The Phases of the Moon', ll. 119–20: 'The burning bow that once could shoot an arrow / Out of the up and down'.

151 *the full moon*: Phase 15, the time of maximum revelation, according to *A Vision*.

156 *those emblems on the sand*: Yeats liked this figure because it suggested that the desert – the whole earth – was a kind of blank page inscribed with a supernatural text. For more exposition of sand-tracing and sand-dancing, see *AV* (1925), pp. 9–11, *AV* (1937), p. 41, and *VPl*, p. 789.

167 *Old fellow-student*: Abd Al-Rabban – see l. 2. This address is somewhat parallel to Yeats's address to the ghost of MacGregor Mathers in 'All Souls' Night', l. 74.

169 *I must buy knowledge with my peace*: compare 'Leda and the Swan', l. 13: 'Did she put on his knowledge with his power'.

174 *That is to age what milk is to a child*: compare 'I see Phantoms ...', l. 40: 'Suffice the ageing man as once the growing boy'.

178 *my fine feathers*: compare 'Among School Children' IV 5–6: 'I ... had pretty plumage once'.

184–85 *all those gyres and cubes and midnight things / Are but a new expression of her body*: 'This refers to the geometrical forms which Robartes describes the Judwali Arabs as making upon the sand for the instruction of their young people, and which, according to tradition, were drawn as described in sleep by the wife of Kusta-ben-Luka' (*VP*, p. 469). Just as Yeats once said of Maud Gonne that his poetry 'shadowed in a glass / What thing her body was' ('A Woman Homer Sung', ll. 11–12), so he now proposes that *A Vision* is but a cubist reconstruction of his wife's body.

Cubism hovers suggestively over the text of *A Vision*: 'the whole philosophy was so expounded in a series of fragments which only displayed their meaning, like one of those child's pictures which are made up out of separate cubes, when all were put together' (*AV* [1925], p. 11); 'now that the system stands out clearly in my imagination I regard [the gyres] as stylistic arrangements of experience comparable to the cubes in the drawing of Wyndham Lewis and to the ovoids in the sculpture of Brancusi' (*AV* [1937], p. 25). Wyndham Lewis appears again in *A Vision* (though he is not named) as the sullen cubist typical of Phase 9 (p. 121); and Lewis is also mentioned among the inhumanly mathematical artists who are 'absorbed in some technical research to the entire exclusion of the personal dream' (*AV* [1925], p. 211). Yeats believed that the geometrical forms of the gyres retained human significance only in so far as they traced a human shape – indeed he seemed to regard *A Vision* as a kind of love-poem, interpretable through 'The Gift of Harun Al-Rashid'.

In 1934 Yeats prophesied the end of an age dominated by reason, the return of a 'myth-haunted', visionary age: 'Perhaps now that the abstract intellect has split the mind into categories, the body into cubes, we may be about to turn back towards the unconscious, the whole, the miraculous' (*VPl*, p. 808; *Ex*, p. 404). 'The Gift of Harun Al-Rashid' can be seen as a recipe for uncubifying *A Vision*, for restoring the supple human body, 'unconscious', 'whole', that lies beneath its figures.

188 *A woman's beauty is a storm-tossed banner*: the poem's ending provides more metaphors for mediumship. For Yeats's note on the banner, see l. 6.

189: this line condenses the following two lines of the original printing: 'Under it armed Wisdom stands, a separate Wisdom / For every separate quality of love' (*VP*, p. 469).

191 *Nor dazzled by the embroidery*: that is, not taking beauty as an end in itself.

193 *the armed man*: the Djinn of l. 136; see also the note to l. 189. This image recalls the end of 'He remembers Forgotten Beauty', where armed men 'Brood her high lonely mysteries'. Such guardians of wisdom as the man in the golden breastplate in 'The Old Stone Cross' and the loyal vassals in 'The Black Tower' are also relevant.

All Souls' Night

The strongest theme of *The Tower* is the poet's labour to engage himself with an image, to construct adequate symbols of life – even the title of the volume suggests this sort of edification. But the volume ends with a counter-theme, present earlier in such poems as 'Nineteen Hundred and Nineteen' III (also similar in metre to 'All Souls' Night'): the soul's effort to disembody itself, to free itself from from every image and symbol. This poem offers some points of comparison with an earlier elegy, 'In Memory of Major Robert Gregory': at the centre of each poem is a trio of ghosts, who while living experimented with various strategies for escape from the natural world, as if in anticipation of their ghostly selves. But whereas the earlier poem moved on to a fourth ghost, that of Robert Gregory, 'All Souls' Night' returns immediately to the poet, who seems to be spiritualizing before the reader's eyes – as if the poem were a funeral elegy for the elegist himself.

Subtitle *Epilogue to 'A Vision'*: both editions of *A Vision* conclude with this poem, as if occult truths are more appropriate to the dead, more keenly felt by them. Yeats did not originally intend this to be the epilogue to the 1925 *A Vision*, but included it shortly before publication (*MAV* II, p. 397).

1 *Christ Church*: a college at Oxford University – Yeats was staying at Oxford when he wrote the poem. For other bells signalling the approach of spirits, see 'Alternative Song for the Severed Head . . .', l. 7.

3 *All Souls' Night*: November 2, when the Catholic faithful pray for the souls of the dead in Purgatory.

14 *mummies in the mummy-cloth*: for mummies, see 'On a Picture of a Black Centaur . . .', l. 7. The relation of a mummy to its winding-cloth suggests the relation of eternity to time – see *The King of the Great Clock Tower* (1935), l. 8, where a musician compares the souls of the dead to 'bobbins where all time is bound and wound'. See also 'Byzantium', l. 11: 'Hades' bobbin bound in mummy-cloth'. The shrouds sewn by the dead in 'Cuchulain Comforted' are reminiscent of these mummy-windings.

21 *Horton*: William Thomas Horton (1864–1919), painter on occult themes, in the tradition of Blake and Audrey Beardsley. A scrap of paper that Horton once sent to Yeats contained a mysterious warning (alluding to the figure from Plato's *Phaedrus* of the white and black horses that pull the Soul's chariot) that helped Yeats to formulate the idea of the anti-self (*MAV* I, p. 11). In *A Vision*'s lunar scheme, Horton was placed at the extremely *primary* Phase 25 (*MAV* I, p. 121). In 1917 Horton became angry with Yeats for republishing his Introduction to Horton's *A Book of Images* while deleting references to Horton (*LTY* II, p. 331).

23 *platonic love*: in the Dedication to *A Vision* (1925), p. x, Yeats alluded to

Horton as one who 'lived through that ... strangest of all adventures – Platonic love.... he gave himself up to all kinds of amorous adventures, until at last, in I think his fiftieth year but when he had still all his physical vigour, he thought "I do not need women but God". Then he and a very good, charming, young fellow-student fell in love with one another and though he could only keep down his passion with the most bitter struggle, they lived together platonically, and this they did ... from a clear sense of something to be attained by what seemed a most needless trampling of the grapes of life. She died, and he survived her but a little time during which he saw her in apparition and attained through her certain of the traditional experiences of the saint'. Yeats also believed that Jonathan Swift, with his 'fakir-like contempt for all human desire' (*Ex*, p. 359), pursued a relation with Stella of 'platonic love' (*Ex*, p. 361).

25 *his lady*: Audrey Locke (1881–1916). Harper thinks that Yeats developed the doctrine of the Over Shadower – the haunting phantom of the beloved (see the note to 'An Image from a Past Life') – from Locke's relation to Horton (*MAV* II, p. 317). In 1934 Ernest Rhys wrote that once Horton 'showed me on the wall a charcoal- or pencil-outline of the shadow of his dead friend, – Audrey Locke. He said one day he found the pale shadow cast clearly & perfectly on the plaster wall, & drew the line round' (*LTY* II, p. 563).

40 *a gold-fish swimming in a bowl*: all heaven is encompassed by one magnified obsessive image. Compare 'The Gift of Harun Al-Rashid', l. 44: 'goldfish in the pool'. In the automatic script for 21 March 1920, Dionertes told Yeats that the goldfish symbolized 'conception – both physical & philosophical' (*MAV* II, p. 389).

41 *Emery*: Florence Farr Emery (1869–1917), English actress. She played in travesty the role of Aleel, the poet-hero of *The Countess Cathleen*, at its first performance in 1899; she also composed chant-settings of Yeats's poems and performed them on the psaltery, an ancient instrument reconstructed by Arnold Dolmetsch (some of these settings are reprinted in *EI*, pp. 21-25). Yeats's seven-year period of celibacy ended in 1903, when he began an affair with her.

46 *a school*: a Buddhist institution in Sri Lanka. Compare John Synge's travelling to 'a most desolate stony place' ('In Memory of Major Robert Gregory' IV 6). 'Florence Farr coming to her fiftieth year, dreading old age and fading beauty, had made a decision we all dreamt of at one time or another, and accepted a position as English teacher in a native school in Ceylon that she might study oriental thought, and had died there' (*AV* [1925], pp. ix-x); 'Florence Farr had accepted a post in a Cingalese girls' school that she might hide her ageing beauty. I have the psaltery Arnold

Dolmetsch designed for her, certain strings are broken, probably nobody will play on it again' (*VPl*, p. 1009). Yeats felt a certain loss of fruition when she abandoned London: Sturge Moore remembered that Yeats called her 'a chalk egg he had been sitting on for years' (see Ronald Schuchard's article in *Yeats: An Annual of Critical and Textual Studies* 2 [1984]: 224). For a less solemn poem inspired by Farr's departure from London, see Pound's 'Portrait d'une Femme' (1912): 'Your mind and you are our Sargasso sea'.

49 *foul years*: she suffered from cancer.

56 *it plunge into the sun*: compare 'There', l. 4: 'There all the planets drop in the Sun'.

58 *Chance and Choice*: see 'Solomon and the Witch', l. 14.

59 *Forget its broken toys*: see 'Certain Artists bring her Dolls and Drawings', l. 11: 'We have naught for death but toys'.

60 *sink into its own delight at last*: compare 'Man and the Echo', l. 36: 'sinks at last into the night'. For the theme of reflexivity, see 'A Prayer for my Daughter', ll. 67–68.

61 *Mathers*: MacGregor Mathers (1854–1918), 'the author of *The Kabbala Unveiled*, and his studies were two only – magic and the theory of war, for he believed himself a born commander ... it was through him mainly that I began certain studies and experiences, that were to convince me that images well up before the mind's eye from a deeper source than conscious or subconscious memory' (*A: FY* 20). He was a diligent student of occult texts and a ferocious leader in the Order of the Golden Dawn – to which Florence Farr also belonged, and to which Yeats tried to induce Horton. The persona Michael Robartes was partly based on Mathers, and a caricature of him appears in Yeats's unfinished novel *The Speckled Bird* I vii and II i. Yeats was bemused by Mathers' absurdity and extravagance, and wrote that he seemed 'a figure in a play of our own composition' (*A: FY* 20). In this poem he is indeed made into an actor in Yeats's supernatural theatre.

63 *of late estranged*: Mathers accused another member of the Order of the Golden Dawn of forging mystical documents; Yeats was on the investigating committee.

64 *half a lunatic, half a knave*: 'MacGregor himself lived in a world of phantoms. He would describe himself as meeting, perhaps in some crowded place, a stranger whom he would distinguish from living men by a certain tension in his heart. These strangers were his teachers.... The break-up [of] his character that was soon to bring his expulsion from my Order had begun' (*Mem*, p. 106); 'he would dress himself in Highland dress ... and his mind brooded upon the ramifications of clans and tartans. Yet I have at moments doubted whether he had seen ... Scotland itself ... He began to foresee ...

the imminence of immense wars ... He imagined a Napoleonic rôle for himself, a Europe transformed according to his fancy, Egypt restored, a Highland Principality' (*A: TG* 18).

81 *names are nothing*: many of Yeats's writings, such as the Leo Africanus MS, speak of the depersonalization of the dead, and the precariousness of any ascription of identity to them.

86–90: the near-repetition of ll. 16–20 suggests the quality of being 'Wound in mind's pondering' (l. 13) or 'Wound in mind's wandering' (l. 99).

95–96 *where the damned have howled away their hearts, / And where the blessed dance*: Yeats could assimilate into his private system certain elements of the Christian hell and heaven by claiming that each dead soul dwells according to his imaginations while on earth of the afterlife: 'as Cornelius Agrippa writes, "We may dream ourselves to be consumed with flame and persecuted by daemons", and certain spirits have complained that they would be hard put to it to arouse those who died, believing they could not awake till a trumpet shrilled' (*M*, p. 354).

THE WINDING STAIR AND OTHER POEMS (1933)

The poems in the previous volume, *The Tower*, were written at the zenith of Yeats's public career, the period when he served as a senator, won the Nobel Prize, and wrote much of his autobiography; the poems of the present volume represent a turning-inward, a concentration. Yeats's health was deteriorating. In 1928 he needed to recuperate from lung congestion in Spain; late in 1929 he suffered first a dangerous lung haemorrhage, then, in Italy, a bout of Malta fever so severe that he made an emergency will, witnessed by Ezra Pound; and the shadow of death lies over many of these poems. In *The Tower*, the time of day was, so to speak, a sunny evening in which the moon was visible; but here the time of day is midnight – a dark field intermitted by a few dazzles that only intensify the darkness.

The Tower and *The Winding Stair and Other Poems* are, to an extent, companion volumes. Some poems in *The Tower* have a kind of twin in the present book: 'Sailing to Byzantium' and 'Byzantium'; 'The Tower' and 'Blood and the Moon'; 'My Table' and 'A Dialogue of Self and Soul'; and the first publication of *The Winding Stair* ended with *A Woman Young and Old*, a sequence parallel to 'A Man Young and Old' at the end of *The Tower*. When, in the early 1920s, Yeats revised his youthful work, he tried to suppress extraneous detail, to introduce a certain 'numbness and dullness ... that all might seem, as it were, remembered with indifference, except some one vivid image' (*A: DP* 15). When, a few years later, Yeats recast some of the themes of *The Tower* into *The Winding Stair and Other Poems*, he took this process of simplifying and intensifying to extreme lengths. Here every ornament, every casual richness of detail, vanishes into a black background, on which a few objects shine with preternatural clarity – tower, sword, flame, metal bird. Instead of the full, wealthy world of *The Tower*, where symbols developed themselves through a slight heightening of a general meaningfulness of landscape and furniture, we have a shrunken and painful universe; instead of a burnished painting in oils, we have stark designs in black and white. The gyres are at their point of maximum tension; and it seems scarcely possible to constitute a human image in a domain where isolated faculties tug and tear, where the season is always the dark of the moon or the full.

The Winding Stair and Other Poems combines two earlier volumes: *The Winding Stair* (1929), which contained the first five poems of the present volume ('In Memory of Eva Gore-Booth . . .' to 'Oil and Blood'), plus *A Woman Young and Old*; and *Words for Music Perhaps and Other Poems* (1932), which contained all the remaining poems (except 'Swift's Epitaph' and 'Crazy Jane talks with the Bishop'). The design of the volume as it now stands (excluding for a moment the long appended sequences *Words for Music Perhaps* and *A Woman Young and Old*) is somewhat circular: at the beginning and end, the poet tries to extricate images of perfection from time's wreck (those of the Gore-Booth sisters in the first poem, that of Maud Gonne in 'Quarrel in Old Age', that of himself in 'Stream and Sun at Glendalough'). In the middle of the volume, however, there is a qualified celebration of the unfinished, the ugly, the time-wrecked – the poet affirms the value of life in all its frenzies and spasms, as if energy were itself delight. Yet the poet is never immune from the lure of timeless glory, the condition of the artifact – and so he runs his helpless course between antinomies, between the blind man's ditch and Byzantium, never able to make a final choice.

This volume struggles continually to constitute a kind of refuge for the poet, an edifice of words. In *The Tower*, Yeats tried to manufacture a verbal equivalent of his own home, Thoor Ballylee – this project continues in the present book, but is supplemented by a variety of other buildings, especially Lady Gregory's mansion (Coole Park) and the Cathedral of Hagia Sophia. All three dwellings seem somewhat precarious: Thoor Ballylee has a waste room at the top ('Blood and the Moon' IV 6); Coole Park, the poet fears, may be demolished ('Coole Park, 1929', l. 26); and even Hagia Sophia seems to lack proper flood control ('Byzantium', l. 40). It is no accident that this volume begins with a poem in which a gazebo is set ablaze. The vehemence of the poet's powers, celebrated in many poems, seems proportional to the general havoc around him.

Dedication: Yeats's friend Edmund Dulac was a painter, designer, and musician – see 'On a Picture of a Black Centaur . . .'

In Memory of Eva Gore-Booth and Con Markiewicz

Yeats had admired the elegance of Eva Gore-Booth (1870–1926) and Constance Gore-Booth Markiewicz (1868–1927) since he met them in 1894; and in this double elegy he laments that that beauty should be compromised by the passage of time. As in the case of Maud Gonne, the poet seems partly to blame the Gore-Booth sisters for their own decay, as if by committing themselves to the political issues of the moment they had deformed themselves into images of temporality. In his study of the drafts of the poem, Stallworthy offers much information about the Gore-Booth sisters (*BL*, p. 165).

I 1 *Lissadell*: the family home of the Gore-Booths, Co. Sligo, built in 1832.

I 4 *one a gazelle*: Eva Gore-Booth – 'I was at once in closer sympathy with ... Eva, whose delicate, gazelle-like beauty reflected a mind far more subtle and distinguished' (*Mem*, p. 78). Yeats thought of becoming her suitor.

I 7–8 *condemned to death, / Pardoned*: Countess Markiewicz was a deputy leader in the Easter 1916 uprising – see 'Easter, 1916', l. 17; her death sentence was commuted to life imprisonment – see 'On a Political Prisoner' – and she was later released.

I 9 *Conspiring among the ignorant*: she fought in the Irish Civil War and became a Member of Parliament.

I 10 *what the younger dreams*: Eva Gore-Booth studied mystical literature and Indian and Neoplatonic philosophy.

I 12 *skeleton-gaunt*: compare 'Among School Children' IV 3: 'Hollow of cheek' (referring to Maud Gonne).

II 6–7 *strike a match ... till time catch*: in a description of a moment of ecstasy in a crowded restaurant (itself versified in 'Vacillation' IV), Yeats wrote that certain 'images from *Anima Mundi*, embodied there and drunk with that sweetness, would, like a country drunkard who has thrown a wisp into his own thatch, burn up time' (*M*, p. 365). For other references to the combustion of time, see 'The Moods', ll. 1–2: 'Time drops in decay, / Like a candle burnt out'. Here this old picturesque motif is strangely literalized, by the precise image of an arsonist taking a match to a gazebo. In an early draft, the line 'till time catch' was followed by: 'Some great bellows to a fire / For widow Nature still / Has those cradles left to fill / And works of intellectual fire' (*BL*, p. 171).

Austin Clarke (who arranged the production of many plays by Yeats) alluded to this poem when he described a fire at the Abbey Theatre: 'Yeats had not dreamed an unstubbed butt, / Ill match, would bring his curtain down' ('The Abbey Theatre Fire').

Fire is an important theme in this volume: see also 'Blood and the Moon' II 18: 'Everything that is not God consumed with intellectual fire'; 'Statistics',

l. 2: 'God's fire'; 'Byzantium', l. 27: 'flames begotten of flame'; 'The Mother of God', l. 1: 'A fallen flare'; and 'Vacillation' I 3: 'A brand, or flaming breath' (and II 1–2: 'A tree there is ... half all glittering flame'; IV 7: 'My body of a sudden blazed'; and VII 4: 'the simplicity of fire').

II 10–11 *We the great gazebo built, / They convicted us of guilt*: Yeats believed that time was only a construction of the human mind, without autonomous reality: 'pure time and pure space ... are abstractions or figments of the mind' (*AV*, p. 71). Compare 'Death', l. 12: 'Man has created death'.

Death

This poem was inspired by the assassination of Kevin O'Higgins (1892–1927), Vice-President and Minister for Justice of the Irish Free State; he was probably murdered in reprisal for his presiding over the execution of 77 civilians captured in the possession of arms. Many of the themes of this poem appear in a letter written to Olivia Shakespear shortly after O'Higgins's death: 'He was our personal friend, as well as the one strong intellect in Irish public life ... A French man of science thinks that we all – including murderers and victims – will and so create the future. I would bring in the dead.... perhaps if we have lived good lives we may be reborn in some peaceful eastern village' (*L*, pp. 726–27). Yeats gave O'Higgins high praise in *On the Boiler* (*Ex*, p. 442), and referred to him in 'Parnell's Funeral' II 8 as the 'sole statesman' of modern Ireland. O'Higgins's picture appears in 'The Municipal Gallery Revisited' I 5–7, 'A soul incapable of remorse or rest'.

4 *Dreading and hoping all*: reincarnation will eventually bring to the soul every conceivable identity, as Yeats explains in 'Fergus and the Druid' and 'Mohini Chatterjee'.

11 *He knows death to the bone*: according to Yeats, O'Higgins told his wife, '"Nobody can expect to live who has done what I have done"' (*L*, p. 809).

12 *Man has created death*: compare 'The Tower' III 28–29: 'Death and life were not / Till man made up the whole'; 'In Memory of Eva Gore-Booth ...' II 10: 'We the great gazebo [time] built'; and 'Vacillation' I 7: 'The body calls it death'. In an early essay on Blake, Yeats wrote that 'love and death and old age are an imaginative art' (*EI*, p. 130). A similar theme appears in a poem by W. J. Turner that Yeats reprinted in *OBMV*, p. 298: 'Nothing exists outside me.... / Death and Birth – ' ('From "The Seven Days of the Sun"' i 7–8).

A Dialogue of Self and Soul

This poem is based on a traditional theme in English poetry, the most famous example of which is Andrew Marvell's 'A Dialogue between the Soul and the Body'; but the strenuous tone of Yeats's poem is far removed from the urbane 'metaphysical' wit of Marvell. Yeats personifies, instead of body and soul, the competing stresses towards subjectivity (the Self) and objectivity (the Soul). In such earlier poems as 'The Tower', Yeats treated the poet's conflicting desires for imaginative engagement with natural life, and for philosophical detachment from it; but here these desires build themselves into sub-personalities, voices in everyman's head. Although Yeats could not have known it, in 1910–11 T. S. Eliot wrote, but did not publish, two poems on similar themes, a 'First Debate between the Body and Soul' and a second debate. Yeats included in *OBMV* Herbert Read's 'Dialogue Between the Body and the Soul of the Murdered Girl'.

The structure of this poem shows how successfully Yeats had internalized the system of *A Vision* (see Introduction XI): this is a gyre-shaped poem, in which the Soul is at its point of maximum intensity at the beginning, incantatory and compelling, while the Self is at its weakest; as the poem progresses the Soul loses confidence and energy and, at last, the power of speech (I 40), while the Self steadily gains until it reaches its climax at the poem's end.

The complex of images and themes gathered around Self and Soul was partly derived from Nietzsche. In the margin of his copy of Nietzsche, which he first read in 1902, Yeats wrote: 'Night (Socrates, Christ): one god – denial of self in the soul turned towards spirit, seeking knowledge. Day (Homer): many gods – affirmation of self, the soul turned from spirit to be its mask and instrument when it seeks life' (Ellmann, *IY*, p. 97, punctuation changed); this is almost a synopsis of the present poem, although in the marginalia Yeats used the term *spirit* instead of *Soul*, and used the term *soul* to mean the totality of the human being. This was a response to Nietzsche's distinction between master and slave moralities – see Otto Bohlmann, *Yeats and Nietzsche*, p. 84.

AE's comment on reading this poem almost suggests that he was himself the model for *Soul*: 'I like best the "Dialogue of Self & Soul". I am on the side of Soul but know that its companion has its own eternal claim, and perhaps when you side with the Self it is only a motion to that fusion of opposites which is the end of wisdom' (*LTY* II, p. 560). Yeats thought of AE as a visionary in whom details were lost, differences minimized: 'He has the religious genius, and it is the essence of that genius that all souls are equal in its eyes. Queen or apple woman, it is all one ... Whereas I have been concerned with men's capacities, with all [that] divides man from man' (*Mem*, p. 130). For more on AE (George Russell), see the Dedication to *Crossways*.

The original title of the poem was 'Sword and Tower': 'I am writing a new tower poem "Sword and Tower", which is a choice of rebirth rather than deliverance from birth. I make my Japanese sword and its silk covering my symbol of life' (*L*, p. 729). Yeats also noted, '*A Dialogue of Self and Soul* was written in the spring of 1928 during a long illness, indeed finished the day before a Cannes doctor told me to stop writing' (*VP*, p. 831).

I 5 *the hidden pole*: compare 'Veronica's Napkin', l. 2: 'Tent-pole of Eden'; also 'He thinks of his Past Greatness . . .', l. 4: 'Pilot Star' (that is, pole-star).

I 7 *That quarter where all thought is done*: according to *A Vision*, the last quarter of the lunar month (Phases 22–28) is marked by an 'Abstraction' that has for its 'object or result the elimination of intellect' (p. 299).

I 10 *Sato's ancient blade*: see 'My Table', l. 2.

I 24 *the crime of death and birth*: compare I 32; and 'Consolation', l. 9: 'the crime of being born'.

I 25 *Montashigi*: according to Jeffares (*NCP*, p. 271), a sword-maker who lived in Osafune in the early fifteenth century.

I 28 *Heart's purple*: 'If I say "white" or "purple" in an ordinary line of poetry, they evoke emotions so exclusively that I cannot say why they move me; but if I bring them into the same sentence with such obvious intellectual symbols as a cross or a crown of thorns, I think of purity and sovereignty' (*EI*, p. 161).

I 28–29 *I set / For emblems*: compare 'My House', l. 30, and 'Blood and the Moon' I 8–9: 'In mockery I have set / A powerful emblem up'. The conscious process of emblem-creation, symbol-making, is an important theme in Yeats's later work.

I 34 *the basin of the mind*: compare 'Ancestral Houses', l. 4: 'the basin spills'; and *A Vision*, p. 285: 'the stream set in motion by the Galilean Symbol has filled its basin, and seems motionless for an instant before it falls over the rim' (another passage in which a pool about to overflow is associated with the instant of poise before a change of gyre).

I 35 *deaf and dumb and blind*: see 'Never Give all the Heart', l. 12. Blindness reappears at II 1 and 19–20.

I 37 Is *from the* Ought, *or* Knower *from the* Known: in the technical terms of *A Vision*, these four entities are, respectively, *Will*, *Mask*, *Creative Mind*, and *Body of Fate* – that is, desire and its object, and intelligence and its object. The Soul is speaking of a condition when the human faculties will no longer be distinct from one another, a condition outside the reincarnative cycle.

I 39 *Only the dead can be forgiven*: the Self contradicts this at II 27.

I 40 *my tongue's a stone*: compare the Introductory Lines to *The Shadowy Waters*, ll. 25–26: '*a chattering tongue / Heavy like stone*'; *The King of the Great Clock Tower* (1935), l. 150: 'there's a stone upon my tongue'; and the speech of an old Aran-islander from 'Away' (1902), a report of one of Yeats's folklore expeditions: '"I know a good many on the island have seen *those* [enchanted people], but they wouldn't say what they're like to look at, for when they speak of them their tongue gets like a stone"' (*UP* II, p. 273; compare *EI*, p. 51). Also compare 'Vacillation' VII, a dialogue of Heart and Soul, where the Soul is 'Struck dumb in the simplicity of fire' (l. 4). Here, the Soul falls silent because it has verged on sacred mysteries beyond articulation in human speech. Yeats himself sometimes felt the same incapacity: 'I tried to describe some vision to Lady Gregory, and to my great surprise could not. I felt a difficulty in articulation and became confused' (*Mem*, p. 128).

II 2 *ditches*: see II 19.

II 5 *ignominy of boyhood*: compare 'A Prayer for my Son', ll. 23-24: 'ignominy / Of flesh and bone'. It seems that, between parts I and II, we have moved from the last quarter of the Great Wheel of reincarnations – the quarter of God – to the first quarter of the lunar month (Phases 2–8) – the quarter of Nature, in which a man slowly extricates himself from a state of complete absorption in the physical world. The Self seems to be speaking partly about the growth of a man in the course of one lifetime, partly about the growth of a man's spirit through many incarnations – Phase 2 is called the Child (*AV*, p. 137).

II 7–8 *The unfinished man* ... *Brought face to face with his own clumsiness*: compare this rapid life-sketch with Yeats's self-descriptions: 'Perplexed by my own shapelessness, my lack of self-possession ...'; 'on passing a tobacconist's I saw ... a lump of meerschaum not yet made into a pipe. She [Maud Gonne] was complete; I was not' (*Mem*, pp. 21, 63).

II 11–13 *disfigured shape / The mirror of malicious eyes / Casts upon his eyes*: 'I have found that if many people accuse one of vanity, of affectation, of ignorance, an ignoble image is created from which the soul frees itself with difficulty, an undiscerned self-loathing'; 'if men speak much ill of you it makes at moments a part of the image of yourself – that is your only support against the world – and that you see yourself too as if with hostile eyes' (*Mem*, pp. 66, 84). For the theme of distorting-mirrors, see 'The Two Trees', l. 21. Also compare Malin's speech in the Prologue to Auden's *The Age of Anxiety* (1947): 'the ego is a dream / Till a neighbour's need by name create it; /Man has no mean; his mirrors distort' (*CP*, p. 347).

II 16 *wintry blast*: compare 'Meru', l. 11: 'winter's dreadful blast'.

II 17 *content to live*: compare 'Words', l. 16: 'content to live'.

II 19 *frog-spawn of a blind man's ditch*: compare Yeats's reference to semen as a 'plaster of ant's eggs' (from a passage mocking Carlyle's impotence, *AV*, p. 116). Compare also 'On a Political Prisoner', ll. 11–12: 'Blind and leader of the blind / Drinking the foul ditch'. A somewhat similar combination – seagull-semen and a ditch – appears in *The Player Queen* (1922) II 118–31, a passage describing the heroine's foul but miraculous birth as a parody of Christ's. (In *Diarmuid and Grania* [1901] III 350, frog-spawn in a pool is mentioned as a sign of pollution.)

In 1937 Yeats more fully explained the theme of transfiguration-in-the-ditch: 'my Christ ... is that Unity of Being Dante compared to a perfectly proportioned human body, Blake's "Imagination", what the Upanishads have named "Self": nor is this unity distant ... but imminent, differing from man to man and age to age, taking upon itself pain and ugliness, "eye of newt, and toe of frog" [*Macbeth* IV i 14]' (*EI*, p. 518).

II 24 *A proud woman*: for example, Maud Gonne.

II 27 *forgive myself the lot!*: according to the Soul (I 39), purgation can be achieved only in death, but the Self, as it moves towards its zenith, is willing to take responsibility for its own salvation.

II 29 *So great a sweetness flows*: the same phrase appears in 'Friends', l. 27.

II 30 *We must laugh*: 'There is in the creative joy an acceptance of what life brings ... which arouses within us, through some sympathy perhaps with all other men, an energy so noble, so powerful, that we laugh aloud and mock, in the terror or the sweetness of our exaltation, at death and oblivion' (*EI*, p. 322).

II 31–32 *We are blest by everything, / Everything we look upon is blest*: the whole volume is full of blessings – compare the first two lines of 'Blood and the Moon'; 'Coole and Ballylee, 1931', ll. 44–45: 'whatever most can bless / The mind of man'; and 'Vacillation' IV 10: 'I was blessèd and could bless'. Also compare the end of *The Cat and the Moon* (1926), where a Holy Man blesses a Lame Beggar and the Lame Beggar rises, throws away his stick, and starts to dance. Yeats wrote to Ethel Mannin that 'Our traditions only permit us to bless, for the arts are an extension of the beatitudes' (*L*, p. 832).

Blood and the Moon

In 'The Tower', Yeats made his home, Thoor Ballylee, an emblem of the imagination's constructive power – its ability to make an edifice of self or civilization. In the present poem, Yeats makes his tower an emblem of the defectiveness of the modern imagination, its loss of connection-making faculty. In 'The Tower', Yeats looked around his neighbourhood and saw in his mind's eye people whose acts could rouse his imagination; but here the poet contemplates distinguished exemplars of eighteenth-century Anglo-Ireland whose powers seem to surpass his own. 'The Tower' ended with a last testament; 'Blood and the Moon' seems to be the work of a poet with nothing but his disdain or helplessness left to bequeath. The image of the tower, formerly a symbol of all human achievement, has dwindled in the moonlight until it is little more than a Tower of Babel, mocking human pretension.

I 1 *Blessed*: compare the last two lines of the previous poem – its mood of ecstatic self-acceptance will soon decline into raillery and wryness.

I 3–6 *A bloody ... power / Rose ... Rose*: the rise of blood (the emblem of Self, or Race, or Subjectivity, or the natural life) towards the moon (the emblem of Soul, or Objectivity, or escape from nature) describes much of the poem's movement.

I 5 *Uttering, mastering it*: 'A civilisation is a struggle to keep self-control' (*AV*, p. 268). As suggested in II 1–3, the tenor of a civilization, the character of its striving, is visibly expressed in its architecture.

I 8–9 *In mockery I have set / A powerful emblem up*: compare II 4; 'My House', l. 30; and 'A Dialogue of Self and Soul' I 28–29: 'all these I set / For emblems'. In a sense the subject of 'Blood and the Moon' is its own poetic vitality, its ability to set up emblems that can achieve an effective derision of the modern age. For the tower as a symbol of a historical era, see a deleted passage from the MS of *A Vision*, describing the new *antithetical* age to come after AD 2000: 'what we symbolise as the Tower [the post-Christian age] inherits all that once belonged to the Catacombs [the Christian age]' (*CEAV [1925]*, notes, p. 64).

I 11–12 *a time / Half dead at the top*: compare IV 6; and 'Three Songs to the Same Tune' III 11 (*VP*, p. 548): 'When nations are empty up there at the top' (and its rewritten version, 'Three Marching Songs' II 21). In modern life, the process of racial utterance and mastery seems to have aborted. Michael Steinman (in *Yeats's Heroic Figures*, p. 115) compares an anecdote about Swift, who pointed to a noble elm, withering above, and said, '"I shall be like that tree, I shall die at top."'

II: the metre of this section, imitating an involved spiral motion, recurs in *Supernatural Songs* II and VII.

II 1 *Alexandria's was a beacon tower*: the Pharos of Alexandria (built *c.* 280 BC), one of the seven wonders of the ancient world.

II 1–2 *Babylon's / An image of the moving heavens*: the Babylonians were noted astronomers – see 'The Dawn', ll. 6–9. A tower that embodies the zodiac suggests the closest possible intimacy between blood and the moon, the great contraries.

II 3 *Shelley had his towers, thought's crowned powers he called them once*: see *Prometheus Unbound* (1820) IV 103, by Percy Bysshe Shelley (1792–1822). Towers are common in Shelley's work – in his essay on Shelley's symbolism, Yeats wrote, 'The contrast between [the tower] and the cave ... suggests a contrast between the mind looking outward upon men and things and the mind looking inward upon itself' (*EI*, p. 87). See also 'The Phases of the Moon', l. 16.

II 6 *Goldsmith and the Dean, Berkeley and Burke*: Oliver Goldsmith (1728–74), poet and dramatist, author of *The Deserted Village* (1770); Jonathan Swift (1667–1745), Dean of St Patrick's Cathedral in Dublin, poet, and author of *A Tale of a Tub* (1704), a satire on institutional Christianity, and *Gulliver's Travels* (1726), a satire on human existence; George Berkeley (1685–1753), idealist philosopher; and Edmund Burke (1729–97), orator and aesthetician on the theme of the sublime (see 'The Tower' III 12). Each embodies a portion of Yeats's own complex of attitudes: Swift embodies Yeats's mockery, Goldsmith his affection for rural life, Berkeley his opinion that the mind creates reality, and Burke his sense that politics should express a race's ideals. These four men, all born in Ireland, preside over the whole of *The Winding Stair and Other Poems*, just as Plato, Plotinus, and Pythagoras presided over *The Tower*. All four reappear in 'The Seven Sages'; a translation of Swift's epitaph is also found in this volume.

When Yeats was young he considered Swift and Berkeley insufficiently Irish to appear on a list of the great Irish books (*UP* I, p. 352); but they came to be among the heroes of his old age. Yeats thought that all four denied the abstraction-ridden philosophy, at once materialistic and unreal, of Locke and other Englishmen: 'Berkeley with his belief in perception, that abstract ideas are mere words, Swift with his love of perfect nature, of the Houyhnhnms, his disbelief in Newton's system and every sort of machine, Goldsmith and his delight in the particulars of common life that shocked his contemporaries, Burke with his conviction that all States not grown slowly like a forest tree are tyrannies, found in England the opposite that stung their own thought into expression and made it lucid' (*EI*, p. 402).

II 8 *the heart ... had dragged him down into mankind*: Yeats may have been thinking of Gulliver's bitter recognition in Book IV of the *Travels* that he was himself a Yahoo, an excrementitious ape. Compare also Aherne's refutation of Christ's commandment of love: '"Jonathan Swift made a soul for the gentlemen of this city by hating his neighbour as himself"' (*M*, p. 301). Yeats later wrote a play, *The Words Upon the Window-Pane* (1934), in which a medium evokes the ghost of Swift, who dwells in a perpetual dream of frustration about the madness latent in himself and in Western history. In 'Parnell's Funeral' II 12, Yeats wrote that Parnell 'enriched his blood' with Swift's 'bitter wisdom'.

II 9 *sipping at the honey-pot of his mind*: Yeats relished Goldsmith's 'picturesque, minute observation' (*Ex*, p. 351); the 'honey-pot' may be related to Goldsmith's periodical *The Bee*.

II 10 *haughtier-headed Burke that proved the State a tree*: 'haughtier' suggests the upward movement on the stair, as we ascend from blood to moon – from Swift to Berkeley. In 'Vacillation' VI there is a tree sprung from human blood, and Burke's tree, in this context, almost seems to grow from the blood of Swift. Yeats often cited Burke's figure of the state as a tree: 'Feed the immature imagination upon that old folk life, and the mature intellect upon Berkeley . . . upon Burke who restored to political thought its sense of history, and Ireland is reborn, potent, armed and wise. Berkeley proved that the world was a vision, and Burke that the State was a tree, no mechanism to be pulled in pieces and put up again, but an oak tree that had grown through centuries' (*SSY*, p. 172; *UP* II, p. 459).

See also Yeats's 1930 Diary: 'A State is organic and has its childhood and maturity and, as Swift saw and Burke did not, its decline' (*Ex*, p. 318); a speech on education (1925), which urges school teachers to teach religion as 'a part of history and of life itself, a part, as it were, of the foliage of Burke's tree' (*UP* II, p. 459); and a speech on Emmet (1904), which conjoins blood and moon: 'A nation is like a great tree and it must lift up its boughs towards the cold moon of noble hate no less than to the sun of love, if its leaves are to be thick enough to shelter the birds of heaven' (*UP* II, p. 323). The decline of the state-tree is suggested in 'Three Marching Songs' II 23: 'What tears down a tree that has nothing within it?'

II 11 *labyrinth*: see 'The Tower' II 96.

II 12 *Cast but dead leaves to mathematical equality*: although Burke was a champion of liberty – he spoke against slavery and deplored the war against American independence – he was no democrat: 'I divine an Irish hatred of abstraction . . . expressed . . . by Burke in his attack upon mathematical democracy' (*Ex*, p. 351). Compare the original version of 'Three Songs to the Same Tune' III 4 (*VP*, p. 547): 'What's equality? – Muck in the yard'.

II 13 *God-appointed Berkeley that proved all things a dream*: Yeats had always been an idealist – in 'Rosa Alchemica' (1896), 'the independent reality of our thoughts . . . was . . . the doctrine from which all true doctrines rose' (*M*, p. 284) – and he came to find that Berkeley gave philosophical prestige to this belief. In the 1930s Yeats argued that the undergraduate Berkeley espoused the heretical belief (recanted later when he became an Anglican bishop) that the thinker who imagined the universe into being was as much mankind as God (*EI*, pp. 406–8; *Ex*, pp. 304, 325); in this poem, however, Yeats seems to suggest that, as the staircase is climbed, human energy, human blood, first flowers into the state, then sublimes into a vision of the divine.

II 14 *pragmatical, preposterous pig*: in 1956 Pound, concerned with the degeneration of Picasso and other modernists into 'marvellous technique and total lack of human value', wrote: 'What Yeats called the "pragmatic pig" had ... triumphed' (*Ezra Pound and the Visual Arts*, ed. Zinnes, p. 178). Also see the note to IV 5–6.

II 16 Saeva Indignatio: savage indignation, a phrase from Swift's Latin epitaph for himself – see 'Swift's Epitaph', l. 2. This stanza offers a rapid summary of the upward movement described in II 9–15.

II 16 *the labourer's hire*: a theme of Goldsmith's.

II 17 *The strength*: what Burke possessed.

II 18 *Everything that is not God consumed with intellectual fire*: the intellectual fire belongs to Berkeley's world-containing mind, burning up the dead materiality of things and promoting them to ideas – in fact Yeats later went so far as to suggest that this fire could consume God as well: 'this light, this intellectual Fire, is that continuity which holds together "the perceptions" ... it is a substitute for the old symbol God ... Descartes, Locke, and Newton took away the world and gave us its excrement instead. Berkeley restored the world' (*Ex*, p. 325). Yeats once reproved Sean O'Casey by telling him that 'Dramatic action is a fire that must burn up everything but itself' (*L*, p. 741). And in 'Ribh Considers Christian Love insufficient', l. 8, Ribh speaks of a hatred that clears the soul 'Of everything that is not mind or sense'.

Compare also the old theme that God is found by world-evacuation, as shown in the story 'Where there is Nothing, there is God' (1897); *Where There is Nothing* (especially a deleted passage from the end of the 1902 version: 'I will go into the sun, for God is in the heart of it, where the flame burns up everything' [*VPl*, p. 1164]); and certain poems in *Responsibilities*, such as 'Paudeen', 'The Three Hermits', and especially 'The Hour Before Dawn' (see l. 103, 'there be nothing but God left'). This theme was common in the mystical texts Yeats studied in his youth: Yeats remembered Madame Blavatsky's prophecy that '"a day will come when ... there shall be nothing but God"' (*UP* I, pp. 300–1). Yeats believed that the function of art was to hasten the Last Judgment by inspiring general conflagration, as Aherne explains in 'The Tables of the Law' (*M*, p. 294; see also *EI*, pp. 140, 339, *L*, p. 741, and *Ex*, p. 340). In a 1910 draft of *The Player Queen*, Yeats wrote a prologue to the mystery play of Noah: 'For you behold in me the patriarch Noah not abashed for all the deluge ... The world, I know, shall be consumed by fire, that is the consuming of all form and images' (Bradford, *WPQ*, pp. 221–22).

III 4 *The blood of innocence has left no stain*: compare IV 9–10. The moon remains immune from contamination by the murders that it appears to provoke – Yeats seems to appeal both to the old notion that the moon causes lunacy, and to his private system, which asserts that the moon's phases govern all human behaviour.

III 11 *we that have shed none*: modern men seem insufficiently bloody and insufficiently lunar – neither powerful nor wise.

IV 3–4 *butterflies ... moths*: old symbols of the soul's metamorphosis at death from the chrysalis of the body; butterflies were commonly depicted on Greek sarcophagi. In *John Sherman* (1891), the heroine receives a brooch showing 'a ladder leaning against the moon and a butterfly climbing up it' (*JSD*, p. 100). In his essay on Berkeley (1931), Yeats mocked abstract models of truth, rigid and static, pre-cut as from cookie-moulds, and added, 'How can we believe in truth that is always moth-like and fluttering and yet can terrify? – A friend and myself, both grown men, talked ourselves once into a terror of a little white moth in Burnham Beeches' (*EI*, p. 400). Also compare 'Tom O'Roughley', ll. 7–8: 'wisdom is a butterfly / And not a gloomy bird of prey'.

IV 5–6 *Is every modern nation like the tower, / Half dead at the top?*: see I 12. Thoor Ballyee terminates in a flat concrete roof surrounded by crumbling battlements; 'Part of the symbolism of *Blood and the Moon* was suggested by the fact that Thoor Ballylee has a waste room at the top and that butterflies come in through the loopholes and die against the window-panes' (*VP*, p. 831). The winding stair seems to halt in mid-spiral. In the eighteenth century, there was a continuum between blood and moon; but in modern times, it seems, the transmission-path has been broken – now blood and moon are not contraries but negations. The waste room in Thoor Ballylee is oddly anticipated in the so-called 'De Burgh' draft of *The Speckled Bird* (*c.* 1900), where a sensitive boy meditates in an old, unused tower, and delights in the stone stairway that winds up to the waste rooms and the battlements on top (*LTMSB*, p. 259). Also see Pound's Cantos: '"half dead at the top" / My dear William B. Y. your 1/2 was too moderate / "pragmatic pig" (if goyim) will serve for 2 thirds of it' (79/487).

IV 7 *wisdom is the property of the dead*: 'the dead are the wisdom of the living' (*AV* [1925], p. 221). Yeats found in Irish folklore the doctrine that the living contribute strength and the dead wisdom: 'though wisdom comes to us from among spirits, the spirits must get physical power from among us' (*UP* II, p. 232); 'strength comes from among men, and wisdom from among gods who are but "shadows"' (*UP* II, p. 282); 'the philosophy of Irish faery lore declares that all power is from the body, all intelligence from the spirit' (*Mem*, p. 166). Compare also 'After Long Silence', l. 7: 'Bodily decrepitude is wisdom'.

IV 12 *When it has looked in glory*: the end of the poem is open – is the moon still a viable goal or governor, or does its glory only mock all human striving? – the poet, being alive, is not wise enough to judge.

Oil and Blood

This poem is a severe simplification of 'Blood and the Moon' – its elaborate contrasting symbols are reduced to a strict dialectic of bodily fluids. The saints' corpses, miraculously free from decay, represent a translation of the human body into the artifice of eternity; while the vampires offer a grotesque literalization of the doctrine that civilization is nourished by human blood.

Here begins a sequence of seven very short poems, perhaps Yeats's closest approach to the minimalism of Pound's poetry around 1913–16 – 'Oil and Blood' even makes use of a technique similar to the overlay effect of Pound's 'In a Station of the Metro' (1913). It is as if naked symbols could constitute a terse speech of their own, almost without words.

2 *Bodies of holy men and women*: compare 'Vacillation' VIII 3: 'The body of Saint Teresa lies undecayed'.

5 *vampires*: Yeats knew Bram Stoker's *Dracula* (1897) and similar tales. In *The Unicorn from the Stars* (1908) I 256–58, a character puts a clause in his will: 'if I die without cause, a holly-stake to be run through my heart the way I will lie easy after burial'.

Veronica's Napkin

According to Christian lore, St Veronica wiped the face of the crucified Christ, and a bloody image of his features was imprinted on the cloth. This is a poem about maps: the poet contrasts the metaphors and symbol-charts that reduce heavenly grandeur to intelligible form with Veronica's cartography of blood. As in 'Wisdom', Yeats contrasts a vision of God's majesty with a vision of God's squalor: the former is desired by the Soul, the latter by the Self.

1 *The Heavenly Circuit*: Plotinus taught, in an essay of this name, that the stars and human souls rotate about God. Amidst a confutation of the materialist position (which assumes that a world of real objects, independent of ourselves, exists beneath our sense-impressions), Yeats used this term as a synonym for the whole complex of subjects and objects in the universe: 'If there is an external "substratum" Whitehead suggests that it is for every "sense-datum" the entire ambient – the 'Heavenly circuit" of Plotinus' (*TSMC*, p. 94). The term also appears in 'First Love', l. 17.

1 *Berenice's Hair*: a warlike queen (d. 221 BC), so mourned by her husband Ptolemy III that he named a constellation after her hair. Compare 'Her Dream', l. 8: 'Berenice's burning hair'; and the last lines of Pope's *The Rape of the Lock* (1714).

2 *Tent-pole*: the earth's axis, extending to the North Star – compare 'He hears

the Cry of the Sedge', ll. 4–5: '*Until the axle break / That keeps the stars in their round*'; and 'A Dialogue of Self and Soul' I 5: 'the hidden pole'. Russell Murphy (*ELN* 23 [June 1986]: 45) quotes Mrs Arthur Strong's description (known to Yeats) of a Roman sarcophagus on which a general is depicted, lying in state beneath a stellated canopy signifying '"the mantle of heaven, the tent of the sky."'

6 *a needle's eye*: compare 'A Needle's Eye', ll. 1–2: 'All the stream that's roaring by / Came out of a needle's eye'.

7 *a different pole*: the Cross of Christ's crucifixion.

Symbols

This is, so to speak, 'A Dialogue of Self and Soul' stripped to its irreducible minimum – compare the relation of 'Oil and Blood' to 'Blood and the Moon'. The first stanza offers an emblem of the Soul, the second and third stanzas offer emblems of the Self, in its masculine and feminine aspects.

2 *A blind hermit*: during a walking trip in Italy, Yeats saw a medieval tower on a mountain and had a sudden vision of 'an old man, erect and a little gaunt, standing in the door of the tower ... He was the poet who had at last ... come to share in the dignity of the saint' (*EI*, p. 291). Compare also the image of the Platonist in his tower, 'The Phases of the Moon', l. 15.

4 *the wandering fool*: in *On Baile's Strand* (1904), Yeats invented a Fool who behaved in a swaggering caricature of the hero Cuchulain. As in 'Blood and the Moon' IV 8, wisdom is incompatible with life.

5–6: quoted in a letter, *DWL*, p. 33.

5 *Gold-sewn silk on the sword-blade*: compare Sato's sword, surrounded by silken embroidery, in 'A Dialogue of Self and Soul' I 9–16 and 'My Table', ll. 2–7.

Spilt Milk

In his description in *A Vision* of Phase 22 – the lunar phase when the desire for objective facts starts to overwhelm every creative impulse of the imagination – Yeats wrote that the *Will* 'has become abstract, and the more it has sought the whole of natural fact, the more abstract it has become. One thinks of some spilt liquid which grows thinner the wider it spreads till at last it is but a film' (p. 158). Thus the subject of this poem (and of the following three) is the loss of imaginative intensity in the modern age.

1–2 *done and thought ... thought and done*: compare 'Vacillation' V 8–9: 'do or say ... say or do'.

The Nineteenth Century and After

Yeats quoted this quatrain in a letter to Olivia Shakespear: 'I have turned from Browning – to me a dangerous influence – to Morris . . . I have come to fear the world's last great poetic period is over'. Then, after the poem, Yeats added: 'The young do not feel like that – George [Yeats] does not, nor Ezra – but men far off feel it – in Japan for instance' (*L*, p. 759). The poem's topic – that loss of genius can itself provide a theme for poetry – is related to that of 'The Circus Animals' Desertion'.

3–4 *The rattle of pebbles on the shore / Under the receding wave*: compare Arnold, 'Dover Beach' (1867), ll. 9–10: 'the grating roar / Of pebbles which the waves draw back' – to which Arnold likened the withdrawal from mankind of the Sea of Faith. Ian F. A. Bell (*Philological Quarterly* 65 [1986]: 337) compares Pound's *Mauberley (1920)* III 44–45: 'delighted with the imaginary / Audition of the phantasmal sea-surge'.

Statistics

This poem curses statisticians as dim and tepid Platonists, whose numerical summaries and charts constitute a kind of parody of the Platonic forms – the divine ideas whose copies make up the material world. As early as 1904 Yeats complained of theatrical critics who wanted to see on stage 'personifications of averages, of statistics' (*Ex*, p. 146).

1 '*Those Platonists are a curse*': compare 'The Tower' III 27: 'cry in Plato's teeth'. For other Platonists, see 'The Phases of the Moon', l. 15.

3 *A diagram*: compare the Babylonian star-charts of 'The Dawn', l. 9 – such computations are typical of an objective, fact-ridden civilization such as our own. Also compare the wise men of 'Nineteen Hundred and Nineteen' V 7, who study calendars instead of watching the seasons. Yeats later wrote of the eighteenth century that it was 'over-rationalised and abstract, more diagram than body' (*Ex*, p. 358).

4 *More women born than men*: a sample of the trivial labours of statisticians.

Three Movements

This is a little parable about the death of imagination in the modern age – a period that, according to *A Vision*, relishes an art that imitates the commonplace and the ugly.

2 *Romantic*: see 'September 1913', l. 7.

The Seven Sages

These seven sages seem to be components of a debate in Yeats's mind, as he tries to define his relationship to four great Anglo-Irishmen of the eighteenth century: 'How much of my reading is to discover the English and Irish originals of my thought, its first language . . . Some of my ancestors may have seen Swift, and probably my Huguenot grandmother who asked burial near Bishop King spoke both to Swift and Berkeley. I have before me an ideal expression in which all that I have, clay and spirit alike, assists' (*Ex*, p. 293). As in *A Vision*, Yeats attempts here to see historical personages as intimate participants in his own inner life.

1 *Burke*: see 'The Tower' III 12.

2 *Grattan*: see 'The Tower' III 12.

5 *the Bishop of Cloyne*: George Berkeley – see 'Blood and the Moon' II 6 and 13. He believed in a panacea called tar-water – a beverage derived from American Indians: 'Had he not been told in America of Indians that cured all kinds of things with a concoction of tar? . . . Could he not lead his reader – especially if that reader drank tar water every morning – from tar to light?' (*Ex*, p. 324; compare *EI*, p. 399).

6 *Stella*: Esther Johnson (d. 1728), Swift's platonic lover.

7 *Whiggery*: to Yeats this term signified much more than a political party – it meant a deadening outlook, coarse and confining, without imagination: 'How convenient if men were but . . . dots, all exactly alike, all pushable, arrangeable . . . Instead of hierarchical society, where all men are different, came democracy; instead of a science [that acknowledges spiritualistic truths] came materialism: all that Whiggish world Swift stared on till he became a raging man' (*Ex*, p. 435).

9 *Swift*: see 'Blood and the Moon' II 6 and 8.

13 *All's Whiggery now*: Yeats believed that the tyranny of the Many (foreseen by Swift) had come to pass in modern democratic Europe – see *Ex*, p. 352. In the following lines the sages explain how the four great Irishmen abide even now as powers against Whiggery, and against the modern world that embodies it.

18 *Roads full of beggars, cattle in the fields*: themes from Goldsmith's *The Deserted Village*.

19 *trefoil*: shamrock – a word Yeats disliked for its suggestion of sentimental Irish caricature. Yeats insisted 'no shamrocks' when asked about a design for a book-cover (*L* I, p. 434), and felt disgust when he saw a bronze medal of himself decorated with shamrocks (*UP* II, p. 487); his senate committee on coin design also was set against shamrocks (*SSY*, p. 161).

25 *as children mimic*: in a speech on education, Yeats stressed a similar affiliation: 'Feed the immature imagination upon that old folk life, and the mature intellect upon Berkeley ... upon Burke' (*SSY*, p. 172).

26 *They understood that wisdom comes of beggary*: for an example, see l. 18. The sages understand the noble achievements of Irish thought as a flowering of dark racial energies – compare the continuum between blood and moon in 'Blood and the Moon' II. For a poem likening classical poets to unlettered lads and madmen, see 'Mad as the Mist and Snow'.

The Crazed Moon

This *Vision*-haunted poem is a parable of existence at gyre's end, in a culture moving through the chaos, violence, ugliness, and abstraction of the last phases of its moon. As in 'The Cat and the Moon', it seems that those who behold the moon intimately reflect the moon's own state – in this case, the moon's exhaustion from overproduction, as if, in these objective times, the moon had used itself up in developing too many objects. Joseph M. Hassett (*Yeats Annual* 5 [1987]: 233–34) cites a relevant passage from Macrobius: 'There is no doubt that the moon is the author and framer of mortal bodies, so much so that some things expand or shrink as it waxes or wanes'.

Mrs Yeats noted in her copy of *CP* (1933) that the MS of this poem (written in 1923) was lost, then found in August 1930.

2 *The moon is staggering in the sky*: Yeats wrote that Shelley likened the moon to 'a "dying lady" who "totters" "out of her chamber led by the insane and feeble wanderings of her fading brain"' (*EI*, p. 92, citing Shelley's fragment 'The Waning Moon'). Compare also Herod, in Wilde's *Salomé*, who speaks of the moon as 'a mad woman who is seeking everywhere for lovers ... She reels through the clouds like a drunken woman' (*Complete Works*, ed. Holland, p. 561).

8 *virginal pride*: perhaps referring to the full moon, a state of visionary perfection uncompromised by the material world.

13 *Fly-catchers of the moon*: compare 'The Statues', l. 18: 'Hamlet thin from eating flies'.

14 *Our hands are blenched*: In *The King's Threshold* (1904), the starving poet has a feverish vision of a leprous moon infecting mankind: 'there he is even now, with his white hand / Thrust out of the blue air, and blessing them / With leprosy' (ll. 662–64; compare ll. 857–59); and in a passage deleted from *The Only Jealousy of Emer*, Fand speaks of 'a last leprous crescent of the moon' (*VPl*, p. 559).

15 *needles of bone*: the contrast between the dance of the second stanza and

the the skeletons of the third recalls the contrast in 'The Double Vision of Michael Robartes' between the dancer of part II, emblematic of the full moon, and the puppets of part I, emblematic of the new moon. Yeats associated skeletons with famishing abstractions (e.g., in *AV*, p. 214).

17 *They are spread wide*: compare (the contemporaneous) 'I see Phantoms ...', ll. 13–14: 'arms and fingers spreading wide / For the embrace of nothing'; also *A Vision*, p. 296: 'Personality is everywhere spreading out its fingers in vain, or grasping with an always more convulsive grasp a world where the predominance of physical science ... of democratic politics ... show that mechanical force will in a moment become supreme'. Like 'Spilt Milk', this poem treats a thinning, weakening, dissolving, clonic civilization, with no goal other than to tear itself apart.

Coole Park, 1929

This poem and the following one – full of well kempt trees, polished furniture, and ceremonious scruples – are reminiscent of the rich textures of many of the poems in *The Tower* (especially 'Ancestral Houses'). The symbols of the two Coole Park poems – the swallows, the swan, the underground stream – seem improvised at leisure from the details of the landscape, unlike the overstressed, glaring emblems in such poems as 'A Dialogue of Self and Soul'. Each poem celebrates the creation of an artificial enclave carved out 'in Nature's spite' (l. 5), a region of unusual ease and conformity to man's will, man's mood, a domain where human personality is effectively inscribed. To some extent Lady Gregory resembles a modern equivalent of the eighteenth-century geniuses praised in 'Blood and the Moon' and 'The Seven Sages' – stately, powerful, and wise – if Yeats and his friends can be the last Augustans as well as the 'last romantics' ('Coole and Ballylee, 1931', l. 41). For a learned discussion of the role of the Big House in Irish literature, see Antony Coleman's article in *Yeats Annual* 3 (1985), pp. 33–52.

2 *an aged woman*: Lady Isabella Augusta Persse Gregory (1852-1932), owner (until 1927) of Coole Park – dramatist, folklorist, and old collaborator and friend of Yeats's.

9 *Hyde*: Dr Douglas Hyde – see 'At the Abbey Theatre', l. 1. Yeats thought his early translations from Gaelic superb, but found his 'ordinary English style' facile and vapid (*A: DP* 17).

11 *one that ruffled in a manly pose*: Yeats himself, according to *A: DP* 23. He saw himself as a man lacking in self-possession, who struggled from youth towards an anti-self.

13 *Synge*: see 'In Memory of Major Robert Gregory' IV 1.

14 *Shawe-Taylor and Hugh Lane*: Lady Gregory's nephews. John Shawe-Taylor (1866–1911), political reformer – Yeats wrote a eulogy for him that used another ornithological image, praising his handsome magnanimity: men such as he, 'copying hawk or leopard, have an energy of swift decision, a power of sudden action, as if their whole body were their brain'. Yeats further suggested that Shawe-Taylor's 'moral genius' complemented Synge's 'aesthetic genius' (*EI*, p. 343, 345). For Hugh Lane, see 'To a Wealthy Man ...'

17 *They came like swallows and like swallows went*: that is, they resemble migratory birds, as the prose draft for this poem specifies. Compare 'Shepherd and Goatherd', l. 62.

18–19 *And yet a woman's powerful character / Could keep a swallow to its first intent*: Lady Gregory's personality exerts a sort of magnetic field, unifying diverse geniuses into a 'dance-like glory' (l. 8) – as if she were an instinctual force, like that which governs the flight of birds. Yeats's prose draft reminded the poet to 'address the swallows flitting in their dream like circles / speak of the rarity of the circumstances, that bring together / such concords of men. each man more than himself / through whom an unknown life speaks. a circle ever returning / into itself' (Stallworthy, *BL*, pp. 180–1).

24 *cut through time*: the achievement fostered at Coole Park is timeless, even if the mansion itself decays – see l. 26.

25 *traveller*: *abi viator* – a common apostrophe on monuments or tombstones – see 'Swift's Epitaph', l. 5, and 'Under Ben Bulben' VI 9.

26 *When all those rooms and passages are gone*: Coole Park was indeed to be torn down, for no good reason, soon after Lady Gregory's death in 1932. Yeats recorded another prophecy of Coole Park's ruin in his 1930 diary (*Ex*, p. 319).

32 *that laurelled head*: Lady Gregory's.

Coole and Ballylee, 1931

This sequel to 'Coole Park, 1929' alters the tragic theme from the ruin of a house to a more intimate ruin – that of Lady Gregory and of Yeats himself. The (imaginary) underground stream that connects his home to Coole Park, some miles away, hints that Thoor Ballylee is a kind of secret outpost of Lady Gregory's charmed land; but the poem's pervasive sense of loss suggests that all charm, tradition, and authority are fragile. This poem originally had seven stanzas – Yeats excised the sixth and published it as 'The Choice'; if that stanza remained here it would give a still darker and more desperate tone to this elegy.

Title: originally 'Coole Park and Ballylee, 1931' – Yeats agreed to his editor Thomas Mark's decision to shorten the title (Finneran, *EYP*, p. 34).

2 *moor-hens*: see 'The Indian upon God', l. 3.

4 *'dark' Raftery's 'cellar'*: Anthony Raftery was a blind (so 'dark') Gaelic local poet – see 'The Tower' II 18. Yeats asked an old man about the meaning of Raftery's line, 'There is a strong cellar in Ballylee': 'He said the strong cellar was the great hole where the river sank underground, and he brought me to a deep pool, where an otter hurried away ...' (*M*, p. 23). This stanza's conjunction of tower and cave hints at certain psychic landscapes that intrigued Yeats in Shelley's poetry – see the note to 'The Double Vision of Michael Robartes' II 2–3.

5 *Run underground*: Yeats had previously written of this underground stream in a stanza deleted from 'My House'.

5–6 *rise ... in Coole demesne*: this revises geographic fact to suit the poet's purpose.

7 *Spread to a lake and drop into a hole*: somewhat reminiscent of the river Alph in Coleridge's 'Kubla Khan' – another soul-scape.

8 *What's water but the generated soul?*: 'I am certain that the water, the water of the seas and of lakes and of mist and rain, has all but made the Irish after its image. Images form themselves in our minds perpetually as if they were reflected in some pool.... Did not the wise Porphyry think that all souls come to be born because of water, and that "even the generation of images in the mind is from water?"' (*M*, p. 80). Note that the following stanzas describe the generation of psychic images and emblems – not only is nature a 'mirror' (l. 13), but the swan seems an emanation of the poet's soul (l. 19).

12 *buskin*: footwear worn by tragic actors in ancient Greece.

14 *the mounting swan*: Yeats wrote to his wife that this swan was 'a symbol of inspiration I think' (Hone, *WBY*, p. 425). If this comment is reliable, then the whole poem prophesies a loss of inspiration and a destruction of long-accreted genius; Pegasus (l. 46) is in any case an inspirational beast. For other swans – often associated with absence and loss – see 'The Wild Swans at Coole'.

16 *The glittering reaches*: compare 'The Tower' III 23.

19 *like the soul*: compare 'Nineteen Hundred and Nineteen' III 1–2: 'Some ... poet / Compares the solitary soul to a swan'.

24 *murdered with a spot of ink*: 'one spot of ink would kill a swan' (*Ex*, p. 90). Compare a line deleted from 'The Circus Animals' Desertion' III: 'A dab of black enhances every white' (Bradford, *YW*, p. 163). Also compare Browning, 'The Worst of It' (1864), ll. 5–6: 'my swan, that a first fleck's fall / On her wonder of white must unswan, undo!'

26 *somebody*: Lady Gregory.

27–29 *Beloved books ... old pictures ... Great rooms*: Yeats wrote a long, reverential description of Coole Park's furnishings in *A: DP* 4 – 'I can remember somebody saying: "Balzac would have given twenty pages to the stairs."'

30 *a last inheritor*: Robert Gregory, Lady Gregory's only son, killed in the Great War – see 'In Memory of Major Robert Gregory'.

40 *Like some poor Arab tribesman and his tent*: without the shaping, focusing force exerted by custom and ceremony (see 'Coole Park, 1929', ll. 18–19), we can only be nomads. Possibly this line was suggested by Stubbs's painting of Arab horses kept by an old owner of Coole Park (*A: DP* 4). Compare 'Ego Dominus Tuus', l. 29: 'a Bedouin's horse-hair roof'.

41 *We were the last romantics*: see 'September 1913', l. 7: 'Romantic Ireland's dead and gone'. Yeats remarked earlier that 'I gather that I am the last Victorian' (*L*, p. 740), and that 'A good poet must, as Henley said of Burns, be the last of a dynasty' (*Ex*, p. 295). Compare 'Fallen Majesty', l. 3: 'some last courtier at a gypsy camping-place'. As early as 1887, Yeats wrote that 'I feel more and more that we shall have a school of Irish poetry – founded on Irish myth and History – a neo-remantic movement' (*L* I, pp. 10–11).

44 *The book of the people*: a phrase used by Raftery: '"This is what I, Raftery, wrote down in the book of the people"' (*Ex*, p. 215); and a reminder of the folklore researches that Yeats and Lady Gregory carried out in the 1890s. An old local man once said of Lady Gregory, '"She has been ... like a serving-maid among us. She is plain and simple, like the Mother of God"' (*A: DP* 4).

46 *all is changed*: for similar declarations, see 'The Wild Swans at Coole', l. 15.

46 *that high horse*: Pegasus – see 'The Fascination of What's Difficult', l. 4. There the winged horse – symbolizing the poetic faculty – was sick; here he seems healthy, but lacking a worthy rider.

47 *Homer*: for other references, see 'A Woman Homer Sung'.

For Anne Gregory

Anne Gregory (b. 1911) was Robert Gregory's daughter. This decorous compliment to Lady Gregory's grandchild lightens (though only briefly) the mood left at the end of the previous poem.

15 *found a text to prove*: compare 'Michael Robartes and the Dancer', l. 43: 'this Latin text'.

16–17 *only God . . . Could love you for yourself alone*: compare 'The Hero, the Girl, and the Fool', l. 16: 'only God has loved us for ourselves'. A haughty queen announces in *A Full Moon in March* (1935), ll. 75–76: 'A lover in railing or in flattery said / God only looks upon me without fear'.

Swift's Epitaph

This is a fairly close translation of the Latin epitaph that Swift wrote for himself – although the first line and the term 'World-besotted' are Yeats's own contribution. This poem helps to explain how Swift continues to exert power after his death (as Yeats described in 'The Seven Sages', l. 20, where 'The tomb of Swift wears' away the modern world): Swift offers himself as a model to be imitated. To some extent Coole Park seems to have followed Swift's model of excellence. This whole poem is quoted in *Ex*, pp. 344–45, to illustrate the 'shudder' that Yeats felt in his spine at hearing an actress play Hofmannsthal's Electra. For more on Swift, see 'Blood and the Moon' II 6 and 8.

1 *Swift has sailed into his rest*: compare 'Sailing to Byzantium' II 7: 'I have sailed the seas'.

2–3 *Savage indignation there / Cannot lacerate his breast*: Yeats quoted a more literal translation of these lines when grieving over Synge's death in 1909: 'is not that epitaph Swift made in Latin for his own tomb more immortal than his pamphlets, perhaps than his great allegory [*Gulliver's Travels*]? – "He has gone where fierce indignation can lacerate his heart no more" ' (*EI*, p. 308); and in *Words upon the Window-Pane* (1934), ll. 139–42: 'he sleeps under the greatest epitaph in history . . . It is almost finer in English than in Latin'; and in a letter to Dorothy Wellesley: 'our ancestor Swift has gone where "fierce indignation can lacerate his heart no more", & we go stark, staring mad' (*DWL*, p. 115). Yeats also wrote that 'Swift's *Epitaph* and Berkeley's *Commonplace Book* are the greatest works of modern Ireland' (*TSMC*, p. 141). Also compare 'Blood and the Moon' II 16, '*Saeva Indignatio*'.

5 *traveller*: see 'Coole Park, 1929', l. 25.

6 *liberty*: 'Liberty depended upon a balance within the State, like that of the "humours" in a human body . . . and for its sake Swift was prepared to sacrifice what seems to the modern man liberty itself' (*Ex*, p. 356).

At Algeciras – A Meditation upon Death

Yeats recuperated from lung congestion in the sunshine of Algeciras, in southern Spain. As in 'Sailing to Byzantium' and 'Swift's Epitaph', Yeats here imagines death as an ocean transit, for which a seaside resort can provide easy metaphors. This poem and 'Mohini Chatterjee' were originally published as two 'Meditations upon Death'.

1 *cattle-birds*: like the 'speckled bird' of 'Shepherd and Goatherd', l. 62, these migratory birds are emblems of the soul's passage from life to death.

4 *the narrow Straits*: the Pillars of Hercules, separating Europe from Africa – the limits of the known world in classical times. Immense flocks of birds migrate over these straits between Europe and Africa – in September 1889 Yeats wrote of 'the season of swifts and swallows. They are now all flying southward, piercing the dew by the Pillars of Hercules' (*LNI*, p. 82).

6 *those mingled seas*: the Mediterranean Sea and the Atlantic Ocean.

11 *Not such as are in Newton's metaphor*: Sir Isaac Newton (1642–1727) compared himself to 'a boy, playing on the seashore, and diverting myself, in now and then finding another pebble or prettier shell than ordinary, while the great ocean of truth lay all undiscovered before me' (David Brewster, *Memoirs ... of Sir Isaac Newton* II, p. 407). When Yeats was a boy these shells had no metaphorical content (compare 'Her Vision in the Wood', l. 31, 'no fabulous symbol'); but as an old man the act of giving seashells to an older friend seems to anticipate the act of presenting one's life work to God. Usually Newton was one of Yeats's villains – see the notes to 'Fragments'.

12 *Rosses*: see 'The Stolen Child', l. 15.

16 *the Great Questioner*: in such poems as 'The Tower' (II 8, 73), the poet saw himself as a questioner; but in this poem, where the imagination is less self-confident, the poet sees himself as someone questioned by a heavenly accuser or judge. Compare 'A First Confession', l. 15: 'those questioning eyes'; and 'The Delphic Oracle upon Plotinus', l. 3: 'Bland Rhadamanthus' (a judge in Hades). For Yeats's provisional use of Christian motifs, see 'A Prayer on Going into My House'.

The Choice

This poem (originally a stanza of 'Coole and Ballylee, 1931) continues the severe self-examination of the previous poem. Yeats had long meditated on the artist's unhappy dilemma: in an 1898 review, he summarized AE's poetry as follows: 'All things are double, for we either choose "the shadowy [i.e., visible] beauty," and our soul weeps, or the invisible beauty ... and the body weeps' (*UP* II, p. 113). And in 1906 Yeats contrasted the artist, who 'identifies himself – to the neglect of his own soul, alas! – with the soul of the world' with the saint, who 'seeks not an eternal art, but his own eternity' (*EI*, p. 286). Most of the intolerable choices described by Yeats are, in one way or another, choices between the body's good and the soul's: in 'A Dialogue of Self and

Soul' and in 'Vacillation' VII, opposing voices – one worldly, the other soulful – clamour for the poet to choose between them; and 'The Three Bushes' makes the relation of man, body, and soul into an erotic triangle. When Yeats imagined a poet whose choice was for the soul's good – the choice opposite to his own – he often thought of AE: as Yeats wrote in 1935, 'My wife said the other night "A.E. was the nearest to a saint you or I will ever meet. You are a better poet but no saint. I suppose one has to choose"' (*DWL*, p. 12).

Yeats thought that the moment of crisis, of choice-making, was governed by forces beyond the human: the anti-self 'brings man again and again to the place of choice, heightening temptation that the choice may be as final as possible' (*M*, p. 361). Compare also 'Under Ben Bulben' III 6–12: 'He completes his partial mind ... Before he can ... choose his mate'.

2 *Perfection of the life, or of the work*: compare 'Words', ll. 15–16: 'I might have thrown poor words away / And been content to live'; also 'What Then?', l. 19: 'Something [that is, work] to perfection brought' (a complaint that the poet has neglected his soul). A draft of 'The Gyres', l. 17, read: 'Perfection of the work, the life the soul!' (Bradford, *YW*, p. 147).

3–4 *must refuse / A heavenly mansion*: compare 'Vacillation' VIII 8–9: 'choose for my belief / What seems most welcome in the tomb'.

7 *an empty purse*: the result of a failed career – the next line shows the result of a 'successful' one.

8 *the day's vanity, the night's remorse*: compare 'Vacillation' V 12: 'My conscience or my vanity appalled'.

Mohini Chatterjee

This poem was originally a companion to 'At Algeciras – A Meditation upon Death'. The Brahmin Mohini Chatterjee (1858–1936) deeply impressed the young Yeats. In 1885 he lectured to the Dublin Hermetic Society; he taught that 'Everything we perceive "including so-called illusions, exists in the external world" ... I learnt it from a Brahman when I was eighteen, and believed it till Blake drove it out of my head. It is early Buddhism and results in the belief, still living in India, that all is a stream which flows on out of human control, one action or thought leading to another, that we ourselves are nothing but a mirror and that deliverance consists in turning the mirror away so that it reflects nothing; the stream will go on but we not know' (*TSMC*, pp. 67–68).

The first stanza of the present poem versifies his doctrine of reincarnation; but in the second stanza the poet makes a considerable modification. Chatterjee taught detachment, passivity, apathy – earthly ambition was vain, for every man comprised a king and slave. But Yeats affirms the value of longing and struggling – strenuous passion is the spring that drives the reincarnative cycle. It is instructive to compare the first stanza of this poem with the juvenile poem 'Kanva on Himself', on an identical theme: 'Now wherefore hast thou tears innumerous? / Hast thou not known all sorrow and delight . . . And as a slave been wakeful in the halls / Of Rajas and Mahrajas beyond number? / Hast thou not ruled among the gilded walls?' (*VP*, pp. 723–24).

5–6 *I have been a king, / I have been a slave*: compare 'Fergus and the Druid', ll. 35–36: 'An old slave . . . A king'.

19 *Grave is heaped on grave*: compare 'Under Ben Bulben' II 9: 'grave-diggers' toil is long'.

24–25 *That such cannonade / May thunder time away*: compare 'That the Night Come', ll. 10–11: 'And the outrageous cannon, / To bundle time away'. For other references to the abolition of time, see 'The Moods', ll. 1–2.

28 *Men dance on deathless feet*: compare 'Nineteen Hundred and Nineteen' II 9: 'All men are dancers'.

Byzantium

This poem was partly inspired by Sturge Moore's letter on the inadequacy of 'Sailing to Byzantium': Moore was 'sceptical as to whether mere liberation from existence has any value or probability as a consummation. I prefer with Wittgenstein, whom I dont understand, to think that nothing at all can be said about ultimates, or reality in an ultimate sense. . . . Your *Sailing to Byzantium*, magnificent as the first three stanzas are, lets me down in the fourth, as such a goldsmith's bird is as much nature as a man's body, especially if it only sings like Homer and Shakespeare of what is past or passing or to come to Lords and Ladies' (*TSMC*, p. 162). Yeats replied that this objection 'showed me that the idea needed exposition' (*TSMC*, p. 164). Moore was alluding to the final proposition of Wittgenstein's *Tractatus* (1921), 'Whereof one cannot speak, thereof one must be silent'; and Yeats's 'Byzantium' pushes speech to its limit in order to point at the unspeakable. Such constructions as 'image, man or shade, / Shade more than man, more image than a shade' (ll. 9–10; compare ll. 17–18) hover among vaguenesses and frustrate the referentiality of language.

This poem's treatment of pictures is as daring as its treatment of words. 'Sailing to Byzantium' proposed two models to describe the soul's condition after death – a glittering mosaic image of a saint and a golden bird; the mosaic saints are the agents of the poet's transformation, the golden bird is an eidolon of the transformed poet. 'Byzantium' offers a more elaborate guided tour of the afterlife – a mummy, a bird made of metal, a self-sustaining flame, a statue – in the hope that a congeries of unnaturalnesses will somehow constitute the genuinely unearthly. Each of these entities seems at once a guide initiating the poet into further mysteries, and an experiment in defining the poet's own eerie shape after he is transfigured by death. Each thing defies, scorns, consumes, or assaults the natural, organic, physical world; amidst these violent assertions of the metaphysical, no image can constitute itself with any durability or precision. The poem presents a succession of fringe-images on the verge of indefiniteness.

In his 1930 diary, Yeats wrote a prose draft: 'Describe Byzantium as it is in the system [of *A Vision*] towards the end of the first Christian millennium. A walking mummy. Flames at the street corners where the soul is purified, birds of hammered gold singing in the golden trees, in the harbour [dolphins], offering their backs to the wailing dead that they may carry them to Paradise' (*Ex*, p. 290). Among Yeats's historical sources were William Gordon Holmes's *The Age of Justinian and Theodora* (1912) and Mrs Arthur Strong's *Apotheosis and After Life* (1915).

1 *The unpurged images of day*: the physical world, full of energy and violence, which shivers away after the gong-blow in l. 4.

3 *night-walkers*: prostitutes.

4 *gong*: compare l. 40; and also 'Nineteen Hundred and Nineteen II 10: 'barbarous clangour of a gong'; 'The Statues', l. 23: 'gong and conch declare the hour to bless'; and 'Alternative Song for the Severed Head . . .', l. 7: '*A slow low note and an iron bell*'. Yeats, remembering the reverberations throughout his life from his first meeting with Maud Gonne, wrote, 'it seems to me that she brought into my life in those days . . . a sound as of a Burmese gong, an overpowering tumult that had yet many pleasant secondary notes' (*Mem*, p. 40).

5 *dome*: that of the Cathedral of Hagia Sophia (Holy Wisdom) – see the note to 'Sailing to Byzantium'.

7 *complexities*: ' "We have no power", said an inhabitant [a dead soul that had achieved beatitude], "except to purify our intention", and when I asked of what, replied: "Of complexity" ' (*AV*, p. 233).

10 *Shade more than man, more image than a shade*: Yeats liked this chiastic ranking-in-threes – compare his description of the poet as 'more type than man, more passion than type' (*EI*, p. 509). For an early example of extremely indefinite supernatural beings, see 'The Poet Pleads with the Elemental Powers', l. 1: 'The powers whose name and shape no living creature knows'.

11 *Hades' bobbin*: the mummy, conceived as a kind of spool upon which its temporal life is rolled – see 'All Souls' Night', l. 13. Yeats thought that 'The soul has a plastic power, and can after death . . . mould it[s vehicle] to any

shape it will by an act of imagination' (*M*, p. 349), and the mummy was often a convenient image. In his account of the dead soul's self-purgation, Yeats wrote that at one point 'the whole cloth is unwound' (*AV* [1925], p. 231). Also compare 'His Bargain', l. 1: 'Plato's spindle'.

12 *the winding path*: Yeats often wrote of the *Hodos Chameliontos*, the road of unintelligible images on which the unwary poet might find himself (see the note to 'To the Rose upon the Rood of Time', l. 21). 'Byzantium' might be considered a journey down the Chameleon Road – the image-production becomes especially furious at the poem's end.

16 *death-in-life and life-in-death*: compare Coleridge, 'The Rime of the Ancient Mariner' (1798), ll. 193–94: 'The Nightmare LIFE-IN-DEATH was she, / Who thicks man's blood with cold; and Tennyson, 'Tears, Idle Tears' (1847), l. 20: 'O Death in Life, the days that are no more!' For Yeats's use of oxymoron in describing the supernatural, see the note to 'The Double Vision of Michael Robartes'.

19 *golden bough*: compare the golden bough of Aeneid VI, the Sibyl's gift to Aeneas, to aid his descent into the underworld.

20 *like the cocks of Hades crow*: compare a passage in 'The Adoration of the Magi' (1897), where an old man, possessed by 'Hermes the Shepherd of the Dead', suddenly crows like a rooster (*M*, pp. 311–12); for other cock-crows, see 'Solomon and the Witch', l. 9. The metal bird of 'Byzantium' seems itself to be a shepherd of the dead, acculturating them to Byzantine hatred of the organic.

21 *scorn*: compare the dolls' derision of human life in 'The Dolls'.

23 *Common bird*: for an earlier poetical bird that resists common birdhood, see Shelley, 'To a Skylark' (1820), l. 2: 'Bird thou never wert'.

24 *mire or blood*: compare 'Her Vision in the Wood', l. 25: 'blood and mire'; and 'The Gyres', l. 10: 'blood and mire'.

27 *flames begotten of flame*: these are spirits, according to an early draft: 'And there is a certain square where tall flames wind and unwind / And in the flames dance spirits, by that their agony made pure / And though they are all folded up in flame / It cannot singe a sleeve' (*BL*, p. 123). (The phrase 'wind and unwind' recalls 'The Withering of the Boughs', l. 13.) This seems similar to the plot of the Noh play *Motomezuka*: 'a [girl's] Ghost tells a Priest of a slight sin which seems a great sin . . . and that she is persecuted by flames. If she but touch a pillar, she says, it bursts into flames, and the Priest who knows that these flames are but her own conscience made visible, tells her that if she cease to believe in them they must cease to exist. She thanks him, but the flames return, for she cannot cease to believe, and the play ends with a dance which is the expression of her agony' (*AV* [1925], p. 225; see also

AV [1937], p. 231, *Ex*, p. 66, *VPl*, p. 777).

But Yeats often used fire to symbolize, not purgation, but the ultimate itself: 'There are two realities, the terrestrial and the condition of fire. All power is from the terrestrial condition . . . there the heterogeneous is, an evil, for evil is the strain one upon another of opposites; but in the condition of fire is all music and all rest' (*M*, pp. 356–57); and in some notes for *A Vision* he posited a 'point in the Zodiac where the whirl becomes a sphere . . . where all fuel has become flame' (Ellmann, *IY*, p. 221).

Yeats used 'Byzantium' to illustrate the conflicting symbolism of fire and water in his poetry: 'That conflict is deep in my subconsciousness, perhaps in everybody's. I dream of clear water . . . then come erotic dreams. Then for weeks perhaps I write poetry with sex for theme. Then comes the reversal – it came when I was young with some dream . . . with a flame in it. Then for weeks I get a symbolism like that in my Byzantium poem . . . with flame for theme. All this may come from the chance that when I was a young man I was accustomed to a Kabalistic ceremony where there were two pillars, one symbolic of water and one of fire' (*DWL*, pp. 86–87). Note the reversion from fire to water in the poem's fifth stanza. For the theme of fire in this volume of poems, see 'In Memory of Eva Gore-Booth . . .' II 6–7. For the rhetoric of self-begetting – useful for evoking the supernatural – see 'A Prayer for my Daughter', ll. 67–68.

33 ***dolphin***: in Neoplatonic mythology, dolphins carry the souls of the newly dead to the Isles of the Blest – see 'News for the Delphic Oracle' II. There were originally dolphins in 'Sailing to Byzantium': 'the foam / Where the dark drowsy fins a moment rise / Of fish, that carry souls to Paradise'; 'O send the Dolphins back & gather me / Into the artifice of eternity' (Stallworthy, *BL*, pp. 96, 100). When the designer of the book cover for *The Winding Stair and Other Poems* was under the misapprehension that Yeats saw all humanity riding on the back of one huge dolphin, Yeats wrote, 'One dolphin, one man. Do you know Raphael's statue of the Dolphin carrying one of the Holy Innocents to Heaven?' (*TSMC*, p. 165).

34–36 *smithies . . . Marbles of the dancing floor*: early drafts show that *Marbles* originally referred to the marble pavement (compare l. 25) of the Forum of Constantine; but then Yeats changed the line to 'The bronze & marble of the emperor' (*BL*, pp. 125, 127), suggesting architecture and statuary (as in 'Elgin marbles'). The poet imagines forges and stone impressing form upon the formless flood of immigrants from the physical world, gathering them into 'the artifice of eternity' ('Sailing to Byzantium' III 8). This poem can be regarded as a foretaste of the initiation-rites that will purge each of us of our flesh, render us stark, inhuman. Compare 'The Statues', ll. 11–12, where Phidias' statues – reifications of number and proportion – attack a watery chaos, 'put down / All Asiatic vague immensities'. (In 'Coole Park, 1929', ll.

17–20, Lady Gregory – possessing an almost superhuman purity of intention – exerts a somewhat similar force on those flighty men whom Yeats compares to swallows.)

37 *Break*: as Vendler notes, this verb has three direct objects ('furies', 'those images', and 'sea'), but, 'Practically speaking, the governing force of the verb "break" is spent long before the end of the stanza is reached' (*YVLP*, p. 118). The syntax struggles with an overwhelming influx of raw energy from the natural world, a flood which threatens to put out all flames and drown all statues.

38–39 *Those images that yet / Fresh images beget*: an early draft reads, 'blind images that yet / Blinder images beget' (*BL*, p. 127). These lines suggest the dangerous reproductive energies of organic creatures – whereas Byzantine entities are self-begetting (l. 27), mundane things teem endlessly, aimlessly. Compare 'Ribh denounces Patrick', which contrasts the general increase of sexual reproduction with the stability of the Divine Trinity. Note also a parallel passage in *A Vision*, describing a kind of art that (unlike Byzantine mosaic or metalwork) seemed to imitate the profusion of the natural world: 'that decoration which seems to undermine our self-control, and is, it seems, of Persian origin, and has for its appropriate symbol a vine whose tendrils climb everywhere and display among their leaves all those strange images of bird and beast, those forms that represent no creature eye has ever seen, yet are begotten one upon the other as if they were themselves living creatures' (p. 281). Also compare Auden, 'United Nations Hymn' (1971): 'Like music, when / Begotten notes / New notes beget' (*CP*, p. 621).

40 *That dolphin-torn, that gong-tormented sea*: natural life, tortured by the conflicting impulses of sexuality (suggested by the dolphins) and of spirituality (suggested by the gong – compare l. 4) – in other words, of Self and of Soul. Compare the rhythm of a phrase from 'The Tragic Theatre' (1910): 'We feel our minds expand convulsively or spread out slowly like some moon-brightened image-crowded sea' (*EI*, p. 245); in the same paragraph Yeats calls tragic art 'the drowner of dykes', a phrase also relevant to the final stanza of 'Byzantium'.

The Mother of God

Here is another of Yeats's attempts at rendering the shock of a god's incarnation, its intimate outrage to mankind – this poem is the *primary* equivalent of 'Leda and the Swan', less brutal but all the uncannier for the ordinariness of Mary's daily life. Pater's essay on Botticelli presents a similar picture of the Virgin: 'she . . . though she holds in her hands the "Desire of all nations", is one of those who are neither for Jehovah nor for His enemies . . . [Botticelli] paints Madonnas, but they shrink from the pressure of the divine child, and plead in unmistakable undertones for a warmer, lower humanity' (*The Renaissance* [1893], ed. Hill, pp. 44, 47). Also compare D. G. Rossetti's 'Mary's Girlhood (*For a Picture*)' (1849), where the young Mary, much encumbered by symbols, feels no fear at all when the Annunciation arrives, only an innocent weepy trust – Yeats discussed the symbolism of this picture in *EI*, p. 147.

Yeats's 'subject' for this poem was: 'The Virgin shrinks from the annunciation. Must she receive "the burning heavens in her womb"? Looks at the child upon her knees at once "with love and dread"' (Bradford, *YW*, p. 115). Yeats rejected as titles 'The Annunciation' ('Annunciation' was once the title of 'Leda and the Swan') and 'Mary Virgin' (*YW*, p. 120).

1 *a fallen flare*: 'the words "a fallen flare through the hollow of an ear" are, I am told, obscure. I had in my memory Byzantine mosaic pictures of the Annunciation, which show a line drawn from a star to the ear of the Virgin. She conceived of the Word, and therefore through the ear a star fell and was born' (*VP*, p. 832). For a second auricular conception, see 'A Nativity', l. 2: 'Another star has shot an ear'.

4 *The terror of all terrors*: compare 'Wisdom' (another Marian poem), l. 20: 'Drove horror from His Mother's breast'; and 'A Nativity', l. 11: 'the woman terror-struck'. In 1926 Yeats wrote an essay on 'The Cherry-Tree Carol', an old poem in which Christ calls out from Mary's womb to a tree, commanding it to bend down and give its fruit; Yeats was indignant that certain contemporary monks wished to suppress the carol: 'There is the whole mystery – God, in the indignity of human birth, all that seemed impossible, blasphemous even, to many early heretical sects ... I can see no reason for the anger of the Christian Brothers, except that they do not believe in the Incarnation. They think they believe in it, but they do not, and its sudden presentation fills them with horror' (*UP* II, pp. 462–63). Yeats's poem, too, tries to restore horror to the miracle – indeed it is a kind of reply to the carol, substituting an impregnation by the ear for a foetus that can speak.

5 *The Heavens in my womb*: for another image of microcosm, see 'Veronica's Napkin'.

15 *bids my hair stand up*: see 'Presences', l. 2: 'As if the hair stood up on my head'.

Vacillation

The theme of this poem is the necessary incompleteness of all human fulfilment – every gratification of a desire leaves some opposing desire all the more famished. By composing this as a sequence of abrupt and jagged poemlets, Yeats imitates the fragmentation and incoherence of life – there is no mediating voice to integrate these bits of philosophy, meditation on symbol, practical advice, and autobiography into a smooth, unitary poem. At the end the poet finds no synthesis or resolution possible; but he does make a tentative choice of one pole over another. As in 'A Dialogue of Self and Soul', the Self (or Heart, as it is called in 'Vacillation' VII) – subjective, violent, sexual – seems to vanquish the Soul – objective, spiritual, disembodied.

Two of Yeats's letters concerning this poem (written to Olivia Shakespear) show the difficulty and doubtfulness of this choice: 'I have begun a longish poem called "Wisdom" [a discarded title] in the attempt to shake off "Crazy Jane" and I begin to think I shall take to religion unless you save me from it' (*L*, p. 788); 'My first denunciation of old age I made in *The Wanderings of Usheen* (end of part I) before I was twenty and the same denunciation comes in the last pages of the book. The swordsman throughout repudiates the saint, but not without vacillation. Is that perhaps the sole theme – Usheen and Patrick – "so get you gone Von Hügel though with blessings on your head" ['Vacillation' VIII 12]?' (*L*, p. 798).

The sections of this poem originally had titles: I 'What is Joy'; II and III [as a single section] 'The Burning Tree'; IV 'Happiness'; V 'Conscience'; VI 'Conquerors'; VII 'A Dialogue'; VIII 'Von Hügel'. In a letter urging Dorothy Wellesley not to include section titles in a multipart poem, Yeats wrote, 'Keep the one general name & put numbers only to the sections – a name pins the butterfly' (*DWL*, p. 61).

I 1 *Between extremities*: compare 'Under Ben Bulben' II 2: 'Between his two eternities'.

I 3–5 *A brand … Comes to destroy / All those antinomies*: Yeats posited a transcendental condition of fire in which all antitheses were resolved into simplicity – see the note to 'Byzantium', l. 27. For the theme of fire in this volume, see 'In Memory of Eva Gore-Booth …' II 6–7.

I 8 *remorse*: one of the stages in the life after death is a reliving of the most intense moments in one's earthly life (*AV*, p. 226); this is sometimes accompanied by the flames of the traditional purgatory (p. 231). Compare a scene in *Purgatory* (1939), where a man looks at the ghosts of his parents embracing: 'If pleasure and remorse must both be there, / Which is the greater?' (ll. 152–53).

I 10 *What is joy?*: the original title of part I. Joy seems precluded both in the furious vacillation of life, and in the purgation of death; and yet the rest of the poem may show that limited joy is indeed possible.

II 1–2: *A tree … half all glittering flame and half all green*: the tree's strange division recapitulates the antithesis of Heart and Soul, or Nature and Fire.

In 'The Celtic Element in Literature' (1902), Yeats found 'the ancient worship of Nature' in a passage from the Welsh epic *Mabinogion*: '"They saw a tall tree by the side of the river, one half of which was in flames from the root to the top, and the other half was green and in full leaf"' (*EI*, p. 176). For another tree that is a kind of diagram of the universe, see 'The Two Trees'.

II 6 *Attis*: a god of Asia Minor, comparable to the Greek Adonis. The earth-mother Cybele fell in love with him, and caused him to castrate himself to ensure his fidelity. According to Frazer's *The Golden Bough*, he was one version of the Nature-god, whose death and resurrection governed the rhythm of the seasons. Compare the 1927 version of *The Resurrection*, ll. 357–60: 'all over Greece, all over Asia Minor ... men have celebrated the death and Resurrection of Attis, or Adonis, or Dionysus' (*VPl*, p. 924).

II 8 *knows not grief*: the priests of Attis engaged in ritual self-castration – perhaps Yeats meant that *castrati* can participate fully neither in the natural world nor in the spiritual one, but suspend themselves artificially between extremes, know neither joy nor grief. 'For in a state of equilibrium there is neither emotion nor sensation' (*AV*, p. 232). For other eunuchs, see 'On those that hated *The Playboy* ...', l. 2.

III 1 *Get all the gold*: compare 'The Witch', l. 1: 'Toil and grow rich'.

III 3 *ram them with the sun*: Yeats liked to quote Ben Jonson's phrase '"So rammed ... with life they can but grow in life with being"' (*M*, p. 360; *Mem*, p. 165) – see *Poetaster* V i 136; compare 'To Dorothy Wellesley', ll. 5–6: 'Rammed full / Of ... silence'; and 'Margot' III 6: 'cram those open eyes with day' (*ASD*, p. 34). A draft of 'The Gift of Harun Al-Rashid' says, 'herself can seem youth's very fountain / So rammed is she with life' (Stallworthy, *BL*, p. 76).

III 8 *children's gratitude or woman's love*: compare *Baile and Aillinn*, l. 40: '*A child's laughter, a woman's kiss*'.

III 9 *Lethean*: Lethe was the river in Hades whose waters made dead souls forget their previous life – compare 'Among School Children' V 4.

III 12 *Test every work of intellect or faith*: compare Michael Robartes' dictum 'Test art, morality, custom, thought, by Thermopylae' (*AV*, p. 52).

III 16 *laughing to the tomb*: compare 'Her Courage', l. 10: 'laughed into the face of Death'.

IV: 'At certain moments, always unforeseen, I become happy ... Perhaps I am sitting in some crowded restaurant, the open book beside me, or closed, my excitement having overbrimmed the page. I look at the strangers near as if I had known them all my life, and it seems strange that I cannot speak to them: everything fills me with affection, I have no longer any fears or any needs; I do not even remember that this happy mood must come to an end. It seems as if the vehicle had suddenly grown pure and far extended' (*M*, p. 364–65). For other ecstatic moments in prosaic settings, see 'An Acre of Grass'.

IV 7 *My body . . . blazed*: compare 'Lapis Lazuli', l. 19: 'Heaven blazing into the head' – an expression of tragic gaiety.

IV 10 *I was blessèd and could bless*: see VIII 12; and 'A Dialogue of Self and Soul' II 31–32.

V 1 *Although the summer sunlight gild*: in both parts IV and V, the poet's emotions are unrelated to his surroundings – joy and sadness are symmetrically unpredictable.

V 4 *intricacy*: compare *The Only Jealousy of Emer* (1919), l. 260: 'Intricacies of blind remorse'.

V 5–6 *I cannot look thereon, / Responsibility so weighs me down*: compare *The Only Jealousy of Emer* (1919), ll. 252–53: 'my memories / Weigh down my hands, abash my eyes'; and 'The Cold Heaven', l. 7: 'I took all the blame out of all sense and reason'.

V 7 *Things said or done*: compare 'Spilt Milk', ll. 1–2 for a similar chiasmus: 'done and thought . . . thought and done'.

V 12 *My conscience or my vanity*: 'the pain of one's own blunders, especially when they hurt one's vanity, never passes away. . . . small acts of years ago are so painful in the memory that often one starts at the presence a little below "the threshold of consciousness" of a thought that remains unknown' (*Mem*, pp. 190–91). Compare 'The Choice', ll. 7–8: 'perplexity . . . Or . . . vanity'.

VI 3 *the great lord of Chou*: from twelfth-century China. The original title of this part was 'Conquerors' – for more conquerors, see 'Her Courage', l. 9.

VI 5 '*Let all things pass away*': compare *The Two Kings*, l. 189: 'Your strength and nobleness will pass away' – a condition prerequisite to love; and *Where There is Nothing* (1902) IV 344-45: 'He [the Christian] must so live that all things shall pass away'. In *A Vision*, p. 219, Yeats noted that he was chilled when Valéry, in 'Le Cimetière Marin', 'rejoices that human life must pass'. (The counter-refrain is found in 'Crazy Jane on God': '*All things remain in God*'.) The shock of this section lies in each conqueror's dismissal of his own achievement – to use the language of 'Blood and the Moon', his sudden reversion from power to wisdom. Each is at once Ozymandias and Shelley.

VI 7 *Babylon*: see 'The Dawn', l. 6; *Nineveh*: see 'Fragments' II 6.

VI 11–12 *From man's blood-sodden heart are sprung / Those branches of the night and day*: compare 'The Rose Tree', ll. 17-18: 'There's nothing but our own red blood / Can make a right Rose Tree'; and 'Two Songs from a Play'

II 15–16: 'Whatever flames upon the night / Man's own resinous heart has fed'. For the theme of man's creation of the universe, see 'The Tower' III 28–31.

VI 13 *Where the gaudy moon is hung*: compare *The Shadowy Waters*, ll. 370–71: 'He has caught the crescent moon out of the sky, / And carries it between us'; and 'Three Marching Songs' III 7–9: '*Robbers had taken his old tambourine / But he took down the moon / And rattled out a tune*'. All three passages seem to allude to a fairy tale from the brothers Grimm, 'The Moon'.

VII 1–2 The Soul ... The Heart: after the alternation between greenery and flame in part II, between family and work in part III, between mania and depression in parts IV and V, and between exultation and dismissal in part VI, this part finally presents the baldest, simplest antinomy, as in 'A Dialogue of Self and Soul'. Yeats quoted a draft of VII in a letter to Olivia Shakespear, in a context suggesting that he wrote it in response to her notion that he would become a bore if he became a religious man (*L*, pp. 789–90).

VII 2 *What, be a singer born and lack a theme?*: in a 1934 review, Samuel Beckett quoted this line to illustrate the contentlessness of recent Irish poetry: 'At the centre there is no theme ... But the circumference is an iridescence of themes – Oisin, Cuchulain, Maeve' (*Disjecta*, p. 71). Compare 'The Circus Animals' Desertion' I 1: 'I sought a theme ... in vain'.

VII 3 *Isaiah's coal*: a seraph touched a live coal to Isaiah's lips, saying 'thine iniquity is taken away, and thy sin purged' (Isaiah 6:7).

VII 4 *Struck dumb*: compare 'A Dialogue of Self and Soul' I 40: 'my tongue's a stone'. In both poems, the Soul is finally hostile to speech, to poetry-writing – only the Heart, or the Self, is confident enough in its relation to the physical world to be able to discover and to manipulate symbols. As III 13 might suggest, the poet regards his role as a poet as fundamental to his being.

VII 4 *the simplicity of fire*: compare 'No Second Troy', l. 7: 'simple as a fire'.

VII 6 *What theme had Homer but original sin?*: '"I prefer", [Lady Gregory] said, "those poems translated by Frank O'Connor because they come out of original sin"' (*OBMV*, p. xv). For other references to Homer, see 'A Woman Homer Sung'.

VIII 1 *Von Hügel*: Baron Friedrich von Hügel (1852–1925) was a Roman Catholic theologian who wrote about the mysticism of the saints. Yeats once cited 'the sincere and noble von Hügel' on the lack of suffering of infants in Limbo (*VPl*, p. 934).

VIII 2 *Accept the miracles of the saints and honour sanctity*: after quoting a draft of part VII of this poem, Yeats explained to Olivia Shakespear the antinomy of Soul and Heart: 'I feel that this is the choice of the saint (St

Theresa's ecstasy, Gandhi's smiling face): comedy; and the heroic choice: Tragedy (Dante, Don Quixote). Live Tragically but be not deceived ... Yet I accept all the miracles. Why should not the old embalmers come back as ghosts and bestow upon the saint all the care once bestowed upon [Pharaoh] Rameses? ... I shall be a sinful man to the end, and think upon my death-bed of all the [sexless] nights I wasted in my youth' (*L*, p. 790).

VIII 3 *Saint Teresa*: Spanish nun (1515–82), whose heart was pierced by an angel's dart in an ecstatic vision celebrated in sculpture by Bernini and in English poetry by Crashaw. Her corpse's miraculous resistance to corruption also appears in 'Oil and Blood', l. 3.

VIII 4 *miraculous oil*: Yeats thought of asking a sceptical philosopher, '"How do you account for the fact that when the Tomb of St. Theresa was opened her body exuded miraculous oil ... ?"' (*TSMC*, p. 122).

VIII 5 *lettered slab*: compare 'Her Dream', l. 4: 'lettered tomb'.

VIII 8–9 *choose for my belief / What seems most welcome in the tomb*: compare 'The Choice', ll. 3–4: 'must refuse / A heavenly mansion'.

VIII 9 *a predestined part*: the poet sees himself, Teresa's embalmers, and Von Hügel as masks worn by eternal actors in a drama – see 'Two Songs from a Play' I 8.

VIII 10: this line originally read, 'I swear to god that I / With fierce un-christened heart shall live in Homer's company' (Bradford, *YW*, p. 129).

VIII 11 *The lion and the honeycomb*: Samson took some honey from a swarm of bees nesting in the carcase of a lion, and posed a riddle to the Philistines: 'Out of the eater came forth meat, and out of the strong came forth sweetness' (Judges 14:14). Compare 'Peace', l. 9: 'All that sweetness amid strength'; 'Ancestral Houses', l. 32: 'take our greatness with our violence'; and 'The Gift of Harun-Al-Rashid', ll. 47–48: 'violent great hearts can lose / Their bitterness and find the honeycomb'. For more on this theme, see 'To a Wealthy Man ...', ll. 25–26.

VIII 12 *blessings*: see IV 10.

Quarrel in Old Age

At the Heart-affirming end of 'Vacillation' Yeats suggested that sweetness grew out of bloodshed, sin, corruption; but in this and in some of the following poems, it seems that sweetness and bitterness coexist, but on different planes of reality.

1 *her*: Maud Gonne's.

3 *blind bitter town*: see 'Words', l. 4: 'this blind bitter land'.

4–5 *incident / Not worth thinking of*: according to Jeffares (*NCP*, p. 305), Maud Gonne quarrelled with Yeats over the treatment of women prisoners on a hunger strike.

12–13 *beyond the curtain / Of distorting days*: the idea that the phenomenal world is a phantom or a veil is common in Blake and Shelley – this poem bears some resemblance to the Conclusion to Shelley's 'The Sensitive-Plant' (1820), some lines of which Yeats quoted in his 1930 diary: 'For love, and beauty, and delight / There is no death nor change; their might / Exceeds our organs' (*Ex*, p. 330). Compare also Tom's notion that death is only a failure of eyesight, in 'Tom the Lunatic', l. 12.

16 *Targeted, trod like Spring*: Yeats called Maud Gonne 'a classical impersonation of the Spring' (*A: FY* 5). *Targeted* means outfitted with a *targe*, or round shield.

The Results of Thought

Like the previous poem, this one attempts to reconstitute the timeless and beautiful from the time-wrecked – the old women discussed here may include Olivia Shakespear and Lady Gregory.

10–12: in one draft Yeats wrote, 'Have found such a deep thought / That I call this back / From insanity / Into their wholesome strength' (Stallworthy, *BL*, p. 214).

13–14 *What images are these, / That turn dull-eyed away*: the decrepit old bodies are dismissed as mere images, defective copies of some eternal referent.

Gratitude to the Unknown Instructors

The unknown instructors are the spirits who taught Yeats the doctrines of *A Vision*.

3 *All things hang like a drop of dew*: compare the 1889 text of *The Wanderings of Oisin*: 'Her eyes were soft as dewdrops hanging / Upon the grass-blades' bending tips' (*VP*, p. 3). Also compare Marvell, 'On a Drop of Dew', ll. 25–26: 'Does, in its pure and circling thoughts, express / The greater Heaven in an Heaven less'.

Remorse for Intemperate Speech

At the end of 'Vacillation', the poet chose Heart over Soul, sinfulness over purity; but this poem shows the danger of that choice, in a land where the heart tends to be depraved by a contagion of hatred. For another expression of self-disgust, see 'Nineteen Hundred and Nineteen' III and IV.

4 *Fit audience*: 'Whitman appealed ... not to the ignorant many, either English or American, but to that audience, "fit though few", which is greater than any nation' (*L* I, p. 416). Compare Milton, *Paradise Lost* VII 30–31: 'still govern thou my Song, / *Urania*, and fit audience find, though few'.

5 *fanatic*: 'I pronounce "fanatic" in what is, I suppose, the older and more Irish way, so that the last line of each stanza contains but two beats' (*VP*, p. 506).

8 *Turn hatred into sport*: Jeffares compares (*NCP*, p. 306) a letter to Olivia Shakespear, 7 Sept. 1927: 'hatred ... is a commonplace here – It lays hold on our class I think more easily than upon the mass of the people. It finds a more complicated and determined conscience to prey upon'.

Stream and Sun at Glendalough

Iseult Gonne and her husband Francis Stuart lived near Glendalough, Co. Wicklow (a valley also mentioned in 'Under the Round Tower', l. 8). This poem is, like 'Vacillation' V, an exercise on an Arnoldian theme – how the mind's operations, such as memory and conscience, prevent men from full participation in the natural world. But here, as in 'A Dialogue of Self and Soul' II 28, the poet casts out remorse, and attains a feeling of union with his atemporal self.

4 *Some stupid thing*: 'the memory of some old quarrel, things lighter than air ... keep the soul from its joy' (*Ex*, p. 200).

7 *But what am I*: compare 'A Prayer for Old Age', l. 7: 'O what am I'.

13 *pierced my body*: see 'The Madness of King Goll', l. 29, for other piercing lights.

15 *Self-born*: for the theme of self-begetting (Yeats's favourite description of the supernatural), see 'A Prayer for my Daughter', ll. 67–68.

WORDS FOR MUSIC PERHAPS (1932)

This is the first of two sequences appended to *The Winding Stair and Other Poems*. The title suggests that Yeats intended these poems as texts for songs; but few composers have so far risen to this challenge, and in fact Yeats himself explained that he gave this title 'no[t] so much that they may be sung as that I may define their kind of emotion to myself. I want them to be all emotion and all impersonal' (*L*, p. 758); ' "For Music" is only a name, nobody will sing them' (*L*, p. 769). Many of these poems do have song-like features – refrains, short lines, stanzaic construction, easy vocabulary – but their 'musical' character lies principally in their emotional directness and their impersonality. Large, free-floating emotions (such as lust, anxiety, self-confidence, loneliness, protectiveness, madness) build around themselves extremely simple masks. These emotions are Moods, in Yeats's technical sense (see 'The Moods') – disembodied intensities that, instead of embedding themselves in Yeats's particular life, remain disembodied, little connected to individuals. Here we have no tower, no Japanese sword, no Maud Gonne, nothing from Yeats's private cache of symbols; instead we have vagrants and crackpots, people with little steadiness of character, little history, people who are nothing except vehicles of songs.

Yeats conceived many of these poems as part of celebration of energy: he wrote that, during his convalescence in the spring of 1929, 'life returned to me as an impression of the uncontrollable energy and daring of the great creators; it seemed to me that but for journalists and criticism, all that evasion and explanation, the world would be torn in pieces. I wrote ... almost all that group of poems, called in memory of those exultant weeks *Words for Music Perhaps*' (*VP*, p. 831). These poems, then, try to eliminate every prosaic component, 'evasion and explanation'; by becoming expressions of sheer force, unimpeded emotion, they approach the condition of music. (For a discussion of the structure of this sequence, see the headnote to *A Woman Young and Old*.)

In the opening poems, given to Crazy Jane, the reader feels that the 'uncontrollable energy' is chiefly sexual in nature. Her dialogues with the bishop suggest something of the dialectic of Self and Soul, of world-affirmation and world-transcendence; but the bishop is a feeble specimen compared to the Soul of 'A Dialogue of Self and Soul' – the bishop seems a mere killjoy, a denier of the flesh, without a positive contribution. It is Crazy Jane who has wisdom about God. Indeed, throughout *Words for Music Perhaps*, the antinomy between Self and Soul seems almost collapsed – bald shivering life enacts some lofty drama of the soul. Some of Yeats's later works, such as the *Supernatural Songs* and *The King of the Great Clock Tower*, prove a similar thesis, that death offers only a more sophisticated and intense, sexy, version of common life.

Yeats wrote that Crazy Jane was more or less founded upon an old woman, a 'local satirist' who lived in a cottage near Gort: '[she has] an amazing power of audacious speech. One of her great performances is a description of how the meanness of a Gort shopkeeper's wife over the price of a glass of porter made her so despair of the human race that she got drunk. The incidents of that drunkenness are of an epic magnificence' (*L*, pp. 785–86). The combination of drunkenness and 'epic magnificence' recalls some of the paradoxes found in the poems themselves – the extremes of bathos and sublimity, foul and fair, seem to meet. Crazy Jane will reappear in 'Three Songs to the One Burden' I 19 and 'Crazy Jane on the Mountain'.

I. Crazy Jane and the Bishop

1 *blasted oak*: for broken trees as a suitable stage-set for old age, see 'The Lamentation of the Old Pensioner', l. 14.

4–5: these lines originally read, 'May call a curse out of the sky / Ere the one or t'other die' (*VP*, p. 508) – Jack's death was the poet's afterthought.

9 *Jack the Journeyman*: in the *The Pot of Broth* (1904), ll. 66-70, a tramp sings a song in which appear these lines: 'I wish you were dead, my gay old man ... So as I'd marry poor Jack the journeyman'. Yeats explained in a note that this text was copied 'from an old woman known as Cracked Mary, who ... sometimes sees unearthly riders on white horses coming through stony fields to her hovel door in the night time' (*VPl*, p. 254). In the first printing of the Crazy Jane poems, the heroine was called Cracked Mary. Crazy Jane's fascination with ghosts may owe something to the Cracked Mary of 1904.

19 *the heron's hunch*: in 'The Old Men of the Twilight' (1897), a flock of herons turns out to be a band of enchanted pedants (*M*, p. 193). In 'The Saint and the Hunchback', a hump is associated with self-suppression.

II. Crazy Jane Reproved

After hearing a reproof from the bishop, Crazy Jane speaks these two stanzas in contradiction: while the bishop's God thunders to show his anger, Crazy Jane's God is indifferent to human sin, much more concerned with small beauties – creating a seashell – than with large effects of storm and terror. This poem is a versification of a passage in 'Ireland after Parnell', in which Yeats deplores the poet who turns to politics – a too-easy, too-blatant use of his talents: 'Is it not certain that the Creator yawns in earthquakes and thunder and other popular displays, but toils in rounding the delicate spiral of a shell? (*A: IP* 14).

2 *dreadful thunder-stones*: compare Shakespeare, *Cymbeline* IV ii 270–71: 'Fear no more ... the all-dreaded thunder-stone'. Yeats also wrote of the thunder-stone in *Sophocles' King Oedipus*, l. 123.

4 *but show that Heaven yawns*: compare *The Wanderings of Oisin* II 205–6: 'with thunder ... God ... speaks His angry mind'.

5–6 *Great Europa played the fool / That changed a lover for a bull*: Zeus assumed the form of a bull in order to abduct Europa – Crazy Jane's point is that a woman is better served by a human lover (like Jack) than by a divine one (like the bishop's loud, overbearing God). Compare *The Player Queen* (1922), II 360-61, where Decima looks at a troupe of actors in animal costumes, and considers them as possible lovers: 'Shall I fancy beast or fowl? / Queen Pasiphae chose a bull'.

7 Fol de rol, fol de rol: Yeats asked Margot Ruddock to read this poem and note the refrain: 'I think when you find words like that in an old ballad, they are meant to be sung to a melody, as [Harry] Partch the Californian musician I told you of sings his "meaningless words". He uses them to break the monotony of monotone. There is no special value in "fol de rol", any meaningless words would do. [Charles] Kingsley [in "Last Poem"] once used "barrum, barrum, barrum, baree". . . . I put "fol de rol" at the end of the stanzas in this poem to make it less didactic, gayer, more clearly a song' (*ASD*, pp. 30–31). Compare 'The Pilgrim', l. 5: 'fol de rol de rolly O'; and the original refrain of 'Colonel Martin': 'Lullabulloo, buloo, buloo'. For the theme of nonsense, see 'Beautiful Lofty Things', l. 6.

8 *To round that shell's elaborate whorl*: compare *The Only Jealousy of Emer* (1919), l. 16, 'A fragile, exquisite, pale shell' – the Musician goes on to ask what supernatural forces 'Dragged into being / This loveliness?' Compare also Tennyson, *Maud* (1855) II 2 i, where the speaker calls a shell 'a work divine . . . With delicate spire and whorl, / How exquisitely minute, / A miracle of design!'

13 *A roaring, ranting journeyman*: Crazy Jane complains that her Jack – as stormy and bullish as the God of the first stanza – lacks ideal delicacy; but the refrain-line seems to dismiss all arguments against Jack as nonsense.

III. Crazy Jane on the Day of Judgment

Here the poet imagines Jane and Jack, still bantering with one another, on the only occasion when full love-satisfaction is possible – the end of time.

3–4 *the whole / Body and soul*: compare 'The Three Bushes', another fable about the hopeless division of love between soul and body. Yeats once intended a stanza for this poem on the theme of the wholeness of the body's sexual sensation: 'See in the night, when we meet in / the dark wood, that you touch all po[r?]tions of / my body – every plane & mound – omit / but one I shall think of Jim or John / or some that might take your place / Love is for wholes [whether of body or souls]' (*'That Black Day': The Manuscripts of 'Crazy Jane on the Day of Judgement'*, ed. David R. Clark, p. 19).

6 *Take the sour*: Judgment Day must comprise sourness and sweetness – another whole. Also compare the Anglican wedding service: 'For richer or for poorer . . .'

13 *hidden*: the condition of natural life is hiddenness, evasion; the condition of Judgment Day is complete exposure, comprehension (l. 18).

17–19 *What true love be? ... If Time were but gone*: compare 'The Hero, the Girl, and the Fool', ll. 24–29: 'When cradle and spool are past ... I think that I may find / A faithful love'.

IV. Crazy Jane and Jack the Journeyman

The theme of this poem is the usefulness of sexual intercourse in promoting the soul's approach to God. If bodily cravings are satisfied, the soul can, at the instant of death, disengage itself from the body and 'leap into the light' (l. 11); but if the body's needs are left unfulfilled, Crazy Jane's ghost will walk earthly roads, and seek the company of Jack. According to *A Vision*, the dead soul is bound to earth by a persistent sensuous phantom of its former body, called the *Husk* (pp. 223–24). Finneran cites Yeats's statement, 'If you don't express yourself ... you walk after you're dead. The great thing is to go empty to your grave' (*EYP*, p. 21).

3–4 *The more I leave the door unlatched / The sooner love is gone*: see 'Two Songs from a Play' II 11: 'Love's pleasure drives his love away'.

5 *love is but a skein*: compare 'The Hero, the Girl, and the Fool', ll. 21–23: 'When thoughts ... Are but loose thread'; 'His Bargain', l. 1: 'Plato's spindle'; 'Ribh at the Tomb of Baile and Aillinn', l. 14: 'whole is joined to whole'; and *The King of the Great Clock Tower* (1935), ll. 6–8: 'lad and lass ... Are bobbins where all time is bound and wound'.

10 *My body in the tomb*: compare 'A Last Confession', l. 15: 'this soul, its body off'.

15 *The skein so bound us ghost to ghost*: see 'Anashuya and Vijaya', ll. 7–10: 'May we two stand, / When we are dead ... With mingling hair'.

18 *Mine would walk being dead*: in other printings this line read, 'Mine must walk when dead' (*VP*, p. 511). Compare Tennyson, *Maud* (1855) I 22 xi: 'My dust would hear her and beat, / Had I lain for a century dead'.

V. Crazy Jane on God

In the previous poem, Crazy Jane discovered God in the exhaustion of the physical world; but in this poem she describes God, not in terms of destitution, but of fullness – God is the storehouse of all things, himself the *Anima Mundi*, the imagination's treasure-trove. As in Hopkins's 'The Leaden Echo and the Golden Echo' (1882), what seems to be fleeting in fact abides with God.

6 All things remain in God: in *A Vision*, Yeats remembered the young Iseult Gonne singing at the edge of the sea, '"O Lord, let something remain"' (p. 220); and, as Ellmann notes (*IY*, p. 277), Yeats summarized Madame Blavatsky on predestination: 'All things past and to come were present in the mind of God and yet all things were free' (Lady Gregory, *Visions and Beliefs* I, p. 277). Also compare 'Tom the Lunatic', l. 16: 'God's unchanging eye'. The contrary refrain appears in 'Vacillation' VI: 'Let all things pass away'.

13–16 *a house ... Suddenly lit up*: Yeats was impressed by several accounts of deserted houses filled with visionary presences: 'the Irish country-woman did see the ruined castle lit up, the bridge across the river dropping; those two Oxford ladies did find themselves in the garden of the Petit Trianon with Marie Antoinette and her courtiers ... All about us there seems to start up a precise inexplicable teeming life' (*Ex*, p. 369). Compare *The King of the Great Clock Tower* (1935), ll. 154–55: 'Castle Dargan's ruin all lit, / Lovely ladies dancing in it'; 'The Curse of Cromwell', ll. 25–26: 'I came upon a great house in the middle of the night, / Its open lighted doorway and its windows all alight'; and *Purgatory* (1939), ll. 176–78: 'My God! The window is lit up / And somebody stands there, although / The floorboards are all burnt away'. A house that contains all its occupants, living and dead, is a metaphor for the divine co-presence of things.

20 *like a road*: the sexual body seems capable of retaining its experiences; it too is a kind of storehouse – see 'Memory'. Note that the road of l. 17 of the previous poem is here demoted to a simile – this is the same sort of trick Yeats often played among the various parts of 'A Man Young and Old'.

VI. Crazy Jane Talks with the Bishop

This poem is notorious for the puns in l. 17. Puns are rare in Yeats's work ('*solid man*' in 'Crazy Jane and the Bishop', ll. 17–18, may be another example), but here they usefully collapse high and low, Love and excrement, into single ambiguous terms. (The mysterious equivalence of Eros and Agape is a common theme in poetry; for another famous modern example, see Auden, 'Lullaby' [1937].) In Yeats's story 'The Death of Hanrahan' (1896) a mad old hag named Winny ceaselessly sings 'I am beautiful ... I am young'; the dying Hanrahan learns that she is in fact an immortal goddess, resident in Winny's empty mind and body (*M*, p. 261). Winny is one of the precursors of the Crazy Jane of this poem; her two-faced appearance is a kind of visual pun, a convergence of extremes.

7 *Fair and foul*: compare Shakespeare, *Macbeth* I iii 38.

15–16 *Love has pitched his mansion in / The place of excrement*: compare Blake, *Jerusalem* (1804) 88:39: 'I will make their places of joy & love, excrementitious' (spoken by the Spectre, a source of discord and division in the universe); and D. H. Lawrence, *Lady Chatterley's Lover* (1928), Chapter XV, where a gamekeeper tells a lady: 'Here tha shits an' here tha pisses: an' I lay my hand on 'em both an' like thee for it'. (Yeats admired the 'forlorn poetry ... something ancient, humble and terrible' [*L*, p. 810] of Mellors' obscenities in this novel.) Note that *pitched* (erected; blackened with tar) is the first of this stanza's puns. Also compare *A Full Moon in March* (1935), ll. 92-93: 'the night of love ... the dung of swine'; and a verse deleted from Decima's song 'Shall I fancy beast or fowl?' in *The Player Queen*: 'the dung is to the fly / What my beauty's to a lover' (Bradford, *WPQ*, p. 334).

17 *sole or whole*: compare *soul* and *hole*. Fragmentation, heartbreak, bitterness are the preconditions to heavenly fullness and coherence.

VII. Crazy Jane Grown Old Looks at the Dancers

This poem originated in a dream, in which a man and a woman were dancing among a crowd of 'strange ragged excited people': 'The man was swinging round his head a weight at the end of a rope or leather thong, and I knew that he did not know whether he would strike her dead or not, and both had their eyes fixed on each other, and both sang their love for one another. I suppose it was Blake's old thought "sexual love is founded upon spiritual hate"' (*L*, p. 758). ('Blake's old thought' is, as Bloom notes [*Yeats*, p. 404], from *Jerusalem* 54:12: 'spiritual Hate, from which springs Sexual Love as iron chains'; see also *M*, p. 336, and 'The Mask', l. 11.) Yeats often considered all peak experiences – orgasm, violent death, spasm of hatred, occult seizure – as interchangeable; this brought forth his doctrine of tragic joy (see 'The Gyres', l. 8).

7 Love is like the lion's tooth: compare *The Shadowy Waters*, l. 459: 'love is war, and there is hatred in it'; 'Solomon and the Witch', l. 24: 'when at last that murder [sexual intercourse] 's over'; 'Her Vision in the Wood', l. 32: 'my heart's victim and its torturer'; and *John Sherman* (1891): 'Perfect love ... is a battle-field where shadows war beside the combatants' (*JSD*, pp. 54–55).

18 *thraneen*: a straw.

VIII. Girl's Song

This poem begins a sequence in which some of the themes of the Crazy Jane series – such as the immanence of eternity in temporal life, and the necessary admixture of love with desolation – are treated from the point of view of sane innocence, instead of mad old age.

11–12 *Saw I an old man young / Or young man old?*: that is, does old age represent the soul's authentic state, or does youth? – the girl (like the boy in the next poem) is perplexed by the body's mutability, since love demands a changeless object.

IX. Young Man's Song

9–10 *She would as bravely show / Did all the fabric fade*: for the theme of the metaphysical endurance of beauty, despite physical age, see 'Quarrel in Old Age' and 'The Death of Hanrahan' (as reported in the note to 'Crazy Jane talks with the Bishop').

12 *Before the world was made*: compare 'Before the World was made'.

X. Her Anxiety

6 Prove that I lie: presumably the girl's heart, which 'cannot lie' (IX 16), will refute her anxieties, as the young man's did in the previous poem.

10–11 *Every touch they give, / Love is nearer death*: compare 'Two Songs from a Play' II 11: 'Love's pleasure drives his love away'.

XI. His Confidence

2–3 *I wrote upon / The corners of this eye*: the young man imagines that his tears inscribe promissory notes on his face – he pays with his misery for 'undying love'. Compare 'His Bargain'.

10–12 *out of rock ... Love leaps upon its course*: compare Exodus 17:6, where Moses smites a rock and water flows forth. As in 'A Memory of Youth', love suddenly springs out of love's despair; this movement will recur in 'Her Dream'.

XII. Love's Loneliness

6 *That protect your blood*: the young man asks the aid and the companionship of his dead ancestors – the continuity of their genetic stock is threatened by the young man's inability to marry the girl.

XIII. Her Dream

In this dream, a miniature version of Pope's *The Rape of the Lock* (1714), love's death suddenly turns into love's transfiguration – compare XI 10–12. This poem (like 'Crazy Jane Grown Old ...') is connected to an actual dream of Yeats's: 'I had a long dream of a woman with her hair on fire. I awoke and lit a candle, and discovered presently from the odour that in doing so I had set my own hair on fire' (*M*, p. 358) – perhaps a too-literal symbol of inspiration.

3 *I had shorn my locks*: an emblem of self-sacrifice associated with a nun's renunciation of the world – but also, in this Popean context, associated with loss of virginity.

4 *lettered tomb*: compare 'Vacillation' VIII 5: 'lettered slab'.

7 *nailed upon the night*: Whitaker compares Henry More's 'The Immortality of the Soul': 'That famous star nail'd down in Cassiopee, / How was it hammer'd in your solid sky?' (*SS*, p. 103).

8 *Berenice's burning hair*: an actual constellation – see 'Veronica's Napkin', l. 1 – here used as a metaphor for the girl's timeless self. Yeats liked this phrase as early as 1902 – 'if we were not accustomed to be stirred by Greek myth, even without remembering it very fully, "Berenice's ever burning hair" would not stir the blood, and especially if it were put in some foreign tongue, losing the resounding "b's" on the way' (*CM*, p. 265). In the automatic script of 4 Nov. 1919 Yeats and the Control Ameritus discussed the meaning of Berenice's hair: Yeats concluded that it meant '"desire & sacrifice" sacrifice of desire ... Hair offered that man may return from dangerous expedition "idealization"' (*MAV* II, p. 345); as Harper notes, Berenice had offered a lock of her hair to the gods, in order to ensure her husband's safe return. Also compare *A Full Moon in March* (1935), ll. 172–76: 'Jill / Had hung his [Jack's] heart on high ... A-twinkle in the sky'.

XIV. His Bargain

1 *Plato's spindle*: Glaucon described the spindle of Necessity – the master control-apparatus of the universe, subdivided like Yeats's gyres into cones spinning inside of cones – in Plato's *Republic* X (616–17); the three Fates who spin and cut the threads of each man's life are the daughters of Necessity, seated near the great spindle. Compare also 'Byzantium', l. 11: 'Hades' bobbin'; 'Crazy Jane and Jack the Journeyman', l. 5: 'love is but a skein'; and 'There', l. 1: 'There all the barrel-hoops are knit'. For references to Plato, see 'The Tower' I 12.

5–6 *Dan and Jerry Lout / Change their loves about*: most people's lives are governed by frantic obedience to the spindle's whirl; but the young monogamist is exempt. They toss about the circumference; he is bound to the centre.

11 *A bargain with that hair*: 'Hafiz cried to his beloved, "I made a bargain

with that brown hair before the beginning of time"' (*EI*, p. 290; *Ex*, p. 301); Diarmuid repeated this cry in *Diarmuid and Grania* (1901) II 218–220: 'Life of my life, I [k]new you before I was born, I made a bargain with this brown hair before the beginning of time'. The girl's hair is stronger than (or equivalent to) Necessity's thread – compare the beloved's hair 'bound and wound / About the stars and moon and sun' in 'He wishes His Beloved were Dead', ll. 9–10. The young man's bargain may be compared with the payment in XI 5.

XV. Three Things

The previous poems dealt with noble and naive lovers, hoping for undying love; this and the following poems show a movement towards emotional complexity – erotic frenzy, mother-love, adultery, old nostalgia, resignation, anger. These songs are sung, not by the romantic leads, but by the chorus and the *comprimarii*.

2 Sang a bone upon the shore: compare Eliot, *Ash-Wednesday* II 48: 'the bones sang, scattered and shining' (this section was published in 1927, two years before Yeats wrote 'Three Things'). According to 'Crazy Jane and Jack the Journeyman', sexual pleasure assisted the soul's disembodiment; here it seems that the woman's extreme satiation reduces her to the state of a chirping bone. According to 'A Prayer for Old Age', l. 4, the best songs are conceived 'in a marrow-bone'. Compare also *The Dreaming of the Bones* (1919), ll. 7–8: 'dizzy dreams can spring / From the dry bones of the dead' (similarly l. 296). In the juvenile 'The Seeker' a shepherd's flute emits a piercing human cry (*VP*, p. 681); in *Calvary* (1920), ll. 34–35, we hear of 'a flute of bone / Taken from a heron's thigh'; and in *The Herne's Egg* (1938) II 21, a flute carved from a heron's thigh summons a priestess. Yeats regarded bones as the characteristic image in modern poetry, just as stars were in the poems of the 1890s (*OBMV*, pp. xix-xx).

11 *all the pleasure that life gave*: compare XIX 11.

17 *stretch and yawn*: Yeats's usual term for sexual languor – see 'On Woman', l. 21, *The Player Queen* (1922) II 363, and 'News for the Delphic Oracle' I 11. David R. Clark, in *Yeats at Songs and Choruses*, p. 44, traces this phrase to Pound's translation of an Arnaut Daniel poem in *The Spirit of Romance* (1910), p. 33; but Clark modifies this opinion in Bradford, *WPQ*, p. 105.

XVI. Lullaby

Yeats quoted a draft of this poem in a letter to Olivia Shakespear, as an example of the perhaps excessive ease and fluency of composition he had achieved in old age (*L*, pp. 760-61); she replied, 'Your lullaby, though very beautiful, is extremely unsuitable for the young! Leda seems to have a peculiar charm for you – personally, I'm so terrified of swans that the idea horrifies me' (*LTY* II, p. 495). In his own letter Yeats introduced the poem with the comment 'A mother sings to her child' – and Mrs Shakespear might well have found it strange that a lullaby addressed to a child would present sleep exclusively in terms of criminal sexual consummation; but, as the preceding poem shows, Yeats thought the pleasures of nursing and of sexual intercourse somewhat equivalent. Again, fair and foul are near of kin. Bradford (*YW*, pp. 101–12) prints many early drafts of this poem.

4 *Paris*: the Trojan prince who abducted Helen of Troy from her Greek husband, thus beginning the Trojan War. In 1935 Yeats wrote to his young lover Margot Ruddock that he valued friendship over love, Penelope over Helen: 'Paris and Helen were Romantic Love, and both were probably fools' (*ASD*, p. 42).

8 *Tristram*: another adulterer, a Cornish knight who fell wildly in love with the Irish princess Iseult when they mistakenly drank a love potion; she was betrothed to Tristram's king, Mark.

14 *Eurotas*: a river in Sparta – Leda was the wife of the Spartan king Tyndareus.

15 *the holy bird*: Zeus, in the form of a swan.

17 *Leda*: see 'Leda and the Swan'. It is remarkable how Yeats has changed the tenor of the earlier poem – which depicts beast-rape in its full terror – to this child's idyll of quiet affection.

XVII. After Long Silence

Yeats sent a copy of this poem to Olivia Shakespear (*L*, p. 772), whom the poem probably concerns. A prose draft appears in Ellmann, *IY*, p. 280, and Bradford, *YW*, p. 209: 'Your hair is white / My hair is white / Come let us talk of love / What other theme do we know / When we were young / We were in love with one another / And therefore ignorant'. As *Words for Music Perhaps* approaches its end, its explicit theme becomes 'Art and Song' (l. 6), as if Yeats were trying to isolate song in its purest state – whether in the wisdom of old age, in the inspiration of classic genius (XVIII), or in the spontaneity of the destitute and mad (XIX-XXIV).

7 *Bodily decrepitude is wisdom*: for a comparable inverse ratio of strength and wisdom, see 'Blood and the Moon' IV 7: 'wisdom is the property of the dead'.

XVIII. Mad as the Mist and Snow

Yeats claimed that this 'mechanical little song' was the first fruit of the sudden reinvigoration that came to him in the spring of 1929, and eventually produced most of *Words for Music Perhaps*: 'life returned to me as an impression of the uncontrollable energy and daring of the great creators' (*VP*, p. 831); and indeed this poem takes such energy and daring as its theme.

7–9 *Horace ... Homer ... Plato ... Tully*: Horace was a Roman poet (65–8 BC), notable for his civilized irony. For Homer, see 'A Woman Homer Sung'; for Plato, see 'The Tower' I 12. Tully: the sententious and dignified Roman philosopher and orator Marcus Tullius Cicero (106–43 BC). In this stanza the poet contrasts the calm, noble books in his library to the winter storm and his own former illiteracy; in the next stanza this division will become untenable.

17 *many-minded*: a translation of *polumetis*, Homer's epithet for Odysseus – one of Ezra Pound's favourite words (see Canto 9/36).

18 Mad as the mist and snow: 'When I began to grow old I could no longer spend all my time amid masterpieces and in trying to make the like. I gave part of every day to mere entertainment, and it seemed when I was ill that great genius was "mad as the mist and snow"' (*Ex*, p. 436). The essential similarity of distinguished genius to beggars or madmen was an old theme in Yeats's work – see 'The Seven Sages', l. 26. In 'The Scholars', l. 12, Yeats contrasted Catullus' passion to the sterility of the philologists who study his work.

XIX. Those Dancing Days are Gone

Here it seems that old age, stripped of all ornament and finery, possesses a kind of wealth in its stark contact with huge simplicities – compare 'Under the Round Tower', l. 13, where a beggar has a vision of 'golden king and silver lady' – that is, the sun and the moon. This poem was originally published with three of the Crazy Jane poems, and the speaker may be a male complement to her.

7–8: ' "The sun in a golden cup" ... though not "The moon in a silver bag", is a quotation from the last of Mr. Ezra Pound's *Cantos*' (*VP*, pp. 830–31). The line by Pound is from Canto 23/107, and is in turn a translation of a line by the Greek poet Stesichorus describing the sunset. Virginia Pruitt (*Colby Library Quarterly* 4 [1981]: 198) compares a passage in Yeats's introduction to *Gods and Fighting Men*: 'When we have drunk the cold cup of the moon's intoxication, we thirst for something beyond ourselves, and the mind flows outward to a natural immensity; but if we have drunk from the hot cup of the sun, our own fullness awakens, we desire little' (*Ex*, p. 26).

XX. 'I Am of Ireland'

'*I am of Ireland* is developed from three or four lines of an Irish fourteenth-century dance song somebody [Frank O'Connor] repeated to me a few years ago' (*VP*, p. 830). When Yeats heard O'Connor reading the old poem, he 'snatched wildly for a piece of paper, and gasped, "Write, write"' (Ellmann, *IY*, p. 280). Yeats's refrain follows the original fairly closely, although '*And time runs on*' is Yeats's addition. Ellmann further notes that, in Yeats's version, the woman is less an Irishwoman than a personification of Ireland (compare the title character in *Cathleen ni Houlihan* [1902]). Only one man hears her singing, and he is too prudent and narrow to accept her invitation; but, like the voluble, semi-divine madwomen in 'The Death of Hanrahan' (1896) and 'A Crazed Dancer', she continues her song, indifferent to its reception. From one perspective, time steadily degrades, mistunes the world; as in 'The Song of the Happy Shepherd', l. 9, Chronos sings a 'cracked tune'. But from another perspective, time is a dance.

21–22 *the kettledrums / And the trumpets*: compare 'That the Night Come', l. 9: 'Trumpet and kettledrum' – another poem about time's rush. For another defective musical instrument, see the broken-down lute in 'A Statesman's Holiday', l. 23.

XXI. The Dancer at Cruachan and Cro-Patrick

In 'An Indian Monk', Yeats contrasted the Russian mystics, indifferent to nature, to the Indian and early Christian mystics, who discovered God's splendour in nature: 'Some Irish saint, whose name I have forgotten, sang, "There is one among the birds that is perfect, one among the fish, one perfect among men"' (*EI*, p. 431; also see pp. 291, 514). (This same sentence appears, almost verbatim, in the unfinished *The Speckled Bird* III iii, as a message imparted during a shared dream of Christ's resurrection, in which appear a crowned eagle, a crowned deer, and a crowned fish [*LTMSB*, pp. 165–66].) The saint may have been 'that blessed Cellach who sang upon his deathbed of bird and beast' (*VP*, p. 837).

4 *Cruachan*: see 'The Hour Before Dawn', l. 4.

5 *Cro-Patrick*: Connemara mountain, object of pilgrimage.

8 *Acclaiming . . . Him*: compare *The King of the Great Clock Tower* (1935), ll. 76–77: 'a sea-mew . . . Yelled Godhead'.

XXII. Tom the Lunatic

Words for Music Perhaps began with a madwoman, Crazy Jane, and comes near its end with a madman, Tom. But to Crazy Jane spiritual truths were deeply embedded in the squalor of the physical world; whereas to Tom the physical world is a phantom about to dissolve.

4 *eyes that had so keen a sight*: this is the conceit, common in Blake and Shelley, that mutability and decay are unreal, the consequences of faulty eyesight. Compare 'Quarrel in Old Age', ll. 12–13: 'the curtain / Of distorting days'; and 'The Delphic Oracle upon Plotinus', l. 5: 'Salt blood blocks his eyes'.

7 *Huddon and Duddon and Daniel O'Leary*: fairy-tale characters whom Yeats also used in his last short story – a 'roaring, ranting crew' (*AV*, p. 32). In the original tale ('Donald and his Neighbours'), Donald O'Nery tricks the hostile Hudden and Dudden, first into killing their own bullocks, then into murdering their own mothers, at last into drowning themselves (*Fairy and Folk Tales*, pp. 270–73).

12 *saw them in a shroud*: death itself is an optical illusion.

15 *Mare or stallion*: compare XXIII 4–5.

16 *God's unchanging eye*: 'it would amuse me to follow these arguments of Ouspensky, that birth and death, spring and summer, and all waxing and waning, are but the appearance that immoveable solids take, as we encircle them' (*CEAV [1925]*, notes, p. 32). Also compare 'Crazy Jane on God', l. 6: '*All things remain in God*'.

18 *In that faith I live or die*: compare the refrain of Rossetti's Villon translation, 'His Mother's Service to Our Lady': 'in this faith I choose to live or die'.

XXIII. Tom at Cruachan

4–5 *The stallion Eternity / Mounted the mare of Time*: compare the tenth of the Proverbs of Hell from Blake's *The Marriage of Heaven and Hell*: 'Eternity is in love with the productions of time'. Mare and stallion can be found in the previous poem, l. 15.

XXIV. Old Tom Again

1 *Things out of perfection sail*: see 'Sailing to Byzantium' II 7.

2 *all their swelling canvas wear*: 'in the faces of Madonnas and holy women painted by Raphael or da Vinci . . . those lips murmur that . . . we came from

no immaturity, but out of our own perfection like ships that "all their swelling canvas wear"' (*EI*, p. 472).

3 *self-begotten*: see 'A Prayer for my Daughter', ll. 67–68.

5 *Building-yard and stormy shore*: where a boat originates and where it founders.

6 *Winding-sheet and swaddling-clothes*: the garments associated with death and birth, here contrasted with the sails of l. 2. Tom asserts that birth is no origin and death no terminus – both are stations on the soul's endless journey.

XXV. The Delphic Oracle upon Plotinus

In the previous poem the soul sailed grandly out of perfection; here the soul swims painfully back into it. Apollo's oracle at Delphi was the most celebrated of the ancient world – for other references, see *The Player Queen* II 491, 542, 552, 579, 'The Gyres', l. 1, and 'News for the Delphic Oracle'. This poem is a witty paraphrase of the Delphic Oracle's reply, when asked about the fate of Plotinus' soul after his death, as Porphyry recorded in his *Life of Plotinus*. Yeats cited broken phrases from the oracle as one of his 'favourite quotations': '"That wave-washed shore ... the golden race of mighty Zeus ... the just Aeacus, Plato, stately Pythagoras, and all the choir of immortal love"' (*EI*, p. 409).

1 *Plotinus*: see 'The Tower' I 12.

3 *Rhadamanthus*: one of the judges in the classical hereafter.

5 *Salt blood blocks his eyes*: compare the distorted eyesight in XXII 4; also *The Wanderings of Oisin* III 51: 'the salt eye of man'; and also the 'salt flakes' on Plotinus' breast in 'News for the Delphic Oracle' I 10.

8–9 *Plato ... Minos ... Pythagoras*: Minos was another of the Hadean judges. For Plato, see 'The Tower' I 12; for Pythagoras, see 'Among School Children' VI 5.

10 *choir of Love*: compare 'News for the Delphic Oracle' I 7: 'choir of love'. *Words for Music Perhaps* can be regarded as a sequence not only for music but about music – in the beginning music is passionately engaged with the foul, sexual world, but by the end music grows increasingly detached, unworldly, paradisiacal.

A WOMAN YOUNG AND OLD (1929)

'*A Woman Young and Old* was written before the publication of *The Tower*, but left out for some reason I cannot recall' (*VP*, p. 831); in the event, this sequence became the second tail depending from *The Winding Stair and Other Poems*, congruent to 'A Man Young and Old' at the end of *The Tower*. 'A Man Young and Old', *Words for Music Perhaps*, and *A Woman Young and Old* – three of Yeats's most important song-cycles – share certain structural features. Yeats explained in a letter to his publisher that *Words for Music Perhaps* is a series of poems leading up to a question from the Delphic oracle, just as 'A Man Young and Old' and *A Woman Young and Old* 'lead up to quotations from Sophocles. The poems in "Words for Music Perhaps" describe first wild loves, then the normal love of boy & girl, then follow poems about love but not love poems, then poems of impersonal ecstasy' (Finneran, *EYP*, p. 18). Each sequence, then, constitutes a gyre, rising from Self to Soul, from sexual passion to the emotion of transcendence.

Like 'A Man Young and Old', this sequence can be seen as a kind of experimental theatre. The man-series presents a minimalist drama improvised from the shifting of a few props on an almost bare stage; the woman-series, on the other hand, derives its effect from the clash of genres: it rapidly moves from artificial drawing-room flirtation (II-IV) to Shakespearean love-duet (VII) to high-Modernist myth-theatre (VIII) to the mummery of old age (X 2) to Sophoclean tragedy (XI). Yeats seems to suggest that a woman's life is a drama of moods too diverse to be encompassed in one theatre.

I. Father and Child

Jeffares notes (*NCP*, p. 325) that this poem is based on the young Anne Yeats's praise of a friend, Fergus Fitzgerald.

8 *Cold as the March wind his eyes*: compare 'Under Ben Bulben' VI 9, '*a cold eye*'.

II. Before the World was made

This poem defends make-up and coquetry in terms familiar from 'The Mask' and *The Player Queen* (1922): the woman claims that the artificial self is authentic, not the natural one.

7–8 *I'm looking for the face I had / Before the world was made*: compare 'Young Man's Song', ll. 11–12: 'No withered crone I saw / Before the world was made'. This phrase is related to a couplet by Mrs Ernest Radford that moved Yeats: 'The love within my heart for thee / Before the world was' (*L* I, p. 253).

13 *Why should he think me cruel?*: compare 'The Mask', l. 11, 'lest you are my enemy'. The woman self-consciously uses the man's responses in order to gauge her success in finding her mask.

III. A First Confession

Yeats quoted a draft of this 'innocent little song' in a letter to Olivia Shakespear (*L*, p. 725–26).

13 *Brightness*: compare the eye-brightening in II 2.

14 *Zodiac*: see VI 3 and 16.

15 *those questioning eyes*: compare 'At Algeciras ...', l. 16: 'the Great Questioner'.

18 *If empty night replies*: compare 'First Love', ll. 16–17: 'Emptier of thought / Than the heavenly circuit of its stars' – this is the parallel passage in 'A Man Young and Old'. The woman may fear that a confrontation with her true lover, or her true self, will paralyse her – whereas playful coquetry leaves her glib and able.

IV. Her Triumph

1 *I did the dragon's will*: compare the allegorizing of the knight's combat with the dragon in 'Michael Robartes and the Dancer', l. 6: 'The half-dead dragon was her thought'. In this poem, too, the dragon seems to represent the woman's wilfulness, her relishing of difficulties she contrived to exasperate her suitors. Also compare *Deirdre* (1907), ll. 163–65: 'Myself wars on myself, for I myself ... Grow dragonish to myself'.

9 *broke the chain*: compare *The Wanderings of Oisin* II 97: 'I burst the chain' – another liberation of a damsel in distress.

10 *St. George or else a pagan Perseus*: both dragon-slayers – Perseus freed Andromeda from dragon-captivity.

12 *a miraculous strange bird shrieks at us*: the woman's sudden liberation from false selves and malicious roles is signalled by a bird's cry – compare the 'most ridiculous little bird' that startles old lovers out of their complacency in 'A Memory of Youth', l. 20, and the orgasmic cockerel-crow in 'Solomon and the Witch', l. 9. Further bird-notes embellish *A Woman Young and Old* at VII 5 and IX 23.

V. Consolation

Yeats sent a draft of this 'not so innocent' song to Olivia Shakespear (*L*, pp. 725–26).

5 *Till I have told the sages*: this impudent advice to advice-givers is similar to that suggested in the title 'News for the Delphic Oracle'.

9 *the crime of being born*: compare 'A Dialogue of Self and Soul' I 24: 'the crime of death and birth'.

VI. Chosen

'I have symbolised a woman's love as the struggle of the darkness to keep the sun from rising from its earthly bed. In the last stanza of The Choice [the original title of this poem] I change the symbol to that of the souls of man and woman ascending through the Zodiac' (*VP*, p. 830). 'In "A First Confession", "The Choice" and "The Parting" I have made use of that symbolic marriage of the Sun and Light with the Earth and Darkness, current in literature since the Renaissance. The sun's northern (not northward) way is his passage under the earth, his sojourn in the bed of love. Earth would bar his way and so prevent the dawn. It was in Blake at times the symbol of the grave' (*BL*, p. 139 – Yeats crossed out the last sentence). In several poems in this sequence the woman seems a queen of night, while her lover is a creature of day, as if sexual and astronomical rhythms were essentially identical. This was an old idea of Yeats's – some of the symbolism in *The Wind among the Reeds* was governed by the conflict between the 'solar hero' and darkness: 'The desire of the woman, the flying darkness, it is all one!' (*VP*, p. 807). Yeats noted in a letter to H. J. C. Grierson that the stanza-form of 'Chosen' was borrowed from Donne's 'A Nocturnall upon S. Lucies day' (*L*, p. 710).

1 *The lot of love is chosen*: as in such poems as 'His Bargain', the soul seems to have committed itself to love from its origin; and to choose love is to choose the whole round of pleasure, suffering, and desertion. Compare also the doctrine that ideal love combines Chance and Choice ('Solomon and the Witch', l. 14).

17 *a learned astrologer*: 'The "learned astrologer" ... was Macrobius ... [see his] comment upon "Scipio's Dream": "... when the sun is in Aquarius, we sacrifice to the Shades, for it is in the sign inimical to human life; and from thence the meeting-place of Zodiac and Milky Way, the descending soul by its defluction is drawn out of the spherical, the sole divine form, into the cone"' (*VP*, p. 831). In *A Vision*, Yeats wrote of a sphere into which all gyres, all dialectics, resolve themselves: 'the *thirteenth sphere* ... is in every man and called by every man his freedom' (p. 302; compare pp. 210 and 240). In 'Chosen' the woman and her lover attain a moment of liberation from time and space, ascend into the realm of the unborn; this freedom (like the chosenness affirmed in ll. 1 and 11) seems to contrast with the general preordination of things, the clockwork Zodiac.

VII. Parting

This aubade is based on Shakespeare, *Romeo and Juliet*:

> *Juliet*. Believe me, love, it was the nightingale.
> *Romeo*. It was the lark, the herald of the morn . . .
> Night's candles are burnt out, and jocund day
> Stands tiptoe on the misty mountain tops.
> I must be gone and live, or stay and die.
> (III v 5–11)

Yeats considered the title 'Breaking Day' for his poem (Stallworthy, *BL*, p. 162).

3 *household spies*: Helen Gardner suggests Donne's twelfth 'Elegie', l. 41, as a source (*BL*, p. 143).

8 *murderous . . . day*: in an early draft Yeats wrote of 'A dragon's winding gullet / That has sucked in the moon, / Rage tooth tusk & bullet / To drive it from its noon' (*BL*, p. 155).

11 *That light is from the moon*: compare the magical confusion of sun and moon in 'The Tower' II 39.

14 *My dark declivities*: compare *The Wanderings of Oisin* I 73: 'gulph of love'.

VIII. Her Vision in the Wood

In this sequence the poet uses several strategies for depicting the heroine as everywoman – for generalizing and intensifying her emotions. One strategy is that of part VI, where the woman and the man are presented in terms of such universal symbols as night and day; and in the present part Yeats reduces his protagonists to their mythic essentials – Venus and Adonis, or Grania and Diarmuid – the woman forever mourning her lover mutilated by a boar. But this poem is not, like 'Leda and the Swan', a depiction of prehistoric events; this is a work in the tradition of Eliot's *The Waste Land* and Joyce's *Ulysses*, in which a vision of antiquity defines some modern, or at least non-mythical, predicament. The woman is less Venus than a withered caricature of her; she seems to step briefly into a stately mythological painting, a smoothly archaic convention of grief, but finds only a heightened version of her own pain.

1 *Dry timber*: for comparisons between trees and old bodies, see 'The Lamentation of the Old Pensioner', l. 14.

2 *At wine-dark midnight in the sacred wood*: compare 'To Dorothy Wellesley', l. 1: 'the moonless midnight of the trees'. For *wine-dark*, see 'Colonus' Praise', l. 2 – the sacred wood is also suggestive of Sophocles' *Oedipus at Colonus*, as if the speaker were a female complement to Oedipus.

7 *I tore my body*: Yeats often wrote of the efficacy of blood in conjuring spirits, in providing them with a body (see *The Player Queen* I 210–16 and *Ex*, p. 366); and by making herself bleed the woman may invoke the vision of the gored man. Also compare *Deirdre* (1907), ll. 364–66: 'tear my face with briars. / O that the creatures of the woods had torn / My body with their claws!'; and *A Full Moon in March* (1935), ll. 107–9: 'my face is pure. / Had it but known the insult of his eyes / I had torn it with these nails'.

9–10 *I held my fingers up, / Stared at the wine-dark nail*: compare 'Cuchulain's Fight with the Sea', l. 7: 'raising arms all raddled with the dye'.

16 *the beast that gave the fatal wound*: in Yeats's and Moore's *Diarmuid and Grania* (1900) I 404–13, the slanderer Conan foretells Diarmuid's 'foul and bloody' death, by the tusks of a bristleless boar. Yeats conceived the boar without bristles as the agent that would destroy the world at the end of time – see 'The Valley of the Black Pig'.

19 *Quattrocento*: the fifteenth century – see 'Among School Children' IV 2.

20 *Mantegna*: Andrea Mantegna (1431–1506), a painter known for beautifully composed scenes of violence (such as the crucifixion of Christ, or the martyrdom of St Sebastian), sometimes depicted from disorienting points of view.

23 *blood-bedabbled*: compare *Deirdre*, ll. 697–98: 'For I will see him / All blood-bedabbled'; *Calvary* (1920), ll. 88–89: 'His dirty / Blood-dabbled feet'.

25 *blood and mire*: compare 'Byzantium', l. 24: 'mire or blood'.

28 *a coin*: compare 'Parnell's Funeral' I 16: 'Sicilian coin'.

31 *no fabulous symbol*: compare 'At Algeciras . . .', l. 11: 'Not such as are in Newton's metaphor'; and 'Parnell's Funeral' I 22–23: 'nor did we play a part / Upon a painted stage when we devoured his heart'.

32 *my heart's victim and its torturer*: compare 'Crazy Jane Grown Old . . .', where the poet describes love as mutual torture. In *The Resurrection* (1931), a procession of transvestites appears, singing and gashing themselves with knives in order to mourn Dionysus' death and to induce him to resurrection, 'imagining themselves . . . at once the god and the Titans that murdered him' (ll. 179–80). Also compare a note to 'Parnell's Funeral', which speaks of a Tibetan ascetic's trance 'where he has seen himself eaten alive and has not yet learned that the eater was himself' (*VP*, p. 835). The extreme intimacy of the woman and her lover – see VI 15 – tends to confuse the subject and object of passion.

IX. A Last Confession

15 *this soul, its body off*: the woman contemplates the paradox that spiritual love is more naked than physical love – death is the ultimate divestiture. Compare X 2, 16–17; the draft cited in the note to 'Sailing to Byzantium' I 1–2; and 'Crazy Jane and Jack the Journeyman', ll. 9–12.

X. Meeting

17 *This beggarly habiliment*: that is, the body – see l. 2 and IX 15.

XI. From the *Antigone*

The hatred of old age expressed in the previous poem is here generalized into a hatred of all things, a vision of universal discord – as if anyone's tragedy were the tragedy of the whole human race. Like Yeats's other versions of Sophocles, this was adapted from Paul Masqueray's French – see 'From *Oedipus at Colonus*'. In the original ode, the chorus of Theban elders deplored the world-bungling power of erotic love; and *A Woman Young and Old* thus investigates the destructive as well as the creative power of sex. Yeats originally wrote this translation in *abab* quatrains, but in February 1928 Pound persuaded him to insert l. 8 directly after l. 1 (see Patrick J. Keane, *Yeats Eliot Review* 8 [1986]: 7) – a disruption of the poem's metre to match the disruption described in the text.

1 *O bitter sweetness*: compare VIII 27. In 'The Adoration of the Magi' (1897; 1925) the dying prostitute – mother of the unicorn who would become the god of the forthcoming violent, *antithetical* age – murmured such strange names of endearment as '"Harsh sweetness", "Dear bitterness", "O solitude", "O terror"' (*M*, p. 314).

6 *Parnassus*: mountain sacred to the Muses.

7–8 *hurl / Heaven and Earth out of their places*: compare 'The Second Coming', ll. 3–4: 'the centre cannot hold; / Mere anarchy is loosed upon the world'.

15 *Oedipus' child*: Antigone.

16 *loveless dust*: Antigone was buried alive as punishment for disobeying Creon's order to leave her brother Polynices unburied.

PARNELL'S FUNERAL AND OTHER POEMS (1935)

Parnell's Funeral and Other Poems is a section of the volume *A Full Moon in March* (1935), also including the play of the same name. The play is a parable, partly based on Wilde's *Salomé* (1893), about a swineherd who attains all physical and metaphysical consummation with his ideal lady only after she has him beheaded. During the early 1930s Yeats tried to apprehend the supernatural through metaphors of extreme violence: decapitation, cannibalism ('Parnell's Funeral'), auto-copulation ('Ribh denounces Patrick'), flagellation ('Whence Had They Come?') – as if only the body's mutilation could provide a sensation intense enough to approximate the soul's keenness of perception. This was a somewhat sterile period in Yeats's creative life:

> I found that I had written no verse for two years; I had never been so long barren . . . Perhaps Coole Park where I had escaped from politics, from all that Dublin talked of, when it was shut, shut me out from my theme; or did the subconscious drama that was my imaginative life end with its owner [Lady Gregory, d. 1932]? I decided to force myself to write . . . In 'At Parnell's Funeral' I rhymed passages from a lecture I had given in America; a poem upon mount Meru came spontaneously, but philosophy is a dangerous theme; then I was barren again. (*VP*, p. 855)

It may be that Yeats used fantasies of erotic vehemence as artificial stimulants to his flagging imaginative energies – the artistic equivalent of the Steinach rejuvenation operation (a kind of vasectomy thought to cure impotence) that Yeats underwent in 1934.

The second poem in this volume was originally 'Three Songs to the Same Tune', later revised, retitled 'Three Marching Songs', and included in *Last Poems.* It is not known whether Yeats would have wished to keep the earlier version in this section; and those readers interested in the order of the poems here would do well to remember this tentative insertion between 'Parnell's Funeral' and 'Alternative Song for the Severed Head . . .'

Parnell's Funeral

This poem is Yeats's most ambitious attempt to present modern Irish politics as an archaic rite or Greek tragedy. Just as Joyce, in *Ulysses* (1922), used the myth of Odysseus to impart a reverberation of old meaning to the unspectacular lives of the common people of Dublin; just as Eliot, in *The Waste Land* (1922), shored up the ruins of the modern city by allusions to the dismemberment and resurrection of the fertility-god, so Yeats discovers, behind the struggles of Irish politicians, the ritual murder and cannibalism that, according to Frazer's *The Golden Bough* (1890), savage tribes practiced to ensure the health of the society.

This poem was originally published as 'A Parnellite at Parnell's Funeral' with an essay separating parts I and II. In this essay Yeats described the character of the last three centuries of Irish history: the eighteenth century –

the Anglo-Ireland of Swift and Berkeley – was proud, cold, intellectual, distinguished; the nineteenth century, influenced by the democratic ideals of the French Revolution, was agrarian, rhetorical, sentimental, insincere; and the modern era, beginning with the death of Parnell in 1891, possessed

> the passion for reality, the satiric genius that informs [Joyce's] *Ulysses*, [Synge's] *The Playboy of the Western World* ... the accumulated hatred of years was suddenly transferred from England to Ireland. James Joyce has no doubt described something remembered from his youth in that dinner table scene in *[A] Portrait of the Artist as a Young Man*, when after a violent quarrel about Parnell and the priests, the host [actually Mr Casey] sobs, his head upon the table; 'My dead King'.
>
> We had passed through an initiation like that of the Tibetan ascetic, who staggers half dead from a trance, where he has seen himself eaten alive and has not yet learned that the eater was himself. (*VP*, p. 835)

(The Tibetan self-eater also appears in *EI*, p. 519; compare *TPU*, p. 78.) Although Yeats does not use the vocabulary of *A Vision*, and *A Vision*'s historical eras do not coincide with the periods described in this essay, it is clear that Yeats is treating Parnell's death as the turning-point of a gyre – a heroic, *antithetical* era is replacing the objective, democratic, tame, *primary* nineteenth century. And yet the new age is miscarrying, failing to be heroic – Ireland is using the resurgence of violent energies against itself, towards its own destruction. Stephen Dedalus in *A Portrait of the Artist* called Ireland 'the old sow that eats her farrow' (p. 203); and Yeats too sees Ireland as a self-cannibal.

Title *Parnell*: see 'To a Shade' – that poem, like this, argues that the age has in Parnell a model for heroic conduct, but it refuses to accept it.

I 1 *the Great Comedian*: Daniel O'Connell – see 'The Three Monuments', l. 4. 'The national character changed, O'Connell the great comedian, left the scene and the tragedian Parnell took his place. When we talked of his [Parnell's] pride; of his apparent impassivity when his hands were full of blood because he had torn them with his nails, the proceeding [preceding?] epoch with its democratic bonhomie, seemed to grin through a horse collar. He was the symbol that made apparent, or made possible ... that epoch's contrary' (*VP*, p. 835). Yeats ascribed O'Connell's bumptiousness partly to his Catholicism: 'All the tragedians [e.g., Parnell, Grattan, Davis] were Protestant – O'Connell was a comedian. He had the gifts of the market place, of the clown at the fair' (*Mem*, p. 213). Yeats similarly contrasted the 'beauty' of 'the great men of the eighteenth century' and of Parnell with the ugliness of O'Connell: 'what have O'Connell and all his seed, breed, and generation but a roaring machine?' (*Ex*, p. 336). Yeats disliked O'Connell for his compromises and temporizing.

I 4 *a brighter star shoots down*: 'I did not go to the funeral ... but my friend [Maud Gonne] went. She told me that evening of the star that fell in broad daylight as Parnell's body was lowered into the grave – was it a collective hallucination or an actual event?' (*VP*, p. 834). Yeats also cited Standish O'Grady's account of Parnell's funeral – the shooting star reminded O'Grady of the flames in the sky, visible throughout northern Europe, when St Columba died.

I 7 *the Cretan barb that pierced a star*: 'I think of the symbolism of the star shot with an arrow, described in the appendix to my book *Autobiographies*. I ask if the fall of a star may not upon occasion, symbolise an accepted sacrifice' (*VP*, p. 834). In the appendix Yeats collected mythological analogies to a vision he had, between sleep and waking, of 'a marvellous naked woman shooting an arrow at a star. She stood like a statue upon a stone pedestal, and the flesh tints of her body seemed to make all human flesh in the contrast seem unhealthy' (*Mem*, p. 100 – compare p. 103; also *L*, p. 266, *M*, p. 340, *A: SB* 6, and 'The Phases of the Moon', ll. 119–20). The woman was, Yeats learned, an image of 'the Mother-Goddess whose representative priestess shot the arrow at the child whose sacrificial death symbolised the death and resurrection of the Tree-spirit, or Apollo. She is pictured upon certain Cretan coins of the fifth century BC as a slightly draped, beautiful woman sitting in the heart of a branching tree ... she is also Artemis' (*A: Notes* II b). The meteor witnessed at Parnell's funeral became, then, a sign that Parnell was himself a kind of god, whose death and rebirth governed historical change. In the automatic script of 9 Jan. 1918, Thomas told Yeats that the beautiful archer of Yeats's vision was a spirit of Phase 15 (*MAV* I, p. 130).

I 12 *A pierced boy, image of a star laid low*: 'The Star goes right back to the Cretan Mother-Goddess. The later Greek form of it was Asterios or Asterion [*aster* is Greek for *star*]. The latter ... is said to be Jupiter's son' (*A: Notes* II d).

I 14 *Cut out his heart*: 'The Cretan Jupiter "made an image of his son in gypsum and placed the boy's heart ... in that part of the figure where the curve of the chest was to be seen ... It may be ... that images were made with a chest cavity to contain the heart of the sacrificed"' (*A: Notes* II c). Yeats liked the conjunction of woman, star, and torn-out heart – compare 'Two Songs from a Play' I 3: 'tear the heart out of his side'; and *A Full Moon in March* (1935), ll. 172–76: 'Jack had a hollow heart, for Jill ... Had hung his heart beyond the hill, / A-twinkle in the sky'.

I 15 *Sicilian coin*: compare 'Her Vision in the Wood', l. 28. Yeats, as chairman of the senate committee on coin design, wrote, 'As the most famous and beautiful coins are the coins of the Greek Colonies, especially of those in Sicily, we decided to send photographs ... to our selected artists'; Yeats further remarked on the 'supernatural energy' that explained the persistence of design-motifs from ancient Sicily to modern Ireland (*SSY*, p. 161, 165).

I 16–23: Yeats quoted this stanza to illustrate how the Irish imagination retreated from the 'sordid scene' of Parnell's downfall into vituperation and satire against Ireland (*VPl*, p. 568; *Ex*, p. 372).

I 17 *strangers murdered Emmet, Fitzgerald, Tone*: Emmet and Fitzgerald were executed by the British as rebels; Tone probably committed suicide in jail after the British captured him – see the Introductory Poem to *Responsibilities*, l. 5, and 'September 1913', ll. 20–21.

I 19 *What matter for the scene*: compare Shakespeare, *Hamlet* II ii 585: 'What's Hecuba to him, or he to Hecuba'. The question 'what matter?' chimes throughout 'The Gyres'; and 'Ribh in Ecstasy' begins with it. The poet accuses Irishmen of treating the downfall of their heroes as a kind of melodrama: 'Blake ... has this description of the playgoer at a "tragic scene": "The soul drinks murder and revenge, and applauds its own holiness" [*Jerusalem* 37 [41]:30] – a description that applies ... to melodrama and its easy victory over our susceptibilities. When we look on at the common drama of murder and sentiment, there is something about it that flatters us. ... Melodrama can make us weep ... but when the curtain has fallen, they leave nothing behind' (*LNI*, pp. 112–13).

I 21 Hysterica passio: hysterical passion – from Lear's cry for self-control in Shakespeare, *King Lear* II iv 57. See also 'A Bronze Head', l. 8, *M*, p. 278, *Mem*, p. 179, and *DWL*, p. 86.

I 21 *dragged this quarry down*: see 'To a Shade', ll. 17–18: 'set / The pack upon him [Parnell]'.

I 22 *None shared our guilt*: the British could not be blamed for Ireland's fury at Parnell after he was accused of adultery.

I 22–23 *nor did we play a part / Upon a painted stage when we devoured his heart*: Parnell's downfall was not a dramatic spectacle in which Ireland was the audience, but a bloody rite in which Ireland was the slaughterer and the slain – 'Ritual, the most powerful form of drama, differs from the ordinary form, because everyone who hears it is also a player' (*Ex*, p. 129). (The opposite doctrine can be found in 'Three Songs to the One Burden' III, which takes the Easter 1916 revolt as a superior sort of play-acting.) Compare the similar rejection of theatre in 'Two Songs from a Play', which turns aside from the 'play' (I 8) or pageant of God's death to a glory that 'Man's own resinous heart has fed' (II 16); and in 'The Circus Animals' Desertion' II 23–24: 'Players and painted stage took all my love / And not those things that they were emblems of'. Also compare the shock of immediacy in 'Her Vision in the Wood', ll. 31–32, when the woman discovers that the gored man was 'no fabulous symbol' but her 'heart's victim and its torturer'.

I 28 *the rhyme rats hear before they die*: ancient Irish poets were thought able to kill rats with rhymes – compare Shakespeare, *As You Like It* III ii 185–86. Yeats seems to feel that only satire retains its efficacy (see *Ex*, p. 372) – poetry is merely a means of extermination.

I 29 *nothing but the nothings*: this systematic evacuation of substance anticipates a quatrain cited in the note to 'The Gyres', l. 22.

I 31 *Whether it be an animal or a man*: compare another poem of self-stripping and self-disgust, 'Nineteen Hundred and Nineteen' IV 3–4: 'Shriek with pleasure if we show ... the weasel's tooth'.

II: this part was originally entitled 'Forty Years Later'.

II 1 *one sentence I unsay*: 'we devoured his heart' (I 23) – in fact, says the poet, no one ate his heart.

II 2 *Had de Valéra eaten Parnell's heart*: Eamon de Valéra (1882–1975) was President of the Irish Free State for many years following his election in 1932. Yeats thought that de Valéra could be compared to 'Mussolini or Hitler', and was impressed with his 'simplicity and honesty' (*L*, p. 806); 'I am told that De Valera has said in private that within three years he will be torn in pieces' (*L*, p. 809). De Valéra is mentioned again in 'A Statesman's Holiday', l. 18. The thirteenth-century troubadour Sordello wrote a plaint for the dead Sir Blancatz, that asked 'that they take his heart out, and have it eaten by the Barons who live un-hearted, then they would have hearts worth something' (Pound, *The Spirit of Romance* [1910], p. 58); there follows a list of many kings who would do well to eat it. In 1936 Auden burlesqued this heart-eating when he wrote to Lord Byron that 'Yeats has helped himself to Parnell's heart' (*English Auden*, p. 198).

II 5 *Cosgrave*: William Cosgrave (1880–1965), de Valéra's predecessor as president (1922–32).

II 8 *O'Higgins*: see 'Death'.

II 9 *O'Duffy*: Eoin O'Duffy (1892–1944), founder of the 'blueshirts', the Irish fascist party, after his dismissal as head of the Irish police in 1933. Like de Valéra and O'Higgins, O'Duffy evidently thought his own destruction likely; Yeats remarked of O'Duffy, 'I did not think him a great man though a pleasant one, but one never knows, his face and mind may harden or clarify' (*L*, p. 813).

II 10 *Their school a crowd, his master solitude*: compare 'The Leaders of the Crowd', ll. 10–11.

II 11 *Swift*: see 'Blood and the Moon' II 6 and 8. 'Blood and the Moon' resembles the present poem in that the poet finds something frustrated, aborted, in modern civilization. Through timidity or daintiness, the resurrection of Parnell's energy has failed. Though Yeats alters to a vegetarian metaphor, it seems that Parnell had eaten Swift's heart, inherited his disciplined pessimism and self-torture; but the inheritance could not be further transmitted.

Alternative Song for the Severed Head in *The King of the Great Clock Tower*

Yeats, when young, disparaged Oscar Wilde's *Salomé* (1893) – '*Salomé* is thoroughly bad' (*TSMC*, p. 8) – but it helped to inspire three of his late plays: the prose version of *The King of the Great Clock Tower* (1934), and the two verse plays into which it split, *The King of the Great Clock Tower* (1935) and *A Full Moon in March* (1935). In all three versions the climax of the play is a song sung by a Stroller's (or Swineherd's) severed head, while a fascinated queen dances with the head. (Like the ritual of the mother-goddess who shoots an arrow at a star in 'Parnell's Funeral', this Salomé-dance was, according to Yeats, a kind of fertility rite: 'it is part of the old ritual of the year: the mother goddess and the slain god' [*VP*, p. 840]). But only in the original prose version does the severed head sing this song – full of unusually intimate reminders of Yeats's poetic career. As in 'The Circus Animals' Desertion', the poet summons the favourite creatures of his imagination – the poet seems himself to have become a tragic character, worthy to join the heroes of his tragic theatre in some heaven of art.

1, 4: these lines originally began, 'Images ride' and 'Out of the grave' (*VP*, p. 549).

2 *Ben Bulben and Knocknarea*: for Ben Bulben, see 'On a Political Prisoner', l. 14; for Knocknarea, see 'The Ballad of Father O'Hart', l. 30.

5 *Rosses*: see 'The Stolen Child', l. 15.

6 *The meet's upon the mountain side*: 'on the southern side of Ben Bulben ... is a small white square in the limestone ... It is the door of Faeryland. In the middle of night it swings open, and the unearthly troop rushes out' (*M*, p. 70).

7 A slow low note and an iron bell: the corresponding refrain-line in the Severed Head's song in the 1935 version is '*A moment more and it tolls midnight*' – there is a sudden accession of Eternity at Time's midnight. Other midnight bells that signal the approach of spirits are found in 'All Souls' Night', l. 1, and the juvenile 'The Phantom Ship', l. 16: 'Slow the chapel bell is tolling as though the dead passed by' (*VP*, p. 718). Compare also the gong-blow of 'Byzantium', l. 4.

9 *Cuchulain that fought night long with the foam*: see the end of 'Cuchulain's Fight with the Sea'; the end of *On Baile's Strand* (1904); and 'The Circus Animals' Desertion' II 18.

11 *Niamh*: the goddess who lured Oisin on a horse-ride over the ocean to paradise – see *The Wanderings of Oisin* I 48.

11 *lad and lass*: Naoise and Deirdre, who, tensely calm, played chess while waiting for Conchubar's murderous arrival – see *Deirdre* (1907), ll. 433–56. In *A Vision* (1925), p. 243, Yeats wrote that during this chess game 'each feels for the other an emotion which has become a supernatural contemplation'. Yeats often associated chess with death or the life after death: the loss of a chess-game symbolizes death or spiritual nullity in the juvenile 'Time and the Witch Vivien' (*VP*, p. 722) and in 'Dhoya' (*JSD*, pp. 123–24); and Yeats wrote that 'even the most wise dead can but arrange their memories as we arrange pieces upon a chess-board' (*M*, p. 359). In a deleted passage from *The Only Jealousy of Emer* (1919), a sea-god 'nods above the board and moves / His chessmen in a dream' (*VPl*, p. 559).

15 *Aleel, his Countess*: Aleel was the love-struck poet in the revised version of *The Countess Cathleen* (1892) – see also 'The Circus Animals' Desertion' II 10.

15–16 *Hanrahan / That seemed but a wild wenching man*: the tattered and half-coherent Hanrahan was the hero of six stories in *The Secret Rose* (1897) and 'Red Hanrahan' (1903) – he seemed but a wild wenching man, but was a poet and visionary as well. Hanrahan also appears in 'The Tower' II 41.

20 *he had feathers instead of hair*: a character from 'The Wisdom of the King' (1895), a story about a disturbingly wise and subtle king, with some hawk blood in him. He thought that everyone grew feathers on his head because his father had commanded all his subjects to tie feathers in their hair, lest his son feel excluded from common humanity; but the boy learned the ruse when he discovered his beloved, featherless, under a bush in the arms of an ordinary man; he stormed away from the kingdom, 'and no man saw him again or heard his voice' (*M*, p. 170). Like most of the stories rehearsed in this song, this parable suggests that the man gifted with imagination endures erotic frustration and finally must vanish from the normal world; the Severed Head sings of a domain in which the disappeared can reappear, and perhaps revel with the objects of their affection.

Two Songs Rewritten for the Tune's Sake

The originals of these songs appear in *The Pot of Broth* (1922 version), ll. 261–79, and *The Player Queen* (1922) II 243–50. These versions differ chiefly in metre. Each song is a piece of abject flattery of a woman: the first is sung by a tramp to a woman whom he wishes to swindle – it presumably represents the common lament of all local men on the day of her wedding; the second is sung by Decima, the Player Queen, to demonstrate to another woman how much her poet-husband loves her – Decima does not yet know that the other woman is her husband's mistress.

I 1 *Paistin Finn*: 'little child of Finn' – the name of a Munster folk tune, to which this version better conforms. 'If [Nancy Price, actress and producer] is going to do *Pot of Broth* . . . tell her that one of the songs, "Paistin Finn" is not quite right for the music. I will send her the correct version' (*ASD*, p. 51).

I 8 *speckled shin*: 'The words "a speckled shin" are familiar to readers of Irish legendary stories in descriptions of old men bent double over the fire' (note after l. 16 of *At the Hawk's Well* [1917]); also see *On Baile's Strand* (1904), l. 228.

II 5 *dreepy*: droopy.

A Prayer for Old Age

Yeats quoted this poem at the end of his Preface to *The King of the Great Clock Tower*: fearing that he had lost his ability to write, he had taken the text of his play to Ezra Pound; 'Next day his judgment came and that in a single word "Putrid"' (*VP*, p. 856). In this poem Yeats rejects an old age of dignity and respectability – his poetry must be ruled by passion and folly, not by the opinions of others, even Pound's. The fool's superiority to the wise man is an old theme of Yeats's – see especially *The Hour-Glass* (1914).

4 *Thinks in a marrow-bone*: for the theme of the Thinking Body, see 'To a Young Beauty', l. 18; also compare 'The Arrow', ll. 1-2: 'this arrow, / Made out of a wild thought, is in my marrow'; 'Three Things', l. 2: '*Sang a bone*'; and 'The Wild Old Wicked Man', l. 41: 'Things hid in their marrow bones'.

7 *O what am I*: compare 'Stream and Sun at Glendalough', l. 7: 'But what am I'.

9 *I pray*: for other prayers, see 'A Prayer on going into my House'.

12 *A foolish, passionate man*: compare the endings of 'The Dawn' and 'The Fisherman', and the personae Yeats used in 'The Wild Old Wicked Man' and 'The Spur'.

Church and State

The original title was 'A Vain Hope'. This is a strong expression of the poet's anti-democratic sentiments: he wishes for a church and a state that retain authority; but he finds a church and a state that have identified themselves with the mob they ought to control.

11–12 *Wine shall run thick ... Bread taste sour*: compare 'The Black Tower', l. 3: 'wine gone sour'. These images of a perverted Eucharist fit the modern church's perversion of responsibility. In the following sequence of poems, the *Supernatural Songs*, Yeats imagines a Christian church more to his taste.

SUPERNATURAL SONGS

These attempts at expressing the inexpressible, or naturalizing the supernatural, differ from some earlier attempts, such as 'Byzantium', in two ways. The first is their explicitly Christian character. Indeed Yeats suggested that these poems were inspired by fantasies of primitive Christianity:

> I associated early Christian Ireland with India; Shri Purohit Swami, protected during his pilgrimage to a remote Himalyan shrine by a strange great dog that disappeared when danger was past, might have been that blessed Cellach who sang upon his deathbed of bird and beast ... every civilization began, no matter what its geographical origin, with Asia ... Saint Patrick must have found in Ireland, for he was not its first missionary, men whose Christianity had come from Egypt, and retained characteristics of those older faiths ... I would consider Ribh, were it not for his ideas about the Trinity, an orthodox man. (*VP*, pp. 837-38)

Similarly Yeats wrote that, in early Irish Christianity, 'Christ was still the half-brother of Dionysus' (*EI*, p. 514). In 1895 the young Yeats hoped to integrate the 'radical truths of Christianity to those of a more ancient world' (*Mem*, p. 124); and in these poems the elderly Yeats tried to display a transcendental strangeness half Hindu, half Christian – the essential shudder that lies at the root of all religions. Ribh can be imagined as Oisin and St Patrick (from *The Wanderings of Oisin*) combined into one persona – one of the many collapses of dialectic visible near the end of Yeats's career.

The second difference lies in their eroticism. In 'Byzantium' Yeats identified the supernatural with purity and flame, the natural with sexuality and water; but in these poems supernatural beings enjoy a kind of sexual intercourse keener and more involved than any possible on earth. The famous motto of Hermes Trismegistus – 'The things below are as the things above' (*EI*, p. 146) – is literalized into a complete sexualizing of the supernatural.

Poems III, IV, VII, and VIII were added to the sequence after its first printing.

I. Ribh at the Tomb of Baile and Aillinn

Baile and Aillinn were ideal lovers who perfected their love in death – '*never yet / Has lover lived, but longed to wive / Like them that are no more alive*' (*Baile and Aillinn*, ll. 205–7). To Ribh, spiritual revelation comes not from Agape but from Eros. A prose draft appears in a letter to Olivia Shakespear: 'a monk reads his breviary at midnight upon the tomb of long-dead lovers on the anniversary of their death, for on that night they are united above the tomb, their embrace being not partial but a conflagration of the entire body and so shedding the light he reads by' (*L*, p. 824). This story is related to the plot of one of Yeats's favourite Noh plays, the *Nishikigi*, where 'ghost-lovers ... come to the priest after death to be married' (*EI*, p. 232); but here it is the lovers who sanctify the priest, not vice-versa. This blank-verse poem is the least songlike of the *Supernatural Songs*; it is a short dramatic monologue, with certain features (elderly speaker, book, instruction to posterity) in common with 'The Gift of Harun Al-Rashid'.

8 *juncture of the apple and the yew*: 'poets found, old writers say, / A yew tree where his body lay; / But a wild apple hid the grass / with its sweet blossom where hers was' (*Baile and Aillinn*, ll. 187–90). Compare the entangled roots of the bushes growing from the tombs of Lady, Lover, and Chambermaid at the end of 'The Three Bushes'.

9 *speak what none have heard*: Ribh tries to speak the nearly unspeakable throughout the sequence – see III 1. He assumes that everyone knows the story of Baile and Aillinn; he will offer an occult sequel to the tale.

14 *whole is joined to whole*: compare the sexual bliss of the dead in *The King of the Great Clock Tower* (1935), ll. 6–8: 'lad and lass, / Nerve touching nerve upon that happy ground, / Are bobbins where all time is bound and wound'. The source of these images is probably Blake's *Jerusalem* (1804) 69:43–44: 'Embraces are Cominglings: from the Head even to the Feet; / And not a pompous High Priest entering by a Secret Place'. Also see 'Crazy Jane and Jack the Journeyman', l. 5: 'love is but a skein'.

15–16 *the intercourse of angels is a light / Where ... both seem lost, consumed*: the dead 'make love in that union which Swedenborg has said is of the whole body and seems from far off an incandescence ... [they run together] and yet without loss of identity' (*M*, p. 356); 'the sexual intercourse of the angels is a conflagration of the whole being' (*L*, p. 805; compare *Ex*, p. 245). Also compare the divine love-conflagration of Aengus and Caer in *The Old Age of Queen Maeve*, ll. 143–44: 'two lovers came out of the air / With bodies made out of soft fire'.

27 *my holy book*: Ribh's breviary; but this book also recalls the 'tablets of thin board, / Made of the apple and the yew' (*Baile and Aillinn*, ll. 195–96), on which poets wrote all known love stories.

II. Ribh denounces Patrick

The poem enlarges and modifies the contrast in 'Byzantium' between self-begetting ('flames begotten of flame', l. 27) and normal sexual reproduction ('Those images that yet / Fresh images beget', ll. 38–39). Ribh claims that these two modes of generation, the supernatural and the natural, are more similar than they appear: both are erotic, even frenzied, although supernatural generation travels on a closed circuit, leads to no increase, no multiplication of entities in the universe. Yeats quoted ll. 4–10 in a letter to Olivia Shakespear, and commented, 'The point of the poem is that we beget and bear because of the incompleteness of our love' (*L*, p. 824). The metre – long-breathed tercets ringed with a single rhyme – is that of part VII and of 'Blood and the Moon' II. The original title was 'Ribh Prefers an Older Theology'.

1–2: these lines vexed Yeats. The first printing reads, 'Abstractions of the Greek philosophy have crazed the man, / Recall his Trinity. A father, mother, child (a daughter or a son)' (*VP*, p. 556); a version sent to Scribner's around 1937, for a proposed edition, reads, 'An abstract Greek absurdity has crazed the man, / A Trinity that is wholly masculine. Man, woman, child (daughter or son)' (Finneran, *PNE*, p. 284). The man in l. 1 is Patrick.

2 *that masculine Trinity*: Father, Son, and Holy Ghost, all male – the concept of trinity promoted by the early Greek church fathers, still accepted by the orthodox.

2 *Man, woman, child*: Ribh's heretical version of the trinity, sexually dimorphic. D. H. Lawrence had a similar notion of trinity – see 'Glad Ghosts' (*Short Stories* III, p. 690).

4 *Natural and supernatural with the self-same ring are wed*: 'I am convinced that in two or three generations it will become generally known that the mechanical theory has no reality, that the natural and supernatural are knit together ... Europeans may find something attractive in a Christ posed against a background not of Judaism but of Druidism' (*EI*, p. 518). For an opposing view, see the 1927 version of *The Resurrection*, ll. 383-89, where a character tries to deny the bodily nature of Christ by saying, 'There can be no contact ... between the corruptible and the incorruptible, and to suggest that God was born of a woman, that He lay in her womb, that she fed Him upon her breast ... is the most terrible blasphemy' (*VPl*, p. 924). Ribh, by contrast, insists on the superior carnality of Godhead.

6 *the Great Smaragdine Tablet*: Hermes Trismegistus, the legendary magician who wrote the Cabbala, was said to have written '"The things below are as the things above"' on an 'Emerald tablet' (*EI*, p. 146).

7 *all increase their kind*: 'And God blessed them, saying, Be fruitful, and multiply' (Genesis 1:22).

8 *When the conflagration of their passion sinks*: Ribh suggests that child-bearing is the result of the incompleteness of orgasm – if passion were perfect we would regenerate ourselves instead of populating the world with defective copies. Compare the Severed Head's derision of ordinary sex in *The King of the Great Clock Tower* (1935), ll 131–32, 138–39: 'Clip and lip and long for more, / Mortal men our abstracts are ... Crossed fingers there in pleasure can / Exceed the nuptial bed of man'.

10 *The mirror-scalèd serpent*: in *John Sherman* (1891), an ornate room begins to 'glimmer like the strange and chaotic colours the mystic Blake imagined upon the scaled serpent of Eden' (*JSD*, p. 97; on p. 135 Finneran identifies Blake's picture as *Satan Watches Adam and Eve*, an illustration to Book IV of *Paradise Lost*); in 'The Twisting of the Rope' (1892), 'it seemed as though the rope of human sorrows changed in his [Hanrahan's] dreams into a vast serpent coiling about him ... till it filled the whole earth and the heavens, and the stars became the glistening of its scales' (*VSR*, p. 204). Multiplicity, then, to Ribh, is Satanic, giddy, suffocating, compared to the simplicity of God. See IV 2, 'There all the serpent-tails are bit'; and the dragons listed in the note to 'The Poet pleads with the Elemental Powers', l. 4. For other references to mirrors, see 'The Two Trees', l. 21.

10 *multiplicity*: compare 'The Coming of Wisdom with Time', l. 1: 'Though leaves are many, the root is one' (in a context suggesting that multiplicity is illusion, unity real).

12 *beget or bear themselves*: for the theme of self-begetting, see 'A Prayer for my Daughter', ll. 67–68. Also compare *The Herne's Egg* (1938) VI 160–64: 'I lay with the Great Herne [God], and he, / Being all a spirit, but begot / His image in the mirror of my spirit, / Being all sufficient to himself / Begot himself'; and 'Ribh in Ecstasy', ll. 5–6.

III. Ribh in Ecstasy

In I, Ribh's text was illuminated by divine sexuality; in II, Ribh developed a theory about it; in this song, he participates in it, at least for a moment.

1 *you understood no word*: compare 'Words', l. 2: 'My darling cannot understand'; and 'Beautiful Lofty Things', l. 6: 'high nonsensical words'.

4 *All happiness in its own cause*: Ribh's soul thus imitates the divine reflexivity – for the theme of self-begetting, see 'A Prayer for my Daughter', ll 67–68.

5–6 *Godhead on Godhead in sexual spasm begot / Godhead*: note the sentence's imitative form: subject, indirect object, and direct object form a circle, a serpent with its tail in its mouth. (A similar rhetoric is found in 'The Statues', l. 22: 'Mirror on mirror mirrored'.) Compare *The Herne's Egg* (1938) VI 160–64, quoted in the note to 'Ribh denounces Patrick', l. 12.

IV. There

This gnomic poem offers four metaphors for the unity into which all discords and antitheses ultimately resolve themselves. For a less triumphant quatrain on the gyres, see the note to 'The Gyres', l. 22.

1 *There all the barrel-hoops are knit*: a startlingly homely image (like many of Yeats's images of the supernatural) of the point of intersection of all the universe's crystalline spheres. According to Plato's *Republic*, the spindle of Necessity is girded like a trireme – see the note to 'His Bargain', l. 1. Compare XII 1: 'Civilisation is hooped together'. Also compare *Where There is Nothing* (1902) V 457–64: 'I will not go out beyond Saturn into the dark. ... O plunge me into the wine barrel, into the wine barrel of God'.

2 *serpent-tails are bit*: the serpent with its tail in its mouth is an old emblem of eternity, or of the eternal recurrence of temporal things; Yeats sometimes used it as a figure for the progress of poetry: 'If it be true that God is a circle whose centre is everywhere, the saint goes to the centre, the poet and the artist to the ring where everything comes round again ... the poet has made his home in the serpent's mouth' (*EI*, pp. 287–88); '[in the Renaissance] poetry [was] moving towards elaboration and intellect, as ours – the serpent's tooth in his own tail again – moves towards simplicity and instinct' (*EI*, p. 356). Also see II 10 ('The mirror-scalèd serpent'); and *The Unicorn from the Stars* (1908) I 408–10, where a character speaks of the enchantment of wandering: 'The roads are the great things, they never come to an end. They are the same as the serpent having his tail swallowed in his own mouth' (compare *Where There is Nothing* [1902] I 359).

3 *There all the gyres converge in one*: 'the gyre or cone ... is in reality a sphere, though to Man, bound to birth and death, it can never seem so, and ... it is the antinomies that force us to find it a cone. Only one symbol exists, though the reflecting mirrors make many appear and all different' (*AV*, p. 240).

4 *There all the planets drop in the Sun*: compare 'All Souls' Night', l. 56, where the soul is whirled about 'Until it plunge into the sun'; and a deleted passage from the end of *Where There is Nothing* (1902 version): 'I will go into the sun, for God is in the heart of it, where the flame burns up everything' (*VPl*, p. 1164). As Whitaker notes (*SS*, p. 118), 'There' is the term Plotinus used (in MacKenna's translation) for the Divine Sphere: 'the sun, There, is all the stars; and every star, again, is all the stars and sun' (*Enneads* I, 125). Compare also the old Hermetic formula that God is a circle whose centre is everywhere and whose circumference nowhere (compare *EI*, p. 287). Elsewhere Yeats wrote that, in Indian astronomy, the moon and the sun alternately swallow each other (*EI*, p. 470).

V. Ribh considers Christian Love insufficient

This poem grew out of a passage of Mrs Yeats's automatic writing (17 Oct. 1933): Dionertes (a Communicator) said to Yeats, '"hate God", we must hate all ideas concerning God that we possess ... if we did not absorption in God would be impossible' (Ellmann, *IY*, p. 283; Bradford, *YW*, p. 135). First Ribh recommends hatred of the things of this world, as a stage in the soul's detachment, an anticipation of the purgation of the dead; then he recommends hatred of God – or, more exactly, hatred of one's conception of God, for every image must be a falsification of imageless truth.

4 *a passion in my own control*: Ribh's insistence on his private mastery of spiritual events recalls that of the proud Judas in *Calvary* (1920).

5 *A sort of besom that can clear the soul*: compare 'Nineteen Hundred and Nineteen' III 22–23: 'a rage / To end all things'.

6 *everything that is not mind*: compare 'Blood and the Moon' II 18: 'Everything that is not God'.

16–17 *Thought is a garment ... trash and tinsel*: compare XII 3: 'man's life is thought'; and 'Michael Robartes and the Dancer', l. 6: 'The half-dead dragon was her thought'. Ribh's metaphor suggests that every metaphor that tries to represent the divine is futile – compare the Commandment, 'Thou shalt not make unto thee any graven image' (Exodus 20:4). Also compare *The King of the Great Clock Tower* (1935), l. 4, where an attendant sings of a lover dwelling in a paradise that is all dancing and no thinking: 'No thought has he, and therefore has no words'. Bloom (*Yeats*, p. 413) compares Blake's *Milton* 41 [48]:3–6: 'To cast off Rational Demonstration by Faith in the Saviour / To cast off the rotten rags of Memory by Inspiration / To cast off Bacon, Locke & Newton from Albion's covering / To take off his filthy garments, & clothe him with Imagination'.

18: this line originally read, 'In hating God she may creep close to God' (*VP*, p. 558).

19 *At stroke of midnight*: compare IX 8.

23 *What can she know*: compare 'Leda and the Swan', l. 13: 'Did she put on his knowledge'.

24 *How can she live till in her blood He live*: in ll. 16–18 Ribh denounces every conception of God; but here he suggests the soul can herself be a kind of embodiment of God. Compare Yeats's sentence, 'Man can embody truth but he cannot know it' (*L*, p. 922).

VI. He and She

Yeats included a draft of this poem in a letter to Olivia Shakespear, and commented 'It is of course my centric myth' (*L*, p. 829) – that is, the myth of *A Vision*, according to which the soul's progress is correlated to the phases of the moon. In IV 4 Ribh imagined a condition in which all planets collapsed into the sun; but here he imagines the usual astronomical stresses of the universe, presented as a dialectic of man and woman, flirting and consummating. The soul (the lunar *She*) approaches towards and retreats from the intolerable light of God (the solar *He*). For other personifications of sun and moon, see 'Under the Round Tower', l. 13: 'golden king and silver lady'.

1–2 *As the moon sidles up / Must she sidle up*: compare 'The Cat and the Moon', ll. 1–2.

3 *As trips the scared moon*: in a 1910 draft of *The Player Queen*, Decima says of Septimus, 'I'd have him think of me all day / And all the night until the scared moon fled / Before his desperate thoughts, and the male sun / Sprang out of bed' (Bradford, *WPQ*, p. 213).

3–6: these lines describe the *primary* phases, the waning of the moon.

8 *I am I, am I*: compare God's name, 'I AM THAT I AM' (Exodus 3:14); also see the note to XII. In ll. 7–12 the waxing soul is approaching Godhead.

VII. What Magic Drum?

This poem may be an attempt to imagine the divine sexual act in which 'Godhead on Godhead in sexual spasm begot / Godhead' (III 5–6). The poet seems deliberately to confuse the reference of the pronouns, suggesting that the participants are little differentiated – God is at once the father, the mother, and the child, caught in a frenzy of self-begetting, an act that is simultaneously coitus, masturbation, and suckling. For the metre, see III.

3 *Drinking joy as it were milk*: for the related pleasures of nursing and intercourse, see 'Three Things' and 'Lullaby'.

4 *what magic drum?*: compare 'A Prayer for my Daughter', l. 15: 'a frenzied drum'.

6 *beast*: compare the apocalyptic animals in the note to 'The Second Coming', l. 21: 'what rough beast'.

6 *its*: the pronominal change from *he* to *it* may suggest the alienness of God from the human mind's categories.

VIII. Whence Had They Come?

In this poem Ribh announces that human sexual response, even the humblest and most intimate, is controlled by superhuman forces – just as, in the preceding poems, Ribh described the eroticism of the divine, so here he describes the divinity of the erotic. This poem universalizes 'Leda and the Swan' – it beholds every sexual act, not just one per millennium, as a kind of divine rape. Zeus seizes Leda from within, by manipulating her appetite, not from outside by force. According to *A Vision*, the Freudian superego is nothing more than the sexual revulsion inspired by unborn spirits who are trying to avoid getting conceived (p. 235) – our sexual lives are in every respect governed by agents of whom we are completely ignorant.

3 *'For ever and for ever'*: Michael Robartes spoke of lovers 'Exhausted by the cry that it [love] can never end' (*AV*, p. 40).

4 *Dramatis Personae*: compare the narrator's dream in 'Rosa Alchemica' (1896): 'I seemed to be a mask . . . Many persons, with eyes so bright and still that I knew them for more than human, came in and tried me on their faces, but at last flung me into a corner' (*M*, pp. 286–87; in *Ex*, p. 56 Yeats spoke of spirits who become 'the *dramatis personae* of our dreams'). Also compare 'the personifying spirits that we had best call but Gates and Gatekeepers, because through their dramatic power they bring our souls to crisis, to Mask and Image, caring not a straw whether we be Juliet going to her wedding, or Cleopatra to her death; for in their eyes nothing has weight but passion' (*A: HC* 9). In *A Vision* (1925), p. 243, Yeats described the continual intervention of spirits in human life: 'the man must receive a violent shock from some crisis created by supernatural dramatisation'. And in 'A Bronze Head', l. 23, Yeats wondered whether Maud Gonne was herself manipulated by a Dramatis Persona in a supernatural theatre: 'a sterner eye looked through her eye'.

7 *The Flagellant*: as in some other poems in this volume, Yeats uses a metaphor of sexual deviation to describe the inspiration for great events; all historical change is the result of a secret sexual drama.

10 *beat down frigid Rome*: compare XII 8: 'good-bye, Rome!' Yeats wrote that Roman civilization was 'rigid and stationary, men fight for centuries with the same sword and spear' (*AV*, p. 277).

12 *world-transforming Charlemagne*: Charlemagne (742–812) is here taken as the demigod of the gyre that undid the classical civilization of Rome. The mathematics of *A Vision* would have conveniently assimilated him if he had flourished around AD 1000; but Charlemagne was crowned emperor in 800, and *A Vision* pointedly avoids discussion of him (p. 283).

IX. The Four Ages of Man

This poem attempts an extreme compression of the symbolic scheme of *A Vision*: in fact it versifies a chart published in *A Vision*, p. 102. Yeats quoted a draft of this poem in a letter to Olivia Shakespear, and added, 'They are the four ages of individual man, but they are also the four ages of civilization' (*L*, p. 826). Yeats also sent Mrs Shakespear some tables of correspondences between the elements, the organs of the body, the faculties of the mind, and history (*L*, pp. 823–25), which may be summarized as follows:

Earth	bowels	Instinct	Early nature-dominated civilization
Water	blood, sex organ	Passion	An armed sexual age, chivalry
Air	lungs	Thought	From Renaissance to end of 19th century
Fire		Soul	The purging away of our civilization by our hatred

Furthermore, these also correspond to the four quarters of the lunar month: first, Phases 1–8, the soul's disengagement from nature, its emerging strength; second, Phases 9–15, the soul's perfection of imagination; third, Phases 16–22, the soul's attempt to master the world through reason, and its compromises with the world; fourth, Phases 23–28, the soul's dismissal of world and reason, its absorption into God.

8 *At stroke of midnight*: compare V 19, and 'Broken Dreams', l. 39.

8 *God shall win*: compare 'The Rose of Battle' (original title: 'They went forth to the Battle, but they always fell'), l. 33: 'defeated in His [God's] wars'.

X. Conjunctions

Like the previous poem, this tries to concentrate the mysteries of *A Vision*. According to its peculiar astrology, the conjunction of the planets Jupiter and Saturn was a signal of an *antithetical* age – in fact Yeats quoted the first two lines of this poem at the end of *A Vision* (p. 302) to illustrate the *antithetical*, aristocratic, violent age that was about to replace the present Christian period, tame and democratic. Similarly, the Mars-Venus conjunction heralded a *primary* age. Yeats built some of this symbolism into 'The Double Vision of Michael Robartes' – see the note to II 2–3.

But these conjunctions also had a personal meaning for Yeats: he quoted this poem in a letter to Olivia Shakespear as a kind of commentary on the characters of his son and daughter – Anne was a 'Mars-Venus personality', Michael a Jupiter-Saturn personality: 'whereas Michael is always thinking about life Anne always thinks of death ... Anne collects skeletons ... When she grows up she will ... have some passionate love affair ... the old association of love and death' (*L*, p. 828).

2 *mummy wheat*: see 'On a Picture of a Black Centaur ...', l. 7. The poet means that the long-extinct *antithetical* age is about to sprout again.

3 *The sword's a cross*: Mars' sword is modified into the crucifix, symbol of the passing *primary* age. Yeats quoted a draft of ll. 3–4, together with 'Symbols', ll. 5–6, in a letter to Dorothy Wellesley, to illustrate how 'war and women ... have always gone together' (*DWL*, p. 33).

XI. A Needle's Eye

For related images of the invisible and nearly unimaginable origin of natural phenomena, see 'His Bargain', l. 1: 'Plato's spindle'; and the quatrain on nothingness printed in the notes to 'The Gyres'.

2 *Came out of a needle's eye*: compare 'Veronica's Napkin', ll. 5–6: 'the magnitude and glory there / Stood in the circuit of a needle's eye'. Also compare Tennyson, *In Memoriam* LXXVI 3–4: 'Where all the starry heavens of space / Are sharpened to a needle's end'; and *Cymbeline* I iii 19. In 1934 AE (alluding to Christ's comparison of the rich man and the camel [Matthew 19:24]) wrote to Yeats, 'I am trying to qualify to pass through the gate which is narrow as the needles eye & I would stick if I had a bulky mind' (*LTY* II, p. 565).

XII. Meru

Meru is the old name of a mountain in Tibet – the 'Golden Peak' of Yeats's early poem 'Anashuya and Vijaya', l. 68, may be the same mountain. In 1934 Yeats wrote an introduction to his friend Shri Purohit Swāmi's translation of *The Holy Mountain* [that is, Mount Meru], an account of a Hindu holy man's ascent into world-renouncing and self-dispossessing: 'Shri Purohit Swāmi ... refused to accompany his friend, who had ... been ordered to seek *Turiyā* ... at Mount Kailās, the legendary Meru; he thought himself unworthy, that he had not freed himself from the world, and could but carry it upon the journey' (*EI*, p. 453). Yeats defined *Turiyā* as 'pure and unimpeded personality, all existence brought into the words: "I am"' (*EI*, p. 462 – compare VI 8: 'I am I, am I'; also Coleridge's definition of imagination as 'a repetition in the finite mind of the eternal act of creation in the infinite I AM' [*Biographia Literaria* XIII]). Yeats conceived Mount Meru as a kind of exit-point from the reincarnative cycles, from the phenomenal world: the sage can 'find some cavern upon Meru, and so pass out of all life' (*EI*, p. 469).

The climax of the 'Supernatural Songs' shows how a naked man can undo the whole fabric of nature, attain such a pitch of disillusionment that supernature is apparent, palpable. Yeats was aware that he was at a verge beyond which all art is vain: 'One remembers the Japanese philosopher's saying, "What the artist perceives through a medium, the saint perceives immediately"' (*EI*, p 462).

1 *Civilisation is hooped together*: compare IV 1: 'There all the barrel-hoops are knit'.

2–3 *the semblance of peace / By manifold illusion*: compare 'Nineteen Hundred and Nineteen' I 9–24, which describes the precarious 'pretty toys' of Western government and law.

5–6 *Ravening ... Ravening*: the state of enlightenment just prior to *Turiyā* is known as the 'ravening tongue ... the man has disappeared as the ... musician into his music' (*EI*, p. 462).

3 *man's life is thought*: compare V 16: 'Thought is a garment'.

7 *the desolation of reality*: see 'Ego Dominus Tuus', l. 48, where Dowson and Lionel Johnson dissipate their lives in order to attain a 'vision of reality'.

8 *good-bye, Rome!*: compare VIII 10.

11 *winter's dreadful blast*: compare 'A Dialogue of Self and Soul' II 16: 'the wintry blast'.

NEW POEMS (1938)

In the 1920s Yeats wrote many poems about political and historical process, from the point of view of suffering mankind; but in the mid-1930s the predominant emotion is not weeping but laughter – an Olympian, half-sublime, half-coarse joviality, akin to the mood of some of Beethoven's later piano sonatas. There is a calculated buffoonery in many of these poems – just as Yeats took pleasure from converting the lofty mythology of *A Vision* into the farce of *The Player Queen* (1922), so he relished describing himself as a 'Wild Old Wicked Man'. The poet seems to sympathize less with Leda, helplessly caught in the coils of history, than with Zeus, travelling through the world in outlandish disguises to satisfy his appetites. The elegiac note is still present, in such poems as 'The Municipal Gallery Re-visited', near the end of this volume; but grief, desperation, rabble-rousing enthusiasm (in such poems as 'Come Gather Round Me Parnellites') all commingle in that strangest of feelings, tragic joy.

The first two poems in this volume expound the concept of tragic joy. This famous oxymoron can be defined as what a man feels when he feels at once everything that he is capable of feeling – a hypothetical apex of emotion comparable to what Freud called the oceanic experience. The doctrine of tragic joy grows out of the more general theme of inappropriate joy or the joy of loss – its antecedents in Yeats's work include the odd blessedness felt by fools and the dispossessed (such as the 'aimless joy' of 'Tom O'Roughley', l. 4, and the self-benediction delivered in the ditch, at the end of 'A Dialogue of Self and Soul'); the general bonfire built by Martin at the end of Act II of *The Unicorn from the Stars* (1908) – 'All nature destroys and laughs'; the 'lonely impulse of delight' felt at the prospect of the plane-crash in 'An Irish Airman Foresees His Death'; and the metaphysical satyriasis of the poems of the previous volume (see its headnote).

The phrase 'tragic joy' appeared in a 1904 *Samhain*, where it already had the sense of unearthly repletion and detachment: tragic heroes 'seek for a life growing always more scornful of everything that is not itself and passing into its own fullness . . . and attaining that fullness, perfectly it may be – and from this is tragic joy and the perfectness of tragedy – when the world itself has slipped away in death' (*Ex*, p. 170). Elsewhere in that publication Yeats argued that the tragic emotion is beyond 'moral judgments': 'This character who delights us may commit murder like Macbeth . . . or betray his country like Coriolanus, and yet we will rejoice in every happiness that comes to him and sorrow at his death as if it were our own' (*Ex*, p. 154).

Tragic joy comprises several aspects:

(1) A fearful optimism about the *antithetical* era to come at AD 2000 – hideous violence will destroy the poet's world, but recreate a hierarchical, aesthetic civilization that cherishes what the poet cherishes. When Yeats wrote that he imagined 'always at my left side just out of the range of the sight, a brazen winged beast that I associated with laughing, ecstatic destruction' (*Ex*, p. 393), he meant it as prophecy of the next age.

(2) The joy of perfecting oneself, the delight in the full exercise of all one's faculties, only possible in the confrontation with irresistible fate, and therefore most likely to be achieved at the point of death. 'The hero [finds his mask] in defeat . . . nor has a shoulder used all its might that an unbreakable gate has never strained' (*M*, p. 337).

(3) The joy of superseding oneself, of passing away, of identifying oneself with the whole human race or with something impersonal, superhuman. Yeats believed that 'character is continuously present in comedy alone', whereas 'tragedy must always be a drowning and breaking of the dykes that separate man from man' (*EI*, pp. 240–41) – the tragic emotion destroys personality, instead of affirming it. This loss of ego is related to the feeling that one has become a mask worn by an actor in some unearthly drama. In fact, at the limit of feeling there is a convergence between (2) and (3): Yeats wrote that the words of Shakespeare's heroes 'move us because their sorrow is not their own at tomb or asp, but for all men's fate. That shaping joy has kept the sorrow pure . . . for the nobleness of the arts is in the mingling

of contraries, the extremity of sorrow, the extremity of joy, perfection of personality, the perfection of its surrender' (*EI*, p. 255).

(4) An exhilaration discovered in destruction, because destruction and creation are the inseparable halves of one process – 'every act of war is an act of creation' (*CEAV [1925]*, Notes, p. 66). Yeats's most notable expression of this unity is a draft of the third part of 'Under Ben Bulben':

when all words are said
And a man is fighting mad,
Something drops from eyes long blind,
He recovers his whole mind,
For an instant stands at ease,
Laughs aloud and seems at peace.
Even the wisest man grows tense
With some sort of violence
Before he can accomplish fate
Know his work or choose his mate
So what's the odds if war must come
From Moscow, from Berlin, or Rome.
Let children should an aeroplane
Some neighbouring city pavement stain,
Or Should the deafening cannon sound
Clasp their hands & dance in a round.
The passing moment makes it sweet
When male & female organ meet
(Stallworthy, *VR*, pp. 163–64)

In this passage, revelation of life's purpose, bombs falling, children at play, and orgasm all converge.

(5) A foretaste of the *Beatitude* experienced by the dead, as they attain integrity and oblivion (*AV*, p. 232). Tragic joy is the emotion felt by a man who glimpses the sphere on the other side of all the gyres of life.

(6) The rapture of inspiration, in which the artist is suddenly placed in immediate contact with his grandest themes: 'There is in the creative joy an acceptance of what life brings, because we have understood the beauty of what it brings, or a hatred of death for what it takes away, which arouses within us, through some sympathy perhaps with all other men, an energy so noble, so powerful, that we laugh aloud and mock, in the terror or the sweetness of our exaltation, at death and oblivion' (*EI*, p. 322). 'In ruin, poetry calls out in joy, / Being the scattering hand, the bursting pod ... God's laughter at the shattering of the world' (*The King's Threshold* [1904], ll. 186-89). Several poems (including 'An Acre of Grass', 'The Wild Old Wicked Man', and 'The Spur') in this volume are prayers for some enabling frenzy or sacred rage, models for stimulating inspiration.

(7) The discovery of dramatic form in ordinary life. The purpose of art, in a sense, is to induce its audience to a shiver of tragic joy; and the drama is particularly well suited, in that it stimulates its spectators to conceive their own lives as a tragic drama. 'The arts are all the bridal chambers of joy. No tragedy is legitimate unless it leads some great character to his final joy' (*Ex*, p. 448). 'The heroes of Shakespeare convey ... the sudden enlargement of their vision, their ecstasy at the approach of death: "She should have died hereafter" [*Macbeth* V v 17], "Of many thousand kisses, the poor last" [*Antony and Cleopatra* IV xv 20], "Absent thee from felicity awhile" [*Hamlet* V ii 358]. They have become God or Mother Goddess... but all must be cold; no actress has ever sobbed when she played Cleopatra ... The supernatural is present, cold winds blow across our hands, upon our faces, the thermometer falls ... I have heard Lady Gregory say ... "Tragedy must be a joy to the man who dies" ... imagination must dance, must be carried beyond feeling into the aboriginal ice' (*EI*, pp. 522–23; compare also *Ex*, p. 163). Tragic joy, then, is a feeling that reaches 'beyond feeling' into the artifice of eternity, the theatre of eternity. To feel it fully entails a kind of transfiguration – 'He who attains Unity of Being ... may even love tragedy' (*AV* [1925], p. 28).

Of course such a pan-sensible feeling cannot last long; and the emotions discovered in the later poems in this volume can be construed as elements generated by the decomposition of tragic joy.

The Gyres

This poem greets the spectacle of civilization's ruin with wild imperatives, interjections, and exclamation marks, as if the poet were determined to outshout the Delphic Oracle. The original title was 'What Matter' – and indeed the poem dismisses all nostalgia and concern for safety in a paean to the irresistible energies of historical change. The gyres of the title are the spinning cones that govern the patterns of recurrence among the millennia – see Introduction XI. This poem is an ode to the whirlwind.

1 *Old Rocky Face*: 'Delphic Oracle', according to a gloss in Mrs Yeats's annotated copy of *Last Poems* (Bradford, *YW*, p. 148) – compare Septimus' allusion in *The Player Queen* (1922) to Delphi as 'that cold, rocky oracle' (II 543), an oracle whose too-chaste counsel he is determined to correct; see also 'The Delphic Oracle upon Plotinus'. Also compare 'Man and the Echo', l. 37: 'O rocky voice', in which the poet addresses an echo of his own voice from a cleft – and the oracle in this poem also may be an echo (ll. 15–16).

2 *Things thought too long can be no longer thought*: compare Pound, Canto 25 (1930): 'what we thought had been thought for too long' (25/118) – a chorus proceeding from a stone pit.

6 *Empedocles*: the Greek philosopher (*c*. 493-*c*. 433 BC), whom Yeats cited as

a key authority for the doctrine of the gyres: 'According to Simplicius . . . the Concord of Empedocles fabricates all things into "an homogeneous sphere", and then Discord separates the elements and so makes the world we inhabit' (*AV*, p. 67).

7 *Hector*: see 'The Phases of the Moon', l. 46.

8 *tragic joy*: see the headnote to this volume.

9 *What matter*: see 'Parnell's Funeral' I 19.

10 *blood and mire*: see 'Byzantium', l. 24: 'mire or blood'.

11 *let no tear drop*: see 'Lapis Lazuli', l. 15: 'Do not break up their lines to weep'. This line originally read, 'Or that those sweaty gangsters live on top' (*YW*, p. 144).

13–14 *For painted forms or boxes of make-up / In ancient tombs I sighed, but not again*: the images and dramatis personae of antiquity are starting to become faintly real, to make themselves felt, as the new *antithetical* age approaches – compare Pound's 'The Return' (quoted in *AV*, pp. 29–30). The poet does not sigh for the past but anticipates the future.

15–16 *Out of Cavern comes a voice / And all it knows is that one word 'Rejoice'*: the Delphic Oracle was concealed in a rocky cavern, but voice and cavern had other associations for Yeats as well. Yeats sometimes identified his anti-self with a cave-dweller, the Wandering Jew Ahasuerus in Shelley's *Hellas* (1821) – both he and Shelley, Yeats thought, were 'gregarious' men fascinated by 'proud and lonely things' – and Yeats quoted in his *Autobiography* a long passage from *Hellas* (ll. 152–85) describing how those seeking the almost inaccessible Jew would make caverns resound with the name 'Ahasuerus!' (*A: FY* 18). Furthermore, Yeats wrote to AE about Ireland's desperate need for practical wisdom: 'Had some young Greek found Shelley's "Ahasuerus" in that shell strewn cavern, the sage would . . . [have] given I think very simple advice . . . fitted perhaps for the next fifty years' (*L*, pp. 666–67). The oracular voice of this poem, then, may be that of the poet's anti-self, and of the anti-self of the whole sick *primary* millennium, boldly foretelling the headier, more vibrant era that will come after AD 2000.

17 *work grow coarse*: compare 'Under Ben Bulben' V 4: 'out of shape from toe to top' (remarked of modern poems) – a section with several points of similarity to this stanza. Also compare Yeats's description of the servile end of the gyre in 'The Phases of the Moon', l. 94, where body and soul assume 'The coarseness of the drudge'.

22 *rich, dark nothing*: compare 'Fragments' II 3–4: 'Out of nothing it came, / Out of the forest loam'; 'I see Phantoms . . .', ll. 13–14: 'Plunges towards nothing . . . the embrace of nothing'; 'Parnell's Funeral' I 29: 'nothing but the nothings'; and a remarkable quatrain (somewhat similar to 'There'

and 'A Needle's Eye') dated 8 May 1938, unpublished until 1983, which states that the gyres not only originate in nothing but end in it:

> What is the explanation of it all?
> What does it look like to a learned man?
> Nothings in nothings whirled, or when he will
> From nowhere unto nowhere nothings run
> (*Yeats Annual* 5 [1987]: 213)

(Compare a journal entry: 'Life is memory of what has never happened and hope for what never will happen' [*Mem*, p 243]; and Yeats's attraction to the Zen Buddhist philosophy in which nothing is real [*TSMC*, p 68].)

Lapis Lazuli

This poem investigates responses to catastrophe, and artistic representations of it. Three possible responses to the coming of world war are found: the hysteria of the women, the gaiety of the artists, and the calm of the sages. But in fact there are only two alternatives: unfocused dithering and tragic joy – for tragic joy is the ultimate response of both artist and sage Yeats compares the two most disparate models of human life that the world's art can offer – Shakespearean tragedy and a Chinese stone-carving; one hectic, busy, ranting, extravagant, the other tranquil, static, abstracted; one a representation of suffering, the other a refuge from it. And yet, they converge on a single vision. The emotion is the same for those in the West who are dying, and those in the East who are watching – for the participants and the audience of the tragic play. Indeed the division between actor and spectator breaks down: the tragic hero's roaring ends in an eerie stillness, simplicity; while the stone figures are unexpectedly animated, involved in the general destruction. The lapis lazuli Chinamen resemble the sages in 'Sailing to Byzantium' III 1, in that they seem to hold out to the poet an attractive vision of translation of mankind into art; but they also resemble the Phidian sculptures of 'Nineteen Hundred and Nineteen' I 1–8 in that they lack immunity from time's ravaging. In 'Lapis Lazuli' the barrier between art and life starts to crumble, and yet art does not appear to lose its potency.

Caption Harry Clifton: a young apprentice-poet who gave to Yeats the lapis lazuli carving as a seventieth-birthday present on 4 July 1935 – 'someone has sent me a present of a great piece carved by some Chinese sculptor into the semblance of a mountain with temple, trees, paths and an ascetic and pupil about to climb the mountain' (*DWL*, p. 8). William H. O'Donnell (*Massachusetts Review* 23 [1982]: 353–54) offers a more exact description: 'This Ch'ien Lung period (1739–1795) "mountain" stands 26.7 cm. (10.5") high ... On the front, three men ascend a mountain path toward a little temple or house. The leader, who is a bearded sage, half turns to face a younger, beardless disciple who follows close behind him. These two men are followed at a respectful distance by a single serving man who carries what may be a lute. The mountain is covered with crags, waterfalls, and pine trees, recognizable by their stylized traditional groups of needles. The mountain scene continues on the back, with more pine trees, a flying crane, and ... a court poem in four, seven-syllable lines'.

1–2 *hysterical women ... are sick of the fiddle-bow*: Whitaker (*SS*, p. 328) compares a passage Yeats wrote in 1908: 'One woman used to repeat as often as possible that to paint pictures or to write poetry in this age was to fiddle while Rome was burning' (*Ex*, p. 239; also see *OBMV*, pp. x-xi).

6 *Aeroplane and Zeppelin*: German Zeppelins bombed London in World War I (*L*, p. 588). Hitler occupied the Rhineland in the year of this poem's composition.

7 *Pitch like King Billy*: a paraphrase of a ballad, 'The Battle of the Boyne', quoted by Jeffares (*NCP*, p. 364): 'King James has pitched his tent between / The lines for to retire / But King William threw his bomb-balls in / And set them all on fire'. (Of course Kaiser Wilhelm, leader of Germany during the Great War, was, like William of Orange, a King Billy.) The odd jocularity of Yeats's line exemplifies the poet's desire to be gay despite all of war's horrors. In an early draft the line about the bomb-balls is followed by more discourse by the 'hysterical women': 'nothing should matter any more / But how to make an end of war / Before populations are blotted out / Galleries museum blown into the air / Civilization beaten flat' (Stallworthy, *VR*, pp. 45–46).

10 *There struts Hamlet, there is Lear*: that is, the ordinary passersby are caught up in a Shakespearean tragedy, of which they may be only half-aware. Not only does Hamlet suffer 'all men's fate' (*EI*, p. 255), but each man suffers Hamlet's – to confront death is to be universalized. The verb *struts* may owe something to the fact that, when Yeats was a boy, he copied the stride of Irving's Hamlet (*A: R* 22). Hamlet is mentioned again as an emaciated intellectual in 'The Statues', l. 19; and Yeats remembered that his father called the dissolute young intellectuals of the 1890s '"the Hamlets of our age"' (*OBMV*, p. x). King Lear will return, as a model for the poet himself, in 'An Acre of Grass', l. 15. Also compare Neville in Woolf's *The Waves* (1931) – a novel Yeats knew: 'It is better ... to read Shakespeare as I read him here in Shaftesbury Avenue. Here's the fool, here's the villain, here in a car comes Cleopatra' (p. 312).

15 *Do not break up their lines to weep*: 'no actress has ever sobbed when she played Cleopatra, even the shallow brain of a producer has never thought of such a thing' (*EI*, p. 523).

16 *Hamlet and Lear are gay*: for the doctrine of tragic joy, see the headnote to this volume.

19 *Black out*: 'it is by the perception of a change [between the sensual and the spiritual], like the sudden "blacking out" of the lights of the stage, that passion creates its most violent sensation' (*A: TG* 13).

19 *Heaven blazing*: compare 'Vacillation' IV 7: 'My body of a sudden blazed'; *Where There is Nothing* (1902) IV ii 268–69: 'When I was meditating, the inside of my head suddenly became all on fire'; and *The Unicorn from the Stars* (1908) II 95–96: 'his head like a blazing tar-barrel'.

29–32 *No handiwork of Callimachus . . . stands*: Yeats considered Callimachus (a sculptor of the fifth century BC) as the leading figure in the movement to Asiatic stylization, following the naturalistic representation of Phidian art (*EI*, p. 225; *AV*, p. 270). For the destruction of Greek art, see 'Nineteen Hundred and Nineteen' I 1–8.

33 *His long lamp-chimney*: 'may one not discover a Persian symbol in that bronze lamp, shaped like a palm [located in the Erechtheum in Athens], known to us by a description in Pausanias? (*AV*, p. 270).

35 *All things fall and are built again*: 'Quae destruxi necesse est omnia reaedificem' (*The Hour-Glass* [1914], l. 346).

44–45 *Every accidental crack or dent / Seems a water-course or an avalanche*: the ravages of time contribute to the carving's aesthetic effect.

47 *plum or cherry-branch*: on the actual carving, all trees are pines.

49–50 *I / Delight to imagine them seated there*: the poet pushes the suggested action on the carving to a conclusion – the stone figures become the characters of an imaginary drama. The distinction between sculpture and theatre, between watcher and participant, breaks down.

52 *On all the tragic scene they stare*: in Arthur Waley's 'The Temple', a translation from Chinese included in Yeats's *OBMV*, a man climbs to a high temple and surveys distant prospects. Also compare *Baile and Aillinn* (1903), l. 168: 'where some huge watcher is'; and Yeats's description of the poet and music critic W. J. Turner: 'the first poet to read a mathematical equation, a musical score, a book of verse, with an equal understanding; he seems to ride in an observation balloon, blue heaven above, earth beneath an abstract pattern' (*OBMV*, p. xxix).

54 *Accomplished fingers begin to play*: see 'To a Friend . . .', ll. 12–14: 'mad fingers play / Amid a place of stone, / Be secret and exult'.

55–56 *Their eyes . . . are gay*: Yeats seems to stress the convergence of the contemplative perspective of the Chinaman and the tragic perspective of those about to be bombed; but in a letter to Dorothy Wellesley about the stone-carving he insisted on the divergence of perspective: 'Ascetic, pupil, hard stone, eternal theme of the sensual east. The heroic cry in the midst of despair. But no, I am wrong, the east has its solutions always and therefore knows nothing of tragedy. It is we, not the east, that must raise the heroic cry' (*DWL*, p. 8).

Imitated from the Japanese

Yeats quoted a draft of this poem in a letter to Dorothy Wellesley: 'I made this poem out of a prose translation of a Japanese Hokku in praise of Spring (*DWL*, p. 116). The source of the original haiku is uncertain.

Sweet Dancer

This poem and 'A Crazed Girl' were inspired by a neurotic poet and actress, Margot Ruddock Collis Lovell (usually known by her maiden name), with whom Yeats was infatuated. He met her in 1934 and coached her in speaking his verse on stage; he wanted her to play the roles of several of his queens, and she did in fact play the real Queen in *The Player Queen* in a London production (*ASD*, pp. 23, 56, 112). In November 1934 he sent her a poem (not published until 1970) entitled 'Margot', in which he marvels at how a young woman's appreciation can glorify his aging body:

I

All famine struck sat I, and then
Those generous eyes on mine were cast,
Sat like other agèd men
Dumbfoundered, gazing on a past
That appeared constructed of
Lost opportunities to love.

II

O how can I that interest hold?
What offer to attentive eyes?
Mind grows young and body old;
When half closed her eye-lid lies
A sort of hidden glory shall
About these stooping shoulders fall.

III

The Age of Miracles renew,
Let me be loved as though still young
Or let me fancy that it's true,

When my brief final years are gone
You shall have time to turn away
And cram those open eyes with day.
(*ASD*, pp. 33–34)

She also sent verse to Yeats, who offered sympathetic criticism.

She suffered a breakdown in 1936, in Barcelona, the day after she visited Yeats in Majorca and read him some of her poems: 'She went out in pouring rain, thought . . . that if she killed herself her verse would live instead of her. Went to the shore to jump in, then thought that she loved life and began to dance . . . [Afterwards in Barcelona she] went mad, climbing out of a window, falling through a baker's roof, breaking a kneecap, hiding in a ship's hold, singing her own poems most of the time. The British consul in Barcelona appealed to me . . . I accepted financial responsibility . . . When her husband wrote it had not been to send money, but to congratulate her on the magnificent publicity' (*L*, p. 856). As in 'A Bronze Head' (concerning Maud Gonne), Yeats passed no clear judgment on the woman's frenzy; it is left open whether the dancer is mad in the psychiatric sense or merely transfigured. Tragic joy, as the extremest of all feelings, may easily terminate in insanity. A draft of this poem is quoted in *DWL*, p. 120.

The Three Bushes

This poem is based on a short unrhymed ballad by Dorothy Wellesley – a matter of lengthy correspondence between her and Yeats (*DWL*, pp. 69–82). The poem fascinated Yeats because of its mysterious sense of the division and collaboration of body and soul in the act of love. It is clear that Dorothy Wellesley was influenced by the myth of Cupid and Psyche, sometimes taken as an allegory of the soul's seduction by erotic love – Cupid made Psyche wear a blindfold so that she could not see her divine lover. Dorothy Wellesley's first stanza (with slight tampering by Yeats) read as follows:

She sent her maid unto the man
   That would her leman be
'O Psyche mimic me at love
   With him I will not lie
'Tis sweetly done, 'tis easy done
   So child make love for me'.
(*DWL*, p. 70)

Just as 'Lapis Lazuli' seeks a state of perfect emotional concentration, synthesized from such contraries as East and West, art and life, so 'The Three Bushes' seeks a state of erotic completeness – a unity of mind and body. The original poem ended with the maid's musing after the death of lady and lover;

Yeats added the intertwining rose-roots over all three graves, symbols of the inextricability of love, body, and soul.

This reworked text itself symbolized to Yeats his own inextricability with Dorothy Wellesley: 'Ah my dear [compare the poem's refrain] how it added to my excitement when I re-made that poem of yours to know it was your poem. I re-made you and myself into a single being. We triumphed over each other and I thought of *The Turtle and the Phoenix*' (*DWL*, p. 82). Shakespeare's 'The Phoenix and the Turtle' discusses the metaphysical oneness of two lovers; it was a 'favourite poem' of Dorothy Wellesley's, and Yeats sent her a book about it (*DWL*, p. 150). For the theme of remaking oneself through art, see 'An Acre of Grass', l. 14.

Caption Michel de Bourdeille: a hoax – in fact the name is probably derived from the French word for hoax, *bourde*; compare also *bordello*.

5 *sing those songs of love*: an early draft makes it clear that the lover is a poet as well as a singer: 'For did you rhyme no more of love / I were to blame young man' (Stallworthy, *VR*, p. 88).

7 *O my dear, O my dear*: in an addendum to *The Hour-Glass* (1914), Yeats translated a Gaelic ballad, the refrain of which is 'O my dear, my dear' (*VP*, p. 779). Also compare 'The Dolls', l. 19: 'My dear, my dear, O dear'.

19–20 *what could I but drop down dead / If I lost my chastity?*: 'The tragedy of sexual intercourse is the perpetual virginity of the soul' (*DWL*, p. 174).

22–23 *you must lie beside him / And let him think me there*: '[someone] said once to George Moore "I wish I had a slave to do this for me. I would not have to think of him afterwards". Your sewing maid gets the same result by being a slave – she had not to think of him afterwards' (*DWL*, p. 81).

24–25: *maybe we are all the same / Where no candles are*: compare *The Player Queen* (1922) II 280–81: 'even I can please a man when there is but one candle' (a gloating line spoken by a man's mistress – a comfortable, physical woman – to his proud beautiful wife; a love-triangle similar to that in 'The Three Bushes').

43–44 *A laughing, crying, sacred song, / A leching song*: compare such oxymorons as 'tragic joy' (see the headnote to this volume).

74–76 *none living can ... Know where its roots began*: compare 'Ribh at the Tomb ...', l. 8: 'juncture of the apple and the yew'. This motif is borrowed from certain versions of the Tristram and Iseult legend, in which a rose and a briar entwine over the dead lovers' grave.

The Lady's First Song

Yeats wrote that this poem was 'supposed to be spoken by the Lady before her two poems addressed to the Chambermaid . . . It is not in itself very good but it will heighten the drama' (*DWL*, p. 105).

2 *Like a dumb beast*: the body seems to assert itself, to revenge itself on the Lady for ignoring it.

The Lady's Second Song

6 *I can strew the sheet*: the Lady's humility and self-abasement – see the preceding poem – have reached such a pitch that she has become her chambermaid's chambermaid.

The Lady's Third Song

3–6: in one draft these lines read, 'If you dare abuse the soul / I must that am his daylight lady / Outrageously abuse the body' (*VR*, p. 100).

10 *A contrapuntal serpent hiss*: during the lover's chaste kisses, the lady feels a counterpoint of unsatisfied sexual desire – just as the chambermaid feels a counterpoint of unsatisfied spiritual yearning during her trysts (l. 12).

12 *labouring*: perhaps a pun.

The Lover's Song

Yeats sent a draft of this to Dorothy Wellesley, and noted that he wrote this poem in order better to explain what he meant by the phrase 'the touch from behind the curtain' (*DWL*, p. 102) in a previous letter, a letter that described reproductions of paintings on his wall: 'Botticelli's "Spring", Gustave Moreau's "Women and Unicorns", Fragonard's "Cup of Life", a beautiful young man and girl running with eager lips towards a cup hel[d] towards them by a winged form. The first & last sense, & the second mystery – the mystery that touches the genitals, a blurred touch through a curtain' (*DWL*, p. 100). If by 'second', Yeats meant the second painting in his list – 'Women and Unicorns' (also described in 'I see Phantoms . . .') – then the 'curtain' might refer to the allegorical disguise of sexual union in Moreau's fantasy of women fondling unicorns. (For other references to touches through curtains, see *UP* I, p. 408: 'a century [the eighteenth] which had set chop-logic in the place of the mysterious power, obscure as a touch from behind a curtain, that had governed "the century of poets" '; and *JSD*, p. 89, where a shallow man is criticized for his inability 'to make his thoughts an allusion to something deeper than themselves. In this he was the reverse of poetical, for poetry is essentially a touch from behind a curtain'.) After quoting this poem, Yeats commented to Wellesley that 'In Fragonard's "Cup of Life" the young man is not in his first youth, his face is lined with thought & that makes that picture too mysterious – a double thirst' (*DWL*, p. 102) – suggesting that the mind's appetites and the body's both seek relief in a woman's love. This poem meditates on the mysterious goal towards which all desires point. Yeats also sent a draft of this poem to another young woman, Ethel Mannin (*L*, p. 867). There are certain parallels between this poem and 'A Drinking Song'.

4 *Now sinks the same rest*: after coition, mind and body are equally sated – in the same way that the bird is exhausted after flight. Compare the Brihadāranyaka-Upanishad: 'But as a falcon or eagle, flying in the sky, wearies, folds its wings, falls into its nest, Self hastens into that sleep, his last resort, where he desires nothing' (*TPU*, pp. 150–51).

The Chambermaid's First Song

When Yeats sent Dorothy Wellesley drafts of this and the next poem, she replied, 'Am much amused about the worm-poem ... but like all women I dislike worms. ... Can you think of something to take the place of the worms?' (*DWL*, p. 106). Yeats, however, refused: 'The "worm" is right, its repulsiveness is right – so are the adjectives – "dull", "limp", "thin", "bare", all suggested by the naked body of the man, & taken with the worm by that body abject & helpless. All suggest her detachment, her "cold breast", her motherlike prayer' (*DWL*, p. 108). Yeats went on to credit Dorothy Wellesley with his new-found ability to write convincing poems using a female persona: 'My dear, my dear – when you crossed the room with that boyish movement, it was no man who looked at you, it was the woman in me. It seems that I can make a woman express herself as never before. I have looked out of her eyes. I have shared her desire' (*DWL*, p. 108; also see pp. 113–14). For Yeats's feeling of consubstantiality with Dorothy Wellesley, see the note to 'The Three Bushes'.

10 *Weak as a worm*: compare 'The Phases of the Moon', l. 49: 'helpless as a worm'.

The Chambermaid's Second Song

See the note to the previous poem.

3: this line originally read, 'His rod, that rose up unfed'; Yeats commented, 'wrongly expressed ... "unfed" being clearly the reverse of true' (*DWL*, pp. 103, 106).

5–6 *His spirit that has fled / Blind as a worm*: this simile of soul and flaccid penis is perhaps Yeats's most daring equation of high and low, in the manner of the Crazy Jane poems. Lady, lover, chambermaid, and poet all contrive to fuse the spiritual and the carnal, seemingly so hopelessly divided. In one draft there were two extra lines before ll. 5–6: 'A shadow has gone to the dead / Thin as a worm' (*DWL*, p. 104).

An Acre of Grass

The setting of this poem is Riversdale, a 'small old house' ('What Then?', l. 12) in Co. Dublin with a garden 'which has some fame among gardeners' (*L*, p. 799), to which the Yeatses moved in 1932, because Thoor Ballylee was far from Dublin, and Lady Gregory's death removed Yeats's incentive for remaining in western Ireland. This is one of many poems in which Yeats contemplated inappropriate settings for inspiration and ecstasy – see the London coffeeshop in 'Vacillation' IV and the various prosaic loci of genius in 'Long-legged Fly'.

5–6 *Midnight, an old house / Where nothing stirs but a mouse*: when Charles Ricketts died in 1931, Yeats felt that 'one of the lights that lit my dark house is gone' (*TSMC*, p. 168). Also compare the half-personified house in *Purgatory* (1939) – burnt-out but subject to bright obsessive replay of the tragic event that occurred there. Also compare two poems Yeats included in *OBMV*: Geoffrey Scott's poem beginning 'What was Solomon's mind? / If he was wise in truth, / 'Twas something hard to find / And delicate: a mouse / Tingling, and small, and smooth, / Hid in vast haunted house'; and Edward Davison's 'In this Dark House': 'Then from the inner gloom / The scratching of a mouse / May echo down my mind / And sound around the room / In this dark house'. Also, the young Yeats quoted with approval William Watson's 'Life without Health', which compares a sick man to a 'home dilapidated' (*LNI*, p. 211).

7 *My temptation is quiet*: 'A poet, when he is growing old, will ask himself if he cannot keep his mask and his vision without new bitterness, new disappointment ... Surely, he may think, now that I have found vision and mask I need not suffer any longer. He will buy perhaps some small old house, where ... he can can dig his garden ... Then he will remember Wordsworth withering into eighty years, honoured and empty-witted, and climb to some waste room and find, forgotten by youth, some bitter crust' (*M*, p. 342). Compare also the last stanza of 'Are You Content'.

9–10 *Neither loose imagination, / Nor the mill of the mind*: as in 'The Circus Animals' Desertion', the poet insists that inspiration must come from the body, not from the mind. In an early draft Yeats wrote, 'Neither loose reverie / Nor those thoughts that grind / Dry bone upon dry bone / Can make the truth known' (Stallworthy, *BL*, p. 218).

11 *rag and bone*: compare 'The Circus Animals' Desertion' III 8: 'foul rag and bone shop'.

14 *Myself must I remake*: Yeats conceived the process of turning oneself into a poet as an exertion on one's person of the same shaping and intensifying force that is needed to make a poem: the poet 'is never the bundle of accident and incoherence that sits down to breakfast; he has been born as an idea, something intended, complete ... he is more type than man, more passion than type' (*EI*, p. 509). Also compare an untitled quatrain from Yeats's 1908 *Collected Works*: 'The friends that have it I do wrong / When ever I remake a song, / Should know what issue is at stake: / It is myself that I remake' (*VP*, p. 778). For the magical identity of the poet and the text he writes, see also the note to 'The Three Bushes'.

15 *Timon and Lear*: see 'Lapis Lazuli', l. 10 – where anyone is susceptible to transformation into a tragic hero.

16 *William Blake*: English poet (1757–1827), whom many considered insane. Yeats and Edwin Ellis published a three-volume edition of his works in 1893. In *A Vision*, pp. 137–40, Blake belongs to Phase 16, just after the full moon – Yeats attributed Blake's violent, incoherent imagination to the desperate attempt to hold together a visionary synthesis that was starting to break apart. Blake reappears in 'Under Ben Bulben' IV 28.

18 *Truth obeyed his call*: compare 'Words', l. 12: 'words obey my call'.

19 *Michael Angelo*: see 'Michael Robartes and the Dancer', l. 32.

22 *Shake the dead*: compare the shaking dead in 'The Black Tower', l. 9.

23 *Forgotten else by mankind*: compare a line from Lionel Johnson's 'The Church of a Dream', quoted by Yeats: 'Alone with Christ, desolate else, left by mankind' (*EI*, p. 493; *UP* II, p. 117).

24 *eagle mind*: compare 'The Hawk', l. 14: 'hawk of the mind'.

What Then?

This 'melancholy biographical poem' (*L*, p. 895) was a contribution to Yeats's high school magazine. Yeats's desire to make a swift lyric summary of his career culminated in 'The Circus Animals' Desertion'.

5 'What then?' sang Plato's ghost: 'all life weighed in the scales of my own life seems to me a preparation for something that never happens' (*A: R* 33); see also the note to 'Among School Children'. Plato's philosophy (see 'The Tower' I 12) gave prestige to ideal forms, and Plato's ghost represents a

further abstraction from common life. This refrain, then, presents an inner voice mocking the vanity of earthly endeavours.

12 *A small old house*: see the note to the previous poem.

19 *Something to perfection brought*: compare 'The Choice', l. 2: 'Perfection of the life, or of the work'. Here the poet has made the second of these choices, and his soul's salvation is in doubt.

Beautiful Lofty Things

The late poems that brood upon the past, such as this and 'The Municipal Gallery Re-visited', differ markedly in character from those that anticipate the future, such as 'The Gyres'. The poems that look ahead tend to be celebrations of anarchy, full of disorderly joy, while the retrospective poems tend to be stately in diction and structure. This poem is unusual in its density of proper names – memorable personages from the poet's past are reduced to a single cameo, vivid against some dark background of confrontation. Another noteworthy feature is its rhythm of repeated words – 'Saints' (ll. 3, 4), 'table' (ll. 5, 7, 9), and 'head' (ll. 1, 4, 11) – the emphasis on heads is appropriate in a poem that resembles a museum.

Title: compare 'A Crazed Girl', l. 7: 'A beautiful lofty thing'.

1 *O'Leary*: see 'September 1913', l. 8.

2 *My father*: John Butler Yeats (1839–1922) confronted a crowd offended by Synge's *The Playboy of the Western World* on 4 Feb. 1907 – 'No man of all literary Dublin dared show his face but my own father, who spoke to . . . that howling mob with sweetness and simplicity' (*A: E* 34; *Mem*, p. 161). As Jeffares notes (*NCP*, p. 380), J. B. Yeats recalled that he said, 'Of course I know Ireland is an island of Saints, but thank God it is also an island of sinners' (*LS*, p. 214).

5 *Standish O'Grady*: Irish historian and man of letters (1846-1928), whose retellings of Irish heroic tales in 'romantic Carlylian prose' Yeats much admired (*A: DP* 5). At a generally drunken dinner in honour of the Irish Literary Theatre (11 May 1899), he 'said in a low penetrating voice: "We have now a literary movement, it is not very important; it will be followed by a political movement, that will not be very important; then must come a military movement, that will be important indeed"' (*A: DP* 11).

6 *high nonsensical words*: for the elderly Yeats's fascination with nonsense, compare 'Crazy Jane Reproved', l. 7: '*Fol de rol*'; 'Ribh in Ecstasy', l. 1: 'What matter that you understood no word!'; 'A Crazed Girl', l. 13: 'No common intelligible sound'; and the note to 'Colonel Martin' I 9.

7 *Augusta Gregory*: Yeats's friend and collaborator in folklore research (1852–

1932). She appeared anonymously in many of Yeats's earlier poems, including 'To a Friend . . .', 'Friends', 'Shepherd and Goatherd', and 'Coole and Ballylee, 1931'; she was the dedicatee of *The Shadowy Waters*; and she is mentioned by name in 'The Municipal Gallery Re-visited' IV 1 and VI 2. In her journal (11 April 1922) she wrote that she showed a threatening tenant 'how easy it would be to shoot me through the unshuttered window' (*Lady Gregory's Journals* I, p. 337).

10 *Maud Gonne at Howth station waiting a train*: this is the only instance in Yeats's poetry of the name of Maud Gonne (1866-1953). At Howth (near Dublin), in August 1891, Yeats first proposed marriage to her; she said 'she would never marry; but in words that had no conventional ring she asked for my friendship. We spent the next day upon the cliff paths at Howth' (*Mem*, p. 46). In a draft for an unwritten poem (*c.* 1897) Yeats also connected Maud Gonne with the railway: 'O my beloved. How happy / I was that day when you / came here from the / railway, and set your hair / aright in my looking glass / . . . I play / with images of the life / you will not give to me o / my cruel one' (Ellmann, *YMM*, p. 161).

11 *Pallas Athena*: see 'A Thought from Propertius', l. 6.

11 *that straight back and arrogant head*: compare 'His Wildness', l. 4: 'so straight a back'; in a 1910 draft of *The Player Queen*, Decima hungers 'for multitudes to see my straight back and high head' (Bradford, *WPQ*, p. 205). For Maud Gonne's goddess-like demeanour, see 'The Arrow' and *A: FY* 5.

A Crazed Girl

This and some of the following poems seem to be addenda to 'Beautiful Lofty Things', extending the catalogue. For Yeats's account of the descent into madness of Margot Ruddock – the Crazed Girl of the title – see the note to 'Sweet Dancer'. The original title of this irregular sonnet was 'At Barcelona', and it was printed in Yeats's introduction to Margot Ruddock's *The Lemon Tree*. Here the crackpot, cracked-kneed poetess becomes a somewhat deformed version of one of Yeats's favourite themes, the Phase 15 dancer – see the note to 'The Double Vision of Michael Robartes' II. Like that earlier dancer, this crazed girl seems to have danced herself beyond the usual categories of things – both are completely self-involved, self-wound.

3 *Her soul in division from itself*: compare 'A Bronze Head', ll. 17–18: 'A vision of terror . . . Had shattered her soul'.

6 *Her knee-cap broken*: compare 'The Tower' II 46: 'broken knees for hire'.

7 *A beautiful lofty thing*: see the previous poem's title.

13 *No common intelligible sound*: 'I was amazed by the tragic magnificence of

some fragments [of Margot Ruddock's poetry]' (*L*, p. 856). For the theme of high nonsense, see 'Beautiful Lofty Things', l. 6. Yeats recommended that the reader of difficult modernist poetry 'should become two people, one a sage ... one a child listening to a poem as irrational as a "Sing a Song of Sixpence"' (*EI*, p. 502).

14 *'O sea-starved hungry sea'*: an actual line by Ruddock: 'I crept into the hold of the boat, a cat came up and looked at me, I started to sing softly ... "Sea-starved, hungry sea, / In a stretched hand humility ... Knowing that the sea is there / Drink deep"' (*ASD*, p. 97). The paradox of a sea starved for itself recalls the reflexive rhetoric Yeats often associated with extreme transcendence – see 'A Prayer for my Daughter', ll. 67–68. Also compare a couplet from the 1889 text of *The Wanderings of Oisin*: 'The sea rolled round, / Crazed with its own interminable sound' (*VP*, p. 30). Other sea-paradoxes include 'laughter from the sea's sad lips' ('The Rose of Battle', l. 19) and 'the murderous innocence of the sea' ('A Prayer for my Daughter', l. 16). It may be relevant that Yeats wrote (in 1934): 'a German psycho-analyst has traced the "mother complex" back to our mother the sea ... to the loneliness of the first crab or crayfish that climbed ashore and turned lizard' (*Ex*, p. 378).

To Dorothy Wellesley

This poem marks another stage in Yeats's textual intimacy with Dorothy Wellesley (1889–1956) – see the note to 'The Three Bushes'. The house and the whole surrounding landscape seem to be extensions of her body's sensuality; and yet radical passion underlies and intensifies all the langorous ease of the woman and the place. The original title was 'To a Friend'; drafts appear in *DWL*, pp. 85–86.

1 *moonless midnight of the trees*: compare 'Her Vision in the Wood', l. 2: 'wine-dark midnight in the sacred wood'.

2 *As though that hand could reach*: compare 'Towards Break of Day', ll. 17–18: 'Nothing that we love over-much / Is ponderable to our touch'.

5–6 *Rammed full / Of ... silence*: see 'Vacillation' III 3: 'ram them with the sun'.

7 *since the horizon's bought strange dogs are still*: Dorothy Wellesley wrote to Yeats, 'I have saved ... this little corner of Sussex from a town of scarlet bungalows. So I now own the lovely ridge opposite'; in a footnote she quoted this line, commenting 'I have never understood ... what he meant by the last half of the line, unless he had a fantastic idea that after buying the few acres I evicted the people who lived on it, together with their dogs!' (*DWL*, p. 53).

13–14 *Neither Content / Nor satisfied Conscience*: for similar antique personifications, see 'A Prayer for my Daughter', l. 80.

16 *The Proud Furies*: 'We have all something within ourselves to batter down and get our power from this fighting. I have never "produced" a play in verse without showing the actors that the passion of the verse comes from the fact that the speakers are holding down violence or madness – "down Hysterica passio [see 'Parnell's Funeral' I 21]". All depends on the completeness of the holding down, on the stirring of the beast underneath. Even my poem "To D. W." should give this impression. The moon, the moonless night, the dark velvet, the sensual silence, the silent room and the violent bright Furies. Without this conflict we have no passion only sentiment and thought' (*DWL*, p. 86). Aeschylus' *Oresteia* describes the process by which the Erinyes, or Furies – primitive spirits of vengeance, or vendetta – are transformed into the Eumenides, the guarantors of legal justice. Yeats often thought of achieved, settled civilization (such as that represented by Dorothy Wellesley's elegant house) as a similar refinement of savage energies – see the note to 'To a Wealthy Man . . .', ll. 25–26.

16 *torch*: Yeats conceived this poem as a dialectic between water (that is, the sensuousness of the opening imagery) and fire: 'About the conflict in "To D. W.", I did not plan it deliberately. That conflict is deep in my subconsciousness, perhaps in everybody's. I dream of clear water ... then come erotic dreams. Then for weeks perhaps I write poetry with sex for theme. Then comes the reversal ... Then for weeks I get a symbolism like that in my Byzantium poem ['Byzantium', l. 27] or in "To D. W." with flame for theme. ... The water is sensation, peace, night, silence, indolence; the fire is passion, tension, day, music, energy' (*DWL*, pp. 86–87).

The Curse of Cromwell

Yeats sent the first six lines of this poem to Dorothy Wellesley, and remarked, 'I am expressing my rage against the intelligentsia by writing about Oliver Cromwell who was the Lennin of his day – I speak through the mouth of some wandering peasant poet in Ireland ... you and I are attacked because the greater part of the English intelligentsia are communists' (*DWL*, pp. 119–20). The persona of peasant balladeer was often attractive to the later Yeats; the following poems treat contemporary politics in a similarly rough and vigorous voice. Yeats seemed to feel relieved from the burden of self-consciousness by the mask of simplicity: 'I write poem after poem, all intended for music, all very simple – as a modern Indian poet has said "no longer the singer but the song"' (*DWL*, p. 123). But elsewhere Yeats wished that he had not hidden himself behind a persona: 'there are moments when hatred poisons my life and I accuse myself of effeminacy because I have not given it adequate expression. It is not enough to have put it into the mouth of a rambling peasant poet' (*EI*, p. 519).

1–2 *You ask what I have found and far and wide I go, / Nothing but Cromwell's house and Cromwell's murderous crew*: Yeats quoted a version of these lines in a letter, and commented, 'My poetry is generally written out of despair ... I see decreasing ability and energy and increasing commonness ... What can I do but cry out, lately in simple peasant songs that hide me from the curious?' (*L*, p. 886).

2 *Cromwell's murderous crew*: Oliver Cromwell (1599–1658) led an anti-royalist rebellion – he beheaded King Charles I and became Lord Protector of a republican government; he remained unpopular among the Irish because he confiscated much land during a military expedition to Ireland. In 1902 Yeats called Cromwell 'the Great Demagogue [who] had come and turned the old house of the noble into "the house of the Poor, the lonely house, the accursed house of Cromwell"' (*EI*, pp. 375–76).

3 *beaten into the clay*: compare 'Under Ben Bulben' V 12. As Ellmann notes (*IY*, p. 194), these lines resemble O'Connor's translation 'Kilcash' (partly written by Yeats, and included in *OBMV*): 'And the great earls where are they? / The earls, the lady, the people / Beaten into the clay'.

4 *where are they?*: the *ubi sunt* of the classical elegy – see *The Wanderings of Oisin* I 126.

6 *His fathers served their fathers before Christ was crucified*: Yeats's favourite example of happy rigidity of hierarchy – the antithesis of communism, which seeks to level all mankind; see the note to 'Three Marching Songs' II 1.

8 What is there left to say?: compare 'Nineteen Hundred and Nineteen' I 43: 'What more is there to say?'

18 *the fox in the old fable*: a stolen fox, concealed in the clothes of a Spartan boy determined to hide his crime, gnawed the thief to death. The poet's knowledge of Ireland's lost greatness similarly gnaws at his vitals.

22 *I am still their servant though all are underground*: compare the 'oath-bound' vassals of 'The Black Tower', determined to be loyal to their buried king. Here the poet seems to envy his masters for being dead.

25–26 *a great house ... Its open lighted doorway and its windows all alight*: see the note to 'Crazy Jane on God', ll. 13-18.

30 *the dogs and horses that understand my talk*: perhaps a hint of the animism associated with the ancient bards – compare the conversation of the Gaelic poet Raftery with a bush (*M*, p. 29).

Roger Casement

Sir Roger Casement (1864–1916) was a former consular officer of the British government who, in 1914, joined Sinn Fein, the Irish revolutionary political party; he travelled to Germany to procure arms for the Irish rebels, but was captured by the British and hanged for treason when he returned by German submarine in 1916. The prosecution used evidence from Casement's diaries showing that he was homosexual. In 1936 Yeats read a demonstration (now thought to be incorrect) that these diaries were forged: 'I am in a rage ... Dr. Maloney ... has proved that the diaries, supposed to prove Casement "a Degenerate" and successfully used to prevent an agitation for his reprieve, were forged. Casement was not a very able man but he was gallant and unselfish, and had surely his right to leave ... an unsullied name' (*L*, p. 867). Yeats hoped that this poem would be popular – 'I shall not be happy until I hear that it is sung by Irish undergraduates at Oxford' (*DWL*, p. 107) – and Yeats did indeed receive wide praise in Ireland (*DWL*, p. 126). When the *Irish Press* paid Yeats for printing this poem, he sent the money to Ethel Mannin as an anonymous contribution for the poor, not for politics – 'I am finished with that for ever' (*L*, p. 884). Casement is also the subject of the next poem, and appears in 'The Municipal Gallery Re-visited' I 3.

1–4: Yeats quoted this stanza in a letter to Dorothy Wellesley, and noted that 'one's verse must be as direct & natural as spoken words' (*DWL*, p. 109); later he told her that this poem 'is, as it should be, an old street ballad & it sings well' (*DWL*, p. 126).

13 *Spring-Rice*: Cecil Arthur Spring-Rice (1859–1918), who became British Ambassador to the U.S. in 1912. Yeats repeated this denunciation in a letter to a newspaper, and claimed that Spring-Rice was 'an honourable, able man' compelled to act against his will (*L*, p. 882).

17 *Tom and Dick*: instead of these anonymities, an early printing mentioned Alfred Noyes, a professor at Princeton – after receiving from Noyes a 'noble letter' of protest, in which Noyes urged the formation of an independent tribunal, including Yeats, to examine the evidence of forgery, Yeats agreed to omit Noyes's name (*L*, p. 882).

24 *in quicklime laid*: the corpses of hanged men were dissolved in quicklime – Oscar Wilde (accused of homosexuality in a court of law, like Casement) expressed his horror at this treatment of the executed in 'The Ballad of Reading Gaol', included in Yeats's *OBMV*.

The Ghost of Roger Casement

This is Yeats's other ballad on Casement; perhaps here the sound of Swift's voice, foretelling the decay of established culture, starts to enter into the cadence of peasant ballad-singer: 'the two Casement ballads ... are meant to support each other. I am fighting in those ballads for what I have been fighting all my life ... our ancestor Swift has gone where "fierce indignation can lacerate his heart no more" [see 'Swift's Epitaph'], & we go stark, staring mad. ... I want to stiffen the back bone of the high hearted and high-minded ... so that they may no longer shrink & hedge, when they face rag merchants ... Indeed before all I want to strengthen myself' (*DWL*, p. 115). Writing in 1937 to Ethel Mannin of his plans to publish another Casement ballad, Yeats assumed an almost ghostly presence himself: 'These ballads of mine though not supremely good are not ephemeral, the young will sing them now and after I am dead. In them I defend a noble-natured man, I do the old work of the poets but I will defend no cause. Get out of the thing, look on with sardonic laughter' (*L*, pp. 881–82).

4 *John Bull and the sea are friends*: John Bull is a personification of the British character – a friend of the sea because of the traditional might of the British navy.

10 beating on the door: Yeats thought of Casement as a spirit prevented from attaining its rest: 'If Casement were a homo-sexual what matter! But if the British Government can with impunity forge evidence to prove him so no unpopular man with a cause will ever be safe. Henceforth he will be denied his last refuge – Martyrdom' (*DWL*, p. 128). Also compare the soldiers' ghosts in 'The Tower' II 72, that 'beat on the board'.

28 *If it lack honesty*: the dishonesty at Casement's trial shows the shakiness of the British Empire.

31 *a village church*: as Jeffares notes (*NCP*, p. 388), the MS of the poem reveals that Yeats was thinking here of Gray's 'Elegy written in a country churchyard' (1751) – the stanza about 'Some mute inglorious Milton', describing the anonymity of the rural dead.

36 *fame and virtue rot*: the precariousness of reputation contrasts with the strong presence of Casement's ghost. Whereas, in 'To a Shade', Parnell's fragile ghost must turn aside from the ignominy of recent politics, Casement's ghost seems an avenging Fury.

The O'Rahilly

This poem can be seen as a populist sequel to 'Easter, 1916' – less a keening over futile courage than an incitement to war. The O'Rahilly (1875–1916) died during the Easter rebellion.

3 *Sing a 'the'*: the definite article indicates the leader of a clan.

9 How goes the weather?: this bland commonplace question may indicate, in this context, a coming storm. Jeffares notes (*NCP*, p. 389) that the original refrain was 'Praise the Proud'.

12 *Pearse and Connolly*: see 'Easter, 1916', ll. 24 and 76.

14 *Kerry men*: the O'Rahilly came from Co. Kerry.

31 *Henry Street*: adjoining the Post Office, the centre of the rebellion.

Come Gather Round Me Parnellites

Yeats sent a draft of this poem to Dorothy Wellesley: 'It has an interesting history . . . Henry Harrison, an old decrepit man, came to see me. As a young Oxford undergraduate fifty years ago he had joined Parnell's party and now had written a book to defend Parnell's memory. . . . He begged me to write something . . . to convince all Parnellites that Parnell had nothing to be ashamed of in [Kitty O'Shea's] love. . . . You will understand the first verse better if you remember that Parnell's most impassioned followers are now very old men' (*DWL*, p. 93). Yeats feared that Wellesley, a staunch Englishwoman, would find the poem politically reprehensible: 'The Parnell Ballad is on a theme which is here looked upon as ancient history. It no more rouses anti-English feelings than a poem upon the battle of Trafalgar arouses anti-French feelings' (*DWL*, p. 130). Like Casement, Parnell was destroyed by presumed sexual irregularity – see the note to 'To a Shade'.

In such poems as 'Parnell's Funeral', it seems that Parnell's downfall, equivalent to the death of a god, desolated Ireland; but in this poem it seems that memories of Parnell tend to promote feelings of warmth, community. The elderly Yeats wrote that Parnell's tragedy liberated the Muses: 'The fall of Parnell had freed imagination from practical politics, from agrarian grievance and political enmity, and turned it to imaginative nationalism, to Gaelic, to the ancient stories, and at last to lyrical poetry and to drama' (*VPl*, p. 957; *Ex*, p. 343).

Title: compare the blind poet's song in 'The Last Gleeman', which begins, 'Gather round me, boys' (*M*, p. 49).

16 *a lass*: Kitty O'Shea – the poet praises the amorousness that Parnell's opponents used to ruin him. Her husband named Parnell as co-respondent in a suit for divorce.

27 *A husband that had sold his wife*: Harrison's book claimed that 'Mrs. O'Shea was a free woman when she met Parnell, O'Shea had been paid to leave her free, and if Parnell had been able to raise £20,000 would have let

himself be divorced instead of Parnell' (*DWL*, p. 93; see also *EI*, pp. 486–90, which includes the text of this poem).

The Wild Old Wicked Man

The wild old wicked man of this poem is a typical persona of the 1930s – just as the sedentary Platonist was typical of his poetry in the 1920s. It is a mask derived from an extreme simplification of a sophisticated poet's old age, until he seems indistinguishable from a beggar-poet – a limit of convergence between the historical Yeats and such wandering minstrels as Raftery or Hanrahan (see the notes to 'The Tower' II). To some extent the wild old wicked man is a male version of Crazy Jane – sex is his major theme – but he is also preoccupied with his own artistic power, his evocation of emotion by contagious magic. According to Mokashi-Punekar (*The Later Phase in the Development of W. B. Yeats*, p. 264), the emotional key to this poem lies in Yeats's unfulfilled plan to travel to India in 1937 with Lady Elizabeth Pelham: 'Lady Betty of whom I [have] seen a good deal has suggested my going to India ... the [Steinach] operation ... though it revived my creative power it revived also sexual desire: and ... in all likelihood will last me until I die. I believe that if I repressed this for any long period I would break down under the strain as did the great Ruskin'. The poem's mood also seems to be foreshadowed in a letter to Dorothy Wellesley: 'Perhaps I lost you then, for part of my sense of solitude was that I felt I would never know that supreme experience of life – that I think possible to the young – to share profound thought & then to touch. I have come out of that darkness a man you have never known – more man of genius, more gay, more miserable.... I have recovered a power of moving the common man I had in my youth' (*DWL*, p. 123). In so far as Yeats's emotional life was centred around his flirtations with young women, the wild old wicked man is a most intimate persona, despite its blatancy and lewdness. It is a mask of simultaneous gaiety and misery, exultation and consciousness of suffering – a proper mask for tragic joy.

5 *Not to die on the straw at home*: compare the slight contempt for domesticity in 'The Rose of Battle', ll. 9–11.

16 *Words I have that can pierce the heart*: this contradicts 'A Song', ll. 7–8: 'Though I have many words, / What woman's satisfied ...?'

30 *Girls down at the seashore*: Jeffares compares (*NCP*, p. 391) Yeats's recollection of a sailor-boy's excited talk of seaside prostitutes (*A: R* 19).

40–41 *touch ... Things hid in their marrow bones*: compare 'A Prayer for Old Age', ll. 3–4: 'He that sings a lasting song / Thinks in a marrow-bone'. The wild old wicked man's speech seems to touch in the literal as well as the figurative sense: his language intensifies physical sensation, deepens shivers. Just as Dorothy Wellesley in 'To Dorothy Wellesley' seemed to create a field of bodily sensuousness around her house, so the wild old wicked man heightens the general carnality of his audience.

43 *warty lads*: Yeats complained to Dorothy Wellesley of certain modern poets who were 'too thoughtful, reasonable & truthful': 'poets were good liars who never forgot that the Muses were women who liked the embrace of gay warty lads ... warts are considered by the Irish peasantry a sign of sexual power' (*DWL*, p. 63).

53 *child hid in the womb*: compare the 'Brave Infant of *Saguntum*' who, during Hannibal's sack of the city, refused to be born (in Ben Jonson's Ode on Cary and Morison [1640], l. 1). Also compare the suffering of the dead babies whose wounds reopen in 'News for the Delphic Oracle' II 3.

55 *stream of lightning*: in a stanza ending with sexual abandon, this bolt from the heavens seems to depict death as a stronger orgasm. Compare 'The Spirit Medium', ll. 17–18: 'An old ghost's thoughts are lightning, / To follow is to die'.

60 *the second-best*: see 'From *Oedipus at Colonus*', ll. 10–12: 'Never to have lived is best ... The second best's a gay goodnight'.

The Great Day

Yeats once wrote 'I am no believer in Milleniums' (*Ex*, p. 336), and this anti-apocalyptic quatrain seems to confirm it. In the 1930s Yeats vacillated between strong prophecies of a new heroic age to come after AD 2000, and rather hesitant and qualified predictions of a new era not dissimilar to the present one: 'We may meet again, not the old simple celebration of life tuned to the highest pitch, neither Homer nor the Greek dramatists, something more deliberate than that, more systematised, more external, more self-conscious, as must be at a second coming' (*Ex*, p. 374). This and the next three poems were originally grouped under the title 'Fragments'. Drafts of this and the next two poems can be found in *DWL*, p. 123 - Yeats commented that the three poems 'give the essence of my politics'.

Parnell

Yeats claimed that this poem 'contains an actual saying of Parnell's' (*DWL*, p. 123).

What Was Lost

This threnody is analogous to 'The Four Ages of Man' – that poem sees each man's life as a series of defeats, this poem sees history as an endless recurrence of defeat.

3 *My king a lost king*: compare 'The Black Tower', l. 13: 'his own right king's forgotten'.

The Spur

Yeats sent a draft of this to Dorothy Wellesley as his 'final apology' (*DWL*, p. 110; compare *L*, p. 872, to Ethel Mannin). In the draft he capitalized Lust and Rage, personifying them as the Muses of a old man. For another poem that explains inspiration physiologically, see 'The Circus Animals' Desertion'.

1 *You think it horrible that lust and rage*: Dorothy Wellesley was somewhat shocked by the phallic brutality of 'The Chambermaid's Second Song'; and she also tried to moderate Yeats's rage over Roger Casement's forged diaries (*DWL*, pp. 106, 108). In a letter quoting a stanza of 'Roger Casement', Yeats replied, 'Forgive all this my dear but I have told you that my poetry all comes from rage or lust' (*DWL*, p. 109).

A Drunken Man's Praise of Sobriety

Drunkenness, like insanity and nonsense-talk in previous poems, may be a low manifestation of tragic joy – see the headnote to this volume. The drunkard sees death as a state of temporary intoxication – and in a sense Yeats would agree with him, for, according to *A Vision*, the dead soul dwells in a condition of confusion or oblivion until rebirth.

10 *dancing like a wave*: compare 'The Fiddler of Dooney', l. 2: 'Folk dance like a wave'. Here the simile seems more sea-sick.

14 *mermaid*: compare 'The Mermaid', where a woman drowns her lover. Here the drunkard seems to ask his dancing partner not to disturb his equilibrium by making him move up and down (towards the grave).

16 *all dead men are drunk*: in *Where There is Nothing* (1902) III 22–24, the visionary hero buys drinks for all the local rabble: 'I said . . . that when we were all dead and in heaven it would be a sort of drunkenness, a sort of ecstasy'. Compare 'All Souls' Night', l. 9, where a ghost intoxicates itself from the fumes rising from a wine-glass; also compare 'The Blessed', ll. 31–32: 'the blessedest soul in the world . . . nods a drunken head'. Yeats wrote that dead spirits summoned by a medium 'are subject to a kind of drunkenness' (*M*, p. 363).

The Pilgrim

Here the poet seems to dismiss all inquiry into religious truth with a nonsense-line. This movement from bitter repentance to frivolity is similar to the movement in 'Lapis Lazuli' from bomb-blasts to gaiety – perhaps the emotion here is the Roman Catholic analogue of tragic joy.

1 *I fasted*: for other fasts, see 'Demon and Beast', l. 48.

5 *fol de rol de rolly O*: compare the refrain of 'Crazy Jane Reproved': '*Fol de rol, fol de rol*'. For the theme of nonsense, see 'Beautiful Lofty Things', l. 6.

6 *Lough Derg*: a small lake where St Patrick fasted and saw a vision – a popular object of pilgrimage. 'If I were four-and-twenty ... I would go – though certainly I am no Catholic and never shall be one – ... to Lough Derg' (*Ex*, p. 266). Yeats followed Ernest Renan in believing that Dante's *Divine Comedy* was partly based on 'visions of Purgatory seen by pilgrims to Lough Derg' (*EI*, p. 185). A picture of a pilgrimage to Lough Derg appears in 'The Municipal Gallery Re-visited' I 2.

9 *that old man beside me, nothing would he say*: compare the hermit in 'The Three Hermits', l. 32, who 'Sang unnoticed like a bird'.

13 *the fires of Purgatory have ate their shapes away*: in Yeats's purgatory the dead lose all individuality (*AV*, p. 234). Compare 'The Spirit Medium', ll. 11–12: 'Some that being dead / Are not individual'; and 'Cuchulain Comforted', ll. 16–17: 'all we do / All must together do'.

16 *A great black ragged bird*: 'I would ... memorialise bishops to open once again that Lough Derg cave of vision once beset by an evil spirit in the form of a long-legged bird with no feathers on its wings' (*Ex*, p. 267). Yeats's wife saw an apparition 'before the birth of our son [of] a great black bird' (*AV*, p. 17). Also compare Browning, ' "Childe Roland to the Dark Tower Came," ' l. 160: 'A great black bird, Apollyon's bosom-friend'.

Colonel Martin

Richard Martin (1754–1834), a famous duellist, held various offices in Co. Galway, including sheriff; he also served in Parliament. Yeats used this story in a lecture in 1910, as an example of the people's delight 'in a striking personality. It showed the mysterious love of that mysterious thing, human nature' (Ellmann, *IY*, pp. 205–6). When Yeats wrote the poem, he again emphasized the mystery: 'It has a curious pathos which I cannot define ... the idea seemed to lie below the threshold of consciousness' (*L*, p. 896–97). Perhaps the story's appeal for Yeats lay in the peculiar immunity from harm conferred on the Colonel by wilful self-dispossession, by spectacular contempt for his own welfare.

I 1–2 *sailing ... Turk*: compare the title 'Sailing to Byzantium'.

I 9 The Colonel went out sailing: the first published refrain was 'Lullabulloo, buloo, buloo, lullabulloo, buloo'. Yeats commented, 'There is a chorus almost without meaning, followed by concertina and whistle' (*L*, p. 897). For meaningless refrains, see 'Crazy Jane Reproved', l. 7.

VI 7–8 *Carry the gold ... Throw it*: in an early draft of *The Player Queen*, Decima makes a similar command: 'Take all that gold and silver and scatter it through the streets of the town. While I am Queen I'll give and give, and when I cannot give, I'll die' (Bradford, *WPQ*, p. 178).

VIII 4 '*Then want before you die*': compare the old ballad 'Edward', ll. 43–45: '"And what wul ye leave to your bairns and your wife?" ... "let them beg thrae life."'

VIII 8 *sea-weed*: sometimes used as field manure – or as food, as in *The King's Threshold* (1904), ll. 285–87.

A Model for the Laureate

The subject of this poem is the abdication of King Edward VIII – like 'Crazy Jane on the Mountain' it expresses Yeats's contempt for modern monarchs. (Other poems, such as 'The Black Tower', attempt to reconstruct a vision of a monarch worthy of devotion.) Yeats sent a draft to Dorothy Wellesley under the title 'A Marriage Ode': 'It is the kind of thing I would have written had I been made Laureate, which is perhaps why I was not made Laureate'. The relation between a king and the kingdom's chief poet had long interested Yeats – it is the subject of *The King's Threshold* (1904).

1 *from China to Peru*: compare Samuel Johnson's *The Vanity of Human Wishes* (1749), ll. 1–2: 'Let observation with extensive view, / Survey mankind, from China to Peru'.

17 *The Muse is mute*: compare 'Crazy Jane on the Mountain', l. 20: 'I kissed a stone' – she had similarly to fall silent when considering the British monarchy. Also compare the sober treatment of the poet's muteness in 'On being asked for a War Poem'.

22–23 *what decent man / Would keep his lover waiting*: part of Yeats's joke is that the King himself did not think his regalia sufficient to keep his lover (Mrs Simpson, later the Duchess of Windsor) waiting.

The Old Stone Cross

The advice here given by the buried captain or king recalls the message of the oracle in 'The Gyres' – he foretells the resurrection of a heroic age, and perhaps (as in 'The Black Tower') his own resurrection. In both the first and last stanza he counsels against crediting the reality of the present age: it is too flimsy, too prevaricating – better to attend to the rumbles of past and future greatness.

Title: Ireland is famous for its stone crosses, some quite large and old; Yeats considered their style to be derived from ancient Greek models – 'our stone crosses got a part of their design from the Painters' Books of Mount Athos' (*VPl*, p. 573). For Yeats's article 'High Crosses of Ireland' (1899), see *UP* II, p. 142.

1 *A statesman is an easy man*: for a statesman who is a very easy man, in fact a strolling musician, see 'A Statesman's Holiday'.

3 *A journalist makes up his lies*: compare the 'drunken journalist' of 'Why should not Old Men be Mad?', l. 4.

7–8 the man ... Under the old stone Cross: compare Denadhach (d. 871), whose epitaph read, '"A pious soldier of the race of Conn lies under hazel crosses at Drumcliff"'; Yeats reported that an old woman saw a vision of this armoured soldier 'still keeping watch, with his ancient piety, over the graveyard' (*M*, pp. 92–93). Also compare 'golden-armed Iollan' in *The Shadowy Waters*, l. 406.

9–10 *this age and the next age / Engender in the ditch*: an allusion to the proximity of the new millennium – just before the switching of gyres there is a time of chaos (*AV*, p. 272). In *The Player Queen* (1922), Decima – the mother of the coming *antithetical* age – was 'born in a ditch between two towns' (II 129–130).

11–12 *No man can know a happy man / From any passing wretch*: it is difficult, during a transitional period, to recognize those who belong to the new gyre.

13 *If Folly link with Elegance*: compare 'My Descendants', ll. 9–12: 'what if my descendants lose the flower / Through ... marriage with a fool?' This line also recalls the premise of *Purgatory* (1939), where the Old Man's high-born mother marries a stable-groom (l. 52).

17 *actors lacking music*: the speaker turns from politics to the theatre in order to emphasize that all history is a drama. Yeats crusaded for decades against the 'realistic' theatre, and especially against actors who tried to normalize their lines to common speech: 'When ... [a] player opened his [mouth], breaking up the verse to make it conversational, jerking his body or his arms that he might seem no austere poetical image but very man, I listened in raging hatred' (*A: FY* 4).

21–22 *what unearthly stuff / Rounds a mighty scene*: compare Prospero in Shakespeare's *The Tempest* IV 156–58: 'We are such stuff / As dreams are made on, and our little life / Is rounded with a sleep'.

The Spirit Medium

In the previous poem a buried man declaims curses and oracles from underground; in this poem the ground is carefully prepared so that other spirits may utter themselves. A spirit medium is usually a person who, during a séance, impersonates the dead; but here the medium is literally the earth itself, as if spirits could construct for themselves bodies of humus or clay – bodies more solid, less provisional or imperfect than the bodies provided by human mediums during séances. In the Introduction to *The Words upon the Window-Pane* (1934) – a play in which a medium evokes the ghost of Swift – Yeats wrote, 'All about us there seems to start up a precise inexplicable teeming life, and the earth becomes once more, not in rhetorical metaphor, but in reality, sacred' (*Ex*, p. 369). The act of gardening seems at once to be a metaphor for the way that spirits take shape in the human mind, and to be something more than a metaphor. This poem may be a dramatic monologue, in which the speaker is someone like Yeats's wife – a gardener as well as a medium; or the speaker may be the poet, whose summoning-of-images uncomfortably resembles mediumship.

4 *Confusion of the bed*: compare 'The Cold Heaven', l. 10: 'Confusion of the death-bed'. Here the ghosts prefer to emerge in the speaker's mind – instead of being reborn.

8 *grope with a dirty hand*: Dorothy Wellesley, much struck by Yeats's indifference to nature, noted that Yeats 'constantly' said, '"Why do you waste your time making your hands dirty just for the sake of a garden?"' (*DWL*, p. 174).

11–12 *Some that being unbegotten / Are not individual*: according to *A Vision*, there are spirits of Phase 1, never incarnate, that are simply dough, plastic to 'whatever image is imprinted upon them' (p. 183); but the spirits of the dead (the 'begotten') also lose their individuality at a certain stage after death – see the note to 'The Pilgrim', l. 13. The speaker seems to fear both the spirits' lack of individuality and their great intelligence (l. 17).

13 *copy some one action*: compare 'Cuchulain Comforted', l. 18, where the dead hero copies the sewing of the other dead.

17 *An old ghost's thoughts are lightning*: Yeats often stressed the superiority, especially the greater speed, of the minds of spirits: 'the thought and its expression may reveal a mind with powers of co-ordination greater and swifter than those of the embodied mind. . . . it has long been known that the hand of the medium can under such influences trace perfect circles' (*AV* [1925], pp. 247–48). Also compare 'The Wild Old Wicked Man', l. 55, where a 'stream of lightning' burns out human suffering.

18 *To follow is to die*: that is, to follow the chain of thought of a spirit is fatal to a mortal man. The poet chooses 'stupidity' (l. 20) instead of this intolerable

intelligence – he cannot know the truth, but he can embody it, make a matrix in which it can appear (to paraphrase *L*, p. 922).

19 *Poetry and music I have banished*: in other poems – such as 'All Souls' Night' and 'The Municipal Gallery Re-visited' – the texts themselves seem to be mediums in which the dead can be embodied.

20–21 *stupidity / Of ... clay*: compare 'Man and the Echo', l. 28: 'body and its stupidity'.

Those Images

Yeats sent a draft of this poem to Dorothy Wellesley, and, in order to explain it, quoted a 'necessary senatorial speech': '"... only by songs, plays, stories can we hold our thirty millions [of Irish] together, keep them one people from New Zealand to California. I have always worked with this purpose in my mind". Yet my dear I am as anarchic as a sparrow' (*DWL*, pp. 142–43); he also suggested that the sentiment was related to that of 'A Model for the Laureate'. Both poems exalt literature over politics – political passions only entangle in lies, abstractions, absurdities, peevishness, and futile toil, while literature is life-giving, athletic, the true agent of community. The five images seem to represent the universals of human experience: the first four (lion and virgin, harlot and child) are emblems of subjectivity and objectivity, experience and innocence, male and female; while the eagle may suggest some proud integrity beyond these antinomies. But it is impossible to reduce the five images to simple meanings – indeed they represent, in a sense, the inexplicability of experience: as early as 1902 Yeats wrote of 'an image that is inexplicable as a wild creature' (*Ex*, p. 93).

2 *The cavern of the mind*: unhealthy abstraction, as opposed to healthy physicality. Bornstein (*YS*, p. 88) derives the phrase from Shelley's 'Speculations on Metaphysics', quoted by Yeats: '"thought ... is like a river, whose rapid and perpetual stream flows outward. ... The caverns of the mind are obscure and shadowy"' (*EI*, p. 85). In 1908 Yeats contrasted scientists and poets: scientists name and number all exterior things, while poets 'are Adams of a different Eden, a more terrible Eden, perhaps, for we must name and number the passions and motives of men' (*Ex*, p. 242).

6 *Moscow or ... Rome*: that is, communism or fascism (and Catholicism). Compare 'Politics', ll. 3–4: 'On Roman or on Russian ... politics'.

7 *Renounce that drudgery*: in one draft this read *Turn from drudgery*, and Yeats commented: 'There must be an accent on "from"' (*L*, p. 896).

8 *Call the Muses home*: compare 'The Tower' I 11: 'bid the Muse go pack'. In 'The Tower' the Muses' enemy is philosophy; here it is politics.

10 *the wild*: as opposed to the 'drudgery' of l. 7. An antithesis between tame and wild can be found in 'Owen Aherne and his Dancers'.

11–12 *lion* ... *virgin* ... *harlot* ... *child*: these apparitions appear in earlier poems: in 'Against Unworthy Praise', l. 20, Yeats spoke of Maud Gonne as 'Half lion, half child'; and in 'Presences', l. 12, the poet's hair stands up at the sight of eerie shapes: 'One is a harlot, and one a child'. These 'Presences' were (though not quite Muses) literary in tendency – indeed they had read the poet's rhymes about unrequited love. In a late essay, Yeats said that psychology was a poor theme for playwrights: 'I delight in active men ... I would have poetry turn its back upon all that modish curiosity, psychology ... I recall an Indian tale: certain men said to the greatest of the sages, "Who are your Masters?" And he replied, "The wind and the harlot, the virgin and the child, the lion and the eagle"' (*EI*, p. 530). (Note that wind appears in l. 4 of this poem.) These images, then, oppose psychology, politics, and abstractions – they are icons of embodiedness, of physical life. Compare also Blake, *Jerusalem* (1804) 61:52: 'Every Harlot was once a Virgin: every Criminal an Infant Love'; and Auden, 'As He Is' (1937), ll. 47–48: 'The lion and the adder, / The adder and the child'.

The Municipal Gallery Re-visited

According to *A Vision*, the soul after death continually redreams the important events of its previous life, 'in the order of their intensity or luminosity' (p. 226). Here the poet seems to find in the pictures at the Municipal Gallery of Modern Art, Dublin, a visible embodiment of this dreaming-back. As in 'A Bronze Head', the museum exhibits become not only a stimulus to memory but a metaphor for it. Not every picture in this poem is clearly identifiable, as if the paintings were endowed with the resonant vagueness of memory; and the leisurely movement from one picture to the next may also imitate memory's drifting. In the previous poem Yeats described universal images, iconic generalities; here he describes the particular images of his emotional crises – and the crises of other Irishmen of his generation.

The first printing of the poem included part of a speech: 'For a long time I had not visited the Municipal Gallery. I went there a week ago and was restored to many friends. I sat down, after a few minutes, overwhelmed with emotion. There were pictures painted by men, now dead, who were once my intimate friends. ... It is said that an Indian ascetic, when he has taken a certain initiation on a mountain [see 'Meru'] in Tibet, is visited by all the Gods. In those rooms of the Municipal Gallery I saw Ireland in spiritual freedom, and the Corots, the Rodins, the Rousseaus were the visiting gods' (*VP*, pp. 839–40).

I 2 *pilgrims*: Sir John Lavery's 'St. Patrick's Purgatory' – set at Lough Derg, like Yeats's 'The Pilgrim'. Lavery also painted pictures of other men mentioned in this stanza – Casement, Griffith, and O'Higgins.

I 3 *Casement*: see 'Roger Casement'.

I 4 *Griffith*: Arthur Griffith (1871–1922), politician and editor of anti-British newspapers.

I 5 *O'Higgins*: see 'Death'.

I 8, II 1–2: these three lines pertain to one painting, Lavery's 'Blessing of the Colours' – that is, the colours of the Irish Free State's flag.

II 3–4 *an Ireland / The poets have imagined, terrible and gay*: 'Ireland not as she is displayed in guide book or history, but, Ireland seen because of the magnificent vitality of her painters, in the glory of her passions' (*VP*, p. 839).

III 5 *Augusta Gregory's son*: Robert Gregory – see 'In Memory of Major Robert Gregory'. His portrait was by Charles Shannon.

III 6 *Hugh Lane, 'onlie begetter'*: see 'To a Wealthy Man . . .'; Lane was the 'onlie begetter' (a term from Shakespeare's dedication to his sonnets) because he was founder of the gallery. His portrait was by John Singer Sargent.

III 7–8 *Hazel Lavery living and dying*: this refers to two paintings by Lavery of his second wife – the first showing her at her easel, the second subtitled 'It is finished'.

III 8 *As though some ballad singer*: this line shows the easy commerce between poetry and painting – appropriate in a poem that versifies pictures.

IV 1 *Mancini's portrait of Lady Gregory*: for Lady Gregory, see 'Beautiful Lofty Things', l. 7; the painter was Antonio Mancini (1852–1930).

IV 2 *Rembrandt*: the Dutch painter (1606–69); Yeats thought that he pitied ugliness instead of cherishing beauty, and emphasized pictorial technique (*AV*, pp. 164–69).

IV 2 *Synge*: see 'In Memory of Major Robert Gregory' IV 1. In *A Vision*, Yeats put Synge and Rembrandt in the same lunar phase (23).

V 2 *that woman . . . that household*: Lady Gregory and Coole Park – the poet sees Coole Park (demolished in 1932) as an extinct gallery of excellence, populated by people, not pictures.

V 3: the meaning is clearer in the first printing: 'Honour had lived so long, their health I found' (*VP*, p. 603).

V 4 *Childless*: compare the Introductory Rhymes to *Responsibilities*, l. 21: '*I have no child*'.

V 5 *Deep-rooted*: compare VII 1: 'that rooted man'.

V 5 *but never foresaw its end*: the antecedent of *its* is *that household*. Originally this line was followed by a line now missing: 'and never foresaw the end / Of all that scholarly generations had held dear' (*VP*, p. 839) – this explains why the stanza only has seven lines.

V 7–VI 1: Edmund Spenser (*c*. 1552–99) mentioned fox and badger in 'The Ruins of Time', ll. 216–17. 'At the end of a long beautiful passage he [Spenser] laments that unworthy men should be in the dead Earl [of Leicester]'s place, and compares them to the fox – an unclean feeder – hiding in the lair "the badger swept" ' (*EI*, p. 359–60; compare p. 260). Coole Park, being destroyed, is immune from fouling. Compare *Deirdre* (1907), ll. 174–75: 'her house has been / The hole of the badger and the den of the fox'.

VI 5 *Antaeus*: a giant who gathered strength by touching the earth – Hercules could defeat him only by lifting him off the ground.

VI 6 *We three alone in modern times*: Donoghue compares a journal entry: 'I must therefore be content to be but artist, one [of] a group, Synge, Lady Gregory – no, there is no other than these' (*Mem*, p. 251). Also compare 'Coole and Ballylee, 1931', l. 41: 'We were the last romantics'.

VI 8 *the noble and the beggar-man*: Jeffares compares (*NCP*, p. 402) Yeats's frequent observation that Lady Gregory 'often quoted the saying of Aristotle: "To think like a wise man, but express oneself like the common people" ' (*Ex*, p. 371).

VII 1 *Synge himself, that rooted man*: see 'In Memory of Major Robert Gregory' IV 1. Yeats thought that Synge had undergone 'an aesthetic transformation, analogous to religious conversion' by living among the primitive Aran islanders (*AV*, p. 167).

VII 2 '*Forgetting human words*': Finneran notes (*PNE*, p. 675) that this is based on Synge's 'Prelude', l. 7 – this poem (included in Yeats's *OBMV*) describes how the poet strayed through the Wicklow countryside 'far from cities' until he 'did but half remember human words'.

VII 3 *You that would judge me*: compare the summoning of judges in the following poem.

VII 8 *my glory was I had such friends*: an expertly turned compliment, but perhaps with a hint of narcissism as well – the pictures on the wall reflect the poet's own glory. In *A Vision* Yeats mentioned how 'my own form might appear in a room full of mirrors' (p. 214) – and in this poem the Municipal Gallery faintly recalls Tennyson's 'The Palace of Art' (1832), where the Soul goes mad from self-reflection.

Are You Content

In the previous poem (VII 3) Yeats asked to be judged in the context of his friends; in this poem he suggests that he judges himself harshly, however others may judge him. Yeats had long felt his inadequacy by the standards of his ancestors – see the note to the Introductory Rhymes to *Responsibilities*. In the final stanza of this poem he again faces the temptation of quiet – the temptation to play the role of sage, to rest on old laurels and bask in ease (see the note to 'An Acre of Grass', l. 7); and again he refuses that role. This poem, then, tries to justify an indecorous life – the life caricatured in 'The Wild Old Wicked Man' – to the highest court of appeal.

Title: Mark and Mrs Yeats added a question mark when editing *Last Poems & Plays* (1940).

8 *I am not content*: 'when I think ... of the anxiety I have given to parents and grandparents, and of the hopes that I have had, all life weighed in the scales of my own life seems to me a preparation for something that never happens' (*A: R* 33).

9 *He that in Sligo at Drumcliff*: Rev. John Yeats, the poet's great-grandfather – see the Introductory Rhymes to *Responsibilities*, l. 5.

11 *That red-headed rector*: Rev. William Butler Yeats, the poet's grandfather (1806–62), Rector of Tullylish. He married Jane Corbet, sister of the owner of Sandymount Castle.

12 *A good man on a horse*: Kelly and Domville note that he was 'Reputedly the best jockey in Ireland in his youth' (*L* I, p. 131).

13 *Sandymount Corbets*: Robert Corbet (d. 1872), Yeats's great-uncle, lived with his mother and aunt at Sandymount Castle (near Dublin), where Yeats was born. In 1930 Yeats recorded a recurrent dream of Sandymount Castle, due to 'The impression on my subconscious ... made in childhood, when my uncle Corbet's bankruptcy and death was a recent tragedy' (*Ex*, p. 319). Yeats used the name John Corbet for a character in *The Words upon the Window-Pane* (1934), a sceptical Cambridge student writing on Swift.

14 *William Pollexfen*: the poet's 'silent and fierce' grandfather – see the Introductory Rhymes to *Responsibilities*, l. 15.

15 *The smuggler Middleton*: another great-grandfather – see the Introductory Rhymes to *Responsibilities*, l. 13. By mentioning the smuggling, Yeats suggests that his judges may be as disreputable by conventional standards as he.

22–23 *What Robert Browning meant / By an old hunter talking with Gods*: Browning (1812–89) wrote in *Pauline* (1833), ll. 323-24, of 'an old hunter / Talking with gods' – this is from a passage based on the young Browning's joy at reading books in his father's library: he participated so intensely in the heroes' adventures that 'I myself went with the tale' (l. 321). This passage meant much to Yeats. In *A Vision* he used Browning's old hunter to exemplify the Mask of a Phase 18 man, such as Goethe or Matthew Arnold – sophisticated men of letters 'worn out by a wisdom held with labour and uncertainty', seeking for their anti-selves 'images of peace' (p. 110). Yeats, belonging to the adjacent Phase 17, could easily take the old hunter as a Mask for himself – but here he refuses this idle dream of simplicity. Yeats also quoted Browning's old hunter in *EI*, p. 409 (as one of his 'favourite quotations', along with the Delphic Oracle's account of Plotinus) and in *Ex*, p. 19. (Some modern scholars have tentatively identified Browning's old hunter as Peleus, to whom Yeats refers in 'News for the Delphic Oracle' III 2, but it is doubtful that Yeats made this connection.)

Yeats wrote little criticism of Browning, but was interested in the possibilities for evasiveness in the dramatic monologue; Yeats also commented, 'To Robert Browning the world was simply a great boarding house in which people come and go in a confused kind of way. The clatter and chatter to him was life, was joy itself. Sometimes the noise and restlessness got too much into his poetry, and ... the verse splintered' (*LNI*, pp. 98–99).

From ON THE BOILER (1939)

On the Boiler (1939) is a flamboyant polemic against modern civilization – Yeats accuses the West of deliberately cultivating imbecility and incoherence, of reducing mankind to some low statistical norm. He suggests that this decline may be reversed by eugenic selection, by better educational methods, and by world war. This little book contains citations from Swift, partly because Yeats's analysis of historical decay was informed by Swift's ideas, and partly because Yeats's persona was related to those laboured, awkwardly forceful, derisive and derisible personae found in such works as *A Tale of a Tub* (1704).

On the Boiler contains three original poems. They were included, evidently without Yeats's warrant, in the posthumous *Last Poems & Plays* (1940); their titles do not appear on the table of contents he prepared shortly before his death for his final volume. But they are attractive poems, easily understood outside their context in *On the Boiler*; and it seems likely that, if Yeats had lived longer, he would have included them in his poetic canon, perhaps in a volume after the one now called *Last Poems*.

Why should not Old Men be Mad?

This poem appears, without a title, at the beginning of *On the Boiler* (*Ex*, p. 407), following Yeats's explanation of the book's name: when Yeats was a boy he used to hear a 'mad ship's carpenter' speaking on top of a large, rusted boiler, 'denounc[ing] his neighbours'. The three poems in this volume all seem to allude to this premise: two describe similarly disaffected people climbing up to a high place – the 'Helen' who climbs on a 'wagonette' (ll. 7–8 of this poem) and Crazy Jane, who climbs a mountain but has become too tired to continue her curses; the third poem describes a statesman who descends to the street, to make himself an easier target for the brickbats of any passing critic.

3 *a sound fly fisher's wrist*: see the note to 'The Fisherman'.

4 *a drunken journalist*: compare 'The Old Stone Cross', l. 3: 'A journalist makes up his lies'.

5–6 *A girl that knew all Dante once / Live to bear children to a dunce*: compare 'Running to Paradise', l. 18: 'many a darling wit's grown dull'. The Dante reader was Iseult Gonne; Yeats also lamented her marriage to Francis Stuart in 'The Death of the Hare'. In 1932 Yeats read a 'strange and exciting' book by Stuart and wondered, 'What an inexplicable thing sexual selection is. Iseult picked this young man, by what seemed half chance, half a mere desire to escape from an impossible life, and when he seemed almost imbecile to his own relations. Now he is her very self made active and visible, her nobility walking and singing' (*L*, p. 800). In a poem addressed to his wife, 'Remembering Yeats', Francis Stuart wrote: 'I wondered would they never go / As under the table I felt your heel / While they spoke high art and quoted a line / From the Purgatorio. / Who was it had known all Dante once? / And why – though why not – had he called me a dunce?'

7–8 *A Helen of social welfare dream / Climb on a wagonette to scream*: probably Maud Gonne, to whom Yeats generally reserved the name Helen. When the foundation stone for the Wolfe Tone monument was laid, there was a procession in which Yeats rode 'with Maud Gonne in a wagonette' (*Mem*, p. 114); according to Hone, Miss Horniman warned Yeats about Maud Gonne: '"The greatest poet ... is always helpless beside a beautiful woman screaming from a cart"' (*WBY*, p. 210).

10 *starve good men and bad advance*: compare 'The Second Coming', ll. 7–8: 'The best lack all conviction, while the worst / Are full of passionate intensity'.

12 *As though upon a lighted screen*: compare Eliot, 'The Love Song of J. Alfred Prufrock' (1915), l. 105: 'as if a magic lantern threw the nerves in patterns on a screen'.

18–19 *what old books tell / And that no better can be had*: compare Swift's defence of the ancient books against the moderns in 'The Battle of the Books' (1704).

Crazy Jane on the Mountain

This is a sequel to the Crazy Jane sequence of 1929–31 (see the headnote to *Words for Music Perhaps*) – Crazy Jane has exhausted herself from her efforts at theology, and now turns to politics. Contemporary with this poem is an essay in which Yeats discussed diction: 'I tried to make the language of poetry coincide with that of passionate, normal speech. I wanted to write in whatever language comes most naturally when we soliloquise, as I do all day long, upon the events of our own lives or of any life where we can see ourselves for the moment. I sometimes compare myself with the mad old slum women I hear denouncing and remembering ... If I spoke my thoughts aloud they might be as angry and as wild' (*EI*, p. 521). The diction of this poem is evidence for this wildness – as Yeats told Dorothy Wellesley, the poem is 'a wild affair' (*DWL*, p. 181), especially the notorious l. 15.

7 *A King had some beautiful cousins*: George V (1865–1936), King of England, whose cousin Tsar Nicholas II was murdered with his family in 1918, in the course of the Russian Revolution. Dorothy Wellesley remembered that Yeats 'considers that George V should have abdicated as a protest when his cousin the Czar was dethroned. "My God!" he said, "in ancient Ireland such conduct as that of George V would have been an impossibility", adding that "the English should have declared war upon their ally Russia in 1917"' (*DWL*, p. 171). In *On the Boiler*, Yeats marvelled that George V was popular because of servile virtues – 'his submission, his correctness' – and noted that George V was the answer of a vast majority of schoolchildren to the question, 'Who was the best man who ever lived?'; Christ came in second place (*Ex*, pp. 442–43). In an unpublished poem from 1929, 'Cracked Mary's Vision', the refrain goes, 'May the devil take King George' (Ellmann, *IY*, p. 102) Also compare the denunciation of the 'modern throne' in 'A Model for the Laureate', l. 18.

15 *Great-bladdered Emer*: When Dorothy Wellesley suggested that 'great-bellied' would be a little more decorous than 'great-bladdered', and still retain the eugenic theme, Yeats exclaimed '"No, I must have bladder!" .. He went on to tell how in the Irish legend all other women were jealous of the Queen's power of retention due to the size of her bladder. This was of great importance as seeming a mark of vigour; also how the Queen was able to make a larger hole in the snow than the other women, so that they were jealous, and set upon her and killed her' (*DWL*, p. 171). In *On the Boiler*, Yeats noted that 'In a fragment from some early version of *The Courting of*

Emer, Emer is chosen for the strength and volume of her bladder' (*Ex*, p. 433). But the old Irish texts seem not to confirm this.

17 *Cuchulain*: see the note to 'Cuchulain's Fight with the Sea'.

20 *I kissed a stone*: see 'The Double Vision of Michael Robartes' III 16, where, as the vision concludes, Michael Robartes 'kissed a stone'. In 'A Model for the Laureate', l. 17, the Muse falls mute when contemplating a modern throne.

A Statesman's Holiday

At the end of *On the Boiler*, Yeats wrote, 'Here in Monte Carlo, where I am writing, somebody talked of a man with a monkey and some sort of stringed instrument, and it has pleased me to imagine him a great politician. I will make him sing to the sort of tune that goes well with my early sentimental poems' (*Ex*, p. 452). The text of this poem follows. Here the great man of modern times – whether statesman, king, general, or industrialist – exposes his true character, that of an organ-grinder, or an organ-grinder's monkey. Here politics becomes, overtly, farce.

Title: 'The Statesman's Holiday' and 'Avalon' were considered; Yeats wrote in the present title on the final page proofs (Finneran, *EYP*, p. 116).

5 *Oscar ruled the table*: probably Oscar Wilde (1854–1900) – 'the dinner table was Wilde's event and made him the greatest talker of his time' (*A: FY* 11).

9–10 *Some knew what ailed the world / But never said a thing*: compare 'The Second Coming', l. 7: 'The best lack all conviction'.

13 Tall dames go walking in grass-green Avalon: compare the juvenile 'Mourn – And Then Onward!', l. 9: 'grass-green plains of Eri' (*VP*, p. 738). Jeffares notes (*NCP*, p. 516) that the refrain read in MS, 'But a Burne-Jones boat and the grass-green island of Avalon'. Avalon was the island to which weeping queens bore the dying King Arthur in a boat (see 'Under the Moon', l. 2). Edward Burne-Jones was a pre-Raphaelite painter famous for his ornate, insipidly beautiful compositions – Yeats once remarked that his knights and ladies are 'faint persons . . . who are never . . . put out of temper' (*A: FY* 12). The statesman, then, sings of a languid, somewhat anaemic dream of past greatness – the opposite of Crazy Jane's vision of great-bowelled antiquity.

15 *the Sack*: one of the prerogatives of the Chancellor of the British House of Lords is a square bag of wool, used as a seat-cushion.

18 *de Valéra*: see 'Parnell's Funeral' II 2.

19 *the King of Greece*: George II (1890–1947), restored to the Greek throne in 1935.

20 *the man who made the motors*: Yeats mentioned Lord Nuffield, whose firm made Morris motor-cars, elsewhere in *On the Boiler* – his philanthropy to Oxford helped to make possible the substitution of 'applied science for ancient wisdom' (*Ex*, p. 423).

23 *its old sole string*: for similarly defective musical instruments, see '"I Am of Ireland,"' ll. 19–26.

28–30 *With any sort of clothes ... old patched shoes*: 'Perhaps all that the masses accept is obsolete – the Orangeman beats his drum every Twelfth of July – perhaps fringes, wigs, furbelows, hoops, patches, stocks, Wellington boots, start up as armed men' (*OBMV*, p. xxxvii).

LAST POEMS (1939)

New Poems was the last of Yeats's formal collections of poetry; but Curtis B. Bradford published a list of poems, prepared by Yeats shortly before his death, which seems to be a table of contents for another volume (also to include the plays *The Death of Cuchulain* and *Purgatory*). This list has no title – *Last Poems* is probably a publisher's convenience. Yeats so arranged this volume that it traces a poet's journey after death, or after some experience akin to death. The book begins with an epitaph. It continues among various purgatories and paradises: some full of the souls of the dead – dead kings, dead warriors, dead philosophers, dead babies; others full of the paraphernalia of transcendental aesthetics, including statues and bronze heads. And it concludes with a kind of rebirth – the poet arrives at his own heart and promises to begin again, composing the heart's themes.

New Poems celebrated, above all, tragic joy. One of the odd features of *Last Poems* is that its poems keep approaching tragic joy, but swerve away from it at the last second. Two of its greatest poems originally included a meditation on tragic joy, but Yeats deleted it in both cases: 'Under Ben Bulben' III once continued into a fierce passage about orgasm and exploding bombs (see the headnote to *New Poems*); and 'The Circus Animals' Desertion' originally concluded as follows:

> O hour of triumph come and make me gay.
> If burnished chariots are put to flight
> Why brood upon old triumph; prepare to die
> Even at the approach of un-imagined night
> Man has the refuge of his gaiety,
> A dab of black enhances every white,
> Tension is but the vigour of the mind,
> Cannon the god and father of mankind.
> (Bradford, *YW*, p. 163)

Instead of this stanza about tragic joy – the exultation in destruction, the vision of death as a kind of epileptic seizure – Yeats substituted the famous stanza about the poet's return to the foul rag and bone shop of the heart. What takes the place of tragic joy is a ferocious humility – a consciousness that the most sublime matters embody themselves in the lowliest, even the filthiest of forms. In one of his last letters Yeats wrote that 'I have found what I wanted When I try to put it all into a phrase I say, "Man can embody truth but he cannot know it"' (*L*, p. 922). Yeats meant *embody* in the most literal manner possible: the truth so profoundly incarnated itself that it became ragged, excrementitious, sexy.

An important feature of this volume is its recapitulatory character: many of Yeats's favourite characters come out for a final bow. However, they are often strangely humbled: Cuchulain has become a seamstress (in 'Cuchulain Comforted'); Oisin has gone to a celestial old-folks' home, where the goddess Niamh appears to be little more than a barmaid (in 'News for the Delphic Oracle'); Maud Gonne has withered into a bronze head. (Similarly, in 'A Crazed Girl' – from *New Poems* – the Phase 15 dancer has deformed herself into a mad poetess with a broken knee; and in 'Crazy Jane on the Mountain' – from *On the Boiler* – Crazy Jane has stopped her discourse on God and turned into a political commentator.) This is another aspect of the same tendency to embodiment: even the noblest, the most unearthly of beings must show itself in an unmistakably human body; and even the feeblest body, even the body of a seventy-three-year-old poet whose health had never been good, must show itself to have a transcendental referent.

Under Ben Bulben

The central theme of this poem is completeness – an idea hammered on at crucial moments (I 9; III 6; IV 16; VI 10). The man of action in III, the painter in IV, the poet in V, and Yeats himself in VI, all move towards a vision of completeness. But this comprehensiveness, this repletion of being, is beheld not as something remote from human life, but as something instinct in human life. Mankind continually recedes from and approaches a state of perfection; and the function of art is to define images of perfection, goals for our self-shaping. The elderly Yeats was fascinated by eugenics – *On the Boiler* (1939) is a long polemic advocating war as an instrument to purify the human race from meanness, misshapenness, and stupidity – and 'Under Ben Bulben' is a eugenic poem: it commands artists to draw a firm bounding-line defining ideal man, it commands poets to assist in the rebirth of an admirable civilization. Yeats wrote much of the poem in catalectic trochaic tetrameter, a metre proper to charms and incantations ('Eye of newt and toe of frog' – *Macbeth* IV i 14); and the metric impulse, combined with the lack of couplet closure created by the frequent off-rhymes, produces within the confines of the poem something of the effect of plenitude and tense structure that the poem advocates.

Prose drafts (under the title 'Creed') are printed by Stallworthy, *VR*, p. 150–58. The second title Yeats tried was 'His Convictions'.

I: this section alleges that both Christian and pagan wisdom affirms a single truth, the immortality of the soul (as described in section II).

I 1 *sages*: Yeats seems initially to have imagined Buddhist and Hindu ascetics as well as Christian monks: 'I believe as did the old sages / who sat under the palm trees / the banyan trees, or among / those snow bound rocks' (*VR*, p. 154). The snowbound rocks recall 'Meru'.

I 2 *the Mareotic Lake*: see 'Demon and Beast', ll 44–45.

I 3 *the Witch of Atlas*: In Shelley's 'The Witch of Atlas' (1820), the beautiful witch sees in the waters of Lake Mareotis 'all human life shadowed upon its waters in shadows that "never are erased but tremble ever" ['The Witch of Atlas' LIX 3]' (*EI*, p. 85). She beheld ultimate reality, the Forms of things reflected in (or refracted through) the waters that symbolize earthly existence. What the sages and visionaries spoke of was the true human image – 'Profane perfection of mankind' (III 16) – later to be envisaged by Phidias, by Michelangelo, and (more faintly) by Blake and by Yeats himself.

I 4 *cocks a-crow*: see 'Solomon and the Witch', l. 9, for birds' cries that herald a new age.

I 5 *those horsemen*: the old family servant Mary Battle saw visionary figures: '"They are fine and dashing-looking, like the men one sees riding their horses ... on the slopes of the mountains with their swords swinging. There is no such race living now, none so finely proportioned"' (*A: HC* 5; compare *M*, p. 58). An early draft of this stanza invoked 'country men / who see the old fighting men / & their fine women coming out / of the mountain, moving from / mountain to mountain' (*VR*, pp. 154–55); compare also the refrain of the next poem: '*From mountain to mountain ride the fierce horsemen*'.

I 6 *Complexion*: 'To those who have seen spirits all skins of human beings appear coarse for long afterwards' (*DWL*, p. 176; also compare *Mem*, p. 100).

I 7 *pale, long-visaged*: common epithets for faeries and goddesses in Yeats's work – for example Echtge in 'Red Hanrahan' (1903) has a 'long pale face' (*M*, p. 220).

I 8 *airs an*: possibly this should read *air in* (see Finneran, *EYP*, p. 75).

I 11 *Ben Bulben*: see 'On a Political Prisoner', l. 14. Yeats wrote of an inaccessible cave high on Ben Bulben, 'the door of Faeryland', from which an 'unearthly troop' rushes out in the middle of the night (*M*, p. 70; compare p. 90).

II 2 *Between his two eternities*: compare 'Vacillation' I 1: 'Between extremities'.

II 3 *That of race and that of soul*: 'This is the proposition on which I write: "There is now overwhelming evidence that man stands between two eternities, that of his family and that of his soul". I apply those beliefs to literature and politics' (*DWL*, p. 166). This dialectic – of immersion into a community vs. withdrawal into solitude – is related to the dialectic of 'A Dialogue of Self and Soul'. For an application to literature, see Yeats's last radio broadcast script: 'I turned my back on foreign themes, decided that the race was more important than the individual, and began my "Wanderings of Oisin"' (*UP* II, p. 509).

Two other passages seem relevant to the dialectic of race and soul: 'To lunar influence belong all thoughts and emotions that were created by the community, by the common people, by nobody knows who, and to the sun all that came from the high disciplined or individual kingly mind' (*Ex*, p. 24; compare *A: SB* 6 and *VPl*, p. 232); '[Balzac's] social order is the creation of two struggles, that of family with family, that of individual with individual' (*Ex*, p. 270; see also p. 273).

II 5 *dies*: all texts (except Finneran's, *PNE*, p. 325) print *die* here; but the indicative seems necessary, since this verb is parallel to *knocks* (II 6). In early drafts the verbs in II 6 and 9 were subjunctive – see *VR*, p. 173.

II 7–8 *A brief parting ... Is the worst man has to fear*: 'There is indeed no great cause why any should fear anything except in the parting' (*UP* II, p. 82).

II 9 *grave-diggers' toil is long*: 'deductions [from popular science] ... compel denial of the immortality of the soul by hiding from the mass of the people that the grave-diggers have no place to bury us but in the human mind' (*Ex*, p. 436). In *The Shadowy Waters*, ll. 430–31, Forgael – identifying himself as a man long dead – claims that 'the grave-diggers ... Have buried nothing but my golden arms'. Also compare 'Mohini Chatterjee', l. 19: 'Grave is heaped on grave' (also concerning reincarnation); and 'In Tara's Halls', l. 17: 'Diggers ... make grave'.

III: a draft of a longer version of this section, moving from the decisive man to bombs, children, and coitus, is cited in the headnote to *New Poems*. A still earlier draft ended with a movement to Sato's sword: 'wisdom enough to choose / his right mate. The wisdom I / seek is written on a sword, mirrored ... on Sato's sword' (*VR*, pp. 155–56). For Sato's sword, see the note to 'My Table', l. 2.

III 1 *Mitchel*: John Mitchel (1815–75) founded in 1843 a newspaper advocating Irish independence; in his *Jail Journal* he prayed for war with England. 'The ... most inspired [of Irish nationalist writers] was John Mitchel, who thundered from his convict hulk ... Mitchel, by the right of his powerful nature and his penal solitude, communed indeed with the Great Gods' (*UP* I, p. 361).

III 2 *'Send war in our time, O Lord!'*: a parody of the well known prayer for peace in our time.

III 12 *Know his work or choose his mate*: work and wife are also paired in 'Vacillation' III.

IV 5 *Make him fill the cradles right*: compare *The King's Threshold* (1904), ll. 128–32: 'the poets hung / Images of the life that was in Eden / About the child-bed of the world, that it, / Looking upon those images, might bear / Triumphant children'; and a couplet deleted from 'In Memory of Eva Gore-Booth ...': 'For widow Nature still / Has those cradles left to fill' (Stallworthy, *BL*, p. 171). Yeats derived from the Aesthetic movement the idea that works of art can exert a shaping force on foetal development: ' "The general esteem for beauty went so far, that the Spartan women set up in their bedchambers a Nireus, a Narcissus, or a Hyacinth, that they might bear beautiful children" ' (Pater, quoting Winckelmann in *The Renaissance* [1893], ed. Hill, p. 166); 'The Greeks ... set in the bride's chamber the statue of Hermes or of Apollo, that she might bear children as lovely as the works of art that she looked at in her rapture or her pain' (Wilde, 'The Decay of Lying', *Complete Works*, ed. Holland, pp. 982–83). Wyndham Lewis also inherited this theme: 'Bertha's was the intellectually-fostered hellenic type of german handsomeness. It would make you think that german mothers must have replicas and photographs of the Venus of Milo in their rooms during the first three months of their pregnancy. Of course they in fact have' (*Tarr* [1918; 1928] I 4).

IV 6 *Measurement*: compare 'The Statues', l. 8: 'a plummet-measured face'.

IV 7 *Forms a stark Egyptian thought*: compare the Egyptian's speech in the 1927 version of *The Resurrection*, ll. 366–69: 'God has form but not body ... but God can communicate with mankind through an illusionary body, such a form as sculptors ... make' (*VPl*, p. 924). Plotinus was born in Egypt, but Yeats may be referring to an anonymous heiratic sculptor, as in the uncollected poem (quoted in the headnote to 'The Statues') that begins 'Let images of basalt, black, immovable, / Chiselled in Egypt ... Represent spirits'.

IV 8 *Phidias*: see 'Nineteen Hundred and Nineteen' I 7.

IV 9 *Michael Angelo*: see 'Michael Robartes and the Dancer', l. 32. In 1915 Yeats wrote an account (using the persona of his anti-self, the explorer Leo Africanus) of the dreamlikeness of the life after death: 'At Rome I had seen Michael Angelo at work upon the scaffolding in the Sistine Chapel, & once I had been in his studio & watched him drawing from the model. The events in life ... were like that model but gradually were so changed, that [they] resembled more what I saw in Adam ... when the scaffolding was taken away' (*Yeats Annual* 1 [1982]: 31). Death, then, exerted the same simplifying and idealizing power on raw life that Michelangelo's art did.

IV 10 *the Sistine Chapel*: a chapel in the Vatican in Rome, built by Pope Sixtus IV. 'Blake ... Nietzsche ... were begotten in the Sistine Chapel and still dream that all can be transformed if they be but emphatic' (*AV*, p. 299).

IV 11 *half-awakened Adam*: in the MS of this poem, Yeats, remembering Michelangelo's own proclivities, wrote 'homo sexual Adam' (*VR*, p. 165). Michelangelo's fresco shows the arms of creator and awakening man outstretched towards each other, their fingers just about to touch – a literal image of the bringing of 'the soul of man to God' (IV 4). The beauty of Adam, in turn, brings the soul of the tourist to God (IV 12). Jeffares notes (*NCP*, p. 405) that when Shaw's *The Black Girl in Search of God* was banned, Yeats took a reproduction of Michelangelo's Adam to the censors to show them their hypocrisy.

IV 13 *her bowels are in heat*: Michelangelo similarly stirs a younger woman in 'Long-legged Fly', ll. 21–22: 'girls at puberty may find / The first Adam in their thought'. For another example of sexual arousal by an image, see 'The Statues', l. 8, where live lips kiss a statue's face.

IV 17 *Quattrocento*: the fifteenth century. According to *A Vision*, pp. 291–92, the artists of the Italian Renaissance achieved around the year 1500 (like Phidias around 500 BC) an accession to maximum beauty, Phase 15 – the heavens opened (IV 26) to mankind.

IV 23 *When sleepers wake and yet still dream*: 'the threshold, between sleeping and waking, where Sphinxes and Chimeras sit open-eyed and where there are always murmurings and whisperings' (*M*, p. 81). As always, the apex of vision is achieved in a liminal state – see 'The Double Vision of Michael Robartes' III 1-3.

IV 26 *Gyres run on*: after the *antithetical* maximum of the Renaissance, 'The gyre ebbs out in order and reason' (*AV*, p. 295).

IV 28 *Calvert and Wilson, Blake and Claude*: for William Blake, see 'An Acre of Grass', l. 16. Edward Calvert (1799–1883) was a disciple of Blake. Richard Wilson (1714–82) was a landscape painter; or Yeats may have meant George Wilson (1848–90), a painter acquainted with J. B. Yeats whom Yeats faintly remembered (*EI*, p. 346). Claude Gellée, called Le Lorrain (1600-82) was the first great landscape painter – his idyllic scenes are often suffused in oblique sunlight. According to Yeats, Swedenborg believed that 'the good are amid smooth grass and garden walks and the clear sunlight of Claude Lorraine' (*Ex*, p. 37). And Yeats thus described Claude's *Mill*: 'Those dancing country-people, those cowherds, resting after the day's work, and that quiet millrace made one think ... of a time when men in every land found poetry and imagination in one another's company and in the day's labour' (*EI*, p. 377).

IV 29 *Palmer's phrase*: Samuel Palmer (1805–81), another disciple of Blake, described Blake's illustrations to Virgil's first eclogue: '"There is in all such a misty and dreamy glimmer as penetrates and kindles the inmost soul ... a drawing aside of the fleshly curtain, and the glimpse which all the most holy, studious saints and sages have enjoyed, of the rest which remains to the people of God"' (*EI*, p. 125, quoting from A. H. Palmer's *The Life and Letters of Samuel Palmer*, pp. 15–16). 'Palmer's phrase' quotes Hebrews 4:9: 'There remaineth therefore a rest to the people of God'; Browning cited this verse in 'Old Pictures in Florence' (1855), l. 175; and Yeats had a monk quote it in a deleted passage from the 1902 version of *Where There is Nothing* V (*VPl*, p. 1145). Also compare *Ex*, p. 44: 'in his [Blake's] boys and girls walking or dancing on smooth grass and in golden light, as in pastoral scenes cut upon wood or copper by his disciples Palmer and Calvert, one notices the peaceful Swedenborgian heaven'. In the context of this poem, such visions are fragile, sheltered, compared to the exuberant Renaissance heaven. (Palmer is also mentioned in 'The Phases of the Moon', l. 17; another phrase of Palmer's that Yeats liked to quote was '"Excess is the essential vivifying spirit ... think always on excess ... make excess more abundantly excessive"' [*EI*, pp. 123, 184].)

V 4 *All out of shape from toe to top*: it seems that the mission of poetry, like that of painting, is to establish the correct proportions of the human body. Compare 'The Statues', l. 29: 'this filthy modern tide'.

V 7–8 *Sing the peasantry ... Hard-riding country gentlemen*: compare Yeats's notion in 'At Galway Races' and 'The Fisherman' that poetry addresses itself to horsemen and fishermen.

V 12 *beaten into the clay*: see 'The Curse of Cromwell', l. 3.

V 13 *seven heroic centuries*: compare *The Dreaming of the Bones* (1919), ll. 98–99: 'mourners for five centuries have carried / Noble or peasant to his burial'.

V 16 *Irishry*: Yeats cited Toynbee's prediction that '"Jewry and Irishry will each fit into its own tiny niche,"' become relegated to unimportance; Yeats commented, 'If Irish literature goes on as my generation planned it, it may do something to keep the "Irishry" living' (*EI*, p. 517).

VI 1 *Under bare Ben Bulben's head*: Pound's parody of this line can be found in Introduction I.

VI 2 *In Drumcliff churchyard Yeats is laid*: this assertion came to pass when Yeats's remains were transported from southern France, where he died.

VI 3 *An ancestor*: Rev. John Yeats, made Rector of Drumcliff in 1805 – see the Introductory Rhymes to *Responsibilities*, l. 5.

VI 5 *an ancient Cross*: compare 'Are You Content', ll. 9–10: 'He that in Sligo at Drumcliff / Set up the old stone Cross'.

VI 8 *these words are cut*: for other poems in which the poem's text is a thematic element, see 'When You Are Old', l. 2.

VI 9–11 Cast a cold eye / On life, on death. / Horseman, pass by!: this epitaph was originally a quatrain, beginning 'Draw rein; draw breath'. Yeats wrote to Dorothy Wellesley that this epitaph was provoked by 'a book of essays about Rilke ... one on Rilkey's ideas about death annoyed me. I wrote [the epitaph] on the margin' (*DWL*, p. 184). As Hone notes (*WBY*, p. 473), Yeats's copy of *R. M. Rilke: Some Aspects of his Mind and Poetry*, ed. William Rose, has no such marginalia. Perhaps what annoyed Yeats in Rilke was his anxious self-engrossment, his lack of 'a cold eye' – Rose's essay (in the above-mentioned book) on 'Rilke and the Conception of Death' stressed that Rilke believed that the death a man dies 'must be familiar to him and not something alien; it must be essentially personal' (p. 57). Yeats also sent his epitaph to Ethel Mannin (*L*, p. 914) and later wrote to her: 'According to Rilke a man's death is born with him and if his life is successful and he escapes mere "mass death" his nature is completed by his final union with it. Rilke gives Hamlet's death as an example' (*L*, p. 917). Yeats had already used Hamlet's death as an example of tragic joy ('Lapis Lazuli', ll. 10, 16) – for Yeats too, life and death could culminate in an integral blaze. 'Under Ben Bulben' contains several echoes of *Hamlet*, including a ghostly command to swear (I v 154) and a grave-digger (V i 35).

VI 9 Cast a cold eye: compare *On Baile's Strand* (1904), l. 506: 'you have a hot heart and a cold eye'; and 'A Bronze Head', l. 23: 'a sterner eye'. This advice seems related to Sri Purohit Swāmi's dictum, '"Act and remain apart from action"' (*L*, p. 806).

VI 11 Horseman, pass by!: for other apostrophes on tombstones, see 'Coole Park, 1929', l. 25. It is significant that a poem that begins with supernatural horsemen should end with this address – almost a challenge. Yeats seems to have attained such a comprehensive view of life and death that he is on equal terms with the unearthly riders of part I.

Three Songs to the One Burden

'Under Ben Bulben' is an elegy for the poet's own funeral, whereas 'Three Songs to the One Burden' is popular entertainment; but despite the differences in diction and sophistication, both poems deplore modern culture – feeble but tenacious – and applaud the resurgence of old energies. 'Under Ben Bulben' is theory, this poem is practice: in I, a violent tinker thrashes common folk; in II, a recluse builds a fence to keep out the plague of commonness; and in III, an actor celebrates warfare – a still higher form of theatre.

I 7 *I take on half a score*: compare *The Wanderings of Oisin* III 164, where the old Oisin returns to a degenerate Ireland, 'a small and a feeble populace'.

I 9 From mountain to mountain ride the fierce horsemen: for Mary Battle's vision of supernatural horsemen, see the note to 'Under Ben Bulben' I 5. The tinker's roaring – like all displays of wild or disciplined strength – foretells a new heroic age. In 1936 Yeats wrote to Ethel Mannin: 'why should I trouble about communism, fascism, liberalism, radicalism, when all . . . are going down stream . . . My rage and that of others like me seems more important – though we may but be the first of the final destroying horde' (*L*, p. 869); 'I am a forerunner of that horde that will some day come down the mountains' (*L*, p. 873).

I 10 *Manannan*: an Irish sea god. In *The Wanderings of Oisin* II 128–36, Oisin finds a sword with Manannan's name on it, and remembers how Manannan 'cried to all / The mightier masters of a mightier race'; Oisin then describes Manannan as a kind of Antichrist.

I 19 *Crazy Jane*: see the headnote to *Words for Music Perhaps*.

I 25 *Throw likely couples into bed*: an expression of Yeats's advocacy of eugenics. In *On the Boiler* Yeats wrote of 'the caste system that has saved the Indian intellect', and he deplored the European governments that 'put quantity before quality . . . accelerate degeneration' by offering 'bounties for the seventh, eighth, or ninth baby' (*Ex*, p. 424).

II 1 *Henry Middleton*: Yeats's eccentric and reclusive cousin, who lived at Rosses Point near Sligo in a house thought to be haunted. His strategy is not to fight the modern world, as the tinker does, but to insulate himself from it, to outlive it. Yeats referred to Middleton in his 1908 Preface to *John Sherman* (1891): 'he who gave me all of Sherman [not based on my own experience] has still the bronze upon his face, and is at this moment, it may be, in his walled garden, wondering, as he did twenty years ago, whether he will ever mend the broken glass of the conservatory' (*JSD*, p. 40).

II 10 *I have locked my gate*: Hone tells that in 1919 Yeats visited Henry Middleton by climbing over the wall and walking into a room 'littered with cheap novels . . . His cousin was there, beautifully dressed . . . "You see", he said . . . "that I am too busy to see anyone"' (*WBY*, p. 22).

II 20 *the Green Lands*: a sandy waste near by the Rosses.

II 25–26 *There's not a pilot on the perch / Knows I have lived so long*: compare *The King of the Great Clock Tower* (1935), ll. 165–67, where a 'wicked, crooked hawthorn tree' says, 'I have stood so long by a gap on the wall / Maybe I shall not die at all'.

III: this song was once entitled, 'An Abbey Player – I meditate upon 1916'.

III 5 *Post Office*: the centre of the Easter rebellion in 1916 – see 'The Statues', l. 26.

III 11 *the player Connolly*: not the labour leader James Connolly, praised in 'Easter, 1916', but Seán Connolly, an actor at the Abbey Theatre shot during the uprising. This song systematically confuses politics and theatre – just as in 'Easter, 1916' Yeats described how the rebels evolved from comedians to tragedians. The Easter rebellion and the Abbey productions are alike antimasques to a greater drama of world-transformation, signalled by the 'fierce horsemen' of the refrain.

III 23: for the textual authority of this line (and of III 16), see Finneran, *EYP*, p. 76.

III 24 *Pearse*: see 'Easter, 1916', l. 24.

III 25–26: see 'The Rose Tree', l. 17.

The Black Tower

This is Yeats's last poem, partly dictated on his deathbed. Like the second of the 'Three Songs to the One Burden', it depicts an attempt to outwait an imbecile civilization – as if *antithetical* heroism and magnificence had dwindled to a single Black Tower, a frontier outpost where soldiers, stiffened almost to icons, stoically await their king's resurrection. Yeats's own tower, Thoor Ballylee, was haunted by the ghosts of Norman soldiers that came 'with loud cry ... To break upon a sleeper's rest / While their great wooden dice beat on the board' ('The Tower' II 70–72); this poem seems to realize these ghosts and their bleak medieval dream.

3 *wine gone sour*: compare 'Church and State', ll. 11–12: 'Wine shall run thick ... Bread taste sour'.

4 *Lack nothing*: the prose draft suggests, in fact, that a miracle provides what the soldiers need: 'The Gods have brought us milk & flesh' (Stallworthy, *BL*, p. 226).

5 *oath-bound men*: compare 'The Curse of Cromwell', l. 22: 'I am still their servant though all are underground'.

6 *Those banners*: that is, the slogans and inane values of the modern state. According to Saul (*Prolegomena*, p. 176), Mrs Yeats said that this is a poem 'on the subject of political propaganda'.

7 stand the dead upright: Finneran quotes (*PNE*, p. 677) a passage from P. W. Joyce's *A Social History of Ancient Ireland* I, p. 551: 'occasionally the bodies of kings and chieftains were buried in a standing posture, arrayed in full battle costume'.

8 winds come: Yeats changed this from *wind comes*, but only in the first refrain; the editor has changed ll. 18 and 28 to agree.

9: in one draft this line read, 'When it blows from the black pig's dyke' (*BL*, p. 232) – an allusion to apocalypse (see 'The Valley of the Black Pig').

9–10 They shake when the winds roar . shake: compare 'An Acre of Grass', l. 22: 'Shake the dead in their shrouds'. The repetition of *shake* recalls a similar repetition in Lionel Johnson's sonnet 'The Church of a Dream', where the images of old saints keep shaking in the wind (*EI*, p 493; *UP* II, p. 117).

13 *his own right king's forgotten*: compare 'What Was Lost', l. 3: 'My king a lost king'.

21 *old cook*: compare 'The Hawk', l. 5: 'The old cook enraged'. Early drafts of 'The Black Tower' call this spry cook 'Old clown Tom' (*BL*, p. 239) – compare such other Toms as 'Tom the Lunatic'.

24 *he's a lying hound*: the tower-dwellers refuse to lose their composure over uncertain hints of the new millennium.

Cuchulain Comforted

This, Yeats's penultimate poem, is 'a kind of sequel' (*L*, p. 922) to Yeats's last play, *The Death of Cuchulain* (1939). (For information on Cuchulain, see the note to 'Cuchulain's Fight with the Sea'.) Having attained every heroic glory, Cuchulain passes into a strange state of abstraction, depersonalization, and oblivion: in *The Death of Cuchulain* his severed head is represented as a black parallelogram, and in this poem the hero and the cowards are enfolded into a single common action. The prose draft makes it clear that the shroud that Cuchulain sews for himself is a substitute for his battle-armour: 'another shade said: "You would be much more comfortable if you would make a shroud and wear it instead of the arms"' (*DWL*, p. 193). In life a man makes a self by brave actions; in death he relinquishes that self.

The metre of this poem is *terza rima*, the metre of Dante's *Divine Comedy*, appropriate in a poem about the Country of the Dead; the most distinguished English poem in this metre is Shelley's last important poem, *The Triumph of Life* (1822), in which a luminous woman dissolves the minds of those who gaze upon her (ll. 382–88) – a poem about the undoing of identity, like Yeats's.

1 *six mortal wounds*: in *The Death of Cuchulain*, ll. 185–95, Conall Caernach kills each of the six men who wounded Cuchulain

13 *make a shroud*: in *The Death of Cuchulain*, ll. 121–24, Aoife anticipates this shroud by wrapping her veil around Cuchulain. The shrouds are also

similar to the mummy-windings Yeats described in earlier poems – see 'All Souls' Night', l. 13.

16 *thread the needles' eye*: compare Dante's famous simile for the band of sodomites staring at the poet in *Inferno* 15: 20–21: 'they knitted their brows at us, as an old tailor does at the eye of his needle'. Also compare 'A Needle's Eye'.

16–17 *all we do / All must together do*: Yeats thought that dead souls lost individuality, became absorbed into groups: 'some spirit once said to me: "We do nothing singly, every act is done by a number at the same instant"' (*AV*, p. 234); 'Hitherto shade has communicated with shade in moments of common memory . . . but now they run together like to like, and their covens and fleets have rhythm and pattern' (*M*, p. 356).

18 *began to sew*: in 'Work' (included by Yeats in *OBMV*), D. H. Lawrence praised the absorption of Hindus sewing long lengths of cloth – 'they clothe themselves in white as a tree clothes itself in its own foliage'.

19 *Now must we sing*: Yeats adopted this reading as a correction of *Now we shall sing*; but possibly he wished to return to the earlier version (Finneran, *EYP*, p. 78).

23 *tunes nor words*: Yeats adopted this reading as a correction of *notes nor words*; but again he may have been unsure which he preferred (Finneran, *EYP*, p. 78).

25 *the throats of birds*: 'Then they began to sing, and they did not sing like men and women, but like linnets that had been stood on a perch and taught by a good singing master' (prose draft, *DWL*, p. 193). The prose draft connects this afterlife to the 'artifice of eternity' in 'Sailing to Byzantium' – a poem with both singing-masters and a supernatural bird. For the theme of a man's spiritual translation into a bird's shape, see the note to 'The Three Hermits'. In a draft of *The Death of Cuchulain*, at the moment when the dead Cuchulain reaches out for his new shape, an attendant whispers, 'Four & twenty black birds – the pie – the six pence – the ry & the pocket – nothing to do with each other an untrue song & yet immortal' (*The Death of Cuchulain: Manuscript Materials*, ed. Philip L. Marcus, p. 93) – as if Mother Goose nonsense approximated the birdsongs of the dead.

Three Marching Songs

These are 'Three Songs to the Same Tune' (1933–34, published in *A Full Moon in March*, directly after 'Parnell's Funeral') rewritten and reordered. 'In politics I have but one passion and one thought, rancour against all who, except under the most dire necessity, disturb public order, a conviction that public order cannot long persist without the rule of educated and able men ... Some months ago that passion laid hold upon me ... While the mood lasted, it seemed that our growing disorder, the fanaticism that inflamed it like some old bullet imbedded in the flesh, was about to turn our noble history into an ignoble farce. For the first time in my life I wanted to write what some crowd in the street might understand and sing' (*VP*, p. 543). Earlier in his life Yeats despised crowd-songs: in 1906 he wrote of 'young men marching down the middle of a street singing an already outworn London music-hall song ... with a rhythm as pronounced and as impersonal as the noise of a machine' (*Ex*, p. 203); and in 1925 he condemned the polemical Shelley (who wrote such rabble-rousers as 'Song to the Men of England' [1819]) when 'out of phase' (*AV*, p. 143).

These songs gave Yeats much trouble, particularly the refrains. Originally all three songs had the same refrain: '*Those fanatics all that we do would undo; / Down the fanatic, down the clown; / Down, down, hammer them down, / Down to the tune of O'Donnell Abu*'. But in *A Full Moon in March*, this was the refrain only of the song that begins 'Grandfather sang it under the gallows'.

I 1 *Remember*: in *A Full Moon in March*, the word *Justify* replaces *Remember* throughout this song.

I 7–10, 17–20, 27–30: in *A Full Moon in March*, the refrain was: '"*Drown all the dogs", said the fierce young woman, "They killed my goose and a cat. / Drown, drown in the water-butt, / Drown all the dogs", said the fierce young woman*' (*VP*, p. 546). The young woman was Mrs Yeats – see *L*, pp. 820–21. Compare Browning, 'Mesmerism' (1855) II 5: 'a cat's in the water-butt' – the epigraph of Pound's 'Mesmerism' (1908). In his own copy of *A Full Moon in March*, Yeats corrected the refrain to '*Go ask the curlew if night has gone / Or if the gangling mind / Still bears and begets its kind / Go ask the curlew if night has gone*' (Edward O'Shea, *Yeats: An Annual of Critical and Textual Studies* 4 [1986]: 124–42).

I 9 time amends old wrong: compare 'Nineteen Hundred and Nineteen' II 6–7: 'the Platonic Year / Whirls out new right and wrong'.

I 20, 30: in most previous texts, this line begins *And all that's*; the editor has regularized the line in conformity with I 10, corrected by Yeats.

I 23 *O'Donnell*: probably Red Hugh O'Donnell (*c.* 1571–1602), who fought with Spain against Queen Elizabeth.

I 24 *both O'Neills*: of the several distinguished warriors named O'Neill, Yeats was almost certainly thinking of Hugh O'Neill (b. *c.* 1540), who fought with Red Hugh O'Donnell against Elizabeth and made an uneasy peace with her and, later, King James: 'Red Hugh allied himself to Hugh O'Neill, the most powerful of the Irish leaders, an Oxford man too, a man of the Renaissance, in [chronicler William] Camden's words "a profound dissembling heart so as many deemed him born either for the great good or ill of his country", and for a few years defeated English armies and shook the power of England' (*EI*, p. 363).

I 25 *Emmet . . . Parnell*: for Emmet, see the Introductory Rhymes to *Responsibilities*, l. 5; for Parnell, see 'To a Shade'.

II 1 *The soldier takes pride*: 'I put into a simple song a commendation of the rule of the able and educated, man's old delight in submission; I wrote round the line "The soldier takes pride in saluting his captain", thinking the while of a Gaelic poet's lament for his lost masters: "My fathers served their fathers before Christ was crucified" [see 'The Curse of Cromwell', l. 6]. I read my songs to friends, they talked to others, those others talked, and now companies march to the words "Blueshirt Abu"' (*VP*, pp. 543–44). '*Down to the tune of O'Donnell Abu*' was part of the original refrain of these songs.

II 4: this line originally read, 'What's equality? – Muck in the yard' (*VP*, p. 547) – compare 'Blood and the Moon' II 12: 'Cast but dead leaves to mathematical equality'.

II 7–10, 17–20, 27–30: in *A Full Moon in March*, the refrain was: '"*Who'd care to dig 'em", said the old, old man, / "Those six feet marked in chalk? / Much I talk, more I walk; / Time I were buried", said the old, old man*' (*VP*, p. 548). According to O'Shea (see the note for the first song's refrain), Yeats corrected the refrain in his own copy of *A Full Moon in March* to '*Remember the saints when night has gone / Night now and much to do, / Night now and a reckless crew; / Remember the saints when night has gone*'.

II 9 airy: '"Airy" may be an old pronunciation of "eerie" often heard in Galway and Sligo' (*VP*, p. 614).

II 12 *The lofty innocence that it has slain*: compare 'The Second Coming', l. 6: 'The ceremony of innocence is drowned'.

II 13–14: for the textual authority of these lines, see Finneran, *EYP*, pp. 80–81.

II 21: this line originally read, 'When nations are empty up there at the top' (*VP*, p. 548) – compare 'Blood and the Moon' IV 5–6: 'Is every modern nation like the tower, / Half dead at the top?'

II 23 *What tears down a tree that has nothing within it?*: most previous editions omit *that*, a possible improvement in rhythm, at the expense of syntax; but Yeats's MS draft of this line in his copy of *A Full Moon in March* has the pronoun, and its omission may have been an oversight. For the figure of the state as a tree, see 'Blood and the Moon' II 10.

II 25 *March wind, and any old tune*: 'My generation . . . came to dislike all rhetoric. . . . People began to imitate old ballads because an old ballad is never rhetorical' (*EI*, p. 497).

III 8–9 he took down the moon / And rattled out a tune: perhaps an allusion to the fairy tale 'The Moon', where the moon is taken piecemeal down from a tree – see the note to 'Vacillation' VI 13. 'Grandfather' dismisses death, by whistling or by beating rhythm at the gallows (as at I 15–16); these executions, these marching songs, are (like all change) synchronized to the phases of the moon.

III 24 *his throat was too small*: compare the throat-change in 'Cuchulain Comforted', l. 25.

In Tara's Halls

The old man's forward thrust, generosity, reverence, pride, disdain, unstooping magnificence, heroic inflexibility, absence of tenderness, and refusal to flinch at the prospect of dying, all reflect the *antithetical* character that Yeats expected to see restored after the millennium. He offers a model of the cold eye cast on life and death at the end of 'Under Ben Bulben'. In such poems as 'The Tower', the poet constructed a verbal edifice to dwell in; now he imagines the construction of a grave.

1 *Tara*: see 'In the Seven Woods', l. 6. In 1906 Douglas Hyde described Tara: 'The great palace where . . . a hundred and thirty-six pagan and six Christian kings had ruled uninterruptedly, the most august spot in all Ireland, where a "truce of God" had always reigned . . . was now to be given up and deserted at the curse of a tonsured monk. . . . It was a blow from which the monarchy of Ireland never recovered' (*Literary History of Ireland*, p. 226). Yeats wrote, 'The hill of Teamhair, or Tara . . . brought before one imaginations, not of heroes . . . but of kings that lived brief and politic lives' (*Ex*, pp. 14–15). Yeats hoped that Tara would be restored by the archaeological authorities (*VPl*, p. 573); and he told the Irish senate that he personally had helped to prevent the mutilation of the ruins at Tara (*SSY*, p. 89).

10 *the man*: another TS reads *the king* (Finneran, *EYP*, p. 82), and (in l. 15) substitutes *women* for *woman*.

12 *the golden plough*: when Martin (in *The Unicorn from the Stars* III 395–98) leaves the stage (after describing world-trampling unicorns), a beggar remarks of him, 'It is maybe to some secret cleft he is going, to get knowledge of the great cure for all things, or of the Plough that was hidden in the old times, the Golden Plough'.

17 *Diggers . . . make grave*: for other grave-diggers, see 'Under Ben Bulben' II 9.

The Statues

This poem is a meditation on idols, on God's co-evolution with man as reflected in divine images. As such it is a sequel to 'The Indian on God', in which the moorfowl sees God as a moorfowl, the lotus sees God as a lotus, and so forth: every civilization creates an image of God suitable for its needs and aspirations. Here mankind is not simply the clay moulded by God's hand, as *A Vision* and such poems as 'Leda and the Swan' may seem to suggest; here God is Himself plastic, malleable to human desire. Pater invited this sort of analysis in his 'Winckelmann': 'Religions ... are modified by whatever modifies [man's] life. They brighten under a bright sky ... they grow intense and shrill in the clefts of human life, where the spirit is narrow and confined, and the stars are visible at noonday' (*The Renaissance* [1893], ed. Hill, pp. 159–60). But a more immediate source for this poem was Yeats's study of Indian philosophy; as Yeats remarked in 'An Indian Monk', 'Nor can a single image, that of Christ, Krishna, or Buddha, represent God to the exclusion of other images' (*EI*, p. 433).

Yeats's prose draft shows his conception of a divine icon continually reshaping itself, growing fat or thin, lax or stern, ugly or beautiful, ruddy or pale, in every way answering man's call, fitting itself to man's purpose: '[I] They went out in broad day or under the moon Moving with dream certainty ... empty faces, measured Pythagorean perfection; only that which is incapable of thought is infinite in passion; only passion sees God. Men were victorious at Salamis, & human victories are nothing, now one up, then another; & only those cold marble forms could drive back the vague, asiatic hoard; beat down multiform Nature with their certainty [II] Weary of victory one was far from all his companions – & sat so long in solitude, that his once athletic body became soft & round incapable of work or war, because his eyes were empty, more empty than the skies at night ... Apolo forgot Pythagoras & took the name of Buddha which was victorious Greece in the asiatic [mode?]. Others had stayed away & ... they saw marble put forth many heads & feet [III] Where are you now. Is it true that you shed the sun-burn & become pale white; Did you appear in the Post Office in 1916 is it True that Pearse called on you by name of Cuchullain Certainly we have need of you. The vague flood is at its Height ... from all four quarters is coming Come back with all your Pythagorean numbers' (Stallworthy, *VR*, pp. 125–26).

Carlyle wrote in *Sartor Resartus* (1831) of the organic nature of symbols, how symbols sprout and grow and decay like living things; and here Yeats describes the strange susceptibility of statues to overweight, sunburn, sexual arousal, as if statues were as alive as the men who make them and contemplate them. This poem take its place in a long line of celebrations of living statues, from the Greek myth of Pygmalion to E. T. A. Hoffmann's 'Der Sandmann' (1817) to Fellini's film *Casanova* (1976) – in 'Men Improve with the Years', Yeats referred to himself as a living statue.

An untitled, uncollected poem of 1934 suggests that God is best represented by the most abstract and hieratic statues – realistic sculptural forms, like the realistic images summoned by mediums, may be too tainted with humanity to embody the supernatural:

> Let images of basalt, black, immovable,
> Chiselled in Egypt, or ovoids of bright steel
> Hammered and polished by Brancusi's hand,
> Represent spirits. If spirits seem to stand
> Before the bodily eyes, speak into the bodily ears,
> They are not present but their messengers.
> Of double nature these, one nature is
> Compounded of accidental phantasies.
> We question; it but answers what we would
> Or as phantasy directs – because they have drunk the blood.
> (*VPl*, p. 969; *Ex*, p. 367)

(For more on secondary personalities or 'messengers' – hybrids half-human, half-superhuman, engendered by spirits on mediums – see the passage on Leo Africanus quoted in the headnote to 'Ego Dominus Tuus'; for more on Egyptian sculpture, see 'Under Ben Bulben' IV 7.) But 'The Statues' is a kind of defence of realism, against abstractionism: those statues that look most like men seem best to inspire, to inform human conduct.

1 *Pythagoras*: see 'Among School Children' VI 5. The poet can claim that Greek statues are reifications of Pythagorean numbers because Greek sculptors used strict ratios to determine the proportions of the body (e.g., the body should be seven times as long as the head – part of the 'canon of Polyclitus'); Yeats wrote in his diary of gymnasts striving to make defective bodies conform to 'that ancient canon which comes down to us from the gymnasium of Greece' (*Mem*, p. 188; *A: DS* 4). Similarly, Pythagoras discovered that musical notes are simple ratios of lengths of a vibrating string. One draft of 'The Statues' is entitled 'Pythagorean Numbers' (*VR*, p. 135).

3 *lacked character*: a commonplace of art historians after Winckelmann. Pater in 'Luca della Robbia' wrote of the monumental insipidity of Greek art: 'that law of the most excellent Greek sculptors, of Pheidias ... prompted them constantly to seek the type in the individual, to abstract and express only what is structural and permanent ... it involved ... the sacrifice of what we call *expression*' (*The Renaissance*, ed. Hill, p. 51–52). Yeats wrote similarly in *A Vision* of 'Grecian eyes gazing at nothing', as opposed to the drilled eyeballs of Roman statues, where 'the delineation of character' is shown in the face (pp. 276–77).

8 *Live lips upon a plummet-measured face*: 'Man is nothing till he is united to an image' (*The Player Queen* [1922], II 480-81) – and a kissed statue represents

such a union quite literally. Yeats sometimes conceived history as a dialectic in which God supplied purity of form and man supplied passion: see the 1927 version of *The Resurrection*, in which the Egyptian sees Christ as a vacant statue and the Hebrew sees Christ as a mere man – the two combine in the real Incarnation. Also see Pater's description of Greek 'statues worn with kissing' (*The Renaissance*, ed. Hill, pp. 162, 429). Yeats once imagined a scene where a statue returns human sexual affection: in *A Full Moon in March* (1935), ll. 180-85, a statue grows animate, descends into mortality – echoing the end of Shakespeare's *The Winter's Tale*: '*Second Attendant*. Why must those holy, haughty feet descend / From emblematic niches, and what hand / Ran that delicate raddle through their white? / My heart is broken, yet must understand. / What do they seek for? Why must they descend? // *First Attendant*. For desecration and the lover's night'.

9 *Greater than Pythagoras*: the Greek sculptors are superior to a mathematician, in that form can exert force on human conduct only when realized in matter.

11–12 *put down / All Asiatic vague immensities*: compare the marbles in 'Byzantium', that break the flood of organic life pouring into Byzantium. Yeats's image of formal Western beauty fighting against Eastern incoherence may derive from Pater: 'in the East from a vagueness, a want of definition, in thought, the matter presented to art is unmanageable, and the forms of sense struggle vainly with it. The many-headed gods of the East ... are at best ... a means of hinting at an idea which art cannot fitly or completely express' (*The Renaissance*, ed. Hill, pp. 163-64).

14 *The many-headed foam at Salamis*: Salamis is an island near Athens, where the Greek navy routed a larger Persian fleet in 480 BC. The foam is many-headed partly because sailors are drowning in it, partly because it symbolizes the multifariousness and unintelligibility of Asia. Yeats liked to speak of the Irish idealist Berkeley's triumph over English materialistic philosophy as the 'Irish Salamis' (*Ex*, pp. 334, 336, 339, 348).

15–16 *Phidias / Gave women dreams and dreams their looking-glass*: for Phidias, see 'Nineteen Hundred and Nineteen' I 7. Yeats here applauds Phidias for imagining an ideal body that human sexual selection can try to realize – Yeats applauded Michelangelo for similar reasons in 'Under Ben Bulben' IV 9. 'Art must once again accept those Greek proportions which carry into plastic art the Pythagorean numbers, those faces which are divine because all there is empty and measured. Europe was not born when Greek galleys defeated the Persian hordes at Salamis; but when the Doric studios sent out those broad-backed marble statues against the multiform, vague, expressive Asiatic sea, they gave to the sexual instinct of Europe its goal, its fixed type.... I recall a Swedish actress ... riding the foam upon a plank towed behind a speed-boat, but one finds it wherever the lucky or the well-born uncover their sunburnt bodies' (*Ex*, p. 451). Yeats implied that the water-skier was beautiful because the mating behaviour of her ancestors was influenced by Phidian standards of bodily perfection.

17 *One image*: Buddha – early carvings of Buddha were in fact based on Greek designs disseminated in India by the armies of Alexander the Great. 'In reading the third stanza remember the influence on modern sculpture and on the great seated Buddha of the sculptors who follow Alexander' (*L*, p. 911). Here the image loses its economy of line, turns flabby, vacuous, innumerate, drifting. Yeats also wrote of Buddha in 'The Double Vision of Michael Robartes' II 3.

19 *Hamlet thin from eating flies*: for Hamlet, see 'Lapis Lazuli', l. 105 – here Yeats takes Hamlet as a intellectual starving from a diet of abstractions, like the shadow-eating Maud Gonne of 'Among School Children' IV 4. In *On the Boiler* Yeats argued that the intellectual Hamlet was a modern caricature – actually Hamlet was 'a medieval man of action' (*Ex*, p. 446). Compare the 1927 version of *The Resurrection*, ll. 124–27: 'Nobody can drive the Roman out, but he eats too much and for that reason he cannot think, and so he lets the Greeks, who are a lean race, do it for him' (*VPl*, p. 910).

19–20 *a fat / Dreamer of the Middle Ages*: Yeats associated this phrase with William Morris, whom Yeats claimed to envy above all men: 'the broad vigorous body [in Watts' portrait of Morris] suggests a mind that has no need of intellect to remain sane, though it give itself to every fantasy: the dreamer of the middle ages. It is "the fool of fairy ...", the resolute European image that yet half remembers Buddha's motionless meditation, and has no trait in common with the wavering, lean image of hungry speculation, that cannot but because of certain famous Hamlets of our stage fill the mind's eye' (*A: FY* 12). Yeats criticized Morris for the lack of tension, the childlikeness, the sloth of his fantasies (*EI*, pp. 60–61) – the contrast in this stanza, then, is between the emaciated, abstract West and the idle, fantastical, complacent East, one too thin, the other too fat, both deviant from Phidian perfection of shape and unity of faculty.

20 *Empty eyeballs*: 'those eyelids of ... India, those veiled or half-veiled eyes weary of world and vision alike' (*AV*, p. 277).

21–22 *knowledge increases unreality ... Mirror on mirror mirrored is all the show*: that is, because the phenomenal world is an illusion (according to Buddha), any engagement with it traps one in hollow images. In *The Hour-Glass* (1914), the Wise Man (a model of Western intellect) teaches that 'truth is learnt / When the intellect's deliberate and cold, / As it were a polished mirror that reflects / An unchanged world' (ll. 379-82) – until the Wise Man sees an Angel who shows him the fallacy of his teaching, proves the unreality of the mind's abstract images of the world; Angels can 'out-stare / The steadiest eyes with their unnatural eyes' (ll. 230–31). Yeats suggested in 'Rosa Alchemica' (1896) that the mind's polished mirror ought to be shattered (*M*, p. 276); and in *On the Boiler* (1939) Yeats also tried to dismiss mental constructions: 'Of late I have tried to understand ... the falsehood that is in all knowledge ... Should we drive it away at last, we must enter the Buddhist monastery in Auden's play [*The Ascent of F6* II i]' (*Ex*, pp. 449–50). For other references to mirrors, see 'The Two Trees', l. 21; for the involved rhetorical form of l. 22, compare 'Ribh in Ecstasy', ll. 5–6: 'Godhead on Godhead ... begot / Godhead'.

23 *gong*: compare 'Byzantium', l. 4. One version of l. 23 read, 'That only Buddha's hand knew how to bless' (*VR*, p. 139) – a line reminiscent of the Buddha in 'The Double Vision of Michael Robartes' II 4: 'Hand lifted up that blest'.

24 *Grimalkin crawls to Buddha's emptiness*: Grimalkin is a name applied to a cat – in *Macbeth* I i 8 a witch summons her familiar with that name. Though Yeats often attributed supernatural power to cats (as in 'The Cat and the Moon'), it is likely that he intended Grimalkin to represent the anxious, famished, intellectual West (according to popular lore, cats, like the Hamlet of l. 19, grow thin from eating flies) crawling to the full but hollow East. Note that in 'The Double Vision of Michael Robartes' II Yeats symbolized the opposition between the faculties of *Will* and *Creative Mind* as an opposition of a soft, desirous Buddha ('those that love are sad') and a Sphinx – another species of cat. The image of Grimalkin crawling to Buddha seems a parody of the Greek adolescents kissing the statues in the first stanza – here there is only a fake synthesis of man and image.

25 *Pearse summoned Cuchulain*: 'Cuchulain is in the last stanza because Pearse and some of his followers had a cult of him. The Government has put a statue of Cuchulain in the rebuilt post office to commemorate this' (*L*, p. 911). For Pearse, the leader of the 1916 rebellion, see 'Easter, 1916', l. 24; for Cuchulain, see the note to 'Cuchulain's Fight with the Sea'.

26 *Post Office*: the centre of the Easter Rebellion of 1916, occupied briefly by Pearse's forces. For other references to the Post Office, see 'Three Songs to the One Burden' III 5, *The Dreaming of the Bones* (1919), l. 44, and *The Death of Cuchulain* (1939), ll. 214–19: 'What stood in the Post Office / With Pearse and Connolly? ... Who thought Cuchulain till it seemed / He stood where they had stood?' In *On the Boiler* Yeats wrote that the descendants of the present Irish ministers 'will constitute our ruling class, and date their origin from the Post Office as American families date theirs from the *Mayflower*' (*Ex*, p. 413).

28 *We Irish*: Yeats was fond of quoting Berkeley's dictum, '"I publish ... to know whether other men have the same idea as we Irishmen"' (*Ex*, pp. 348,

300, 333; *EI*, p. 396; *UP* II, pp. 458, 484).

28 *that ancient sect*: Yeats thought that Ireland and Greece were the European lands with the richest and oldest mythologies – 'we Irish poets ... reject every folk art that does not go back to Olympus' (*EI*, p. 516).

29–30 *this filthy modern tide ... its formless spawning fury*: compare the denunciation of modern art in 'Under Ben Bulben' V 4: 'All out of shape from toe to top'. (For Yeats's own rejection of free verse in favour of traditional verse-shapes, see *EI*, p. 522.) Shapeless modern images recall the distended Buddha of l. 18; in contrast to these undisciplined images, the disciplined image of Cuchulain becomes a source of energy for the rebels. In the unfinished novel *The Speckled Bird* II i, a character (partly based on MacGregor Mathers) goes to the British Museum and measures his own muscles, kept in shape by athletic training, against those of Greek statues; he claims that men once looked like those heroic images, but now human bodies are growing more and more miserable – and without the statues the world would get much worse (*LTMSB*, p. 114).

31 *proper dark*: 'When I stand upon O'Connell Bridge in the half-light and notice that discordant architecture, all those electric signs, where modern heterogeneity has taken physical form, a vague hatred comes up out of my own dark' (*EI*, p. 526).

32 *a plummet-measured face*: Yeats in fact disliked the statue of Cuchulain, sculpted by Oliver Sheppard (no Phidias) and placed in the Dublin Post Office as a memorial to the Easter rebels: 'Some of the best known of the young men who got themselves killed in 1916 had the Irish legendary hero Cuchulain so much in their minds that the Government has celebrated the event with a bad statue' (*Scattering Branches*, ed. Stephen Gwynn, p. 53). But Yeats liked the idea of putting such a statue there: in *The Death of Cuchulain* (1939), a harlot sings of Pearse's summoning of Cuchulain's presence during the Easter Rebellion: 'A statue's there to mark the place, / By Oliver Sheppard done' (ll. 224–25). Bloom notes (*Yeats*, p. 445) the oddly Yeats-like scene in Beckett's *Murphy* (1938), chapter 4, where a mad shabby teacher of Greek philosophy beats his head against the buttocks of the statue of Cuchulain.

News for the Delphic Oracle

At the end of 'The Statues', men are stiffened and strengthened through contact with an image; in this poem images are softened through contact with men. This poem marks a turning-point in the volume: the preceding poems define the goals of human conduct and beauty, attained through warfare and eugenics, both means for purifying and intensifying the race. But this and several following poems take transcendent images and re-orient, humanize them in the matrix of common life. If men and ultimate things are to grow coincident, to touch one another (as Adam touches God on the Sistine Chapel in 'Under Ben Bulben' IV 11, or the adolescents kiss statues in 'The Statues', l. 8), then men will have to strive beyond the usual limits, and their paradigms will have to bend down, accommodate themselves to human frailty. 'News for the Delphic Oracle' describes such a regression to earth.

In 'The Delphic Oracle on Plotinus', Yeats summarized the oracle's account of the soul of the dead Plotinus, swimming from earth to the Isles of the Blest. In this poem he has reached his destination – and has found himself in a celestial home for decayed actors and musicians. This C-major pseudo-heaven – too calm, too insipid – is a deliberately rickety construction, and soon starts to fall apart. Just as, in 'Byzantium', heaven was threatened by a flood of the waters of generation, so here the Isles of the Blest seem about to be torn apart by sexual energies roiling the surrounding waters. The first stanza concerns the senile, the second concerns murdered babies, and the third concerns a foetus – Yeats sometimes thought that the dead re-live their lives backward ('He grows younger every second', according to 'Shepherd and Goatherd', l. 89), and the structure of this poem demonstrates such a reverse chronology.

Yeats wrote the first few lines of this poem in the back of his copy of Milton's poetry; and the poem is in part a parody of Milton's 'On the Morning of Christ's Nativity' (1629). Milton described the morning of Christ's birth as a general hush: 'The Winds, with wonder whist, / Smoothly the waters kiss't' (ll. 64-65); this enforced calm leads to a stilling of the Delphic Oracle: 'The Oracles are dumb / No voice or hideous hum / Runs through the arched roof in words deceiving' (ll. 173–75); the silence is broken only by the angels' ravishing hymn to Christ, 'the mighty *Pan*' (l. 89). Yeats's joke is to substitute the brutish earthly Pan for the heavenly Pan, so that Milton's pious hymn is subverted into a Bacchanale. 'Berkeley in his youth described the *summum bonum* and the reality of Heaven as physical pleasure' (*EI*, p. 410), and 'News for the Delphic Oracle' imagines the reality of Heaven along similar lines.

Spenser was as important a source as Milton. Yeats wrote of Spenser that 'He was not passionate ... He is a poet of the delighted senses, and his song becomes most beautiful when he writes of ... lovely effeminate islands' (*EI*, p. 370); and the languid paradise of the first stanza owes something to Spenser's islands of Phaedria and Acrasia (*The Faerie Queene* II vi, xii), as Yeats understood them. The structure of 'News for the Delphic Oracle' also echoes that of Spenser's Garden of Adonis (*FQ* III vi) – Yeats, describing the secret paganism of Spenser's ostensibly Christian imagination, wrote that 'it is pagan Venus and her lover Adonis who create the forms of all living things and send them out into the world' (*EI*, p. 366). Yeats compared the *Anima Mundi* – where the general human imagination stores all images – to Spenser's Garden of Adonis (*M*, p. 352); and this poem can be read as an allegory of the descent of images to earth from some comatose heaven. Spenser's artfully indolent islands and gardens also helped Yeats to imagine the islands in *The Wanderings of Oisin* (1889), his first important success; and the present poem is a kind of sequel to that narrative, in which the battered and ferocious Oisin at last finds rest, or a mockery of rest, on a fourth island. This poem thus closes a circle in Yeats's career.

I 1 *golden codgers*: an impudent description of the denizens of heaven – a diction in keeping with the playful arrogance of the title.

I 5 *Man-picker*: a term Yeats used elsewhere to describe a bar-maid with an illegitimate child (*Ex*, p. 433). Yeats here delights in debunking Niamh, the divine heroine of his *The Wanderings of Oisin* – a man-picker who plucked Oisin from Ireland and carried him on horseback over the ocean to three enchanted islands.

I 7 *choir of love*: see 'The Delphic Oracle upon Plotinus', l. 10.

I 8 *Pythagoras*: see 'Among School Children' VI 5. Note the deliberate incongruity of a heaven that includes *primary* philosophers and *antithetical* heroes alike. A similar effect is found in 'Her Courage', l. 6, where the poet places Mabel Beardsley in a heaven that includes Diarmuid and 'some old cardinal'.

I 9 *Plotinus*: see 'The Tower' I 12.

I 10 *salt flakes*: possibly an allusion to Plotinus' leprosy. Compare the 'Salt blood' that blocks Plotinus' eyes in 'The Delphic Oracle upon Plotinus', l. 5.

I 11 *stretched and yawned*: Yeats's code-words for sexual languor, bizarre in this context – see 'Three Things', l. 17.

II 1 *dolphin*: in Neoplatonic mythology, dolphins carried the souls of the dead to the Isles of the Blest – see 'Byzantium', l. 33. As Jeffares notes (*NCP*, p. 417), a fresco (School of Raphael) in the Papal Apartments at the Castel S. Angelo, Rome, shows similar sea-scapes.

II 3 *Innocents*: the babies slaughtered by King Herod in his attempt to kill the infant Christ (Matthew 2:16) – compare *The Land of Heart's Desire* (1894), l. 363: 'The Holy Martyrs and the Innocents'; 'A Prayer for my Son', l. 26; and *TSMC*, p. 165: 'Do you know Raphael's statue of the Dolphin carrying one of the Holy Innocents to Heaven?' In 'The Wild Old Wicked Man', l. 53, the poet speaks of the suffering of the 'child hid in the womb'. In so far as the paradise of the first two stanzas of this poem consists only of old men and babies, it is anticipated in William Morris's *The Water of the Wondrous Isles* (1895), where there is an Isle of the Old and the Young.

II 5 *The ecstatic waters laugh*: this redounding from torture to laughter suggests the emotion Yeats called tragic joy – see the headnote to *New Poems*.

Compare 'His Dream', ll. 17–18: 'Crying amid the glittering sea ... ecstatic breath'.

II 8 *dolphins plunge*: compare *John Sherman* (1891): 'Seagulls ... plunged ... a porpoise showed now and then, his fin and back gleaming' (*JSD*, p. 102).

II 9 *some cliff-sheltered bay*: a similarly eerie landscape, also attended by dolphins, is found in Pound's Canto 17, which Yeats included in *OBMV*.

III 1 *nymph*: compare 'The Realists', ll. 4–5: 'the dolphin-drawn / Sea-nymphs'.

III 2 *Peleus on Thetis*: the mortal Peleus begot Achilles on the nymph Thetis.

III 5 *Thetis' belly listens*: the unborn Achilles (see 'Her Courage', l. 9), already sensitive to the fierce drama of mortal life. This conceit may come from the Cherry Tree Carol, an old poem in which Christ pipes up from inside Mary's womb, and orders a cherry tree to present his mother with fruit – Yeats ridiculed some of the Catholic clergy for taking offence at this carol (*UP* II, p. 462). A painting by Poussin, 'The Marriage of Peleus and Thetis' (now called 'Acis and Galatea'), in the National Gallery, Dublin, seems to supply several details in this poem.

III 7 *Pan*: the Greek nature-god, master of nymphs, satyrs, and all nature-spirits; his name means *all* in Greek. The death of Pan (recorded by Plutarch) was long associated with the passing of the pagan world and the birth of Christ. Pound used this legend in 'Pan is Dead' (1912); here Pan's 'Intolerable music' may represent the resurrection of *antithetical* energies after the long bland Christian era. Compare Yeats's juvenile *The Island of Statues* (1885) II iii 300–4, where a man paralysed into a statue comes to life and remembers antiquity: 'As here I came I saw god Pan. He played / An oaten pipe unto a listening fawn ... Doth he still dwell within the woody shade ...?' (*VP*, p. 678).

III 10 *bum*: the lowest point of Yeats's diction.

III 11 *Flash fishlike*: compare such grotesque amphibians as the fish-formed slave-traders in Pound's Canto 2, and as the Caliban of Shakespeare's *The Tempest* (1611) and Browning's 'Caliban upon Setebos' (1864) – often taken as an emblem of Nature. This poem may be read as Nature's victory over Art, a countermyth to 'Byzantium'.

Long-legged Fly

This poem investigates the mysterious origin of great deeds and great works of art. An earlier poem on this theme, 'Mad as the Mist and Snow', stressed the wild passion that lay behind works that today seem settled, composed, dignified; this poem makes the opposite argument – violent, world-transforming acts begin in a strange stillness, improvisatory and receptive. By imagining the biographical context of inspiration, Yeats here anticipates the method of 'The Circus Animals' Desertion'.

5 *Caesar*: Julius Caesar (63 BC–AD 14), who extended the boundaries of Roman control in his wars against the barbarian Gauls.

9 Like a long-legged fly: as W. E. Rogers has noted (*Concerning Poetry* 8 [1975]: 11–21), this simile is related to a passage in Coleridge's *Biographia Literaria* VII: 'Most of my readers will have observed a small water-insect on the surface of rivulets, which throws a cinque-spotted shadow fringed with prismatic colours on the sunny bottom of the brook; and will have noticed, how the little animal *wins* its way up against the stream, by alternate pulses of active and passive motion, now resisting the current, and now yielding to it ... This is no unapt emblem of the mind's self-experience in the act of thinking'. Also compare Pope, *An Essay on Man* (1733) I 217: 'The spider's touch, how exquisitely fine!' – another image of preternatural sensitivity to imperceptible vibrations.

11 *the topless towers*: see the note to 'When Helen Lived', l. 8.

15 *part woman, three parts child*: see 'Against Unworthy Praise', l. 20 (where Maud Gonne is 'Half lion, half child') for other divisions of the female subject.

21–22 *girls at puberty may find / The first Adam*: compare 'Under Ben Bulben' IV 13, where Michelangelo's Adam arouses a tourist 'Till her bowels are in heat'.

26 *Michael Angelo*: see 'Michael Robartes and the Dancer', l. 32.

A Bronze Head

This is the culmination of a thirty-years' series of poems, beginning with 'The Arrow', on the theme of Maud Gonne's aging. The bust of Maud Gonne mentioned in the title is a plaster cast, painted bronze, by Lawrence Campbell, in the Municipal Gallery of Dublin – no ideal image, but a portrait of a wrinkled, elderly woman. (This shows another aspect of the convergence of man and image found in 'The Statues': an image is carefully deformed until it matches a human being.) The poet wonders how Maud Gonne, once beautiful and (in private) gentle, could have turned into this stark inhuman icon, and he finds two competing explanations, one mundane, psychological – terror drove Maud Gonne mad, distorted her being; and the other supernatural – she was possessed by a spirit from beyond the grave, appropriately imaged as a bronze head. In his later prose Yeats often deplored psychology: he wrote that tragic joy 'has certainly no place in the modern psychological study of suffering' (*Ex*, p. 296), and that 'I would have poetry turn its back upon all that modish curiosity, psychology' (*EI*, p. 530). And yet in his own poetry Yeats was fascinated by psychology – particularly in 'The Circus Animals' Desertion', an almost Freudian dissertation on creativity. Here the psychological and the occult theories of behaviour attain a strange coexistence: 'maybe substance can be composite' (l. 12), and maybe Freud and Madame Blavatsky can be reconciled.

In such poems as this and 'Hound Voice', Yeats experimented with *rime royale* – a stanza one line shorter than his usual *ottava rima*. The text of this poem is unsettled – for a useful table of variant readings, see Finneran, *EYP*, p. 86.

4, 8 *great tomb-haunter ... dark tomb-haunter*: in the context of 'a bird's round eye' (l. 2), this epithet seems an image of a raven or a vulture. Yeats once referred to Maud Gonne's 'sybilline old age' (*UP* II, p. 488), and (like the Cumaean Sibyl who speaks in the epigraph to Eliot's *The Waste Land*), she seems to be withering, death-obsessed, yet immortal. Jeffares notes (*NCP*, p. 419) that Maud Gonne was rarely seen in public in her later years, except to visit graveyards on political occasions, all dressed in black. In the 1890s a young man told Yeats his vision of an empty tomb, which Yeats interpreted in the light of his concern that the ill Maud Gonne was dying: 'Have I sought on earth what I should seek beyond the grave?' (*Mem*, p. 71); and in 1910 Yeats himself dreamed of Maud Gonne's tombstone (*Mem*, p. 238).

5 *there*: in her eyes.

7 Hysterica passio: see 'Parnell's Funeral' I 21.

10 *a most gentle woman*: Yeats considered Maud Gonne's outer nature was violent, but her inner nature was 'gentle and passive and full of charming fantasy' (*Mem*, p. 124).

11 *Which of her forms*: that is, the young, luminous woman or the 'dark tomb-haunter'. If 'substance can be composite', then both forms are correct.

12 *composite*: compare 'Michael Robartes and the Dancer', l. 44: 'blest souls are not composite' – that is, divided into body and soul.

13 *McTaggart*: the philosopher J. M. E. McTaggart (1866–1925). As Finneran notes (*EYP*, pp. 89–90), his *The Nature of Existence* showed that all substances are compound, that a man is the summation of a series of selves altering through time. (Thus the poet can see his beloved from either the physical or the metaphysical point of view.) Yeats thought that McTaggart had made the doctrine of reincarnation 'the foundation of the first English systematic philosophy' (*EI*, p. 417; see also pp. 402, 406) and cited McTaggart's belief that Hegel accepted the truth of reincarnation (*Ex*, p. 396).

14 *hold*: some drafts read *held*; but *hold* seems preferable, as an infinitive preceded by an implied *can*, parallel to *can be* (l. 12).

18 *shattered her soul*: compare 'A Crazed Girl', l. 3: 'Her soul in division from itself'. In the 1890s Yeats believed that Maud Gonne was troubled by an evil spirit: 'She had been priestess in a temple somewhere in Egypt and under the influence of a certain priest who was her lover gave false oracles for money, and because of this the personality of that life had split off from the soul and remained a half-living shadow' (*Mem*, p. 49). Thus her 'schizophrenia' might have an occult as well as a psychiatric explanation. Also note Yeats's belief 'that Maud Gonne had a strong subconscious conviction that her soul was lost' (*Mem*, p. 62).

20 *I had grown wild*: propinquity seems to cause a contagion of terror.

23 *a sterner eye*: compare 'Under Ben Bulben' VI 9: '*Cast a cold eye*'. This division of Maud Gonne between furious actor (in stanza 3) and detached watcher (stanza 4) recalls the contrast between the streetcorner Hamlets and the Chinamen in 'Lapis Lazuli'. For the theme of men who are manipulated by the personages in a supernatural drama, see 'Whence Had They Come?', l. 4: 'Ignorant what Dramatis Personae spake'.

25 *gangling stocks grown great, great stocks run dry*: 'The danger is that there will be no war . . . that the European civilisation, like those older civilisations that saw the triumph of their gangrel stocks, will accept decay' (*Ex*, p. 425).

26 *pearls all pitched into a sty*: 'neither cast ye your pearls before swine' (Matthew 7:6).

28 *what was left for massacre to save*: compare 'September 1913', ll. 14–15: 'what, God help us, could they save? / Romantic Ireland's dead and gone'.

A Stick of Incense

The theme of this cryptic quatrain resembles that of 'Long-legged Fly': the greatest events originate in small impalpable things. As Yeats wrote in 'The Symbolism of Poetry' (1900), 'I am certainly never sure, when I hear of some war, or of some religious excitement . . . that it has not all happened because of something that a boy piped in Thessaly' (*EI*, p. 158). But here the poet seems less respectful: Christianity may have altered the world, but its provenance seems trivial, almost fatuous.

Title: the incense is presumably one of the gifts of the Magi.

2 *empty tomb or Virgin womb*: 'the next civilisation may be born, not from a virgin's womb, nor a tomb without a body, not from a void, but of our own rich experience' (*Ex*, p. 437). Yeats disliked the abstractness of Christianity, its gnostic character.

3 *Joseph*: his peripheral role in the conception of Christ has sometimes made him a figure of coarse fun through the ages. Yeats rarely mentioned him

elsewhere, though in the so-called 'Leroy' version of the unfinished *The Speckled Bird*, there is a madman who beats children with an old parasol, which he says was given to him by St. Joseph (*LTMSB*, p. 236); also see *The Island of Statues* II iii 266 (*VP*, p. 676).

Hound Voice

This paean to the hunter's life is congruous with such earlier poems as *The Wanderings of Oisin* I, 'The Ballad of the Foxhunter', and 'The Fisherman'; and with such later poems as 'The Black Tower' it shares the premise of an isolated band that rejects the contemporary world. Its praise of hounds is, however, unusual; as Dorothy Wellesley noted, 'I do not think that Yeats cared for dogs' (*DWL*, p. 145).

3 *boredom of the desk*: compare 'The Tower' III 60: 'This sedentary trade'.

7 *their hidden name – 'hound voice'*: the canine note that obtrudes in the human voice is reminiscent of 'Cuchulain Comforted', l. 25: 'They ... had the throats of birds'.

18 *Stumbling upon the blood-dark track*: compare Pound, 'The Return' (1912): 'See, they return; ah, see the tentative / Movements, and the slow feet ... Gods of the winged shoe! / With them the silver hounds / sniffing the trace of air! ... These were the souls of blood' (quoted in *AV*, pp. 29–30). Yeats took Pound's poem as a prophecy of the return of the pagan gods, imagined as huntsmen, trying to manifest themselves in a Christian world.

19 *Then stumbling*: the TSS read *That stumbling* – but see the Note on the Text.

21 *chants of victory amid the encircling hounds*: at the end of *The Wanderings of Oisin*, the old hero imagines a war of the pagans against the Christian heaven, ending in triumph; but, he says, even if they fail, he will be content if he can dwell with his hounds (III 223).

John Kinsella's Lament for Mrs. Mary Moore

The preceding poem celebrated rustic dignity and ceremony; this one celebrates rustic earthiness. A draft can be found in *DWL*, pp. 182–83. One of Finneran's most interesting discoveries is an unpublished letter to F. R. Higgins (Yeats's collaborator on a series of *Broadsides* for the Cuala Press), which gives a series of corrections to this poem (*EYP*, p. 94); these corrections regularize the rhythm by adding an unstressed syllable before catalectic lines. Yeats made these corrections 'to make it more suitable for singing'; but, since it is not certain that Yeats wished the song-version to replace the more emphatic, abrupt, and plaintive version previously published, the editor has thought it best to print the earlier text.

I 11–12 *What shall I do for pretty girls / Now my old bawd is dead?*: Yeats quoted this refrain in a letter, and noted, 'I have just thought of a chorus for a ballad. A strong farmer is mourning over the shortness of life and changing times' (*L*, p. 912). In *A Vision*, Yeats wrote that Christ's predecessor (2000 BC) 'careful of heroic men alone ... mourned over the shortness of time' (p. 285).

II 9–10 *she put a skin / On everything she said*: Finneran notes (*PNE*, p. 679) that *put a skin* is an Irish idiom for *polish* or *make plausible*. This phrase may also pertain to the embodiedness of Mary Moore's discourse – compare the woman whose friendship 'covers all he has brought / As with her flesh and bone' ('On Woman', ll. 5–6).

III 10 *plucks the trees for bread*: compare 'The Man who Dreamed of Faeryland', l. 23: 'the sun and moon were in the fruit'.

High Talk

Goethe wrote of his *Faust*, a poem that took his whole life to write, that what began as tragedy, ended as opera; and, similiarly, some of the final poems of Yeats's final volume show a strange levity, almost lightheadedness. Yeats was always fascinated by the processes of artistic composition; but in 'High Talk', 'A Nativity', and 'The Circus Animals' Desertion', Yeats seems to go backstage to the poet's workshop, where the elements of his craft are all too plainly visible. Many of Yeats's earlier poems show the artist as prophet, sage, spirit-summoner, enchanter, or oracle; but in these last poems the genius shows himself as a clown, the magus shows himself as a magician, eager to expose the mirrors, wires, and smoke-bombs that enable his conjuring. 'High Talk' is itself a kind of circus-trick, walking effortlessly on the tight-rope between the sublime and the bathetic.

1 *stilts*: in his first surviving letter, the eleven-year-old Yeats noted, 'I am getting stilts' (*L* I, p. 3). Here stilts provide a metaphor for the poet's elevation of diction and loftiness of thought, as the title suggests. 'Then in 1900 everybody [among poets] got down off his stilts; henceforth nobody drank absinthe with his black coffee; nobody went mad; nobody committed suicide; nobody joined the Catholic church' (*OBMV*, p. xi-xii). The generation of poets that followed Yeats also tended to disapprove of poets' attempts to elevate themselves: 'Whenever a modern poet raises his voice, he makes me feel embarrassed, like a man wearing a wig or elevator shoes' (Auden, *Secondary Worlds*, p. 116). Compare 'The Circus Animals' Desertion' I 7: 'Those stilted boys'.

3 *mine were but fifteen foot*: the shrinking of the stilts parallels Yeats's myth of the diminishing capacities of imaginative men towards the end of a millennium (*AV* [1925], pp. 211–13).

8 *I take to chisel and plane*: here the poet reconstructs his stilts – in 'The Circus Animals' Desertion' III 7, he is content to be ladderless.

11 *All metaphor, Malachi, stilts and all*: as the poet hoists himself out of ordinary life by means of his tropes, he attains such a level of artifice that the metaphor-maker himself becomes a metaphor. Compare the poet's self-transformations in 'Sailing to Byzantium' IV (where he turns into a golden bird) and in the quatrain quoted in the note to 'An Acre of Grass', l. 14 (where he identifies himself with the texts of his poems).

11 *A barnacle goose*: a bird also associated with metamorphoses – because they were thought to originate from barnacles, they were legally fish, and medieval monks could eat them on fast days. In *The Green Helmet* (1910), l. 270, Cuchulain compares his death-eager soul to a barnacle goose; and in 'The Crucifixion of the Outcast' (1894), the gleeman prays, ' "O great grass-barnacles, tarry a little, and mayhap my soul will travel with you to the waste places of the shore and to the ungovernable sea!" ' (*M*, p. 153). Other barnacle geese appear in *The Wanderings of Oisin* III 156 and 'Beggar to Beggar Cried', l. 20.

14 *sea-horses*: compare 'Colonus' Praise', l. 32: 'horses of the sea' – horses were sacred to Poseidon; also 'The Circus Animals' Desertion' II 2: 'sea-rider'. 'High Talk' ends with a circus-parade of images, an impressive incoherence: the poet's figures of speech have become so elevated that they seem to have lost their referents, to mean nothing at all.

The Apparitions

Yeats told Virginia Woolf in 1934 that he had personally seen supernatural visions: 'His coat hanger advanced across the room one night. Then a coat on it, illuminated: then a hand in it' (Woolf, *Diary* IV, p. 256; compare her *Letters* V, p. 341, which adds details of 'a child's hand, and a message about an unborn baby in Greek'). Vita Sackville-West wrote to her husband: 'Virginia gave me an imitation of Yeats telling her why he was occult. He had been confirmed in this theory because he saw a coat-hanger emerge from his cupboard and travel across the foot of his bed; next night it emerged again, clothed in one of his jackets; the third night, a hand emerged from one of the cuffs; the fourth night – "Ah! Mrs Woolf, that would be a long story; enough to say I finally recovered my potency" ' (Harold Nicolson, *Diary* I, p. 188). Bradford notes that in a MS book Yeats described this apparition as 'extraordinarily terrifying' (*Dolmen Press Yeats Centenary Papers* [1965], p. 174), but in this poem the apparition seems deliberately commonplace. If, as Freud thought, the uncanny is merely a dislocation of the familiar, this is Yeats's most uncanny poem: its terror lies in a vision of death as a coat that outlasts its owner.

17–21 *joy ... Night*: compare 'Man and the Echo', l 42: 'joy or night'.

A Nativity

In 'Wisdom' Yeats described the contrast between the humble manger where Christ was born and the magnificent images of that manger in Christian art. In this poem – a catechism of the Second Coming, not the first – the humility, the abjection disappear entirely: the new god's birth is decorated, scripted, acted, and directed by the most flamboyant theatrical geniuses. No extraneous or incongruous element is allowed to intrude on the scene; rain, insects, stray rustics are all dismissed to permit greater concentration on the chief event. Yeats often thought of history as a species of theatre (see 'Two Songs from a Play' I 8); and it seems that the artists mentioned in this poem – all masters of the grand gesture – are the demiurges of historical change. The line between history and art has nearly vanished.

2 *Another star has shot an ear*: see 'The Mother of God', ll. 1-2: 'a fallen flare / Through the hollow of an ear'.

4 *Delacroix*: Eugène Delacroix (1798–1863), French Romantic painter, noted for elegantly bold compositions. In praise of Ricketts' visionary but unpopular paintings, Yeats wrote, 'Ricketts made pictures that suggest Delacroix by their colour and remind us by their theatrical composition that Talma once invoked the thunderbolt' (*Ex*, p. 418). In the same passage Yeats mentioned Botticelli, whose painting of the Nativity in the National Gallery, London, suggests an effort at angelic stage-contrivance of Christ's birth.

6 *Landor*: see 'To a Young Beauty', l. 18. Landor's classical, epigrammatic manner made him a suitable poet for the *antithetical*, neo-heroic age to come. Indeed the terse style of this poem may partly imitate Landor's.

7–8 *What brushes fly and moth aside? / Irving and his plume of pride*: in his last broadcast script Yeats quoted these lines, preceded by this commentary: 'Some people say I have an affected manner, and if that is true ... it is because my father took me when I was ten or eleven to Irving's famous "Hamlet". Years afterwards I walked the Dublin streets when nobody was looking ... with that strut ... Two months ago, describing the Second Coming, I wrote this couplet' (*UP* II, p. 507). (Yeats also mentioned his imitation of the stride of Irving's Hamlet in *A: R* 22; and Yeats contrasted Irving's method of acting with that of actors who simply copy from life in *Ex*, p. 256.) Yeats seems to align his personality as well as his art with those of the artists mentioned in this poem.

8 *Irving*: Sir Henry Irving (1838–1905), British actor.

10 *Talma*: François Joseph Talma (1763–1826), French tragedian. Yeats wrote that Frank Fay, the Abbey Theatre actor and manager, belonged to 'that school of Talma which permits an actor . . . to throw up an arm calling down the thunderbolts of Heaven, instead of seeming to pick up pins from the floor' (*EI*, p. 529). The angry Old Man who serves as Prologue to *The Death of Cuchulain* (1939) claims to be 'the son of Talma', 'out of date like the antiquated romantic stuff' of the Cuchulain myth itself.

11 *terror-struck*: compare 'The Mother of God', l. 4: 'The terror of all terrors'.

12 *Can there be mercy in that look?*: mercy and pity are traits associated with the Christian age (*AV*, p. 275); the newborn Antichrist is not likely to be merciful.

Man and the Echo

In an early draft the speaker was labelled, not *Man*, but *Poet* (Stallworthy, *VR*, p. 60); and indeed this is a somewhat autobiographical poem. The poet's mood – dismal self-interrogation – is anticipated in such poems as 'Vacillation' V. But here he receives brief replies to his brooding queries: he addresses his own words (ll. 11–16), and his words echo back to him, as if his old speeches and poems had a voice of their own, a private oracle full of black counsel. At the end, however, the poet seems to break out of this involution, this dark self-preoccupation, and to respond to the sensuous world around him. This poem and 'The Circus Animals' Desertion' are companion pieces, in that the poet here listens to his works as if they constituted a voice from beyond the grave, while in the following poem he listens to his works as if they constituted a message from his own heart.

Title: the addition of 'The' before 'Man and the Echo' in *Last Poems and Two Plays* (1939) is probably the work of Mark and Mrs Yeats (Finneran, *EYP*, p. 97).

1 *Alt*: a glen on the side of Knocknarea, a mountain near Sligo. Yeats wrote about a cave on the side of another local mountain, Ben Bulben, thought to be the entrance to the spirit world (*M*, p. 70); and this rock-cleft also seems to serve as an access-point to relevation. Compare *The Unicorn from the Stars* (1908) III 396–97: 'maybe to some secret cleft he is going, to get knowledge of the great cure for all things'.

11 *that play*: *Cathleen ni Houlihan* (1902), in which a beautiful personification of Ireland (played by Maud Gonne) encouraged bloody revolt. The play had been granted a licence for performance only after Yeats officially declared that it was not written to affect popular opinion of England (*Ex*, p. 199).

'Connolly carries in procession a coffin with the words "British Empire" upon it, and police and mob fight for its ownership ... an old woman killed by baton blows ... I count the links in the chain of responsibility, run them across my fingers, and wonder if any link there is from my workshop' (*A: SB* 5). In a senate speech Yeats spoke of Synge's and Goethe's guilt from suicides evidently inspired by their work (*SSY*, p. 52).

12 *Certain men*: probably the leaders of the Easter 1916 Rebellion; Yeats may also have been thinking of 'the player Connolly' ('Three Songs to the One Burden' III 11), an actor from the Abbey Theatre, one of the first men shot in the Rebellion. Compare Paul Muldoon's '7 Middagh Street' (1987): 'If Yeats had saved his pencil-lead / would certain men have stayed in bed?'

14 *that woman*: probably Margot Ruddock – see the note to 'Sweet Dancer'. Originally there were both a woman and a man: 'did my spoken words perplex / That man that woman now a wreck' (Stallworthy, *VR*, p. 63).

16 *a house*: probably Coole Park – see 'Coole Park, 1929'.

19 *Lie down and die*: the Echo's preoccupation with death and night may suggest a kinship between the Echo and the Soul of 'A Dialogue of Self and Soul' – another dialogue-poem. The echo-device is very old – a familiar example in English poetry is George Herbert's 'Heaven' (1633).

22 *bodkin*: a dagger, alluding to Hamlet's soliloquy on suicide, *Hamlet* III i 76. In a description of the terrors of the afterlife, Yeats wrote that 'when Hamlet refused the bare bodkin because of what dreams may come, it was from no literary fancy' (*M*, p. 355).

28 *Body and its stupidity*: compare 'Shepherd and Goatherd', l. 83: 'stupor of youth'; and 'The Spirit Medium', ll. 20–21: 'stupidity / Of ... clay'. The body's inertia or narcosis is also suggested in 'To Ireland in the Coming Times', l. 22: '*only body's laid asleep*'.

31 *all's arranged in one clear view*: 'The dead ... perceive, although they are still but living in their memories, harmonies, symbols, and patterns, as though all were being refashioned by an artist' (*M*, pp. 355–56).

36 *sinks at last into the night*: compare *The Hour-Glass* (1914), ll. 599–600: 'We perish into God and sink away / Into reality – the rest's a dream'; and 'All Souls' Night', l. 60: 'sink into its own delight at last'.

37 *O rocky voice*: compare 'The Gyres', l. 1: 'Old Rocky Face' – an epithet for the Delphic Oracle.

37–38 *voice ... rejoice*: Auden imitated this rhyme in 'In Memory of W. B. Yeats' III (1939): 'With your unconstraining voice / Still persuade us to rejoice' – in these lines, written in a Yeatsian metre, Auden seems to play the role of Echo, while Yeats plays the role of Man.

45 *A stricken rabbit is crying out*: 'I . . . shot at birds with a muzzle-loading pistol until somebody shot a rabbit and I heard it squeal. From that on I would kill nothing' (*A: R* 10).

The Circus Animals' Desertion

In his old age Yeats often urged the artist to express himself, not as he actually is, but in some simplified and intensified form: the poet 'is never the bundle of accident and incoherence that sits down to breakfast; he has been reborn as an idea, something intended, complete . . . he is more type than man'; 'all that is personal soon rots; it must be packed in ice or salt . . . If I wrote of personal love or sorrow in free verse, or in any rhythm that left it unchanged, amid all its accidence, I would be full of self-contempt because of my egotism and indiscretion' (*EI*, p. 509, 522). This is the final development of the doctrine of the Mask: the poet presents less an anti-self than a stylized self, made shapely in conformity to old principles of verbal form.

But 'The Circus Animals' Desertion' shows that Yeats wished not only to construct such a self but to deconstruct it, to reduce it to the 'bundle of accident and incoherence' from which it sprang. ('News for the Delphic Oracle' shows a corresponding desire to deconstruct paradise – the ideal place – as well as the ideal self.) The self that sits down to breakfast and the self revealed in poems and plays exist in a difficult, shifting equilibrium; together these selves constitute the whole man. As Yeats once wrote, 'the myth becomes a biography . . . the biography changed into a myth' (*AV* [1925], pp. 185, 214). In this poem Yeats's myth of his identity, so carefully formulated through his career, breaks down into naked self-expression. For earlier poems on anti-mythological themes, see the note to 'Reconciliation'. The anti-mythological movement of this poem partly follows that of a poem of Synge's: 'Adieu, sweet Angus, Maeve and Fand, / Ye plumed yet skinny Shee, / That poets played with hand in hand / To learn their ecstasy. // We'll search in Red Dan Sally's ditch' (*Collected Works* I, p. 38).

Among the titles that Yeats rejected for his poem are 'Tragic Toys'; 'Despair'; and 'On the lack of a theme'.

I 1 *I sought a theme and sought for it in vain*: 'I begin to feel a difficulty in finding themes' (*L*, p. 668); 'For five weeks I could not write a line, and then the poem came and a new mass of themes' (*DWL*, p. 148); 'We cannot discover our subject-matter by deliberate intellect' (*EI*, p. 289). Also compare 'Vacillation' VII 2: 'What, be a singer born and lack a theme?' For earlier examples of meta-poetry – poetry about writing poetry – see 'All Things Can Tempt Me', 'A Coat', 'Lines Written in Dejection', and 'The Tower' I.

I 4 *heart*: all references to *heart* were added to the poem in its final drafts

(*YW*, p. 164). The final stanza's association of heart and detritus is anticipated in the 1927 version of *The Resurrection*, ll. 292–94: 'What is the heart but corruption, change, death? It is gloomy, dark ignorant and terrible' (*VPl*, p. 920).

I 6 *circus animals*: poetic themes and devices that reliably please an audience, somewhat overfamiliar to the elderly poet who has long employed them. After a 1937 radio broadcast turned into a fiasco, Yeats wrote, 'Perhaps my old bundle of poet's tricks is useless' (*L*, p. 879).

I 7 *stilted boys*: compare 'High Talk', l. 1, where stilts are metaphors for the poet's elevation of style. *Stilted* (in the sense of trite) is also insinuated.

I 8 *lion and woman*: in 'Against Unworthy Praise', l. 20, Yeats called Maud Gonne 'Half lion, half child', and in 'Those Images' Yeats enumerated lion, virgin, and harlot as three of five seminal images. But here they are demoted to star-turns in Yeats's circus.

II 2 *sea-rider Oisin*: Yeats's first success, *The Wanderings of Oisin* (1889), tells how the goddess Niamh lured Oisin to gallop over the sea to three false paradises, each an attempt to extrapolate partial pleasure into total bliss. Compare the sea-horses of 'High Talk', l. 14.

II 2 *led by the nose*: the hero is himself reduced to the state of one of the circus-ponies of the first stanza.

II 4 *Vain gaiety, vain battle, vain repose*: 'Oisin needs an interpriter. There are three incompatable things which man is always seeking – infinite feeling, infinite battle, infinite repose – hence the three islands' (*L* I, p. 141).

II 6 *adorn old songs or courtly shows*: 'when I had finished *The Wanderings of Oisin*, dissatisfied with its yellow and its dull green ... I deliberately reshaped my style, deliberately sought out an impression as of cold light and tumbling clouds. I cast off traditional metaphors and loosened my rhythm' (*A: R* 17); 'after *The Wanderings of Usheen*, I had simplified my style by filling my imagination with country stories' (*A: SB* 6).

II 8 *starved for the bosom of his fairy bride*: the poet regards the poem as a gaudy sublimation of his wayward sexual desire. In the juvenile 'The Danaan Quicken Tree' (1893), Yeats dramatized a young poet's voyage to the dangerous and seductive island of Innisfree, 'Where Niam heads the revelry' (*VP*, p. 743).

II 9 *a counter-truth*: in *The Wanderings of Oisin*, a dream brought forth an imaginary woman; in *The Countess Cathleen* (1892), a real woman, Maud Gonne, 'brought forth a dream' (II 15).

II 10 *The Countess Cathleen*: a play partly based on a Faust-like legend of a noblewoman who sold her soul to the Devil in order to feed her starving peasants, and partly based on Maud Gonne's struggle to feed the populace of Donegal during a famine (Yeats quoted part of her eloquent speech on famine in *LNI*, pp. 151–52). 'I told [Maud Gonne] after meeting her in London I had come to understand the tale of a woman selling her soul to buy food for a starving people as a symbol ... of her soul that had seemed so incapable of rest' (*Mem*, p. 47). This deconstruction of his play into an allegory of his emotional life is anticipated in *The Old Age of Queen Maeve*, ll. 134–35, which claims that Maud Gonne is the secret subject of all mythology of proud queens: 'there is no high story about queens / In any ancient book but tells of you'.

II 11 *pity-crazed*: compare 'Human Dignity', ll. 1–4 (also referring to Maud Gonne): 'her kindness ... is the same for all'.

II 12 *masterful*: a key word – compare III 1. Aesthetic contrivance smoothes and prettifies all that is rich, jagged, unsatisfying in human life. The hate-crazed Maud Gonne, eager for violence against England, metamorphoses into the 'pity-crazed' (II 11) Countess, and a noble ending is imposed on inconclusive reality – angels fight with devils for the Countess's soul, and carry it to heaven.

II 16 *This dream itself had all my thought and love*: again there is a deflection from life to fantasy. Yeats concluded that *The Countess Cathleen* 'was not ... more than a piece of tapestry' (*A: DP* 10).

II 17 *the Fool and Blind Man*: characters in *On Baile's Strand* (1904), respectively representing strength and wisdom (or body and soul); they feed themselves by collaborating on minor thefts. The Fool is a parody of the hero Cuchulain, and the Blind Man a parody of the crafty High King, Conchubar, who binds Cuchulain to his service. Yeats may mention these shadow-relations here because they hint at the farce latent in high tragedy. In the mythology of *A Vision*, the Fool came to represent the *antithetical* gyre and the Blind Man the *primary* – 'Life drifts between a fool and a blind man / To the end, and nobody can know his end' (*On Baile's Strand*, ll. 623–24); compare the poem 'Symbols'.

II 18 *Cuchulain fought the ungovernable sea*: at the play's climax, Cuchulain, driven mad by the sudden realization that Conchubar has manipulated him into killing his son, takes his sword against the sea. (Yeats also told this story in 'Cuchulain's Fight with the Sea'.) In all the drafts of this line, the sea is called *invulnerable*, not *ungovernable*, and Bradford speculates that *ungovernable* is a misprint (*YW*, pp. 161–62). Compare 'Cuchulain's Fight with the Sea', l. 86: 'fought with the invulnerable tide'; *Fighting the Waves* (1929), l. 231: 'invulnerable body' (of a sea-goddess); *The Death of Cuchulain* (1939), ll. 138–39: 'I fought against the sea. / *Aoife*. I seemed invulnerable'; and 'The Crucifixion of the Outcast' (1894): 'the ungovernable sea' (*M*, p. 153).

II 19 *Heart mysteries there*: Yeats might have found the legend of Cuchulain relevant to his personal life in a number of ways; for example, Yeats struggled for years against his own father's rationalism and scepticism – they once quarrelled so violently that John Butler Yeats 'broke the glass in a picture with the back of my head' (*Mem*, p. 19).

II 21 *Character isolated by a deed*: in 1904 Yeats wrote of tragedy, 'An action is taken out of all other actions ... The characters that are involved in it are freed from everything that is not part of that action ... an eddy of life purified from everything but itself' (*Ex*, pp. 153–54; compare *EI*, p. 530). But according to this poem, such concentration, such abstraction from mundane life, are slightly sinister, famishing.

II 23–24 *Players and painted stage took all my love / And not those things that they were emblems of*: the sensuous charms of the spectacle seduce the poet away from its inner meaning, its psychological truth – the vehicle overwhelms the tenor. Compare two earlier passages about the inadequacy of theatre, 'Reconciliation', ll. 6–7: 'Helmets, and swords, and half-forgotten things / That were like memories of you'; and 'Parnell's Funeral' I 22–23: 'nor did we play a part / Upon a painted stage when we devoured his heart'. In his last essay on the drama, Yeats repeated Matthew Arnold's complaint in his 1853 Preface against psychological dramas, dramas of passive suffering: 'I had begun to get rid of everything that is not, whether in lyric or dramatic poetry, in some sense character in action ... I delight in active men ... I would have poetry turn its back upon all that modish curiosity, psychology' (*EI*, p. 530). But Yeats here suggests that the psychology of the playwright is the truest theme of his plays.

III: a completely different draft of this stanza, based on the theme of tragic joy, is cited the headnote to *Last Poems* – in that stanza all the toys, circus acts, and images vanish into 'unimagined night' (Bradford, *YW*, p. 163).

III 1 *images*: a draft of this line enumerates them: 'The faery woman, Cathleen, Fool and Blind Man' (*YW*, p. 164).

III 3 *A mound of refuse*: Yeats believed that transcendent images could become real by means of blood – 'until they have been fed with the blood they are ... shadows' (*The Player Queen* I 213-14); and here Yeats discovers that the beautiful images of his art have incarnated themselves by feeding on the humblest, most grotesque matter.

III 5 *that raving slut*: 'I tried to make the language of poetry coincide with that of passionate, normal speech ... I sometimes compare myself with the mad old slum women I hear denouncing and remembering' (*EI*, p. 521). A draft of III 5–6 read, 'that raving slut / Called Heart and Company' (*YW*, p. 165).

III 6 *my ladder's gone*: compare the shrinking stilts in 'High Talk', ll. 3–4.

III 8 *rag and bone shop*: Yeats's most abject term for the *Anima Mundi*, the imagination's storehouse of images, now relocated in a private slum. Yeats once thought that his symbols – the matter of his art – were taken from some celestial public domain; but now he has come to agree with Carlyle, who argued in *Sartor Resartus* (1831) that symbols were earthly, indeed subject to decay: 'are not the tatters and rags of superannuated worn-out symbols (in this Rag-fair of a World) dropping off everywhere . . . ?' But Yeats here speaks less of the rot of used-up symbols than of their messy origins. In the 1910s Pound often spoke of the poet as an incoherent quarry of themes: 'I myself am a rag-bag, a mass of sights and citations, but I will not beat down life for the sake of a model' (*Pavannes and Divagations*, p. 102; compare *Three Cantos* [1917] I 5). Also compare C. Day Lewis, 'Few Things can more inflame' (included by Yeats in *OBMV*): 'Phrase-making, dress-making – / Distinction's hard to find . . . time trundles this one to the rag-and-bone man'.

Yeats earlier wrote of rags in *Where There is Nothing* IV ii 422–23: 'One by one I am plucking off the rags and tatters of the world'; and 'An Acre of Grass', ll. 10–11: 'the mill of the mind / Consuming its rag and bone'. But now the poet puts rags on, instead of taking them off. In a sense the end of this poem reverses the curriculum of poetry prescribed by Blake, in *Milton* (1804) 41 [48]:4–7: 'To cast off the rotten rags of Memory by Inspiration . . . To take off his filthy garments, & clothe him with Imagination / To cast aside from Poetry, all that is not Inspiration'.

Auden used this line of Yeats's to illustrate the lack of relation 'between the moral quality of a maker's life and the aesthetic value of the works he makes': 'every artist knows that the sources of his art are what Yeats called "the foul rag-and-bone shop of the heart", its lusts, its hatreds, its envies' (*Secondary Worlds*, p. 135).

Politics

This poem was inspired by an article in the *Yale Review* (Spring 1938) by the American poet Archibald MacLeish, who praised Yeats's poetry and cited the passage from Thomas Mann (the German novelist, 1875–1955) used as this poem's epigraph. Yeats sent a draft of this poem to Dorothy Wellesley, and commented that MacLeish's article 'commends me above other modern poets because my language is "public" . . . It goes on to say that, owing to my age and my relation to Ireland, I was unable to use this "public" language on what it evidently considered the right public material. The enclosed little poem is my reply . . . No artesian well of the intellect can find the poetic theme' (*DWL*, p. 163). As this last sentence shows, 'Politics', like 'The Circus Animals' Desertion', is a meditation on the propriety of themes for poems. Its placement at the end of Yeats's last volume of poems makes it a kind of valediction: and it fulfils this role, first by dismissing every topical theme in favour of the most universal, and second by its deliberate appeal to one of the oldest and most famous lyrics in modern English, the anonymous 'Westron Wind': 'Westron winde, when wilt thou blow, / The smalle raine downe can raine? / Christ if my love were in my armes, / And I in my bed againe'.

1–2 *How can I ... My attention fix*: compare 'On Being Asked for a War Poem'.

3–4 *On Roman or on Russian ... politics*: compare 'Those Images', l. 6: 'To Moscow or to Rome'.

11–12 *O that I were young again / And held her in my arms*: compare 'Men Improve with the Years', ll. 14–15: 'O would that we had met / When I had my burning youth!'

ACKNOWLEDGMENTS

The publishers and editor wish to thank the following for permission to reproduce copyright material:

A. P. Watt Ltd on behalf of Michael B. Yeats for 'Reprisals', first published in 1948; three stanzas from the early drafts of 'A Prayer for my Daughter', not published in the final version; an unpublished draft of the third part of 'Under Ben Bulben'; 'Margot'; a stanza originally included in 'The Circus Animals' Desertion'; a prose draft of 'The Statues'; and the quatrain on nothingness, dated 8 May 1938, but unpublished until 1983.

A. P. Watt Limited on behalf of Michael B. Yeats and Macmillan (London) Ltd for extracts from *Memoirs* by W. B. Yeats.

Oxford University Press for extracts from *Letters on Poetry from W. B. Yeats to Dorothy Wellesley*; *The Letters of W. B. Yeats*; *The Collected Letters of W. B. Yeats*, vol. I, 1865–95; *W. B. Yeats and T. Sturge Moore: Their Correspondence, 1901–37*.

The editor also wishes to thank Jocelyn Burton of J. M. Dent & Sons Ltd for her wise consideration of the text and for her many kindnesses.

INDEX OF TITLES

INDEX OF FIRST LINES

ABOUT THE EDITOR

DANIEL ALBRIGHT is Professor of English at the University of Rochester, NY. His publications include *The Myth against Myth: A Study of Yeats's Imagination in Old Age*; *Representation and the Imagination: Beckett, Kafka, Nabokov, and Schoenberg*; *Tennyson: The Muses' Tug-of-War* and *Stravinsky: The Music-Box and the Nightingale.*

This book is set in EHRHARDT. The precise origin of the typeface is unclear. Most of the founts were probably cut by the Hungarian punch-cutter Nicholas Kis for the Ehrhardt foundry in Leipzig, where they were left for sale in 1689. In 1938 the Monotype foundry produced the modern version.

Luton Sixth Form College
Learning Resources Centre
WITHDRAWN